D1072212

CONNECTICUT FOR THE UNION

The Role of the State in the Civil War

CONNECTICUT FOR THE UNION

The Role of the State in the Civil War

by JOHN NIVEN

New Haven and London, Yale University Press, 1965

Designed by John O. C. McCrillis,
set in Garamond type,
and printed in the United States of America by
Vail-Ballou Press, Inc., Binghamton, N.Y.

Library of Congress catalog card number: 65-11186

Published with assistance from
The Putnam Prospect Foundation.

WHEN the Connecticut Legislature established the State Civil War Centennial Commission in 1960, it spelled out the duties and powers of that Commission. Included was the mandate to inaugurate, direct, and secure the publication of an official history of Connecticut's role in the War for the Union.

This particular assignment was undertaken by the Chairman of the Commission serving as administrator and the Chairman of the Commission's Publications Committee serving as editor. The latter, in his search for a competent historian to write the book, found a scholar who satisfied all the desirable criteria: he had been raised in Connecticut and had received his education there until the taking of his M.A. and Ph.D. degrees in history under Allan Nevins at Columbia University; and that doctoral degree had been awarded for a dissertation dealing with the economic and social developments of Connecticut during the period 1860–75. This man also knew war at first hand, having served in the amphibious forces of the United States Navy in the European and Pacific theaters of operations.

John Niven has made a noteworthy contribution to the historiography of his state, with the perspective of the professional historian who never loses sight of the fact that Connecticut's role was part of a national struggle to justify Abraham Lincoln's faith in an indestructible Union.

(signed) Albert D. Putnam, *Chairman, Connecticut Civil War Centennial Commission*

Rollin G. Osterweis, *Chairman, The Publications Committee of the Connecticut Civil War Centennial Commission*

FOREWORD

THIS is a book well worth the talent and painstaking labor that John Niven has poured into it, for it tells a unique story.

When we think of the antebellum history of Connecticut, a vision of striking coherence and solidarity rises before our eyes. Connecticut had character. Larger and better endowed states, like New York and Virginia, offer a richer panoply of names. Massachusetts, as not merely elder sister of Connecticut but leader of all New England, can boast of a more spacious history. But the record of most states seems miscellaneous and heterogeneous when compared with that of Connecticut. In unity of temper and intensity of self-consciousness the little "republic," as she called herself in a memorable Act of October 1776, long held a place beside that other stubbornly independent little commonwealth, South Carolina. Both cherished an indomitable spirit. Both were essentially conservative. The two great differences were that in Connecticut economic enterprise steadily undermined the political and social conservatism; and in Connecticut the sense of loyalty to the nation grew stronger decade by decade.

In oldtime Connecticut, so steadfast, so closely knit, so well unified in temper and purpose, groups and families seemed to count far more than individuals. We find ourselves, as we read her history, fastening on one generic name after another. The remarkable body of Trumbulls was led out by the redoubtable Revolutionary governor to whom Washington used to appeal in hours of perplexity with "Let us hear what Brother Jonathan says"; and adorned no less by the artist John Trumbull, before whose picture of the Declaration of Independence in the Capitol generations have stood in unequivocal awe. We think of the many Wolcotts, among them Oliver the Signer and that other Oliver who was head of the Treasury after Hamilton, a thorn in the flesh of John Adams, and a governor whose annual re-election for ten years helped give Connecticut its name as a land of steady habits. We think of the long line of Dwights. Greatest among them was the Timothy Dwight who wrote that unread epic, "The Conquest of Canaan," who gave Yale one of its longest administrations, and whose published works ("occasionally animated") filled thirteen octavo volumes; and there were numerous other Dwights.

We think, too, of Lyman Beecher, the fighting clergyman who had thirteen children, nearly all distinguished, not least among them the Harriet Beecher Stowe who dealt slavery its shrewdest blow. We think of Eli Whitney, whose cotton gin gave slavery its wide grip and whose firearms helped destroy that hold. We think of Benjamin Silliman, who helped usher in the age of coal and petroleum, and of the other Sillimans; of Noah Porter and the other Porters; and of Ellsworth Huntington and the other Huntingtons. Where is a state that is more of one texture, and more closely held together by an array of family clans?

Such a state, full of machine shops, of metal-working establishments, and of mills great and small—full, above all, of ingenious mechanics and industrious laborers—was certain to make its weight felt in the Civil War. Direction was given its war effort, as Mr. Niven clearly shows, by an unusual roster of leaders. Foremost among them was Gideon Welles, the Neptune of the Navy, as Lincoln termed him, who, with Gustavus V. Fox, created by 1864 not only a body of warships unrivaled in the world but a fleet of nearly five hundred blockading vessels; and Welles can be credited also for an unwavering support of Lincoln against both the disloyal men of the time and the intemperate radicals who tried to break the Administration down by such measures as the Wade-Davis Bill. Almost equally valuable to the government was the indefatigable war governor, who if not quite another Jonathan Trumbull was one of the Northern executives on whom Lincoln chiefly relied. In earlier days he had been repeatedly elected mayor of Norwich; now he was re-elected governor every year from 1858, until in 1866 he refused to stand again. It was in large part because of his exertions that Connecticut always exceeded her quota for the armed services, with the help of some "Yankee ciphering." Many weeks before Sumter he had warned the militia that their service might be needed at any minute, and on his own responsibility he had ordered the quartermaster officers to buy equipment for five thousand men.

Connecticut, where every man thought for himself, and where the progressive towns and cities differed sharply from the conservative rural areas, had never been a monolithic state politically. On the contrary, it was closely divided in election after election. In the spring of 1861 Buckingham was returned to the state house by the narrow vote of 43,012 to 41,103. But in fundamental loyalty to the Union, as Mr. Niven's narrative shows, the unity of Connecticut majorities was always adequate. When in the days of this close election Buckingham went beyond his legal authority to call for a regiment of volunteers, the response was electrifying; fifty-four companies appeared instead of ten. Town meetings not only poured in their contributions of men but voted contributions of money to support the families of volunteers; the cities did even better; and Buckingham departed for Washington to get the Administration to take three regiments instead of one. In later elections the story was much the same. Especially striking here is the narrative of the election of 1863, when the Peace Democrat Thomas H. Seymour, who had proclaimed that the South could never be defeated, made a tremendous plunge for the governorship. His party filled the countryside with its peace banners, but it went down ignominiously.

Patriots of the time liked to boast that Connecticut gave the Union cause its first four eminent martyrs, Elmer Ellsworth, Theodore Winthrop, General Nathaniel Lyon, and James H. Ward of the Potomac gunboat flotilla. These men were at least of Connecticut stock. The state also gave the Union Andrew H. Foote, who moved the river flotilla upon Henry and Donelson, and a goodly list of generals, of whom John Sedgwick, Darius N. Couch, and Joseph R. Hawley stand pre-eminent. The chief heroes of the state, however, as Mr. Niven well says, were the men who laid down their lives for the Union and the cause of human freedom. A population of 461,000, sending more than thirty regiments of infantry, cavalry, and artillery to war, lost nearly 1,200 officers and men killed in action, some 700 others mortally wounded, and more than 3,300 dead of disease. And how great a burden of mutilation and debility, of sorrow and family impoverishment, fell upon the towns of the state!

This well-stored and many-sided volume offers materials upon which writers will be glad to levy. It contains instruction for the social historian, the economic historian, the political historian, and the technological historian—not to mention the military expert. Connecticut was fortunate long ago in a writer of fiction, John W. DeForest, who dealt with the wartime and postwar scene. Now she is fortunate in a writer who has given us one of the fullest, best proportioned, and most penetrating of all the state records of the war.

Allan Nevins

PREFACE

ANY ATTEMPT to delineate the role of a single state during the Civil War raises a problem of organization. How, one must ask, was the role of this state different from that of other states? Why is it profitable to focus upon one particular piece of territory, to consider the particular view rather than the overview? Moreover, does not such an approach lend itself to distortion, to an exaggeration of the parochial over the general?

It is difficult, if not impossible, to correct for this prismatic effect in dealing with local history on a meaningful basis. But the microscopic technique still has its virtues, particularly for close study of the Civil War period. As many historians of the War have pointed out, a few Northern states, as well as Southern, shouldered the major responsibility of supporting their respective war efforts. In such a loosely organized country as the United States in 1861, the concept of states rights not only was a dominant political force but had important economic and social connotations. Thus at the risk of magnifying the local and the unique, it has seemed appropriate to chart the role of a single state—Connecticut—as if she were engaged in her own war with the Confederacy together with her allies, the other loyal states of the Union. In this way it was possible to do justice to Connecticut's individual contribution yet at the same time to examine critically the impact of war and industrial change on her people and their institutions.

This book could not have been written without the continuing assistance and support of many friends and colleagues. I owe an enormous debt of gratitude to Allan Nevins, who first suggested the topic and who has given generously of his time in reading and criticizing the manuscript. Rollin Osterweis of Yale University, in the double role of warm friend and demanding editor, saved me from many foolish errors of fact and interpretation. For generous support of the project and keen interest in its development, I am deeply indebted to Albert Putnam, Chairman of the Connecticut Civil War Centennial Commission. A historian of the Civil War and a Connecticut man in the deepest sense, he more than any one else has made this book possible. I should like to thank also my colleagues, Douglass Adair, Edwin Fussell, Albert Friedman, and French Fogle of the Claremont Graduate School, George Wickes of Harvey Mudd College, Sidney Mead of the State University of Iowa, Leland Carlson of the Southern California School of Theology, Denis Strong of the University of California at Riverside, and Alan Brownsword of California State College at Long Beach, who read all or parts of the manuscript.

For invaluable assistance in the research phases of this volume, I must express my deep appreciation to Thompson Harlow, Director of the Connecticut Historical Society, Howard Gotlieb, formerly Curator of Historical Manuscripts at Yale, Ralph Thomas, Curator of the New Haven Colony Historical Society, Donald Poulin, War Records Librarian at the Connecticut State Library, Calvin Simkin of the Travelers' Insurance Co., and the staffs of the Huntington Library, the New York Public Library, the New York Historical Society, the Library of Congress, and the Honnold Library.

Mrs. Orin Tramz, secretary for the departments of English and History at the Claremont Graduate School, helped in the typing of the manuscript, as did my wife, Elizabeth Thomson Niven, who also bore the brunt of first listener during the formative stages of the writing.

Charles Staurovsky drafted the maps, and I am indeed grateful for his assistance.

J. N.

Claremont, California
November 17, 1964

CONTENTS

LIST OF ILLUSTRATIONS

MAPS

ABBREVIATIONS

CHS	Connecticut Historical Society
CSL	Connecticut State Library
HL	Huntington Library
LC	Library of Congress
MHA	Marine Historical Association
NYHS	New York Historical Society
OR	*Official Records of the Union and Confederate Armies*
PDLC	*Public Documents of the Legislature of Connecticut*
SL	Sterling Library

PART ONE

The Rising of the People

1. THE LAND OF STEADY HABITS

MARCH is an unpredictable month in Connecticut. Not infrequently the changeable temperature may range fifty degrees in twenty-four hours; and there may be sunshine, snow, hail, and rain all in one afternoon. March 7, 1860, was just such a day in the busy manufacturing town of Meriden. Intermittent rain and sleet during the daylight hours had converted Meriden's unpaved streets into deeply rutted quagmires. As night came on, the rain stopped; but the damp air was cold and raw. Despite the dreary weather, the town had a festive appearance. A Republican parade and rally had been planned, and the streets were jammed with townsmen and visitors, many of whom bore kerosene torches.

Precisely at 7 P.M. Meriden's two-pounder brass election cannon barked out the signal for the procession to form. The town's cornet band struck up the new and popular "Yellow Rose of Texas,"[1] and a thousand cheering men began the march to the railroad depot to greet the speaker of the evening who was coming up from New Haven on a special train. At 8 P.M. the bunting-draped locomotive with six cars came in sight. With many whistle blasts, puffs of smoke and steam, and sudden brakings it eased itself to the platform, where it was immediately surrounded by enthusiastic citizens. The cars unloaded another 600 torchbearers and two more cornet bands, compounding the crush around the platform. Young Orville Platt, Meriden's popular assemblyman, with the assistance of the three bandmasters, finally managed to get the happy throng lined up behind the carriages reserved for the notables. Heedless of the ankle-deep mud, some 2,000 marchers splashed through the main streets to Meriden's town hall. Sprays of roman candles and rockets arched their route, while scores of bonfires along the way

1. The three most popular new tunes were "Dixie," "The Yellow Rose of Texas," and "The Babbling Brook." *Hartford Courant* (Jan. 2, 1861).

made a colorful contrast to the pale yellow sputtering flame of the moving torches. Abraham Lincoln had arrived in Meriden.

This was to be the third speech Lincoln would make in Connecticut, yet the initial enthusiasm was the greatest he had experienced since his arrival in New York nine days before. Clearly his reputation as an interesting speaker had preceded him to Meriden. At Hartford the audience had been more curious than enthusiastic at first. His reception in New Haven had been cordial but nothing as compared with the roaring welcome he got in Meriden. Lincoln, tired out from his ordeal of nine speeches in nine days and worried about the problem of fresh material, could not help being heartened at the obvious success of his tour. The *New Haven Palladium* estimated that 3,000 people were jammed into the hall. With every aisle filled and all standing room taken up, the doors were thrown open so that the 300 or so outside could catch a phrase or two from the rostrum.

Lincoln delivered much the same speech he had given in New Haven, and though many in the audience had read it in the *Palladium,* they "seemed to hang on every word." [2] Despite the orator's grotesque appearance, his high clear voice with its Southern drawl, his occasional awkward gesture,[3] he carried the audience with him from beginning to end. Every familiar joke brought down the house, every important phrase drew deafening applause. Where his humor had amused the more sophisticated audiences of Hartford and New Haven, it convulsed his Meriden audience of farmers and workingmen. If the logic and the innate conservatism of his stand on slavery had reassured the city folk, his emphasis that the West belonged to free white labor, not to black slave labor, was what Meriden factory hands and farmers' sons wanted to hear. Draw a line around the slaveholding South, he seemed to say, and quarantine slavery where it had existed historically. "The new territories," he stated, "are the newly-made bed to which our children are to go, and it lies with the nation to say whether they shall have snakes mixed up with them or not." [4] It made no difference to the audi-

2. *New Haven Palladium* (March 8, 1860); *Hartford Courant* (March 8, 1860).

3. Richard M. Devens, *American Progress, or the Great Events of the Greatest Century* (Chicago, 1882), p. 471.

4. Roy P. Basler, ed., *The Collected Works of Abraham Lincoln, 4* (New Brunswick, Rutgers University Press, 1953–55), p. 18.

ence that Lincoln drew a careful distinction between the Negro and slavery. The citizens of Meriden heard what they wanted to hear, and that was best expressed by the *Hartford Courant* five days after Lincoln's speech. "Ours is the WHITE MAN'S PARTY, for the interests of FREE WHITES; the Democrats are fighting for more niggers and slavery." [5]

For a Westerner who had never before visited New England, Lincoln demonstrated a shrewd understanding of the Connecticut mind. His speeches had just the right amount of high-minded idealism mixed with common sense. They were conservative in argument, but at the same time presented a novel solution; they were concrete instead of abstract, and well calculated to suit both the agrarian and the labor elements in the local population. While Lincoln seemed to acknowledge Connecticut's traditional conservatism, he had responded also to the evidences of rapid industrial change. On the surface the state was still "the Land of Steady Habits," still the butt of music-hall burlesque and Southern satire, a state where wooden nutmegs and wooden pumpkin seeds were said to be the major products, and where Lydia Sigourney, P. T. Barnum, and Henry Ward Beecher dispensed an original mixture of Arcady, larceny, and piety. But quite apart from popular humor at the state's expense, the sharp stereotype of the inventive Connecticut Yankee, with his close-set eyes fixed on the main chance, was starting to fade. Underneath the tough, unyielding character of the state, the folding and faulting of new economic forces were heaving up against the social order. This Lincoln had recognized and had adroitly used.

Although a majority of Connecticut's population in 1860 was engaged in agriculture and lived in rural areas, the most populous counties of the state had been importing foodstuffs for more than thirty years. Hartford county, for example, had not been agriculturally self-sufficient since 1820.[6] Yet forty years later the net worth of Connecticut farms was a substantial sum—said to be in excess of $92,000,000 [7]—while the capital invested in industry was

5. *Hartford Courant* (March 13, 1860).

6. John M. Niles, "Oration Pronounced before the Agricultural Society of Hartford," 1841 (HL).

7. Ninth Census, 1870, *The Statistics of the Wealth and Industry*, 3, 86, table III.

probably in the neighborhood of $150,000,000. Though the industrial plant represented a much higher share of the state's net worth in 1860, only 14 per cent of the population gained their livelihood from manufacturing.[8] To be sure, a considerable amount of the farm economy was closely integrated with manufacturing. Such important cash crops as animal fodder or tobacco, the breeding of draft animals, and the growing dairy industry all found their principal markets in the dynamic economy of cities and factory towns.[9]

Increasing specialization was influencing agricultural techniques, but it had made little impression on traditional attitudes. The conservative, parochial outlook of the agrarian, though on the defensive, saw to it that Connecticut remained the land of steady habits. Hardworking, frugal, narrow, as suspicious of innovation as of new neighbors, naïve and at the same time shrewd, the average Connecticut farmer of 1860 stubbornly stuck to his family acres, while his overworked sons and daughters dreamed of adventure in Hartford or New Haven (did they dare dream of New York?) and escaped at the first opportunity. David Osborne was just such an example of Connecticut yeomanry. Born in East Windsor in 1780, he was married in 1808 to the daughter of a neighboring farmer. The Osbornes, both in good health in 1863, had never traveled more than forty miles from home, and then only once, in 1823, when Osborne went on horseback to Middletown. Neither he nor his wife had ever ridden in a stagecoach, a steamboat, or a railroad car. For seventy-five years he had worked from sunup to sundown on the farm every day except Sunday; and his wife, besides her household chores, had contributed to the farm economy by raising without assistance one hundred bushels of onions a year for the past twenty years.[10] Thousands of David Osbornes lived and worked in the Connecticut of 1860, thousands whose sons would soon invoke

8. Ninth Census, 1870, ibid., 3, 392, 393, table VIIIa; *The Statistics of Population*, 1, 17 Table II.

9. See, for example, the rise in horse population between 1850 and 1860, from 26,879 to 49,515; or the increase in the hay crops from 516,131 tons to 562,445 tons. Hay was the most valuable cash crop in 1861, followed closely by corn and oats. *Report of the Commissioner of Agriculture, 1862*, pp. 561, 565.

10. *Hartford Courant* (Dec. 3, 1863).

patriotism to provide them with their passport from drudgery and boredom. And few of those farmers' sons who escaped rebel bullets and Southern fevers would remain permanently on the homestead. The Osbornes still managed to stamp their character and steady habits on their native state, but in a generation their predominating influence would be gone. Such legacy as they bequeathed may yet in 1965 be seen in the stone walls running through thickets of black birch and bull briers or in the occasional old apple tree amid scrub oak and swamp maple. Two hundred years of back-breaking labor and careful husbandry had left scarcely a trace.

When Lincoln spoke at Meriden, the state had a population of 460,000, most of whom were native-born Protestants.[11] The Congregational Church, with its spiritual center at Yale, still dominated the religious life of Connecticut. Under the enlightened leadership of Theodore Dwight Woolsey and Leonard Bacon of New Haven, and the intellectual Horace Bushnell of Hartford, Connecticut Congregationalism had been considerably purged of its narrow Calvinist theology. Since the fierce doctrinal disputes between the Taylorites and the Tylerites of the early thirties, the Church had cautiously made itself more responsive to the secular needs of society. Bacon preached the concept of Christian stewardship to New Haven's bustling business community, and Bushnell asserted freedom of the will, a doctrine that well suited the entrepreneurial instincts of Hartford bankers and insurance men. On such controversial issues of the day as slavery, the Congregational clergy were particularly circumspect. Bacon held perhaps the most radical view in that he preached abolition, but at the same time it had to be legal abolition. He would have no truck with William Lloyd Garrison and his abolition zealots, and he resigned his coeditorship of the *New York Independent* in part because he felt that the journal was being moved into the Garrison camp.[12] A bit of brimstone still stuck to the pages of Yale's *New Englander*, where such articles as "Original Sin: The State of the Question" or "The Congregational

11. Eighth Census, 1860, *Population of the United States*, p. 41, table IV; Report of the Committee on Home Evangelization, "The Home Heathen and How to Reach Them," *New Englander*, 18 (1860), 1012–13.

12. Leonard Bacon to Henry Bowen, 1859 (Bacon Papers, SL).

Polity and a Biblical Theology?" appeared during 1860. But the major emphasis of the journal was toward history, literature, and current politics, reflecting the more liberal tastes of the growing cities rather than the more orthodox attitudes of the countryside New Haven in 1860 was a narrow little world, as John W. DeForest has observed, but it was cosmopolitan when compared with a village like East Granby. Although Yale was still on the side of steady habits, Jonathan Edwards was no longer infallible, even when speaking ex cathedra on faith and morals.

Also competing for the minds, if not the souls, of the citizenry were the Baptists in the southeast, the Episcopalians in Hartford and in Fairfield counties, and the Methodists fairly well distributed throughout the state.[13] Since the eighteenth century the membership and influence of these churches had slowly and steadily grown at the expense of Congregationalism. Both Episcopalians and Methodists had succeeded during the early thirties in establishing colleges at Hartford and Middletown, despite the long and bitter opposition of Yale. In 1860 Connecticut's Episcopal Bishop Thomas Brownell enjoyed the distinction of being the presiding bishop of the nation There can be no doubt that the activities of these opposing Protestant churches had played a part in modifying the extreme Calvinism of the Connecticut Congregational Church.

If the various Protestant churches had differences among themselves, they still represented Yankee supremacy and tended to form a common front against a most disturbing element in Connecticut society—the European immigrant. There always had been a trickle of immigrants into the state, but more foreigners arrived and settled in Connecticut during the ten-year period between 1850 and 1860 than in its entire previous existence as a colony and a state.

John Hooker, the eminent Connecticut lawyer and charter member of Hartford's Nook Farm group, has related how rare the immigrant was in the Connecticut of the early thirties. The digging of the Farmington canal, according to Hooker, brought the first Irishmen to Connecticut. "I remember well," he said, "the first one I saw. I was on my way to school when I met him. He stopped me and said to me in a brogue I could hardly understand, 'Do you know who I am?' I told him I did not. 'Well,' said he, 'I am a wild

13. *New Englander, 18,* 1014.

rishman just over.' I told of this when I got home as I would if I ıad seen a wild zebra in the street." [14]

Somewhat over 80,000 inhabitants, or approximately 17 per cent ›f the total population, were foreign born in 1860. Most of these (79 ›er cent) were Irish and Roman Catholic, and the remainder were ıbout equally divided between English and Germans.[15] Since most ›f the newcomers crowded into existing urban areas, which made ittle or no provision for their accommodation, they either occupied ›vercrowded tenements or built themselves shanty towns out of liscarded lumber and any other scrap material they could find. /ery soon the pleasant tree-shaded little cities of Hartford, New Haven, Norwich, and New London became encircled by squalid lums from which crime and disease frequently spilled into the inest residential areas. Over 30 per cent of Hartford's population ınd nearly 27 per cent of New Haven's in 1860 were foreign born, ›rincipally Irish.[16]

A majority of the immigrants were at the bottom of the socio-conomic ladder, but a surprising number quickly made an impres-ive mark on the social, economic, and political life of the cities and arger towns. Patrick Maher, who had emigrated from Ireland in 848, was a successful mason-builder in New Haven, and Timothy Ryan, also Irish born, was a practicing lawyer in Waterbury.[17] ewis Osterweis, a native of Bavaria, who had moved his tobacco ›usiness from Iowa to New Haven in 1858, organized the first full-scale cigar factory in the state in May 1860.[18] Hartford's Irish-›orn Thomas McManus, an ambitious young lawyer, had just been ppointed one of the six police commissioners of the city.[19] Alex-ınder and Hugh Harbison, natives of County Armagh, Ireland,

14. John Hooker, *Some Reminiscences of a Long Life; with a Few Articles on Moral nd Social Subjects of Present Interest* (Hartford, 1899), p. 17.

15. Eighth Census, *Population of the United States in 1860*, pp. 39–41, tables III, V.

16. Ibid., p. 41.

17. Rollin G. Osterweis, *Three Centuries of New Haven, 1638–1938* (New Haven, 953), p. 285; Thomas H. Murray, *History of the Ninth Regiment Connecticut Volun-eer Infantry, "The Irish Regiment," in the War of the Rebellion, 1861–65* (New Haven, 903), pp. 351, 352.

18. Osterweis, p. 255.

19. Thomas F. Weaver, *Historical Sketch of the Police Service of Hartford* (Hartford, 901), p. 43.

were to open one of the largest groceries in Hartford just before th attack on Fort Sumter.[20] On Centinel Hill near the Harbisons' store Gerson Fox, a German immigrant, had been operating a dry good business since 1847. Bearing his name and managed by his descend ants, that store was to become the dominant enterprise of its kin in twentieth-century Connecticut.

Outside the cities and factory towns, the popular image of th Irishmen as quarrelsome, shiftless, and intemperate simply did no square with the facts. In the country town of Sharon, Litchfiel County, one of the local Congregational ministers estimated th foreign-born population to be 300, chiefly Irish. "They are generall industrious," he reported, "and as they accumulate means seem t buy land and own a homestead."[21] The pastor of the Congrega tional church in Newtown, a man noted for his "exact and thoroug observation," had warm praise for the 119 Irish families who ha settled in his flourishing town just east of Danbury. "There is n class of people in this community more industrious," he stated "Eighty-one of these families own real estate and it is a commo remark, that they stand ready to buy up all the land thrown on th market in the town. As fast as our American families fall int decay and are obliged to sell their property, the Irish catch it up They buy poor land and by hard work improve it; and they bu good land and keep it good. It is a constant marvel to me to see ho fast they are getting on in the world."[22] What dismayed the Con gregational ministers who surveyed 120 of the 170 towns in th state was that "the religious neglect and degeneracy are in town and parishes almost exclusively agricultural, containing no village of considerable size and no considerable admixture of foreign ers."[23] They estimated that one-third of the native American rura population never attended church, while in the urban, manufactur ing areas only one-sixth were nonchurchgoers.[24]

Indeed, it seems possible that the industry and land-purchasin habits of Irish immigrants in rural areas may have been an impor tant factor in arousing the nativist hostility that infected Connecti

20. Ibid., 137.
21. *New Englander*, 18, 1009; see pp. 1015–18.
22. Ibid., p. 1015.
23. Ibid., p. 1013.
24. Ibid., p. 1014.

it during the middle fifties. Although the Native American or
now-Nothing movement had, as a political party, become extinct
y 1860, its leaders continued to be a troublesome faction within
ie Republican party. A majority of the state's population still
sented deeply the intrusion of the newcomers. The wave of immi-
ration had been too sudden and too strong. Ethnically, in 1850
onnecticut had been one of the most homogeneous states in the
nion.[25] By 1860 one out of every six residents was foreign born.
he Irish bore the brunt of popular antagonism. Their Roman
atholic religion was highly suspect in Calvinist-oriented, Protes-
nt communities. The sharp increase in drunkenness and crime for
hich they were held responsible seemed to threaten hallowed insti-
itions. Moreover, the tendency of most Irish to vote the Demo-
atic ticket was creating a serious political problem for the Repub-
cans, as it had for the Whigs earlier. It had been this political
anger which had given impetus to the formation of the American
arty out of the remnants of Connecticut's Whig organization in
ie middle fifties.

Supported by a statewide network of secret lodges, the Ameri-
ans capitalized on the desire of conservatives everywhere to raise
a issue which would divert the public from the potentially disrup-
ve slavery question. In the elections of 1855 and 1856 they cared the state, and it was only with the greatest difficulty that the
epublicans managed to gain American support for Frémont. Dur-
ig the Know-Nothing administration of William T. Minor in
855, the legislature revised the registry and voting laws of the
ate. Ostensibly, these reforms were aimed at purifying the ballot
ox, but practically, they denied the privilege of suffrage to many
ish residents. In addition, the legislature disbanded all Irish militia
ompanies. More galling than these official actions was a dramatic
se in community discrimination instigated by the Know-Nothing
dges and press. Events on the national scene, however, skillfully
xploited by resourceful Republican leaders such as Gideon Welles
nd William A. Buckingham, who had been elected as the first
epublican governor in 1858, managed to shift public attention
way from Know-Nothing intolerance. But mutual bitterness and
istrust between the native majority and the foreign-born minor-

25. Odell Shepard, *Connecticut Past and Present* (New York, 1939), p. 291.

ity was very much apparent in 1860. Significantly, Lincoln ha
avoided any direct comment on this troublesome political and eco
nomic issue. His emphasis on free labor—the right to strike—an
particularly on the right to move to free white territories in th
West was sound political doctrine for both defensive Yankees an
ambitious Irishmen.

The ethnic conflict of the fifties had indeed promoted tension
within the state, but this was merely the outward and visible sig
of underlying economic change. Steady habits had been unde
steady attack for almost a decade. The countryside ranged itsel
against the cities; city fought city; county competed agains
county, and region against region. Connecticut had reached th
take-off stage in its transition from farm to factory. Industry an
transportation were sufficiently developed to enhance local interest
but were not extensive enough to merge these in the over-all inter
est of the state. The railroad net, for example, was not only incom
plete but not far enough advanced technologically to overcome th
combined opposition of river and sound steamboats and the locali
ties they served. Insufficient capital was being generated by indus
try and agriculture to sustain the rapid economic growth devise
by strong entrepreneurial forces. Moreover, home industries, unt
the depression of 1857, had to compete with the new West for loca
money. Connecticut's geographic position between the rival metro
politan areas of New York and Boston also promoted internal divi
sions, even as it hastened industrial development. Local entrepre
neurs looked to these urban centers for outside capital and market
ing services, and as a result were strongly influenced by the atti
tudes of the Boston and New York business communities. By 186
New York City had extended its influence over the southern coun
ties of the state. The carriage industry in New Haven, the bras
industry in the Naugatuck valley, and the hat industry in Dan
bury were all more or less dependent upon New York City credi
sources and distribution agents. Through the commercial and fi
nancial houses of the great metropolis, these industries were close
integrated into the Southern market structure. Hartford, Tollan
and Windham counties inclined toward the Boston orbit. The cit
of Hartford was at this time more of a financial than a manufactur

ng center and tended to merge its economic interests with Boston a competition with Wall Street. While certain powerful Hartford ounty industries—fire arms, gun powder, and carpets—also had ies with New York and the Southern market, the predominant nsurance companies and banks were more concerned with business nd investment opportunities at home or in the West. They were articularly involved in the textile industry of eastern Connecticut, s were certain Boston and Providence capitalists.[26] Thus the hisoric competition between Hartford and New Haven was as much he result of outside influence as it was of local pretensions and ivalries.

Culturally and politically, the frequent intervention of New ork and Boston interests in what may be described as Connectiut's internal affairs had bred a fierce pride among the citizenry, an lmost strident insistence on their own particular and unique idenity. Connecticut citizens of the fifties and sixties, even the newly rrived immigrants, were strongly attached to the virtues, fancied r otherwise, of their home state. Outspoken in its defense, quick to esent any criticism of its institutions, they wanted their state to ollow an independent course. The long political career of Gideon Velles, Hartford's most distinguished citizen, was primarily conerned with making Connecticut's voice heard in national affairs. A tates' righter all his life, Welles had only disdain for what he egarded as New Englandism promoted by Boston and serving Boson's interests.[27] Conversely Leonard Bacon, William T. Eustis, and . W. S. Dutton, who spoke for the Congregational clergy of New Iaven, warned their parishioners against the corrupting materialist ulture of New York. All, at one time or another, published articles n the *New Englander,* stressing Connecticut history, its own paricular heritage, and its particular sense of dedication to ancient uritan ideals.

Thus while accepting eagerly the pottage offered by rich and owerful neighbors, the state seemed desperately anxious to preerve its integrity. Connecticut in 1860 was not a satellite of Boston s was its eastern neighbor, Rhode Island, nor had it fallen victim

26. Frances M. Caulkins, *History of Norwich* (Hartford, 1866), pp. 610–21.

27. Gideon Welles to Sam Houston, n.d., Feb. 1855 (Welles Papers, LC).

to the dynamism of New York City. Cultural and political stat rights still maintained a precarious ascendancy.[28] The economi bootstrap, however, had worn too thin to support the weight o expansive industry. And as the industrial function was rapidly be coming the major force in Connecticut life, so the cultural an political form of society would follow in its image.

But behind all this buoyant enthusiasm and drive, the entrepre neurs were insecure. They had received a sharp jolt in the depressio that followed the financial crisis of 1857. Hartford banks and in surance companies that had invested in Western lands suddenl found their assets seriously impaired.[29] Factories in the Hartfor area, textile mills in eastern Connecticut, and the hat industry i Danbury all went on reduced time.[30] Throughout the state spo radic strikes occurred; none was successful, but all bespoke commu nity hardship and unrest.

By March 1858 most of the cotton mills along the Norwich an Worcester Railroad had resumed full-time operations. Wages, how ever, had been cut 20 per cent.[31] Railroads, most of which ha heavy capital debts, were immediately affected by the industria slowdown. Some of the newer lines, such as the Shore Line and th New Haven and Northhampton, went into receivership; and earn ings of the established roads were reduced sharply.[32] The onl bright spots in the Connecticut economy had been the sewing ma chine industry in Bridgeport and New Haven's carriage industry which had manufactured over 7,000 vehicles valued at $1,613,15c principally for the Southern market, during 1857.[33] Wheeler an Wilson, the largest sewing machine factory in the state and nation increased its output by 57 per cent during 1858 and more tha doubled it again during 1859.[34]

By the spring of 1860 recovery was well advanced, though in dustrial production and wages had not yet reached predepressio

28. Horace Bushnell, *Speech for Connecticut, Being an Historical Estimate of the Stat Delivered before the Legislature and Other Invited Guests* (Hartford, 1851), p. 15.

29. *Hartford Courant* (May 29, 1860).

30. Ibid. (March 8, March 20, April 13, 1858).

31. Ibid. (March 20, 1858).

32. "Eighth Annual Report of the Railroad Commission," *PDLC* (May Sess., 1861)

33. *Hartford Courant* (Jan. 20, 1858).

34. Wheeler and Wilson manufactured 4,591 machines in 1857; 7,978 in 1858; an 21,306 in 1859. Ibid. (Jan. 28, 1860).

vels. The sober attitude of the business community was reflected ı the money market, where capital was in good supply but not for ›eculative investment. "The past trade season," noted the *Hart-ord Courant*, "was remarkably free from speculation. Articles have ›een purchased for consumption but not for a rise." [35] Just as busi-.ess seemed to be headed for prosperous times, John Brown's raid ıcreased the political tension between North and South. Connect-:cut manufacturers and bankers were instantly concerned and ıeir attitudes were communicated to press and pulpit. The two :ading abolitionists in the state, Leonard Bacon and Joseph Haw-:y, editor of the *Hartford Press*, quickly denounced Brown's ction. Bacon felt that Brown had usurped the function of govern-ıent. "He who interposes with any other than a moral influence, ıakes war," declared the New Haven minister. "Let all who love ıeir country . . . avoid all fellowship with men who would abol-h slavery by arms in the hands of invaders, or in the hands of aves," he solemnly concluded.[36] Joseph Hawley was more careful f his public utterance but no less explicit. "He [John Brown] ommitted a crime against a noble cause in starting an insurrec-on," he wrote his father, the Reverend Francis Hawley.[37] If Con-ecticut businessmen were worried about the implications of John rown's raid, they were even more dismayed by the threat of outhern economic boycott. The fact that a Collinsville toolmaker .ad manufactured pikes for Brown was given wide currency in the outhern press, and "black Republican" Connecticut manufactur-rs had been singled out by such fire-eaters as governors Letcher of 'irginia and Gist of South Carolina for special economic reprisal.[38]

Most Connecticut businessmen were so disturbed by the possibil-y of sanctions that they eagerly accepted the idea of a state manu-acturers' convention where they might adopt measures of appease-ıent. Every leading banker and industrialist in the state, irrespec-ıve of party, met in convention at Meriden on January 18, 1860. . majority of the delegates had hoped that the meeting would be

35. Ibid. (May 29, 1860).

36. Leonard Bacon, "The Moral of Harper's Ferry," *New Englander*, 17 (1859), pp. 078.

37. Hawley to Rev. Francis Hawley, March 4, 1860 (J. R. Hawley Papers, LC).

38. Oswald Garrison Villard, *John Brown: A Biography, 1800–1859* (New York, 929), pp. 283–85.

nonpartisan; but as soon as organization was completed, it divided on political lines. Although all members condemned abolitionists, a minority would not be blackmailed into abject submission. A H. D. Smith, a Southington manufacturer, remarked heatedly, "I never will say to the South that I will give them my principles if they will buy my goods." He was bitterly opposed by John C. Palmer superintendent of Sharps' Hartford rifle factory. Palmer, together with such eminent Connecticut businessmen as W. H. Perry of Wheeler and Wilson, the Coe brothers of the Naugatuck brass industry, Charles Parker, the famed Meriden manufacturer, and G. M. Landers of New Britain hardware, supported resolutions that complied with all Southern political demands. They condemned John Brown's raid as "a monstrous crime," repudiated "the doctrine of a 'higher law' as a snare and delusion practically absurd and revolting," and condemned abolitionists and indeed any agitation on the slavery question as "Phararasaical [sic] and meddling." Important representatives of every important industry in the state signed their names to these resolutions.[39]

Yet Connecticut manufacturers were still uneasy about possible economic sanctions. And Abraham Lincoln sought to allay their fears when he spoke in the state six weeks later. "You have not lost that trade," he told his Connecticut audiences, ". . . your factories have not struck work, neither those where they make anything for coats, nor for shirts, nor for ladies' dresses."[40] What Lincoln said was true. Southern sanctions which had seemed so threatening in December had dissolved with the spring thaw. Information had been received that the South would market the largest cotton crop in its history. The Southern market was brisk for carriages, fine leather goods, coarse cotton, and hardware. Sharps', Colt's, and Whitney's factories had received substantial orders from various Southern states. Colt's, for example, had a $50,000 order from the state of Virginia to re-equip its militia.[41] Connecticut resort hotels had as many Southern guests as in previous seasons. By mid-June, Sachem's Head Hotel on the Long Island Sound was crowded with rich Southerners who mingled easily with fashionable folk from New York and

39. *Hartford Courant* (Jan. 19, 1860).
40. Basler, *Lincoln*, 4, 25.
41. *New Haven Journal and Courier* (March 7, 1860).

Philadelphia.[42] Connecticut industrialists, as they took stock of their situation during the summer of 1860, were cautiously optimistic about the future, and tended to discount the fulminations of Southern leaders as so much gasconade induced by warm weather and ardent spirits. The depression of 1857 was safely behind them; John Brown's raid was but an insane action of a bigoted madman; Southern boycotts had failed to materialize. They had experienced a decade of unparalleled economic growth during which the population of the state had doubled and the output of the industrial plants had increased about 90 per cent.[43] True, the Kansas situation was troublesome and the national organization of the Democratic party appeared to be breaking up; but the Republican party, at least as represented by Lincoln, Edward Bates, and Cassius Clay, seemed to be following a moderate course. And that party in Connecticut was headed by a successful businessman who was noted for his caution. Massachusetts and South Carolina agitators disturbed the confidence of few Connecticut manufacturers as they planned for the spring trade of 1861.

But the steady habits of the business community were not quite the same as those of the ambitious farmers' sons and factory hands. If the manufacturer had a vested interest in the status quo and the Southern market, the young people in country and city were vitally interested in the future of the West. For many the West was and would be a dream, but no Southern grandee with his hordes of Negro slaves would be permitted to destroy it without a challenge. Commenting on the scarcity of good farm hands in the Connecticut of 1860, Donald G. Mitchell, the popular essayist, attributed this to the lure of the West. "American blood is fast," he wrote, "and fast blood is impatient with a hoe among small carrots." [44]

42. *Hartford Courant* (June 25, 1860).

43. Ninth Census, 1870, *The Statistics of Wealth and Industry*, 3, 393, table VIIIa.

44. Donald G. Mitchell, "Hints about Farming," *New Englander*, *18* (1860), 900.

2. CRISIS: 1861

DURING the first week of January 1860 Democratic politiciar from all over New England converged on the quiet Clarendo Hotel in New York City. They had come in response to an invita tion from ex-President Franklin Pierce, who was anxious about th state of national politics and the spring elections in New Hampshir and Connecticut. Pierce also wanted to sound out the Yankee Dem ocratic leaders on the possibility of nominating Jefferson Davis a the party's candidate for the forthcoming presidential election. Among the first to arrive was Thomas Hart Seymour, a tall, digni fied gentleman from Hartford, Connecticut, his military bearin and slim figure cleverly emphasized by the craftsmanship of Henr Poole, of Savile Row, Napoleon III's personal tailor.[2] Seymour ha just arrived in the United States after four years as American minis ter to Russia. Pierce, Seymour, and Jefferson Davis were old friend from Mexican War days. The ex-President was not surprised, there fore, when Seymour warmly supported Davis as the presidenti nominee.[3]

As Pierce had put it when he suggested Davis, "our people ar looking for 'the coming man.' A man really fitted for this emer gency by his ability, courage, broad statesmanship and patriotism. The ex-President was extremely bitter about Northern abolitionist and Republicans. He predicted that if the Union were broken up bloodshed would inevitably follow, not only between the sectior but within the North as well. At the end of the meeting, as he bad his Connecticut friend goodbye, Pierce impressed upon Seymou the necessity to "overthrow political abolitionism" in the sprin

1. Pierce to Jefferson Davis, Jan. 6, 1860 (*Hartford Courant,* Sept. 22, 1863).
2. Seymour Papers, account rendered by Henry Poole, Aug. 6, 1859 (CHS).
3. *Hartford Courant* (Sept. 22, 1863).

ction. "You must repeal that unconstitutional and obnoxious ersonal liberty] law," he said vehemently.[4]

Seymour went home to a state that was beginning to quicken th intense political excitement. Everyone sensed that the Con- cticut election would be regarded as a significant test of strength tween the two great parties in the industrial North. With so ich at stake, the Democratic high command welcomed the secret vis candidacy as an objective that would give an underlying ise of purpose to their state campaign. Such powers as Isaac ucey, Buchanan's Navy secretary, Alfred E. Burr of the *Hart- d Times,* Minott Osborne of the *New Haven Register,* William Pomeroy of the *Bridgeport Farmer,* and the Ingersoll clan of w Haven, all agreed with the Pierce-Seymour estimate of Davis' ailability. The Mississippi Senator, they thought, would be the n most likely to carry both Southern ultras and Unionists, and the same time attract many Northern conservative votes. It was ential, however, that the Democrats win in the state election; d in order to do so, they needed a strong gubernatorial candidate o could rally conservative men irrespective of party. Of all the ominent Democrats in the state, Seymour had the best chance of ing this. He was personally on the best of terms with former ngressman James T. Pratt, Stephen A. Douglas' chief lieutenant Connecticut. Pratt, an unstable garrulous individual, was deeply lebted to Seymour for past services.[5] It seemed likely that Pratt d his following could be persuaded to support Seymour, who had en out of the country during the Buchanan Administration's ault on Douglas.[6] At any rate, Seymour agreed to be a candidate.[7]

The state convention, smoothly controlled by the *Times-Regis-* group, managed to nominate Seymour on the first ballot with- t any serious opposition.[8] Although conservative Democratic iders had privately resolved to seek repeal of Connecticut's Per- nal Liberty Law, publicly they were silent on the issue. They opted a platform that breathed union sentiment, supported the

4. Ibid.

5. Pratt to Thomas H. Seymour, July 17, 1855 (Thomas Hart Seymour Papers, CHS).

6. *Hartford Courant* (Feb. 16, 1860).

7. Jarlath Robert Lane, *A Political History of Connecticut during the Civil War* Vashington, 1941), p. 115.

8. *Hartford Times* (Feb. 16, 1860).

national administration and the Cincinnati Platform, and co demned John Brown's raid. The Republicans had renominat Buckingham and also had written a conciliatory platform—whic however, condemned unsparingly the extension of slavery into t territories. They too attacked John Brown's raid as outlawry, y balanced their criticism with an explicit censure of Southern fora into Kansas.[9]

Outwardly, Republican leaders seemed supremely confiden united behind their platform and their popular Governor with h record of two previous victories; but actually they were deep concerned about the future. The outcome of the manufacture meeting at Meriden had been a severe blow, and in an effort placate businessmen they had underscored a protective tariff plan which had been included in their platform.[10] Republicans we even more disturbed when an expected bolt of the Douglas Dem crats failed to materialize. They were faced with what appeared be a united party devoted to its leader and running hard on platform that had been carefully framed for voters with stead habits. When Republican leaders contrasted the bitter factionalis and the imperfect organization of their own party with the appa ent unity of their opponents, they could not help being dismaye Yet every effort to produce solidarity within Republican ranks cr ated new tensions in some other area. These were perhaps merely t growing pains of a new political organization; but time was ru ning out for the Republican party in 1860.

The most serious division was the mutual dislike and distru between the old-line Whigs and the anti-Nebraska Democrat Gideon Welles, who had the double distinction of being a found of both the Democratic and Republican parties in the state, w extremely bitter about the tendency of former Whigs to discrim nate against former Democrats. In a draft of a letter he had writte in 1859 to United States Senator Lafayette Foster, Welles remarke that "since the Presidential election there has been a dispositio with many to revive the Whig party on living issues." [11] A prou sensitive, and ambitious man, he felt that his suggestions had bee

9. *Hartford Courant* (Jan. 26, 1860).

10. Ibid.

11. Welles to Lafayette S. Foster, n.d., 1859 (Welles Papers, HL).

scarded and that he had been persecuted simply because of his emocratic antecedents. "I confess I am becoming tired of it," 'elles wrote. "I will go and vote while it avails, which under such anagement cannot be long, but I do not feel inclined to labor with uch zeal under such circumstances." [12] What had particularly censed the Hartford journalist-politician was a tendency he saw nong former Whigs to neglect principles for political expediency. f course, there is ample reason to believe that Welles, always a hot rtisan, could not distinguish between the Whigs he had fought ;ainst so bitterly in the hard-cider campaign of 1840 and the 'higs who joined the Republican party in 1856.

Yet it was undeniable that former old-line Whigs in the Republi- n party were soft on "Know-Nothingism," and not necessarily :cause they believed in its principles. Ex-Whigs James F. Babcock, litor of the *New Haven Palladium,* and Nehemiah D. Sperry, a 'ew Haven real estate speculator, were perhaps the most promi- :nt politicians of this variety. Both ambitious for office, they had :aded a movement in 1857 to change the name of the party from epublican to American-Republican.[13] Their activities had irri- .ted such prominent Know-Nothings as Orris S. Ferry, who re- nted being used for blatant personal preferment.[14] Welles harged that "real Republican issues were suppressed in order to corporate a Know-Nothing element in the Resolutions" and that ll foreign-born Republicans as well as "men of Democratic anteced- nt" had been "proscribed except for lesser positions." [15] A fur- her grievance of ex-Democrats and Free Soilers was that former Whigs had monopolized all of the prestigious offices won by the epublicans since 1856.[16] "You are right in saying that the radical)emocrats and Free Soilers are the soul of the Republicans," wrote arnest, intense Joseph R. Hawley to his father. "The old Whig :aders never had either principles or brains. They smashed their wn party—Greeley would bury our party in two years." [17]

In the state elections of 1858 and 1859 the Republicans may

12. Ibid.
13. Welles to A. N. Clark, 1859, undated draft (ibid.).
14. Orris S. Ferry to Hawley, Jan. 25, 1860 (Hawley Papers).
15. Welles to Clark, 1859 (Welles Papers, HL).
16. Ibid.
17. Hawley to Rev. Francis Hawley, March 11, 1860 (ibid.).

have been divided, but they were in better shape than their adve saries. They had profited from the deeply disruptive feud b tween[18] the Douglas supporters and the Administration machi in the state. In addition, the Democrats had chosen a weak canc date to head their ticket, the erratic Douglas Democrat James Pratt, in 1858 and 1859.[19] Civil War in Kansas and the depressi of 1857 had also hurt them. By 1860, however, the Democrats Connecticut had regained much lost ground. The depression w over; Kansas seemed destined to become a free state. Despite Sout ern intransigence, many important Connecticut manufacture were in a conservative, appeasing mood with respect to the Sout Most important, the Democrats were not only united behind the leader, Thomas H. Seymour, but for the first time in three yea were more than adequately supplied with campaign funds from t New York and Boston financial community.[20] It would appe that the only substantial resource of the Republican party in t state was Governor William A. Buckingham of Norwich. Now his fifty-sixth year, Buckingham was a short, stocky man who ruddy, regular features, white hair, and full sideburns gave him t appearance of a bluff-hearty English country squire. But there w nothing casual about his erect posture and neatness of dress, whi his deep-set bright blue eyes mirrored a certain strength of purpo and dignity.[21]

Born in Lebanon, Connecticut, Buckingham was the son of substantial farmer who had moved to this pleasant country tow from Saybrook. Though he knew heavy labor as only a Connect cut farm boy in the early years of the nineteenth century unde stood that phrase, he also knew the simple secure life of the sel sufficient farm family—"the brick meeting house," the primar school (in which he taught a term), the orderly discipline of deepl religious parents.

Apprenticed to a surveyor, Buckingham decided against this pro fession, and finally, at the age of nineteen, entered his uncle's dr goods store in Norwich. Here he showed strong aptitude for bus

18. Lane, pp. 98–99, 103–04.

19. Ibid.

20. *Springfield Republican* (March 26, 1860).

21. Samuel G. Buckingham, *The Life of William A. Buckingham, the War Governor c Connecticut* (Springfield, 1894), pp. 444–86.

ess and, with family encouragement, soon struck out for himself. or twenty years he operated the most successful dry goods store in orwich, which was fast developing into the farming and industrial center of eastern Connecticut. In 1848 he had the foresight to vest all of his capital in the new rubber industry, then slipping ut of the careless hands of Charles Goodyear. The principal organer of the Hayward Rubber Company in nearby Colchester, Buckgham managed this business so successfully that by 1856 he was a ch man.

Though still active in the affairs of Hayward, he entered state olitics that year as a Republican elector for Frémont. Nominated r governor on the Republican ticket in 1858 over such influential ntenders as Gideon Welles, Hartford's most influential politician, uckingham had won easily on his business record and his known oderate politics. Re-elected in 1859, he proved to be a capable, if ber, executive, whose sturdy conservatism appealed to both the rm and the business community as the state rode out the depreson of 1857. Buckingham had been a Whig prior to his affiliation ith the Republican party, and on national issues was known as an tremely cautious public man. Unlike many of his Whig colagues, he had never associated with the Know-Nothings, but he d not alienated them either.[22] If anyone could hold together the scordant elements of the party, Buckingham was the man.

Even this asset seemed slender indeed when pitted against the emocratic nominee. In personality, Thomas Hart Seymour was rtainly Buckingham's superior. Tall, genial, an excellent orator d debater, Seymour had had long public experience and familiar- with other lands and customs. All this made for a savoir faire at Buckingham could never hope to match.[23] A few trips to ratoga and Worcester, as well as to New York and Boston, had en the extent of Buckingham's travels outside his native state. ymour had been a colonel in the Mexican War, during which he d led the charge on Chapultepec. A congressman in his twenties, ur times governor of the state, he had just returned after serving United States minister to Russia. Differences in education beveen the two contestants were even more marked. Buckingham

22. *Springfield Republican* (Jan. 15, 1858); Lane, pp. 94–96.
23. Buckingham, pp. 47–48.

had a common school education; Seymour was a practicing law
yer.[24] The Democratic nominee was idolized by the conservati
party leaders and the rank and file, an affection that would remai
long after his death. Buckingham was not the master of his party i
1860, nor would he ever in subsequent years enjoy undisputed lea
ership. He would always stand as a bridge between such conserva
tives as United States Senator and party boss James Dixon, and suc
ambitious radicals-to-be as Mark Howard and Joseph R. Hawle

The Republican leadership in the state, distracted with its inte
nal feuds yet fully aware of the election's importance on the na
tional scene, desperately sought outside assistance. This w
promptly and generously given. Cassius Clay, the blustering Ken
tucky Republican, spoke at Hartford on February 25.[25] Lincol
made six speeches in the state in early March, and on his return t
Illinois he urged Senator Lyman Trumbull to help out. "They ar
having a desperate struggle in Connecticut," he wrote Trum
bull, ". . . the fiendish attempt now being made upon Connecticu
must not be allowed to succeed."[26] But something more tha
speeches had been needed, something dynamic enough to generate
higher level of enthusiasm in the party and among the people.
half-dozen kerosene torches, several yards of cambric cloth, a quick
witted Hartford banker, and a phrase-making editor provided th
correct formula. Spontaneously, the young men of the party, nc
the bickering leaders, applied it with vigor and imagination.

The Hartford County Republican Committee had arranged
torchlight parade to escort Cassius Clay from Mayor T. M. Allyn
home to Touro Hall, where he was to make the opening speech i
the state campaign. A group of clerks from Talcott and Post's dr
goods store, who had equipped themselves with kerosene torche
found to their dismay that the oil was leaking out and staining thei
clothes. As the parade reached the store, they dashed in and cu
lengths of cheap, black cambric cloth, which they draped ove
their heads and shoulders before rejoining the parade. Hartfor
banker George P. Bissell, who was parade marshal, noticed thei
dramatic appearance in the flickering smoky light of the torche

24. Ibid.
25. Ibid., p. 49.
26. Basler, *Lincoln*, *4*, 13, 34.

NEW-YORK ILLUSTRATED NEWS.

No. 40.—Vol. II. NEW-YORK, SATURDAY, AUGUST 11, 1860. Price Six Cents.

OPEN THIS PAPER WITH CARE BEFORE YOU CUT IT.

CONTENTS OF THIS WEEK'S NEWS.

Torchlight Procession and Banquet of the "Wide Awakes," at Hartford, Conn.

FOUNDERS AND OFFICERS OF THE "WIDE AWAKES" OF HARTFORD.

THE "SAVANNAH BLUES."

FUNERAL OF PRINCE JEROME NAPOLEON, AT PARIS.

THE JAPANESE SWINDLE.

INSIGNIA OF THE "WIDE AWAKES."

OFFICERS OF THE GRAND COMMANDERY OF KNIGHTS TEMPLAR, WASHINGTON, NO. 1.

Sketches of the Sicilian Revolution—View of a House in which Twenty-two Persons perished during the Bombardment—View of the Barricade in Toledo street, Palermo—Destruction of the Fort Castello-a-mare, at Palermo, by Garibaldi's Volunteers.

BY OUR SPECIAL ARTIST, TH. NAST, ESQ., NOW AT PALERMO.

DEPARTURE OF THE GREAT EASTERN FOR CAPE MAY.

VENEANCE OF ST. LOUIS AGAINST THE BROTHELS.

FOUNDERS AND OFFICERS OF THE "WIDE AWAKES" OF HARTFORD, CONN.—(See page 218.)

1. Young Connecticut in the campaign of 1860: Captain James S. Chalker (standing, third from right). Collection of J. Doyle Dewitt.

e sent them to the head of the procession, where they attracted e attention of an interested bystander, William Fuller, city editor the *Hartford Courant*. When Fuller wrote up the Clay speech, alluded to the striking appearance of these young men, whom he bbed "Wide Awakes." The phrase caught on first in Hartford, ere it led to the formation of the Wide Awakes, a semimilitary ung men's group. For the modest sum of $1.75, total cost of uipment—oil cloth cap, cape, and a kerosene torch—any young publican could join the Wide Awakes, with their meetings, ills, parades, and the exciting sense of actual participation in the mpaign.[27] There was even the added thrill of mild danger. ordes of young, pugnacious Irishmen dogged all Republican pades, where they caused as much disturbance as possible. Sometimes ese hecklers were paid a few cents each by Democratic ward ders, but generally they needed no financial encouragement. It is sheer delight for them to heave bricks into the ranks or wrench rches from Yankee foes. The military organization of the Wide wakes from the beginning had been aimed at preserving order d securing protection for the marchers.[28]

Wide Awake companies were quickly organized all over the ate. At least seven of them escorted Lincoln when he made his eriden speech on March 7.[29] By mid-summer they were a feature all state Republican rallies, and the idea had been picked up by epublican organizations in other states throughout the North and e West.

This was what the campaign needed: a device to arouse the youth Connecticut, who then communicated their exuberance, as only ung people can do, to the stolid mass of conservative citizenry in e land of steady habits. The Democrats quickly countered with eymour Clubs" and even adopted torches, capes, and caps of a fferent style, but they were never able to duplicate the enthusiasm spired by the Wide Awake organization, nor match the magic of s name. If the young Republicans in Connecticut had not seized e initiative and added such a dynamic dimension to the cam-

27. *Hartford Courant* (March 3, 1860); Oscar W. Firkins, *Cyrus Northrop, a Memoir* linneapolis, 1925), p. 174.

28. J. Doyle Dewitt, "Lincoln in Hartford" (Hartford, 1962), p. 13; *Hartford Count* (March 3, 1860).

29. *Hartford Courant* (March 9, 1860).

paign, it is probable that the Democrats would have won. As it w Buckingham defeated Seymour by the narrow margin of 541 vo out of the 88,395 cast. By Connecticut standards, the turnout been enormous, almost 10,000 more votes cast than in the elect of 1859.[30] Seymour carried all the cities except Norwich and N London, but lost heavily in eastern Connecticut and in the coun towns and villages.[31] Republicans also won a good working maj ity in both houses of the legislature, ensuring the re-election Lafayette Foster to the United States Senate.[32]

As soon as it was certain that the state ticket and the legislat were safely Republican, aspiring politicians began to plan for national convention. The *New Haven Palladium* editor, James Babcock, who had entertained Lincoln at his home in New Hav was one of the first to support the Illinoisian as the Republi candidate for president. Writing to Lincoln on April 8, Babc said that he had heard his name "mentioned more freely than e in connection with the Chicago nomination." [33] The *Palladium* e tor requested a list of Lincoln's confidential "friends" with wh he might open a political correspondence. Lincoln sent him the and the wily Babcock made good use of letters from David Da Senator James W. Grimes of Iowa, and the popular Ohio congr man Samuel R. Curtis, to boost Lincoln's candidacy.[34]

Lincoln's speeches in New York and Connecticut had mad strong impression, but few influential Republicans were ready accept him as the party's candidate. Horace Greeley, who was s porting Edward Bates of Missouri at this time, persuaded many t such a compromise candidate was needed.[35] In late March for Whig senator Truman Smith of Stamford, Bates' manager in state, was convinced that the entire Connecticut delegation wo go for the Missouri conservative.[36] Smith was overly optimis

30. Buckingham, *Life*, p. 51.

31. Ibid.

32. Ibid., p. 53.

33. Babcock to Abraham Lincoln, April 8, 1860 (R. T. Lincoln Papers, LC).

34. Basler, *Lincoln*, *4*, 34.

35. Babcock to Lincoln, April 8, 1860 (Lincoln Papers); Hawley to Francis Haw March 4, 1860 (Hawley Papers).

36. Howard K. Beale, ed., *The Diary of Edward Bates 1859–1866*, *4*, Annual Repor the American Historical Association for the Year 1930 (Washington, 1933), p. 114.

Gideon Welles, who would head the delegation, was still uncommitted. Although sympathetic to Bates' conservatism, Welles habitually distrusted old-time Whigs. He and most of his influential Hartford friends were inclined toward Salmon P. Chase or John C. Frémont.[37] When the Democratic party split at Charleston and it became possible for the Republicans to nominate a less conservative candidate, the Connecticut delegation characteristically moved the other way. If the Bates candidacy had been weakened by the rupture in the Democratic party, it was strengthened in Connecticut.[38] William H. Seward, the leading candidate, was applauded for his antislavery stand but was condemned for his free-spending financial policies and his critical attitude of state rights. Moreover, all Connecticut Republicans who had been Democrats would never accept what they regarded as Seward's ultra-Whig tendencies. Salmon P. Chase of Ohio also had some support, particularly among younger Republicans like Joseph R. Hawley of the *Hartford Press*, who preferred Chase, with Frémont as a second choice.[39] The Connecticut delegation was friendly toward Lincoln, a sentiment that Babcock was able to exploit; yet only two out of the twelve delegates at Chicago, E. S. Tweedy of Danbury and George H. Noble of New Milford, voted for Lincoln on all ballots.[40]

Republicans seemed satisfied, if not warmly enthusiastic, with the nomination of Lincoln and of Hannibal Hamlin of Maine as his running mate. Governor Buckingham summed up the popular attitude in his brief note of congratulations to Lincoln. He hoped to see an honest government that would "not impinge upon the national rights of any section of our common country." [41] Considering the factional nature of the party before the spring election, it was surprisingly well unified in its support of the national ticket and platform. Even the Abolitionists fell into line. Indeed, one of their spokesmen fervently defended Lincoln when he came under attack by Wendell Phillips in early July. Phillips had publicly stigmatized Lincoln as "a slave hound and a knave!" [42] Joseph R. Hawley, who

37. Bissell to Welles, n.d., 1860 (Welles Papers, HL).
38. Ibid.; Lane, *Connecticut*, pp. 129–30.
39. Hawley to Francis Hawley, March 4, 1860 (Hawley Papers).
40. F. Wildman to Hawley, Jan. 19, 1861 (ibid.).
41. Buckingham to Lincoln, May 21, 1860 (Lincoln Papers).
42. Hawley to Wendell Phillips, July 17, 1860 (Hawley Papers).

was on intimate terms with the Abolitionists of Hartford, rebuked Phillips in a highly emotional letter. After stating that he had been an Abolitionist since early youth, Hawley wrote, "this is the first time I have felt really insulted, grossly wronged, and felt as if no gentleman would have done it." "I know Mr. Lincoln," the angry young editor continued, "he is not quite up to my standards, but he has always been ahead of his neighbors; he has fought gallantly, honorably and unselfishly." [43] Lincoln was perhaps not up to the standards of many Connecticut Republicans, but they were not about to jeopardize a certain victory that would bring with it the coveted spoils of office. After the failure of Democratic leaders to restore harmony among the factions, and the emergence of the Douglas, Breckenridge, and Bell candidacies, it had become obvious that the Republicans would carry the state in the presidential election. Therefore, little effort was expended by party leaders to push the campaign. Democrats fought bitterly among themselves. Thomas H. Seymour headed the Breckenridge group, and James T. Pratt, tardily aware of the anti-Douglas conspiracy, struck back with all the fury of his splenetic nature.[44]

While their elders busied themselves in working out a proper division of the expected patronage, young Republicans shouldered the major burden of the campaign. The 26-year-old Cyrus Northrop, for example, besides being secretary of the Connecticut Wide Awakes and party chief in Fairfield County, superintended all local political meetings, printed and distributed all handbills, posters, and ballots for the election in every town of the county, and paid all the election expenses with the money he had been allocated by the state central committee. In addition to these chores, which Northrop performed without staff, he spoke two or three times a week at political rallies and somehow found time to prepare for his bar examinations.[45] During July he and other state officers of the Wide Awakes arranged the most spectacular event of the campaign, a torchlight parade in Hartford of more than 2,000 members from all over the northeast. On this occasion, fortunately, the

43. Ibid.

44. Lane, pp. 136–37.

45. Firkins, *Northrop*, pp. 174–75.

young Republicans were assisted by the national and state committees and the city merchants, who cooperated in putting on one of the most gaudy fireworks displays Hartford had ever seen.[46]

As had been assumed, Lincoln won handily. The total vote cast was 77,292, 11,000 less than the vote cast in the state election. But Lincoln received 43,792, only 676 votes behind Buckingham's total of the previous April. At least 10,000 Democrats failed to go to the polls in November. Those who did cast ballots were split principally between Douglas and Breckenridge, with the Illinois Senator receiving 15,522 votes, while the ultra Southern candidate polled 14,641. John Bell, the border states' candidate, received 1,485 votes—1,852 having been cast for fusion, Douglas and Bell. Lincoln had a majority of 10,292 over the combined opposition.[47] A disturbing factor, though one not recognized at the time, was the unusually large Breckenridge vote. Since the most distinguished Democrats in the state—Thomas H., Origen S., and Daniel M. Seymour, the Burrs of the *Hartford Times,* Minott Osborne of the *New Haven Register,* and the Ingersolls of New Haven—were all avowed Breckenridge supporters, Southern ultras could count on numerous highly articulate allies within the very stronghold of their Northern enemies.

An earnest of pro-Southern intent was given by Daniel M. Seymour of Hartford, a cousin of Colonel Seymour. On November 20, 1860, exactly one month before South Carolina seceded, Seymour wrote Governor Gist of South Carolina, enclosing his personal check for $1,000 to be invested for him in the new 6 per cent state bonds. These had been approved by the legislature to provide funds for the arming of South Carolina. Praising the Governor's action in calling for a secession convention, Seymour said that "compromises will be offered to cheat her [South Carolina] into surrender of those rights, but as a friend to liberty, I beg of her never to surrender." Clearly he thought that the bold action of separation would force "the cringing North not only to make amends but give her stronger guarantees, such as may not hereafter be misconstrued, that the rights of the sovereign states shall be again in-

46. *New York Illustrated News* (Aug. 11, 1860).
47. *New Haven Palladium* (Nov. 10, 1860).

volved."[48] At the time Seymour wrote to Gist, an extra session of the South Carolina legislature had just adjourned after having approved the call for a secession convention, ordering out 10,000 volunteers to resist, if necessary, Federal authority and appropriating a million dollars to arm and equip them.

Such precipitate action following Lincoln's election seemed to confirm Southern threats. But only the Breckenridge Democrats took South Carolina's action seriously. The *Hartford Times* and the *New Haven Register* immediately adopted a tone of crisis and demanded broad concessions to the South. These newspapers were particularly concerned with Connecticut's Personal Liberty Law. They urged instant repeal by a special session of the legislature to be convoked for that purpose. Their warnings, however, were discounted as the fulminations of a defeated political faction. Most Connecticut citizens were unaware of the extent of the crisis. And despite the financial flurries that followed the actual secession of South Carolina on December 20, they still refused to believe that the Union was in serious danger. There had been similar threats in 1832, 1850, and 1856; each time the nation had pulled through. Many conservative businessmen felt somewhat abashed at their panic action following John Brown's raid. Significantly, even those manufacturers who were active Democrats did not press for another Meriden convention, nor did they make any public expression of alarm. If a majority of the people seemed disposed to let events take their course at this stage, political leaders, who were closer to the actual situation, recognized that some sort of showdown was imminent.

The younger element among the Republicans, perhaps overly influenced by Lincoln's mandate in Connecticut, welcomed this with a kind of grim satisfaction. Enjoying the excitement of the crisis, consulting and being consulted, they were always ready to stiffen the backbones of their seniors at home or in Washington. The momentum of the campaign would simply not be stopped by Lincoln's election. Young Republicans were in a dangerous mood. For once they were involved in an issue that was important and exciting, one that commanded a large measure of public accept-

48. Seymour to William H. Gist, Nov. 30, 1860; Gist to Seymour, Dec. 7, 1860. *Hartford Courant* (March 30, 1865).

ance. What a relief from the humdrum of a small Connecticut city or a country town to participate in such great events, to face down the arrogant Southerner, to live again the thrill of marching with 2,000 comrades in a torchlight parade. Their high-spirited attitude was reckless, totally un-Connecticut, even belligerent, but highly infectious. It stirred the more responsible senior citizens as they had not been stirred since the days of Andrew Jackson.

Hawley and young Charles Dudley Warner, who had recently joined the staff of the *Press*, reveled in the atmosphere of gathering tension. Day and night the cluttered *Press* office was thronged with Republican political and social bigwigs. Tall, white-bearded Gideon Welles spent a large part of each day there, now commanding the attention of the group in his quiet, logical way, now recalling the party battles of his youth, now engaged in his incessant writing at a corner table. Smooth-faced, ruddy Calvin Day, one of the richest men in Hartford, and dark, nervous Mark Howard, already a leading figure in local insurance circles, were frequent visitors. Everyone brought in some part of his daily correspondence to be eagerly and confidentially discussed by all. Through all the hubbub Hawley and Warner not only put out the paper but found time to conduct their own voluminous correspondence. And they enjoyed it hugely. In New Haven, Cyrus Northrop divided his attention between the offices of the *Palladium* and the *Journal and Courier*, writing what he called his "torpedoes" for both papers.[49]

In Washington, Connecticut's youthful representatives (average age: 36) were nearly as eager for a showdown as their friends at home. Two of the delegation, Alfred A. Burnham and John W. Woodruff, voted against the resolution, raising a committee of 33 to consider measures of conciliation.[50] Nor could it be said that those who voted for it were in any mood to appease the South. Representative Orris S. Ferry of Norwalk supported the resolution but reassured a worried Hawley that "we must not compromise one iota of the Chicago platform." "We have got three things to do," Ferry explained to the *Press* editor, "first, to do right; second, to

49. Firkins, p. 186; "A Memoir of Joseph R. Hawley and Arthur Shipman," *Hartford Times* (Jan. 28, 1832).

50. W. A. Croffut and John M. Morris, *The Military and Civil History of Connecticut during the War of 1861–65* (New York, 1868), p. 32.

overthrow forever the power of slavery; third, to save the Republic. The President is a traitor; traitors are in the Senate; traitors are in the House." [51] The older senators, both former Whigs, were far more disposed to compromise. James Dixon, in particular, stated on the floor of the Senate that "my constituents are ready to make any sacrifice which a reasonable man can ask or an honorable man grant." Hot-tempered Representative Dwight Loomis of Windham County was certain that Dixon would stretch his definition of "honorable" to the limit.[52] Indeed, all of Dixon's efforts to seek an abatement of the crisis through concession were bitterly assailed by most Republicans at home. Only the *Hartford Courant,* whose editor, A. N. Clark, was deeply indebted to the Senator, defended his actions in seeking some variation of the Crittenden Compromise that would be acceptable to the hostile sections. David Bartlett, a Hartford Republican, wrote his friend James Beekman of New York that Dixon "was a gentleman and a Christian, but in times like the present it would not do for all our statesmen to be as gentle as he—as mild and compliant as he." [53]

Rumors of treason and compromise in Washington during January 1861 roused most Connecticut Republicans to a high pitch of anxiety and anger. All varieties of Republican thought joined in attacking the weak and fumbling Buchanan Administration. Some feared that the lame duck President would deliver the Federal government to the South; others felt that the President and his alleged Southern allies would frustrate Lincoln's inauguration. Most, however, deplored his failure to exert leadership. When Buchanan asked the American people to pray for the Union, David Bartlett stigmatized him as "a poor, miserable old man." [54] And Gideon Welles wrote in his diary, "wretched man! Most of our public troubles are to be attributed to his weakness and wilful perversity." [55] Despite his contempt for the lame-duck Buchanan Administration, Welles, at the request of Senator Foster, wrote his former associate Isaac Toucey, Secretary of the Navy, "urging him

51. Orris S. Ferry to Hawley, Dec. 31, 1860 (Hawley Papers).
52. Dwight Loomis to Hawley, Dec. 17, 1860 (ibid.).
53. David E. Bartlett to Beekman, Jan. 2, 1861 (James Beekman Papers, NYHS).
54. Ibid.
55. Gideon Welles, Diary (unpublished), Jan. 4, 1861 (Welles Papers, HL).

to do right and stand by his country while treason is at work."[56] Welles had not even spoken with Toucey for six years and had little confidence that his letter would accomplish anything. "He is no statesman," concluded the diarist tartly, "but a narrow-minded partisan."[57]

While Welles and others kept up a constant correspondence with the decision makers in Washington, Joseph Hawley impulsively determined to visit the national capital for an on-the-spot evaluation of the crisis. "My very soul was sick with the rumors of compromise and I wanted to talk a little of God's truth *right at* the men who are preparing it or likely to be drawn into the treachery," the young editor wrote his father.[58] His expenses paid by a group of Hartford Republicans, Hawley left Saturday noon, January 4, traveled all night, arriving in Washington at six o'clock Sunday morning. Without sleep, except fitful dozing in the stuffy, jolting railroad car, Hawley immediately began a round of visits with congressmen that lasted until midnight. He saw Henry Wilson, John Sherman, and Charles Sumner; he had a long talk with Representative Bingham of Ohio, whom he thought "a true man," and with a half-dozen other congressmen. Finally, he buttonholed Thurlow Weed. At first "the Dictator" of New York State politics was attracted to this earnest, energetic young editor and exuded all of his formidable charm. But Hawley was appalled at Weed's compromising views. "Thurlow Weed is the most dangerous foe to liberty that lives in this country," he wrote, "he is either scared to death or a bought traitor." Weed was busily promoting his version of the so-called border state compromise, which would strengthen the Fugitive Slave Law and restore the Missouri Compromise line dividing free and slave states.[59] He soon realized that he had caught a tartar in young Hawley, who told him bluntly that such appeasement "would smash the party" and accused him of merely making a "good record against secession" rather than doing anything to prevent it. Anger flashed from the eyes of the New York

56. Lafayette Foster to Welles, Jan. 3, 1860; Welles to Toucey, Jan. 4, 1860 (Welles Papers, LC).

57. Diary, Jan. 5, 1861.

58. Hawley to Francis Hawley, Jan. 7, 1861 (Hawley Papers).

59. Glyndon G. Van Dusen, *Thurlow Weed, Wizard of the Lobby* (Boston, 1947), p. 266.

State political boss, and the two men parted under strained circumstances. The impetuous Hawley had much to learn about political tactics and would soon regret his caustic comments to such a powerful figure. But at the time, he regarded it as his duty to face down anyone, however powerful politically, who was attempting conciliation. Even Senator John Sherman of Ohio came under suspicion of "playing a deep politician's game," of secretly engineering compromise. "I wonder that God does not sink this city," Hawley declared vehemently.[60]

Typical of the hard line being pushed by young Republicans was the attitude of Isaac Bromley, 27-year-old editor of the *Norwich Bulletin.* Handling his pen like a cavalry saber, Bromley hacked at the compromise measures with a great deal of vehemence but with little finesse. In a *Bulletin* editorial of January 12 he declared that the compromise proposed treating with "armed traitors," giving slavery a broad belt of territory, and stimulating "the appetite of the South for yet greater demands." Nevertheless when the Crittenden Compromise finally failed and the only course appeared to be complete surrender to the South on all points, including slavery in the territories, even temperate Republicans such as James Dixon dropped their appeasing attitude.[61]

The sudden stiffening of Buchanan's position with respect to the demands of the South Carolina commissioners embarrassed Connecticut's Breckenridge Democrats. They had taken their cue from the President's State of the Union address to the Second Session of the 36th Congress. Throughout December the editorial columns of the *Times, Register,* and *Norwich Aurora* argued that while secession might be unconstitutional, it was impossible to coerce a sovereign state. When five more Southern states adopted ordinances of secession during early January 1861, and Buchanan still refused to give up Federal property in South Carolina, they began to agitate for a peaceful dissolution of the Union. Burr, Osborne, and William S. Pomeroy of the *Bridgeport Farmer* thought that secession was a temporary, local phenomenon brought about by Republican intransigence—merely a partisan tactic, a bargaining position that would teach their political opponents the facts of life. Public opin-

60. Hawley to Francis Hawley, Jan. 7, 1861 (Hawley Papers).

61. Lane, *Connecticut,* pp. 149–50.

ion, these Breckenridge editors asserted, would soon force the Northern Republicans to modify their stand and let the seceded states return to the Union on their own terms. To such extreme Democrats time was the important factor to develop the realities of the situation; "fratricidal war" was absolutely unthinkable. In an effort to impress Congress with their views, they supervised the sending of "peace" petitions from almost every city and town in the state.[62]

From Norwich, Governor Buckingham viewed the political crisis with a mounting concern. Though not in complete accord with the extremists of his own party, the Governor had become disgusted with Buchanan's constitutional scruples and wavering course of action. John A. Rockwell, an old friend of Buckingham and a former Whig congressman who had represented Connecticut's second district during the Mexican War, urged the Governor to call a special session of the legislature for repeal of the Personal Liberty Law. Rockwell, now a Republican and a Washington lobbyist, reflected the traditional fears of conservatives. The Governor politely rejected Rockwell's suggestion. His stand was both practical and moderate but unyielding on principles. "I do not believe it [the General Assembly] would repeal the law," the Governor replied, "for to many members it would appear to be yielding to the threatening attitude of the South." "Even if it were repealed," he argued, "that would not calm the tempest for the grievances of the South lie deeper." The issue, to Buckingham, was the Southern contention that the Federal government must defend slavery in the territories, a stand fraught with "greater evils to our community than the terrible calamities of revolution and disunion which now threaten us." [63]

Writing Lincoln two days after Christmas 1860 to recommend Gideon Welles for the cabinet, Buckingham urged a strong nationalist administration and hoped that the President-elect would be able "to execute the laws all over our land in spite of the combinations of states." When he looked over what he had written, the Governor crossed out the word "states" and substituted "trai-

62. *Congressional Globe*, 36th Congress, 2d Sess. 1860–61, part 1, pp. 698–992; part 2, pp. 993–1264.

63. Buckingham to John H. Rockwell, Dec. 8, 1860 (John A. Rockwell Papers, HL).

tors."[64] Convictions were rapidly forming in his mind, and events were only serving to harden them. Buckingham's response to the tensions of early January indicated that he was evaluating the crisis carefully and was almost, though not entirely, committed to the inevitability of conflict. Major Robert Anderson's evacuation of Federal troops from Fort Moultrie to Fort Sumter in Charleston Harbor, and the firing on the *Star of the West* on January 9 as she vainly tried to provision the Fort, made him angry—so angry, in fact, that when he received the request of ex-President Tyler that Connecticut send delegates to a peace conference at Washington, his first thought was "no."[65] But the Governor was prudent. As a businessman he distrusted judgments made in an emotional state; as a careful politician he would not take sole responsibility for such an important decision. Though doubting the efficacy of any more conferences, he decided to seek advice. "What do you think of the expediency of appointing commissioners to the convention of the Fourth instant?" the Governor telegraphed Gideon Welles. An equally cautious Welles sounded out Calvin Day, Mark Howard, and Joseph Hawley before he telegraphed his reply: "It will be well to have the state represented." Welles later learned that Buckingham had not received an official invitation to send commissioners. "Had I known this fact, I doubt if I should have so promptly advised the appointment," he recorded in his diary; yet, on further reflection, he concluded that the conference would at least demonstrate to the border states that the North was acting in good faith, exploring all avenues of a peaceful solution.[66]

Acting upon Welles' advice, the Governor chose six delegates, not one of whom held extreme views. Two ex-governors—Roger S. Baldwin of New Haven, immensely respected, a Unionist but a conservative, and Chauncey F. Cleveland, a former Democrat—headed the group.[67] Other delegates were Douglas Democrats Charles J. McCurdy of Lyme and James T. Pratt, now thoroughly estranged from the Seymour group; these men were balanced by two moderate Republicans, Robbins Battell and Amos Treat.[68]

64. Buckingham to Lincoln, Dec. 28, 1860 (Lincoln Papers).
65. Lane, p. 151.
66. Diary, Feb. 3–4, 1861.
67. Croffut and Morris, *Connecticut*, pp. 34–35.
68. Ibid.

Governor Buckingham gave the delegation strict instructions that narrowed the limits of compromise to a razor's edge. They were to be conciliatory; they were, however, to maintain the dignity and authority of the government; and they were to give no sanction to measures that would force the government into new guarantees of slavery. In fact, going further, Buckingham defined slavery as a "principle subversive of the foundations of a free government." Thus the Connecticut delegation, if it followed instructions, was well nigh powerless at the onset to meet upon any middle ground.[69] Despite this handicap, Baldwin at Washington strenuously urged a national convention to propose amendments to the Constitution, a proposition that was rejected, thirteen states to five.[70] Thereafter, the Connecticut delegates voted against all convention proposals.[71]

When Buckingham reported to the legislature in May on Connecticut's participation, he stressed the facts that the deliberations of the peace convention were held without authority of law and that he had been unable to find any circumstances requiring that the General Assembly be called to consider it.[72] The Governor's conscience was clear. He had sent delegates, he was a man of peace; and what was even more comforting, his instructions to the Connecticut delegates would not be public property until the event had become ancient history, as in fact it was when he told the legislature about it.

As early as February 1861, Connecticut Republicans had temporarily settled their differences and closed ranks, and were awaiting the inauguration of Abraham Lincoln. Waverers had been brought into line. Spurred on by the determination of their younger colleagues, seasoned party leaders seemed to have accepted the belligerent symbol of the Wide Awakes. At the other extreme, the hard core of Breckenridge Democrats were obstinate defenders of the seceded states. Thomas H. Seymour had not been dubbed "the hero of Chapultepec" for shirking what he regarded as his duty. Inevitably, such intense friction descended from newspaper name-calling

69. Buckingham Papers, 1860 (CSL).
70. Croffut and Morris, p. 35.
71. Ibid.
72. *Senate Journal* (May Sess., 1861).

to personal innuendo. Close friends who happened to differ in politics could now no longer tolerate even social connections.

On February 11 Gideon Welles met Charles F. Pond on Main Street in Hartford. Pond, one of the city's richest men, was a successful railroad promoter, private banker, and inveterate Democrat. Formerly, the two had been close friends, but their relationship had been strained by politics. In the course of their conversation Pond noted "that men would not go from here south to fight." "What do you mean by that remark?" asked Welles sharply. "Do you mean that men from here would not go south or anywhere to support the Constitution and Union and enforce the laws? Will they go north to fight and not south? If there is an insurrection in Portsmouth, New Hampshire, will not men go from here if necessary to suppress the traitors or rebels?" Pond refused to answer and shifted his comments to Congress, which he described as traitorous. "In what respect are members of Congress traitors?" inquired Welles. "Because they did not settle their difficulties by voting for the Crittenden Compromise," Pond answered. "That would increase the difficulties," said Welles, "for I should despise them if they would vote for it and so would those who elected them." "Do you not approve of the Compromise?" asked Pond. "I have only contempt for it," was the icy reply. Accustomed to deference and respect for his opinion, Pond reddened with anger. Without another word, he turned his back and marched away.[73]

It had been just over a year since Thomas Seymour and Franklin Pierce had made their plans to place Jefferson Davis in the White House. They had then been important figures in a great national political organization. In Connecticut, at least, their opponents, crippled by factionalism, had seemed ripe for defeat. Now, Seymour and his associates represented a mere faction of a party that no longer existed. The power they thought they held had been warped and weakened in the fierce firestorm of sectional controversy; the prestige and respect they had once enjoyed in the community had been blackened. Ambitious Republicans with a sure instinct for the jugular were not above using the political crisis to menace their status. For the time being at least, conservative Democrats were fast becoming social pariahs in a community which they

73. Welles, Diary, Feb. 11, 1861.

had ruled economically, if not always politically, for the past quarter of a century. As Welles put it, Pond and his fellow Democrats "exhibit the animus of a class—wealthy . . . and proud who assume tone but are partisans to the verge of treason." [74]

Looking back on the campaigns of 1860, Sheldon B. Thorpe of North Haven, a sergeant in the 15th Connecticut Volunteers, decided that "Providence had had many a lad in training . . . and they who marched in the uniformed ranks of the 'Wide-Awakes' of that year, learned a drill that was of inestimable service to them and others in the ranks of the Union Army." [75] In Connecticut the Republicans were "wide awake," and if war were to result, most seemed ready to shoulder the responsibility, ready to bear the consequence.

74. Ibid.

75. Sheldon B. Thorpe, *The History of the Fifteenth Connecticut Volunteers in the War for the Defense of the Union, 1861–1865* (New Haven, 1893), pp. 14–15.

3. FORT SUMTER

ON JANUARY 17, 1861, eight days after the Sumter relief ship *Star of the West* had been turned back by the batteries of Fort Moultrie and Castle Pinckney, Governor Buckingham issued an emergency proclamation. In reviewing the actions of the seceded states,[1] the Governor considered them frankly to be both traitorous and irrational. He felt that conflict was quite possible, and he alerted the people to the possibility that the active services of the state militia might be required in the near future. With bold language, Buckingham hoped to awaken the people. He would minimize, if possible, the certain confusion that would follow a sudden outbreak of hostilities.[2] Without consulting anyone, he ordered the state's quartermaster general to begin purchasing equipment for 5,000 men.[3]

A rapidly deteriorating situation in the deep South argued the correctness of the Governor's course. That he had delayed so long was the result of his instinctive caution. He knew that the powerful Democratic press would attack any policy of preparedness, and he also knew that those pressing for action in his own party did not as yet represent a majority opinion.[4] As the Governor had expected, the *New Haven Register*, speaking for the Breckenridge Democrats, reacted strongly to the proclamation. "We trust," it said, "that he [the Governor] is not so far lost to common sense as to suppose the people of this state are disposed to draw the sword to compel seceding states to return to the Union! The idea is preposterous and the threat conveyed by such Chinese rub-dubbing is ridiculous." [5]

1. *Hartford Courant* (Jan. 17, 1861).
2. Buckingham, *Life,* p. 131.
3. Croffut and Morris, p. 34.
4. *New Haven Register* (Jan. 31, 1861).
5. Ibid. (Jan. 17, 1861).

Although conservative Democrats chose to ignore it, Southern agents had been placing large orders for some time in Connecticut arms factories and powder works.[6] As early as June 1860 W. L. Sykes, adjutant general of Mississippi, had concluded a contract with Eli Whitney, Jr., for the delivery of 1,500 rifles with bayonets, 1,000 of which were to be delivered by December 1, 1860. This particular contract was never fulfilled, because the samples Whitney shipped were not up to contract specifications.[7] On December 29, 1860, however, Whitney did ship eight wagonloads of pistols and carbines to his New York agency for sale to Southern customers.[8] Samuel Colt, whose political arguments were confined to the drawing room when business was concerned, put his huge Hartford factory on a twenty-hour, two-shift basis.[9] It was common knowledge that Colt's—and Sharps', also of Hartford—had more Southern orders than they could handle.[10] On November 19, for example, John C. Palmer, superintendent of Sharps', shipped 180 cases of carbines and 40,000 cartridges to the state of Georgia,[11] and during February 1861 the public learned that large Alabama and Georgia orders for firearms were being filled at the Whitneyville factory of Eli Whitney, Jr. When the *New Haven Journal and Courier* smoked this information out, enough pressure was brought to bear on Whitney to force that close-mouthed gentleman to publish a notice in the New Haven papers. Whitney stated vaguely that he was "doing nothing that would not bear a thorough investigation." "But," exclaimed the *Courier*, "cases of muskets consigned to gentlemen of Richmond, Virginia, continue to make their unmistakable appearance at the Adams Express Company in the New Haven depot." [12] John Forsyth, one of the Confederate commissioners seeking to treat with the United States government, was particularly active as a purchasing agent for arms and ammunition. In early April 1861 he ordered for immediate delivery

6. *Hartford Courant* (Dec. 10, 1860).
7. War of the Rebellion, *OR*, Ser. IV, 1, 62–63.
8. *Hartford Courant* (Dec. 31, 1860).
9. Ibid.
10. *Norwich Courier* (Jan. 30, 1861).
11. *Hartford Courant* (Nov. 20, 1860).
12. *New Haven Journal and Courier* (Feb. 3, 4, 1861); *Norwich Bulletin* (Feb. 5, 7, 8, 1861).

2,000 new Colt army pistols at $25 each, and 2,000 Sharps' rifles at $22.50 each.[13]

Gunpowder manufacturers also did a heavy and profitable business with various Southern state governments during the winter of 1860–61. Governor Pickens of South Carolina purchased 300,000 pounds of powder from the Hazard Powder Company of Hazardville, Connecticut, in late January 1861.[14] On February 21 Jefferson Davis, recently inaugurated as provisional President of the Confederacy, instructed Captain Raphael Semmes to visit the Hazard Powder Company and purchase as much powder as possible. "You will probably be able to obtain cannon and musket powder, the former to be of the coarsest grain," President Davis advised. In addition, Davis authorized Semmes to employ Augustus Hazard "for the establishment of a powder mill at some point in the limits of our territory." [15] Semmes met the Connecticut powder manufacturer during March and purchased one ton of large grain powder.[16] Shortly thereafter John Forsyth learned that Hazard was willing to sell 200–300 tons of powder for twenty cents a pound. Confederate Secretary of War Leroy P. Walker sanctioned its purchase "if the powder has been tested and is cannon powder." On April 7, 1861, Forsyth concluded satisfactory arrangements with Hazard, purchasing 200 tons of his best cannon powder for $80,000.[17] No one bothered to note the following week that good Connecticut powder had battered the walls and casemates of Fort Sumter.

Business acquaintances of Buckingham in the Norwich vicinity had already decided that they had better secure raw cotton while it was still in supply; and from early December until the attack on Sumter, they kept all the coasters to that city busy bringing the staple into Norwich, where it was freighted to points north along the Norwich and Worcester Railroad.[18] The brisk demand caused price spirals, and those who bought for speculation became the first

13. *OR*, Ser. IV, *1*, 212–13.

14. Charles E. Cauthen, *South Carolina Goes to War, 1860–65* (Chapel Hill, 1950), p. 116; *OR*, Ser. I, *6*, 268–69.

15. Davis to Raphael Semmes, Feb. 21, 1861; *OR*, Ser. IV, *1*, 106–07.

16. L. P. Walker to Semmes, April 1, 1861; *OR*, Ser. IV, *1*, 202.

17. *OR*, Ser. IV, *1*, 216.

18. *Norwich Courier* (Jan. 26, 1861).

var profiteers in the state.[19] Where some profited from the secession, others were not so fortunate. A fishing fleet from Mystic was seized off the coast of Florida, confiscated under an old statute, and the Mystic men imprisoned. They were eventually released after paying a nominal fine, but their brief detention caused considerable excitement and a flurry of correspondence between Governor Buckingham and the Florida state authorities.[20]

Little daily incidents, too, brought secession and possibilities of war closer to the general public. New Haven citizens awoke one morning in early January to see a huge South Carolina palmetto flag waving from the ramparts of Fort Hale, a crumbling, abandoned defense work, at the mouth of New Haven harbor. Hoisted on a fifty-foot staff, the flag was visible for miles. For a brief period, some New Haven alarmists predicted that the port would be blockaded or even the city attacked by a filibustering expedition. City authorities, though doubting that New Haven was in any immediate danger, decided to take no chances. They ordered out a company of the New Haven Greys, who reconnoitered its vacant ramparts and concluded that the flag had been only a Yale student prank.[21]

Two weeks later, less jittery New Haven residents laughed when they saw three Negroes with large secession badges parading on the green. This rustic jeer at Southern pretensions provoked instant retaliation. The same evening several Southern students managed to tie another large palmetto flag to the steeple of Yale's Alumni Hall.[22] A dry goods merchant in New Haven exploited the popular interest: to advertise his goods, he featured South Carolina and secession in his *Palladium* advertisement.[23] And Isaac Bromley, editor of the *Norwich Bulletin,* captured the imagination of the public by sending a penholder made from the wood of Benedict Arnold's birthplace, with the inscription, "1780 speaks to 1861," to Jefferson Davis, new president of the Confederacy.[24] The populace, therefore, was not unduly shocked when the Governor issued,

19. Ibid.
20. Ibid. (Jan. 12, 1861).
21. *New Haven Journal and Courier* (Jan. 7, 1861).
22. Ibid. (Jan. 23, 1861).
23. *New Haven Palladium* (Jan. 3, 1861).
24. *Norwich Courier* (Jan. 3, 1861).

on January 26, his General Orders No. 227, directing that militia units be filled and careful arms and equipment inspection undertaken immediately.[25]

In the midst of the excitement came the party nominations and elections. The Democrats, meeting in convention on February 6 with the news before them of the Montgomery, Alabama, convention, regarded secession as a *fait accompli.*[26] Peace at any price became their credo; coercion, a pernicious doctrine.[27] The convention from the first to the last was dominated by Breckenridge Democrats under the leadership of unyielding William W. Eaton, a faithful lieutenant of Seymour and a Hartford lawyer of strong convictions.[28] Douglas Democrats attended the convention, but their candidates, John T. Wait of Norwich and Henry Deming of Hartford, never had a chance.[29] In party maneuvering, Eaton and Seymour and the Burrs of the *Hartford Times* were an unbeatable combination.[30] Their choice, James C. Loomis, a more moderate Peace Democrat and a highly respected citizen of Bridgeport, was nominated with little difficulty. The Republicans again nominated Buckingham to run on a platform calling for strong measures, including coercion, to maintain "the supreme and perpetual authority of the national government." [31] The campaign was hotly joined, and the issues were clear enough to bring out a large vote on April 2.[32] Loomis proved to have been a popular choice, at least as far as the Douglas Democrats were concerned. Buckingham won by only a 2,000 vote majority.[33]

Despite the relatively narrow victory, a majority of the people seemed to be solidly behind the new President. George P. Bissell, the Hartford banker, reflected the sense of relief prevailing among Connecticut Republicans that Lincoln was developing a firm policy toward the Confederacy. After the long limbo of the Buchanan

25. *Norwich Bulletin* (Jan. 26, 1861).
26. Lane, *History of Connecticut,* pp. 154–56.
27. Ibid.
28. James G. Wilson and John Fiske, eds., *Appelton's Cyclopedia of American Biography, 1888–89,* 2 (New York, 1889), 296.
29. Lane, pp. 154–56.
30. Ibid.
31. Croffut and Morris, *History of Connecticut,* 37.
32. Lane, pp. 157–67.
33. Ibid. See Lloyd W. Fowler, "No Backward Step," *CHS Bulletin,* 27 (1962), 3–5.

Administration, they were encouraged by rumors in the press that the government would support Fort Sumter and also Fort Pickens, off Pensacola, Florida. As Bissell put it, "all hands are delighted with the activity and the prospect of a stand at last being taken." [34] Bits and pieces of information which filtered out of Washington were just enough to heighten the romantic sensibilities of a public that was thrilling to the mystery of Wilkie Collins' *Woman in White*. "The secrecy of the movement," wrote Bissell, "adds a charm to the whole affair and we feel that Mr. L. has something of Old Hickory about him." [35] An air of expectancy, of gathering tension, hung over Connecticut during these early weeks of the Lincoln Administration.

Most conservatives had become resigned to an end of the Union as they had known it. And to many of these the Union was more than just a system of government, a democracy, a republic; it was a symbol of the expectations of their youth, now slipping away, never to be regained. For such as they, this impending tragedy had universal proportions. Unlike the young and vigorous Republicans—Bissell, Hawley, Northrop, Warner, or Alfred Terry of New Haven—despairing Democrats felt no charm of adventure, no spice of excitement, no cocky determination to show the arrogant Southerner what the God-fearing Yankee could do. Repudiated at the polls, ostracized socially, they could only wait and hope, though they knew in their hearts that the eleventh-hour reprieve would never come.

Friday, April 12, was a raw, storm-lashed day.[36] Streaks of rain and wind blown in fitful gusts whipped telegraph wires and interfered with transmission.[37] By early morning the news that Sumter had been under attack since 4:30 A.M. was known along the line of the New York and New Haven Railroad, and a little later the news had reached New London and Norwich by way of the Shore Line road.[38] At the same time Hartford telegraphers in the New Haven and Hartford depot were relaying the news.[39] Almost immedi-

34. Bissell to Welles, April 9, 1861 (Welles Papers, HL).
35. Ibid.
36. *Norwich Bulletin* (April 13, 1861).
37. Ibid.
38. *New London Daily Star* (April 13, 1861).
39. *Hartford Courant* (April 13, 1861).

ately, excited people began to crowd into the various newspape offices clamoring for bulletins. From 1 P.M. until about 5 in th evening, transmission was uninterrupted and most newspaper pro prietors got out four editions of extras.[40] Despite the rain, anxiou crowds hovered around newspaper and telegraph offices for th latest news. The storm increased in intensity, and all Saturday nigh transmission was intermittent.[41] Sunday dawned clear and beauti ful, the kind of perfect day in early spring when one instinctively looks for crocuses or snow drops in the garden.[42] The worse ha come to pass. Now, it was no longer necessary to ponder, to ques tion, to argue what course should be taken. To most of the peopl the duty to preserve the Union even by force of arms now seeme plain: the opposition was reduced to a handful of hard-core Demo crats, who were willing to risk their reputations and their property for their principles.[43] Even they would fight in defense of Wash ington or against any invasion of a loyal state, but they were stead fast in opposition to any attack upon the South that involved mor than the recapture of Fort Sumter.[44]

On Sunday ministers all over the state took for their sermor texts appropriate chapters from Elijah and demanded war.[45] In New Britain, war meetings were announced for Monday evening.[46] The aged prejudice against Sunday newspapers was waived but the presses could not satisfy the appetite for news. The *Hartford Post*, a Douglas paper, even sold its special editions in Hartford churches,[47] and the *New Haven Palladium* disposed of 8,000 extr copies.[48]

"The traitors are firing on Sumter!" and "Anderson answers gun for gun!" had been the first messages posted outside the telegraph and newspaper offices. And the crowds thrilled to the brave defense against heavy odds. When it was learned that Major Anderson had surrendered, patriotic emotion scaled the heights of romantic hy-

40. Ibid.
41. Ibid. (April 15, 1861).
42. Croffut and Morris, p. 39.
43. Ibid., pp. 40–41.
44. *Hartford Times, New Haven Register* (April 15, 1861).
45. Croffut and Morris, pp. 39–40.
46. Ibid.
47. *Hartford Evening Post* (April 15, 1861).
48. *New Haven Palladium* (April 15, 1861).

perbole. The desire to avenge the nation's honor, to expunge this nsult to the flag, temporarily submerged the Union concept beneath tidal wave of Northern nationalism. On Monday, April 15, the President issued his call for 75,000 troops to be drawn from the nilitia of the loyal states. This went over the telegraph and was published in the Tuesday morning papers throughout the state.[49] But even before receipt of the proclamation, voluntary war meetngs were being organized, enlistments being taken, cornet bands nd fife and drum corps dinning their martial messages. Spreadagle speeches in a setting of flags and bunting stirred the patriotic motions of the public as if all the 4th of July celebrations since 790 had been rolled into one. Drab meeting halls and nondescript treets concealed their ugliness behind a façade of color—streamers, osettes, bunting, flags—the blue, white, and gold of Connecticut, nd the red, white, and blue of the Stars and Stripes. Everything seemed to be happening spontaneously. There had been no direction, no organization, not even suggestions from the press. It was clearly a rising of the people. Spearheaded by the young men and women who organized themselves into volunteer teams for war work or volunteer militia companies, the state was transformed overnight into a hive of military activity. Without this spectacular outpouring of volunteer effort, it would have taken months for Connecticut to come to the aid of the embattled Federal government.

The state administration was unprepared; the militia had been a laughing stock for thirty years; the militia laws, as then constituted, could not be enforced; arsenals were in disrepair, equipment obsolete.[50] In the entire state there were but 1,020 army muskets of Mexican War vintage, and 2,000 percussion muskets, heavy, unreliable, practically useless as weapons.[51] Ammunition was also in short supply: only 50,000 ball cartridges had been purchased since December 1860. Thirty pieces of artillery, all smooth-bore napoleons, were owned by the state, but there were no caissons, harnesses, or baggage wagons. Governor Buckingham had done as much as he

49. Buckingham, *Life,* p. 122.

50. Croffut and Morris, p. 56.

51. "Governor's Annual Message to the Legislature of Connecticut," *PDLC* (May Sess., 1861).

dared to put the militia in some state of readiness and to purchase some equipment, but he had been hampered by constitutional provisions.[52] The legislature of Connecticut, under the provisions of the state constitution of 1818, reserved to itself all powers over the militia. Consequently, the executive department had no choice but to fall back on voluntary workers, even as the Federal government at this time was completely dependent on the loyal states.

What was lacking in direction and coordination was supplied by zeal in all walks of society. Homes, shops, and factories gave uniform material freely, though the quality and types of cloth were as varied as the colors were striking. With such a prodigious output and plenty of manpower willing and eager to enlist, the organization of just one regiment, Connecticut's quota, was too easy. In fact, the first regiment of Connecticut volunteers, three-months men, was fully organized in three days. In three weeks' time fifty-four full companies, or nearly six full regiments, had been mustered for service. The Governor then induced a reluctant War Department to accept two additional three-months regiments on condition that two more would be enlisted for three years.

On May 3, when the President called for a second installment of 42,000 volunteers, Buckingham announced the formation of the 4th and 5th Regiments for three years' service. These were quickly filled up, and according to the state adjutant general "not less than 2,000 men from Connecticut enlisted in other states or in the regular army and navy." [53] Upon the state administration fell the task of providing equipment, selecting camp sites, and organizing a commissary to feed 6,000 men and a paymaster's department to pay them. The state could expect no help at this time from Washington. On the contrary, the national government was making frantic demands for troops to defend the capital from what was thought to be an imminent invasion.

Now that war had come, Governor Buckingham acted with vigor. His first concern was an adequate supply of money to finance the war effort. A special session of the General Assembly might be called and an appropriation rushed through, but this

52. William T. Davis, ed., *The New England States, Their Constitutional, Judicial, Educational, Commercial, Professional and Industrial History* (Boston, 1897), I, 464.

53. Croffut and Morris, p. 71.

would have wasted a week at least. Judging from the Washington telegrams, a week's delay might be fatal. On Monday morning, April 16, he borrowed $50,000 from the Thames Bank of Norwich on his own promise to pay.[54] Actually, Buckingham had no need for concern. Practically every bank in the state offered ample funds, even before his action had become public.[55]

The personal staff of the Governor consisted of political appointees serving merely for the prestige, and was therefore largely inept. Adjutant General Joseph D. Williams early proved himself unable to cope with the problems involved. Since Buckingham had little knowledge of military affairs, he leaned heavily on a fellow townsman and former West Pointer, Daniel Tyler. The 62-year-old Tyler was offered and accepted command of the 1st Connecticut Regiment, with orders to set up a training camp for the 1st and 2nd Regiments in New Haven.[56]

When Tyler arrived there, he decided to lease the Armstrong lot behind the New Haven Hospital on a temporary basis, after rejecting other offers of better sites from owners who wanted to charge admission to watch the parades. His first order was to institute an iron discipline over the raw recruits, which he administered with a harshness and severity perhaps usual with seasoned troops but not suitable to untrained volunteers.

Indeed, everything at New Haven, except discipline, was in short supply. Tents were scarce and became overcrowded when they had to accommodate nine men.[57] For cooking facilities, one portable light stove, scarcely adequate for ten men, had to do for a company of 200 men.[58] Yet each day brought more men. Recruits were quartered at the armory of General William H. Russell's Military School; and when this temporary shelter was filled to capacity, they bunked at the Yale Alumni Hall, under the stern gaze of former Yale presidents and professors, whose portraits lined the walls.[59] Within a week Tyler found a suitable camp site for the

54. Ibid., p. 58.
55. Ibid.
56. Ibid., p. 70. Tyler resigned his regular army commission after the Mexican War.
57. *New Haven Journal and Courier* (April 30, 1861).
58. *New Haven Palladium* (April 30, 1861).
59. *Norwich Courier* (May 1, 1861). Troops concentrated at Hartford were experiencing similar difficulties. *Hartford Press* (May 2, 1861).

two regiments at Brewster's park, in the western suburbs of th
city. At Hartford an improvised camp was set up for the 3r
Regiment on the fair grounds, in open country, two miles fro
the State House.[60]

Tyler relied at this time on General Russell, who made availab
the services of his well-trained cadets. No one, least of all the unmil
itary volunteers, found it embarrassing to be drilled by Russe
cadets, most of whom were mere boys from twelve to fiftee
years of age. Every day these stripling taskmasters, very earnest i
their blue uniforms, white belts, bandoliers, and pillbox cap
marched and countermarched their sweating, stumbling compani
on the New Haven green.[61]

Citizens who visited the New Haven camps were invariably im
pressed by the tall clean-shaven Tyler, who never relaxed his stif
military posture as he strolled through the uneven ranks of th
drilling recruits. Tyler was a spare individual with hard eyes an
impassive features that rarely betrayed the impatience he must hav
felt with the antics of untried men and volunteer officers. Afte
supervising the first stage of the organization of the 1st and 2n
Regiments, he was offered and accepted command of the state mili
tia with the rank of a brigadier general.[62] Over all the recruits h
maintained strict control; his cure for discontent was work-dri
from five in the morning to five at night.[63] The Tyler regime
combined with the general disorganization caused much grum
bling, particularly over the food and quarters. Bad morale quickl
resulted in a temporary desertion of fifty men from the 1st Regi
ment to New Haven for a decent meal.[64] Tyler acted with hi
accustomed severity: courts martial were held, some privates ex
pelled from the regiment, and all noncommissioned officers broke
to the ranks.[65] Discipline was restored, but the insubordination o
the soldiers created enough unfavorable publicity to focus criticism
upon Buckingham's Administration.

60. Croffut and Morris, p. 68.

61. *New Haven Register* (Sept. 30, 1923; Oct. 15, 1961).

62. "Governor's Annual Message, 1862," *PDLC* (May Sess., 1862), p. 8; Croffut an
Morris, p. 70.

63. *Norwich Courier* (April 30, 1861).

64. Croffut and Morris, p. 62.

65. Ibid.

On May 4 a mass meeting of indignant Danbury citizens ap-ointed a committee to investigate the hardship of recruits at New Iaven, especially their alleged lack of food.[66] The committee vis-ed New Haven and found the complaints well grounded. Then, it alled on Quartermaster General John M. Hathaway, who rejected eir evidence as unwarranted hearsay. As a result, another citizens' ass meeting unanimously voted to present the report to the legis-ture.[67] Danbury was not alone in complaining: the *New Haven ournal and Courier* was a persistent critic. In fact, the soldiers lways had a ready audience in their home towns and willing ears in e legislature when complaints were mentioned.[68] The 3rd Regi-ent was so clamorous in its complaints about poor rations that uckingham himself made a personal inspection of its commissary. Ie found everything in order and thought that the rations were oth wholesome and plentiful. Orville H. Platt, a rising young Re-ublican, disputed the Governor's conclusions. Claiming that Buck-igham had been deceived, he charged that the regimental quarter-aster had sold the rations and provided in their place inedible ubstitutes. Platt pushed a legislative investigation which proved his oint, despite the obvious discomforture of the state administra-ion. Constant surveillance by self-appointed town or legislative quisitors played havoc with discipline and accomplished more arm than good.

Actually, the poor food was only in part attributable to an inex-erienced commissariat. True, Hathaway had contracted with a upplier to furnish food for the 1st Regiment at thirty cents a head er day. And the supplier had promptly arranged with subcontrac-ors to furnish rations on a twenty-cent per capita basis. Thus he ecured a substantial sum for doing relatively nothing.[69] Yet Jo-eph Hawley, ex-editor of the *Hartford Press,* who was a captain in he 1st Regiment, maintained it was not the quantity or quality of he food that was at fault. He put the blame on the inexperience of he men in drawing and trading rations and in preparing them. Vriting from New Haven to Warner of the *Press,* Hawley de-

66. *New Haven Journal and Courier* (May 7, 1861).
67. Ibid.
68. See *Journal of the Senate* (May Sess., 1861), for memorials introduced.
69. Letters to editor, *Norwich Courier* (May 9, 1861).

scribed a typical day's ration: "today our Company was entitled t
pork and beans, our Sergeant took only 26 lbs. of pork and wit
the remainder he bought of the contractor 40 lbs. of fresh codfis
and a supply of onions and potatoes, giving a good chowder fo
dinner and having pork enough for supper and breakfast. And s
on through the ration. Our Sergeant bought a good ham this morn
ing, with the soap and candles he had not drawn." [70]

In the meantime, delays, confusion, and lack of organizatio
were irritating many who were eager to see Connecticut troops i
the field. These were days not only of high patriotic ardor but o
very real concern regarding the safety of Washington. Enthusiasti
citizens were thrilled when the 6th Massachusetts Regiment passe
through the state on April 18. Nearly 3,000 Hartford resident
were on hand to greet the Massachusetts troops when their specia
train of nineteen cars arrived at the city depot at 2:15 in th
morning. An equal number of New Haven residents serenade
them when they stopped briefly in that city two hours later. The
came the dispatch that the regiment was being mobbed in Balti
more; and suddenly all communication with Washington was cu
off.

Governor Buckingham was at his home in Norwich when th
telegraph office in New York City advised that the Washington
Baltimore line had been cut. Assuming the capital city was about t
be attacked, Buckingham decided that he must convey at once t
the President and the War Department written assurance of Con
necticut military support. He also wanted an eye-witness apprais
of the situation for policy guidance in the state's military build-u
For such an important mission the Governor selected his son-in
law, William A. Aiken, who left Norwich on April 22. Despite th
difficulties of traveling through Maryland, Aiken made good tim
arriving in Washington at 10 P.M. two days later. As the tire
travel-worn courier from Connecticut rode in a hack through th
city to the War Department, he was appalled at "the unbroke
silence of its hotels and apparent desolation of its streets." Aike
reached Scott's headquarters at 11 P.M. and found the aged, agitate
Commanding General at his desk attended by only two members o

70. *Hartford Press*, quoted in *New Haven Palladium* (May 6, 1861).

his personal staff. Aiken introduced himself and handed Scott the Governor's letter. The General broke the seal, scanned the letter, and startled Aiken by immediately leaping up. From his majestic six-foot, six-inch bulk, Scott looked directly down on his young visitor and said with emotion, "Sir, you are the first man I have seen with a written dispatch for three days; I have sent men out every day to get intelligence of the northern troops; not one of them has returned. Where are the troops?" Obviously laboring under great strain, Scott asked question after question. Aiken concluded from the interview that the situation was indeed critical. His opinion was further confirmed when some time later he spoke with Secretary of War Simon Cameron in his bedchamber. According to Cameron, the District was completely surrounded by the enemy.

The following day Aiken visited the President and presented Buckingham's letter of encouragement. As he recalled the interview,

> No office seekers were besieging the presence that day. I met no delay. Mr. Lincoln was alone, seated in his business room upstairs, looking towards Arlington Heights through an open window. Against the casement stood a very long spy glass or telescope which he had obviously just been using. I gave him all the information I could from what I had seen and heard on my journey. He seemed depressed beyond measure as he asked slowly and with measured emphasis, "What *is* the North about? *Do* they know our condition?" "No," I answered, "they certainly did not know when I left."

After further conversation, Aiken mentioned that though he had plenty of New York City bank notes, they had proved absolutely worthless in Washington. "I remarked to the President," said Aiken, "that I hadn't a cent, though my pocket was full. . . . He instantly understood and kindly put me in possession of such an amount of specie as I desired." [71]

Just as Aiken was leaving Washington for home on April 25, the 7th New York in full battle dress arrived at the Baltimore station. The sight of their gray jackets and shining rifles restored a measure

71. Croffut and Morris, pp. 840–41.

of confidence not only to Aiken but to the loyal citizens in th capital. During his arduous trip through Maryland he had not see one American flag.[72]

At home, anxiety over the situation in the Washington-Balti more area was intensified by the abundance of rumors that tappe their way over the telegraph lines from New York. A heightenin sense of frustration found its relief in the bellicose editorials of th Republican press and the angry comments of loyal citizens. "W propose to go through Baltimore," exploded brusque George Bisse "and will lay your infernal city in ashes if a gun is fired. That's th kind of talk that the people want and they will back it up." [73] Th state experienced a great sense of relief when Mrs. Gideon Welles, a 8 P.M. on April 25, received word from her brother, R. C. Hal quartermaster general of Pennsylvania, that Washington wa safe.[74] The following day Aiken arrived in Norwich and person ally confirmed the good news. There was no question of the ardo and loyalty of most Connecticut citizens. Unfortunately, warlik spirit was but a partial antidote for unpreparedness.

New Haven, which had been the scene of the first military activ ity, where troops drilled on the green as well as in camp, was th first city to demand quick dispatch of Connecticut troops.[75] Th *Norwich Bulletin,* speaking for the Governor, responded on May and explained carefully the folly of sending untrained men t Washington.[76] But by the first week of May, Massachusetts an New York troops had reached the beleagered capital. Criticism o Connecticut's apparent sloth was being heard out of the state, an impatient demands for action within the state would not be si lenced with explanations, however sound.[77] Finally, on May sixty-four horses and 16 wagons for the 1st Regiment arrived i New Haven; and two days later the 1st Connecticut Regimen ready for embarkation, marched down a flag-decorated Chap Street escorted by the Governor's horse guards and the city po

72. Ibid.
73. George P. Bissell to Welles, April 24, 1861 (Welles Papers, HL).
74. *Hartford Courant* (April 26, 1861).
75. *New Haven Journal and Courier* (April 23, 1861).
76. *Norwich Bulletin* (May 2, 1861).
77. *New York Daily Tribune* (May 6, 1861).

ce.[78] It was dark when the regiment reached Long Wharf, where ne steamer *Bienville* was waiting. At a few minutes after 11 'clock, beneath a colorful canopy of streaming rockets, the over-aded little vessel (780 men, wagons, horses, and full camp equip-nent) made its way cautiously out of the dark harbor. The next ay the 2nd Regiment embarked on the *Cahawba;* and two weeks iter the 3rd Connecticut, which had been delayed by strife among s officers, got underway for Washington.[79] The troops were carcely trained at all. Their uniforms and personal equipment, xcept for rifles, were poor,[80] their tents and camp equipment of ndifferent quality.[81] They left behind a host of problems that vere to occupy the legislature, the Governor, and the people for a rueling four years.

Governor Buckingham was handicapped by a lack of complete uthority, a legislature attuned to local pride and jealousy, and a ress which at times was recklessly irresponsible. He was further edeviled at first by an accounting system that did not provide dequate controls over profligacy and dishonesty. Any move he nade was looked upon with suspicion, but none with more doubts han his appointments to high military and civil positions. It can-not be said that the Governor himself was above local pride, or that is appointments were free of political implications. Usually these wo factors were balanced in his mind, but when he made an ap-pointment without due consideration of politics, he invariably got nto trouble. His appointment of Colonel Daniel Tyler had been he *cause célèbre.*

In the first place, Tyler was a Norwich man, and New Haven nd Hartford felt slighted. Nor were these cities mollified when prominent citizens of both were given commands of other state egiments, because at the same time Tyler was given over-all com-mand. Furthermore, Tyler disdained politicians, a fatal error at this ime of groping leadership, and he had grave personal faults as well.

78. *New Haven Palladium* (May 8, 1861).

79. Croffut and Morris, p. 68. The *Cahawba* and the *Bienville,* which carried the egiments, were sound steamers chartered for the state by Henry B. Norton, a Norwich usinessman.

80. Ibid., p. 67.

81. *Hartford Courant* (May 21, 1861).

Treating his subordinates with the professional's contempt for the amateur, he might have been able to command respect from his officers and men, but never devotion; and actually, he inspired a hatred that threatened to boil over in the 3rd Regiment.

When Colonel John H. Arnold, commanding officer of the 3rd, resigned because of his inability to preserve discipline, his high-spirited deputy, Lieutenant Colonel Allen G. Brady of Torrington, assumed command. Citing militia regulations, he refused to relinquish his position when ordered by General Tyler to hand over command to the able disciplinarian Lieutenant Colonel John L. Chatfield of the 1st Regiment. The General, as usual, acted harshly. Brushing aside the opinion of the regiment, which was devoted to Brady, Tyler had him arrested and very nearly precipitated a mutiny.[82] In this instance Buckingham defended his general against adverse public opinion, though he revoked Brady's arrest for insubordination, and permitted him to be honorably mustered out at the close of the 3rd's enlistment. But when Samuel Colt, the commanding officer of the 5th Regiment, three-year volunteers, rode roughshod over the opinion of his regiment, the Governor sided with the men's complaints against arbitrary authority.

One week after the attack on Fort Sumter, Colt had telegraphed Buckingham, offering to the state free of charge 1,000 of his revolving rifles with bayonets and associated equipment. These would be used to arm a regiment which Colt asked permission to raise and command. He also offered the services of the Colt Guard, a private drill organization, composed of his own employees, to assist in training the volunteers. Buckingham, apparently unaware of Colt's difficult personality, accepted the offer. Colt began the enlistment of what was termed "the First Regiment of Colt's Revolving Rifles of Connecticut" on May 10. The arms maker then began a series of highhanded measures which very soon forced the issue as to whether the Colonel or the Governor was to have ultimate authority.

At first the overworked Buckingham delegated to Colt the power to appoint his own officers, rather than have them elected by the men. Then he agreed to Colt's stipulation that recruits had to

82. *New Haven Journal and Courier* (June 14, 1861).

be five feet, seven inches, or over. When the impetuous Colonel, without consulting the volunteers, exerted pressure on Washington to have his regiment accepted as a regular army unit with a five-year enlistment, the Governor finally decided that he would have to take some action.[83] It was none too soon.

The entire regiment had become disgusted at Colt's arbitrary course in appointing and dismissing officers. The men regarded a five-year regular army enlistment as a violation of their enlistment contract and were quite prepared to return to their homes. Buckingham suggested to Colt that a regimental plebiscite be taken. The arms maker not only rejected this but gratuitously accused the Governor of improper motives.[84] For once, the deliberate Buckingham lost his temper. In a cold fury he revoked Colt's commission and disbanded the regiment. Well over half its complement returned home. Those who remained, however, became the nucleus of the 5th Regiment of three-year volunteers, which was organized under the command of Congressman Orris S. Ferry.[85]

Both the Tyler and Colt episodes were given wide publicity in the press and contributed to a growing uneasiness among the people regarding the state's war effort. Much of this was expressed in a mounting concern for the welfare of the volunteers and a suspicion that some officers of the Buckingham Administration were not acting in the best interests of the state. It was inevitable that such community protests would be voiced by members of the legislature.

As soon as the General Assembly convened in early May, numerous special committees were appointed to investigate the administration's conduct of the war. Most of the inquiries were centered on the operations of the quartermaster department, whose head, John M. Hathaway, had already come under fire for speculating with the volunteers' ration allowance. Buckingham managed to head off an investigation into the procurement of knapsacks, which the recruits had criticized as being too heavy and awkward. And he saw to it that the committee investigating the complaints of the 4th Regi-

83. Ibid. (June 11, 1861); *Norwich Bulletin* (June 13, 1861); Edwin E. Marvin, *The Fifth Regiment Connecticut Volunteers: A History Compiled from Diaries and Official Reports* (Hartford, 1899), pp. 2–19.

84. *Hartford Courant* (June 1–15, 1861).

85. Croffut and Morris, pp. 73–74.

ment reported that "it [was] unwise to interfere with the stric discipline of military life." [86] He was unable, however, to circum vent a searching investigation of uniform procurement, which wa again to reflect on the policies of Quartermaster General Hathaway

Hathaway had purchased from New Haven contractors 500 uni form suits of broadcloth; Hartford citizens furnished 200 coats o the same material at no charge.[87] After this promising start in pro curement, he delayed a week before completing his purchase order By then, supplies of broadcloth had vanished in Connecticut, as result of buying by other states and the Federal government.[88] Th remainder of the uniforms were cut from blue satinet, a cheap rough material often manufactured from reclaimed or second grade wool, and woven on a cotton warp. Though fairly servicea ble, it was coarse, and heavy without the protective qualities of th superior cassimeres and broadcloths. In fact, satinet was little bette than that inferior material known as cassinet or, more commonly Negro cloth, which New England mills had manufactured for th plantation trade.[89] For want of anything better, 1,300 pairs o trousers, 800 coats, and 500 gray overcoats made of satinet wer supplied to the 1st, 2nd, and 3rd Regiments.[90] These uniform were purchased for the state by contractors to whom Hathaway had entrusted the entire uniform procurement. Though a legislativ committee of investigation did not charge that collusion had been practiced, it found that a large portion of the uniforms were defec tive in both quality and workmanship, and that some were worth less.[91]

Other members of the legislature were far more critical of pro curement than the Joint Special Committee. James Gallagher, Democrat and representative from New Haven, who would soon b called "the volunteers' friend" because of his interest in their wel fare, condemned the report as a whitewash of thieves and grafters He said he had shown a pair of the satinet trousers to a Hartfor

86. *Senate Journal* (June 7, 1861).

87. "Report of the Joint Special Committee," *Connecticut Legislature* (May Sess 1861); *New Haven Register* (June 13, 1861).

88. Ibid.

89. Arthur H. Cole, *The American Woolen Manufacture* (Cambridge, 1926), *I*, 200–0

90. "Report of Joint Special Committee," *Connecticut Legislature* (May Sess., 1861)

91. Ibid.

tailor and had been told that they were not worth eighty cents. "Volunteer officers," continued Gallagher, "wouldn't give ten cents a pair for them." The committee, however, refused to censure anyone, maintaining stoutly that uniforms had been furnished at $7.50 each, which it claimed was $1.90 less than any other bidder had offered.[92] Although the legislature accepted this estimate of the situation, Connecticut regiments had not been in Washington a month before their uniforms were in shreds.

Resort to cheap material such as shoddy in these early hectic days was perhaps justifiable, but textile manufacturers, who found it easy to furnish inferior goods at high prices if they possessed influence in Hartford and Washington, continued to supply the army with them. Complaints from soldiers and visitors to the front, both official and unofficial, soon made the word "shoddy" a term of contempt. In vain did manufacturers try to substitute the more innocuous term "flocked material"; shoddy was one of those euphemisms that the public simply would not forget. The uproar was sufficient to cause the introduction of a bill in the legislature during the May session of 1863 to prohibit the manufacture of shoddy. In the Senate the bill was immediately referred to the Judiciary Committee, where shoddy manufacturers secured an adverse report, and the matter was dropped without debate on May 26.[93] The following day the House Committee, which had been subjected to similar influence, also rejected the bill.[94] House Judiciary Committee Chairman John T. Adams of Norwich, who was the legislative spokesman for the Sprague cotton interests, stated that "the committee thought it not advisable to embarrass the operation of the trade; that shoddy perhaps filled a place in the market and answered a good purpose." [95]

While special legislative committees were examining all phases of the state effort, the legislature was undertaking to provide for the social and economic dislocation caused by the departure of heads of families for the front. A bounty bill, giving all state volunteers $10 a month in addition to their army pay, as a family allotment, was

92. *New Haven Journal and Courier* (June 15, 1861).
93. *Hartford Courant* (May 27, 1863).
94. Ibid. (May 29, 1863).
95. Ibid.

brought before both houses of the legislature very early in the session.[96] Since the bounty was for three-months regiments only, the outlay of $30 for each man seemed modest enough and the measure was quickly passed. When Democratic members of the legislature proposed to add the new three-year volunteer regiments to the list, enthusiasm was somewhat dampened. Still, no member of the legislature would admit what many felt—that here was an expense which might well get out of hand. Enemies of the proposal introduced statistics tending to show that Connecticut could not afford to be too generous. Typical of this stingy attitude was the remark of Elisha Carpenter, a Republican representative from Killingly, who said: "We should make ample provisions for the volunteers in full view of the ability of the State to pay when pay day comes. It would cost in all nearly $100,000 for one regiment and $1,000,000 for ten regiments. This would be a large sum for us to pay." [97] Nevertheless, many, if not a majority, were worried about the families of volunteers. The sudden dislocation was already beginning to work a real hardship. $11 a month (later raised to $13), the regular army pay for a private, was barely enough to supply a soldier's personal needs. With living costs rising each month in an inflation economy, soldiers' dependents suffered want.[98] By June 20, after exhaustive argument, an acceptable military bounty bill was finally framed in the House. It provided for a bounty of $30 a year to each volunteer, and $6 monthly to his wife or dependent, with $2 allowed for each child under ten years, a maximum of $10 to be alloted each family.[99]

Although the legislature had provided support for soldiers' families, and had passed a good deal of legislation necessary to building up the military establishment, it failed conspicuously to provide an adequate pool of manpower for future or extraordinary demands. To a considerable extent, this failure was the result of the conservative manpower policy followed by the Federal government during these early confused months of the war. President Lincoln had

96. Ibid. (June 8, 1861).

97. *Norwich Bulletin* (May 12, 13, 1861).

98. *Hartford Courant* (May 8, 1861).

99. Ibid. (June 21, 1861).

made a second call for 42,000 volunteers,[1] but responding to the opinion of the War Department, and doubtless sharing the dominant sentiment that the war would be a short one, he advised the states that their quota did not have to be met.[2] In fact, his proclamation implied that it would be better to curtail volunteering rather than exceed the desired number.

Considering the state of the nation, this was scarcely a valid excuse for again neglecting to develop an adequate militia. When Connecticut had been caught napping by the attack on Sumter, the excuse had been an archaic, faulty militia law. The Governor had strongly recommended a new law in his annual message, and public opinion was overwhelmingly in favor.[3] Most responsible citizens considered that such a law should claim first place in importance at the session.[4] But any militia law without teeth was impossible to enforce, and a law that provided for compulsory enlistment of able-bodied males in the army age groups was too much like a draft. Few members of the legislature at this time, or for any time during the war years, dared to include the requisite clauses. Doubtless, a majority felt that nothing should be done to curtail the patriotic spirit.

A new bill, permitting the Governor to draft citizens into the militia, was finally passed on July 1. It included a number of crippling features, however. The Governor was delegated the power to draft men from the inactive militia to the active; but militia draftees would not be liable for Federal service except on direct requisition of the President and governor, and then their length of service was limited to three months.[5] Anyone so drafted could avoid service by paying a $10 fine.[6] Moreover, the legislature retained the feature that militia members had to buy their own uniforms, a further deterrent to enlistment. In an attempt to encourage volunteering, the new law permitted the governor to draft men for Federal

1. Fred A. Shannon, *The Organization and Administration of the Union Army 1861–65* (Cleveland, 1928), *I*, 35.
2. Ibid.
3. *New Haven Palladium* (May 3, 1861); *Norwich Bulletin* (May 3, 1861).
4. *Norwich Bulletin* (May 3, 1861).
5. *New Haven Palladium* (July 2, 1861).
6. *Public Acts* (May Sess., 1861), chap. 65.

service from the inactive militia if quotas were not met, and as an additional incentive, the state and the towns were authorized to pay bounties—bounties payable only to volunteers, not to draftees.[7] Some improvements were made on the administration of the militia. The law provided for a rapid mobilization if the state were actually invaded. For the first time in almost fifty years, accurate and up-to-date rolls of all men between the ages of 18 and 45 were to be prepared by town selectmen and transmitted to the adjutant general.[8]

Considering the time taken to frame a militia law, the state still had no effective home defense organization when the legislature adjourned in July. The Governor would again have to resort to volunteers when the Federal government called upon him for troops. This happened much faster than anyone had anticipated. The defeat of the Union army at Bull Run on July 21 jolted Northern opinion out of its state of complacency. Everyone had assumed that when the Federal army moved into the Confederacy, a few skirmishes would scatter the Southerners and bring a sudden end to the rebellion. Governor Buckingham had never shared these expectations. From the beginning of hostilities, he kept more or less constant pressure on a reluctant War Department to accept more troops. As a wise executive, he believed in being prepared for setbacks. Assuming that the enthusiasm of the people might not always be so fervid, he was eager to fill up as many regiments as possible. Well before Bull Run he was worried about replacements for the three-months regiments when their enlistments expired. He had also very quickly decided that no realistic planning or policy guidance could ever be expected from Simon Cameron's chaotic War Department. Accordingly, he had done his best, purchasing in a scarcity market, to accumulate at the state arsenal uniforms, blankets, rifles, ammunition, wagons, tents, and other items of military equipment.[9]

When Buckingham called for the enlistment of four three-year regiments, the 6th, 7th, 8th, and 9th Connecticut Volunteers,

7. Ibid.

8. Ibid. The *Norwich Courier* said: "The active Militia are for State not United States service. If a draft were ordered for men to serve in the United States Army, it would be made from the inactive and not from the active Militia."

9. Croffut and Morris, pp. 121, 141; Buckingham, *Life*, p. 187.

sufficient supplies were on hand to uniform, equip, and encamp three of them. The 9th Regiment, the last to be organized, was the most poorly equipped—no rifles and only partial uniforms of the poorest quality. Other regiments, however, received adequate arms and equipment before departure for the South. In addition, the state had enough cannon and associated equipment on hand to organize a light battery, despite the fact that four batteries had already been supplied to the Federal government.[10] Horses, harnesses, carbines, sabers, and uniforms were also available to equip one battalion of cavalry. As a result, Buckingham decided to petition the War Department for authority to enlist an artillery battery and cavalry battalion as a part of the state's quota. After much needless correspondence with the War Department, he finally got permission in early September to organize these units.[11]

As Buckingham suspected, enthusiasm for enlistment had subsided considerably. Casualty figures from Bull Run and enlistment for three years instead of three months had produced a sobering effect. More importantly, unemployment, which had increased during the business uncertainties of the secession crisis, had almost disappeared. Recruiting for volunteer regiments would now compete with recruiting for labor by rapidly expanding war industries. Scarce agricultural labor, in short supply before the war, was fully engaged in gathering in the harvest. The Governor was faced with a difficult job, but thanks to the three-months regiments, recruiting proved easier than he had anticipated. Even the most bitter Breckenridge Democrats must have been moved by the physical appearance of these regiments when they returned home after the disgrace of Bull Run.

The 1st Connecticut, for example, arrived at New Haven on July 28. Thousands of New Haven citizens were on hand when the men disembarked from the sound steamer *Elm City*. Everyone was shocked at the condition of the troops. They had departed three months before with bright, new uniforms, an imposing martial display; they returned tired, dusty, and literally in rags. Governor

10. *OR*, Ser. III, *1*, 466.

11. Croffut and Morris, *Connecticut*, p. 137; Herbert W. Beecher, *History of the First Light Battery Connecticut Volunteers, 1861–1865. Personal Records and Reminiscences* (New York, 1901), *1*, 26.

Buckingham, who greeted them on Long Wharf, was moved to tears at their condition. At half past ten, with the dignified Governor at their head, the strange, even outlandish, procession began moving through densely crowded streets to the State House on the green. Up East Street to Wooster, up Wooster to Olive, up Olive to Chapel, they marched. Many were wearing captured Confederate zouave uniforms, others had made trousers out of blankets, but they all marched with heads high, conscious that at least they had fought well at Bull Run.[12]

When it became known that most of the three-months men would re-enlist for three years, a new surge of patriotic emotion swept the state. Less spectacular than the response to the Sumter attack, it was better organized and more deliberate in its impact. Over 100 veterans fanned out over Connecticut and did such a systematic job of recruiting that within one month six new regiments, a light artillery battery, and a cavalry battalion had been formed.[13] Governor Buckingham, constantly on the move, presided at huge war meetings in every city and in most of the larger towns of the state. As they had done three months earlier, rich men pledged money to support the families of volunteers. But it was the veterans of the three-months regiments who recruited, organized, and trained these new troops. Popular, able Alfred H. Terry and equally popular Joseph R. Hawley were a strong team in filling up and whipping into shape the 7th Regiment. Building on a solid base of three-months men who had re-enlisted, they soon had a well-disciplined regiment assembled at Oyster Point, near New Haven.[14] Colonel John L. Chatfield, who had been commanding officer of the 3rd Regiment, assisted by members of his former command, was equally successful in raising the 6th Regiment, which also encamped at New Haven.[15]

Determined this time not to lose the impetus of the recruiting drive, Buckingham decided to accept all companies offered. After

12. *New Haven Palladium* (July 29, 1861).

13. Croffut and Morris, p. 102.

14. Stephen W. Walkley, comp., *History of the Seventh Connecticut Volunteer Infantry, Hawley's Brigade, Terry's Division, Tenth Army Corps, 1861–1865* (Hartford, 1905), p. 13.

15. Charles K. Cadwell, *The Old Sixth Regiment, Its War Record, 1861–65* (New Haven, 1875), p. 11.

securing the necessary legislation from a special session of the General Assembly, he expanded the state organization to include two additional regiments, or eight in all. The 1st Light Battery and 1st Cavalry Battalion proved popular from the outset. Within one month both units were filled,[16] but it became increasingly difficult to complete recruiting for the last three regiments of infantry, the 11th, 12th, and 13th, even though all had a nucleus of three-months veterans and all boasted influential commanding officers. The 13th, for example, was not even organized until the late fall of 1861. Finally, with the monetary inducements of state and national bounties, which now totaled $130 for each volunteer, the 13th was brought up to strength by March of 1862.[17]

It was soon obvious that if a volunteer was interested in being properly equipped, adequately fed, and decently sheltered, he had better enlist in a regiment whose field officers had some military experience and knew their way around state political circles. The best combination, of course, was to serve under a commanding officer who enjoyed a close relationship with the Governor. Edward Harland, who received command of the 8th Regiment, was just such an individual. A well-to-do Norwich lawyer, Harland had been a close friend of Buckingham for years. He had been a company commander in the 3rd Regiment, had handled his company well at Bull Run, and had gained a reputation of being extremely solicitous for the welfare of his men. Harland did not disappoint his admirers. The 8th was the best equipped of all Connecticut regiments sent to the front during 1861.[18]

In sad contrast was the condition of the 9th (Irish) Regiment, organized by Thomas W. Cahill of New Haven. Despite the fact that most Connecticut Irishmen had voted the straight Breckenridge ticket, no ethnic group had been more patriotic after Sumter. Thomas H. Murray, historian of the 9th, has estimated that between 7,000 and 8,000 men of Irish descent enlisted in Connecticut regiments during the war, and that an additional large number enlisted in regiments of other states. No alleged disloyalty, therefore, can be offered as an excuse for the failure of the state adminis-

16. Croffut and Morris, *Connecticut*, pp. 137–38.
17. Ibid., p. 156.
18. Ibid., p. 124.

tration to equip the 9th. Either Colonel Cahill and his staff were lax in pressing state authorities for proper arms and equipment or dishonesty was practiced by responsible officials.

Initially, Buckingham had been most enthusiastic at Cahill's proposal to enlist an Irish regiment as other states were doing at this time. The Governor had stood by Cahill when strong Know-Nothing elements in New Haven demanded publicly that he revoke the organization of an Irish regiment.[19] And he had initiated prompt action in the legislature to remove the old Know-Nothing laws which had disbanded Irish militia companies.[20] Cahill himself was a highly respected member not only of the New Haven Irish community but of the business community as well. A partner in a large New Haven masonry concern, he had been twice elected to the Common Council and was serving his third term as a city alderman.[21] Cahill's staff, Lieutenant Colonel Richard Fitzgibbon and Major Frederick Frye, were both veterans of Bull Run, as were many of the enlisted men. With such a fine nucleus, the 9th should have been a popular regiment. But the lack of proper military equipment from the outset gave the 9th a bad name and made it extremely difficult to fill up the ranks. During its entire stay in New Haven the state issued one shoddy, blue uniform to each of the Irish troops. They received no rifles, a minimum of personal equipment, and only about half were lucky enough to draw the clumsy state-issue cowhide shoes known variously as "tan yards," "gunboats," and "gubbies." Recruited principally from the New Haven area, the 9th, in addition to its reputation of being the poorest equipped of the state regiments, was also regarded as "the most turbulent." [22]

The genial Cahill preferred not to impose a strict discipline until his men had become better acquainted with military life. Because of their high spirits and their wretched material condition, this was probably a wise decision. Unfortunately, Cahill's easy-going regime had repercussions in the community. These exuberant, ragged, roistering volunteers taxed the best efforts of New Haven's inade-

19. Carroll J. Noonan, *Nativism in Connecticut, 1820–1860* (Washington, 1938), pp. 205–06.

20. *Norwich Aurora* (Jan. 10, 1861); Murray, *Ninth Regiment*, p. 27.

21. Murray, p. 322.

22. *OR*, Ser. III (I), p. 653.

quate police force. Buckingham was much relieved when General Benjamin Butler, who was seeking Connecticut regiments for his New England brigade, offered to take the 9th.[23] The Governor quickly authorized the necessary transfer, and the Irish Regiment was shipped off to Lowell, to the terror or delight of the local factory girls when they heard the cry "Connecticut over the fence." [24]

With the exception of the 9th, all the three-year regiments were fairly well equipped when they left the state. Uniforms were still poorly cut and indifferently stitched, and would last about one month under ordinary field conditions. Arms were perhaps above the average standard for volunteer regiments. Flank companies were armed with Sharps' rifles, and most of the remainder were issued rifled Enfields. A few companies, however, still carried heavy, inaccurate, smooth-bore muskets.[25]

The administration had made strenuous efforts to provide adequate camp facilities in the state. At Oyster Point, New Haven, the Quartermaster General constructed large "A" frame wooden barracks, which housed the 6th, 7th, and 9th Regiments quite comfortably. Similar barracks were built outside of Hartford for regiments concentrated in that area. But even in planning for the shelter of the soldiers, measures of false economy ruled. Not enough barracks were built to house all the regiments.

The 13th was quartered at Durham and Booth's empty carriage factory in New Haven, an old, three-story firetrap, poorly ventilated and only partially heated by a capricious steam piping system. The volunteers were jammed into storage rooms with rough wooden shelves one above the other for bunks. During the severe winter of 1861–62 pneumonia, measles, and smallpox flared up. Fortunately, the smallpox cases were detected early, and isolation was handled so carefully that the disease did not spread. The troops were unaware of the outbreak. Yet twelve members of the 13th Regiment died of infectious disease before it left for the front.[26]

23. Ibid.

24. Murray, p. 51.

25. Croffut and Morris, p. 121.

26. Ibid., p. 155, lists ten to twelve who died. Homer B. Sprague, *History of the Thirteenth Infantry Regiment of Connecticut Volunteers during the Great Rebellion* (Hartford, 1867), pp. 28–29, lists nine.

The fact that Henry Birge, a Norwich merchant and nephew of Governor Buckingham, was commanding officer of the 13th, did not help the regiment with respect to quarters. But Birge was eminently successful in securing the very best equipment the state could supply, even to the extent of custom-tailored dark blue trousers in place of the regulation sky blue.[27] Not all regiments and units were quartered in structures. The 10th and 12th, and the 1st Light Battery, shivered in tents of the James patent, similar to Sibley tents in that the central supporting pole was hollow and acted as a chimney for a cast-iron stove.[28]

Despite the experience of the 9th and the 13th, camp conditions had improved since the hectic days of the first call for troops. Food was better and was better prepared, and what was lacking in the state rations was more than made up by the attentions of civilians. But discipline, so little understood by those who have to conform to it yet so important to over-all comfort, cleanliness, and general morale, was, if anything, more relaxed in the three-year regiments. The letdown after Bull Run had demanded that companies be recruited on a community basis, which meant that the three-year regiments had a high percentage of friends and relatives within their ranks. The close, informal friendships of youth did not yield rapidly to any impersonal military pattern. It was probably best that officers did not insist upon rigid military discipline, at least in the initial phase of converting raw farm boys and factory workers into efficient soldiers.

Patriotism in 1861 was a fragile thing. No complicated apparatus of the state or nation operated that could command resigned obedience to the national will. Nothing more than friendship and respect for community leaders, nothing more than a vague desire for adventure, a rejection of narrow, parochial living, had prompted the signing of the rolls. Discipline had to mature slowly; it had to be handled expertly; and it was doubly hard when it was administered by close friends or relatives. Thus, while officers kept up appearances in camp for the benefit of visitors, there was a considerable amount of drunkenness, of horseplay—sometimes with fatal consequences—and of rowdiness when on liberty. With the

27. Sprague, p. 31.
28. Croffut and Morris, p. 144.

exception of their attitude toward the Irish 9th Regiment, the community bore the tumult with forbearance, but it was with a sense of relief as well as sorrow when the boys departed.[29] Although grumbling over food and discipline continued to make its occasional appearance in the press, the volunteers would look back on their camp life at home as a delightful, carefree period. Their hardships were really to begin when the state turned them over to Federal control.

During 1861 Connecticut had made a substantial manpower contribution in the support of the Union. Three regiments of three-month volunteers, then ten additional regiments of three-year volunteers, for a total of approximately 12,000 infantry, had joined the armies of the Union. In addition, the state had turned over to the Federal government a cavalry battalion, a light artillery battery —all fully equipped—and ordnance equivalent to four batteries.[30] A sum of $2,000,000 had been raised for military expenditures, well over $100,000 of which had been contributed by private sources; state funds were being paid to help support soldiers' families; and tons of books, pamphlets, clothing, and medical supplies were being collected from the community for the comfort of the volunteers. Even frequent legislative investigations on the conduct of the war effort, though they accomplished little, did focus attention on contractors, and thus made for more honest procurement. True, the Governor cut down investigation when he could, but he also corrected the evils when they were pointed out and encouraged the sending of complaints to him rather than to the legislature.[31]

This distrust of the legislature and the absence of any sound liaison between it and the Governor had resulted in the breakdown of that body. By the end of the session a good many Connecticut citizens were exasperated with its apparent desire to do nothing but argue. Business that had been disposed of was brought up again and amended; bills and resolutions passing one house were rejected by the other. Despite the practice of employing joint committees, much proposed and necessary legislation followed a course aptly described by the *New Haven Register:* "Passage by the House,

29. Murray, pp. 47, 48.
30. *OR*, Ser. III, *1*, 783–84.
31. *Norwich Bulletin* (June 15, 1861).

rejection by the Senate, the House amends, the Senate insists, a conference committee is appointed, and finally both Houses reject its report and the bill dies."[32] Besides the endless wrangling between the two houses, the legislature wasted much time with minutiae that in most states would have been delegated to the courts and the executive department. Divorce petitions, prison pardons, even changes of name might come under its surveillance, and in some instances it regulated the disposition of trusts and estates.[33]

In a first burst of enthusiasm the legislature had distinguished itself by accomplishing a great deal of necessary work. Thereafter, little was done. If it had not been for the spontaneous work of the townsfolk, Connecticut might not have furnished combat troops until 1862. Individual citizens volunteered labor, money, and raw materials before the cumbersome machinery of the state could function effectively. War meetings, independently organized, not only assumed but fulfilled these important duties with ability and a high degree of efficiency. From family cellars and garrets, from manufacturers' warehouses, and from countless small shops came an endless stream of cloth to be made into uniforms, undergarments, bandages, and blankets; iron for cannon balls; food of all descriptions; and money to supplement state bounties. It was clearly a rising of the people. Had this not occurred, the state administration during the first year of the conflict would have faced an unmanageable chaos. But devotion to the Union had converted a majority of the people into a solid auxiliary that supported the nation during the first perilous year, and gave it time to build a long-term war program.[34]

32. *New Haven Register* (July 4, 1861).

33. Davis, *The New England States, I,* 464.

34. Croffut and Morris, chaps. 2, 3.

4. MANPOWER: 1862–1865

The city reporter of the *Norwich Bulletin* concluded that just about everyone in Norwich had turned out to honor the Governor on his departure for New Haven and his fifth inauguration as chief magistrate and captain general of the Republic of Connecticut.[1] Somewhat careworn after a year of heavy responsibilities, Buckingham was cheered by this spontaneous expression of regard from his friends and neighbors. Equally encouraging was the popular applause that greeted him when he left the train at the East Haven depot. Accompanied by the colorful horse and foot guard and by various other gaily bedecked military units, he mounted a magnificent black Morgan and began the four-mile ride to the State House on the green. New Haven store fronts, private dwellings, and public buildings were bright with bunting. Despite a year of civil war, the bells in all the church towers and the brass napoleons on the green sounded the traditional election-day salute.

The state government needed this measure of public reassurance. Although the electorate had given the Governor a resounding vote of confidence in the spring election just past, it had been a difficult year. His administration had been subjected to constant criticism not only from state-rights Democrats but from loyal Republicans as well. Buckingham had been much relieved when Colonel Daniel Tyler was promoted by General Scott to command the Connecticut Brigade. But when he made the parallel state appointment for Tyler, he was roundly attacked by the New Haven press. Buckingham, who had learned much from the Colt and Brady episodes during the first months of the war, ignored the tirade and indeed all criticism of his field officer appointments except those which seemed to involve grave political danger.

One year of wartime responsibilities had made a surprisingly as-

1. *Norwich Bulletin* (May 3, 1862).

tute politician out of a cautious businessman. The stresses of mobilizing an unprepared people had also developed qualities of leadership which he exerted in a quiet but forceful manner. The Governor had made mistakes and would continue to make them through difficult months ahead. But he managed to learn from each blunder and never persisted in the path of error for the sake of mere personal pride or pique, as his brilliant contemporary, Governor John A. Andrew of Massachusetts was so prone to do.

Buckingham also recognized the symbolic importance of his position. No war governor was more indefatigable than he in visiting Connecticut soldiers at training camps in the state or in actual theaters of operations. He was always the chief speaker at war meetings in the cities and larger towns; he participated in camp prayer meetings whenever possible; and he made it a point to answer personally all direct inquiries from Connecticut soldiers in the field. His offices in the state houses at New Haven and Hartford were always open to citizens and as a result were invariably crowded. Yet the Governor still found time to conduct a substantial official correspondence with Washington—some 310 letters or telegrams during the year 1861 [2]—and with other war governors as well as local and national political figures.[3] Constantly shuttling between the two Connecticut capitals of Hartford and New Haven and the three national centers of Boston, New York, and Washington, he put in a twelve-hour day, seven-day week schedule during the war years. With not a quarter of the staff personnel enjoyed by Governors Andrew of Massachusetts, Morgan of New York, or Curtin of Pennsylvania, Buckingham was able to cope with the constant pressures and multiplying complexities of raising, equipping, and caring for an army of some 50,000 men.

The first two months of Buckingham's 1862 term were relatively calm ones. With the exception of the Bull Run defeat, the first year of the war had been quite successful for the armed forces of the Union. The War Department, as a result, had suspended recruiting in the loyal states on April 3, 1862. Relieved of this heavy burden, Buckingham was able to turn his attention to various problems of a purely administrative nature that were hampering the war effort.

2. OR, Ser. III, *1*, 978.

3. See Buckingham letter books (CSL).

There was a pressing need to correlate widely diversified war activities under responsible heads, to remove dishonest or incompetent officials, and, especially, to prize more powers out of the iron grip of the legislature, whose frequent assumption of plenary authority seriously interfered with the work of the state administration and whose reputation for inefficiency was notorious.

Governor Buckingham accomplished a far-reaching and needful reform when he prevailed upon the legislature in June 1862 to delegate to him, the state comptroller, and the state treasurer, the power to settle military claims.[4] For two sessions the legislature had been attempting to handle them with an ineffectual committee apparatus. Claims had become mixed up with personal favoritism and politics. This caused endless debate and recrimination. Though the usual fears of a "Connecticut regency" were voiced, the grant of powers was made.[5] Henceforth, Governor Buckingham was able to institute an orderly and fair reckoning in all departments, saving time and money.

The Governor showed commendable leadership in the military claims reform, but he seems to have been blind for some time to the misconduct of his quartermaster general, John M. Hathaway. During the late summer of 1861, however, he had finally become aware of the Quartermaster's official misconduct and immediately secured his resignation.[6] The Governor made an interim appointment which was not satisfactory, and then, on January 16, 1862, chose his son-in-law, William A. Aiken, a competent man whom he could trust. Aiken was to serve in this capacity for the remainder of the war.[7]

Hathaway had been appointed to the office in 1857, when it was merely an ornamental dignity.[8] He had had neither the training nor the honesty required for his position when it became, next to the governorship, the most important in the state. The mounting war effort demanded that the quartermaster appoint assistants for the procurement of supplies and equipment. Hathaway hired as

4. *New Haven Palladium* (June 15, 1862).
5. Ibid. (June 14, June 15, 1862).
6. "Governor's Message," *PDLC* (May Sess., 1862).
7. Croffut and Morris, *History of Connecticut*, p. 80.
8. "Governor's Message," *PDLC* (May Sess., 1862).

deputies men of easy virtue, who accepted bribes and padded accounts.[9] The Quartermaster himself accepted a substantial bribe from the secretary of Sharps' Rifle Company, and when this became public knowledge made no effort to return it. He also charged to the state a considerable sum for board to which he was not entitled.[10] The facts about Hathaway and his principal assistant, John Goodrich, were unearthed by the House Committee on Military Affairs, whose chairman was the sharp-eyed, testy War-Democrat and former member of Congress James T. Pratt of Wethersfield. Pratt, at times, cut a ridiculous figure and bungled important jobs, such as his attempted reorganization of the militia; but he was a fearless investigator and did not spare Hathaway, though the exposure embarrassed the administration.[11]

Nor was Hathaway the only corrupt individual in the Buckingham administration. State Treasurer G. W. Coite, by various accounting devices, was able in four years to defraud the state of approximately $12,000 in cash and perhaps three times this amount from the marketing of state bonds. Though it was well known that he was a poor man when elected to the office, and his official salary was only $800 a year, no suspicion seems to have been even aroused among critical Democrats at his frequent entertainments during legislative sessions.[12] An openly dishonest deal of Coite's was the sale of 984 shares of state-owned bank stock to personal friends in Middletown for ten dollars a share under the market price; though reported in the press, it aroused only a little public grumbling and no censure from the Governor or responsible party leaders.[13] It was not until 1867, when the Democratic administration of James E. English came into power, that the Treasurer's operations were discovered.[14] Though the state treasurer was an elective officer, Governor Buckingham deserves some criticism for his ignorance of Coite's conduct or, if he knew about it, for his failure to take necessary steps to bar the Treasurer from renomination. Nei-

9. *New Haven Palladium* (July 1, 1862).

10. Ibid.

11. Croffut and Morris, pp. 187–88.

12. *Norwich Advertizer* (June 1, 1867).

13. *Hartford Courant* (Oct. 26, 1865). $9,540 was lost to the state by Coite's private transaction.

14. *Norwich Advertizer* (June 1, 1867).

ıer Hathaway nor Coite was prosecuted by the state for his lar-enies. Coite eventually paid back the actual cash he had stolen; Iathaway escaped even this.[15]

Once Buckingham had strengthened his administration in the rucial area of procurement, he turned his attention to the man-ower problem. First, he endeavored to develop an adequate militia orce, and then, as the Union suffered a series of military disasters uring late 1862 and early 1863, he devoted himself to the recruit-ıent and training of new regiments. As far as the militia was oncerned, the Governor had to admit defeat. He even resorted to a ıilitia draft, which was a complete failure; he tried repeatedly, but nsuccessfully, to secure an adequate militia law from the General ssembly. In the raising of new volunteer regiments or in the send-ıg of replacements to veteran units, Buckingham was more suc-essful, though after 1862 he had to contend with faltering morale nd partisan opposition.

The persistent manpower problem claimed a large share of Buck-ıgham's time and energy, but he did not neglect his responsibility ɔ provide services for the Connecticut troops in the field. He ıaintained a network of state agents, who constantly visited the ɔldiers, bringing parcels from home, caring for and transporting he wounded, advancing small loans, even settling arrears in pay vith sight drafts on Buckingham's personal accounts. The Gover-or, however, relied heavily on the support of private citizens—the ons of Connecticut in New York City, the Connecticut Soldiers' elief Association in Washington, D.C., the Connecticut Chap-ıins' Aid Association, local women's aid groups, and, indeed, any-ne who wanted to help out. Buckingham encouraged such patri-tic activities because he felt that they boosted home-front morale nd, more importantly, because the General Assembly refused to ppropriate sufficient funds for the purpose.

These two areas then—military manpower and soldier welfare—laimed the principal attention of the state government and its ɔyal citizens during the war. The record contains both success and ailure, high-minded patriotism and narrow-minded self-interest, ourage and weakness, a minimum of planning and organization, nd a maximum of confusion and spontaneous individual effort.

15. Ibid. (Aug. 3, 1867).

Yet a pattern of authority runs through the apparent chaos
wartime Connecticut, the action and counteraction, the incredib
sacrifice and equally incredible selfishness. For the fact remains th
somehow, during four hard years, large numbers of people who h
never worked together before were joined in a common cause. Th
achievement was due largely to the common sense of their leade
especially the Governor, who set the example of personal devotio
and who, recognizing the naïve individualism of the people, s
about to harness their strengths while tolerating their weakness

During the spring of 1862 the Federal government had indicat
that it would undertake full responsibility for the future recru
ment, organization, and equipment of the army. Congress h
granted the President authority to recruit 500,000 soldiers for t
duration, and the newly appointed General-in-Chief George
McClellan persuaded him to accomplish this by Federal recru
ment.[16] But just before the Peninsular campaign in the spring
1862, Secretary of War Stanton had this system revoked. The go
ernors were again required to assume primary responsibility f
military manpower, and they were to be plagued with this assig
ment for the next three years.[17]

Buckingham had taken advantage of a lull in the business of t
legislative session to escape his busy office in New Haven. He w
resting at his Norwich home when an urgent telegram from Adj
tant General Lorenzo Thomas was relayed to him from Hartfor
"Raise one regiment immediately. Do everything in your power
urge enlistments," Thomas had telegraphed.[18] Buckingham repli
immediately that he would give the directive his "earnest atte
tion," but he was deeply disturbed. Such an abrupt change of p
icy was more characteristic of Simon Cameron's circumlocuti
office, not the supposedly efficient War Department of Edw
Stanton and General McClellan. Moreover, the Governor knew th
it would be just as difficult to raise one regiment as to raise six. H
serious was the situation? The only information he had was th
McDowell's army had left Washington to join McClellan's co
mand. But Buckingham did not have to wait long for the answ

16. Shannon, *Union Army*, I, 265; Croffut and Morris, p. 240.
17. Lane, *History of Connecticut*, p. 209; Croffut and Morris, p. 245.
18. *OR*, Ser. III, 2, 61.

ee, taking advantage of McClellan's involvement in the Peninsula, ad sent Stonewall Jackson down the Shenandoah Valley toward arpers Ferry and the undefended city of Washington. General athaniel Banks' small army in the valley seemed marked for de-ruction.

The telegrams from Washington took on a frantic tone. How far ould the Governor go? The state had just received a Krupp can-on which it had ordered through Henry S. Sanford, United States inister to Belgium; and it had a complete light artillery battery a hand. These the Governor promptly offered to Stanton, who cepted the Krupp gun but politely refused the battery. At the me time, Buckingham issued orders for the formation of the 14th egiment; but even before a company organization could be devel-ed, the crisis evaporated. Banks, reinforced by Frémont, managed extricate his army; Lincoln recalled McDowell; and McClellan nally began to bring sufficient pressure on Lee to force a recall of ackson's menacing army.

For two weeks nothing except routine communications came out Washington; then suddenly Stanton sent out a peremptory re-uest for troops to all loyal governors. By this time Buckingham, erplexed with his difficulties in recruiting for the 14th Regiment, tempted to clarify the situation. He wrote Stanton on June 18: If you want 2000 or 3000 troops for three months' service, I have o doubt I can raise them in a very few days if you can show our tizens that a necessity exists for such service."[19] No reply came om the War Department, which had now become wholly in-olved with McClellan's sanguinary retreat from the Peninsula. ndeed, the Governor did not learn of the perilous state of affairs ntil he received a telegram on June 30 from the governor of New ork, E. D. Morgan. Morgan asked if he would be willing to join he governors of the loyal states" in requesting the President to ll for additional troops.[20] Morgan was acting as an intermediary or William H. Seward, whom the President had sent to New York ith a draft memorial to be signed by the governors and a draft sponse in the form of a Presidential proclamation. This was the nd of positive policy Buckingham had been seeking vainly for

19. Ibid., p. 163.
20. Ibid., pp. 181–87.

more than a month. His reaction was a prompt and enthusiast agreement.[21]

The "Memorial from the Loyal Governors" and Lincoln's call fc 300,000 three-year volunteers were published in Connecticut pa pers on July 2.[22] On the following day the public read what was or of Buckingham's more eloquent proclamations. Brief as were all c the Governor's messages, this one was charged with emotion, y free of bombast. "Prompt and decisive action," he said, "will b economy in men and money . . . Close your manufactories an work shops, turn aside from your farms and your businesses, leav for a while your families and homes, meet face to face the enemi of your liberties." [23] Connecticut's quota as set forth by the Pres dent was 7,145 men. Accordingly, the Governor called for th formation of "six or more regiments." The state had already raise 15,000 soldiers, or about 6 per cent of its total male population; i war industries were booming; labor was scarce; and heavy Unio casualties in all theaters of operation had depressed public moral

Buckingham realized at once that a major effort would have t be developed. A methodical man, he made careful plans, whic involved the maximum use of persuasion on the community level– patriotism, social acceptance, money, mass meetings, the press. H most original contribution, however, was his encouragement c local war committees composed of opinion leaders in every tow and city. The state was divided into recruiting districts, accordin to population density. In each district a war committee, generall the one located in the largest population center, was designated t coordinate the activities of local bodies. In addition, the Governc informally delegated to these committees important executive pow ers. They would be responsible not only for recruiting in the districts but in calculating their districts' share of the quota. Com mittees were also empowered to arrest deserters. But most impor tant, Buckingham agreed to accept the district war committee nomination for field officers of the new regiments.[24] Such valuab appointments at their disposal, he reasoned, would add to the com

21. Ibid., p. 187.
22. Buckingham, *Life*, p. 249.
23. Ibid.
24. Croffut and Morris, p. 227.

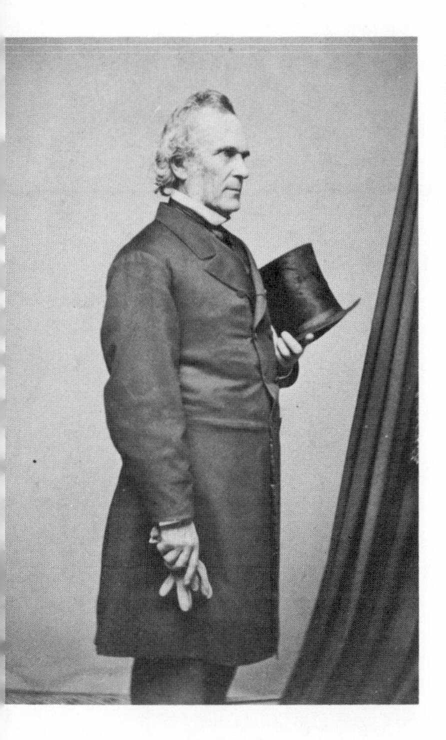

2. Businessman-politician and able administrator: William A. Buckingham, Civil War Governor of Connecticut. Connecticut Historical Society.

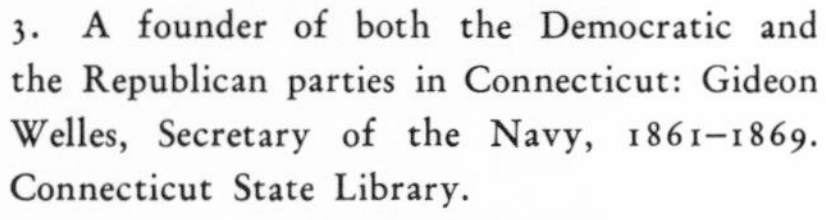

3. A founder of both the Democratic and the Republican parties in Connecticut: Gideon Welles, Secretary of the Navy, 1861–1869. Connecticut State Library.

4. Brave and bitter reactionary: Thomas Hart Seymour, leader of the disloyal opposition. Connecticut State Library.

ıittees' prestige and make their activities more effective. He as-
umed that local community leaders were in a better position than
e to make proper selections. What hot partisan of locality could
harge the Governor with discrimination or favoritism, if his own
var committee had nominated the regimental commander? Paral-
ling Buckingham's action, town meetings from time to time
vould provide war committees with additional powers, such as the
isbursing of bounties, the hiring of substitutes, and the payment
f commutation fees.

The war committee system was imperfect in many ways. Origi-
ally nonpartisan, it had become, when finally discarded in 1864,
n instrument of the Republican party. Moreover, some war com-
nittees tended to construe their authority rather broadly in areas
ouching civil liberties. For example, James G. Batterson, a member
f the Hartford war committee, constituted himself a one-man
igilante force: he arrested alleged deserters and had them jailed;
lacarded the city of Hartford with lists of "sneaks and renegades,"
requently on mere hearsay evidence; and utilized town funds as
xpenses in scouring New England for substitutes. In this regard
Batterson seems to have received approval from the committee. At
ny rate, he visited Vermont and New York in December 1863 and
ecruited 691 men for Hartford's quota, at the average cost of
49.82 per man.[25]

On the whole, the war committee system worked quite well. This
vas largely the result of the organizing ability of the businessmen
vho staffed the committees on the community level. Men who
vere accustomed to devoting their spare time to civic improvement
nd who accepted the doctrine of Christian stewardship were zeal-
us in contributing their time, money, and experience to the raising
f troops. Accustomed as they were to keeping in touch with their
olleagues in other towns and cities throughout the state, their busi-
ess channels of communication helped to coordinate effort.[26] The
ommittees disbursed several million dollars of town funds without
hint of corruption. During the heavy recruiting drives of the late
ummer of 1862 they worked long hours without pay to enlist
olunteers and provide for their families. Without this or a similar

25. *Hartford Courant* (Dec. 20, 1864).
26. Croffut and Morris, chap. 15; passim.

system the Governor would never have been able to meet the con stant manpower demands of the next two years.

While Buckingham was developing his recruiting plans, Senatc James Dixon arrived in Hartford and let it be known that he ha come at the request of the President to acquaint the public with th gravity of the military situation.[27] He then met with the Governc and Adjutant General Williams and briefed them on the collapse c the Peninsular campaign. Governor Buckingham had little pe sonal or political respect for the rather pretentious Dixon. Eve now, the two men were skirmishing for control of the party in th state, a contest that would eventually split Connecticut Republi cans into two bitterly hostile camps. But for the time being the acted as a team in considering how best to fill the state's quot rapidly. Dixon concurred heartily in Buckingham's policy of wa committees, and both agreed that every effort should be made t enlist prominent Peace Democrats in the forthcoming citizen ralli planned for every city and major town in the state. For the nex fortnight the two political rivals traveled together and spoke fron the same platform at all mass meetings. Appealing to the opposi tion, they managed to include on every program a prominent repre sentative of the local Peace Democrats. Minott Osborne, editor c the *New Haven Register* and an outspoken critic of the war, joine Dixon and Buckingham on the stage of the Music Hall at Ne Haven's meeting. Alfred E. Burr of the *Hartford Times* an Thomas H. Seymour were elected vice-presidents of the Hartfor rally.

The New Haven meeting of July 8, which opened the recruitin drive, was an outstanding success. Commodore Foote, home o leave, presided over the gathering. Everyone was deeply touche when the grizzled old hero of forts Henry and Donelson swun himself on crutches to the center of the stage. Sufficient recrui were secured on the spot to form the nucleus of the 15th Regi ment.[28] But it was the Hartford meeting that set the style an tone of the recruiting drive. Inveterate Democrat William J. Ham mersley, Hartford's mayor, was chosen by acclamation to act the presiding officer. Buckingham and Dixon made major addresse

27. *Hartford Courant* (July 7, 1862).
28. *New Haven Register* (July 9, 1862).

and then a number of community leaders followed with short, impassioned remarks. These speakers, perhaps stirred by the emo-ion of the crowd or the crisis facing the nation, instinctively adopted a revivalist style of oratory with questions from the ros-trum and massive responses from the audience. Studded with such phrases as "War! War to the knife! Knife to the hilt!" the speeches whipped the meeting into a patriotic frenzy. Young men jumped up and came forward to enlist; rich men pledged funds; business concerns offered their employees a continuation of wages during ervice. Enlistment seemed a patriotic sacrament, the war a crusade, the South a land of evil. In Bridgeport nine days later the revival echnique got a second trial with similar results. William D. Bishop, Fairfield County's leading Peace Democrat, made the principal peech and asked for a private subscription to promote enlistment. $20,000 was pledged in five minutes. Elias Howe, Jr., heir to the ewing machine fortune, started a wave of enlistments when he made a public declaration of his faith in the Union by signing the rolls as a private.[29] Publicized through the press and through the tate-wide network of war committees, the patriotic revival swept Connecticut.[30]

But the Governor and the local war committees were too experi-enced in the ways of the community to put their trust entirely in the patriotic impulse. A state bounty of $90 to each volunteer was pushed through the General Assembly.[31] Following the legislature's example, local war meetings voted bounties ranging from $50 to $200, as they had been empowered to do under the 1861 militia aw.[32] Thus began the policy of competitive bidding by towns, which was to lead to confusion in enrollment and bounty jumping as manpower became increasingly scarce. At this stage, however, carefully organized war meetings and monetary incentive were sufficient to make the recruiting campaign the most successful to be undertaken in the state. After only 45 days of intensive effort, 3,036 men had volunteered, almost 1,000 more than the quota.[33] Eight full regiments of infantry and one light battery had been

29. *Bridgeport Standard* (July 18, 1862).

30. *Hartford Courant* (July 23, 1862).

31. Croffut and Morris, p. 224.

32. Lane, *Connecticut,* p. 204.

33. Croffut and Morris, p. 224.

organized under the direction of General Daniel Tyler, whose services the Governor had secured from the War Department.

Just when the recruiting campaign was gaining momentum, Buckingham was confronted with another demand for volunteers to be recruited for nine months' service. General John Pope, who had replaced McClellan, was badly defeated by Lee and Stonewall Jackson at the second battle of Bull Run. Washington was again in a state of crisis, and Lincoln issued a second call for 300,000 men. At the same time, older three-year regiments, whose ranks had been depleted by sickness and enemy action, began clamoring for fresh recruits, and their arguments were most appealing to potential volunteers. An officer of the 8th Regiment wrote the *Courant* that recruits "would fare better on regular rations, clothing, etc., for it takes a while for Quartermasters and Colonels to get posted up and learn what soldiers are entitled to, and how to get it. As far as safety is concerned, it is better to serve under an experienced Colonel." [34]

Technically, Connecticut's quota of seven nine-months volunteer regiments would be recruited into the militia, but since the men would be drawn from the inactive militia rolls, the three-months restriction did not apply. The governors were authorized to draft men if that should become necessary. With the painful memory of January's militia draft fiasco still fresh in his mind, Buckingham was most reluctant to fill Connecticut's new quota by draft. Yet he did not flinch from informing the public that a draft might be necessary if the nine-months regiments were not up to full strength by August 15, 1862. Then he pushed every effort to enlist volunteers, working through war committees and bringing to his aid powerful newspaper support. Despite the double burden, he secured a high degree of cooperation; but there was a limit to what could be obtained by financial inducements, speeches, and patriotic editorials. As the August 15th deadline approached with unfilled quotas, the manpower potential began to melt away. Men of draft age soon learned that the easiest and cheapest way of escaping military service was to get a certificate of medical disability.

Medical ethics in Connecticut at this time were of the most casual sort. For as little as $35, Dr. Beckwith, a Litchfield examiner,

34. *Hartford Courant* (Aug. 8, 1862).

issued exemption certificates, though prices were usually much higher than this.[35] Even such an honest physician as Dr. P. W. Ellsworth of Hartford granted certificates to 600 of the 1,600 men he had examined.[36] The war committees, the press, and mass meetings attacked such draft evasion. Many of the newspapers published lists of those who had secured certificates, together with their alleged disabilities. And Beckwith was the subject of several critical editorials in the *Litchfield Enquirer*. The *New Haven Palladium* declared that the frauds had been "wholesale" and that some towns, "which have furnished few volunteers will escape a draft, while towns that have been most patriotic . . . are likely to be the most serious sufferers from the draft." [37] Public indignation eventually forced the medical profession to cut down its issuance of certificates, but not before at least 1,000 potential recruits had utilized this means to slip through the draft.

Many who had been refused a medical exemption or who were too poor to hire a substitute as provided under draft regulations left for Canada.[38] One day before the draft deadline, James G. Batterson, secretary of the Hartford war committee, announced in the Hartford papers that "anyone who has information of the departure of any man to Canada to avoid the coming draft, will serve his country by reporting the name of the renegade to the War Committee of this city." [39] The *New Haven Journal and Courier* reported that "a member of the New Haven Common Council joins the sneaks and goes to Canada." [40]

Buckingham, still hoping that volunteer enlistments would fill up the nine-months quota, postponed the draft three times.[41] By the first of September, with the state quota only one-half filled, he finally set the date for September 10. Resistance had been freely predicted in the Democratic press, and Buckingham alerted the various ornamental militia companies to be prepared for any eventuality—a needless precaution as it turned out, for 1,212 men were

35. Croffut and Morris, p. 242.
36. *Hartford Courant* (Aug. 22, 1862).
37. *New Haven Palladium* (Aug. 26, 1862).
38. *OR*, Ser. III, 2, 334.
39. *Hartford Courant* (Aug. 14, 1862).
40. *New Haven Journal and Courier*, reprinted in *Norwich Courier* (Aug. 21, 1862).
41. Lane, p. 207.

enrolled with no disturbance.[42] The public may not have bee enthusiastic, but it seemed resigned to compulsory measures.

The most significant indicator of declining patriotism was th substitute mania. At least a month before the scheduled draft, me of means who anticipated being called were scurrying about i search of available manpower. It was noticed sarcastically that sub stitute seekers could be roughly divided into three categories: tho who felt themselves indispensable to the management of their en terprise, those who were afraid of military service and were ric enough to hire a replacement, and those "whose patriotism is goo first rate, as long as they are not drafted." [43] In response to th demand, the price for substitutes rose sharply. A. N. Clark, th *Courant* editor, heard of one case where $2,000 was offered. H deplored the tendency to bid up the market before it was learne who would be drafted. "Such competition," he warned, "will onl tend to raise prices of substitutes so high that only men of ind pendent fortunes will be able to obtain them." [44]

Like the anxious businessmen, the *Courant* editor was anticipa ing a sellers' market after the draft. His prediction was quickl verified. From now until the end of the war, the substitute busine was to be one of the most lively enterprises in the state. A rash substitute brokers suddenly appeared in every city and town, an bounty jumping between towns became a distinct occupation f agile opportunists. The danger of possible arrest for desertion adde an element of illicit adventure for those who preferred to take t risk at home and get paid for it.

One of the most brazen of bounty jumpers was Robert O. Vo berg of Barkhamstead. Just before the draft was made, Vosbe went to Hartford, where he opened a recruiting office and manag to enlist a number of men under the pretense of paying each one $200 private bounty. For his services the Governor awarded him lieutenant's commission. Soon afterward Buckingham revoked Vo berg's commission for misconduct. When notified of this action b the adjutant general, the ex-lieutenant sold his recruits to oth recruiting officers at $10 a head and then sold his own services to

42. *Hartford Courant* (Sept. 12, 1862).
43. *Hartford Courant* (Aug. 11, 1862).
44. Ibid.

Hartford draftee for $450. Sworn into the service, he collected his town bounty of $200 and fled the state. He was captured, however, near the Canadian border and spent the rest of the war in the old Capitol Prison in Washington.[45] As the demand far outstripped the supply, not a few of the more adventurous were tempted to speculate in futures. A Wesleyan College student, taking advantage of a day's time lag between sale and enlistment, sold himself as a substitute to a drafted man for $300, but before taking the oath he managed to buy another substitute for $200. He achieved this minor miracle by sending a friend to wave the cash around the dram shops of New Haven's slum area, while he remained in the enlistment line.[46] Others, who found the local supply of substitutes relatively scarce, hastened to the shore-front areas of New York City and Brooklyn, where manpower for a price was still plentiful. So many Connecticut brokers and draftees were operating in the New York City vicinity during September and October that community leaders became alarmed about their own quotas. The *New York Express* demanded indignantly that city authorities stop "the large number of drafted Connecticut men from paying as high as $300 and with only nine months of service," for substitutes.[47]

The public, except presumably those who had hired substitutes, was outraged by the business[48] and promptly decided that the draft itself had been the cause of it all. What remained of a united party front, so solid during the July recruiting drive, fell apart.[49] The state-rights Democrats gained many who had previously supported the Union cause. If the draft had been an outstanding success, this might have justified the damage done to the morale of the state and its troops in the field. Unfortunately, it had been a complete failure. A typical example of how it failed to operate can be seen in the town of Fairfield. On September 10, 62 men were drafted to fill Fairfield's quota. The first selectman took them to New Haven, where they were given physical examinations. All were accepted for military service. On their return to Fairfield, 5 of

45. *Hartford Courant* (Nov. 10, 1862).
46. *Middleton Sentinel and Witness* (Sept. 24, 1862).
47. *New York Express* (Oct. 11, 1863).
48. *Hartford Courant* (Oct. 1, 1862).
49. *New Haven Register* (Nov. 17, 18, 1862).

the draftees purchased substitutes for prices ranging from $300 to $500. These 5 substitutes were the only ones who entered the service; the balance of 57 men bought medical exemptions in New Haven at an average cost of $75 each.[50] In fact, medical exemptions and desertions so reduced the ranks of drafted men that out of 1,212 conscripted, a mere 135 were actually mustered as nine-months volunteers, and 81 of these deserted after arriving at camp, leaving a net gain of 44 men.[51]

Surely, 44 men were a poor showing for all the excitement, not to mention the expense of setting up the draft machinery.[52] On the day set for the draft approximately 85 per cent of Connecticut's quota had been filled by volunteers. Despite heavy Connecticut casualties at Antietam, it would seem to have been a worth-while risk to try another two weeks of intensive recruiting. The War Department had delegated such power to the governors.[53] Buckingham could have delayed a draft as long as he deemed it necessary. He was not under any extraordinary pressure to dispatch all nine-months regiments at once; he knew that the people were generally hostile to a draft they regarded as an example of European militarism. Predraft experiences with medical exemption certificates had demonstrated that he could not count on the honesty of the medical profession. As a good administrator, Buckingham must have known that the state had not created proper policing arrangements to guard against desertion. In December 1862 the *Hartford Courant* estimated that "at least 1,000 deserters were at home in this state. Some are daily arrested and are no sooner put under guard at Fort Trumbull [New London] than they escape again." [54] There were not enough state officers or Federal provost marshals to arrest deserters, and members of the various war committees helped informally in this unpleasant and dangerous task. James G. Batterson, of the Hartford war committee, was worth a score of provost marshals in tracking down deserters. On November 3, for example, he returned to Hartford with John B. Hinch-

50. *Danbury Times* (Oct. 17, 1862).

51. "Governor's Message," *PDLC* (Spec. Sess., Dec. 1862), pp. 7–8.

52. Ibid., p. 36.

53. Buckingham to Gov. Israel Washburn, Jr., et al., Aug. 27, 1862 (*OR*, Ser. II, 2, p. 471).

54. *Hartford Courant* (Dec. 22, 1862).

nan, a deserter from the 25th Connecticut Volunteers, whom he ıad personally arrested at a tavern on Elizabeth Street in New ľork City.[55]

Assailed by the Democrats and conservative Republicans for or- lering the draft, Buckingham came under bitter attack from the adicals of his own party for not requesting authority to raise Negro regiments. In response to a critical query on the subject rom a Winsted radical, Buckingham said: "It seems to me that the ime may yet come when a regiment of colored men may be profit- ıbly employed. But now, if a company . . . should be introduced nto a regiment, a regiment into a brigade, it would create so much ınpleasant feeling and irritation that more evil than good would esult." [56] One wonders why such caution was not manifest in his lraft decision, especially since Negro regiments would have made a lraft unnecessary. Of the Connecticut Negroes eager to enlist, here were enough to make up at least one full regiment. Another rear of draft complications and the Governor's fears of racial prob- ems were to resolve themselves. He was to authorize Negro regi- nents in 1863.[57]

By then, Connecticut had supplied roughly 35,000 men to the ırmed forces of the Union, well over half its able-bodied manpower etween the ages of 18 and 40.[58] The strain had become severe ndeed. Lack of military success, heavy casualities, the bitter after- nath of the 1862 draft, the imminence of future calls—these had come close to cracking the morale of the home front. But more everses lay ahead, and even men of high courage and patriotism vere beginning to wonder how much more the people could tand.[59]

It had been hoped that a majority of the nine-months regiments vould re-enlist for three years. Both Federal and state governments ffered bounties, which at first were set at a total of $502. In November 1863 the state raised its bounty to $300, and towns were

55. Ibid. (Nov. 5, 1862).

56. *Norwich Bulletin* (Aug. 27, 1862).

57. Lane, *Connecticut*, p. 256.

58. "Adjutant General's Office Report," New Haven, 1863.

59. See appropriate entries in John T. Morse, ed., *Diary of Gideon Welles, Secretary of he Navy under Lincoln and Johnson* (Boston, 1911), *1*, chap. 6; Beale, *Bates Diary*, hap. 5.

forbidden to offer any additional financial inducements. But th
nine-months regiments had in most cases been severely handled
Many had been rushed into such bloody engagements as Antietan
and Fredericksburg without training or adequate arms. When th
War Department finally got around to mustering them out, the
had already served a year or more. Their morale was low, few re
enlisted, and the whole project was given up in favor of new re
cruiting drives to fill up the old three-year regiments with a Federa
draft of the enrolled militia if quotas were not met.

On March 3, 1863, Congress passed the first Federal Conscrip
tion Act, which divided the nation into districts, assigning each
proportional quota. A draft would now be a certainty in thos
districts that furnished insufficient volunteers. The new law imme
diately generated a storm of criticism from conservatives, wh
viewed it as an unwarranted invasion of states' rights, and eve
from radicals, who were frankly dismayed because it permitted th
hiring of substitutes or the payment of $300 as an alternative t
military service. To such ardent nationalists this seemed a blatan
discrimination in favor of the wealthy.[60] Critics of the class fea
tures in the law were not surprised at the July draft riots in Ne
York and Boston. "The poor," gravely pronounced the conserva
tive Democratic *Norwich Aurora,* "will never allow the rich man'
money to be an equivalent for their blood." [61]

The New York draft riot made a profound impression in Con
necticut, where it was already obvious that volunteer recruitmen
would not supply the quotas. Buckingham was determined to pre
vent a similar outbreak. At the risk of exceeding his constitutiona
authority, he removed rifles and ammunition from the state arsena
and distributed them secretly among ten responsible citizens in th
various counties. Significantly, those towns along the railroad rout
from New York received the largest number of weapons.[62] Onl
then did the Governor deem it safe to proceed with the draft
which went forward without disorder on July 18.[63]

Well before the draft deadline, hundreds of able-bodied men ha

60. *Hartford Press* (July 12, 1863).

61. *Norwich Aurora* (July 15, 1863).

62. He dispatched 275 out of total 715 muskets to individuals in Stamford, Norwalk and Derby. Croffut and Morris, *Connecticut,* p. 458.

63. Lane, pp. 247–48.

ːft the state. As early as July 1 the railroads had added extra cars o accommodate such a sharp increase in traffic.[64] But at least as ıany came in as departed. Anticipating a good market for substiutes from the rich industrial towns and cities, New York riffraff, liens from Canada and from Europe, and Negroes from all over he North circulated through the counties looking for the highest idders. Some came individually, some were brought in by zealous own agents; but brokers, many of whom were gifted swindlers, nported a majority of the would-be substitutes.

Meanwhile, town authorities had been studying the commutation eatures of the draft law. In an effort to stop the towns from ankrupting themselves in competitive bidding, the 1862 legislaure had expressly forbidden them to offer bounties. But canny electmen discovered a loophole in the act that permitted towns, ities, or boroughs to make appropriations "for the purpose of enouraging the enlistment of volunteers."[65] Why not "encourage" drafted man with the commutation fee which he could either pay o the government or utilize as part payment for a substitute? Almost every town in the state utilized this device, or, under the uise of supporting a volunteer's family, appropriated commutaion funds. The state government had to acquiesce. Indeed, the pecial legislative session of November 1863 actually adopted the levice when it raised the state bounty to $300.

Few drafted men, however, would risk the mere payment of the ee, because it was unclear whether this would exempt them only for he present call or for the duration of the war. It was generally considered safer to hire a substitute who was obligated for three ears' service, and to use the state bounty and the town allotment o defray most of the costs.[66] As in the earlier state draft, the ubstitute business enjoyed boom times. Even an occasional Negro esident, who found himself on the draft list, availed himself of the ubstitute market. William Bowen, a Negro carpenter of Farmingon, sent a white substitute to the front in August 1863.[67] Out of he 11,539 men who were drafted, 8,000 were exempted on various

64. *Hartford Courant* (July 13, 1863).
65. Ibid. (July 21, 1863).
66. For example, Hartford furnished 245 substitutes and only 19 paid the commutaion fee. *Hartford Courant* (Nov. 26, 1862).
67. Ibid. (Aug. 25, 1863).

grounds. Only 248 principals entered the service, together with 2,248 substitutes, 400 of whom promptly deserted.[68]

The whole substitute and deserter problem would have been farcical had it not pointed to a tragic coarsening in the moral fiber of the state. In their desperate effort to escape service, substitutes fired the conscript camp at New Haven, jumped off moving trains,[69] overpowered guards at New Haven and New London, and deserted en masse. The New Haven breakout occurred on July 28, when thirty-five substitutes fanned out like a flock of partridges over the countryside. Twenty-one were eventually recaptured, but not before one deserter was killed and another seriously wounded.[70] Federal authorities enforcing the draft were, if anything, less efficient than state officials had been. In a squad of 127 conscripts sent under guard from New Haven to Baltimore, 60 wriggled through railroad car windows en route.[71] And when the troopship *Cambria* went on the rocks at Hell Gate, 125 conscripts aboard, who were replacements for the 15th Connecticut Volunteers, dared the treacherous currents to escape military duty. Some 15 were drowned.[72]

During the fall and winter of 1863–64 the President issued additional calls for a total of 500,000 troops, and in March 1864 he called for 200,000 more. New Federal legislation had dropped the controversial commutation feature; drafting for one year's service was also authorized if volunteers did not fill up the quotas after fifty days from date of requisition.[73] The Federal government assumed all responsibility for recruiting and demonstrated promptly that it could not cope with the substitute evil. Many of the recruiting officers were openly dishonest. The entire recruiting organization for the 4th Congressional District,[74] including the provost marshal and the examining surgeon, were court-martialed and dismissed from the service for fraudulent activities.[75] In other dis-

68. Croffut and Morris, p. 459.
69. *New Haven Palladium* (Aug. 18, 1863).
70. *New Haven Journal and Courier* (July 29, 1863).
71. *Hartford Courant* (Jan. 30, 1864).
72. Ibid. (Dec. 20, 1864).
73. Ibid. (July 7, 1864).
74. New Haven County.
75. *New Haven Palladium* (Sept. 20, 1863).

tricts, if the army officers were not corrupt, their authorized agents were. Some accepted as much as a $100 commission from town selectmen for each substitute they placed on a town's quota. Prices for substitutes had now reached $700, from which the principal could deduct the $300 state bounty.[76] With Federal bounty and various town allotments (paid in many cases despite apparent violation of state law) a substitute could realize well over $1,000 upon enlistment.[77]

Negroes had been counted on town quotas since midsummer of 1863; and tempted by the Negro manpower resources of the South, the Governor had sent agents to the various theaters of operations with funds and authority to enroll recruits. In addition, the agents were to be paid $300 by each principal for recruiting expenses.[78] The overworked Buckingham did not exercise his customary care in the selection of these agents. Thus a majority of the 1,114 Negroes recruited were defrauded of their state bounty.[79] Towns were also active in recruiting Negroes, and these, too, were frequently swindled out of their bounties by unscrupulous brokers and agents.

From midsummer of 1863 until the end of the war the only significant recruiting of Connecticut citizens was to be found in the re-enlistment of veteran three-year regiments whose terms of service had expired. A corporal's guard of residents, principally Negroes, tempted by high bounties and substitute fees, had volunteered; the rest were nonresidents. In all, Connecticut sent 3,849 substitutes into the army during 1864; [80] 3,347 veterans re-enlisted; [81] and about 2,000 Negroes of the 29th and 30th Regiments went to the front.[82] Despite heavy pressure for more troops during the year, the state managed to convince the War Department that it had met its quota. This feat had been achieved through a wind-

76. *Hartford Courant* (Nov. 15, 1864).

77. Ibid. (Aug. 6, 1864).

78. "General Orders #5," July 1, 1864. Adjutant General's Office, New Haven,1865.

79. House, Jan. 14, 1865; Senate, Jan. 16, 1865. *Hartford Courant* (Jan. 17, 1865); "Governor's Message," PDLC (Special Session, Jan. 1865), pp. 12–15.

80. Croffut and Morris, p. 634.

81. Ibid., p. 462.

82. *Record of Service of Connecticut Men in the Army and Navy of the United States during the War of the Rebellion*, comp. Adjutant General's Office (Hartford, 1889), pp. 861–91.

fall of additional manpower that could be counted and some hard work on the part of the war committees.

New England governors for the past two years had been pressing the Lincoln Administration to count navy enlistments on state quotas. Finally, in mid-1864, Congress enacted the necessary legislation and the adjutant general credited some 2,000 navy men to Connecticut's quota.[83] Meanwhile, the war committees, which had been relieved of their recruiting duties, were engaged in making exact tabulations of deferments. Every medical certificate, every essential war-worker deferment, every alien deposition was collected. From this and other data new quotas were calculated, which considerably scaled down the War Department estimate. In Hartford County alone the war committee secured a quota credit of 2,598 men.[84] Confronted with such a mass of documentation, the army adjutant general had no recourse but to accept the state's evaluation. No men were furnished the hard-pressed armies; but this did not seem to concern the home folk, who regarded quota correction as simple justice and one of the outstanding achievements of the war committees.

It was not so regarded in the army. A soldier wrote the *Hartford Courant* in August 1864 that the obsession with quotas at home was injuring morale. "When the government issues a new appeal for men," he said, "the great effort in New England seems to be to prove by Yankee 'ciphering' that it has been already met, not to supply what it demands—to furnish excuses not soldiers—to show by some new count of veterans, or some addition of stolen names from another town—or some other iniquitous and shameful means that Hartford, or New Haven, or Barkhamstead, is already far ahead of the quota." [85] That muscular Christian, Henry Clay Trumbull, chaplain of the 10th Connecticut Volunteers, was unsparing in his criticism of slackers at home. "Selectmen and war committees may boast of their adroitness in shaving off a draft," he wrote, "but the poor soldier who moves forward in a new fight, unsupported, and meets defeat instead of seeing victory, will have no thanks for those who have left him to suffer or to die alone." [86]

83. Ibid., pp. 919–49.
84. *Hartford Courant* (Aug. 5, 1864).
85. Ibid. (Aug. 9, 1864).
86. Ibid. (Sept. 19, 1864).

As far as substitutes were concerned, veterans were as disgusted with the principals at home who sent them as they were with the low morals of the substitutes themselves. Almost all Connecticut regiments from late 1863 until the war's end received an average of 200 substitutes as replacements. Well over 50 per cent of these mercenaries deserted, some three or four times. The fact that most of them had absolutely no patriotic motives was bad enough, but when they bragged about all the money they had received for their services and then deserted at the first opportunity, it was difficult for the underpaid, underfed veterans to contain their rage. Those veterans who still cherished Unionist ideals were shocked at the callous contempt shown for soldiering that was implicit in the type of men sent forward as substitutes.

Captain Samuel Fiske of the 14th Connecticut had this to say about substitute purchasers: "We hold nobody to be your proper companions, but shoulder hitters, plug uglies, dead rabbits, and all manner of vile vagabonds, the refuse of our cities, the ruffians from our penitentiaries, whom we are accordingly caressing, coaxing and bribing to go to you in our places." [87] General Joseph R. Hawley was equally outspoken in his condemnation of filling the quota without filling the army. He denounced the policy of the war committees as "reckless, cowardly, quota-filling madness." The "very best men are needed in soldiering, as in any other serious and dangerous work," he said vehemently, "the idea that material of the sort now sent us, though inexpressibly vile and piratical, is the best timber for soldiers, I often hear intimated and suggested; and nothing but the knowledge it is not so intended prevents me from receiving and resenting it as a stinging personal insult." [88]

Army critics of the extravagant bounty-substitute system were severely attacked by many prominent Connecticut citizens.[89] The very vehemence of the counterblasts suggests strongly that the truth hurt many of the stay-at-home patriots. For no impartial observer could ignore the desertions in the state and en route, the crimes committed by substitutes, the bounty-jumping, and the all-pervasive air of graft and bribery which had clung to the substitute

87. Samuel Fiske, *Mr. Dunn Browne's Experiences in the Army* (New York, 1866), p. 238.

88. Croffut and Morris, p. 635.

89. Ibid., p. 636.

trade since mid-1863. Nor could any able-bodied civilian ignore completely the fact that he was evading military service. Young and vigorous Cyrus Northrop, who, as editor of the *New Haven Palladium,* had considered Trumbull's and Fiske's criticism of substitutes to be irresponsible, never in postwar years would explain why he did not enlist, but contented himself with war work at home and in Washington. When it was suggested that his health might have been the cause, Northrop replied hastily: "No, no, it had nothing to do with my health," and said no more on the subject. His biographer has concluded that "there the matter rested, and there it must rest for us." [90]

The record of Connecticut may not have been completely creditable in supplying troops, and a spirit of sacrifice was certainly lacking in the somber days after heavy Union defeats, but support of the soldiers in the field and solicitude for their comfort and care did much to redress the balance. On those occasions when the Army supply service broke down, the state rushed whatever was necessary to its regiments. One of the greatest contributions Connecticut made to final victory was the constant attention paid to the morale of its troops and the care of its wounded during the long series of bloody battles from the Peninsular campaign through the siege of Petersberg.

Shortly after the battle of Fredericksburg, a dispatch by the Washington correspondent of the *New York Evening Post* was widely copied in the Connecticut press.[91] Of all the military units the correspondent had seen in the vicinity of Washington, the worst clothed and most wretched were three Connecticut regiments: no knapsacks since the battle of Antietam, not even blankets or overcoats in the savage winter weather.[92] The *Hartford Press* quoted a letter from the 17th Connecticut stating that many of the men were without shoes.[93]

With commendable speed, members of both houses passed a joint resolution authorizing the appointment of four agents to proceed to Fredericksburg and do whatever was required for the material

90. Firkins, *Cyrus Northrop,* p. 176.
91. *Hartford Courant* (Dec. 15, 1862).
92. *Norwich Courier* (Dec. 18, 1862).
93. *Hartford Press* (Dec. 15, 1862).

wants of the soldiers. Before the Governor had selected the delegations, several members volunteered to leave that evening for the front.[94] They were accompanied by two Hartford physicians who had been retained by Elliot Beardsley, a well-to-do member of the legislature, to care for Connecticut wounded.[95]

Inadequate clothing was not the only hardship endured by Connecticut troops in the dark days following Fredericksburg. Most had not been paid for the past six or seven months, and thus had been unable to supplement their meager rations with trifling luxuries from the sutlers' wagons. Again, as in the spring of 1861, the state shouldered a burden which rightfully was the responsibility of the Federal government. Both Governor and legislature made available private and public resources, and if these emergency funds had not come in time, low morale might well have resulted in mutiny.[96] But volunteer local groups rendered the most important soldier welfare services. Every town and city had a soldiers' aid society, supported entirely by private contributions of clothing, preserved food, medical supplies, and money to defray any expenses. During the spring of 1861, when the makeshift army commissary broke down completely in attempting to feed the flood of troops entering the Washington area, rations of Connecticut soldiers would have been reduced to starvation levels if they had not received food packages from friends, families, and communities. Individuals all over the state had worked to collect and transport clothing and food for the front. Men like Elisha Slocum of Norwich and Alfred Walker and Thomas Trowbridge of New Haven gathered clothing, made train arrangements, accompanied the supplies to Washington, and personally distributed them. Twice a month during the year Slocum carried never less than 1500 pounds of parcels to the front.[97] The Hartford and New Haven Steamboat Company transported supplies from Hartford to New York free of charge, and the Hartford insurance companies insured the goods without

94. *Hartford Courant* (Dec. 16, 1862).

95. Ibid. (Dec. 20, 1862). Governor Buckingham appointed the following members: Lyman Coe, Senator of the 5th District, Dr. Samuel T. Salisbury, Rep. from Plymouth, Dr. T. B. Townsend of New Haven, and Orlando J. Hodge of Colebrook. Ibid. (Dec. 17, 1862).

96. House, Dec. 18, 1862; Senate, Dec. 19, 1862. Ibid. (Dec. 19, 1862).

97. *Norwich Courier* (July 4, Dec. 10, 1861).

payment of premium.[98] When Negro regiments were raised in 1863, the colored women of Bridgeport, New Haven, and Hartford organized soldiers' aid societies for Negro troops.[99]

Some of the larger, more prosperous societies like those in New Haven and Hartford employed their own agents to superintend collection, shipment, and distribution of supplies. Generally, such agents coordinated their activities with the Sanitary Commission in Washington, though their prime objective was to aid Connecticut troops. Virgil Cornish, agent for the Hartford society, acted in this dual capacity. He went directly to the Antietam battlefield with several wagonloads of supplies, and then made the rounds of the hospitals in the Washington area. His stout carpetbag, stuffed with stationery, stamps, bitters, liquid rennet, cologne, oranges, and pickles, Cornish gave to sick and wounded soldiers without regard to state designation. But he never forgot to emphasize where it came from. "As they receive the several gifts," he related, "they say, 'Good for Connecticut, good for Hartford and the Association.' " "In this ward," Cornish continued, "are some Connecticut boys, but I cannot pass by one from Massachusetts or Delaware. The Delaware boy says, 'I wish Delaware was as attentive to her soldiers as Connecticut is.' I gave him a bottle of Preston salts, remarking at the same time whenever you start the cork, remember to let Connecticut take a sniff at it with you, and that Delaware and Connecticut are one in putting down this infernal rebellion.' 'I'll do it,' he says, 'good for old Connecticut.' "[1]

The soldiers' aid societies were particularly zealous in shipping traditional foods to the troops for holiday celebrations. Thanksgiving and Christmas were always the occasion for community drives to collect poultry, pies, fruit, both fresh and preserved, and other delicacies. Bridgeport, for example, shipped by the steamer *Arago* 471 barrels, 181 boxes, 20 half-barrels, 4 kegs, 1 firkin, and 1 bale of food and clothing to Connecticut troops on the Carolina coast for Christmas 1863.[2] If the troops in the field did not always receive the foodstuffs, this was not the fault of the societies, for they

98. *Hartford Courant* (Feb. 11, 1865).
99. *Bridgeport Standard* (Oct. 2, 1863).

1. *Hartford Courant* (Nov. 1, 1862).
2. *Bridgeport Standard* (Dec. 22, 1863).

made every effort, including the charter of special vessels, employment of agents, and the attention of the state's congressional delegation, to expedite delivery and guard against theft en route.

During the winter of 1863–64 scurvy assumed epidemic proportions in the Union army. The Sanitary Commission and the Army Medical Corps made frantic pleas for fresh vegetables, and all soldiers' aid societies in Connecticut responded. Bridgeport was the leader in this effort, though supplies came from all over the state. Within ten days 700 barrels of vegetables had been collected and shipped free of charge to Washington, where the Navy Department took over transportation. Society agents, however, accompanied the produce, which was distributed to eleven Connecticut regiments, the 1st Light Battery, and the 1st North Carolina (Colored) Regiment.[3]

Despite the efforts of these patriotic citizens, the first year of the war found no organization of effort or correlation of goods with needs. The New Haven Soldiers' Aid Society was not organized until the autumn of 1862,[4] but when it finally got under way it coordinated the activities of all the towns in the county. Unlike other societies, the New Haven group from the beginning acted as the state organization of the Sanitary Commission, and the supplies it collected were sent forward for general distribution. Utilizing the Governor's and the Treasurer's offices in the New Haven State House as operating headquarters when the legislature was not in session, the New Haven society directed hundreds of lady volunteers who rolled bandages, picked lint, and made pillowcases, sheets, and underclothing in the representative's hall of the General Assembly.[5] Soldiers' aid societies sent immense quantities of bandages and other hospital supplies to the Army Medical Corps.

When the Sanitary Commission, in June 1862, called upon the loosely organized societies for hospital supplies, the materials sent spelled much in devotion and zeal but little in unified effort or conformity to actual needs. Dozens of boxes of pepper, innumerable eyeshades, 600 pincushions, and even bags of rope were typical of the consignments. Of much wider variety was the assortment of

3. Croffut and Morris, p. 465.
4. Osterweis, *New Haven*, p. 325.
5. Croffut and Morris, p. 471.

hospital supplies. The medical officer in charge of the 11th Connecticut regimental hospital received 1,000 pillowcases and a dozen sheets. Such was the penalty of misguided effort.[6] In this instance the Sanitary Commission was to blame, but in countless others it was the complete absence of proper administrative apparatus that defeated the best of intentions.

However, late in 1862 Frederick Law Olmsted, Hartford-born journalist and landscape architect, thoroughly reorganized the Sanitary Commission, centralizing collection and distribution of supplies and coordinating voluntary contributions with actual military needs. At first Olmsted encountered strong opposition to his essential reform measures. The Army Medical Corps, relying on the British Crimean War experience, opposed his assumption of any power, while the people of Connecticut, in common with those of other states, were wary about contributing to a general agency.[7] Furthermore, local agencies had finally organized themselves and had set up a "Connecticut Soldiers' Relief Association" in Washington. Gideon Welles, overwhelmed by his Navy Department labors, for a time headed the Association, to be followed as chairman by the semiretired Admiral Foote.[8] Both Welles and Foote felt they could distribute to Connecticut soldiers through the Association more advantageously than through the Sanitary Commission; [9] their well-meant state patriotism, however, created considerable duplication of effort.[10]

The Association continued throughout the war, and when Foote died in 1863, the Rev. W. A. Benedict succeeded him. Though primarily concerned with the physical needs of Connecticut troops, the Association, especially when headed by Benedict, provided allotment and claim services to Connecticut troops. With pay accounts usually several months behind, a medical discharge for wounds or sickness often meant a claim for back pay against the government. Accurate records of all Connecticut men discharged were kept by the Association, and claims were automatically processed. By special arrangements with the paymaster general, the As-

6. *Norwich Courier* (June 5, 1862).
7. Croffut and Morris, p. 151.
8. *Norwich Courier* (Dec. 18, 1862).
9. Croffut and Morris, pp. 464–73.
10. Ibid., p. 838.

sociation also maintained an allotment service of great convenience to the soldiers.[11]

Despite the preference of Connecticut citizens for contributing through their own agencies and to their own soldiers and hospitals, the Sanitary Commission made great headway. By 1863 local soldiers' aid societies were well integrated with the Sanitary Commission structure. Reserve stocks of medical and other supplies had been accumulated for emergency use and were available on call from Washington.

Individual citizens during the first year of the war also assumed responsibility for looking after the spiritual and social needs of Connecticut soldiers. The war was only a month old when Leonard Bacon formed the Chaplain's Aid Commission and infused into it the vigor of his strong personality.[12] Almost every clergyman and man of wealth in the state contributed liberally. Soon every three-month Connecticut regiment and then the early three-year regiments were supplied with a chapel, tents, and portable libraries.[13] Tents were large, with a seating capacity of 250, and were much appreciated by the volunteers, who used them as a camp social center as well as for divine services.[14] Portable libraries were most popular. Connecticut soldiers particularly enjoyed Dickens, Maria Edgeworth, and T. S. Arthur, and "Army and Navy Melodies" were in much demand for group singing. The Commission collected used Connecticut and New York periodicals and newspapers, which were sent in bundles to the soldiers.[15] Though the Chaplain's Aid Commission was wholly Protestant and heavily Congregational, it provided the 9th (Irish) Regiment with Roman Catholic pamphlets and papers in a fine spirit of tolerance that contrasted strongly with the Know-Nothingism of a few years earlier.[16] Eventually, the tract societies were able to handle the distribution of books and papers, including thousands of instructional pamphlets for the Negroes.[17] By July 1862 the need for the Commis-

11. "Governor's Annual Message," *PDLC* (May Sess., 1865), 3, pp. 14–16.
12. Croffut and Morris, p. 183.
13. Ibid.
14. *Hartford Courant* (June 7, 1862).
15. Ibid. (Jan. 18, 1862).
16. Ibid.
17. Ibid. (Jan. 13, 1862).

sion had ceased, and the organization was dissolved.[18] For almost a year it had supplied an important military welfare service, which Washington had ignored completely.

Care of the wounded as the war intensified after 1862 imposed yet another burden upon both the state government and the people. Thousands of Union casualties were moved into the makeshift hospitals around Washington and Baltimore, threatening to submerge completely the antiquated, inadequate army medical services. Civilians who visited the army hospitals were shocked at what they saw and filled their home newspapers with graphic descriptions of suffering and neglect. Governor Buckingham reacted promptly to their criticisms. During the winter of 1862–63 he appointed Dr. W. H. Coggswell of Plainfield and Dr. W. M. White of Fair Haven as state medical commissioners to investigate hospital conditions. The result of their work and that of other official and unofficial reports from Connecticut observers led the Governor to enlarge New Haven's "Knight" hospital, which at this time was being operated jointly under state and Federal aegis.[19]

The state government and the local aid societies did what they could to improve medical conditions, but unfortunately there was little that could be done in the only area that counted—the state of the medical art. Medicine and surgery were on the brink of revolutionary change, but such vitally important knowledge as the germ theory of disease, antisepsis, blood transfusions, and treatment of shock was all in the future. Even anesthesia, which was standard practice in surgery, had not as yet developed a systematic doctrine. Dr. Nathan Mayer, surgeon of the 11th and later the 16th Connecticut, relied on untrained infantrymen to begin chloroform anesthesia, which he then completed in preparation for operating.[20]

Accepted treatment for wounds was whiskey and morphine, if available, followed by probing with unclean instruments or dirty fingers. In arm and leg wounds, if bone damage were slight and the foreign body could be extracted, medical care was apt to consist of ice water dripped on the wound and liberal doses of whiskey. As

18. Ibid.

19. Ibid. (Feb. 21, 1863).

20. Stanley B. Weld, *Connecticut Physicians in the Civil War*, Connecticut Civil War Centennial Commission (Hartford, 1963), p. 13.

DeForest described it, "whiskey was the internal panacea of the hospital, as iced water was the outward one. Every time that the surgeon visited the four [wounded] officers he sent a nurse for four milk punches and if they wanted other stimulants, such as claret or porter, they could have them for the asking."[21] If bone damage were severe or if the foreign body could not be withdrawn, instant amputation was the prescribed technique—hence the cart-loads of limbs and the pools of blood which gave the appearance of abattoirs to emergency medical facilities under field conditions. Body wounds were almost invariably fatal, and nothing was done for the victim beyond easing his pain with narcotics and whiskey.

Dietary, pulmonary, and other infectious diseases were more or less endemic in the Connecticut regiments, as they were throughout the Army. A steady diet of salt pork, salt beef, hardtack, and coffee produced scurvy and dysentery. Contaminated water and unsanitary field conditions made typhoid and typhus a constant threat. Winter exposure brought pneumonia, and summer marches exposed everyone to bouts of malaria or epidemics of yellow fever. Scurvy and, to a more limited extent, dysentery, among Connecticut troops, were eventually brought under control by shipments of onions, cabbages, and other fresh vegetables from the Sanitary Commission and the soldiers' aid societies. Malaria was also effectively controlled by quinine, with which Connecticut surgeons seem to have been well supplied. But for other diseases the remedies were limited to such well-known purgatives as calomel, castor oil, and various herbal medicines. Nathan Mayer, the 24-year-old German-Jewish-born surgeon, even used calomel and castor oil to combat a yellow fever epidemic at New Berne, North Carolina, during the summer of 1864. Mayer, who had received his medical training in Europe and at the Cincinnati College of Medicine, treated typhoid with fresh milk and beer, and smallpox with whiskey.[22] On the march this popular physician and surgeon dispensed quinine, morphine, and whiskey to sick soldiers. "In one pocket, I carried quinine, in the other morphine and whiskey in my canteen," he wrote. "The quinine—Weightmann's—was cottony, the morphine

21. John W. DeForest, *Miss Ravenel's Conversion from Secession to Loyalty* (New York, Harper, 1939), p. 264.

22. *The Universal Jewish Encyclopedia*, 7 (New York, 1942), 425; Weld, pp. 11–12.

a fine powder. They licked from my hand and the men carried water in their canteens to wash it down." [23]

During the first year of the war most of the troops' medical needs were met by the states and by the individual efforts of regimental surgeons. In 1861 the Army surgeon general had only a skeleton staff; no separate ambulance corps existed, no trained nurses, medical corpsmen, nor any adequate general hospital facilities. The slender stocks of medicines and surgical instruments were soon exhausted in attempting to fill the needs of the rapidly expanding volunteer army. In this emergency Governor Buckingham supplied funds to the regimental surgeons, while the various soldiers' aid societies assisted with voluntary contributions. Thus Connecticut regiments were adequately supplied until the purveyor general and the Sanitary Commission were able to discharge their responsibilities beginning in early 1862.[24]

The hospital shortage, however, was a chronic problem throughout the war, particularly on the regimental level. Dr. Francis Bacon, surgeon of the 7th Connecticut, demonstrated that the medical staff had to be ingenious improvisers as well as physicians and surgeons. Bacon used rubber blankets to patch the holes in the medical tents that were "flimsy speculator's ware at best," and heated 32-pound shot for warmth. He wrote Georgeanna Woolsey that each patient was put to bed with a warm cannon ball at his feet and that a "radiant stack of cherry red balls" in the center of the tent floor served as a space heater. "This is troublesome and laborious to manage, however," remarked Bacon, "and we greatly need some little sheet iron stoves." [25] Dr. Nathan Mayer was another ingenious improviser not only in establishing hospital facilities but in securing supplies and in training nurses. Faced with serious outbreaks of typhoid and smallpox at New Berne, North Carolina, he moved his patients out of their dirty barracks and into tents. Then he organized "a corps of nurses from the rough material of our boys." "I assure you," he wrote in his *Reminiscences of the Civil War*, "they were not bad." The "American has a faculty

23. Weld, p. 13.

24. Ibid., pp. 3–4.

25. Georgeanna Woolsey Bacon and Eliza Woolsey Howland, *Letters of a Family during the War for the Union, 1861–1865* I (New Haven, 1899), pp. 222–25.

and these country boys carried out my Munich ideas better than they deserved." Mayer's next requirement was the procurement of certain sickroom supplies that were used in Germany for the care of such patients. "In an ambulance," he related, "I headed into the enemy's country and brought in several cows, put them in charge of a man from Pomfret . . . and had milk for my typhoids better than Borden condensed which was supplied in cans. I went into New Berne and unearthed some kegs of beer—in a German tinner's shop—paid for them out of the hospital fund, and stimulated my patients Munich fashion." [26] Bacon and Mayer were representative of the medical officers attached to the Connecticut regiments, all of whom were by education, training, and skill superior to the average Union army doctor. Of the 148 medical men who served in the army of the state, 98 per cent were college trained, most at Yale's medical department. Moreover, a majority were older men who had practiced their profession before joining military service.

Despite the efforts of such able doctors as Bacon and Mayer, Connecticut regimental hospitals were dreary, uncomfortable places at best, always short of supplies and trained attendants. Most were similar to one that was described by a visiting member of the Hartford Soldier's Aid Society in the winter of 1861. It was located in a ramshackle three-story frame house, almost bare of furnishings. The 105 sick and wounded patients slept on the floors with their uniform coats for covering, as there were no beds and few blankets.[27] Both state and Federal governments, however, made strenuous efforts to develop adequate general hospital facilities. The great army hospitals which sprang up around Washington seem to have been clean and well administered though never adequate for the thousands of wounded that poured in upon them. The old "state" hospital in New Haven, initially conceived as a medical facility for Connecticut regiments, and always during the war given careful attention by the Governor, was designated as a United States Army Hospital in 1862. Renamed the "Knight" Hospital in honor of New Haven's revered Dr. Jonathan Knight,[28] its appearance and interior arrangements were typical of the better

26. Weld, pp. 11–12.

27. *Hartford Courant* (Dec. 9, 1861).

28. Weld, p. 9; Osterweis, *New Haven,* p. 326.

army hospitals during the war. The main building, in "the Grecian architectural mode," had been constructed in 1830 and had a capacity in excess of 100 beds. In 1862 two temporary "A" frame barracks were built, and subsequently tent pavilions were added, bringing the capacity of the Knight up to 1,500 beds. The unpainted wooden barracks presented a rude, austere appearance, but the interior walls were painted white and were well maintained. Each barracks was divided into four wards that accommodated more than 200 patients. Two rows of wooden bedsteads—eighteen inches high—lined the walls, leaving a passageway in the center. At the foot of each bed stood a spittoon, "teaching . . . the men a lesson of neatness," according to an interested observer. In addition, the patient was provided with a chair, a washstand, a shelf above his head for personal effects, and a tin identification holder that contained his name, place of residence, company, regiment, and diagnosis. Beds were equipped with straw mattresses on which were two sheets and two blankets. Hospital regulations required that the sheets be changed once a week.[29] The Knight records indicate that 25,340 cases were treated at the hospital during the war.[30]

It is safe to say that a majority of the sick or wounded Connecticut soldiers were treated, at least initially, in far worse surroundings. Mayer, for example, performed most of his amputations and other surgery in tumbledown sheds and barns on operating tables improvised from doors, rough planks, or logs. Springless ambulances, which jolted over rutted dirt or plank roads, tortured the wounded men. DeForest has described such a trip from Port Hudson to Springfield Landing. "So nearly supernatural in its horror, was the burden of anguish which filled that long train of jolting wagons," he wrote, "that it seemed at times to his fevered imagination as if he were out of this world, and journeying in the realms of eternal torment." [31] To be sure, much of the misery suffered by sick or wounded soldiers must be attributed to the undeveloped state of medical and surgical knowledge during the war. But inattention to the procurement of proper ambulances, which certainly could have been designed and constructed, and to adequate long

29. *Hartford Courant* (Feb. 6, 1863).

30. Weld, p. 9.

31. DeForest, *Miss Ravenel's Conversion*, p. 262.

distance transportation for the wounded was the result of chaotic, improvised medical organization in the field.

The Connecticut wounded, whenever possible, were brought home under the direction of the Governor's personal agent in New York, John Almy, and his volunteer staff, the Sons of Connecticut Association. Once Almy had taken over, the invalids were assured of better treatment. The appointment of a New York agent was one of Buckingham's more important acts, and his choice of Almy could not have been wiser. Throughout the difficult days, without accepting any wages, this selfless individual performed all the difficult tasks of funneling Connecticut troops through the city, and was especially diligent in protecting them from unscrupulous traders.[32] More than once, his personal attention to details spared the volunteers some of the hardships involved in ocean trips to the theater of operations.

When the transport carrying the 13th Connecticut took on water in New York City, a profiteer supplied it in filthy oil casks. If these had been accepted, the troops would have been deprived of water for the remainder of the trip. But Almy discovered the fraud. Within a few hours he had the contractor behind bars, and the regiment was supplied with clean water in clear casks. Almy was also a friend, indeed the only friend, on whom many sick or wounded country boys could count when they were dumped by army transport in New York City. In April 1862, 300 disabled veterans of the battle of Roanoke arrived in the city. Sixty of them were members of Connecticut regiments. Penniless and ragged, they had not been paid for over six months and had no means of getting home. Almy immediately took charge. He applied to the army paymaster's office in the city, and when he learned that it was without funds for this purpose he telegraphed directly to Secretary Stanton, who replied that he would forward $10,000 for special emergency payment.[33]

The work of Almy and the Sons of Connecticut in New York emphasizes the important responsibilities of the Northern states in support of military activities. Connecticut's Washington and New York agencies, staffed with volunteers and supported by private

32. *Norwich Courier* (March 20, 1862).

33. *New Haven Journal and Courier* (April 11, 1862).

and state funds, maintained a web of agents who performed significant welfare services for the troops and their families. Certainly, the course pursued by Connecticut and by Buckingham in support of the Union, if open to criticism with respect to military manpower, was above reproach in providing essential services to its troops in the field.

PART TWO

A Thousand Circling Camps

5. AU REVOIR HERE OR HEREAFTER

WHEN THE EIGHTEENTH CONNECTICUT joined General Robert Milroy's division of the 8th Corps at Winchester, Virginia, it had never seen an armed enemy soldier. The men had been on guard duty in the Washington-Baltimore area since their muster into Federal service six months before. Exactly three weeks after joining Milroy's force on May 24, 1863, the 18th Connecticut had ceased to exist as an organized unit. Thirty-one of its members were dead, including one company commander; 44 were wounded, including 4 company commanders; its commanding officer, second in command, and 522 other officers and men were prisoners of war.

Twice the regiment had charged in an effort to break through General Jubal Early's 30,000 Confederate troops, which had surrounded Winchester. Then, completely cut off, short of ammunition, exhausted from forty-eight hours of constant combat, the commanding officer of the 18th—angular, bewhiskered William G. Ely—surrendered the regiment. He offered what was left of his sword, the hilt and about six inches of blade (it had been shattered by a musket ball), to Confederate General Walker. "When was this done, Colonel?" Walker inquired politely. "This morning, sir, in the fight," replied Ely. "You deserve to keep this, here are the marks of bravery and honor," said Walker. "I will give orders that it be returned to you."[1] Ahead lay twenty-one months in various Southern prisons for most, eventual exchange for Colonel Ely and six officers, and a dozen hard fights for the remnant that escaped Winchester. In all, the 18th was to suffer over 300 casualties, a full third of its original strength.

The 18th was a typical Connecticut three-year regiment. Eighty-five per cent of its complement was native-born, the remainder

1. William C. Walker, *History of the Eighteenth Regiment Connecticut Volunteers in the War for the Union* (Norwich, 1875), p. 118.

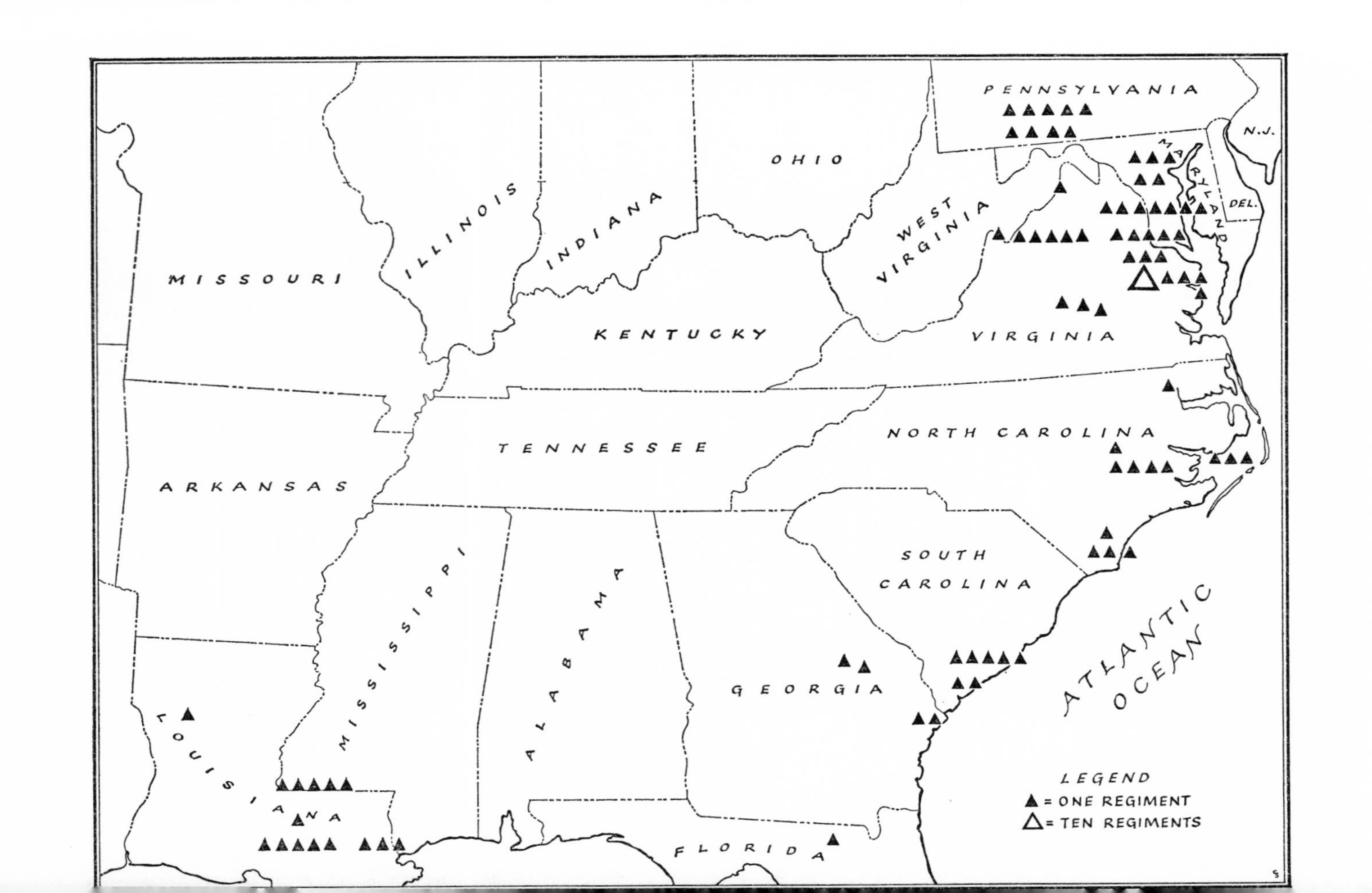
PENNSYLVANIA
N.J.
MARYLAND
DEL.
OHIO
WEST VIRGINIA
VIRGINIA
MISSOURI
ILLINOIS
INDIANA
KENTUCKY
TENNESSEE
NORTH CAROLINA
ARKANSAS
SOUTH CAROLINA
MISSISSIPPI
ALABAMA
GEORGIA
LOUISIANA
FLORIDA
ATLANTIC OCEAN
LEGEND
▲ = ONE REGIMENT
△ = TEN REGIMENTS

principally of Irish birth. Farmers and farmers' sons formed the largest occupational group, some 35 per cent, closely followed by factory workers, about 30 per cent. Slightly over half the regiment were married men, and 80 per cent were over 20 years of age.[2] Colonel William G. Ely, commanding officer, had been trained as a civil engineer. In April 1861 he was assistant superintendent of the Rogers locomotive works in Paterson, New Jersey. A man of personal courage and conviction, he had returned to his native state and enlisted as a private in the 1st Connecticut Volunteers. Ely was second in command of the 6th when he was offered and accepted the colonelcy of the 18th.[3] As commanding officer he was a firm believer in setting an example for the men. And like so many factory managers converted to military command, he was a thoroughgoing paternalist in his dealings with the regiment. The officers of the 18th were all community leaders, ambitious young lawyers, journalists, skilled tradesmen. With one exception they were residents of the larger towns or small cities of eastern Connecticut.[4] Officers had recruited their own companies and had known most of their men personally before the war.

Each enlisted man had received an average bounty of $100 from his town, $100 from the Federal government, and $90 from the state.[5] If he was married and had children, he received, in addition to his army pay of $13 a month, a maximum state allowance of $10 a month. A uniform allowance was also granted to enlisted men. Officers received pay ranging from $45 a month for second lieutenant to $95 for full colonel. They were eligible for bounties but were required to pay for their rations and customarily supported a body-servant.

In 1862 total income for a private, including bounties and pay, was sufficient to support a family of five for a year at a modest living standard. For those of the 18th who were factory workers, bounties and pay prorated over one year would have been roughly equivalent to their civilian wages. For those who came from a farm background, income from military service frequently meant an

2. Ibid., p. 17.

3. Duane H. Hurd, ed., *History of New London County, Connecticut, with Biographical Sketches of Many of its Pioneers and Prominent Men* (Philadelphia, 1882), p. 111.

4. One officer was from Hartford County.

5. Croffut and Morris, *History of Connecticut*, p. 224.

increase in family purchasing power. However, if the enlisted man happened to be a farm owner and operator with minor children, as many were, army pay and bounties did not compensate for the loss of his management and labor. Agricultural commodity prices were rising, it was true, but the hard-scrabble acres that covered most of the state needed careful management if they were to support a family and allow for continuing investments in stock, fertilizer, and equipment that would maintain minimum productivity.

Surely, bounties could not have been a prime inducement to the volunteers in the 18th Regiment; and regiments formed earlier were not even granted these. When bounties and substitute fees rose high enough to provide a real incentive, they were to attract no better material than thugs, thieves, the lame and the halt, if not the blind. Why then did the men enlist? Why, after enlistment, did so many raw troops display such personal bravery, such response to command? How was it that those who did not die of disease and exposure were able to endure what we, in the twentieth century, would regard as unspeakable food, frightful camp and hospital conditions, and utterly exhausting marches and countermarches? How did they manage to fight it out to the end when they knew that many of their general officers were incompetent or reckless of human life or both? What was the stimulus that kept them going when they were perfectly aware that there were slackers at home who provided bounty-jumping deserters for substitutes? And what of the speculators, who were making money everywhere at the expense of an enlisted man's comfort and even his life? Yet manage they did. Some straggled, some wrote angry letters home, more learned to drink and swear. But there were no mutinies in the Connecticut three-year regiments, very few desertions, except among the substitutes, and rarely disrespect for officers.

Patriotic revivals, conducted by respected community leaders, had been important factors in the original enlistment of the three-year regiments. Connecticut communities were neighborly places, but class lines were more clearly defined than today. When the leading men of the cities and towns asked for recruits, they were generally successful, at least through the year 1862. In a tiny factory village like Voluntown, for example, Ira Briggs, owner-manager of the sole cotton mill, conducted war meetings which resulted in thirty-eight enlistments. Briggs was the most important man in Voluntown. Almost everyone worked in his Beachdale mill, lived in Beachdale-owned tenements, and traded at the Beachdale-owned company store. Briggs was a self-made man, a driver, as any small manufacturer had to be if he was to succeed in the Connecticut of the early sixties, yet he was neighborly and matter of fact in his relations with the workers.[6]

When Ira Briggs spoke for the Union, it meant more than just another patriotic speech to his spinners and weavers. Perhaps Briggs evoked in some empathic fashion a vicarious kinship with his overworked, underpaid men, in which they were able to identify themselves with him, with his success, with his prominence. But we can imagine that he really captured the imagination of his audience when he promised the young workers an escape from their hard, monotonous life to a glorious crusade. Suddenly there must have seemed a way out of all the daily problems, all the labor, all the boredom of life in a dreary mill town. Briggs, the owner, who gave or withheld the daily bread, the figure of authority, had voiced his personal concern and had asked the young men of Voluntown to share it with him. Scenes like this were duplicated all over the state with more of a flourish, more distinguished orators, and larger audiences in the cities, but with the same message, the same images, the same close rapport between the great ones on the dais and the workers and clerks in the audience. The great religious revival that had begun in 1857 merged into the patriotic revivals of 1861 and 1862. These were to fill up the ranks of the 18th Connecticut and seven more three-year regiments in record time.

Yet the social environment had to be just right for such emotional appeals to take hold as vigorously as they did. And once the recruiting drives of 1862 had gathered up the impressionable young men—the adventurous, the patriotic, the discontented—revivalist techniques would lose their appeal. Meanwhile, they accomplished their purpose by making a clean sweep of the best potential military manpower still remaining in the state. Tough, ambitious, frustrated individuals, they enjoyed military life at first as a welcome relief from the farm, the mill, or the dry goods store. And their character

6. Hurd, pp. 748–49.

and stamina were strong enough to keep them in the ranks long after the glamour had worn off.

Society in Connecticut betrayed a kind of disorientation that stemmed from the tensions and the uncertainties of the incomplete industrial state. Old and comforting landmarks were receding, yet the further shore was still a smudge along the horizon, more to be imagined than perceived. To the young and ambitious, this neutral ground, this becoming rather than being, seemed in some vague way to represent opportunity; and they were eager to leave behind what remained of older constraints and limitations, to push on with the course. The nascent nationalism of the North, stimulated by the transportation and communication advances of the industrial revolution, was already a power in the land. But much of the naïveté, the simplicity, the parochialism of the old order remained—just enough, in fact, for young men to see in a volunteer army and a great patriotic war in "foreign" places an acceptable means of escape from a life which suddenly seemed hard, narrow, and commonplace.

The new order was crude, brash, demanding, though the paternalism of the early industrial revolution had not as yet given way to the impersonal factory system that was to characterize the postwar period. It had, however, become progressively less benevolent. As factories grew larger and machinery more sophisticated in the 1850s, entrepreneurs were faced with increasing capital outlays, which, in turn, put higher premiums on the use of property, plant, and equipment. Moreover, in a highly competitive market, where profit margins had to be shaved expertly for survival, capital for improvement and expansion was difficult to generate. Management tended to speed up production and, if possible, hold down fixed charges. Sixty-five to seventy hours of labor each week were considered the normal schedule, while the factory managers, in their desperate efforts to keep down overhead, crowded more and more machinery into their mills.[7]

7. John R. Commons, et al., eds., *A Documentary History of American Industrial Society, 8* (Cleveland, 1910), 161–62; A. J. Y. Brown, *The American Economy* (New York, 1951), p. 54; Melvin T. Copeland, *The Cotton Manufacturing Industry in the United States* (Cambridge, 1917), p. 10.

In appearance and in function many of these mills and factories reflected the capital scarcity of the times. They were rickety, poorly ventilated wooden, stone, or brick buildings, most dating back to the 1820s. Interior levels, in some instances, were supported so inadequately that the addition of tons of new machinery caused the collapse of an entire floor, precipitating workers, machinery, belts, pulleys, and bales of raw and finished materials down to the next level. Such overcrowding of the mills and speed-up of the machinery had other unpleasant or dangerous aspects. Factory aisles between the whirling, unguarded machinery were narrow and meandering. Workers had to squeeze through sidewise or maneuver themselves around corners. Many a girl was scalped by catching her long hair on the edge of a whizzing shuttle; many a worker was drawn into the machinery by missing a step or slipping on grease-soaked floors.[8] Most factories were firetraps, full of oil-soaked waste and overheated machinery.[9] Fire escapes, even in the most modern mill, were the exception rather than rule; emergency exits were few. The state had few laws governing factory inspection or fire prevention, and insurance companies had not as yet developed sufficient experience to insist on certain standards with respect to inflammable materials, boiler inspection, or the like.[10] An industrial accident that permanently incapacitated the principal wage earner spelled economic tragedy to a worker's family, though mill owners usually accepted some responsibility and the community helped. In addition, most workingmen did have some cooperative arrangement to insure against death or disability. Financial aid, however, was scant and, of course, temporary.

In times of economic stress wages were always cut sharply. During the depression of 1857, for example, Connecticut mill workers received drastic cuts in wages, but commodity prices were not reduced proportionately until a year later.[11] Even in prosperous years like 1851, a highly paid skilled worker with a family of five made about $10 a week, slightly less per week than what his family

8. Commons, 7, 133–35.

9. *Hartford Courant* (Aug. 14, 1858).

10. Norris G. Osborn, ed., *History of Connecticut in Monographic Form*, 2 (New York, 1925), pp. 200, 228.

11. Commons, 8, pp. 314–15.

needed for food, shelter, and clothing. And the food for such a worker, as outlined in the *New York Tribune,* was high on cheap, monotonous, starchy products, flour and potatoes; low on meat, milk, butter, eggs, and cheese. The *Tribune* diet listed two pounds of butcher's meat per day, or an average of six ounces of meat for each member of the family. It made no provision in its budget for leisure, amusement, or even such trifling delicacies as a pudding for dessert. In the mill towns of Connecticut the average wage was $5 per week, considerably less than in New York City.[12] Fresh meat appeared on the table perhaps twice a week; and the family diet consisted principally of dried beans, bread, potatoes, cheap salt fish, and salt pork. From 1851 to 1858 the purchasing power of the workers remained approximately the same. Some improvement occurred between 1858 and 1860, but only because widespread unemployment had reduced living costs.[13]

A worker's life in the cities of Connecticut was little better, although two of the skilled trades had established unions, which offered some protection to their members; and a chronic shortage of skilled workers curtailed the more vicious aspects of the technological speed-up. But for every skilled worker ten were semiskilled or unskilled. Whether a young man lived in a succession of Connecticut mill-town tenements or in the rapidly developing urban industrial slums, his standard of living was low, his opportunity for advancement narrow, but his physical endurance was apt to be fairly high. If he could survive until his mid-twenties the epidemics of typhoid fever, dysentery, and typhus in the summer, or the winter complaints of tuberculosis and pneumonia, and still work a 72-hour week in the factories, he could stand considerable hardship. To many, army life in 1861 and through most of 1862 must not have seemed excessively hard or even particularly danger-

12. Norman J. Ware, *The Industrial Worker, 1840–1860: The Reaction of American Industrial Society to the Advance of the Industrial Revolution* (Boston, 1924), p. 31; Commons, 8, 227. Indeed, Robert Layer's estimate of weekly earnings in the New England cotton mills during the decade of the '50s averaged about $3.75 a week. Robert G. Layer *Earnings of Cotton Mill Operatives, 1825–1914* (Cambridge, 1955), pp. 26–27.

13. Ware, p. 33; Felicia J. Deyrup, *Arms Makers of the Connecticut Valley: A Regional Study of the Economic Development of the Small Arms Industry* (Northampton, 1948), p. 242.

ous until the blood baths of Antietam and Fredericksburg dispelled this particular notion. And by then Connecticut had enlisted almost all the native manpower it would ever recruit.

Farm life was rugged too. Whatever the romanticizers have said about the charm and beauty of the rural scene, the average young Connecticut farmer or farmer's son of the 1850s found little time to rhapsodize on the psychic benefits of the agrarian idyll. It took an enormous amount of man and beast hours to wrest a living out of the average Connecticut farm. During the spring, summer, and fall, when the countryside was at its loveliest, farmers were busiest with their crops. Grueling, back-breaking labor, six days a week, was absolutely essential. Farm machinery, just beginning to appear, would not materially lighten the farmers' burden until well into the postwar period. The innate conservation of the countryside and the high cost of such equipment ruled against wide use, but more important was the fact that most Connecticut cash crops—dairy, tobacco, orchard products, and potatoes—still required traditional farm labor techniques.

The long harsh winters were times of heavy work too—animal care, woodcutting for family use and extra income, ice-cutting, and endless repairs of farm equipment. An isolated Connecticut farm looks charming in a Currier and Ives winter scene or in a colorful Prang's chromo, but it was a bleak and uncomfortable place, with icy drafts, unheated bedrooms, and no conveniences. Cyrus Northrop described Ridgefield, a typical Connecticut farm community, in the winter of 1858. "No one there," he wrote in his diary, "all desolate—trees naked—grass dead—houses dreary and cold—church solemn and desolate—everything like a deserted village. Oh, give me the city in the winter—the city where is life—where men move and you see them and if one dies, it does not seem as if . . . the graveyard had swallowed the entire place." [14]

A farm family's diet was generally more plentiful and varied than that of a mill worker. Connecticut farms, even those that specialized in tobacco culture, raised most of the family foodstuffs. Salted mutton, pork, and codfish were staples, together with turnips, potatoes, cabbages, and hull corn (a kind of hominy) and

14. Firkins, *Cyrus Northrop*, p. 13.

dried beans. Some poultry was raised, mainly for eggs but not for meat, because chickens and turkeys consumed too much expensive grain. Since the salted meats and the root crops were replenished but once a year, farmers' families were used to the distinct flavors of sprouted, moldy potatoes, soft, acrid turnips, and strong, stringy meat. Fresh meat was always something of a luxury, to be indulged on infrequent Sundays and holidays, and briefly at slaughtering time in the fall. Smoked meat was also considered expensive and seldom appeared on farm tables. Farm boys, like factory workers, were certainly well prepared for the army diet. They were also used to hard work and were healthier than the town and city volunteers, except in one important respect. The relative isolation in which they lived made them highly susceptible to such childhood diseases as measles, mumps, and chicken pox, and they seemed less able to cope with the infectious diseases like dysentery and pulmonary disorders that swept through the army camps.[15]

Life on the farm for most of the young men during this period of changing social values was, if anything, more restrictive than life in the mill town and infinitely more sterile than city life. Travel into the outside world, beyond their native village or marketing place, was reserved for very special occasions. It was a question of time and money, interchangeable factors to the subsistence farmer. Stagecoaches, the only means of public transportation for a majority of Connecticut farmers, were too expensive to be used for social trips. Wagons and teams could be better employed at home, and so could the man-hours consumed in travel when it took an entire day to make a ten-mile round trip. Factory workers at least traveled about in search of work in slack seasons; farmers were almost as closely tied down to their native region as feudal serfs.

Social life centered around the church, remembered with distaste by most young men of the period, and politics, remembered with great affection. John Hooker, who belonged to a town family in the agricultural community of Farmington, writing fifty years afterward, still recalled the icy atmosphere of the local church, the uncomfortable box pews, the minister in his overcoat, waving his

15. George W. Adams, *Doctors in Blue: The Medical History of the Union Army in the Civil War* (New York, 1952), p. 15.

arms around "a good deal to keep himself warm, thus making his delivery more impressive." [16] Donald Grant Mitchell, the humorist, (Ik Marvel), also of a town family thought that the sermons of those days were very long for children.[17] His entire childhood in the late 1820s was dominated by a distaste for the compulsory Bible-reading, chapter after chapter, and "then the drill in the catechism, with reasons 'annexed' and the long hours at church, seeming to listen, but not listening to the sermons." [18]

Mitchell, the son of a prosperous minister and grandson of a rich lawyer and judge, had enjoyed a privileged youth. Cyrus Northrop, who came of an average farm family, spent four hours every Sunday attending three services. His laconic remark was "Sunday, not much of a day of rest," but he did look forward to the customary after-church dinner of "nicely browned salt shad with potatoes." The Northrop family never had a supper meal on Sunday.[19] But if Northrop and Hooker found church very dismal indeed, they found the political campaigns and the town meetings of their youth most exciting. "Lindenwold [sic], the fox's hole," sang the Ridgefield farmers in 1844, "the coons all laugh to hear it told, Ha, Ha, Ha, such a nominee, as James K. Polk of Tennessee." When the news finally filtered through that Polk had beaten Clay, the ten-year-old Northrop broke down and wept.[20] In between state and national election campaigns, town meetings were the only other source of prime entertainment and interest. "The selectmen," as John Hooker remembered, "were allowed one dollar a day for the time actually spent in the town business and were held to a very strict account of what they had done to earn the money. I remember one of the farmers who was opposing some outlay . . . remarking that 'if you touch a man's pocket, you touch him all over.' " [21]

To the hard-working, credulous farm boys, whose principal reading had been the Bible and the weekly edition of the Hartford, New Haven, or New York dailies, and whose main entertainment

16. Hooker, *Reminiscences*, p. 12.

17. Waldo H. Dunn, *The Life of Donald Grant Mitchell, "Ik Marvel"* (New York, 1922), p. 27.

18. Ibid.

19. Firkins, p. 40.

20. Ibid., p. 34.

21. Hooker, p. 21.

was politics, the increasing political tension of the late 1850s must have been exciting. The semimilitary Wide Awake campaign of the Republicans, which they carried into the countryside, was a first-rate emotional outlet for these sensation-starved young folk. Even the grim and practical head of the family relaxed his relentless authority. For once, the young men could use the team to travel to town and join the parade. When the war came, the Connecticut countryside had been well primed with a volatile mixture of restlessness and escapism. And much the same kind of restless spirit was evident among the young urban members of the upper classes.

If emerging industry was polarizing Connecticut society, we might expect that it would exert the greatest stress on the leadership group in the cities and larger towns. For this group, in these places, was planning and executing the revolution. Not consciously, but intuitively, community leaders were responding to the technological possibilities of the period. They could feel material success in their bones; but as hard as they worked (and they worked harder perhaps than the farmers and the mill hands), progress seemed exasperatingly slow and difficult. Capital was short, skilled labor scarce and hard to handle, competition strong, markets capricious. Nor were the entrepreneurs themselves immune to the opposite attraction of older values. Almost against their will, as they drove on, they seemed to be making business decisions and social judgments that subtly disturbed ingrained ethics and morals. It was all somewhat troubling to the capitalists directly involved. But for those on the periphery, the college-trained youth, the aspiring clerks, the junior partners, the young lawyers, all who had the ambition and the insight but as yet neither the opportunity nor the responsibility, Connecticut urban life must have appeared incredibly bleak and restrictive.

Some, like Dexter Wright, a Meriden lawyer and soon to be commanding officer of the 15th Regiment, escaped to California during the 1849 gold rush. Some like John Hooker or Stephen Kellogg, who was to command the 2nd Connecticut Heavy Artillery, shipped before the mast; but because of family ties, many simply would not make individual decisions involving such a radical departure from accustomed pursuits. These would have to be made for them, and were when society decreed that military service was both a duty and an honor. Meanwhile, they stayed at home and reduced their frustrations by work, or sought relaxation in such work-oriented endeavors as militia companies, politics, and religious revivals. And even in these tedious avocations they were pathetically circumscribed by an unyielding social and moral code.

During the winter of 1851–52 that rough-hewn old Presbyterian evangelist Charles G. Finney, himself Connecticut-born, visited Hartford to conduct a religious revival. Only the young people were responsive to his appeals for public conversion. In the course of his prayer meetings he converted over 600, thereby creating a perplexing problem for the venerable Joel Hawes, pastor of Hartford's First Congregational Church. Hawes was stirred by the zeal of Hartford youth but was afraid it would vanish as soon as the young people joined the church congregation. "What shall we do with these young converts?" Hawes asked Finney. "If we receive them to our churches, where we have so many elderly men and women who are always expected to take the lead in everything, their modesty will make them fall behind . . . and they will live as they have lived and be inefficient as they have been." Finney suggested a young people's missionary society outside the churches. When the Congregational clergy accepted his proposal, the new converts conducted the most extensive and successful revival the city had ever witnessed.[22]

Polite society tended to be dominated by the Congregational Church, which still clung with a kind of awesome persistency to the patriarchal doctrines of Calvinism as expounded by Jonathan Edwards. What had once given form, substance, and integrity to an ordered society had by the 1850s sought refuge in social convention. Such an elegant young observer as rich and aristocratic John William DeForest, soon to be the captain of Company I, 12th Connecticut, described its workings early in 1861 in New Haven. "New Boston [New Haven] is not a lively nor a sociable place . . . the city is divided into more than the ordinary cliques and coteries and they are hedged from each other by an unusually thorny spirit of repulsion," he wrote.[23] Farmers and factory work-

22. Charles G. Finney, *Memoirs of Rev. Charles G. Finney: Written by Himself* (New York, 1876), pp. 417–19.

23. DeForest, *Miss Ravenel's Conversion,* p. 14.

ers at their simple social functions—barn raisings, quilting bees, or river excursions—at least managed to enjoy an occasional robust frolic. But the dreary afternoon dinner parties that DeForest detested, with the pristine decanter of sherry brought from the family medicine cabinet, provided thin entertainment for a generation that was covertly peeping into the haut-monde rompings of France's Second Empire as reported by interested British observers or into such shockers as *Madame Bovary* and Eugène Sue's *Mysteries of Paris*. "Colonel," asked DeForest's New Haven-bred hero, Colburne, of Carter, the second in command of the 2nd Barataria (Connecticut) Volunteers, "wouldn't you like to go on a pic-nic?" "Pic-nic?—political thing? Why, yes; think I ought to like it; help along our regiment?" "No, no; not political . . . I mean an affair of young ladies, beaux, baskets, paper parcels, sandwiches, cold tongue, biscuits and lemonade." [24]

DeForest was one of those rare individuals among Connecticut's upper classes who had decided upon a writing career. Well traveled, cosmopolitan, he had prior to the war divided his time between New Haven and Charleston, South Carolina. Alfred Howe Terry, an acquaintance whose lineage in Connecticut terms was every bit as illustrious, and whose inherited fortune was ample for a life of ease, more accurately typifies the frustrations of the able and ambitious young man in prewar urban society.

Terry was thirty-four years old in 1861. He had been practicing law in New Haven for the past twelve years.[25] An excellent trial lawyer, with a fine personality, impeccable family connections, and a huge capacity for work, he was still unable after five years of practice to make much of a career at the New Haven bar. Terry had been happy to accept the clerkship of the County Superior Court when it became vacant in 1854—an honorable position but scarcely a challenge to a man of his talents and energy.[26] While performing his court duties and carrying on his law practice, Terry devoted long hours to drill and instruction of the Connecticut militia. This must have been a particularly thankless task, since the

24. Ibid., p. 24.

25. Wilson and Fiske, *Appleton's*, 6, 65.

26. Allen Johnson, ed., *Dictionary of American Biography*, 18 (New York, 1928), 378.

Connecticut militia had long since degenerated into an ill-equipped, Graustarkian affair, fit only for a colorful show on state occasions. Had there been no war, Terry might have ended his career as an obscure superior court judge. However, within three years he was to be a major general and the hero of Fort Fisher.

The New Haven of 1860 had some possibilities for a novelist with satire in mind, but it was scarcely a promising place for the display of youthful talent. In its commercial as well as its social life, this little city of 40,000 still lingered in the pale blue twilight of genteel Calvinism. Yet not a stone's throw from Yale College sprawled the Tontine Hotel, where commercial travelers, promoters, and politicians drank whiskey punches and smoked "segars." And not four blocks from the campus, the working-class tenements and dram shops were still roaring with life when long before sunrise Yale's ex-president Jeremiah Day, who had graduated from college during Washington's Administration, slipped through his garden gate for his daily trip to chapel, where he offered a tremulous prayer for restless students and all backsliders.[27]

Other Connecticut cities and towns were perhaps less convention-ridden than New Haven. The differences in outlook between Hartford and New Haven, for instance, are best understood by the fact that one was dominated by Yale and the other by banks and insurance companies. Textile magnates were beginning to secularize Norwich society. Shipping interests and the Baptist Church promoted liberal tendencies in New London, while the Methodists of Middletown had been traditionally more responsive to change than their Congregational brethren in New Haven. But it was all a question of degree. Career opportunities for young men of good family and education were severely limited everywhere. Social life was hedged all about with traditional restrictions still geared largely to the needs of the older generation. The new industrial economy was inadequate in 1860 to provide rapid advancement for the qualified and energetic young man.

Joseph Hawley of Hartford, one year older than Terry and soon to serve as his faithful lieutenant, gained prominence earlier. In this he was fortunate to have been associated with two powerful and talented individuals, Gideon Welles and John M. Niles, who had

27. Dunn, p. 47.

gained state and national stature rebelling against the status quo in Jackson's day. In 1856 they were both engaged in their last rebellion—the cause of Free Soil and the Republican party. Detecting a kindred spirit and impressive forensic talents in the 29-year-old Hawley, they made him editor of the first Republican daily in the state, the *Hartford Evening Press*. But even rebels must conform to age and experience. Though Hawley occasionally stepped out of bounds, Welles and his rich Hartford friends exercised a firm control over the *Press's* editorial policy. From the first day of his editorship until the day he marched off as a company commander of the 3rd Connecticut, Hawley averaged an eighty-hour weekly stint in the *Press* office, broken only by a few hours off on Saturday afternoon and evening after the edition had gone to press. "I board at the U.S. Hotel near the office," he wrote his father in March 1860, "my only social relaxation is taking supper Saturday afternoon and spending the evening at Hooker's with our minister, Mr. Burton." [28] For all this dedication and labor, Hawley's share of the paper's profits for the year amounted to $800.[29]

A majority of the officers who recruited and led the Connecticut volunteers were not so well educated, nor did they have the career potential of Hawley, Terry, or DeForest. But they shared a similar urban environment,[30] and a surprisingly high proportion had received the equivalent of a high-school education or better. Most were young men of some prominence in their communities; all were eager, used to hard work, determined to broaden their limited horizons. Some, like Joseph Converse, were unusually sensitive to the problems and possibilities of their generation. Converse, a quiet, rather distant individual, came from the semirural factory town of Windsor Locks. Well read, gifted with a pleasant prose style and with good powers of description, he had hoped for a writing career. Lack of funds had kept him from entering college, but in addition to his work on the family farm he continued his writing as a local correspondent for the *Hartford Press*. When the war came, Converse was one of the first to enlist from Windsor Locks. His intelligence and ability were instantly recognized when he was made first

28. Hawley to Francis Hawley, March 4, 1860 (Hawley Papers).
29. Hooker to Hawley, March 10, 1862 (ibid.).
30. Croffut and Morris, *Connecticut*, pp. 225–27.

sergeant of Company C of the 1st Connecticut. After Bull Run he was commissioned a second lieutenant in the 11th, and eventually rose to the rank of major in that regiment. During the next two years of army life Converse repeatedly questioned the basis of American society. As his good friend and fellow iconoclast Dr. Nathan Mayer of Hartford wrote of him in the summer of 1864, "He fully realized the state of transition which the present age and our nation is in, and his satire flashed up broad and indignant against the fetters that yet are timidly thrown around us, because the clear aim and the result of our progress can not now be foreseen." [31] Converse and his impatient Connecticut comrades were outward bound and not particularly concerned whether a course had been charted. For him the journey would end in an unmarked grave at Cold Harbor, but in 1861 he was in no mood to speculate on the nameless perils of the future.

Charles Russell of Derby was quite another brand of zealot, though if anything more determined than Converse. In April 1861 Russell was 32 years old and was working as a foreman in Edward Shelton's tack factory at Derby. His educational opportunities had been meager—district schools in New Haven and Derby. When he was 13 he began his apprenticeship in tack-making, while at the same time he participated in the village lyceum and borrowed books for self-improvement, which he read with a desperate persistence. Like Terry, he soon found an outlet in the local militia company, the Derby Blues, where he displayed such leadership qualities that he became a captain before he had reached 20. A real hothead in politics, Russell plunged enthusiastically into the political ferment of 1860: he commanded the Derby Wide Awakes and, drawing on his lyceum training, made several speeches at rallies for Lincoln and Hamlin. On one of these occasions, when asked "What will be the condition of things in 1864?" he replied casually, "Before that day, this country will run red with blood; I see it, believe it and I tremble that the notes of preparation are not already sounding in our ears." [32] Russell was to welcome the conflict with savage zest. He enlisted his entire company of the Derby Blues in the 2nd

31. Ibid., p. 598.

32. Samuel Orcutt, *The History of the Old Town of Derby, Connecticut, 1642–1880, with Biographies and Genealogies* (Springfield, 1880), pp. 640, 641.

Connecticut on the day Sumter surrendered. After the first battle of Bull Run, during which he was Terry's adjutant, Russell was given command of the 10th Connecticut and was killed instantly at the head of his regiment in the final assault at Roanoke Island.

Undoubtedly, one of the compelling motives for volunteering was that it represented a socially acceptable means of rebelling against hearth and home, that symbol of authority, that reason for the apparent futility of daily life. But whatever the Articles of War had to say about discipline, even the most unruly soldier or the most democratic officer recognized the need for some system of command and obedience.

Connecticut troops were recruited from a society where paternalism still ruled. It was to be expected then that the familiar would be carried over into the recruitment, organization, and leadership of the volunteer regiments. Finding themselves suddenly in positions of authority, the young officers dealt with their enlisted men in the same fashion that they or their fathers had handled family situations or business problems. Likewise, the enlisted men had been conditioned to accept such a relationship, even if they had chafed under its restrictions at home. Since the state had no military tradition and its citizens believed implicitly in individual freedom, the kind of noblesse oblige instinctively applied by officers was probably the only way discipline could have been maintained, at least for the first two years of the war. Private William Warren of the 17th Regiment has described this relationship vividly: "Captain sometimes gets to talking to one of the boys and pretty soon the whole company will be around him and if he would talk all night I don't believe the boys would go to bed for he is just like a father." Warren's captain was James E. Moore of Danbury. He was killed on the first day of Gettysburg. A young, restless small businessman, he had been a color-bearer in the Mexican War and commanded Company I of the 3rd Connecticut at Bull Run.[33]

The system worked, but it did not measure up to the professional military standards of the day. Camps tended to be dirty, disease-ridden places. Some drunkenness, much horseplay, and always poorly prepared food were but a few of the penalties paid for this individualistic officer-man relationship. In battle, military paternal-

33. William Warren, MS Diary, April 1863 (SL).

ism seemed to work better, but it put an excessive premium on officer leadership. Where each enlisted man had a personal tie with his company officers and a personal identification with his regimental commander, those who led had to be in the most exposed position. They had to set the example, which meant fulfilling a symbolic as well as a military role. Who would not follow twice wounded Colonel Chatfield of the 6th when he seized the ragged colors from a dying color-bearer and leaped upon the outer works of Fort Wagner? [34] Unfortunately, if the officers did not measure up to both of their demanding roles, the entire organization would dissolve, as happened frequently during the early years of the war.

Until the volunteer army had painfully developed a professional tradition of its own, excessive paternalism was the only method that could have worked. Connecticut regiments, like those of other states, mirrored a cross section of society. They exhibited all the incipient strengths and all the glaring weaknesses of a state and nation in transition. For the first two years of the war Connecticut's citizen army inevitably followed the pattern of the society from which it sprang. It seems a paradox that a changing social order, which had bred restlessness, frustration, and a passionate yet unrequited desire for escape, should have projected itself onto the battlefield. Yet the paradox is more apparent than real if one considers that there was no substitute for the remembered and the experienced in an unfamiliar situation.

Connecticut society in 1861, and indeed society throughout the entire North, could not have accepted the modern notion of total warfare any more than it could have understood modern industrial organization. This was amply demonstrated by the amateurish reliance upon volunteers and the abysmal draft failures of 1862 and 1863, the comparative tolerance of war-profiteering, political favoritism, and the like. Nor initially could Connecticut society and its military arm have sustained for any extended length of time the more modern, professionalized butchery that Grant utilized for final victory. This was perhaps the single most important reason why Connecticut volunteers and their friends and relations at home supported McClellan with such vehemence during the early years of the conflict. McClellan fitted perfectly into the apex of the

34. Croffut and Morris, pp. 445, 446.

paternalist socio-military system, and there had to be a McClellan before the nation and the Army woud follow a Grant.

On June 27, 1861, the 23-year-old Willie Lusk of Norwich scribbled a note to his cousin Louisa Thompson. In his eagerness to enlist he would not wait for a vacancy in one of the Connecticut three-months regiments, and had just been accepted in the 79th New York. Lusk came from one of the most prominent families in southeastern Connecticut. The son of a rich, Connecticut-born New York City merchant, he had recently returned from Germany, where he had gone to study medicine at Berlin and Heidelberg.[35] The opportunity for education and travel, however, had not altered his youthful idealism or romantic enthusiasm. "Think, Cousin Lou," he wrote, "I am going to see real danger, real privation, real work—not as a mere Carpet Knight, talking valorously to girls, but going forth in all humility to help to conquer in the name of God and my Country." Lusk closed his note with a dashing postscript that voiced the devil-may-care sentiments of most adventure-hungry young officers. "Hurrah! Off in ten minutes, so *au revoir* here or hereafter," he tossed off gallantly.[36] Lusk was not to find the Army as gloriously romantic as he had imagined.

But the Danbury farmer's son, Private William Warren, after seven months of campaigning, still thought military life was wonderful. "The longer I stay, the better I like it," Warren noted in his diary. "Edgar Knapp went out on picket for three days. He said he never enjoyed himself better. War is not near so bad as folks make it out to be . . . How can a man be homesick for we have music all times a day. I never enjoyed better health than since I have been in the army, nor ever weighed more, 152 pounds." [37]

Each in his own way, the cultivated, privileged Lusk and the uncultivated, underprivileged Warren were responding to the amorphous dynamism of Connecticut society in 1861. Lusk, the youthful idealist, sought for a higher meaning to his life than the aimless pleasures of European junkets or the local gossip of Norwich salons. Warren, the wide-eyed farmer's son, more limited in outlook

35. William T. Lusk, *War Letters of William Thompson Lusk* (New York, 1911), vii, 13.

36. Ibid., p. 47.

37. William Warren, MS *Diary*, April, 1863 (SL).

yet more practical, merely sought some experience beyond the narrow circle of farm life. For a young man who had probably heard band music only once a year at the Danbury Fair, such a simple pleasure as daily serenades from an indifferent regimental band must have been a rare treat indeed. What matter if the band gave a ragged performance; Warren had no basis for comparison and the important thing was that it played for the soldiers "all times a day."

Lusk and Warren symbolize the restless yearnings, the naïve illusions, the frustrations that had been building up among the young people of the state since the early 1850s. Vaguely dissatisfied with life at home, they and their comrades had sought emotional outlets in prewar militia companies, Wide Awake parades, and spirited politics. When Sumter was attacked, they threw themselves with ardor into the patriotic revivals of 1861 and 1862. Most found army life exciting and adventurous at first, and as their youthful exuberance was drained off by the successive Union defeats, they gained a tough professional attitude toward soldiering that would eventually win the war. "If we cannot conquer," cried Captain Fiske, after the battle of Fredericksburg, "in Heaven's name, let us find it out, and make peace and go home; and if we can conquer, let us do it before in general bankruptcy and wreck of things, victory and defeat become of equal value to us!" [38]

Initially, McClellan had no firmer supporters than these Connecticut boys, and they were slow to admit his shortcomings. As late as December 22, 1862, William Lusk was to say, "Let Lincoln turn his talents to splitting rails, I prefer George McClellan to Abraham Lincoln as the Commander-in-chief of the Army." [39] These were the officers and men who formed the hard core of Connecticut's army, who were to walk and fight and die in seven rebel states and two loyal ones. Mistreated by a careless government, mishandled by incompetent commanders, most were to retain their spirit and their loyalty to regiment, state, and nation, in that order; and after three difficult and dangerous years, they were to re-enlist for the duration.

38. Fiske, *Mr. Dunn Browne*, p. 89.
39. Lusk, p. 256.

6. THE UNION FOREVER

WALT WHITMAN stood on Maryland Avenue watching the defeated, disorderly mob that had been the Union Army straggle over Long Bridge into Washington. It was the day after the disaster at Bull Run, and the good, not yet so gray, poet was shocked to the very depths of his being. Later, during his prowlings through the streets of the city, he stopped at Willard's Hotel. The bar was crowded with officers who had abandoned their men. "Bull Run is your work," the angry poet raged in his journal. "Had you been half or one-tenth worthy your men, this would never have happen'd." [1]

Whitman was only partly right. Until panic enveloped the untrained troops, the Union Army had fought bravely, if amateurishly. It had even carried out General Irwin McDowell's elaborate flanking movement, a complex maneuver that a more experienced commander would never have attempted with green troops. Moreover, some elements of the Army were still fighting a rear-guard action in good order at the very time that Whitman was privately castigating the barflies in Willard's. Among these was the Connecticut brigade.

The Connecticut regiments had been a part of McDowell's first division, commanded by their old martinet drill instructor, Daniel Tyler. "Old Dan" had come far since he had drilled the 1st Connecticut on the New Haven green three months before. General Scott had been impressed by his handling of the Connecticut regiments in Washington, and he was, of course, familiar with Tyler's professional reputation as an artillerist, engineer, and businessman. Had it been possible for Scott and McDowell to talk frankly with any of the Connecticut regimental commanders, they might have

1. Walt Whitman, *Prose Works, 1892*, ed. Floyd Stovall (New York, 1963), I, 28.

hesitated in assigning Tyler such important field responsibilities. Gruff and pedantic, he had the kind of engineering mind that gloried in detail and preparation but was utterly incapable of rapid improvising to meet unexpected conditions. And behind his brusque façade Tyler was a sensitive, highly emotional man. Two days before the battle he had blundered into a premature engagement with Beauregard's main force at Blackburn's ford. Although casualties were light, the Confederates mauled one of Tyler's brigades. This action hurt the morale of his entire division and shook Tyler's confidence in himself and his troops. Yet much depended upon the new brigadier if McDowell's battle plan was to succeed.

The plan called for Tyler's division, which was out in front, to make a vigorous demonstration at the stone bridge across Bull Run, while a full third of the Union Army swung far around to the right and attacked the extreme flank of the enemy. When the flanking movement had reached a point roughly opposite Tyler, he was to launch a direct attack, affect a junction, and sweep Beauregard from the field. Success of the plan called for rapid execution and prompt coordination. Beauregard had been reinforced and was at this time planning a similar flank attack on McDowell. His strength was concentrated on the Union left, opposite Blackburn's Ford, where Tyler had launched his disastrous reconaissance in force. Only about 5,000 Confederate troops were entrenched opposite the stone bridge, and the remainder of Beauregard's army was from ten to fifteen miles away.

Tyler spent so much time lining up his troops that the flanking force behind was held up for three hours. Then, his demonstration, which began at 6 A.M., was so weak that it failed to screen the flanking operation. Later, when ordered by McDowell to deliver his crucial assault, Tyler delayed an hour and only one of his brigades (W. T. Sherman's) was of material assistance in the critical assault upon the Henry Heights. Schenk's brigade and four batteries of regular artillery never moved from their position east of the Run until they were caught up in the headlong retreat toward Washington.

Tyler himself accompanied Colonel Erasmus Keyes' brigade, composed of the three Connecticut regiments and the 2nd Maine. Instead of following Sherman, he sent the brigade cautiously up the

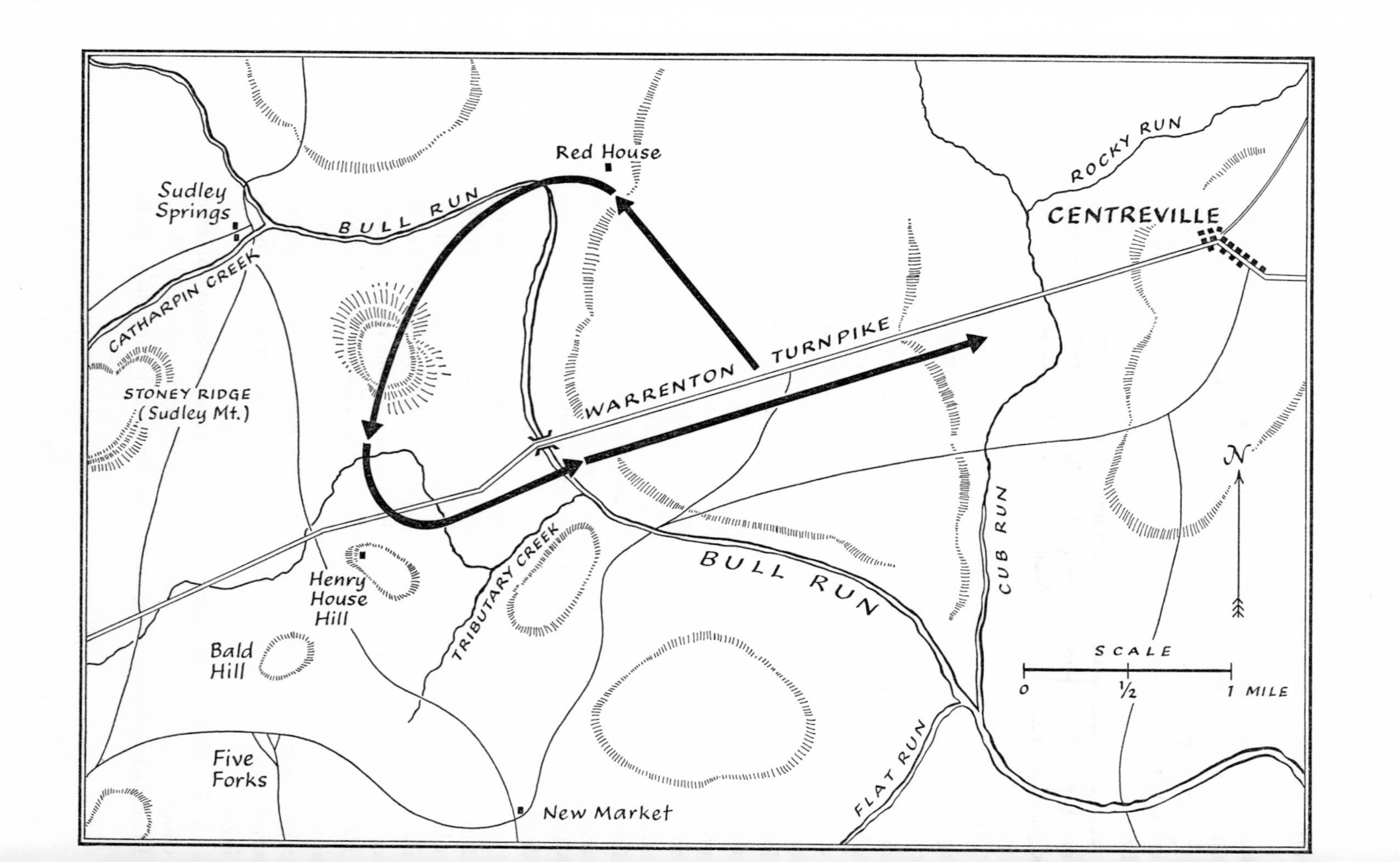

Red House
Sudley Springs
BULL RUN
CATHARPIN CREEK
STONEY RIDGE
(Sudley Mt.)
ROCKY RUN
CENTREVILLE
WARRENTON TURNPIKE
N
Henry House Hill
TRIBUTARY CREEK
BULL RUN
CUB RUN
Bald Hill
SCALE
0
1/2
1 MILE
Five Forks
New Market
FLAT RUN

estern slope of the Heights, where it was promptly stopped cold y an artillery battery posted near a small farmhouse owned by a Ir. Robinson. Though the enemy artillery was in a strong position, determined assault by Tyler's more than 3,000 men would have vamped it. However, the overly cautious General ordered only wo regiments to attack, the 3rd Connecticut and the 2nd Maine. When these were repulsed by the eight Confederate cannon firing anister, Tyler spent the remainder of the afternoon attempting to utflank the battery. He was still engaged in marching and coun-ermarching his regiments when ordered to retreat. Down the slope marched the three Connecticut regiments and the 2nd Maine. As hey crested a small rise that shielded the meadow and the stone ridge from view, they saw the plain and the Run jammed with oldiers—half of McDowell's army in full retreat.

It was a great credit to the Connecticut officers and men that hey did not stampede when they saw this horrifying spectacle. General Tyler, for once, acted with vigor. He detached a battalion f the 2nd Maine and rode off in search of Schenk's brigade to stablish a rear-guard action. Unable to find Schenk, he did run nto Ayres' splendid battery, of thirty-pounder Parrott guns, un-mbered and waiting for orders. This he promptly put into action, nd with the support of the Maine infantry battalion conducted a emblance of rear guard that partially covered the retreat across the Run. Tyler finally discovered Schenk with the remnants of his rigade at Cub Run, a stream halfway between Bull Run and Mc-Dowell's former headquarters at Centreville. He was not to see his Connecticut troops until the next morning, when they marched nto Fort Corcoran on the outskirts of Washington, in good order nd with six prisoners.

Meanwhile, with Tyler out of the picture, Keyes ordered his rigade to skirt the Warrenton pike, by now choked with the tragglers of a beaten army. Colonels Terry, Burnham, and Chat-eld already had their regiments in close order, and they forded the tream just below the stone bridge without difficulty or confusion. When the Connecticut brigade reached the plain between Bull Run nd Cub Run, almost in unison the orders rang out to form a line f companies, with rifle companies on the flank. Up and down the anks rushed the tired officers, checking to make sure that muskets and rifles were loaded and capped. Soaked with rain and swea dirty, hot, and scared, these 2,500 Connecticut and Maine volu teers managed to keep their ranks steady, a small block of order an cohesion surrounded by vast chaos. But would they hold attacked?

Not a mile away to the west, just visible through the heav drizzle, a regiment of enemy cavalry was forming for the char which its commander assumed would break through to Centrevill Colonel Keyes ordered the brigade to face by the rear rank. Th order was carried out with commendable speed, and the warning hold fire was given automatically. It took something more tha courage for these green troops to stand while 800 galloping, yellin horsemen bore down on them. But somehow they did hold until th cavalry was within a hundred yards, and then, unable to restra themselves further, they opened fire. Though the volley was ragge it was massive, and it broke the charge completely. The enti enemy regiment was thrown into a confused and disorderly retrea It was here that six dazed, unhorsed Confederate cavalrymen we taken prisoners.[2]

If the Connecticut brigade had been merely a collection of cred ulous young citizens in uniform, it was now made up of soldiers o better still, officer material. These men had broken an enemy ca alry charge at close range, a final test of their ninety-day trainin course; they had been under fire, had suffered casualties (68 kille and wounded), and had taken prisoners. When they marched int their camp, the Connecticut regiments had been moving constantl for 36 hours. On the way back they picked up and brought in th tents and equipment of three regiments, as well as two abandone cannon and their own equipment. Bull Run climaxed their militar indoctrination course. Over 400 officers and men of the Connecti cut brigade would provide the officer backbone for future regi ments. They were Connecticut's "ninety-day wonders" of the Civ War. It should be noted also that over 500 officers and men of th three-months regiments would serve later as noncommissioned offi cers. About one-third of the total three-months personnel, there fore, would apply their training and battle experience to the organ

2. Robert U. Johnson and Charles C. Buel, ed., *Battles and Leaders of the Civil Wa* (New York, 1884–87), I, 167–93.

zation, training, and leadership of the new regiments. These men vere to prove indispensable to Connecticut's military effort, not nly for their services in whipping green recruits into shape and in eading them into battle but also in sustaining their morale through he incredible hardships and dangers which lay ahead.[3]

The campaign participation of the Connecticut regiments illus-rates in microcosm the painful, sanguinary groping of the Union oward an over-all strategy and a professional tactic. Connecticut egiments were to fight with all the major armies in all significant heaters of operations; they were to be involved in all important xpeditions. On a tactical level Connecticut regiments were to uffer as much at the hands of incompetent brigade and division fficers as the Union armies did from blundering army command-rs. It was their misfortune to be mishandled by some of the very vorst general officers that the war produced—men such as Benham, Butler, and Banks, or the feckless Milroy. Occasionally bad general-hip would result in dire circumstances—the capture of almost the ntire 18th Regiment at Winchester in 1862 or the 16th at Plym-uth, North Carolina, in 1864, the slaughter of two untrained Connecticut regiments at Antietam, the frightful frontal assault of he Second Heavy Artillery at Cold Harbor, or the terrible casual-ies at Port Hudson. But more frequently, poor tactical leadership vas to impose unnecessary hardships on the daily lives of the volun-eers.

Incompetent brigade and division commanders generally paid cant attention to logistics; their men often went hungry, simply ecause the general commanding had not made adequate provision or supply, food, uniforms, and especially shoes, which would be ised up in a week or so of hard campaigning. When the Irish 9th Regiment assigned to Butler's New Orleans expedition was dropped ff at Ship Island, Louisiana, nearly half the men were shoeless and hirtless; many were without blankets, coats, and trousers. Some companies had to drill in their long-handle underwear.[4] For several weeks after Antietam, at least half of Harland's Connecticut bri-gade was barefoot and all were ragged, despite the enormous quan-tities of quartermaster's supplies in the Washington area. Long in-

3. Croffut and Morris, *History of Connecticut*, pp. 93–100.

4. Murray, *Ninth Regiment*, p. 63.

tervals between pay days were especially exasperating to the soldiers. "Nearly five months' pay is now due our regiment," wrote a soldier of the 12th from Thibodaux, Louisiana, in November 1862. "The men are entirely without funds not even enough money to buy a paper of tobacco." Rations in the field, never plentiful or wholesome, were generally so bad that even non-discriminating farm boys complained. A sergeant of the 16th wrote: "the hard crackers that we got last was full of worms and bugs, and not much at that. You wish I was at home; so do I, if they don't use us no better . . . I should like it if they would give us enough to eat . . . after drilling for two hours, we have just got our rations, and the hard crackers we got is full of worms as long as a half an inch; it's God's truth." The *Courant* editor in commenting on this letter stated that government rations were ample and that "the fault rests with the officers of the regiment whose business it is to see that the food is good and abundant." [5] Captain Samuel Fiske of the 14th had the same bitter criticism for regimental and brigade staff who neglected their duties. "The men feel that they are treated like dogs," he asserted; ". . . their wants are not attended to, their feelings are not regarded. They are neglected when they are sick, and are left to die with little care or sympathy manifested in their behalf." [6]

Nothing bore down so hard on the volunteers as the continuous unnecessary marching and countermarching that resulted from inadequate staff work at the brigade and division level. DeForest has described such a march, on which the 12th Connecticut did 87 miles in 76 hours through the steaming humidity of a southern Louisiana summer. Their only food on this marathon was hardtack and coffee. At the conclusion of the march DeForest wrote, "if the enemy had been there we could not have fought him nor run away from him . . . God alone knows why we marched thus; our commander [Banks] has probably forgotten." [7] It would appear that the more incompetent the commander, the more he drove his

5. *Hartford Courant* (Dec. 3, 1863).

6. Fiske, *Mr. Dunn Browne*, p. 86.

7. John W. DeForest, *A Volunteer's Adventures: A Union Captain's Record of the Civil War*, ed. James H. Croushore (New Haven, 1946), pp. 99–102.

ıen. DeForest, who had marched with "cavalry Sheridan," con-
idered Banks "the most merciless marcher of men that I ever
new." [8] Indeed, the problem of whether this unit should be at this
lace or that place at this time or that time seems to have baffled the
est efforts of many zealous tacticians, who, for better or for worse,
referred to order the men out and then ponder the problem after-
vard. Of course, military intelligence was primitive and communi-
ation slow, but orders of ambiguous meaning drawn up on the
pur of the moment and executed impetuously showed as little
onsideration for the safety of the troops as it did for the military
bjective to be gained.

The 6th Regiment had just such an experience early in 1862,
vhen General Thomas W. Sherman, commander at Port Royal, de-
ided to bypass Fort Pulaski and make a quick thrust at Savannah
hrough Wassaw Sound, without either proper reconnaissance or
aval coordination. Dyspeptic "Uncle Tim" Sherman ordered Gen-
ral H. G. Wright's brigade to make the amphibious operation. As a
art of this brigade, the 6th was hastily embarked on an improvised
roop carrier, the *Cosmopolitan*, a tiny river ferry too small to
ccommodate the regiment. The inevitable storm set in, and Com-
nodore Samuel DuPont's fleet, together with transports, was kept
t anchor in Port Royal Harbor for a week. For another two weeks
he 6th was confined in its floating pest-house, while DuPont edged
is way up the Wassaw Sound inlets, only to find that they were
oo shallow for his gunboats. The expedition was called off. Mean-
vhile, the men of the 6th had suffered under deplorable conditions.
They had slept on the deck of the *Cosmopolitan*, which was so
rowded that once everyone was settled for the night, no one could
nove from his allotted position. Rancid salt pork and moldy salt
unk with verminous hardtack was the only food for officers and
nen. Because the water barrels had formerly contained kerosene oil,
he water was unfit to drink. With no sanitary facilities, filth and
ody lice were everywhere. Contagious diseases broke out and an
verage of five men a day died.[9] Had Sherman reconnoitered Tybee
Island on the eastern side of Wassaw Sound, as he was to do when

8. Ibid., p. 99.
9. Cadwell, *Sixth Regiment*, pp. 30–32.

the expedition returned, he would have found it abandoned by the enemy. Wright's brigade could have encamped there in relative safety and health while the fleet scouted the inlets.

Any military movement that involved transportation either by rail or ship was apt to be a trying experience. Those Connecticut regiments that went South by rail from New York City were generally jammed into windowless boxcars or cattle cars, only partially cleansed after the animals had been transported. The boys did what they could to improve the situation by smashing holes in the boxcars with their rifle butts or wrenching off boards from the cattle cars to scrape out the manure. Those units that went by ship frequently fared worse. The voyage of the 1st Light Battery from new York to Port Royal, South Carolina, was typical of the casual way Army authorities arranged for ship transportation. The battery, consisting of 156 men, 12 cannon with complete equipment, and 160 horses, was ordered aboard a Black Ball packet, the *Ellwood Walter,* in late January 1862. They had built their own berths and stalls for the horses from a pile of frozen lumber stacked on the dock. Then they loaded their batteries and ammunition. After several days' delay because of bad weather, the *Ellwood Walter* finally put to sea. Off Cape Hatteras the packet ran into winter gales that persisted all the way to Hilton Head. The rolling of the ship frightened the horses and kept them in a perpetual lather; many developed horse distemper or pneumonia. Every day several animals died. It was imperative that the stiffened, stinking carcasses be removed quickly, but the companionways were so narrow that the dead horses could not be hauled up by ordinary means. Private Mark Hall, a butcher by trade, suggested that the carcasses be dismembered by sharp axes. This solved the problem. There was no solution, however, to the heavy effluvia of the sick and dead horses that permeated the entire ship. Yet the animals had to be fed and watered, the carcasses removed, and the temporary stables cleansed. Shifts of battery members descended into the reeking holds and did the job despite the fact that most of the workers were so seasick or ill with animal-contracted diseases that they could hardly stand. The men endured these noisome, squalid surroundings for two weeks without losing their sense of humor or their high spirits. Corporal Herbert Beecher quotes one of his comrades as saying, "our horses were between decks and one of these, a little mare, was known as 'the cheerful kicker.' Every lunge that the vessel would give caused her to squeal and kick around. I remember how at every roll of the ship, comrade Frank Thompson would say 'there we go Pa, we shall never see Ma again, shall we, Pa.' "[10]

Despite chaotic organization and untrained or incompetent personnel in key positions, the Lincoln Administration embarked on an ambitious war strategy that demanded up to 3,000 miles in supply lines and offensive operations all along the coast of the Confederacy. After the defeat of Bull Run, the President realized that it would take a great deal more than a brief summer campaign to achieve victory. While General George McClellan was putting together an army in Washington, for operations in Virginia, Lincoln and his advisers adapted elements of General Scott's "anaconda" plan, which envisaged a slow, naval strangulation of the South.

The Union Navy, at this time, though far more powerful than the Confederate, was unable to maintain more than a token blockade. Merchant ships were being collected frantically and converted to naval use. Northern shipyards, including those of Connecticut, were crowded with government orders. But all this took time. It would be at least a year before the fleet was large enough for even a partially effective blockade. This meant that the Navy had to take maximum advantage of the Southern coastal topography.

From the Virginia capes to northern Florida, the Southern coastline was a deeply serrated fringe of river mouths, tidal inlets, bays, shifting sand bars, and marshy islands. Through this maze, shallow-draft, speedy Confederate blockade runners were able to travel in comparative safety from the few patrolling Union cruisers. It was, in short, a magnificent inland waterway system with scores of entry points for ocean traffic and substantial protection for coastwise shipment of supplies, men, and munitions among the four most populous states of the Confederacy. But in the absence of sea power, one of its greatest strengths—the large protected inland sounds—was also a grave weakness to the Confederacy. For these were invariably dominated by relatively narrow channels which, if seized, would not only cut off Confederate traffic at its sources but turn over all the communication advantages of the inland water-

10. Beecher, *First Light Battery*, I, 78.

way system to the Union. Fewer ships would be needed in the blockading fleet, while the deep inlets and navigable rivers would simplify military operations into the interior.

A second major objective in the tightening of the blockade was the seizure of the port of New Orleans and control of the lower Mississippi River system, which led deep into the heart of the Confederacy. The seven principal approaches or passes to New Orleans through the Mississippi Delta were also a complex of bayous, islands, and sand bars. Here, too, Confederate blockade runners, with so many choices for exit or entry, found it a simple matter to confuse the blockading vessels. Both Navy and Army were not as yet ready in the fall of 1861 to undertake such a difficult operation as the capture of New Orleans. But anticipating the need for a staging area prior to an assault, the Navy seized undefended Ship Island, a sandy waste about forty miles northeast of the major passes to the delta.

Meanwhile, the first operation against the south Atlantic coast had been most successful. In August 1861 Flag Officer Silas Stringham had captured the Confederate forts guarding Hatteras Inlet. This secured control of Pamlico Sound, the largest protected body of water south of Chesapeake Bay.

Port Royal, South Carolina, the next objective, would be far more difficult because of its strategic importance and its close proximity to the cities of Savannah and Charleston. Both Navy and Army planned their mission with a care unusual in this early stage of the war. Samuel F. DuPont, the naval commander, evolved a novel tactical maneuver which would enable him to bring the two forts guarding Port Royal Harbor under continuous broadsides from both front and flank. And the Army, recognizing the amphibious character of the operation, chose regiments from states that had a seafaring tradition. Thus, among the 12,000 men who made up General Sherman's expedition, there was a high percentage of New Englanders familiar with boat-handling and other naval techniques. Another army consideration in its choice of manpower was the expectation of siege work.

In addition to the forts opposite Port Royal, the expedition would also be confronted with Fort Pulaski, which guarded Savannah and the powerful works surrounding Charleston. The brilliant engineering officer Quincy A. Gillmore was accordingly selected to be engineer-chief of the expedition. Since those states with a seafaring tradition were also among the most highly industrialized, it was assumed that many of the men would have the requisite mechanical skills for siege operations. In both respects the choice of the Connecticut 6th and 7th Regiments was a wise one.

After a hazardous voyage, during which DuPont's fleet was scattered by a gale of near hurricane force, the expedition finally concentrated off Port Royal. From their transports the two Connecticut regiments had a superb view of the successful five-hour bombardment. On November 7, 1861, they were landed by lighter—or, rather, dropped in waist-high surf—but they reached shore without mishap. Formed into companies, the Connecticut regiments marched into the wrecked, abandoned Fort Walker on Hilton Head Island as if "on dress parade." [11] Even those soldiers who had been at Bull Run were startled by the destruction they witnessed in the Fort. Dead and wounded soldiers, horses and mules, lay in heaps. Private Charles Cadwell of New Haven recalled that "many of the dead were literally torn to atoms and some were half buried where they fell; guns were dismounted, army wagons smashed . . . knapsacks, blankets and rifles lay in confusion all around." [12] This was a sobering experience for the young Connecticut soldiers. Soaked to the skin, fearing an enemy counterattack, they were unable to sleep that night. The next day they were kept busy burying the dead, collecting abandoned equipment, and bringing in supplies. It was not until the third day, when both regiments were ordered out for reconnaissance, that the volunteers were able to observe this strange land, so delightfully different from far-off Connecticut.

Hilton Head was one of the fertile sea islands which had grown rich on the cultivation of long staple cotton. The countryside was green and fragrant—the cotton fields awaiting a second picking, the orange trees heavy with ripe fruit, fig trees, palmettos, mossy live oaks, gently waving fields of sugar cane. It was frosty November in the harsh Connecticut hills, but here all was warm and bright as a rare June day in the North. The island had been aban-

11. Walkley, *Seventh Connecticut,* p. 28.
12. Cadwell, pp. 27–28.

doned; even the Negro population had fled. The soldiers appropriated oranges, sugar cane, cattle, pigs, and fowl; they dug up yams and for several days feasted sumptuously. For most, who had never been more than thirty miles from home in their entire lives, Hilton Head was a stimulating experience. They would never have quite the same outlook as before, nor would the thousands of other Connecticut boys to follow them into this land of enchantment and fresh sensation, those who were to sail with General Burnside for Roanoke Island, or those soon to accompany Butler to New Orleans, and later, Banks to Port Hudson. It would all contribute to what might be called the Americanization of the Connecticut youth. Some would never escape the lure of the South or the West; most would return home after the war; but the sturdy old commonwealth their fathers knew and cherished above all would be to them merged into a newer, broader concept of the nation.

For two months the 6th and 7th remained on Hilton Head, enjoying camp life while the build-up of Union forces continued; then they suddenly experienced the rough edge of Southern life. Both regiments were ordered to erect siege batteries for the reduction of Fort Pulaski.

Pulaski had been constructed by the Federal government in the 1840s under the supervision of Connecticut-born Joseph K. F. Mansfield. Situated on Cockspur Island in the Savannah River, the Fort had cost over a million dollars and was considered to be one of the most modern harbor defense works in the world. In 1862 it was armed with forty-eight guns, most of heavy caliber.[13] But Gillmore persuaded General Sherman that he could reduce Pulaski with newly developed rifled guns and heavy siege mortars from batteries erected on the north shore of Tybee Island. Other batteries would be built on the south shore of Jones Island and on Bird Island on the north bank of the Savannah River, west of the Fort, to cut off any naval reinforcement from Savannah.[14] The islands were little more than hummocks of mud (at some places twelve feet deep) and marsh grass. Quite often covered with water at high tide, they were infested with mosquitoes and fleas which no netting or blanket could keep out.

13. Johnson and Buel, *Battles and Leaders*, 2, 10.
14. Ibid., p. 4.

In order to ensure maximum impact and accuracy from the batteries, Gillmore ordered that they be built as close as possible to the beach facing Pulaski. He decided that the range for his heavy 13-inch mortars would be 3,400 yards from the walls of the Fort; columbiads, rifles, and lighter mortars were to be emplaced from 3,100 to 1,650 yards. In all, Gillmore planned to use thirty-six pieces of ordnance ranging from 13-inch siege mortars that weighed 8½ tons down to one-ton James rifles. Ordnance and supplies had to be hauled 2½ miles to emplacement, and the last mile was open marsh, where every movement could be easily observed from the Fort.[15] All labor had to be done at night, and the evidence had to be carefully covered with marsh grass before dawn. For security reasons, Gillmore would not permit horses to be used. Thus the 7th Regiment, which did most of the work, hauled the heavy equipment by muscle power over corduroy roads they had constructed. As many as 250 men were needed to drag the 13-inch monsters on sling carts whose wheel diameters were twice a man's height. Orders were given by whistles and only whispering was permitted.[16] Fort Pulaski mounted twenty heavy guns on its Tybee face. Had the garrison discovered early enough what was going on, not a mile and a half away, it could have made the position untenable. Yet only occasional rounds were fired from the Fort until Gillmore's Tybee batteries began regular siege bombardment. Jones Island was even muddier than Tybee, but the 6th Regiment managed to build a mud fort there, which the sun soon baked hard, and to mount upon it nine heavy guns.

Tortured by insects, the men worked day after day in knee-deep mud and water. Finally, on April 9, everything was ready except fuse plugs for the 10-inch mortars, which had been neglected in the rush of preparation. Lieutenant Horace Porter, the ordnance officer, assuming that all Yankees were whittlers by instinct, assigned to the 6th and 7th Regiments the job of carving several thousand wooden plugs. On one of his rounds Porter asked a private of the 6th what the regiment thought of its light occupation. The Connecticut boy replied, "thank ye, Leftenant, we're undergoin' a con-

15. R. B. Lattimore, *Fort Pulaski, Historical Handbook,* No. 18 (Washington, 1954), p. 29.

16. Walkley, p. 41.

sid'able degree o' comfort." [17] On the 10th the eleven batteries on Tybee were armed and awaiting orders. Some 400 men and 18 officers of the 7th manned five of the six mortar batteries, the 46th New York, the 3rd Rhode Island Volunteer Artillery, and 100 sailors from DuPont's flagship, the U.S.S. *Wabash*, manned the other 21 guns; Colonel Alfred H. Terry of the 7th was in over-all command.[18] With the exception of the sailors, none of the siege force personnel had any prior experience handling heavy artillery; indeed, most were infantrymen whose training had consisted of a few hours of loading and aiming exercises when they were not at work constructing the batteries.

Just after sunrise Major General David Hunter, who had replaced Sherman in command of the Department of the South, sent Lieutenant James Wilson under a flag of truce to demand surrender of the Fort. Pulaski's 25-year-old commanding officer, Connecticut-born Colonel Charles H. Olmsted, rejected Hunter's ultimatum. At precisely 7:45, Captain Oliver S. Sanford of Meriden fired the first shell, a 13-inch mortar, at Pulaski. On it he had written " a nutmeg from Connecticut; can you furnish a grater?" By 9:30 all the Tybee batteries were in operation and the Fort was responding. Colonels Hawley and Terry, acting as observers for the Union bombardment, corrected the aim of the gunners and relayed information on counterbattery fire. "Sometimes we called out, 'ten incher,' " Hawley wrote, "as a certain big Columbiad, on the southwest angle of the Fort let off; sometimes 'Pocket pistol!' or 'Little rifle!' as a small, sharp, accurate Blakeley gun on the ramparts fired. We got so that we knew where each gun was trained and could tell by the sound where the shot was going." [19] Despite their lack of training, the would-be artillerists from Connecticut managed to get a shell off from each mortar every fifteen minutes. According to Gillmore, the mortars were "carefully and fairly served," but, unfortunately, not more than 10 per cent fell within the Fort.[20]

After four hours of bombardment it was evident that the rifled

17. Johnson and Buel, *Battles and Leaders*, 2, 7.
18. Ibid., p. 2.
19. Croffut and Morris, *Connecticut*, p. 196.
20. Johnson and Buel, *Battles and Leaders*, 2, 9.

5. "Never at fault when serious work was to be done": John Sedgwick, Major General, U.S. Volunteers. Connecticut State Library.

6. Fortifications expert: Joseph K. F. Mansfield, Major General, U.S. Volunteers. Connecticut State Library.

7. "The Hero of Fort Fisher": Major General Alfred H. Terry, U.S. Volunteers. Sterling Library. Yale University.

8. Impetuous idealist: Brevet-Major General Joseph R. Hawley, U.S. Volunteers. Collection of Miss Roswell Hawley and Mrs. Marion Coudert.

guns were eating away the scarp of the Fort. Hawley observed that by early afternoon there were four or five holes close together, one of them an estimated twelve feet in diameter. "Now and then," he wrote, "a cartload of masonry rolled down." [21] The ebullient Hawley was almost beside himself with excitement as the gun captains jumped up on the mud banks and yelled, " 'No. 1, fire!' 'No. 2, fire!' 'No. 3, fire!' 'No. 4, fire!' " [22] By nightfall, when firing ceased, a large break in the southeast walls could be seen with the naked eye. After six hours of bombardment on the following day, the entire wall facing Tybee had collapsed into the moat. Union gunners then began to direct their fire at the north magazine, which could be clearly seen through the ruins. At 2 P.M., Colonel Olmsted surrendered what was left of the Fort. Some 4,275 rounds of shot and shell had been fired at Pulaski during the seventeen-hour bombardment, but almost all the damage had been done by three James rifles—two 84 pounders and one 64 pounder.[23]

The Civil War had many such surprises for traditional military and naval thinking. That an improvised band of artillerists from an average distance of two miles could in seventeen hours demolish one of the most modern fortresses in the world forced drastic changes in doctrine. Ordnance experts and military engineers in Europe and America could not ignore the accuracy or the proven capacity of these new weapons. In its symbolic context Pulaski demonstrated vividly the power potential of the industrializing North, its capacity to alter abruptly and violently the classic engineering concepts of the old order, and the society that had generated them. But the agents of the revolution were not given to such speculations. They were more interested in the straw hats, the ice, and the fresh meat that a grateful government thoughtfully provided for their welfare.[24] Other rewards were bestowed. Gillmore and Terry were made brigadier generals; Hawley was promoted to full colonel and given command of the 7th. General Hunter and his assistant, Connecticut-born Brigadier General Henry W. Ben-

21. Croffut and Morris, p. 196.
22. Ibid.
23. Lattimore, p. 36.
24. Walkley, pp. 46–47.

ham, received warm praise from the government for a tactical operation which had been planned by their predecessor, General Sherman.

Although Sherman had never been popular with the troops, Hunter and Benham soon made them yearn for the days of "Uncle Tim." The flailing energy of the sixty-year-old Hunter, with his drooping white mustache and tiny goatee, made their lives miserable. Benham, an egotistical West Pointer whose unhappy childhood would seem to have permanently warped his personality, treated officers and men with cold contempt. The Pulaski surrender had stimulated the ambition of the generals for further success. Now that Savannah had been bottled up, Benham, in particular, was full of plans for a daring descent on Charleston. For the time being, Hunter had submerged himself in the Negro problem and permitted Benham an unusual degree of freedom. But he warned the impetuous officer that the forces available were not strong enough for anything more than a reconnaissance, and explicitly ordered him not to bring on an engagement. It is not clear what Benham's objective was. He had only about 10,000 men, and though he talked about capturing Charleston, and though he was densely egotistical, even he would not have tried such a foolhardy operation. Probably he had some thought of flanking the fortifications guarding the southern approaches to Charleston, which might then be reduced by a combined Army-Navy assault. At least this was the direction his badly mismanaged expedition—or "excursion," as the troops called it—eventually took.

Benham divided his force into three divisions, one commanded by the short, bearded Isaac Stevens, one by the able, courtly Horatio G. Wright, and one by himself. The 6th Regiment was attached to Wright's division; the 7th and the 1st Connecticut Light Battery (the latter a high spirited outfit composed mainly of Guilford boys who were frequently the despair of Alfred Rockwell, their earnest young captain) were assigned to Stevens. When Benham consolidated his three divisions on the south shore of James Island, near Charleston, he should have attacked promptly and in an area where he would have received artillery support from Union gunboats in the Stono River. Instead, he delayed an entire week making feeble robes of the Charleston defenses. Then, against the advice of his ivision commanders, he ordered a full-scale frontal assault on what vas to prove the strongest point in the enemy line, a newly con- tructed earthwork in front of the village of Secessionville.

The fort stood on a rise and was so situated between two con- erging marshes that if a direct assault was made, the front would arrow down to 200 yards, scarcely enough room to deploy one egiment.[25] All of the hard ground leading up to the fort was a eeply rutted cotton field, most difficult for men to charge across. seven-foot moat and an intricate complex of rifle pits surrounded t; and a sixty-foot tower on the right flank of the fort gave the arrison excellent observation for several miles in all directions. ny frontal assault would have seemed to be doomed, yet there was bare possibility that it might succeed if Benham's troops achieved omplete surprise.

At first, fortune favored the foolhardy. Stevens' division, which vas to lead the attack at 4:00 A.M., came up promptly and over- vhelmed the Confederate pickets. By 4:30 his right wing had eached the main works. Then everything went wrong. The gar- ison, by now alerted, opened at point-blank range from six artil- ery pieces and 1,000 muskets. In the center of the earthworks the onfederates had mounted a 15-inch coast defense howitzer, which hey loaded with glass bottles, old chain, spikes, horseshoes, and vhatever other miscellaneous scrap iron they had available. At very discharge of this monster, great gaps were blown in the ightly packed blue lines.

The 7th Connecticut charged through the inferno until it was riefly disorganized by a deep ditch about 200 yards from the face f the fort. But several companies held their ranks and the rest ame up quickly. Officers waived the no-firing command and per- nitted the men to pick off Confederate sharpshooters and gunners n the parapet. Hawley seemed everywhere at once. He rallied the egiment around the colors, dressed it under heavy fire, and moved t again to the attack, this time by the right flank. The 1st Light attery had meanwhile roared into action. Its howitzer section, two uns, opened on the fort from a range of 500 yards, exploding

25. *OR*, Ser. I, 5, 211.

canister and spherical case over the heads of the defenders. Within minutes one James rifle from the right section had bounced int supporting position and opened fire.

Most of the 6th Regiment remained with Wright's division in reserve, but two companies had been lent to Hawley and wer moving forward for a second attack when General Stevens ordere all assaulting troops to fall back 1,200 yards and regroup behind thick hedge. Then the 7th was ordered forward again on the double quick. As soon as Hawley's regiment got to within 500 yards of th fort Stevens shouted at Rockwell, of the 1st Light Battery, "Con-necticut boys go in and the day is ours." Whips and spurs goade the horses to a gallop. Heavy guns, caissons, and limbers dance over the deeply rutted field as the horses made their steeplechas dash. Private Edward Griswold has described the wild ride: "W had to cross a cotton field, some 800 yards, and the enemy wa raking that field with cannonades, and the seacoast howitzer tha had been taken from the Government . . . the cannoneers wer not mounted . . . Corporal Scranton mounted one of the limber and sitting astride, managed to hold on. I grasped the muzzle of th gun, with my thumb over the sight pin. How those horses went!" [2 The guns were planted in the ranks of the 7th, and Hawle himself acted as spotter. "We worked the guns lively," said Privat Griswold, "and most of the time in a stooping position." [27] Cor-poral Thomas M. Lord of New Haven, on his knees swearing con-stantly as he loaded, touched the barrel of the howitzer. "By God," he cried, "it is so hot it sizzes." [28] Miraculously, not one member o the battery was hit by the assorted missiles that were cutting dow the ranks of the infantrymen. With no room for maneuver, th Union line [29] attempted the impossible task of pinning dow enemy artillerists with musket and light artillery fire. At this poin General Stevens gave up and ordered a retreat. Withdrawal wa orderly, but it did not stop until it reached the protection of th gunboats on the Stono. Benham had fed 6,600 men into this trape-zoidal death trap.

26. Beecher, *First Light Battery*, 1, 151.
27. Ibid., p. 152.
28. Ibid.
29. *OR*, Ser. I, 5, 211.

During the twenty-five minutes of action at Secessionville, 763 men had been killed or wounded, a very high casualty rate for that period of the war.[30] The 7th alone had eighty-three casualties out of the 600 who went in. After the battle Captain William T. Lusk of the 79th New York, which had sustained over 100 casualties, lashed Benham unmercifully in a letter he wrote his uncle, John Adams, a prominent resident of Norwich. "Let there be no mercy shown to one who shows no mercy," he said, indicting the hapless General. "He must be crushed at once or we are all lost . . . I will not enumerate half the examples of imbecility he has shown, or the wickedness of which he has been guilty. The last act is too real." [31] Lusk did not have long to wait. Hunter had Benham placed under arrest for disobedience to positive orders and sent North.[32]

Two more expeditions were to occupy the 6th and 7th Regiments during the remainder of 1862. The first, an amphibious raid on an enemy fort at St. Johns Bluff in Florida, was simply a walking feat through miles of snake-infested swamp.[33] The second operation, an attempt to cut the Charleston-Savannah Railroad, was another impromptu affair, which accomplished nothing but cost 340 Union casualties at Pocataligo, a village ten miles east of the rail line. Among the killed and wounded were sixty-seven Connecticut boys, including the commander of the 6th, Colonel Chatfield, and his deputy, Lieutenant Colonel Speidel.[34]

While the thinly held Department of the South was endeavoring with scant success to extend its beachheads from the Sea Islands, the 8th, 10th, and 11th Connecticut under General Burnside were invading a part of the North Carolina coast to the north. The presumed seafaring and mechanical skills of Connecticut soldiers had again been the criteria for their selection in the planned amphibious operation.[35] On January 9, 1862, the North Carolina expedition of eighty vessels had set sail from Annapolis. Although Burnside thought the fleet presented a fine appearance, it was in reality a motley collection of sailing craft, ferryboats and sound steamers,

30. Cadwell, *Sixth Regiment*, p. 43.
31. Lusk, *War Letters*, pp. 153–54.
32. Hazard Stevens, *The Life of Isaac Ingalls Stevens* (Boston, 1900), p. 399.
33. Walkley, *Seventh Connecticut*, pp. 57–58.
34. Croffut and Morris, *Connecticut*, p. 305.
35. Johnson and Buel, *Battles and Leaders*, 2, 234.

3. Secessionville, June 16, 1862. Elements of the 6th, the 7th, and 1st Light Batter were attached to Isaac Stevens' brigade.

the sweepings of Northern harbors.[36] Naval authorities had asserted that most of the vessels were unseaworthy, a prediction that was to be borne out when fifteen were lost before the fleet gained the comparative safety of Pamlico Sound. For the 3,000 Connecticut boys who marched aboard their makeshift transports, this was to be a first experience with real military hardship; and what an experience it would be.

Whoever had been responsible for transportation had blithely assumed a two-day trip to Cape Hatteras and ignored the probability of bad weather off the stormy Virginia capes. Six hundred soldiers of the 10th were jammed into the hold of the Raritan Bay steamer *New Brunswick;* their bunks of unplaned boards in tiers were six feet long, thirteen inches wide, and eighteen inches high. But the six companies of the 8th who were assigned to an ancient bark, the *J. P. Brookman,* had no bunks at all. Those who were fortunate enough to sleep on the deck in January weather were far better off than those who were sent down to the hold, where the filthy, years'-old corruption of the sloshing unventilated bilges seemed to poison the lungs with every breath. As for the 11th, it had been split up between the tiny propeller *Sentinel* and the dirty old bark *Voltigeur,* whose rotten shrouds soon gave way off Hatteras. Out of control, the *Voltigeur* went on the beach; and for twenty-three days, while she was pounded to pieces in the surf, Colonel Henry Kingsbury and five companies of the 11th were stranded aboard her in imminent peril of drowning, before a Navy tug finally rescued them.[37]

For three dismal weeks, Burnside's fleet was blasted by North Atlantic gales off Hatteras Inlet. Benjamin S. Pardee of Hamden, a captain in the 10th, vividly described the long misery aboard the transports: "the skies black unpromising; the surf beating sullenly the solemn requiem of the lost; sickness on all the vessels; epidemics rapidly extending; deaths frequent; no comforts for the sick; scanty food for the well; water, tainted with kerosene, served out in limited quantities." [38] By February 4 Commodore Louis M. Goldsborough had scoured an eight-foot channel through the bar or

36. Ibid., p. 235.
37. Croffut and Morris, p. 164.
38. Ibid., p. 104.

"swash" across Hatteras Inlet, and the fleet which had been milling about outside finally entered Pamlico Sound.[39] Three days later, it was in Roanoke Sound, and the Navy escort began bombardment of the enemy forts on Roanoke Island in preparation for the infantry assault.[40]

"Dirty, muddy, swampy, brackish, diseased and deathful Roanoke!" as Lieutenant Colonel Albert Drake of the 10th described it,[41] was Burnside's first objective. This island, ten miles long and about two miles wide, commanded the narrow entrance to Albemarle Sound. The only solid ground on marshy Roanoke was a narrow causeway running north-south like a spine through its center. Almost in the middle of the island, 3,000 Confederate troops and a three-gun battery were entrenched on a high point athwart the causeway, about one mile from the water's edge. Goldsborough's fleet drove off a Confederate flotilla but was unable to silence the fort. A muddy beach was found below the forts, however, and 7,500 Union troops landed under gunboat cover without difficulty between 4 P.M. and 10 P.M.[42] Both the 8th and 10th were attached to Brigadier General John G. Foster's brigade, but just before the general assault at dawn of the next day, Burnside sent the 8th Regiment off to the left flank as a reserve force in case the enemy should attempt a turning movement.[43] There it remained, much to the disgust of its members, during the entire action. The balance of Foster's brigade was ordered to make a frontal demonstration along the causeway, while the other two brigades under generals John Parke and Jesse Reno sought a way through the marshes on either flank of the Confederate line.

The 9th New York and the 25th Massachusetts, the first units to charge up the causeway, were swept back with heavy losses by point-blank artillery and musket fire. It was now the 10th's turn. "An aide came to us with the order, 'Advance the 10th,' " related Captain Pardee, "Colonel Russell pressed his lips firmly together and said, 'we are going under fire, captain. Forward, solidly,

39. Johnson and Buel, *Battles and Leaders*, 2, 235.

40. Ibid., p. 236.

41. Croffut and Morris, p. 170.

42. Johnson and Buel, *Battles and Leaders*, 1, 642.

43. Croffut and Morris, p. 165.

quickly' . . . we saw the smoke and flashes from the redoubt. At last we were under fire." [44]

The men of the 10th Connecticut, neatly outfitted in their gray satinet overcoats, edged up to within 150 yards of the fort and, standing as if on parade, began firing at will. For nearly an hour the regiment blazed away at the entrenched enemy. Then one of General Foster's aides rode up and ordered them to cease fire and lie down. All sought whatever protection was available—logs, stumps, even bushes. But Colonel Russell remained standing, a conspicuous figure with his old Derby Blues militia cap pushed back from his high forehead, his naked sword held at parade rest, as he watched for the expected flank attack of the other brigades. Apparently satisfied that he could still observe the field from cover, he accepted the repeated requests of those near him and, without sheathing his sword, stretched out on the ground. A few moments later a chance musket shot went through his shoulder and heart; he died instantly.

While Russell's body was being carried to the rear, cheering on the left indicated that the Confederate right flank had been broken. Foster immediately ordered a general advance. The 10th, now commanded by the impetuous Lieutenant Colonel Albert W. Drake, rose up and charged the entrenchments, which they entered almost simultaneously with the troops of the flanking brigades. The 10th Connecticut had suffered 56 casualties during its brief time under fire, more than any other regiment engaged, but the fruits of victory for once were substantial. Albemarle Sound had been secured, and with its fall Norfolk and the Gosport Navy Yard were vulnerable to an amphibious attack from the south. In addition, 2,675 enemy officers and men had been cornered on the northern tip of the island and forced to surrender.[45]

Burnside's force was now in an excellent position to move north through Currituck Sound against Norfolk or strike south against New Berne and Beaufort. McClellan's Peninsular campaign was in the advance planning stage at this time, so it was decided that more would be accomplished if Burnside moved against New Berne. This

44. Ibid., pp. 165–66.

45. Johnson and Buel, *Battles and Leaders*, I, 644.

busy little city was not only a sizable port but the terminus of the Atlanta and North Carolina Railroad, which joined the Welden and Petersburg line at Goldsboro, sixty miles to the northeast. The Welden Railroad was the only direct line between Richmond and the South Atlantic states; a vigorous move in its direction would threaten Confederate communications and thus be of significant assistance to McClellan. Moreover, if New Berne were taken then Beaufort and Fort Macon could be seized from the rear, bringing all of Bogue and Core sounds under Union control. An amphibious expedition had just taken the small Florida ports of Fernandina, St. Augustine, and Jacksonville. Should New Berne and Beaufort fall to Burnside, then only Wilmington, North Carolina, and Charleston, South Carolina, on the Atlantic Coast, would be available for blockade running; and both of these ports would be comparatively easy to watch.

Burnside moved leisurely. It was more than a month after the surrender of Roanoke before the 8th and 10th Regiments were at sea, headed for the Neuse River entrance to New Berne. The makeshift fleet got up as far as Slocum's Creek, sixteen miles below the city, and stuck fast on the mud flats near the shore. Here, the 11th Connecticut, which had been shipwrecked off the swash, joined the expedition. Early on March 13, under cover of Goldsborough's gunboats, the soldiers began to disembark. Small tugs towed troop-laden ships, boats, and old coal barges as far as they could toward shore; and when they stranded, the soldiers jumped off, wading the rest of the distance.[46] Despite the mud and the cold penetrating rain, the Connecticut boys were in good spirits. After landing, they marched twelve miles through the swampy woods on a circuitous route toward New Berne, while the gunboats kept abreast of them, spraying the south bank of the Neuse with grape and canister. Soaked through, the troops finally bivouacked for the night within two miles of the enemy line and roughly parallel to it. It rained steadily all night, with the moisture freezing on the ground, so that next morning the camp area resembled a frozen sponge. Colonel Drake, suffering from the tubercular infection that would kill him within three months' time, assumed that at least a hundred men of

46. Croffut and Morris, p. 170.

his command would be sick from exposure. He was astonished when all reported fit and eager for duty.[47]

Potentially, the New Berne fortifications were strong ones. The enemy's first defense position ran from the river's edge to the railroad line. Behind this was another earthwork mounting four 24-pounders. Four miles beyond lay Fort Thompson, with thirteen heavy guns and the main defenses, a line of breastworks that extended for a mile and a quarter to the railroad. On the opposite side of the railroad for another half mile rifle pits and short trenches had been dug; these were flanked with field artillery batteries. Between each position, ditches and felled tree trunks added to the natural obstructions of the marshy ground. In all, 8,000 Confederate troops manned the defenses, which bristled with 41 heavy guns and 19 field pieces. The Union force of 13 infantry regiments had an effective strength of 12,000 men and 8 pieces of field artillery.[48]

Burnside decided to employ tactics similar to those which had proved so successful on Roanoke. Deploying Reno's brigade to the left of the railroad line, and Foster's to the right, he placed Parke's in the center to act as a reserve which could be swung to the support of either flank or could make a frontal assault. As the division went into position, the 11th was just behind the 8th at the tail end of Parke's brigade, and the 10th at the extreme left of Foster's brigade, next to the railroad.

Foster's brigade advanced first through dripping woods that Captain Pardee thought were as "quiet as the morning of a New England sabbath." [49] The men had not gone far, however, when everyone was startled by the roar of a cannon just ahead and the crash of a heavy tree limb that had been neatly sliced off by a rifled projectile. Adjutant Henry Ward Camp of the 10th described the passage of the shot as a "loud, swift whiz," like someone tearing "a thousand yards of canvas from one end to the other at a single pull." [50] Almost immediately afterward scores of artillery balls and shells from the as yet unseen enemy began shrieking over the heads

47. Ibid., p. 171.

48. Johnson and Buel, *Battles and Leaders*, 1, 648–51.

49. Croffut and Morris, p. 172.

50. Henry C. Trumbull, *The Knightly Soldier: A Biography of Major Henry Ward Camp, Tenth Connecticut Volunteers* (New York, 1865), p. 70.

of the advancing troops. Ordered to lie down behind a slight crest, Camp wrote that "the men of the 10th didn't wait to hear the orders twice. I never saw a crowd drop so suddenly as they did." [51] After twenty minutes, when enemy fire slackened, the 10th was ordered up to the edge of the woods, where they were to form a line of battle and open fire. They accomplished this maneuver quickly, without being noticed by the enemy. Before any orders could be given, the companies on the right opened fire; other companies followed until, "wild with excitement," the entire regiment was shooting, "half of them without taking aim." [52] After the first few volleys, however, the men listened to orders and aimed carefully and deliberately at the breastworks 200 yards in front.

Meanwhile, Reno's brigade was attacking on the extreme right flank. The 8th and two Rhode Island regiments had been ordered up along the rail line to the clearing in front of the breastworks. Colonel Rodman of the 4th Rhode Island, observing the break the railroad made in the enemy entrenchments, requested permission to charge through and flank the main enemy line. Permission was granted and 2,700 New England soldiers with fixed bayonets burst out into the clearing. At a rapid walk they reached the earthworks before Confederate artillery could be swung around. Facing right with parade-ground precision, up the steep embankment they went, overrunning six artillery pieces and directing a heavy ragged fire on the right flank of the Confederate line. Young Colonel Drake, his face flushed with fever, had the blue and white Connecticut flag planted on the commanding point of the earthworks. Rodman followed with the Rhode Island flag, while the regimental color-bearers rushed forward with the Stars and Stripes. As Drake has described it, "we fired until they were dead silenced—not a gun in reply." Then General Foster ordered his brigade forward. The 11th Connecticut, which had replaced the 27th Massachusetts in Foster's brigade, charged across the clearing with the 10th and three Massachusetts regiments. Gaining the face of the redoubt, they added their fire to that of the three flanking regiments. What was left of the Confederate line now broke completely and fled. While Parke's and Foster's brigade were driving the Confederates

51. Ibid., p. 71.
52. Ibid., p. 72.

from their main defenses, the appearance of the American flag in the enemy works on the far left showed that Reno's attack had also succeeded.[53]

The sudden collapse of the Confederate defenders so disorganized Burnside's forces that by the time the regiments had lined up for pursuit, the enemy had retreated through New Berne, burned the bridge across the River Trent, and made good their escape. But they left behind 578 in killed, wounded, and prisoners, 1,000 stand of rifles, tons of army and naval stores, 66 pieces of artillery, and of course their city of New Berne.

Burnside's little army had performed magnificently: his tactics had been admirable, and brigade and regimental commands had worked smoothly and efficiently. The confident commanding general now moved rapidly to capture Beaufort and Macon. Four days after the fall of New Berne, Parke was marching his brigade south toward these objectives. Carolina City, Morehead City, and Beaufort fell without a shot, but Macon, a large, antiquated stone block fortress on the northern tip of Bogue Island, across the Beaufort Channel, rejected Parke's demands for surrender. Mounting 67 guns and garrisoned by 500 troops, Macon could prove a difficult proposition. Not at all daunted, Parke spent the remainder of March and the first three weeks in April in developing siege operations. By April 23 a part of his brigade, including the 8th, had moved over to Bogue Island and driven the Confederate pickets into the fort. The news of Pulaski's fall under the devastating impact of rifled cannon had traveled quickly to Beaufort and greatly simplified Parke's job. On April 25 his three siege batteries, puny when compared with Gillmore's monsters at Pulaski, began bombardment. After ten hours, with ramparts caved in and seventeen of its cannon dismounted, Macon surrendered.[54]

With the fall of Macon, Burnside would seem to have expended all his energy. General Robert E. Lee, who was now commanding the Army of Virginia, had reacted to the capture of New Berne by sending General Theophilus Holmes with 9,000 men to guard the vital rail junction at Goldsboro. But Burnside made no move in this direction. For the next two months the 8th, 10th, and 11th were

53. Croffut and Morris, p. 173.
54. Ibid., p. 654.

encamped near New Berne with little to do but read "hoary magazines that had come in boxes of Sanitary or Soldiers' Aid clubs." In July the 8th and 11th Regiments sailed north to join the Army of the Potomac, and the 10th remained on garrison duty at New Berne.

While Connecticut regiments were helping to bring the coastal areas of Georgia and North Carolina under Union control, the 9th (Irish), 12th, and 13th Volunteers were landing on Ship Island, about fifty miles east of the approaches to New Orleans, in preparation for the last of the great amphibious assaults planned during 1861. They were a part of Major General Benjamin F. Butler's New England division, which had been designated for the capture of New Orleans. Apart from the usual discomforts and improvisations of combined operations, these troops had seen little action. The capture of New Orleans had been a Navy show all the way. No bloody engagements, such as Roanoke Island or Secessionville, marred the military occupation of New Orleans and its environs. The Connecticut boys at Ship Island heard the distant rumble of Lieutenant David Porter's 13-inch mortars bombarding forts Jackson and St. Philip sixty miles away. Then they were sent up to the head of the passes, some seven miles below the forts, where their transports anchored. "We smoked and read novels," wrote DeForest; "we yawned often and slept a great deal; in short, we behaved as people do in the tediums of peace, anything to kill time." [55] New Orleans surrendered on April 29, and the following day the small steamer *Matanzas*, with the 9th aboard, and the propeller *E. W. Farley*, with the 12th, glided up the river past "the long green moundlike earthworks of Fort St. Philip" and "the mouldy old brickwork of Fort Jackson." [56]

The Connecticut boys crowded the rail as the *Farley* followed the winding course of the Mississippi. Full of wonder and interest, they watched the constantly changing exotic scene. Dark green cypress forests in the distance formed an unusual contrast to the fields of sugar cane and corn. Blossoming orange groves and magnolia trees surrounded the occasional white plantation house, bringing a sense of richness and variety to the flat countryside. During the river trip

55. DeForest, *A Volunteer's Adventures*, p. 15.
56. Ibid.

they saw very few people on the banks; even Negroes were scarce. And when a small tugboat pushed the *Farley* into her dock at New Orleans that evening, "the city was dark and quiet." But the following day, when the 9th and 12th disembarked, "thousands of people [had] gathered along the docks to stare in silence," as the blue uniformed regiments with fixed bayonets formed up on the levee. Then the crowd found its voice. "The roughs, the low women and the ragged urchins continue to hoot, jeer, swear and call us evil names," wrote DeForest. Under strict orders, the soldiers with their muskets near at hand were outwardly indifferent as they went through their duties of setting up a temporary camp on the levee.

For the next two weeks Butler's 18,000 troops poured into the city and fanned out into strategic areas to combat expected riots or enemy counterattacks. The 9th and 12th Connecticut were sent to Camp Parapet, a muddy, unfinished Confederate fort, north of the city. Colonel Cahill of New Haven commanded the 9th, and Lieutenant Colonel Ledyard Colburne of Derby replaced Colonel Henry Deming as commanding officer of the 12th. Butler had assigned the fat, gouty Deming to the command of all forces in the city. An ex-Democratic Mayor of Hartford, he was a pleasant, highly cultured man who was much better suited to a desk job than to the active command of a regiment. As a reward for the careful attention Colonel Henry W. Birge had paid to the uniforms, appearance, and drill of the 13th, Butler assigned it to the Custom House as his personal provost guard.

The stout, cross-eyed Butler may have appeared ridiculous when he bounced along St. Charles Street on horseback, accompanied by his 13th Connecticut bodyguard, but he soon demonstrated that he could cope with any would-be rioters. New Orleans was seething with violence. Captain Homer Sprague of the 13th wrote that Butler "had perhaps the most villainous set of rascals to deal with that ever disgraced and endangered a city. Deserters from the Confederate Army, deserters from the Union Army, foreign rogues from the four quarters of the world, gamblers, 'fancy men,' thieves, cut throats . . . the city to a man, yea, to a woman, was hostile to Federal rule." Colonel Birge, whose brief army experience would seem to have uncovered a latent strain of profanity, remarked bluntly that "every Union man is a drunk and every Union woman is a whore."

Butler acted promptly and energetically. Relying on his military power, he clamped martial law upon the city. In short order, he had exacted sullen obedience from the population. He was less successful, however, in dealing with insults and snubs to Union troops, especially from the middle- and upper-class females. One Saturday evening during the early stages of the occupation, Colonel Henry Deming went down to the levee to escort Flag Officer David Farragut to a dinner party. While the two distinguished officers in full uniform were walking arm in arm up Magazine Street, the contents of a chamber pot were emptied on them from the balcony above.[57] As Butler dryly remarked about this shameful episode, "a city could hardly be said to be under good government where such things were permitted or attempted by any class of its inhabitants."[58] This and previous insults prompted the commanding general to publish his famous or infamous order stating that any New Orleans lady who was found guilty of insulting the Union military would be arrested and penalized as a prostitute. To the outraged South, he was instantly stigmatized as "Beast" Butler, an epithet which neither disturbed nor deterred him. "The order executed itself," said Butler.[59]

Despite the obvious rudeness of the civilian population, the officers and men of the 13th enjoyed themselves thoroughly during the four months of their provost duties in the Crescent City. Everyone had a Negro servant from among the thousands of runaway slaves who came into the city claiming the protection of the Army. For army rations or clothing, the soldiers were able to purchase a variety of personal services from the liberated Negroes. Although at first Butler tried to put a stop to these practices, he finally gave up and acting under the provisions of the second Confiscation Act, permitted employment of runaway Negroes as free laborers.

Officers of the 13th and, indeed, whenever they could get away, officers of the 9th and 12th, reveled in the comforts of the city.

57. Benjamin F. Butler, *Autobiography and Personal Reminiscences of Major-General Benjamin F. Butler; Butler's Book* (Boston, 1892), p. 417.

58. Ibid.

59. Ibid., p. 414.

Butler had permitted a remarkably free hand to the officer personnel of his favorite regiment. Every one of them found comfortable, even luxurious billets in the abandoned homes of the New Orleans aristocracy; and there was much plundering of wine cellars and *objets d'art*. One day in early June, DeForest, on an errand in New Orleans, chanced to meet Colonel Birge, who promptly invited him to dinner. "You would have considered it a decent meal," he wrote his wife, "and I marvelled at it as a luxurious one. Just think of claret; also of sparkling Isabella, served in coffee cups for lack of glasses; also wine sauce on the pudding and *café noir* as a final." [60] In September, DeForest again spent the night with officers of the 13th. "Of course I was not indignantly surprised to find the field officers grandly lodged and abounding in foraged claret. But I really was disgusted at receiving an even more luxurious hospitality from a mere lieutenant," he wrote.[61] The "mere lieutenant" was William M. Grosvenor, formerly local editor of the *New Haven Palladium*. Grosvenor's quarters were in a small luxurious town house equipped with $15,000 worth of imported French furniture and knickknacks. "The cellar is well stocked with madeira and burgundy, some of the vintages being twenty years old," related DeForest. "He told me that in one day he and his friends drank 46 bottles. I found the burgundy soured and corky, although he did not know it, the barbarian; but the sauterne which he served iced for breakfast, was in good condition and of superior quality." [62] Captain Sprague has described Grosvenor as a man with "an iron constitution" and "unwonted energy." Both of these qualities must have been severely tested during his vinous tour of duty in New Orleans.[63]

If the 13th was wallowing in unaccustomed luxury, the 9th and 12th were barely existing at Camp Parapet. The constant torrential rains not only kept their undrained campground a bog of knee-deep gumbo but streamed through the "numerous rents and holes in the mouldy, rotten canvas" of their tents. Those who were not sick were frequently drunk, a condition that the officers tended to

60. DeForest, *A Volunteer's Adventures*, p. 26.

61. Ibid., p. 48.

62. Ibid., pp. 48–50.

63. Homer B. Sprague, *History of the 13th Infantry Regiment of Connecticut Volunteers* (Hartford, 1876), p. 13.

excuse. "You must understand," wrote DeForest, "that many of my men are city toughs, in part Irish; also that they are desperate with malaria, with the monotony of their life and with their incessant discomforts." [64] Almost, it would seem, as retribution for the absence of the human enemy were the unseen, more deadly fevers that rose out of the pestilential swamps to strike the 9th and the 12th. Nearly every officer and man came down with "swamp fever"—probably malaria—dysentery, typhoid, and other infectious diseases. When the 12th finally went into action during the Lafourche campaign, a bare 600 men would answer the roll out of the 1,000 who had sailed with Butler.[65]

The 9th Regiment suffered even more severely. Fifty of its Irish lads had died and were buried at Ship Island; many more sickened at Camp Parapet; but their worst experience occurred when they were sent up the river in June to help dig a canal across the Vicksburg peninsula. Week after week they labored in the mud and swamp with nothing to eat but pork and hardtack, and nothing to drink but muddy water out of the Mississippi. They ran out of quinine and could not get medical supplies or even food from New Orleans. During the month of July 153 soldiers of the 9th died of malaria and other virulent diseases.[66] "We could not give a funeral escort to the dead," wrote Captain Lawrence O'Brien, "the few who were able to do guard and picket duty could not attend to any extra duty." [67] Yet sick as they all were, they gave a good account of themselves in repelling a Confederate attack on the city of Baton Rouge by General John C. Breckenridge. The 9th had been rushed down the river from Vicksburg to reinforce other Union regiments holding the former capital of Louisiana. Early in the Confederate attack the Union commander, Brigadier General Thomas Williams, was killed. Cahill of the 9th, senior ranking Colonel, took charge and handled with courage and skill the 2,500 Union troops who manned the defenses.

Baton Rouge was the first serious brush with the enemy for any of Butler's Connecticut troops, but their New Orleans sojourn

64. DeForest, *A Volunteer's Adventures*, p. 41.
65. Ibid., p. 27.
66. Murray, *Ninth Regiment*, p. 109.
67. Ibid., p. 111.

was rapidly coming to an end. All looked forward to a change. For the 12th, anything seemed better than the monotony and mud of Camp Parapet. Even the 13th had grown acutely sensitive to its nickname—"Butler's pets"—and was quite willing to exchange the savored fleshpots of New Orleans for the as yet unsavored excitement of facing an actual enemy.

In October, the 12th and 13th, under General Godfrey Weitzel, participated in the brief Lafourche campaign against the young Louisiana militia general Jean Mouton. Although the campaign was relatively bloodless (Weitzel's tactics were good, Mouton's force was largely undisciplined militia), the two Connecticut regiments had their baptism of fire and suffered some casualties. More than that, they had been exposed to the rigors of forced marches in enemy territory, and for the first time they knew what it was like to operate without a commissary. In all respects they stood up well. DeForest, who had been worried about his own reaction as well as that of his company when it first came under fire, was somewhat surprised that fear was not "an abiding impression but comes and goes like that of pain." [68] Similarly Captain Sprague of the 13th said that while the men had great confidence in General Weitzel and Colonel Birge, they were quite unsure of themselves. "We were little more than a quarter of a mile from the rebel line, and had not yet fired a bullet, when the enemy's infantry opened upon us with a rattle like the discharge of an endless string of fire crackers," related Sprague. He added that the rifle bullets and musket balls, "invisible messengers, came humming and singing in our ears and striking a man here and there with a quick chuck! that sounded far uglier" than the cannonballs and shells which could be seen in flight and dodged.[69]

The outnumbered Confederates were driven from the field. After marching down the bayou and not encountering any of the enemy, Weitzel's brigade encamped near the village of Thibodaux. Since supplies had long since given out, foraging became a matter of necessity. Adjutant Grosvenor of the 13th, "that barbarian" who didn't know the difference between a soured burgundy and a proper bottle at New Orleans, easily adapted himself to the necessi-

68. DeForest, *A Volunteer's Adventures*, p. 59.
69. Sprague, p. 87.

ties of the moment. Almost every day, with a Negro to handle the mules, he ploughed up sweet potatoes for his half-starved regiment.[70] The 12th and 13th existed under such conditions until December 1862, when Nathaniel P. Banks, "the bobbin boy of Waltham," now a major general, relieved Butler in command of the Union forces in Louisiana. Banks, a political general like Butler, had many faults, but he did not lack energy. Indeed, if anything, Banks was too energetic, as the Connecticut regiments would soon discover to their dismay. Banks' appointment in Louisiana and Gillmore's replacement of Hunter in the South Atlantic coastal theater presaged a more active exploitation of the scattered Union beachheads.

The first phase of the amphibious war had come to an end. Almost 8,000 Connecticut troops had participated in these operations, which had cut the flood of foreign supplies into the Confederacy down to a trickle, had seriously interfered with the enemy's north-south communication, and had seized New Orleans, the commercial capital of the Confederacy. Charleston and Wilmington, in the Carolinas, and Mobile, Alabama, were the only ocean ports of any consequence left to the enemy. The most important objective of the second phase in the blockade strategy would be to seize these cities or to cut their communications with the North. Along the Mississippi, as 1862 ended, only Vicksburg and Port Hudson remained to guard Confederate supply lines with Texas. And both were coming under massive attack.

Over 2,000 Connecticut soldiers had been killed or wounded, or had died of disease, during the first phase of the amphibious war. 3,000 more would become casualties in the second, bloodier phase. The coastal operations of 1861–62 may have seemed a sideshow to the strategists in Washington, but to the Connecticut boys involved and their folks at home this endless succession of bitter little engagements, these endless marches through endless Southern swamps, were the real faces of war in its worst aspect. "I should like to have a share in the grand blows of the army of the east," wrote Henry Ward Camp from New Berne. "Our out-of-the-way performances down here don't seem to amount to much by themselves; and yet we've had sharp work . . . The list of casualties

70. Ibid., p. 94.

ooks small alongside of what you read of in the great battles of the Vest; yet when you come to compare the numbers engaged, we lost s many in four hours at New Berne as they did in two days at 'ittsburg Landing or in three at Fort Donelson." [71] Camp would ain his share of glory as well as his death fighting in the big show round Richmond. But it would take another year of increasingly itter slogging in the forgotten war along the Mississippi River and he Carolina coast before these Connecticut regiments would find hat the Army of the Potomac had its own particular style of ardship and danger.

71. Trumbull, *Knightly Soldier*, p. 81.

7. THE FORGOTTEN WAR

AFTER TWO YEARS of bitter warfare the Confederacy seemed stronger than ever. Outgeneraled and out maneuvered, the massive blue-clad legions were now standing on the defensive to protect the soil of Pennsylvania. The critical Northern audience, observing the titanic struggle in Virginia, was growing fearful and restive.

Yet despite the apparent strength of Lee's army, the Confederacy was in trouble. The people of the North could not see it; even the Lincoln Administration despaired of a peace with victory; but the average Union soldier knew that eventually the material might of the North would crush the rebellion. He could not help contrasting the equipment of his army with the threadbare condition of the enemy. From his vantage point as a prisoner of war after the battle of Chancellorsville, Captain Samuel Fiske of the 14th Connecticut never doubted that the North would win: "Their [the Confederacy's] artillery horses are poor starved frames of beasts, tied on to their carriages and caissons with odds and ends of rope and strips of rawhide. Their supply and ammunition trains look like a congregation of all the crippled California emigrant trains that ever escaped off the desert, out of the clutches of the rampaging Comanche Indians." [1]

Fiske paid tribute to the fighting qualities of the men in tattered gray, but he regarded spirit and endurance as no substitute for the hard facts of material supremacy. Thus, at the height of its military power in Virginia, the Confederacy was losing the crucial battle for the supply not only of munitions from abroad but of food, animals, and other essentials from within its own territory. These were the impressive dividends the North had already earned from the victories along the Southern coastline during the first year of the war.

If Washington after 1862 relegated these theaters to a subordi-

1. Fiske, *Mr. Dunn Browne*, p. 151.

ate position, Richmond did not. The next eighteen months were) be a frustrating period for the Union invaders. Gone were earlier ncertainties when the Confederacy failed to support adequately ıe defense of New Orleans, Port Royal, and New Berne. Drawing eavily on its slender resources, the Confederacy strengthened such ey positions as Vicksburg, Port Hudson, Mobile, Charleston, and Vilmington. And it reacted strenuously to any Union move on vital ommunications, especially those in North Carolina, Florida, or orthern Louisiana. Operating on interior lines in all areas, Confed- rate forces were constantly on the lookout for an opening that ould enable them to sweep the invaders into the sea. Attacks and ounterattacks in scores of engagements rarely involving more than o,000 men were to mark the second phase of the amphibious war. ı a region of swamps, fevers, guerrillas, and bristling fortresses, ourteen Connecticut regiments were to struggle from December 862 until April 1864. Always playing a minor role as far as na- onal attention was concerned, but fighting and dying neverthe- ss, they helped to cut down the vital stream of the bacon and ornmeal, horses, mules, munitions, and men that powered the rmy of Virginia.

An early indicator of the Confederacy's mounting concern for ıe security of its internal supply line was Richmond's vigorous sponse to J. G. Foster's raid in late November 1862. General Fos- r, the new commander at New Berne, made a sudden dash deep ıto North Carolina. This bold foray had caught the Confederates ff guard. Large quantities of essential supplies were destroyed and ommunications with Virginia briefly disrupted before he returned) his base. The authorities at Raleigh and Richmond had reacted romptly to the threat. Lee rushed a division of troops to Golds- oro, and Governor Zebulon Vance sent forward a large body of ate militia. The success of Foster's raid had likewise impressed Gen- al Ambrose Burnside, who had just replaced McClellan as com- ıander of the Army of the Potomac. Burnside reasoned that if the ıajor effort against Lee at Fredericksburg should prove successful, would be useful to have a strong Union force across one of Lee's rincipal supply routes. During the first week of December he rdered Foster to seize the rail junction at Goldsboro. Four days fter receiving Burnside's orders, Foster, with 12,000 men and an

artillery train of fifty pieces, was marching west from New Bern
The 10th Connecticut, commanded by acting Colonel Robert Leg
gett of New London, had been assigned to his reserve brigade. O
the third day out, just as the division reached the village of Kinsto
bridge, about half way to Goldsboro, the enemy made a stand fro
a carefully prepared position—the usual combination of a rise dom
inating swampy approaches with a bridged stream in their rea
When his advance brigade failed to carry the enemy position, Fos
ter ordered his reserve brigade to charge through it and carry th
hill.

For thirty minutes the struggle went on at distances of from 5
to 150 yards while the 10th worked its way into the most advance
position of the attacking line. The defenders, who by now wer
short of ammunition, suddenly broke ranks, jogged down the sid
of the hill across Kinston Bridge, which they fired, and through
cornfield on the opposite side of the stream. Caught up in th
excitement of the battle, the 10th pressed them hard, actually tak
ing 150 prisoners. Forward across the burning bridge the Connecti
cut soldiers ran, heads down through the heavy smoke up to th
edge of the cornfield. So intent were the men of the 10th on driv
ing the disorganized foe that they failed to note the telltale glint
ings of bayoneted muskets on their immediate left. A deafenin
roar of musketry at point-blank range brought the regiment to it
senses, as whole squads were bowled over by the impact of 500 bal
and buck charges from a range of forty yards. It had been flanke
by a Texas regiment, and before Foster's main force could come u
almost a third of the 10th had fallen; some having been hit a
many as three times.[2]

Relentlessly, Foster pushed ahead against increasing oppositio
until he reached the railroad junction near Goldsboro. The impor
tant bridge across the Tar River was burned and several miles o
tracks destroyed. In danger of being encircled by superior forces, h
called off the advance and retreated to New Berne.

Foster had again demonstrated the feasibility of cutting off Vir
ginia from the Deep South, but instead of reinforcing him for
large-scale invasion of North Carolina, Washington decided t
move on Charleston. This decision had been prompted more b
political than by military reasons, for Charleston and Fort Sumte

2. *Hartford Courant* (Dec. 27, 1862).

vere potent symbols to both North and South. The 10th Regiment ested briefly at New Berne and was then sent to St. Helena Island, orth of Hilton Head, where an army was being concentrated for he attack on Charleston. In March 1863 it was part of the force hat seized Seabrook's Island, a garden spot off the South Carolina oast, thirty miles south of Fort Sumter. Here the regiment settled nto camp routine and waited for the next assignment.

As always in military life, whenever a soldier has made himself omfortable in his temporary surroundings, headquarters seems erversely determined to remind him that there is a war to be won. or several days Adjutant Henry Ward Camp and his friend haplain Henry C. Trumbull, both of the 10th, had been planning New England clam chowder party at Seabrook's. It had taken onsiderable effort to assemble the necessary ingredients. Soldiers of he 10th had found clams on the tidal flats; government-issue salt ork, and potatoes just received from the North, were available. amp had saved several cans of Borden's condensed milk. Even ome onions, the most scarce and necessary item, were "borrowed" rom the Sanitary Commission's antiscurvy stores. And, of course, here was plenty of hardtack, another essential to the New England alate. Thus, on a warm Monday evening in early July, a pleasant inner was in progress at the 10th's field and staff mess-tent. A ight offshore breeze billowed the mosquito netting over the en-rance. The candles flickered in their sockets of empty condensed nilk tins. Outside, the warm Southern night seemed ablaze with ireflies. Huge green and yellow moths fluttered thickly around the ent pole, their compound eyes glowing like so many red jewels as hey caught the candlelight. Around a table made of a half-dozen verturned hardtack boxes, nine Union officers sat in their suspend-rs and shirt sleeves and gave themselves up to the hearty pleasure f clam chowder.

The group had just finished dinner when an orderly pushed aside he netting, saluted General Thomas Stevenson, one of the guests, nd handed him orders from General Gillmore to embark his bri-ade on the large ocean steamer *Ben deFord,* which was scheduled o arrive at Seabrook's during the night. Everyone present knew hat something big was in the wind when Stevenson read the con-lusion of the orders—"Light marching order, forty rounds of am-nunition in the cartridge boxes, ten days rations, shelter tents for the men." It would have to be Charleston. When Camp took the orders around to company commanders, one of the young lieutenants performed "the wildest kind of Pawnee war dance; just about half crazy with delight." [3] Few Connecticut soldiers gave much thought to the dangers that lay ahead; and it is well they did not The approaches to Charleston had been heavily fortified: any movement against the city was sure to entail heavy casualties Within ten days time one of Camp's dinner guests, Commander Rodgers, would be dead; another, Lieutenant Colonel Leggett of the 10th, would lose a leg in the Morris Island trenches; Camp himself and Chaplain Trumbull would be prisoners of war.

Charleston harbor had a narrow entrance partially blocked by a tricky sand bar. The city was guarded on the north by Fort Moultrie on low-lying Sullivan Island, and on the south by Battery Gregg and Fort Wagner on Morris Island, another swampy hummock. Between the two islands lay Fort Sumter, within easy supporting range of either position. South of Morris and separated from it by Light House Inlet lay the long, narrow wasteland of Folly Island. To the west of both islands the much larger James Island reached to within a mile of Charleston. Three hundred and eighty cannon of all calibers had been distributed throughout the harbor defenses. Some 12,000 troops manned the various forts and earthworks, but only about 6,500 men were available for the outer defense lines on James, Morris, and Sullivan islands.[4] Gillmore's strategy recalled his earlier operations against Fort Pulaski. First, he would seize Folly Island, which he knew to be lightly held, and use it as a base of operations against Morris. Once Morris had been taken, heavy Union guns would reduce Sumter and Fort Johnson on nearby James Island. The fleet could then enter the harbor and take Charleston as Farragut had taken New Orleans. To accomplish this, Gillmore concentrated a force of 12,000 men, which he divided into two divisions, the first commanded by Truman Seymour and the second by Alfred H. Terry.[5]

In the opening phases of the Charleston operation, the 10th Con-

3. Trumbull, *Knightly Soldier*, p. 138.

4. Johnson and Buel, *Battles and Leaders*, 4, 22.

5. Estimates of the Confederate forces in Charleston vicinity range from 6,500 to 18,000; Union forces from 11,000 to 16,000. Ibid., p. 75.

ıecticut and the 1st Light Battery were assigned to Terry's divi-
ion, while the 6th Connecticut and one battalion of the 7th, under
.ieutenant Colonel Daniel Rodman, operated under General Sey-
nour. On April 30 the 6th and 7th landed on Folly Island, which
vas occupied without difficulty, Confederate forces retreating across
.ight House Inlet to Morris Island. Gillmore decided that the outer
lefenses of Morris Island were too strong for an unsupported as-
ault, even with fleet bombardment from the ocean side. Thus the
ith and 7th found themselves in their familiar role of constructing
ıeavy masked batteries that would shell the opposite shore about
;oo yards distant. It was a repetition of their labors at Tybee.
Working only at night under the cover of the scrubby sand hills,
hey emplaced forty-eight pieces of heavy ordnance. Beauregard,
he Confederate commander, was not fooled, but he was confused
bout Gillmore's intentions. Would the major attack be made
gainst Morris or against James? Regarding James Island as the
nore feasible route for an assault on the city, the Confederate
ommander was worried about its defenses. Gillmore was also eye-
ng James Island, though not as a major objective. A diversionary
novement on James, he thought, might draw off the enemy re-
erves, throw Beauregard off balance, and assure the success of the
najor assault on Morris.

The Folly batteries were finally ready on July 8. After assuring
ıimself that a landing on James would not entail extraordinary
isks, the methodical Gillmore ordered Terry to make the diversion
ınder the cover of the gunboat *Pawnee,* which was to take up
tation in the Stono River, south of the island. On the afternoon of
'uly 8 Terry's understrength division of 3,800 men began an unop-
›osed landing on James.[6] The next evening he ordered his entire
livision to make a demonstration toward the old battlefield of Se-
essionville. For three days his troops held their positions near the
Confederate defense lines, while pickets skirmished with the enemy.
On the evening of the third day he withdrew his force under cover
›f the gunboats and returned to Folly Island. Terry's diversion had
›een highly successful. Beauregard had shifted all but 400 men,

6. A confusion in times and dates of the James landing exists between Trumbull and
Gillmore. Gillmore's account I have deemed more reliable, and have used as the source. See
ohnson and Buel, *Battles and Leaders,* 4, 57.

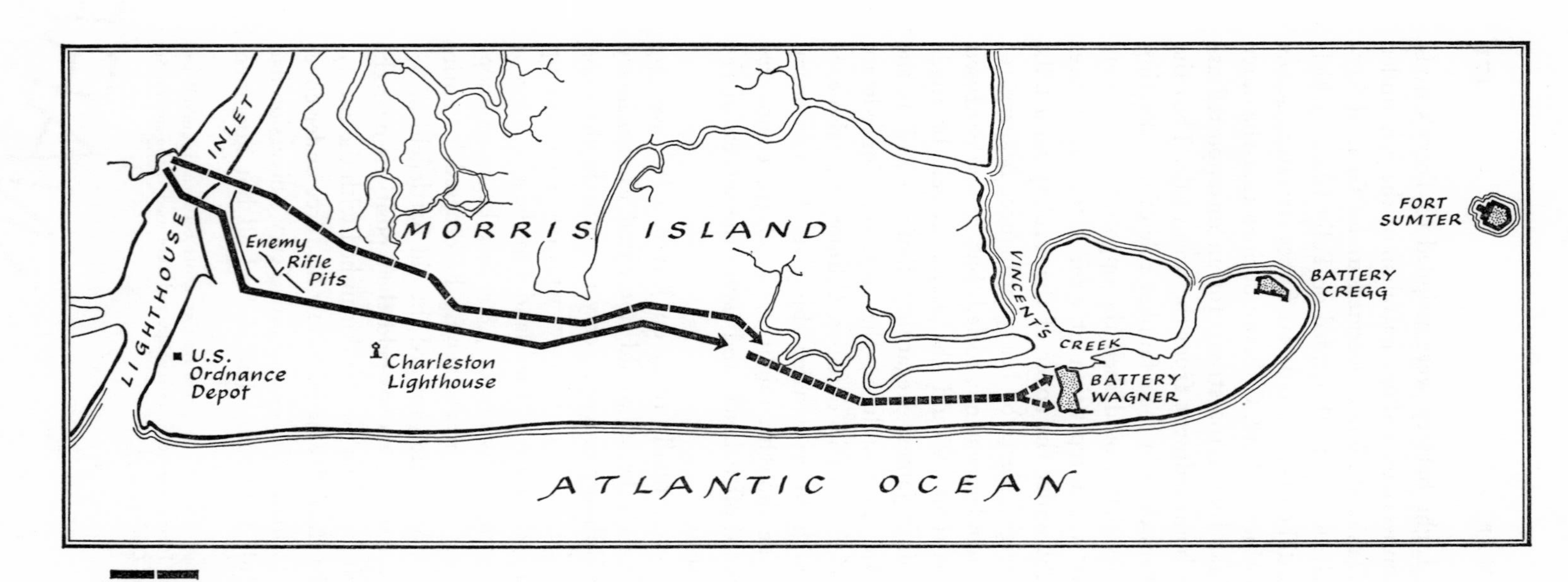

4. Operations against Fort Wagner, July 10–Sept. 6, 1863. Top: route of 7th Connecticut. Middle: route of 6th Connecticut. Bottom: route of infantry assaults on the Fort.

principally artillerists, from the outer defenses of Morris to meet an expected attack on James Island.[7]

While Terry was moving on Secessionville, General Strong's brigade, of Seymour's division—some 2,500 men—embarked in whaleboats and rowed for Light House Inlet. With the 6th and 7th in the lead, the flotilla reached its position on the east side of the Inlet about 3 A.M. on July 10. Screened from Morris by shoulder-high marsh grass, they waited silently for Gillmore's bombardment. Just before sunrise the masked batteries of Folly erupted with a sheet of flame as every gun was touched off simultaneously. A few minutes later four Navy monitors, like some bizarre sea creatures, slowly materialized out of the early morning mist and added their heavy Dahlgren projectiles to the land-based mortar and cannon shells. For two hours Gillmore continued the barrage but was unable to silence the carefully protected enemy batteries. At 7 A.M. he ordered a cease fire, and then signaled Strong to make an assault.

The Morris defenders had also seen the signal, and as soon as Strong's whaleboat flotilla emerged from its concealment, they raked it with grape and canister from eleven artillery pieces. Strangely enough, only one boat, carrying soldiers of the 6th, was hit, despite the fact that the narrow inlet was jammed with targets. But it was unnerving for the Union troops to row through the water spouts, doused with spray from scores of near misses. At one point General Strong's boat was enveloped by two well-directed rounds of grapeshot. Lieutenant Colonel Rodman, whose boat was nearby, shouted through the din to Strong, requesting that he be allowed to charge that particular battery with his battalion of the 7th. Strong hesitated for a moment, shaken by the perilous position of his troops, and then merely said, "Go!" Rodman, who was six feet tall, stood up in the stern, pointed his sword toward the shore, and ordered his Connecticut boys to pull with all their might. Within minutes they had grounded on Morris, leaped out on the sandy shore, and formed a line of battle. No orders were given, the men knew instinctively what to do. Skirmishers went forward on the double-quick, rapidly clearing the first line of rifle pits, and then carrying the second, while enemy gunners struggled to slew around an eight-inch howitzer. Company I seized the already

7. Ibid., p. 14.

loaded howitzer, traversed it another 45 degrees, and managed to explode two canister shells over the retreating enemy before they reached the safety of Fort Wagner.[8]

Meanwhile, Colonel Chatfield, observing Rodman's advance, ordered the whaleboats of the 6th to make for the shore on the right of the 7th, directly in front of another Confederate battery. Every boat got through to the beach without a casualty. Not even waiting for the boats to strand, the men of the 6th jumped off into knee-deep water and with fixed bayonets swarmed up the sand dunes in front of the battery. So rapid was the assault that the Confederates got off only one more round. Poorly aimed, the solid shot and shells struck the beach ahead of the advancing troops, and ricocheted harmlessly over their heads. With a cheer, they poured into the battery and captured 125 Confederates and a South Carolina regimental flag that bore the inscription, "Pocotaligo, Oct. 22, 1862." Chatfield, who had been wounded at that battle, seized the flag and waved it in the direction of the retreating foe. The 6th scrambled after them, overrunning line after line of rifle pits until it got within 300 yards of Fort Wagner, where the men were forced back by heavy artillery fire. Strong quickly followed up Rodman and Chatfield's successes, and by 9 A.M. all but forts Wagner and Gregg on the narrow neck of Morris were securely in Union hands. Losses were comparatively light.[9] Strong's brigade, in two hours of fighting, had captured eleven artillery pieces, several hundred prisoners, and large quantities of arms and ammunition. Thus far, the operations had been well planned and executed. Had Gillmore followed up his initial advantage and stormed Wagner and Gregg, he probably would have taken them. The forts were undermanned and their defenders demoralized by their defeat on the beaches. But the Union commander had expected a much tougher resistance on Morris; he was unprepared for an immediate follow-up to his quick and easy victory. The attack would be delayed for twenty-four hours, a lapse of judgment in an otherwise model operation that would cost hundreds of lives and months of

8. Walkley, *Seventh Connecticut*, pp. 73, 74.

9. The 6th Regiment had ten casualties; there is no mention of any in the 7th. *Record of Service of Connecticut Men in the Army and Navy of the United States during the War of the Rebellion*, comp. Adjutant General's Office (Hartford, 1889), p. 258.

laborious siege operations, only to fail in its ultimate objective—the capture of Charleston.

To the Union troops in front of it, Wagner appeared much like the rest of Morris Island—a series of irregular, low sand hills. To the practiced eye of Gillmore, however, it was a formidable work indeed. Constructed almost entirely of sand, it was largely impervious to artillery fire. Even when a gun was dismounted or a parapet shattered, repairs could be made quickly and easily. Beauregard had built a huge bombproof shelter behind its ramparts, where the garrison could remain in almost perfect safety during bombardment. In addition, the shelter contained a large number of mobile field artillery pieces which could be run into position ready for action within a few minutes. The Fort itself was 800 feet long; it was armed with eleven heavy guns in fixed emplacements. Though a small portion of the western ramparts was incomplete, Wagner stretched completely across the narrow neck of Morris Island from sea to harbor. To make matters even more difficult for an assault, the sand-strip approach to Wagner had been worn away by the heavy storms of the past spring. It was approximately one-third the width Gillmore's charts indicated. Assaulting troops would have to move across 1,000 yards of open ground on a front of 100 feet, only two feet above high water.

At 2:30 A.M. on July 11 the officers of Rodman's command ordered their sleepy young men to fall in with muskets loaded and bayonets fixed. General Strong spoke to them briefly, announcing that they would form a part of the combat team chosen to assault Wagner at dawn. Briefly, Strong outlined their mission. They were to move forward silently until the enemy pickets opened fire; then they were to rush into the Fort. He promised prompt support and closed his little speech with the now familiar injunction, "if you fire, aim low, but don't stop to fire; trust in God and give them the bayonet." Private Stephen Walkley of Company A recalled that "when I learned what we were to do my knees shook so that I thought I should drop." [10] While they waited for the order to attack, Rodman and his officers moved among the men reassuring them with jokes and casual remarks. Finally, the fateful order, "Forward the 7th!" As the men started to move, they gained confi-

10. Walkley, p. 75.

dence, and when the enemy pickets opened fire, the battalion charged. Its impetus was slowed down temporarily by a fusillade of musket fire from the ramparts, but the officers quickly got the men moving again. At a run the 7th went over the outer work, splashed through a foot of water in the moat, and rushed up the face of the Fort, where the panting infantrymen were pinned down by heavy musket fire under the sandbag parapet. Here they dueled with Confederate sharpshooters as they waited for the promised support before attempting to scale the last obstacle.

Support never came. The 76th Pennsylvania and the 9th Maine, which were to follow the 7th and then fan out to the right and left, waited too long after the first fire from Wagner before they charged. This gave the garrison enough time to rush out of its shelter and man the walls in full strength. When the 76th resumed its charge to the right and the 9th Maine behind rushed to the left, both regiments were met with the concentrated fire of a thousand muskets and three heavy artillery pieces double-shotted with case and canister. Both regiments were shattered and dispersed. Until now, the 7th had been lucky. Shielded by the parapet, the men were able to hold their own with few casualties. But when the supporting columns were driven off, their position instantly changed to one of great peril. If they stayed where they were, they would be overwhelmed; if they charged the parapet, they would be butchered; if they retreated, they would have to run a gamut of full garrison fire. Despite the awful risk, Rodman decided that retreat offered the best alternative. At the Colonel's order, the battalion dashed from its cover down Wagner's face and up the reverse side of the moat. Perfect line-on targets against the morning sky, they were cut down by the dozen at point-blank range. Back and forth through the dead and wounded strode Rodman, lending a hand here, encouraging the frightened there. It was inevitable that he would be hit; and he soon went down with a musket ball in his side. Lieutenant Charles Greene of Killingly rushed to help him. As he lifted Rodman up, the Colonel was shot again in the leg. Then Greene was felled by a Minié ball. By this time, dead and wounded Connecticut boys were strewn all the way from Wagner's ditch to within a few yards of the advance Union rifle pits. General Strong, who was observing the ordeal of the 7th, was heard to murmur, "Ah, my brave fellows, you deserved a better fate." [11] Only 88 men of the battalion responded to roll call after arrival in camp. Rodman had led 10 officers and 185 men in the Wagner assault; 103 had been killed, wounded, or were missing.

Gillmore had not yet given up hope of a direct assault, but he decided that Wagner would have to be softened up by heavy bombardment from both land and sea. Union troops, working at night, built five sand batteries within 1,700 yards of the Fort. In five days they had emplaced 14 mortars and 27 rifled guns, all of which bore upon Wagner's land face. Everything was ready by the 18th, and at noon on that day 60 guns from land and sea opened fire, pouring shot and shell into the Confederate works for eight hours. Sergeant Charles Cadwell of the 6th was particularly impressed by the naval bombardment. The *New Ironsides,* Dahlgren's flag, and five monitors had moved to within 300 yards of Wagner's sea face, where they fired enough shot, in Cadwell's opinion, to have established "several first class iron foundries." [12] Well before the bombardment stopped, Wagner's batteries had ceased firing, though the guns from Gregg, Sumter, and Moultrie, and the James Island batteries, continued blasting away at the fleet. Summer twilight was just approaching when Gillmore ended the shelling and signaled General Seymour to make another assault. Unfortunately, a sharp-eyed Confederate, who had emerged from the Wagner's bombproof precisely at this time, saw the signal and understood its meaning. He signaled Sumter and Gregg that an attack was underway and alerted Wagner's garrison, which had remained safely in its shelter during the bombardment.

Over 5,000 Union troops were now in motion, with the 54th Massachusetts (Negro), under Colonel Robert Shaw, in the lead, followed closely by the gallant Chatfield and the 6th Connecticut. Confederate harbor batteries soon opened on the advancing troops, the burning fuses of their shells describing lazy red arcs in the gathering dusk. Adjutant Camp, who was standing on a sand hill just behind the Union outposts with his friend Chaplain Trumbull, has described the assault as "a few minutes of comparative silence, and then a burst of flame from the walls of the fort—otherwise

11. Ibid., p. 77.
12. Cadwell, *Sixth Regiment,* p. 71.

indistinguishable in the darkness—and the sharp crackle of musketry . . . Heavy discharges of artillery followed in rapid succession, flashing like heat lightning; while the little jets of fire from
the rifles made a sparkling frieze along the dark parapet." [13]

The garrison had waited until the Union troops were within clos
range; then, guided by the flashes of their exploding shells which li
up the narrow sand strip, the Confederates opened a concentrate
musket and artillery fire on the 54th. Despite Shaw's franti
efforts to move them forward, his Negro troops hesitated, as th
76th had a week before, and broke for the rear, pouring throug
the ranks of the 6th. Chatfield, however, kept his troops in hand
Through a shower of musket balls and canister shot the 6th wen
up over the abatis, down into the moat, and up onto the parapet
Nor did the men stop here: they leaped down into the first line o
casemates and bombproofs before they fired their first shot. Her
under the blue and white flag of Connecticut—already staine
with the blood of its dead German-born color-bearer, Gustav d
Bouge—men of the 6th held out for three hours, skillfully improvising Confederate dugouts for their own defense.[14]

Meanwhile, Shaw had rallied the Negro soldiers of the 54th an
they managed to reach the parapet to the left of where the 6th ha
clawed its way into Wagner. But Colonel Shaw, on whom thei
spirit depended, was killed; and remnants of the regiment dribble
back to Union lines, leaving a jumble of dead and wounded black
soldiers and white officers. The troops behind them, who were
jammed into the narrow space of the attacking front, were als
scattered and demoralized as they attempted to work their way
along Wagner's face. General Seymour, the division commander
was severely wounded; Strong, mortally. Chatfield of the 6th ha
been an early casualty, wounded in hand and leg—injuries tha
would soon cause his death.[15] Leaderless and unsupported, the 6t
finally was compelled to withdraw from its salient. So choked wa
the moat with dead and wounded of their own and other regiment
that the survivors had to squelch over bodies as they made thei
way back. It was a grisly sequel to the 7th's ordeal, with heavy

13. Trumbull, *Knightly Soldier,* pp. 153–54.

14. Cadwell, p. 73.

15. Croffut and Morris, *History of Connecticut,* p. 445.

casualties right back to the advance line of Union rifle pits. In all, 141 officers and men out of the 300 who made the charge were killed, wounded, or missing. The 10th Regiment had been kept in reserve and did not participate in the second assault. But Adjutant Camp and Chaplain Trumbull, who had volunteered to assist in bringing in the wounded, misunderstood the truce arrangements and were taken prisoners.[16]

There was no rest for the weary battle-shaken troops. Gillmore began a methodical construction of siege lines, which eventually pushed heavy Union batteries and entrenchments to within 500 yards of the Confederate positions. His primary objective, the reduction of Fort Sumter, had not changed. If he could not take Wagner, he would fire over it at Sumter two miles away. The range was twice as far as it had been at Pulaski a year before, but such improvements had been made in heavy ordnance since then that Gillmore was confident his rifled projectiles would reduce the Fort. Another thousand Connecticut troops joined the siege forces during late July and early August. Hawley brought the second battalion of the 7th from Florida to Morris. The 17th Connecticut, commanded by Colonel William H. Noble of Bridgeport, arrived on August 12 and manned the trenches before Wagner. All of these troops, besides guarding against attacks, spent their nights constructing batteries and digging trenches.

On August 17 the first rifled projectile was fired at Sumter, and by the 19th eighteen heavy guns were pounding the Fort at the rate of 450 rounds a day. Three companies of the 7th served the mortar and rifle batteries, and a fourth company, with an eight-inch Parrott rifle known as the "Swamp Angel," lobbed shells into the city of Charleston several miles away. After seven days of constant bombardment from land batteries and naval units, Sumter had become a mound of debris. What guns had not been destroyed were removed by Beauregard, who realized that the Fort could not withstand Gillmore's heavy rifled ordnance. While the bombardment of Sumter was under way, Gillmore inched his entrenchments ever closer to Wagner, which Beauregard had decided to hold at all costs until he completed his second Charleston defense line. By the evening of September 6, when Union trenches had enfiladed the entire

16. Trumbull, pp. 156–57.

south face of the Fort, Beauregard ordered the evacuation of both Wagner and Gregg. On the following day the Stars and Stripes floated over two of the most stubbornly defended fixed fortifications in the Confederacy. For all the months of labor, all the deaths and injuries, all the tons of shot and shell that had been poured into those sandy wastes, the Union forces had gained nothing of a decisive nature. Charleston remained in Confederate hands, its fortifications, if anything, stronger than before. Blockade runners continued to slip in and out of the harbor until the city fell to Sherman's army late in 1864. From 20,000 to 30,000 Union soldiers had been tied up for six months by 1,000 indomitable defenders and a quantity of Carolina sand.

After the fall of Wagner and Gregg, the 7th went south to Hilton Head and the 6th to St. Helena Island. There they rested and received substitute replacements, most of whom proved a sore trial to the veterans. About half the 7th Regiment re-enlisted for the duration of the war and went home for a thirty-day leave. The balance of Connecticut troops remained at Folly and Morris, where they formed part of the Union defenses in the Charleston vicinity. In November, Hawley left for the North, where he purchased for the 7th, on his own signature, 400 of the new Spencer seven-shot repeating rifles and a large quantity of metallic cartridges. The regiment, now numbering 375 men, was fully equipped with these novel weapons by January 1864.

Both Gillmore and his first division commander, Truman Seymour, were impressed with the rifles and the way the 7th handled them. Thus, when President Lincoln suggested an invasion of north Florida, one of Gillmore's first operations orders was the assignment of the 7th to the expedition. Gillmore did this with the knowledge that the regiment, as then constituted, was composed entirely of veterans whose term of enlistment was almost up, or new substitutes of doubtful quality.[17]

A presidential election would be held in 1864, and Lincoln was seeking a second term. The President had received what he considered reliable information that a large part of Florida's population was loyal to the Union; he had also learned that it was lightly held by the enemy. The possibility of seizing an entire Confederate state

17. Croffut and Morris, p. 510.

and converting it into a loyal one would not only assist Lincoln's candidacy but provide another significant test of his tentative reconstruction policies. Moreover, an invasion could be justified on the grounds of military expediency. Florida was an important source of Confederate food supply; and its communications with Georgia seemed temptingly vulnerable to attack through the port of Jacksonville. The fact that the Confederates in Georgia could use these same communications to rush reinforcements to any threatened point in the interior of Florida seems not to have concerned Lincoln, nor even at first the high command in the Department of the South.

As soon as the invading force of 5,000 men landed at Jacksonville, Seymour began to have qualms about his mission and about the supposed loyalty of the Floridians. Gillmore, nevertheless, ordered him to cut the principal rail connection between Florida and Georgia. At the same time, from his headquarters at Port Royal, Gillmore issued a proclamation that Florida was now a free state under the protection of Union troops.[18] Seymour was in a quandary until he learned from presumably reliable sources that the enemy forces were about equal to his own. He decided to move west according to the original plan, and wrote Gillmore to that effect. It was now the turn of the Commanding General to play the cautious role. Gillmore replied with a prompt negative, but Seymour, now beyond the reach of telegraph, did not receive the message in time.

Confederate skirmishers fell back before his troops until they approached the village of Olustee on the morning of February 27. Here opposition suddenly stiffened. Union cavalry probed the Confederate position, reporting back that enemy infantry and artillery were strongly posted in a pine woods directly across the line of Union advance. Seymour hurried his artillery up to shell the center of the Confederate position. Then he ordered Hawley, who was commanding his advance brigade, to storm its right flank.

Hawley's brigade, consisting of the 7th Connecticut, the 7th New Hampshire, and the 8th United States, a Negro regiment, was in a flank formation with the Connecticut troops in the center to the left of the Union artillery. Confident of their superior firepower, the men of the 7th went forward on the double, firing as

18. Johnson and Buel, *Battles and Leaders*, 4, 77.

they ran—"the discharges of their seven shooters making a continuous roll like the musketry of a whole brigade."[19] Five Confederate regiments supported by artillery gave way slowly before the 7th's impetuous advance. Captain Benjamin F. Skinner of Danbury, acting regimental commander, never doubting that the rest of the brigade would support him, pushed the enemy line back to its entrenchments. The murderous Spencers had proved their worth, but they had also consumed ammunition at a fearful rate. With only about one magazine load of cartridges left per man, and no support in sight, Skinner had little choice but to fall back. This was done in good order, and when the 7th New Hampshire was met coming forward, the Connecticut troops divided to the right and left to let them through. Meanwhile, the entire Confederate line had consolidated and was advancing. Some 4,000 Confederates hit the 7th New Hampshire and the 8th United States, with shattering impact. Hawley tried desperately to rally his troops, but in vain. They came streaming back, exposing the division's artillery, which now began to suffer heavy casualties. If the Confederates had not exhausted their ammunition, Seymour would have lost all his cannon.

By now the 7th Connecticut had received a fresh supply of ammunition and was ordered forward in the center to assist in holding the line.[20] They reached their assigned position just as a Confederate brigade was rushing forward. "Now boys, give them the seven shooters," shouted Hawley, who was with his old regiment. Again the Spencer's heavy firepower dissolved the yipping ranks of gray as each Connecticut boy pumped out an average of ten shots a minute. The enemy line wavered and was pinned down and held until elements of Seymour's 2nd and 3rd Brigades came up to support the flanks.[21] For three hours the blue and the gray shot it out at close range. Seymour's reserve brigades were gradually flanked and driven back with heavy casualties. The Union commander had no choice but to order a general withdrawal. Had the Confederates followed up their advantage, they would have captured Seymour's entire force.[22] Over one-third of the Union divi-

19. Letter of Hawley, quoted in Croffut and Morris, p. 508.
20. Joseph R. Hawley in Johnson and Buel, *Battles and Leaders*, 4, 79.
21. Walkley, *Seventh Connecticut*, p. 122.
22. Croffut and Morris, p. 509.

sion were casualties, and the remainder too dispirited to offer much resistance. Throughout the night the beaten troops made their way east. "It was a weary, woeful march," wrote Hawley. "The poor fellows dragged themselves along on foot, or bestrode mules, supported by their comrades on either side." [23] For the next two months Seymour's badly mauled division rested at Jacksonville under the protection of Dahlgren's fleet. As transportation became available, regiments were shipped North, and finally by mid-April, the 7th left Florida for the Army of the James.[24]

The Olustee expedition seems to have been badly conceived from the start. It would appear that Gillmore had doubts about it because he did not assign sufficient forces to guarantee Federal superiority; nor did he maintain sufficient pressure on the Confederates in Georgia and South Carolina to inhibit their reinforcement of northern Florida. Both Seymour and Gillmore appreciated the dangers, but neither individual was able to communicate his opinions to the other. Gillmore apparently did not dare advise the President on this score. He did not suggest that Lincoln's information regarding the supposed loyalty of Florida may have been in error, even after Seymour had warned him that there were few Union supporters in the state.[25]

Seward and Stanton had been informed of the proposed expedition, but the rest of the Cabinet were kept in the dark. Welles suspected that something was afoot when the President's private secretary, John Hay, was sent off to Gillmore's headquarters on a secret mission.[26] His suspicions were confirmed when he was advised that the Navy was to cooperate in a Florida expedition. On the Washington level the disaster was shrouded in secrecy.[27] When the War Department learned of Seymour's defeat, Stanton clamped a strict censorship on all news from Florida. Welles, who had learned about it from Seward, criticized this policy in his diary. As the testy naval secretary wrote, "this suppressing of a plump and plain fact, already accomplished, because unfortunate, is not wise."

23. Ibid., p. 510.

24. Walkley, p. 124.

25. Johnson and Buel, *Battles and Leaders*, 4, 76.

26. Hay was commissioned an army major and supplied with loyalty oath blanks. General Samuel S. Jones, C.S.A., in *Battles and Leaders*, 4, 76, quotes Lincoln to Gillmore, Jan. 13, 1864.

27. Morse, *Welles Diary*, 2, 531–32.

But perhaps it *was* wise. Had the facts been published, the newspapers probably would have asked embarrassing questions, and then the troops involved might have discovered that they had been used as mere pawns in a high political game. For those men of the 7th Connecticut who had only a few months to go before discharge, this would have been a disheartening disclosure indeed. Olustee was another one of those bitter little engagements that had claimed Connecticut lives. "One of the side shows of the great war," wrote Hawley years after the event, "But the loss on the Union side was proportionately about three times as great as at Buena Vista." And then somewhat wryly he concluded, "I suppose it did help to whittle away the great rebellion." [28]

As Kinston bridge, Wagner, and Olustee had shown, Confederate power south of the Virginia capes was strong enough to cope with any serious Union effort to break out of its coastal footholds. Indeed, at times it was strong enough to go on the offensive whenever an opportunity occurred to catch the Union commanders off balance. The Davis government by late 1863 was desperately anxious to break the Atlantic blockade and to drive off Union foragers in the rich agricultural districts of southern Virginia and North Carolina. It was only a question of time before the Confederates would make a serious attempt to recover the North Carolina coast above Wilmington. Early in 1864 the military situation favored such an operation. Union forces in North Carolina were split up into three separate garrisons, guarding the ports of New Berne on the Neuse River, Washington on the Pamlico, and Plymouth on the Roanoke. These ports, about thirty miles apart, had the additional protection of river gunboats, an unknown quantity because the Confederates had nearly completed a powerful ironclad ram, the *Albemarle,* on the Roanoke River sixty miles upstream from Plymouth. When operations in northern Virginia came to a standstill during the winter of 1863–64, Lee was finally in a position to spare some men. Accordingly, in January 1864 he ordered General Robert H. Hoke to take a division into North Carolina and cooperate with the *Albemarle* against the various Union garrisons.

On the same day that Lee ordered Hoke's division south, the 15th and 16th Connecticut sailed from Portsmouth to reinforce the

28. Johnson and Buel, *Battles and Leaders, 4,* 80.

Union garrison at Plymouth.[29] The 15th then went to New Berne; and during February the 16th was also sent there from Plymouth to assist in its defense against Hoke, who by now had 10,000 men poised for attack. But Hoke's gray horde melted away into the interior, and the 16th returned to Plymouth under the genial command of Connecticut-born Brigadier General Henry W. Wessels. The men counted themselves luckier than their comrades of the 15th and the 21st, who had inherited as their commander at New Berne General John J. Peck, a fussy, timorous West Pointer, who had made their lives miserable during Longstreet's siege of Suffolk, Virginia, some months before. Their glee at being delivered from Peck's whimseys and caprices would be short-lived. The *Albemarle* had been completed and Hoke was ready to move. Plymouth was to be the initial objective.

Major General Benjamin F. Butler, new commander of the Army of the James, had been concerned at the dispersal of Union forces in North Carolina. Butler was not much of a strategist, yet even he recognized that the isolated garrisons of Washington and Plymouth would be easy pickings for Hoke if local naval supremacy were achieved by the Confederates. Moreover, he felt that if New Berne were held securely, the two lesser ports would be of little assistance to blockade runners. Butler recommended to Lincoln and Halleck that Washington and Plymouth be evacuated;[30] and General Grant, when he assumed command of the Union armies in March, recommended the same action. Lincoln, who had rejected Butler's proposal, was still considering Grant's when the Confederates struck.[31]

During the first week of April, Wessels learned that Hoke was moving his division toward Plymouth. On the 13th he received positive information that the *Albemarle* was ready to descend the river.[32] Although the naval commander present, C. W. Flusser, thought that his two gunboats could handle the ram, he failed to convince Wessels. That prudent officer telegraphed Peck at New Berne and Butler at Fortress Monroe for reinforcements. Butler,

29. Croffut and Morris, p. 482.

30. Butler, *Butler's Book*, p. 635.

31. Adam Badeau, *Military History of General Grant* (New York, 1881), 2, 56–57.

32. Bernard F. Blakeslee, *History of the Sixteenth Connecticut Volunteers* (Hartford, 1875), p. 54.

speaking for Peck, refused the request,[33] although he could have easily sent him the garrison at Washington.[34]

Hoke's division of 10,000 men attacked Plymouth on Sunday, April 17. Throughout the day the garrison of 1,600 managed to fight off all attacks with a fury born of desperation. "It was very evident to us," recalled Lieutenant Blakeslee, "that we must either be killed or go to 'Libby.' "[35] Early the next day Hoke brought up his artillery and for twelve hours blasted the forts and redoubts that surrounded the town. At eleven that night the Confederates, after two vicious attacks on the outer works, finally captured them, though not before suffering heavy casualties from the stubborn defenders, who tossed hand grenades into the tightly packed Confederate ranks. While this furious engagement was going on, the men of the 16th who were holding a fortified line at the right and left of the main defensive position were startled by heavy explosions that lit up the flooded Roanoke only 200 yards away. There a macabre spectacle was revealed as the strange turtle-like *Albemarle*, spouting fire from her eight-inch rifles, grappled with two Union gunboats, the *Southfield* and the *Miami*, chained together by their intrepid commander. The *Albemarle* rammed the *Southfield* and separated her from the *Miami*. As the Connecticut boys watched, the *Southfield* sank, nearly pulling the *Albemarle* down with her. At this point, one of the *Miami's* heavy shot, rebounding from the *Albemarle's* sloping side, destroyed her own bridge and killed her courageous captain, Flusser. The *Miami's* executive officer, who now took over, veered off and sailed his fast ship out into the sound.[36]

Wessels was now abandoned to an overwhelming enemy force supported by a formidable ironclad. For two more agonizing days he held out, losing one strong point after another. Finally, at noon on the 20th, he surrendered. His stout defense had cost the enemy about 1,900 casualties, substantially more than his entire garrison.[37] This was the last battle of the war for the 16th. Within

33. Butler, *Butler's Book*, p. 635.

34. Badeau, p. 56.

35. Blakeslee, p. 55.

36. Johnson and Buel, *Battles and Leaders*, 4, 627.

37. Blakeslee, p. 67.

twenty-four hours, the 400 Connecticut boys who had accounted for 500 Confederate casualties in thirty minutes were on their way to Andersonville. Approximately half of them would never return.[38]

Operations along the South Atlantic coast during 1863 and 1864 had added no luster to Union generalship nor to high strategy as conceived in Washington. True, Confederate resistance had stiffened. But Gillmore's ponderous assaults on Wagner had reaped negligible results; and politics had been primarily responsible for the tragedies of Olustee and Plymouth. While the Union victories of 1862 were being frittered away in Florida and the Carolinas, operations in the lower Mississippi were also floundering in much the same morass of inept command and political interference.

By the spring of 1863 General Nathaniel P. Banks had collected in the New Orleans area an army of 30,000 men, of whom at least half were raw nine-months militia troops. He had also collected (not by his own choosing) a sizable group of general-officer misfits sent him from other commands. Despite the dubious military reputation of Banks and the uncertain quality of his troops, Lincoln ordered him to accomplish a mission of great importance. Banks' army was to act as the southern arm of a pincer movement that would clear the Mississippi Valley of enemy troops; Grant's army, the northern arm, was to move south on Vicksburg. Banks would follow the river north, forcing the Confederates to fight on two fronts. Barring Banks' way was the Confederate river stronghold of Port Hudson and a small army under General Dick Taylor.

Port Hudson, 135 miles north of New Orleans, was a position of great natural strength. Perched on a sheer bluff which rose seventy-five feet from the river, it was protected on the land side by a series of heavily wooded steep ravines. Despite these natural obstacles, Banks probably could have taken Port Hudson if he had moved against it promptly. As late as January 1863 the fortress was still unfinished and undermanned.[39] But the Massachusetts General immersed himself in administrative details and in the training of his

38. Ibid., pp. 58, 59, 107.

39. Fred H. Harrington, *Fighting Politician, Major General N. P. Banks* (Philadelphia, 1948), p. 119.

nine-months regiments. When he was ready to move, the Confederates were ready to receive him. They had completed almost five miles of fortifications and had brought the garrison up to 12,000 men, more than enough to cope with Banks' entire army; for the rule of thumb during the Civil War was that one man behind a breastwork was worth three in the open field.

Port Hudson did have one significant weakness, however. With naval supremacy on the river and in the bayous, it could be cut off and starved out. When Banks learned that the Port Hudson garrison was too strong for assault, he adopted this strategy. The Navy scouted out a safe all-water route through the Bayou Atchafalaya which would carry his army north of Port Hudson to the mouth of the Red River, where it could cross the Mississippi and come in behind the fortress. But after Farragut's costly passage of the fort and Banks' own blundering attempt at a land diversion, the Massachusetts General changed his plans. Always eager to improve his tarnished military reputation, Banks had little taste for tedious, unexciting siege operations. He knew that General Dick Taylor in western Louisiana had only about 5,000 men. Why not bag him and earn a cheap sensational victory? Banks turned aside from Port Hudson and sent 15,000 troops east on a two-pronged assault up the Bayou Teche and through Grand Lake to encircle Taylor.

Over 4,000 Connecticut troops had been assigned to Banks' command. In addition to the veteran 12th and 13th Regiments, the 24th, 25th, 26th, and 28th (nine-months) Regiments had arrived during December 1862. For the expedition against Taylor, Banks was chary about using nine-months men, because of their poor training and generally bad morale. But he had been impressed by the appearance of the 25th and especially by the vigor of its commanding officer, Hartford banker George P. Bissell. The 25th was ordered to General Cuvier Grover's division along with the 13th Connecticut. Colonel Birge of the 13th was made brigade commander.[40] The 12th was assigned to Weitzel's division, while the remainder of the Connecticut boys stayed in the New Orleans area.

On April 11 Grover's division moved up the Atchafalaya and Weitzel's started up the Teche. Two days later Grover reached the

40. Sprague, *13th Infantry Regiment*, p. 99.

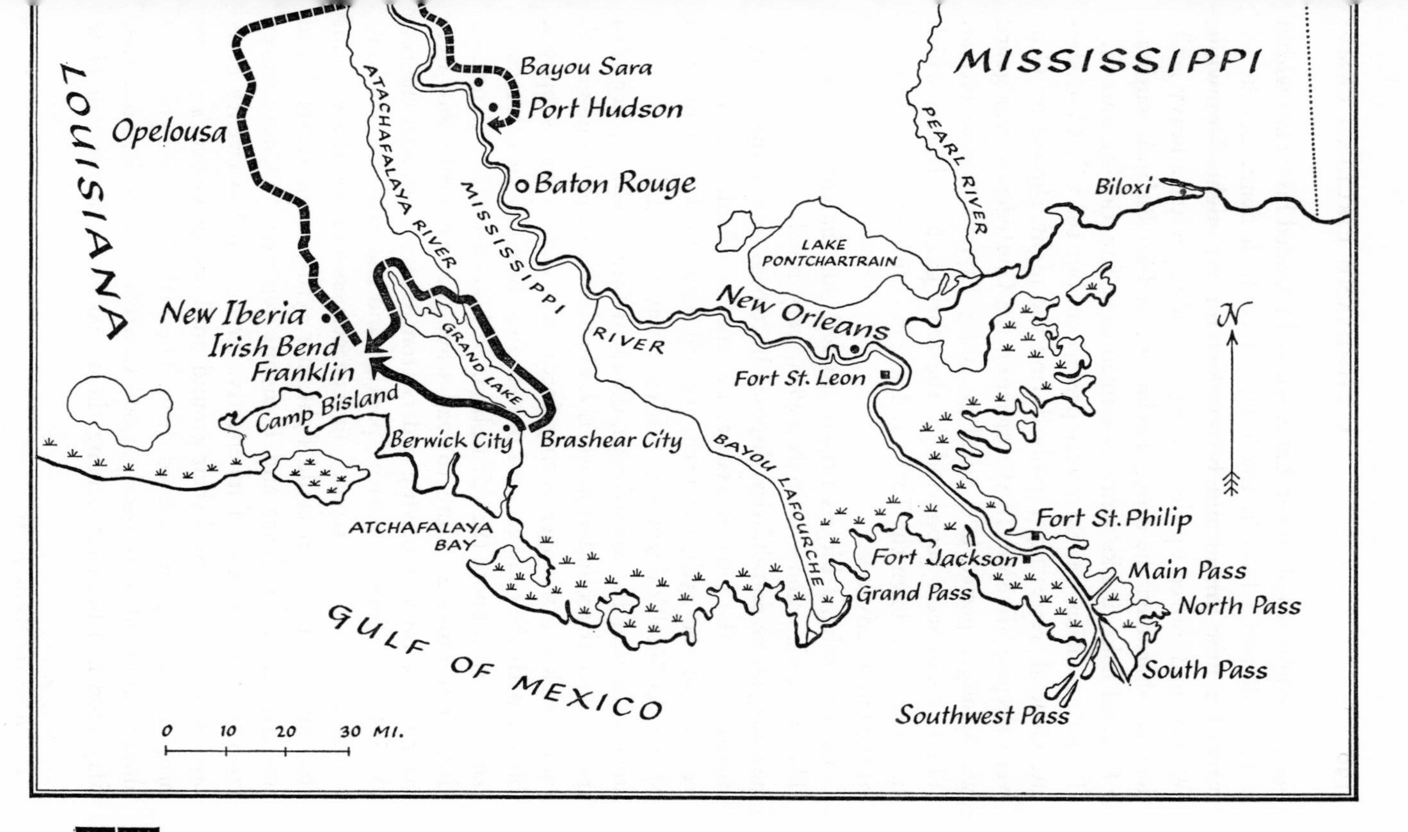

5. Nathaniel Banks' campaign in eastern Louisiana and Mississippi, March–May 1863. Top: Grover's march on Irish Bend. Middle: Weitzel's march on Camp Bisland and Irish Bend. Bottom: Banks' march on Port Hudson.

northernmost tip of Grand Lake, where he landed his troops within a few miles of a loop in the Teche called Irish Bend. Grover advanced a mile inland and bivouacked for the night. Meanwhile, Weitzel had moved up the Teche on schedule. After a heavy artillery bombardment he drove Taylor out of Fort Bisland, southeast of Grand Lake. Banks' strategy seemed to be functioning smoothly. Taylor's position was extremely precarious, but the wily Confederate General, retreating rapidly during the night, slipped by Grover's sleeping division. In the morning the Confederate rear guard was strongly posted in a wood guarding Taylor's line of retreat. These troops were supported by the rebel gunboat *Diana,* which had just come down the Teche and was in position to rake the flank of the Union advance.

Grover ordered Birge's brigade to feel out the enemy position. The energetic colonel from Norwich, very much conscious of his new brigade responsibilities, disposed his troops in a triangular formation with the untried 25th at the apex, its flanks protected by veterans of the 13th, the 15th, the 9th New York, and the 26th Maine. As Bissell's skirmishers felt their way through the waist-high sugar cane near the woods' edge, the silent forest suddenly began to sputter with the sound of musketry. Hundreds of tiny white smoke-puffs marked a stronger enemy force than Grover had supposed. Bissell, with the coolness of a professional, brought his other companies up to support the skirmishers. At his order, the 25th opened fire, front ranks kneeling to load while the rear ranks shot over their heads. Birge, receiving orders from Grover, directed the rest of his brigade into supporting position and the battle became general along a half-mile front.[41] In its eagerness to show the veterans that nine-months men could fight, the 25th pressed forward and was flanked by a Texas and Louisiana regiment.[42] Under heavy cross fire, 25 per cent of its effective strength fell in twenty minutes. Yet the men stood their ground until one of Grover's reserve brigades came up and rescued them. The 13th also at one point was almost surrounded by nearly 3,000 Confederates. In five minutes, fifty men had been hit, among them two Frank Stanleys of New

41. Ibid., p. 112.
42. Croffut and Morris, p. 405.

Britain;[43] but they too were supported just in time by a fresh brigade and the advance continued.[44] It was now late afternoon, and Birge's brigade had been under fire for eleven hours when Weitzel's fresh division finally appeared. Banks threw it against Taylor's flank, which promptly caved in. The Confederate commander had had enough. His supply wagons well beyond Banks' reach, he ordered the destruction of the *Diana* and retreated to the west along the road his men had defended so valiantly.

Banks hailed the battle of Irish Bend as a great victory for the Union.[45] No one could deny that the Massachusetts General had won the battle, and for the moment even the tired troops had a word of praise for their handsome commander. But when Banks had them up at dawn driving them after the retreating enemy, his brief popularity began to fade. After five days of forced marches deep into western Louisiana without being able to corner Taylor, the men had become openly contemptuous of their commander. Whatever had been gained at Fort Bisland and Irish Bend, they felt, had been lost in this fruitless exhausting pursuit. Bad morale degenerated into looting, despite strict orders forbidding it. At one point, acting Colonel Alexander Warner of the 13th and his entire regimental staff were placed under arrest for not controlling their men.[46] Early in May 1863 Washington called a halt to Banks' "eccentric operations." He received peremptory orders from Halleck to withdraw and concentrate on Port Hudson. By the 25th Banks' army was in the rear of the fortress; its outer works had been driven in; and his troops had taken over the enemy camp.[47]

Port Hudson was not quite so formidable as it had been two months before. Grant's pressure on Vicksburg had forced the Confederates to draw off nearly half the garrison, but Major General Frank Gardner, the enemy commander, still had 7,000 veteran troops and 50 well-protected heavy cannon. Infantry and artillery covered every approach to the fort. Dense underbrush, steep ravines, and felled trees made it difficult to launch a coordinated

43. Ibid., p. 406.

44. Sprague, p. 114.

45. Harrington, *Banks*, p. 120.

46. Sprague, p. 128.

47. Johnson and Buel, *Battles and Leaders*, 3, 593.

attack even with expert staff work and crack troops. Banks had neither. By all odds, logic should have demanded regular siege operations. The fort was completely cut off, and the heavy guns of the fleet in the river, when added to Banks' splendid artillery, gave the Union forces an overwhelming predominance in firepower. Banks, however, was worried about Joseph E. Johnston's army to the northeast, a needless fear because it could not abandon the Vicksburg area. Moreover, there was always the possibility that a quick thrust would be successful and would earn Banks the national fame he craved. Without proper reconnaissance, the ambitious General ordered an all-out assault on the 27th.

The Union forces, numbering about 14,000 men,[48] had been grouped into four divisions, with Weitzel on the right, Grover next, Christopher C. Augur in the center, and Thomas W. Sherman on the left. The 13th, 24th, and 25th Connecticut were with Grover's division, the 12th with Weitzel, and the 26th with Sherman. The 28th had just arrived and did not take part in the assault. Of the nine-months regiments involved, only the 25th had seen action. All the division commanders were West Pointers, well seasoned in battle tactics. Though none were brilliant general officers, they were dependable. Unfortunately, Banks failed to specify either the timing or the mode of attack. Despite the obvious difficulties of the terrain and the strength of the fort itself, he left all details of coordination and communication to the individual judgments of his division commanders.

Weitzel began the attack in the early morning. His division, formed in two lines, slipped and stumbled up a steep grade through a thick forest of magnolia trees. So dense was the foliage that the regiments quickly lost touch with each other. After twenty minutes of hard climbing, the men of the 12th began to hear the steady booming of artillery fire ahead. A few moments more and they reached a flat crest overlooking a wide ravine. Then, as if a curtain had been suddenly lifted, a vivid battle panorama appeared before them. Across the ravine, crowning a high bluff, was the Confederate position, an uneven, dirty yellow line, partially obscured by heavy, drifting smoke. Working its way down into the gorge ahead was one of Weitzel's advance brigades. For fifteen minutes the men

48. Ibid., pp. 598, 599.

of the 12th waited, dodging cannon balls and shells while Colonel Warner tried to find a general who would tell him what to do. Several men were hit by shrapnel or grapeshot. Captain DeForest was momentarily blinded and deafened by a shell that burst over his right shoulder. "It seemed to me," he recalled, "that, if I had lifted my hand, I could have reached the halo of smoke and black specks; but all the fragments hummed rearward."[49] Warner never found Weitzel, but did find General William Dwight, who told him that the 12th was a mile to the right of its brigade. "It doesn't need you," said Dwight, "better turn to the left and occupy a gap there."

Elsewhere along the Union line, the same command confusion was appallingly evident. Grover had coordinated his attack with Weitzel, but hearing no sound of battle on his left, ordered his men to take cover and engage in skirmishing. The 13th, 24th, and 25th, which had been in the first line of Grover's division, needed no urging. They spent the rest of the day behind stumps or fallen trees, while shells from both sides passed continuously overhead.[50]

Augur and Sherman did not move until early afternoon—and then, only after Banks had personally ordered them to do so. Both attacks failed completely. Augur's division became entangled in the felled trees and heavy brush; and Sherman's was battered to pieces by concentrated artillery and musket fire while it tried to cross four parallel lines of stout split-rail fences. During the advance the 26th maintained discipline even after losing its commanding officer, Thomas G. Kingsley, who had been severely wounded, and over one-quarter of its effective strength.[51] When Banks called off the attack, almost 2,000 officers and men had been killed or wounded. With less than half of the attacking force, Confederate General Gardner had been able to concentrate his garrison and repel each division in detail. Banks was not to repeat the blunder of uncoordinated attacks, but the heavy Union loss was far too high a price to pay for furthering his military education. Despite the fact that Port Hudson stood revealed as well-nigh impervious to direct assault, he was determined to try again. For the next two weeks,

49. DeForest, *A Volunteer's Adventures*, 109.
50. Croffut and Morris, pp. 409–411.
51. Ibid., p. 411.

however, he pushed regular siege operations from Union positions, which ran in as close as 150 yards from the fort.

This was dangerous, dirty, fatiguing work. Most of Banks' entrenchments were merely hastily improvised breastworks in front of wooded ravines overlooked by the enemy garrison. Both sides settled down to a sharpshooting match; and though the soldiers soon developed a sixth sense for survival, everyone expected that sooner or later his luck would run out. Regiments manned these advanced positions on a rotation basis, twenty-four hours in the trenches, forty-eight hours off. Relief duty, at least for the men of the 12th, meant only that they were not shooting; they were still exposed to Confederate fire without even the doubtful pleasure of returning it. From fifty to sixty men of the 12th were killed or wounded in the trenches during the forty-five day siege of Port Hudson—many of these in the relief area. When Captain DeForest admired a little hut just being vacated by Lieutenant Clark of his relief company, Clark replied, "It looks nice, but it isn't all my fancy painted it." He then explained how a rifle bullet had pierced the leading editorial of a paper he had been reading. Soon afterward, DeForest himself had a narrow escape from a cannon ball while sitting beside Clark's hut. He was just recovering from the shock of this when his company sergeant, only a few feet away, was killed instantly by a rifle shot. "So much for the advantages of the shanty which Lieutenant Clark had put up, after due thought as to selecting a safe location," commented DeForest.[52]

After two weeks of trench warfare, the restless Banks ordered a large-scale night reconnaissance. His object was to draw the fort's artillery fire so that the various batteries could be located and silenced by counterbattery fire in preparation for another assault. For reasons of his own, Banks did not divulge the real purpose of the mission to the troops who would participate. They were merely ordered to seize Port Hudson's outer works. When they had done so, they would be supported by a general advance. Seven companies of the 12th were selected to attack an apron of the fort in front of their entrenchments. It was known that two enemy regiments and several heavy caliber artillery pieces defended this position. Since the total strength of the seven companies did not exceed 200 men,

52. DeForest, *A Volunteer's Adventures*, pp. 119, 120.

the regimental commander regarded Banks' orders as complete madness.[53] But with that kind of resignation which comes when men have lived so long with danger and death, the officers of the 13th made their preparations. "No one spoke aloud," recalled De-Forest; "there was a very little whispering; the suspense was sombre, heavy and hateful." The only sound that came as the small band climbed the breastworks and filed out into the dark, sultry night was the measured clicking of bayonets against canteens.[54] Even this light sound was enough to alert the garrison. The Connecticut boys had not gone more than fifty yards into the ravine when the apron above them exploded into action.

The garrison threw in everything it had—grape, canister, solid shot, buckshot, musket balls, and rifle bullets. So abrupt and so heavy was the enemy fire that the men were dazed. While Lieutenant Stephen Ball of New Haven leaned against a sapling, trying to get his bearings, it was struck six times. Within ten minutes almost half of the little force had been killed or wounded and the rest were scattered over the ravine, each man for himself, desperately clawing for some protection from the searching fire of the garrison. All night—a night of thunderstorms and sporadic shooting—the wretched Connecticut boys shivered behind their rocks and stumps. At dawn they were recalled and had the unnerving experience of leaving their protection and scrambling back to their trenches under full view of an Alabama regiment. This time luck was with them. On the return only one man was hit, and he not seriously. The night reconnaissance had located two enemy cannon, which were put out of action. But the then novel tactic of using men to draw out artillery fire destroyed what little respect the troops still had for Banks [55]—an injury to morale that would have serious consequences when he ordered his second major assault four days later.

Everyone knew that something was planned when all of the Union batteries and ships opened fire on June 13. The terrific bombardment went on for two hours and then suddenly stopped. While the Connecticut men in the trenches wondered what would happen

53. Ibid., p. 125.
54. Ibid.
55. Ibid., pp. 130–132.

next, they saw several Union officers going toward Confederate lines under a flag of truce. Banks had decided to demand surrender before launching the attack. Gardner promptly refused. After this brief period of noise and activity, the Port Hudson siege returned to its accustomed routine. Duty regiments resumed their sharp-shooting, and relief regiments ate their meager meals of hardtack and coffee and went to sleep, many perhaps musing on the strange ways of commanding generals.

If the trenches seemed relatively quiet, headquarters was bustling with activity. Banks would not repeat his mistake of May 27: he had taken particular care to write out explicit instructions for his division commanders. The plans called for a dawn assault on the left and center of the Confederate works. Except for the battered 25th, which was kept in reserve, and six regiments of the 28th assigned to the center, all the Connecticut troops were ordered to the right wing.[56] For the attack on the right, Banks planned to use a so-called "covered way" that relief regiments had scooped out of a natural ravine during the past three weeks. This trench, one-half mile long, six feet deep, and ten feet wide, had been extended to within eighty yards of the fort. It offered scant protection from Confederate sharpshooters above, and it debouched directly in front of one of the strongest points in the enemy line. Known in the military parlance of the times as a "priest cap," this position was actually a triangular bastion with its legs pointed toward the Union lines. Any frontal attack must face cross fire all the way. The priest cap topped a steep rise; along its base was a wide ditch of stagnant water from four to five feet deep. Just beyond the ditch ran a gully conforming roughly to the bastion and approximately thirty yards below it. Banks' faulty reconnaissance had not discovered this hidden ravine, nor had it assessed properly the strength of the priest cap.

At 1 A.M. on Sunday, June 14, the Irish sergeant major of the 12th, John Mullen, moved silently among the sleeping soldiers of the regiment. As he came to each company commander, he awakened him gently and whispered instructions. A few minutes of sleepy stumbling, and 300 tired officers and men were walking through the humid night. After several miles of twisting and turn-

56. Croffut and Morris, p. 412. At this time the 25th could muster only 95 effective

ng through the dark forest, they finally reached the vicinity of the
overed way, where Lieutenant Colonel Frank Peck called the com-
any commanders together for a briefing. The 12th and the 75th
New York were to lead the attack, fan out as skirmishers at the
ottom of the priest cap, and cover the main assault. For several
ours, the Connecticut men marched and countermarched, directed
y staff officers who were obviously ignorant of the terrain. During
his mix-up, five companies were left behind as the regiment
roped its way after the 75th New York in the covered way.[57]

Dawn was just breaking, but a heavy fog from the river reduced
isibility to a few feet. When the 75th New York reached the exit
f the trench and filed out rapidly along a rain gully, it was hit
vith a withering cross fire from the priest cap. Gardner had sus-
ected an attack from this quarter. Musket and artillery had been
ighted at the precise range and target angle. The garrison pumped
hot and shell blindly but effectively into the New Yorkers as they
ried to form a line of skirmishers. A few companies managed to
vade across the moat and tumble into the hidden ravine above, but
he remainder of the regiment reeled back into the covered way,
vhere it caused immediate confusion among the troops who were
ollowing. Confederate artillery now began spraying the covered
vay with case and canister. At this point over 4,000 men were
ammed into the narrow trench. Five companies of the 12th, which
vere right behind the 75th, managed to break out of the confusion
nd the slaughter, only to lose their way in the roaring inferno
utside. As DeForest described it, "around us was a chaos of fog
nd smoke, with yelling men rushing through it in various direc-
ons . . . while the Southern crossfire seemed to storm in from all
uarters." [58] Meanwhile, the 24th Connecticut had struggled out
f the trench. Each man had been loaded with two thirty-pound
ags of cotton to bridge the ditch. The cotton was never used for
his purpose but did come in handy for an improvised breastwork
vhich was hastily put together on a knoll in front of the moat,
bout 100 yards below the fort.

Behind the 24th, 100 men of the 28th, who had been issued hand
renades, lost their company organization in the general confusion.

57. DeForest, *A Volunteer's Adventures*, p. 134.
58. Ibid., p. 135.

Individual soldiers trickled out of the trench, but few got close enough to throw their grenades. Those who did were soon picked off by the garrison as the fog began to lift. Some kind of order was now being established in the trench. Lieutenant Colonel Selden, commanding the 26th, got his regiment clear and it worked around to the extreme left in an effort to bypass the priest cap. The regiment had already suffered heavy casualties when two heavy artillery shells exploding almost simultaneously killed or wounded 22 men.[59] Pinned down in a shallow ravine, the 26th regiment remained all day under the broiling sun, slowly being shot to pieces.[60] Faithful Sergeant-Major Mullen of the 12th finally found his lost companies and directed them through the moat to a knoll in front of the hidden ravine, where they joined their regiment. Here, with just enough protection to shelter them from the vicious cross fire, Colonel Peck and his men watched the hopeless charge of the right wing's reserve.

Banks, through Weitzel, had ordered Colonel Richard E. Holcomb of the 1st Louisiana, now acting as a brigade commander, to make the assault. Holcomb's brigade consisted of his own regiment, the 13th Connecticut, one Maine, and several New York regiments—in all about 1,500 men. When the newly organized 1st Louisiana reached the exit of the covered way, the men balked at the appalling scene of death and destruction. By now, dead and wounded of a dozen regiments—all tumbled together like jackstraws—carpeted the rough ground outside the trench. Hand grenades, bags of cotton, bayonets, muskets, pieces of uniform and equipment, and parts of human bodies were scattered everywhere. Holcomb, who had been a Connecticut railroad contractor before the war, was a remarkably direct and forceful man.[61] Climbing up on a stump, he roared at his frightened men in the rough, coarse language of the construction boss.[62] Only about fifty soldiers responded to his harangue; and it is quite probable that if five companies of the 13th, his old regiment, had not come up at this time, there would have been no assault.

59. Croffut and Morris, p. 414.
60. Ibid.
61. Sprague, *13th Infantry*, pp. 12–13.
62. Ibid., p. 152.

The 13th, like all the reserve regiments, had been ensnarled in the covered way. But the left wing of the regiment under Captain Homer Sprague was still intact. With a vigorous cheer, the men signified their willingness to follow their former major. The example of the 13th restored a measure of morale to the brigade. About 800 soldiers, "an unsteady mass of men of different regiments," as Sprague described them, climbed up over the log breastworks of the trench and began the treacherous climb toward the fort. The rest of the brigade could not be moved. Holcomb had chosen an unfortunate route. The garrison held its fire until his sweating troops were within 150 yards of the crest. Just as the doughty Connecticut colonel jumped up on a boulder and waved his sword for the charge, 1,000 Arkansas and Louisiana riflemen started shooting. No one could stand up to that fusillade. Most were shot down at once, among them Colonel Holcomb. A mere handful, rolling, crawling, and somersaulting down the slope, managed somehow to escape injury. These joined other troops on the right, who had taken refuge in the hidden ravine.

The assault in the center had already failed, but Banks was still determined to push on with the attack. By 10 A.M., at heavy cost, he had worked another 500 men into the ravine. Counting the remnants of the first assault, Banks now had approximately 1,500 soldiers in the ravine from 30 to 150 yards below the ramparts. Their situation was uncomfortable and dangerous. The hot summer sun of Louisiana beat down upon them. Their canteens were empty; ammunition was running low; the enemy was methodically searching out every exposed point in the crowded ravine. Everyone feared a counterattack from the numerically superior garrison, which could have easily captured the whole lot. Yet again and again came peremptory orders from Banks to attack. As they wondered what to do, commanding officers of the various regiments tended to congregate in an informal conference. Colonel Nathaniel Hubbard of the 159th New York offered to follow but would not lead an attack. "I regard it as a perfect slaughter pen," he said. Colonel Simon Jerard, of the 22nd Maine, was even more explicit. "If General Banks wants to go in there, let *him* go in and be damned," Jerard said bluntly, "I won't slaughter my men that way." Lieutenant Colonel Nicholas Day of the 131st New York summed up the general attitude: "I started out this morning with the determination to be a hell of a fellow! I've been a hell of a fellow long enough. If any one else wants to be a hell of a fellow, I've no objections." [63] Afterward, Hubbard and Jerard were to be court-martialed and dishonorably discharged for disobedience to orders. Almost 2,000 troops, one-third of the attacking force, were killed or wounded before Banks called off the attack.

For the rest of the day three Connecticut regiments, the 12th, 13th, and 24th, were among those Union troops who held the most advanced positions. In the afternoon, at great risk, a little hardtack and coffee was brought up. "It was a strange meal," wrote DeForest, "not but what the fare was familiar enough, but the surroundings were universally dismal." One incident, however, had its amusing overtones. Near him on a stump sat a Connecticut private chewing on a piece of hardtack while a comrade gingerly probed for a buckshot in his skull with a jackknife. "God damn it! Can't you start it," groaned the wounded man, "Dig in like hell." [64] During the night both the 12th and 13th were ordered back to their original positions. For three days more, the 24th held its cotton-bag-protected salient, now strengthened with clay and logs. Then, they too were ordered back and the siege again settled into routine.

Banks planned one more assault to be undertaken by 1,000 volunteers. Colonel Birge promptly offered himself as its commander and was accepted. Though everyone recognized that this would probably be another hopeless slaughter, 225 enlisted men and 16 officers of the 13th volunteered; 30 to 40 volunteered from the 12th. DeForest observed that they were "a curious medley as to character, some of them being our very best and bravest men, while others were mere rapscallions whose object was probably to get the whiskey ration." [65] No more than a corporal's guard could be recruited from the other Connecticut regiments. The nine-months men evidently had had enough of gallantry and more than enough of Banks. Fortunately, the surrender of Vicksburg occurred just

63. Sprague, pp. 156–57.

64. DeForest, *A Volunteer's Adventures*, p. 141.

65. Ibid., p. 145.

efore the planned assault. The Confederate position at Port Hud-on was now untenable. Gardner did not need much urging to ccept the plain facts. He surrendered his starving garrison on July . When the news of Vicksburg's fall reached the trenches, every oldier cheered himself hoarse. "What are you yelling about?" asked n Alabama sharpshooter from across the ravine in front of the 2th's position. "Vicksburg has gone up," answered twenty mem-ers of Company I in unison. "Hell!" he replied.

The forty-five day siege had been a fearful experience for the Connecticut troops. Early in the siege they had lost all confidence n Banks' leadership. After listening to one of the commanding eneral's morale-boosting speeches before the surrender, the men of he 12th refused to cheer him, but stood in sullen silence until the mbarrassed Banks mounted his horse and rode away. The heat, the ilth, the constant racket of artillery and small arms, the lack of ood and even water, mass slaughter in ill-coordinated assaults; wift, silent death or injury every day from the hidden snipers; ppeals, threats, broken promises from the vainglorious Banks—hese had been Port Hudson. The psychic wounds went deep. As DeForest remarked on the vicious trench warfare: "the spring is lways bent, the nerves never have a chance to recuperate; the lasticity of courage is slowly worn out." [66]

The 13th Connecticut had already—as its designation suggested—gained the reputation of being an unlucky regiment. It was to articipate in Banks' last disaster, the Red River expedition, and hen was to suffer heavy casualties in Sheridan's operations against Early in the Shenandoah Valley. After this, what was left of the egiment was to be assigned provost duty in Georgia and was not to e released until May 1866, having served continuously for almost our and a half years.[67] A majority of the veterans in the 13th, owever, remained surprisingly cheerful through it all. Most of hem had volunteered for Banks' last desperate assault on Port Hudson, from which they had received a timely reprieve, and most f them re-enlisted as veterans after their original enlistments ex-ired. Entitled to a thirty-day leave at home for their patriotic

66. Ibid., p. 116.

67. *Record of Service*, p. 511.

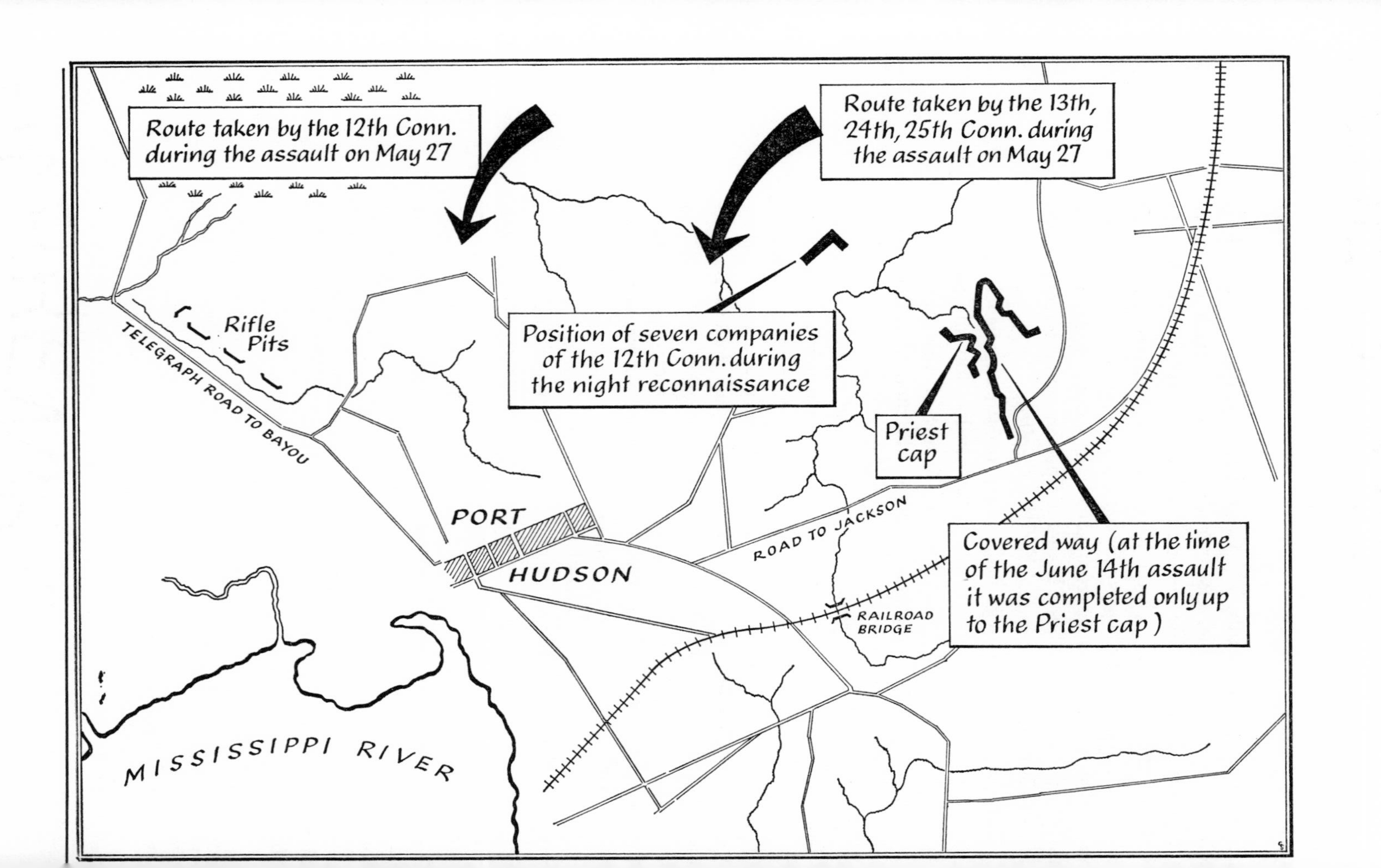
Route taken by the 12th Conn.
during the assault on May 27
Route taken by the 13th,
24th, 25th Conn. during
the assault on May 27
Rifle
Pits
TELEGRAPH ROAD TO BAYOU
Position of seven companies
of the 12th Conn. during
the night reconnaissance
Priest
cap
PORT
HUDSON
ROAD TO JACKSON
RAILROAD
BRIDGE
Covered way (at the time
of the June 14th assault
it was completed only up
to the Priest cap)
MISSISSIPPI RIVER

gesture, the veterans of the 13th were callously ignored by General Banks. They were kept in the field a good six months beyond their promised time for furlough before he grudgingly released them.[68]

The 12th was luckier. After skirmishing with Dick Taylor's army in western Louisiana, those who re-enlisted got their home leave without undue delay. They, too, were reassigned to Sheridan's army in the Shenandoah Valley, where, if the generalship was better, the danger was no less intense. The nine-months regiments returned to Connecticut and were discharged—their depleted ranks testifying to the awful casualties and hardships of the Louisiana campaign. No holiday mood marked the somber crowds that gathered for the return of Hartford's 25th nine-months Volunteers. Seven officers and 188 men marched down Asylum Street from the railroad station, a pitiful remnant of the spick and span regiment, 811 strong, that had marched off so proudly not ten months before. Many of the missing 600 were in hospitals, and were to straggle back home singly or in small groups, but ninety would never return.[69] Though the 25th had lost more than any of the nine-months regiments, all bore the scars of Banks' ill-fated operations. Even the 23rd, which had escaped the major campaigns in the Department of the Gulf during 1863, buried 55 of its men in Louisiana.[70]

The Red River campaign closed out large-scale operations in the Gulf theater. Confederate forces would hold out in western Louisiana and in Texas until the end of the war. Indeed Port Hudson, as poorly conducted as the siege had been, was the only significant Union victory in the Deep South until Sherman's march to the sea during the summer of 1864. Inept command, politically dominated strategy, unhealthful climate, difficult terrain, and stubborn resistance had been more than enough to check the individual courage and astonishing hardihood of the Union troops involved. Yet the constant pressure on the enemy's north-south supply lines achieved results. If brilliant military successes were lacking, replacements and supplies for Lee's hard-pressed army were reduced substantially. For nearly three years a major portion of Connecticut's military manpower had been engaged in this generally dirty and for-

68. Sprague, pp. 217–18.
69. *Record of Service,* p. 806.
70. Ibid., p. 773.

gotten war stretching from the Carolinas to the eastern border of Texas. Now the scene would change. Connecticut troops from all over the Deep South were being concentrated in Virginia for the final contest of the war. They, too, would serve in the big show in which many other Connecticut regiments had been fighting since the fall of 1861.

8. "ONLY THE OFFICERS GOT LICKED"

ON THE EVENING OF JUNE 23RD, 1864, the men of the 1st Connecticut Light Battery lounged at their brass twelve-pounders, smoking and yarning. As usual they complained about the war and blamed it on their commander, Benjamin Butler, known variously as "old jelly bag" and "the emperor," not to mention coarser epithets.

It was unusually still, warm with a light breeze that wrinkled the muddy James River beneath them. Far off to the southwest, the steeples of Petersburg could just be seen, as a spectacular sunset touched their tips with fire. Downstream a United States Navy monitor lay at anchor—squat and ugly—jarring the peaceful symmetry of a Virginia summer evening. Working crews were still busy patching shot holes in her smokestack with pieces of sheet iron. The tapping of their hammers carried faintly on the breeze. To the farmer boys of the battery the sound was oddly reminiscent of home, of mending rakes and mowing machines, of riveting handles on scythes. It would soon be haying season in Connecticut.

While they lounged and talked, a short dusty soldier, walking beside his horse, approached. Private Edward Griswold sprang up and saluted. The soldier asked politely about an annoying Confederate battery across the river. As soon as he rode on, Griswold asked excitedly, "Boys, do you know what that is?" One of the artillerymen idly answered, "an orderly." "Not so," replied Griswold, "his orderly will soon follow; that is General Grant." [1] In a few moments the orderly followed, also dressed as a private. Even then his skeptical comrades, who had only seen Grant once at a distance, when he accompanied the President on a review some months before, refused to believe him. But they agreed that if "the Emperor [General Butler] with his suit [sic] followed, then it would be

1. Beecher, *First Light Battery,* 2, 504.

Grant, sure." [2] In a short time, with jingling of spurs and slapping of dress sabers, the paunchy Butler appeared at the head of his 200-man staff. They cantered along the path that Grant and his orderly had taken. "We got away quick," related Griswold, "as we were always afraid of arrest for some unknown cause, if *he* happened along." Everyone decided that it *was* Grant after all, and that Butler and his "suit" with all their "gilt and feathers" looked just like the governor's inaugural parade back home.[3]

Intuitively, the men of the light battery had recognized Grant as a professional and Butler as an amateur. Wise in the ways of personal survival, they would still tolerate the prospect of death or injury if they were confident in their commander. For the Army of the Potomac had finally realized that Napoleonic maxims would not win the war. Grant had commanded the Army for only eight weeks; he had made tragic mistakes, but the rank and file saw in him the way out of an awful situation, the only guarantee that eventually they would be home for good. In the light battery's contempt for Butler's pomp, and its approval of Grant's quiet competence, it was rejecting the old order of things—the fifes and drums, the martial display, the glories of a warrior's death which had once moved the men to a religious ardor. So it was with other Connecticut regiments in the Army of the Potomac. Captain Samuel Fiske, ruminating about the presidential campaign of 1864, decided that being an ex-President must be "the least desirable thing in the whole world." But, he wrote, "for McClellan now the case is different. It might be a comfort to him even to become an ex-President" [4]—harsh words, indeed, for the man who once dramatized the spirit of martial youth, yet commanded the humble respect and support of the President himself. Before he enlisted as a private in the 14th Connecticut, the Reverend Samuel Fiske had prayed for McClellan from his pulpit in Madison, and had praised his soldierly qualities in many a stirring sermon.

The McClellan symbol had been essential at the time. It sustained the raw Connecticut volunteer while he learned to fight. It stiffened the home front too, providing cohesion until the public

2. Ibid., p. 505.
3. Ibid.
4. Fiske, *Mr. Dunn Browne,* pp. 364–65.

learned enough about war to pay the price for peace with victory. After the Peninsular campaign, McClellan was through with a majority of the Connecticut public, but the volunteers supported him until well after Antietam. Voicing a prevalent attitude, Captain William Lusk of Norwich said in late 1862 that the Army simply did not trust Lincoln's judgment. "Pope, Sigel, Frémont and the whole batch of our political generals are objects of honest terror to every soldier in the Union Army," he wrote his cousin, Horace Barnard.[5] The army was aware of McClellan's limitations, but it was not ready to cut the cord. "We of the army are jealous of McClellan's reputation," Lusk continued, "and fear the possibility of losing him." [6] As their confidence in McClellan dwindled, their confidence in themselves, in their ability to fight and win, grew steadily. Sometime during the slaughter at Fredericksburg or the bloody confusion of Chancellorsville, they too cast off their romantic notions about war as casually as they had once discarded their burdensome knapsacks before the first battle of Bull Run. But in the springtime of the war, the state and the nation idolized their handsome young commander.

Connecticut troops first met General McClellan in October 1861. The 5th Connecticut, commanded by Orris S. Ferry of Norwalk, was in western Maryland at the time. Still an undisciplined, devil-may-care crowd of Connecticut boys who seemed accidentally to be in uniform, they were assigned to Banks' army in the Shenandoah Valley. Incredibly naïve and provincial, the men of the 5th had been surprised at the Pennsylvania Dutch. How was it, they asked, that "so many white folks, living so near Connecticut and looking so much like Connecticut Yankees . . . could speak so little good English?" [7] The hospitable Pennsylvanians offered them such local delicacies as cottage cheese, sauerkraut, and smoked sausage. The Connecticut boys balked at this strange fare and would accept only bread and milk.[8] As callow as they were, they took instinctively to McClellan when he assumed personal command of Banks' withdrawal in western Maryland.[9] In the months

5. Lusk, *War Letters,* p. 214.
6. Ibid.
7. Marvin, *Fifth Regiment,* p. 29.
8. Ibid.
9. Ibid., p. 42.

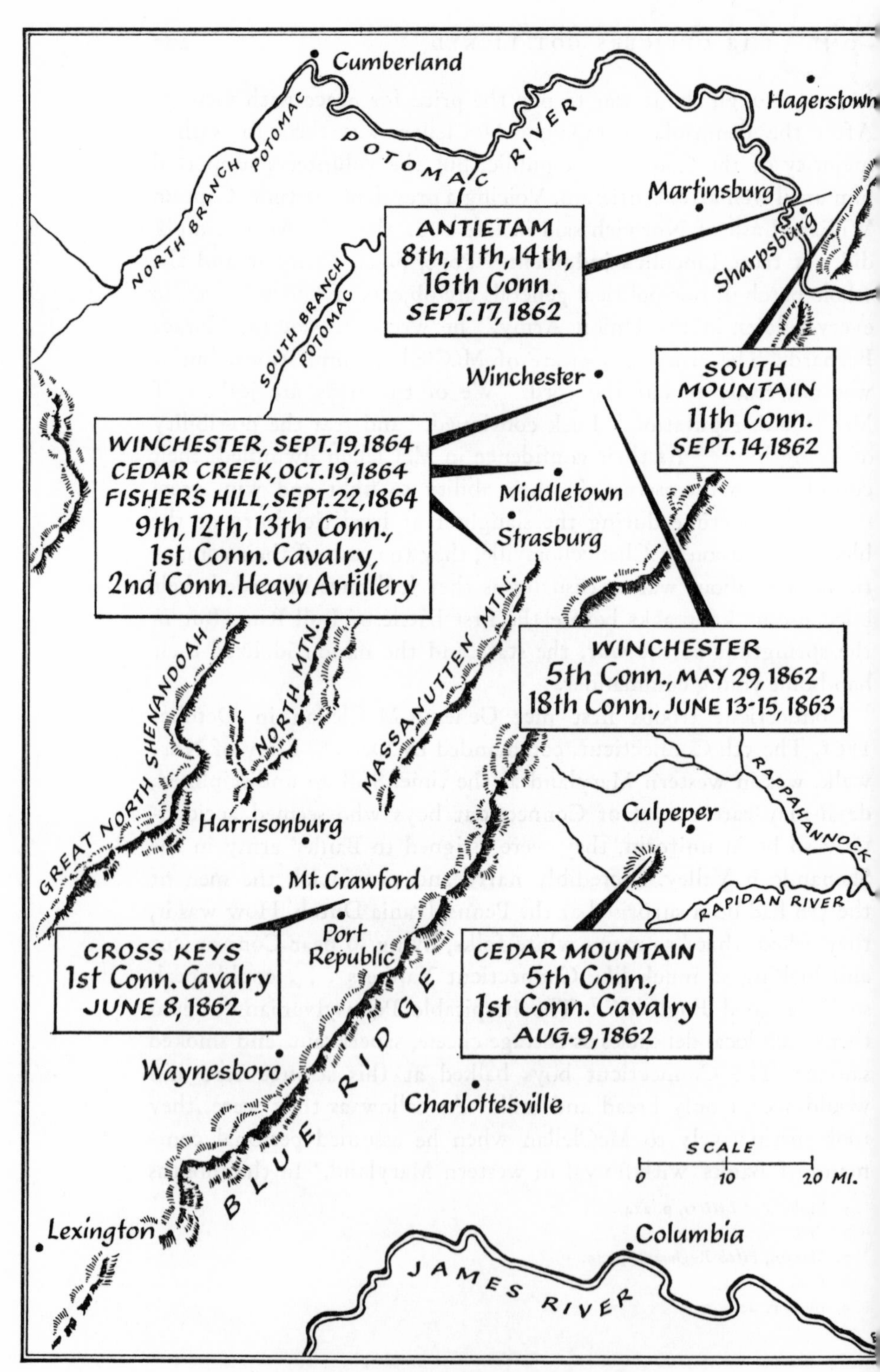

7. Connecticut troops in the Shenandoah Valley, 1862–64.

ahead, as they were repeatedly punished by Stonewall Jackson, they remembered McClellan's "calm and confident demeanor,"[10] and appreciated his systematic rebuilding of the demoralized Army after Second Bull Run.[11]

Banks' sparring with Jackson in the Shenandoah Valley was a confusion of occasional skirmishes, hard marches, and wretched rations. All this ended abruptly in late May 1862, when Jackson suddenly dashed up the Luray Valley with an army of 16,000 men and moved to encircle Banks' army of 8,000 at Front Royal and Strasburg. Jackson's attack achieved almost total surprise. The confused Union General ordered a retreat along the turnpike to Winchester, twenty miles to the north. Badly mismanaged, this movement soon degenerated into a panic-stricken route: the road to Winchester was jammed for miles with wagons, ambulances, Negroes, Unionist civilians, army stragglers, and prostitutes.[12]

The 5th, now commanded by Colonel George D. Chapman of Hartford, arrived in Winchester in the early evening without knapsacks or overcoats.[13] Assigned to Banks' rear-guard brigade, the men spent a cold night lying in a wet meadow watching Jackson's campfires and listening to the noise of his camp. Though all knew that the morrow would bring their first major battle, the volunteers welcomed the opportunity. The fact that they had been called upon to act as rear guard of the army gave them a sense of superiority over the rabble who had fled wild-eyed down the road.

When it was light enough, Jackson's artillery, posted in the hills overlooking the turnpike, opened up on the camp. Gulping hot coffee, the men of the 5th had just formed a line of battle when the Confederate infantry began to drive in their pickets. Chapman held his men in check until the enemy was well within musket range, and then ordered a volley that was coordinated with the fire of the entire brigade. Jackson's men fell back, rallied, and advanced again. By now, all the regiments were firing at will. For three hours

10. Ibid.

11. Ibid., p. 236.

12. Harrington, *Banks,* pp. 75, 76.

13. Marvin, *Fifth Regiment,* pp. 94–95.

the infantry battle went on, during which the Union brigade organization finally broke down under the immense pressure of Jackson's army. The 5th was nearly surrounded when orders came through for a retreat. Chapman managed to avoid encirclement, and had his regiment safely into Maryland late that night.[14]

Jackson pursued Banks to the Potomac and then turned back to deal with two Union armies (Frémont's and Shield's) that had been ordered by President Lincoln to cut him off. The 5th, in common with all of Banks' command, had been physically exhausted by the battle of Winchester and the long retreat. It was not until June 3 that they were able to move, and by June 9 they were again in the Winchester area. For the next month the 5th, now a part of General John Pope's new command, was marched aimlessly around the Shenandoah Valley. This was their first introduction to Pope's generalship, and they were not impressed.

August 9 found the regiment at Culpeper Court House, a village in northwestern Virginia, on the Orange and Alexandria Railroad. Jackson's army was known to be in the vicinity, and Banks, now a corps commander, was ordered to delay the Confederates until Pope had consolidated his forces. As the 5th marched through Culpeper, it was jeered at by the townsmen. "Old Jack will give you all you want," said one Confederate sympathizer to the overloaded, perspiring Connecticut boys. "You'll be whippee'd out o'yere right smart." [15] Prophetic words, but few of the volunteers paid any attention as they crowded around the town pump, where an obliging full colonel drew water for their benefit.[16]

The 5th bivouacked for the night seven miles south of Culpeper, near a stream called Cedar Run. In front of its camp, scarcely two miles away across open corn and wheat fields, loomed Cedar Mountain, a steep, partially wooded hill, some 600 feet high. On its slopes the men could see Confederate horsemen and an occasional artillery battery being wheeled into position. Next morning clouds of dust, stretching off to the southwest, indicated that a large enemy detachment was moving in their direction up the Orange Road. This was A. P. Hill's division, which Lee had sent to rein-

14. Ibid., p. 143.
15. Ibid., p. 151.
16. Ibid., p. 152.

force Jackson. Banks' corps, a mere 8,000 men, was now faced by a Confederate force of 24,000,[17] which held a strong position in the woods in front of Cedar Mountain, well supported by two miles of artillery. A prudent commander in Banks' position would have scouted out the Confederate strength carefully and, after estimating its character, retreated to Culpeper, where he could have been reinforced by two Union corps, McDowell's and Sigel's. But Banks had been ordered by Pope to attack if Jackson advanced, and he was eager to retrieve his military reputation, clouded by the pell-mell retreat from Winchester.

Both sides spent the morning and a greater part of the afternoon establishing their positions. Though Jackson gained the advantage of high wooded ground, he bunched his troops on the left, leaving his right to be defended by Dick Ewell's understrength division of three brigades. Opposing Jackson's right was Banks' strongest division, commanded by capable Christopher C. Augur. On his left Alpheus "Pap" Williams commanded Samuel Crawford's and G. H. Gordon's brigades, supported by George Bayard's cavalry. Had Banks attacked Ewell, he might have rolled up Jackson's flank, gained Cedar Mountain, and driven Jackson from the field. But when the Massachusetts General spotted the cautious advance of General C. S. Winder's division on Jackson's left, he ordered Crawford's brigade to attack and then threw his entire corps against the strongest part of the line.

The 5th had just joined Crawford's brigade when Banks ordered it to advance. Colonel Chapman gave his men a few words of encouragement, hoped they would be a credit to their state—and then shouted "Fix bayonets and charge, charge, charge and yell!" The men of the 5th tore down a split-rail fence in front of them and started through a stubble field toward a line of trees over 200 yards away. They had not gone more than fifty feet when they were swept with a heavy volley of musket fire from both front and right flank.[18] By the time the 5th had covered half the distance, it had been hit by three volleys; yet the men struggled on, keeping a semblance of alignment with other regiments. When the Connecticut boys reached the woods, they were confronted with a log fence,

17. Johnson and Buel, *Battles and Leaders,* 2, 459.
18. Marvin, p. 158.

and while attempting to tear it down, came under the concentrated fire of seven enemy regiments. It was claimed that fifty men of the 5th were shot down in three minutes.[19] The rest managed to get over the fence and among the enemy, followed on their right by other regiments of Crawford's and Gordon's brigades, while on their immediate left Augur's entire division had smashed into Winder's right.

For a few minutes the blue and the gray were engaged in a wild melee of swinging gun butts, thrusting bayonets, and point-blank shooting from rifles and revolvers. Lieutenant William Rockwell of New Haven shot six of the enemy with his Colt pistol, yet escaped injury. Next to him, Adjutant Heber Smith of Hartford was killed instantly by six musket balls. And Lieutenant Henry M. Dutton of New Haven, son of the former governor, was riddled by a volley of musketry. But the impact of more than 5,000 charging Union troops was more than Winder's division could stand. His three brigades broke and fell back on Hill's fresh division, which was moving in to support them. Meanwhile, Ewell's division, which had been pinned down by Banks' artillery, began closing in from the right when the Union gunners shifted fire to support the attack. Jackson rallied Winder's scattered division in time to assist Hill's advance and repel Bayard's heroic cavalry charge.

Banks' corps had spent itself, yet it fought stubbornly and maintained its organization as it retreated. Tall, hearty Major Edward Blake of New Haven, a grandnephew of Eli Whitney, staggered back and fell dead. He had worn his new dress uniform into battle, and from the beginning of the attack, had been a conspicuous target. Colonel Chapman, armed only with his dress sword, was captured. By now the 5th had but two line officers left; the rest were either casualties or prisoners. Seven color-bearers had been shot down and the regimental flag captured. Darkness saved what was left of the 5th and, indeed, what remained of Banks' spirited corps. The 5th Connecticut had lost 40 per cent of its effective strength: 48 officers and men had been killed, 67 wounded, and 64 captured.[20] Only one other Connecticut regiment would suffer such losses in proportion to its men engaged—the 2nd Heavy Artillery

19. Ibid., p. 160.
20. Ibid., p. 175.

at Cold Harbor. Though Cedar Mountain must be considered a Confederate victory, it was not without some benefit to the Union. Banks' soldiers demonstrated that Union troops were as tough and brave as their opponents. The 5th Connecticut may have lost its colors and its Colonel, but it had helped in routing, even if only temporarily, the famed Stonewall brigade.

For the next month the men of the 5th were caught up in the confusion of Pope's army as it marched over Fauquier and Prince William counties, Virginia, while Lee, Jackson, and Longstreet closed in. The regiment escaped the bloody engagements that culminated in Pope's heavy defeat at the Second Bull Run, but it shared in the general breakdown of Union morale.[21] Therefore, the 5th and, indeed, all the dispirited Union forces in northeastern Virginia welcomed McClellan's return to command. In the reorganization of the army that followed, it received a new corps commander, that stalwart professional soldier from Middletown, Connecticut, J. K. F. Mansfield. The men of the 5th were pleased at the change, for they had come to regard Banks as "unlucky in war." [22] And then seeming to confirm their change of luck, they were spared the slaughter pens of Antietam, which claimed the life of General Mansfield and decimated four Connecticut regiments.

The 5th was on provost duty at Frederick, Maryland, when the 16th Connecticut passed through the town heading for the front.[23] They had just missed the 14th, which was already nearing Antietam Creek. The 14th and 16th were new regiments, untrained even in the manual of arms, much less in the complex maneuvers of a regiment in battle. Dwight W. Morris, commanding officer of the 14th, was a man of vigorous personality and impressive whiskers, but he had no military experience. A prominent Bridgeport lawyer and politician, he owed his position to the Fairfield County war committee. What little drill the 14th had received had been handled by its lieutenant colonel, Sanford Perkins, a veteran of the Peninsular campaign. This had been sandwiched between long marches and tiresome trips on dirty trains and ferry boats. The 16th had a more experienced commanding officer: Frank

21. Ibid., p. 235.
22. Ibid., p. 236.
23. Ibid., p. 237.

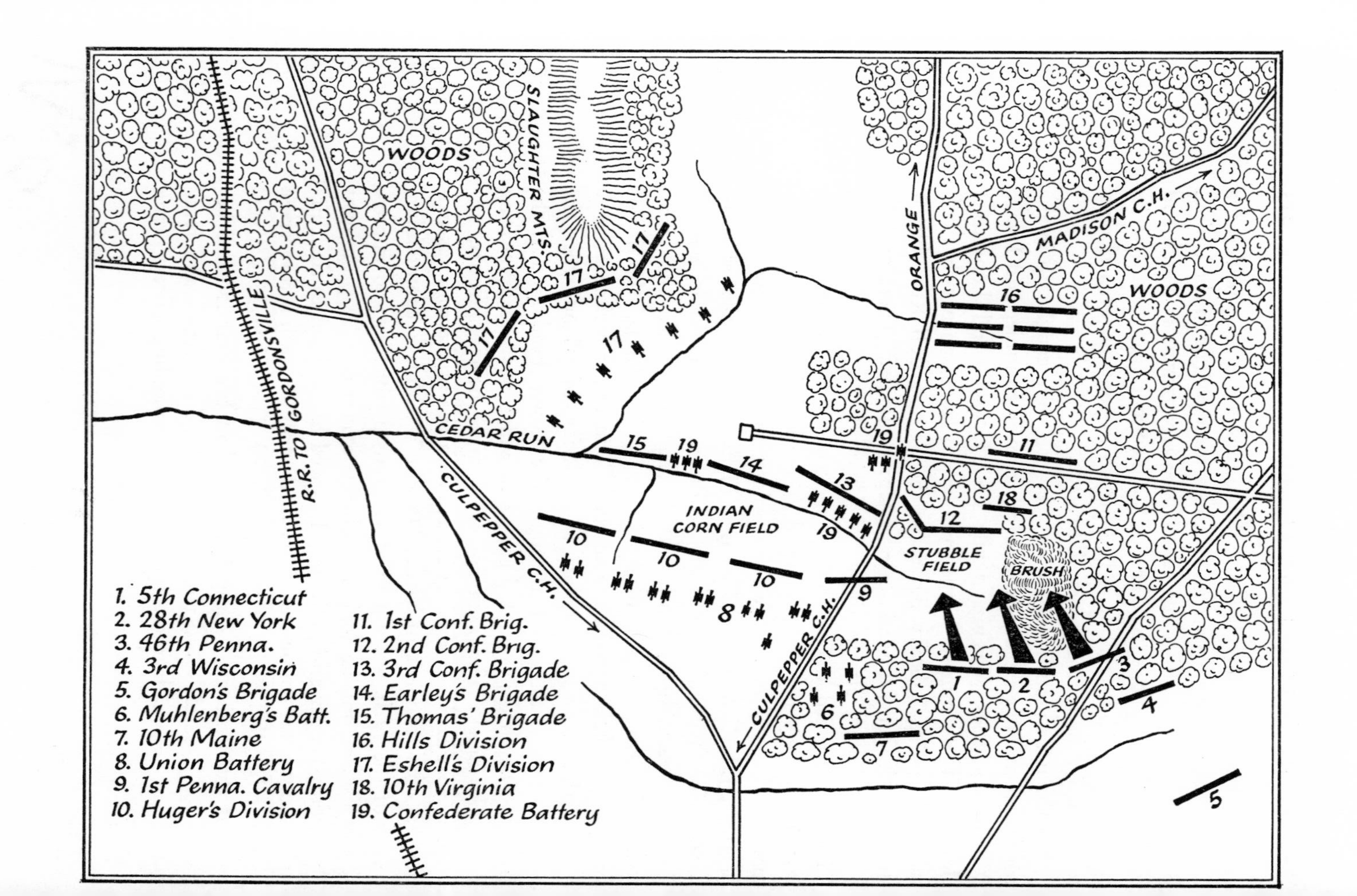
WOODS
SLAUGHTER MTS.
CEDAR RUN
R.R. TO GORDONSVILLE
CULPEPPER C.H.
ORANGE
MADISON C.H.
WOODS
INDIAN CORN FIELD
STUBBLE FIELD
BRUSH
1. 5th Connecticut
2. 28th New York
3. 46th Penna.
4. 3rd Wisconsin
5. Gordon's Brigade
6. Muhlenberg's Batt.
7. 10th Maine
8. Union Battery
9. 1st Penna. Cavalry
10. Huger's Division
11. 1st Conf. Brig.
12. 2nd Conf. Brig.
13. 3rd Conf. Brigade
14. Earley's Brigade
15. Thomas' Brigade
16. Hills Division
17. Eshell's Division
18. 10th Virginia
19. Confederate Battery

Beach of Hartford, a regular army man, a strict disciplinarian, and a conscientious drillmaster, but he had not as yet given his regiment battalion drill.[24]

After Pope's defeat Lee decided to invade Maryland and adopted the audacious policy of dividing his army in order to capture the isolated Union garrison at Harpers Ferry. As McClellan moved northwest from Washington to protect eastern Maryland and Pennsylvania, he had the amazing good fortune to secure a copy of Lee's operational plans. These disclosed that the Army of the Potomac was in an excellent position to crush the Confederate forces in detail. "Little Mac" accordingly started his army west, but moved so slowly that Lee was able to concentrate all his divisions, except Jackson's command, squarely in front of the Union advance. And Jackson's men, having taken Harpers Ferry, were coming up fast.

The 14th had been assigned to a new brigade in General William H. French's 2nd Corps, together with an equally untrained New York and Pennsylvania regiment. Since Colonel Morris was senior, he was made acting brigade commander. It is not surprising that the Connecticut boys were tense and bewildered during their march through Maryland. How much, they wondered, could a middle-aged Bridgeport lawyer know about brigade tactics when he had not even drilled a regiment? One thing, however, was reassuring to the raw recruits of the 14th and that was the sheer size of the Army of the Potomac. "There are about a thousand acres of soldiers visible from this point; and we have passed miles and miles of army wagons on our way up the Potomac," wrote Samuel Fiske, of Company G.[25]

The men of the 16th were also confused at their abrupt transition from civilian life to the unknown perils of combat. Five days after being sworn into service,[26] the regiment was hurrying north through Maryland, and for the next week averaged fifteen miles a day of hard, hot, dusty marching. By September 16 it had joined[27] Edward Harland's brigade of Burnside's corps. "Ned" Harland of Norwich was a capable, experienced officer. A favorite of Burnside,

24. Croffut and Morris, *History of Connecticut,* p. 271.

25. Fiske, *Mr. Dunn Browne,* p. 41.

26. Blakeslee, *Sixteenth Connecticut Volunteers,* p. 7.

27. Ibid., p. 11

he had been given command of a new brigade composed of the 4th Rhode Island, and the 8th, the 11th, and now the 16th Connecticut.

Beach found Harland's brigade encamped on a meadow near the stone bridge over Antietam Creek. In plain view, not more than 100 feet away, was the Confederate position along the slopes of the west bank. The men loaded their muskets for the first time and settled down in the drizzling rain. During the night one of the nervous Connecticut boys accidentally discharged his musket. "In a second," recalled Bernard Blakeslee, then a corporal in Company H, "the troops were on their feet with arms at the 'ready' and as they stood peering into the darkness ahead, you could hear both lines of battle spring to arms for miles." [28] The 16th had been in service twenty-three days.

At dawn, September 17, 1862, McClellan's army of 70,000 men lined up near Antietam Creek. On the extreme right, west of the stream, was Joseph Hooker's 1st Corps, with Mansfield's 12th Corps behind it. Edwin Sumner's 2nd Corps on the east bank was further south; Fitz-John Porter, commanding the 5th Corps, held the center opposite the village of Sharpsburg. Burnside's 9th Corps was on the left. Lee had established his position in and around the town of Sharpsburg. On the right, opposing Burnside, Lee's position overlooked Antietam Creek, then swung west and north along a sunken road and on both sides of the Hagerstown turnpike up to the edge of a forty-acre cornfield. In all, Lee was to have about 35,000 men when A. P. Hill's division arrived from Harpers Ferry. The Potomac River was at his back. If he were defeated, there would be no escape.

McClellan had an enormous advantage over his opponent in manpower and in artillery. He planned to launch a major attack on the right, where his artillery, massed on the hills along the east bank of the Antietam, could lend support. While maximum pressure was being exerted here, Burnside would attack on the left. Should either or both of Lee's flanks be turned, McClellan would throw Porter's fresh corps against the center of the Confederate line. The plan was logical but demanded close coordination between the three corps on the right—Hooker's, Mansfield's, and Sumner's—and Burnside's on

28. Ibid., p. 12.

the left. Otherwise, Lee could unbalance his line, and smash each attacking corps in detail.

The Army of the Potomac had been reorganized after the Second Bull Run defeat. Corps, division, and brigade commanders had not worked together long enough to establish prompt lines of communication and coordination. Green troops like the 14th and 16th Connecticut made proper deployment, on the regimental and brigade level, extremely difficult. Finally, McClellan had as usual overestimated the strength of Lee's forces. It could be expected that at the first indication of serious trouble he would hold his reserve back and go on the defensive.

Before dawn the 14th was moving forward with French's division. As the Connecticut boys neared Antietam Creek, they heard Hooker's attack on the Confederate left and McClellan's long-range artillery shells pounding enemy positions on the high ground around a little white box of a building known as the Dunker church. At 8 A.M., while the 14th was wading over a ford of the Antietam, Mansfield's corps had come to Hooker's support and was blasted out of a forty-acre cornfield north of the church. One hour later, French's division reached the edge of East Wood, a forest belt east of the Hagerstown road. To the right and dead ahead, the parklike woods, gentle hills and valleys, and fields of corn were obscured by smoke from the musketry and artillery of half a dozen engagements. Elements of Mansfield's corps were fighting around the Miller farmhouse and the Dunker church. The lead division of their corps, Sedgwick's, had just been attacked on its front, left flank, and rear by two Confederate divisions under Jubal Early, and was streaming back across the Hagerstown Pike. Woods and fields were filled with stragglers and dead and wounded men from three Union corps.

Though shaken by this awful scene and the unaccustomed racket of the battle, the 14th followed the brigade ahead between the handsome farmhouse of William Roulette and the blazing Mumma house, into a large field of ripening corn.[29] For a few moments the regiment was concealed from the enemy, but as soon as the men

29. Charles D. Page, *History of the Fourteenth Regiment, Connecticut Volunteer Infantry* (Meriden, 1906), p. 36.

emerged from the corn, they were swept by "a perfect tempest of musketry," and almost at the same time a Maryland regiment shouting "skedaddle" recoiled on them. But steady Sanford Perkins managed to control a threatened stampede and get his men back into formation. With presence of mind he ordered them to fire at will, though they could not see the enemy. "A thin cloud of smoke," about 200 yards directly ahead, was all that marked the Confederate position along a sunken road, henceforth to be known as "bloody lane." With very little protection except its own cornfield, the 14th was in a nasty position, but the order to fire had steadied the men's nerves. Many had never shot a musket before, and the business of loading, capping, and firing their weapons kept them too busy to be scared. No one bothered to coordinate the fire of the regiment.[30] Sergeant John Pelton of Company B, unable to get off a round without shooting someone in front, began firing from the hip, holding his heavy Springfield at a 45-degree angle. After several shots, one of his men shouted over the racket, "John, are you bombarding them?" This query convulsed the entire company; and it was only with some difficulty that Captain Elijah Gibbon restored order. For two hours the 14th remained in its exposed position, gradually dissolving into squads and sections as the soldiers sought whatever cover they could find. Then General Israel Richardson's fresh division came up on their left, beat off two desperate Confederate counterattacks, and enfiladed bloody lane. Musket firing in front of the 14th slackened and ceased. Perkins had formed up his regiment and was about to move it forward when Colonel Morris ordered him to the left, where D. H. Hill's last counterattack threatened to break the Union line. Under constant shell fire, the 14th helped to stabilize the line.

Lee had committed his last reserves. General William B. Franklin's fresh corps was already on the field, moving up to join Richardson and French. Had Franklin attacked, Lee's left flank would have caved, and in all probability his army would have been destroyed. But General Sumner refused to commit Franklin. Badly shaken by the carnage of the day, Sumner convinced McClellan to go on the defensive. The boys of the 14th would have agreed with Sumner had their opinions been asked. To them the day had been

30. Ibid., p. 44.

one of incredible confusion. "Troops didn't know what they were supposed to do," wrote Samuel Fiske, "Generals were the scarcest imaginable article . . . we neither saw nor heard anything of our division commander after starting on our first charge early in the morning, but went in and came out here and there promiscuously, according to our own ideas through the whole day." [31] Yet the sardonic Fiske thought the 14th had fought well. After the first shock of battle and the first careless fumbling with unfamiliar weapons, he noted that most fired "with precision and deliberation, though some shut their eyes and fired up into the air." [32] The relative composure of the 14th under fire was not characteristic, unfortunately, of other green regiments in McClellan's army. On the far left the 16th had been unable to cope with the changing fortunes of battle.

Burnside had been ordered to attack at the same time as the corps on the right. Apparently baffled by the problem of the stone bridge across Antietam Creek, he did little but launch two abortive attacks and shell Confederate positions on the opposite side. Any crossing of the bridge was bound to be smothered by enemy fire. To its left the creek made a deep bend to the east: the tongue of land, thus enclosed, had steep wooded banks which overlooked and flanked the bridge and, curving north, commanded the approaches. These slopes were guarded by an entire division of seasoned Confederate troops, well supported by artillery. About 10 A.M., when it appeared that the Union right had been crushed, McClellan sent Burnside peremptory orders to advance. Burnside still assumed that strong enemy forces opposed him, but actually Lee had withdrawn all but one brigade of infantry and two batteries of artillery from the immediate vicinity of the bridge. These twelve guns and 2,500 sharpshooters had more than enough firepower, however, to sweep the stone bridge and its approaches.

In preparation for the attack, the 11th Connecticut was detached from Harland's brigade and sent forward to pin down enemy marksmen on the opposite shore. In case the assault should fail, Burnside had ordered General Isaac Rodman's third division south along the creek, where a ford had been reported. The Antietam was

31. Fiske, *Mr. Dunn Browne,* p. 47.
32. Ibid., p. 48.

fordable practically along is entire length, but no one had tested its depth until Rodman's men, including the 8th and 16th Connecticut of Harland's brigade waded across easily about one mile south of the bridge.

Colonel Henry Kingsbury of the 11th divided his regiment into two battalions: Lieutenant Colonel Griffin Stedman, on the right, was to cover the bridge from a hill that overlooked its eastern approaches. Kingsbury, moving in from the left, would hold the approaches. Under heavy fire, Stedman accomplished his mission and threw two companies under Captain John Griswold of Lyme forward as skirmishers. Griswold interpreted his task as effecting a lodgment on the opposite shore, plunged into the Antietam, and began wading through waist-deep water. He was shot in the chest in midstream, and fell mortally wounded on the west bank, thus proving with his life that the creek could be forded. His two companies had already fallen back, half of their number dead or wounded. Meanwhile Kingsbury had pushed his battalion up to the bridge, where he deployed it on a skirmish line. Confederate artillery now opened a point-blank fire with case and canister. Kingsbury was wounded in the foot; seconds later a canister shot went through his leg. While being helped back, he was wounded again in the shoulder and then mortally in the stomach. Both battalions of the 11th were firing rapidly now and were managing to pick off Confederate artillerymen. Then with a wild cheer, the 51st New York and 51st Pennsylvania poured through them down onto the bridge, across it, and into the enemy on the other side. Behind them came a full division. Once the west bank had been gained, the Confederate brigade and its artillery took to their heels. The battle of the stone bridge was over.

Rodman's division, which had crossed the Antietam earlier moved against the southern slopes, but it was checked by Confederate artillery until the bridge was forced. It was not until one o'clock that the two forces joined and not until 3:00 that Burnside started moving his corps toward Sharpsburg. He fought his way toward the village along the high ground west of the stream, slowly overcoming stubborn resistance from D. R. Jones' division. Harland's brigade, minus the 11th Connecticut, was on Burnside's extreme left. During the advance, the 16th and the 4th Rhode Island

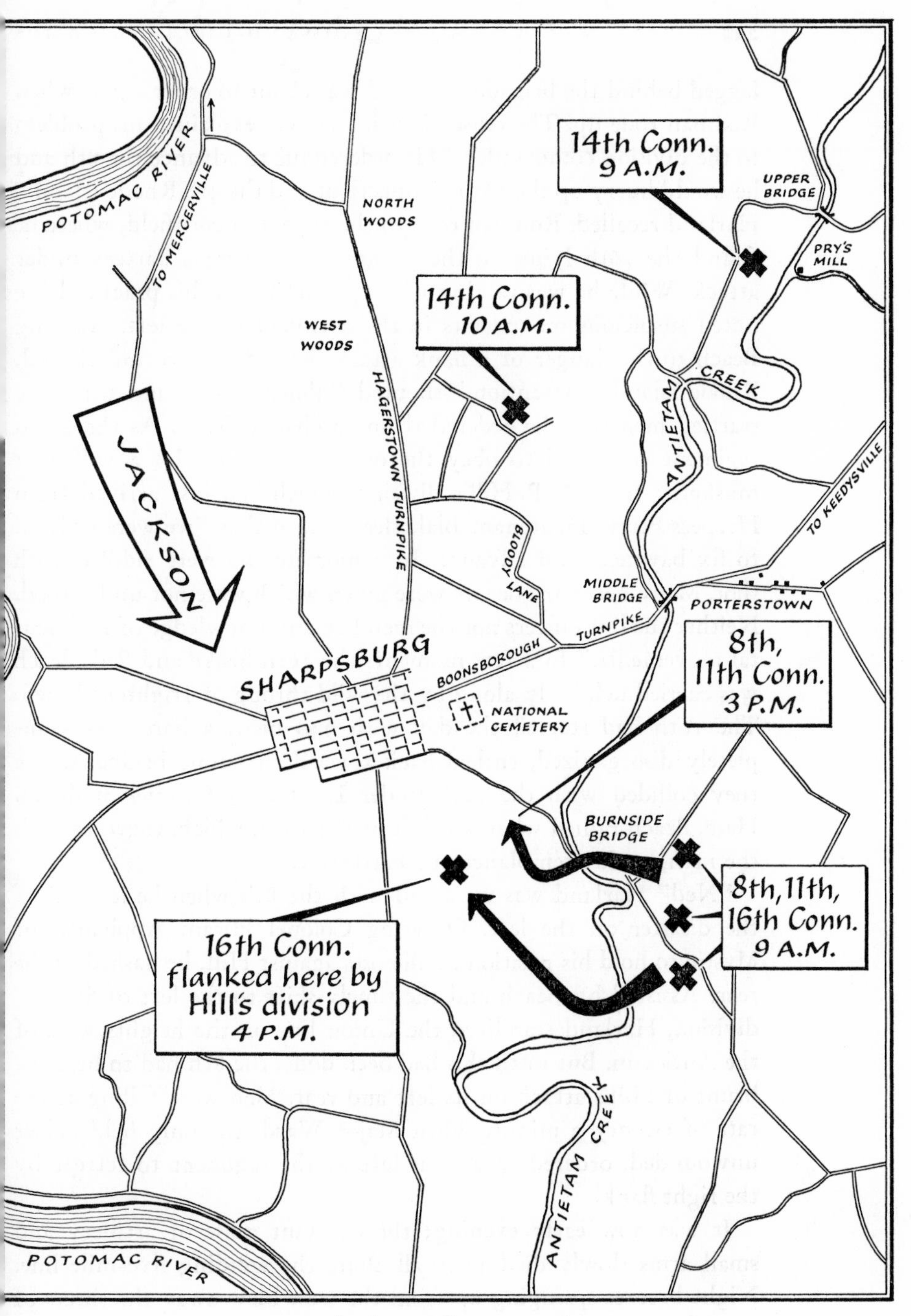

9. Antietam, Sept. 17, 1862.

lagged behind the brigade. Harland was about to order a halt when Rodman rode up. The tense Norwich lawyer explained his problem to the division commander. "He ordered me to advance the 8th and he would hurry up the 16th Connecticut and the 4th Rhode Island," Harland recalled. Rodman rode to the edge of a cornfield, where he found the 16th lying on the ground supporting a battery under attack. While he was talking with Colonel Beach, his practiced eye noted suspicious movements in the cornfield to the left. Alerting Beach to the danger of a flank attack, he rode off to find the 4th Rhode Island. "Attention," shouted Colonel Beach; and when the startled men rose, he ordered them to change front. As the green regiment struggled to obey the order, it was hit by a volley of musketry from A. P. Hill's division, which had just arrived from Harpers Ferry. Lieutenant Blakeslee recalled that "we were ordered to fix bayonets and advance. In a moment we were riddled with shot. Many necessary orders were given which were not understood. Neither the line officers nor the men had any knowledge of regimental movements." In a few moments the 16th broke and fled. Beach was carried helplessly along by the wild throng of frightened men. The 16th had started the day with 940 men; a bare 200, completely disorganized, rushed back toward the stone bridge, where they collided with the 11th under Lieutenant Colonel Stedman. Here, Beach rallied what was left of the 16th, which, together with the 11th, made a semblance of a battle line.[33]

"Ned" Harland was up ahead with the 8th when he learned of the disaster on the left. Ordering Colonel Hiram Appleman of Mystic to hold his position at all costs against Hill, he dashed to the rear. Assisted by Beach and the timely shift to the left of Sturgis' division, Harland stabilized the Union line on the heights west of the Antietam. But until this had been done, the 8th had to bear the brunt of Hill's attack on its left and rear. Men were falling at the rate of twenty a minute when Major Ward, the only field officer unwounded, ordered what was left of the regiment to retreat by the right flank.

It was now early evening; the constant noise of artillery and small arms slowly died away all along the winding five-mile line. Night breezes springing up from the west blew away the sheets of

33. Blakeslee, *Sixteenth Connecticut*, p. 17; Croffut and Morris, *Connecticut*, p. 274.

acrid smoke which had hung low over the countryside all day. Exhausted, grimy troops on both sides lay down where they were and slept with their fouled rifles loaded and capped beside them. But the dark, silent fields and woods remained alive with furtive movement for hours, as chaplains and special details crawled about in search of the wounded.[34] Despite these medical aid patrols, thousands lay in the field all night. Many were picked up the next day, when Lee's pickets fell back; but many more would not be discovered for several days. Burial squads searching for bodies found wounded men still alive under fences, in thickets, and among rocks where they had crawled for shelter. Every conceivable kind of structure behind the lines was pressed into makeshift hospitals, and when these were filled, the wounded were laid in rows on straw outside, their only protection an army blanket. When bandages gave out, the field surgeons used fresh corn leaves.[35] B. F. Blakeslee of the 16th has described the primitive surgical facilities: "In a room 12 feet by 20 feet a bloody table stood and around it five surgeons. A wounded man was laid on the table and it took but a few seconds for them to decide what to do and but a few minutes to do it. The amputated limbs were thrown out of the window. In forty-eight hours there were as many as two cart loads of amputated legs, feet, arms, and hands in the pile." [36]

Stragglers, the dazed, and those simply lost wandered back for days. Others, who had made off at the first sound of firing, also began returning. "The vile, obscene, blasphemous swaggerers of our regiment, the thieves and drunkards and rowdies of the regiment generally," Fiske called them. Some 75 to 100, he estimated, had slipped away from the 14th before Antietam, "and came sneaking back for days after the battle with cock and bull stories of being forced into hospital service and care of the wounded." [37] All Connecticut regiments had been badly cut up. Both the 8th and 16th Regiments had lost, either in killed or wounded, 50 per cent of their effective strength; the 11th and 14th had nearly 300 casualties out of about 1,300 engaged. Heavy losses in commissioned offi-

34. Croffut and Morris, p. 274.

35. Ibid.

36. Blakeslee, p. 19.

37. Fiske, p. 58.

cers (well over one-third were killed or wounded) had temporarily broken down regimental organization.[38] Few of the Connecticut boys were eager to fight again on the morrow. Private Hincks of the least injured 14th regiment said that "tired, hungry, cold and dirty as we were, we did not personally have much of the 'on to Richmond' feeling and personally were not anxious to renew the contest, but all day we expected the order and had it come, no doubt would have done our duty."[39]

The six-month period after Antietam marked the lowest point in the morale of the Army of the Potomac. To the Connecticut troops —over 5,000 of them—it was a dreary period when, as Samuel Fiske observed, "war, certainly as conducted on the principles of the present one, proves its own best antidote." The men wasted little time mourning the departure of McClellan, or praising the appointment of Burnside as commander. The cold, rainy weather, the red Virginia mud, the smoky fires of green wood, and scanty, half-cooked rations all contributed to dampen any enthusiasm they may have felt for their new general.[40]

Seven Connecticut regiments were involved in Burnside's fruitless assault at Fredericksburg, but only the 14th and the untried 27th, a nine-months regiment, participated in the bloody attacks on Marye's Height. The 14th had been in the first charge of French's division and had littered that perilous slope with a full quarter of its number. Hancock's division, with the 27th in its ranks, had followed in the second attack. The 27th was made up largely of young farmers who had enlisted after harvest, assuming that they would be home in time for the next.[41] They had not, however, considered Marye's Height or the fact that they would be armed with defective Austrian rifles. As the regiment was preparing to advance, its brigade commander, Colonel Samuel Zook, looked over the wretched weapons (some without locks) and told the raw volunteers: "Boys, if you cannot discharge them, you can use the bayonet."[42] In the end it probably made little difference.

38. Croffut and Morris, pp. 275–83.

39. Page, *Fourteenth Regiment,* p. 47.

40. Croffut and Morris, p. 290.

41. Ibid., p. 245.

42. *Hartford Courant* (Jan. 13, 1863).

Hancock's division got a few feet beyond French's, where it too was pinned down about 100 yards from Longstreet's riflemen. When the farmer boys of the 27th crawled back that night from Marye's Height, a full third of their number were casualties.

After Fredericksburg the Army of the Potomac wallowed in mud at its winter camp at Falmouth, Virginia: Everything was in confusion, a dismal, dirty world of mud, cold rain and half rations. It used up all of a man's energy, it seemed, merely to keep alive, what with "coughs, colds, consumptions, rheumatism and fevers; a row of unmarked graves, all along the track of the Army." [43] Yet few of the Connecticut boys criticized the hapless Burnside, even though they regarded him as unfit to lead the army.[44] Typically, Fiske sympathized with "our noble Burnside," while blaming McClellan "who kept us two months in inactivity after the battle of Antietam in the most beautiful and precious time of the whole year." [45]

Connecticut troops were indifferent to Hooker when he took over in January 1863.[46] But they were agreeably surprised at the new commander's concern for the welfare of the army. Rations improved and so did their distribution. The mountains of shoes and other quartermaster supplies that had been accumulating in Washington found their way to the soldiers. Camps were cleaned up. Supplies of fresh vegetables came through to the scurvy-stricken volunteers. Paymasters made their appearances, distributing as much as six months' back pay to the Connecticut regiments. Sutlers did a heavy business in "wooden ginger cakes, brandy [vinegar] peaches and cast iron pies" at the usual exorbitant prices.[47] Morale rose so rapidly at Falmouth that officers and men rediscovered their sense of humor. Company G of the 14th had a stuttering teamster nicknamed "Uncas," who fancied himself a spiritualist. To the great delight of the men, he would go into trances on request and give stuttering speeches on "didactic subjects." The entire regiment roared with laughter when Lieutenant Fred Sey-

43. Fiske, p. 117.
44. Ibid.
45. Ibid.
46. Lusk, *War Letters*, p. 274.
47. Page, p. 111.

mour asked him after one of his séances "to take a drink in his spiritual not his material character." [48]

In late April came signs of a major campaign. Thousands of army mules were brought up to carry blankets and shelter tents; miles of cattle were driven along for fresh beef. Reveille was sounded for the 5th, 17th, and 20th Connecticut at 3 A.M. on April 27, and the men fell into line for eight days' rations. All that they knew, including the corps commanders—George C. Meade of the 5th, O. O. Howard of the 11th, and Henry W. Slocum of the 12th—was that the route of the march lay west along the north bank of the Rappahannock to Kelly's Ford 25 miles away.[49]

At 10 A.M. the two corps had started. It was a beautiful day and the Connecticut boys were in good humor. The 5th was fed up with provost duty, which had been its mission since Cedar Mountain, while the 20th, which had barely smelt gunpowder smoke at a brief skirmish some months before, was anxious to achieve the enviable status of veterans. Both regiments marched with "Pap" Williams' division of the 12th Corps. The 17th Connecticut, attached to the 11th Corps, was also eager to join the ranks of fighting men. It had seen no combat since it had been mustered into the Army of the Potomac six months before.

On the next day, April 28, the 14th and 27th left Falmouth with Darius Couch's 2nd Corps. They marched four miles to the west, going into position opposite Bank's Ford, where they remained hidden from the enemy on the south side of the Rappahannock. Then in response to urgent orders from Hooker, the corps moved west to United States Ford, followed within 24 hours by the 3rd Corps under Daniel E. Sickles.

After the three advance corps had concentrated at Kelly's Ford on the evening of the 28th, Hooker briefed his commanders. They were to cross the Rappahannock, brush aside whatever Confederate pickets might be on the opposite bank, and head east for Fredericksburg. Slocum and Howard were to take their corps south, then east, and cross the Rapidan at Germanna Ford. Meade was to ford the river at Ely's five miles further downstream. The three corps

48. Ibid., p. 112.

49. Johnson and Buel, *Battles and Leaders*, 3, 157.

would concentrate in the vicinity of Chancellorsville, a brick mansion in the Wilderness where three roads led to Fredericksburg. This movement, if successful, would uncover United States Ford across the Rappahannock. Couch's two divisions at Bank's Ford and Sickles' 3rd Corps would then be ordered up. Both would cross the river at that point, an easy day's march from Fredericksburg. John Sedgwick with the 6th Corps and John F. Reynolds with the 1st Corps had been ordered to demonstrate in front of Fredericksburg so that Lee would be kept in the dark regarding Hooker's intentions as long as possible. It was presumed that with five army corps at his rear Lee would be forced out of his heavily fortified positions. The Confederate commander would either have to fight Hooker on the open ground between the city and the Wilderness or fall back on Richmond. If he chose to fight, Sedgwick and Reynolds would be ordered to cross the Rappahannock, take Fredericksburg, and move in on Lee's rear. Hooker's was an excellent plan, one of the best battle plans of the war. Of course, it meant dividing his army along exterior lines, but his superiority in manpower was so great that this would entail no great hazard.

For three days Hooker's ambitious end run operated with precision. By the morning of May 1 he had 73,000 men around Chancellorsville. According to plan, Hooker sent Meade with two divisions to the left along the River Road toward Fredericksburg. In the center Hancock's division of the 2nd Corps, and Sykes' division, moved east along the Rappahannock Turnpike, while on the right Slocum's corps, with Howard's behind, advanced along the Plank Road. Lee, who had finally understood Hooker's strategy, left 10,000 men to oppose Sedgwick and concentrated the balance of his army in front of the Union center and right. Hooker's advance divisions encountered Lee's force just at the eastern edge of the Wilderness, where a lively engagement opened immediately. The 5th Connecticut was under severe artillery fire for two hours but, protected by the rolling countryside, suffered no casualties. To the left the 27th, with Hancock's division, helped repulse an enemy advance on the flank of Sykes' division. Union troops all along the line were holding strong positions in open country.

The stage was set for Hooker to move forward with his overwhelming superiority in manpower. With some luck and proper deployment of his troops he should have been able to gain a decisive victory. Yet for some unaccountable reason "Fighting Joe" lost his nerve and ordered all his corps back to Chancellorsville. For the remainder of that crucial day and far into the night, Union troops worked with axes and spades, bayonets, and even tin cups and plates [50] to convert the Chancellorsville area into a fortified camp. Unfortunately, Hooker assumed that the forest on his right formed an impenetrable natural barrier against the advance of large bodies of enemy troops. His breastworks and abatis covered the left and center of his line, but his right, defended by O. O. Howard's 11th Corps, was up in the air. The Wilderness, where Hooker proposed to make his stand, was a gloomy, tangled thicket of second growth —which ruled out the proper emplacement of artillery except in such key areas as Hazel Hill to the right of Hooker's line or in the open fields around the Chancellor house. Dense brush also made it difficult to coordinate infantry action. Even company commanders found it impossible to keep track of their men.

Hooker established his headquarters at the Chancellor mansion. The 11th Corps on the far right was spread out along the turnpike facing south; on its right, forming a blunt wedge, were the corps of Slocum and Couch. Meade's 5th Corps extended on the left along Mineral Spring Run to the Rappahannock. Sickles' corps in the center was held in reserve. Lee and Jackson probed Hooker's line throughout the day of May 1, and soon discovered the weakness on its right. With supreme audacity, or perhaps contempt, Lee divided his army. He ordered Jackson with 24,000 men across the front of the Union Army to the Brock Road and up the Brock Road to Wilderness tavern, which would put it squarely on Howard's flank.

Meanwhile, Hooker strengthened his lines by putting Sickles' corps on the right between the 11th and 12th Corps. After Jackson's troops had passed his front, for several hours Sickles suggested a reconnaissance in force. Headquarters, which was under the impression that Lee was retreating, agreed to this proposal. When Sickles' corps swung out to engage Jackson, the 12th, on its left, shifted to the right to cover the line. During this maneuver the 5th and 20th left their breastworks, made their way across Hazel Hill, and went into position facing southeast.

50. Croffut and Morris, *Connecticut*, p. 364.

Despite a stream of reports warning of probable flank attack, Howard refused to take even elementary precautions. The 17th Connecticut, stationed at the extreme right, was still facing south when Jackson's force hit it from the west in the early evening. Like the unfortunate 16th Connecticut at Antietam, the 17th had never seen action. But its sober colonel, Bridgeport businessman William H. Noble, had had at least sufficient opportunity to drill the regiment adequately in battle maneuvers. When Jackson struck, two companies of the 17th were on picket to the south. They were quickly overwhelmed, though most of the men got back to their regiment. Colonel Noble, his long, sad face and lugubrious white-streaked whiskers making him look even more anxious than he was, somehow got his regiment facing toward the west. The men actually fired several volleys into the faces of the screaming rebel host, before they fled toward Chancellorsville. The disorganized regiment did not stop until it reached a line of rifle pits near army headquarters, and then only because the men were winded. Yet their brief stand, during which the regiment lost its colonel (badly wounded) and lieutenant colonel (killed) and suffered a hundred casualties, bought enough time for Adolphus Bushbeck's brigade on its left to change front. Bushbeck, in turn, was able to check Jackson for a crucial thirty minutes, while Howard and Hooker threw together a defense line that would hold temporarily. While officers were frantically working to establish a new line, genial John McCarthy of New Haven lined up his 14th Regiment brass band and marched it into the no-man's land west of the Chancellor house. For twenty minutes amid exploding shells, wild-eyed stragglers, and cursing, saber-spanking officers on horseback, the cornets, horns, fifes, and drums sounded out the National Anthem, "The Red, White and Blue," and "Yankee Doodle." Two of the musicians were hit by shrapnel, but went on playing. "They never played better," a Pennsylvania colonel thought, "its effect upon the men was magical . . . Its strains were clear and thrilling for a moment, then smothered by that fearful din, an instant later sounding bold and clear again." [51]

In some areas of the Wilderness the woods and brush were so thick that they muffled all sound more than a mile away. When the

51. Page, *Fourteenth Regiment,* p. 121.

11th Corps caved in, the 5th Connecticut was moving slowly back to its old position, unaware of the panic on the right. The brigade commander, General Joseph Knipe, had lost his way several times, and darkness had fallen before the regiment approached the breastworks it had built two nights before. Suddenly out of the gloom came a sheet of bright flame, so close that it illuminated the entire column. A Confederate brigade had captured their breastworks and opened at 100 yards range. Fortunately, the enemy's massive volley was high, but in the confusion that followed, Colonel Packer and twenty members of the 5th were captured. The rest made a dash for the Chancellor house.[52] Although the brigade was completely disorganized, the energetic Knipe managed to sort it out and launch a counterattack. This was taken in both front and flank by two Confederate brigades, "and again the whole line hunted the rear very lively." The 5th held together, however, and helped establish a new brigade line some 700 yards to the south of their old breastworks. Confederate troops were now between it and Hooker's headquarters. In the morning the badly shot-up 5th was relieved by the 20th Connecticut. The men moved out of the front line into a reserve area, where presently they were subjected to enfilading artillery fire from Stuart's artillery on the heights of Hazel Grove.

Like the 5th, the 20th had been moving back to its former breastworks when the 11th Corps was crushed. Being further to the left, the 20th had reached its old position without mishap. But Jackson's second massive attack at 8 P.M., which rolled over Knipe's brigade, came pounding up to their position. Relatively secure behind their log bulwarks, the boys of the 20th sent volley after volley practically into the faces of Jackson's ragged soldiers, who it seemed were everywhere in the heavy brush ahead. The scene reminded Lieutenant Colonel Philo Buckingham of Dante's *Inferno:* "red flashes from the muskets and pieces of artillery, lighted up the woods; and as the smoke settles . . . you could see underneath the sulphurous canopy, men begrimed with smoke and smeared with blood flowing from their wounds, stalking about like fiends." [53]

Bad as it was that night, it was worse the next day. The men

52. Marvin, *Fifth Regiment*, pp. 252–53.
53. Croffut and Morris, p. 365.

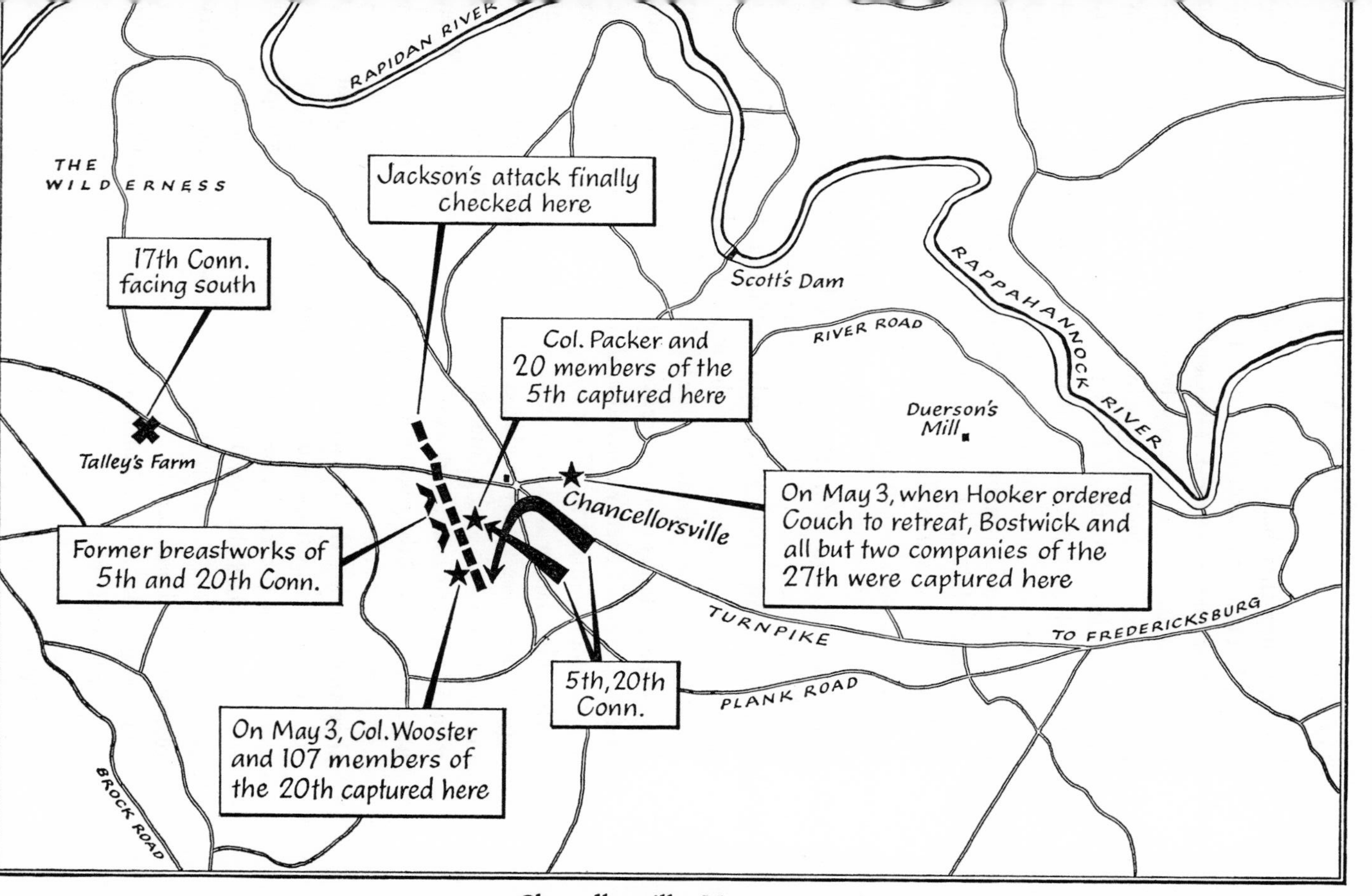
RAPIDAN RIVER
THE WILDERNESS
Jackson's attack finally checked here
17th Conn. facing south
Scott's Dam
RAPPAHANNOCK RIVER
RIVER ROAD
Col. Packer and 20 members of the 5th captured here
Duerson's Mill
Talley's Farm
Chancellorsville
On May 3, when Hooker ordered Couch to retreat, Bostwick and all but two companies of the 27th were captured here
Former breastworks of 5th and 20th Conn.
TURNPIKE
TO FREDERICKSBURG
5th, 20th Conn.
PLANK ROAD
On May 3, Col. Wooster and 107 members of the 20th captured here
BROCK ROAD

10. Chancellorsville, May 1–4, 1863.

cheered when they heard from Confederate prisoners that Jackson and A. P. Hill were wounded, but J. E. B. Stuart, who took over, proved he could strike hard. The Confederate Army was still split in two, and it had taken a heavy beating. With 50,000 fresh troops guarding his rear, Hooker was in an excellent position to hit the flanks of either or both of Lee's forces with crushing power. And Sedgwick still sat opposite Fredericksburg with almost three times as many men as his opponent. Yet Hooker seemed incapable of judgment. Five Union infantry divisions would have to stand off Lee's army, while nine more Union divisions remained immobile within a mile or two of the firing line.

Early Sunday morning, May 3, Stuart began his attack on the right. At the same time, Anderson and McClaws moved against the Union center and left. Massed Confederate artillery along the Hazel Grove heights rolled shells and solid shot up and down Sickles' and Slocum's lines. For nearly five hours the men of the 20th held out with their brigade at the extreme right of Slocum's line. By this time the persistent Confederates had worked their way around both flanks of its entrenched position. Colonel Samuel Ross of Hartford had been wounded and had been replaced by Lieutenant Colonel William B. Wooster, a lawyer and entrepreneur from Derby. This dapper little officer of precise habits was now dirty and ragged, his close-set eyes glazed with fatigue, his neat burnsides matted with sweat and grime. Wooster was not much of a military man, but he was brave and stubborn—perhaps too stubborn. When he finally ordered the regiment to retreat, it was too late for himself and 107 officers and men of the 20th, all of whom were captured as they were leaving the breastworks. The rest of the regiment had to run through cross fire—musketry from both flanks, grapeshot and canister from the front. Seventy-five men went down before the regiment reached the new Union line. Meanwhile, near total disaster had befallen the 27th Regiment—those farmer boys who had planned to be home for the 1863 harvest.

During Jackson's and Stuart's attack on the right, the 27th, with other units of Hancock's division—about 400 men in all—was holding an advanced position on the left of the perimeter. At 9:30 A.M., May 3, Hooker, who had been injured in the fighting, ordered Couch, his second in command, to pull the entire army back

9. Where the 2nd Connecticut Heavy Artillery spent much of the war: a part of the defenses of Washington, D.C., redoubt "A" near Fort Lyon, Virginia. Connecticut State Library.

10. Regimental headquarters field and staff, 20th Connecticut: dapper Lieutenant Colonel William B. Wooster (fifth from left). Connecticut State Library.

oward the Rappahannock. The first indication that the 27th had of a change in the line was when several dozen artillery shells fired from their rear burst over their lines. At the same time, the men aw Confederate troops working into the woods on their right and eft. Worried about his flanks, Colonel Richard Bostwick sent Maor James Coburn to Hancock for reinforcements. Coburn had gone only 1,000 yards when he was captured.

After ten minutes the shelling stopped; far down the road the men saw a Confederate officer waving a white flag. As Lieutenant Winthrop Sheldon of Company H recalled the scene: "the rebel—a all rough specimen, and yet with the manner of a gentleman—announced himself as Lieutenant Bailey of a Georgia regiment." Bailey told Bostwick that the regiment was completely surrounded and demanded its surrender. The Colonel was not convinced. He ent Lieutenant Colonel Henry Merwin of New Haven through the woods to the rear. When Merwin reported that Bailey's assertion was true, Bostwick decided that further resistance was hopeless. With the exception of D and F companies on detached duty, the 7th Regiment was soon on its way to Libby.

The capture of the 27th closed out active fighting at Chancellorsville for the Connecticut regiments. Hooker continued his reeat across the Rappahannock to the old mud camp at Falmouth. Lee turned to deal with Sedgwick, but that wily Connecticut Yankee managed to elude him and rejoin Hooker. The Chancellorsville campaign, which had started under such bright auspices, had utterly collapsed. It was another heavy defeat, made more tragic or the Army of the Potomac by the long lines of bedraggled Union prisoners (among them over 500 Connecticut boys), and the housands of wounded whom Hooker had left on the field. But few among the rank and file would admit that Union soldiers were nferior to Confederate. Walking down the company street at the oth Regiment's camp, Captain Sanford Chaffee of Company B overheard a private say: "It was only the officers that got licked, we wasn't."[54] These boys and 1,200 more from the Nutmeg State would give a good account of themselves at Gettysburg.

54. John W. Storrs, *The Twentieth Connecticut, a Regimental History* (Ansonia, 886), p. 57.

9. IRON NUTMEGS

THOUGH the Army of the Potomac was much smaller than it ha
ever been, observers felt that it now represented a hard core o
fighting men.[1] Whether accurate or not, the Connecticut regi
ments that marched north with Meade into Pennsylvania durin
June 1863 had been reduced to about one-third of normal strength
Most were now commanded by lieutenant colonels or major
though oddly enough the smallest regiment, the 27th, with only 7
enlisted men present for duty, had the fullest complement of fiel
grade officers.[2]

The first Connecticut regiment to see action at Gettysburg wa
the 17th. When Howard's 11th corps arrived northwest of th
town on July 1, Union troops were being forced back by the supe
rior numbers of A. P. Hill and Dick Ewell. The 17th was sen
forward as corps skirmishers, while Howard probed the Confeder
ate line on Oak Hill, a height that commanded Gettysburg fro
the northwest. Lieutenant Colonel Douglas Fowler, commandin
the 17th, divided his regiment, giving the left wing to Major Alle
G. Brady—that high-spirited officer who had clashed with Da
Tyler before First Bull Run. No sooner had Fowler made the
dispositions than Jubal Early's corps, 10,000 strong, hit the 17th o
its right flank, and smashed it in one blast of musketry. Fowler wa
killed instantly, and so was Captain James E. Moore of Danbury
Private Warren's father image. Warren himself was so dazed tha
he was swept up by the yelling Confederates as if he were an anima
driven by beaters. War, he had suddenly discovered, was no
merely band concerts "all times a day." Howard's troops, badl
beaten, streamed back through the streets of Gettysburg to Ceme

1. Fiske, *Mr. Dunn Browne,* p. 180.
2. Croffut and Morris, *History of Connecticut,* p. 378.

tery Hill, one mile south, where the one-armed General had prudently planted his corps artillery and one division of infantry. This reserve force managed to check further Confederate advances.

Meanwhile Sickles' 3rd Corps and Slocum's 12th Corps, which had responded to Howard's urgent call for reinforcements, were pouring into the Cemetery Hill positions. By the evening of July 1 the Army of the Potomac, except for Sedgwick's 6th Corps, was entrenched along the heights south of Gettysburg. That evening the Commanding General arrived and inspected the Union position. New in command and cautious by temperament, Meade was painfully conscious of his responsibilities. He had not intended to make a fight of it at Gettysburg, but after examining the army's position and noting its defensive strength, he decided against retreat.

Meade's army was drawn up south of Gettysburg, and commanded three major north-south highways: Emmitsburg Road to the west, Taneytown Road in the center, and the Baltimore Pike to the east. Like a fishhook, Meade's position curved north, then south and east around Cemetery Hill to Culp's Hill. The shank lay south along Cemetery Ridge, two miles of high land that ended in two outcroppings, Big Round Top and Little Round Top, at the extreme south. At the time of Meade's inspection the strategic Round Tops, which overlooked the end of the shank, were unoccupied, but they were secured in the nick of time on the following day. Culp's Hill and Cemetery Ridge commanded all approaches from the east and from the west. Stone walls and boulders along their crests gave solid protection to infantry and artillery. More importantly, the Army of the Potomac was situated so that any portion of the line could be easily and quickly reinforced. Connecticut troops were stationed on the right of the Union line, along the curve and barb of the hook. The 5th and 20th, which were brigaded together, held rifle pits they had dug around the base of Culp's Hill. On Cemetery Hill the 17th held a stone wall near the entrance gate to Gettysburg cemetery. The 14th and 27th were also strongly posted behind stone walls on Cemetery Ridge, about one mile south of the Hill. East of Cemetery Ridge, between it and Culp's Hill, the 2nd Connecticut Light Battery was planted in the reserve artillery park, whose 200 guns were commanded by near-sighted, conscientious Robert O. Tyler of Hartford, formerly commander of the 1st Connecticut Heavy Artillery, now the trusted deputy of Meade's artillery chief, Henry Hunt.

Lee, like Meade, had not intended to fight at Gettysburg. After his victory on the first day, however, he was in no mood to retreat without first trying to convert the situation into another Chancellorsville. By the next morning his three corps roughly conformed to the Union line, with Ewell at the left in front of Cemetery Hill and Culp's Hill, A. P. Hill along Seminary Ridge across the valley to the west, and Longstreet opposite the Round Tops. Mistaking the Emmitsburg Road for the main Union line, farther to the east, Lee ordered Longstreet to attack Meade's left, turn it, and roll up the flank of the Union Army. At the same time, Ewell from the north was to close in on Cemetery Hill and Culp's Hill, cutting off Meade's line of retreat southeast along the Baltimore Turnpike. To complete the rout of the Union Army, A. P. Hill would then attack the main Union position on Cemetery Hill.

Meanwhile, Sickles, misinterpreting Meade's instructions, moved his corps forward from the vicinity of the Round Tops to the Emmitsburg Road in a salient position, with its point centered on a peach orchard in the valley between the two armies. Though Lee had mistaken the position of the Union line, Sickles' rash move corrected his error. Longstreet would be able to attack Sickles' salient from the front and both flanks. Meade recognized the danger as soon as he rode up to Sickles' position in the late afternoon. But as Longstreet had already started his attack, all the furious Meade could do was conform his army to the new line. He threw the 5th Corps, under George Sykes, behind Sickles, moved Hancock's corps south, and hurried Slocum over from Culp's Hill to back up Sykes when it seemed that Longstreet's attack might overwhelm the Union left.

While Sickles' corps was under attack, Hancock on the right advanced his corps into a wheatfield to lend support. Rushing forward with it was the remnant of the 27th—75 men behind their youthful Lieutenant Colonel Henry C. Merwin. Longstreet's tough, veteran marksmen waited until the advance divisions were 25 yards away, then shot at knee level through the wheat stalks. Merwin pitched headlong, with a mortal wound in the chest. This gentle, quiet, thoughtful young man lived long enough to whisper, "my poor regiment is suffering fearfully." [3] Merwin's dying comment exactly stated the condition of the 27th and, indeed, of Hancock's entire corps. For a few minutes the men had been able to drive the enemy from their front, only to be taken in the flank by fresh Confederate troops. Under heavy cross fire, Hancock's corps retreated to its former position, but not before the tiny 27th had lost 38 men.

The appearance of Slocum's fresh corps forced Longstreet to give way; at sunset firing on the left died down, only to start again on the extreme right at Culp's Hill. Ewell was attacking the one Union brigade that held this crucial strong point. The 5th and 20th, with Slocum's corps, were rushed back to their old positions and found them occupied by thousands of enemy soldiers. Through Colonel Packer's mind flashed that dreadful moment at Chancellorsville when he and the advance companies of the 5th, returning to their breastworks, had been "gobbled up" by the enemy who had arrived first. Much to the Colonel's relief, this time "Old Pap" Williams had his division well in hand; the 5th fell back to a protected position along the Baltimore Turnpike. During the night Meade assigned a newly arrived Maryland brigade to support him. In addition, twenty-four pieces of artillery were placed to cover all possible avenues of Confederate attack. While Ewell's left was attacking the base of Culp's Hill, his right was attempting to seize Cemetery Hill from the east. Here the 17th was involved in a fierce seven-hour engagement with the famous Louisiana Tigers back and forth in front of the Hill. But Early's troops had been severely handled in their repeated attacks, and when a fresh Union brigade delivered a heavy counterattack, they broke and fled through the ravine that separated Culp's and Cemetery Hill.

The humid night of July 2 had been an anxious one for the Army of the Potomac, from the commanding general down to the perpetually frightened teamsters. It was particularly trying for the 20th on Culp's Hill. The men had stumbled into Ewell's pickets when they went for water from a small stream they had used the day before. This encounter developed into a sharp fire fight before the two lines disengaged. Nervous pickets on both sides saw to it

3. Winthrop D. Sheldon, *The Twenty-Seventh, a Regimental History* (New Haven, 1866), p. 91.

that the men got little sleep.[4] At dawn Slocum's corps was ready for action; its artillery opened on the Confederate positions. The cannonade lasted an hour; then the first and second divisions were ordered to attack. With the 20th on the left, the first division scrambled over its stone wall redoubt and jogged down Culp's Hill into Rock Creek Valley. Ewell's men, who were on the point of making their own attack, were ready. They broke the attack, only to be thrown back themselves by the corps artillery, firing 12-pounder shells on a flat trajectory over the Union infantrymen. Several burst in the ranks. Shrapnel tore both arms off Private George Warner, which inspired nervous, peppery Colonel Wooster to send word that if the artillery did not correct its aim he would order his regiment to turn around and charge it. Back and forth for seven hours the Battle on Culp's Hill raged, with the 20th in the thick of it, until sheer weight of numbers forced Ewell across Rock Creek. Culp's Hill was now securely in Union hands.

On Cemetery Ridge the 14th and 27th also spent a wakeful night. Arnold's Rhode Island battery, a few feet to their left, apparently eager to expend its ammunition, kept them awake, and when the battery fell silent, the noisy attack on Cemetery Hill brought the regiment to the ready again. At 4 A.M. two companies of the 14th were sent forward as skirmishers, and then early in the morning four additional companies were ordered to capture and destroy the sharpshooter-infested barn of William Bliss. This sanguinary little exercise cost 62 casualties, including 10 dead, out of the 100 men involved. After the Bliss barn skirmish, the 14th, now reduced to 100 men, sprawled behind the stone wall on Cemetery Ridge, waiting with the rest of Meade's army for Lee's next move. At approximately 1 P.M. they saw puffs of smoke from the Confederate signal guns on Seminary Ridge and were deafened as 130 enemy cannon opened fire. All of the men lay flat on their stomachs, close together, instinctively seeking mutual protection, as the storm of solid shot and shell skimmed over their heads or hit the ledge in front and ricocheted with ear-splitting screams. Arnold's battery, which had been cursed by the tired men the night before, replied steadily for one hour, despite heavy casualties. Quartermaster Sergeant Hincks, who was lying directly in front of one of the

4. Storrs, *Twentieth Connecticut*, p. 91.

cannon with his arm thrown over a comrade, remembered wondering what Arnold could be shooting at. The smoke in the valley was so thick it blotted out the sun. Behind the wall no one moved or spoke but the Rhode Island gunners. Hincks saw the indescribable confusion to the rear, where "brigades . . . had lost their way in the blinding sulphurous canopy and were flying hither and thither, trying to escape the storm of bursting shot and shell which filled the air." Suddenly a fence rail hit by a solid shot went spinning into the air: it looked like a drumstick spun by a fancy drummer at a dress parade.[5]

The cannonade stopped as suddenly as it had begun, and at the same time the sun broke through the smoke. This was a signal for the men to rise, stretch their cramped legs, and shake their heads to clear the ringing in their ears. "In our inexperience," said Hincks, "[we] thought the battle was over, but Major Ellis was better posted than we. 'No,' said he, 'they mean to charge with all their infantry.' " Slowly before the eyes of the Union troops a magnificent pageant of war materialized. First one line, looking from that distance like toy soldiers, emerged from the woods at the base of Seminary Ridge, then a second, a third, and finally a fourth—15,000 men were advancing across the valley. As they neared, the men of the 14th were spellbound with admiration. "As far as the eye could reach," wrote Major Ellis, "could be seen the advancing troops, their gay war flags fluttering in the gentle summer breeze, while their sabers and bayonets flashed and glistened in the mid-day sun." [6]

The men of the 14th were warned not to fire a shot until the enemy had reached the Emmitsburg Road, which at that point swung in directly below Cemetery Ridge. They quietly checked their Springfields and Sharps, made little piles of cartridges, prayed, or pulled out battered daguerreotypes of loved ones. Private Joseph L. Pierce of the 14th, the only Chinaman in the Army of the Potomac, carefully stuffed his long queue down the back of his dirty uniform shirt and pulled lightly on the breech of his Sharps to double check its load.

By now Arnold's battery had opened again, this time joined by

5. Page, *Fourteenth Regiment,* p. 150.

6. Ibid., p. 151.

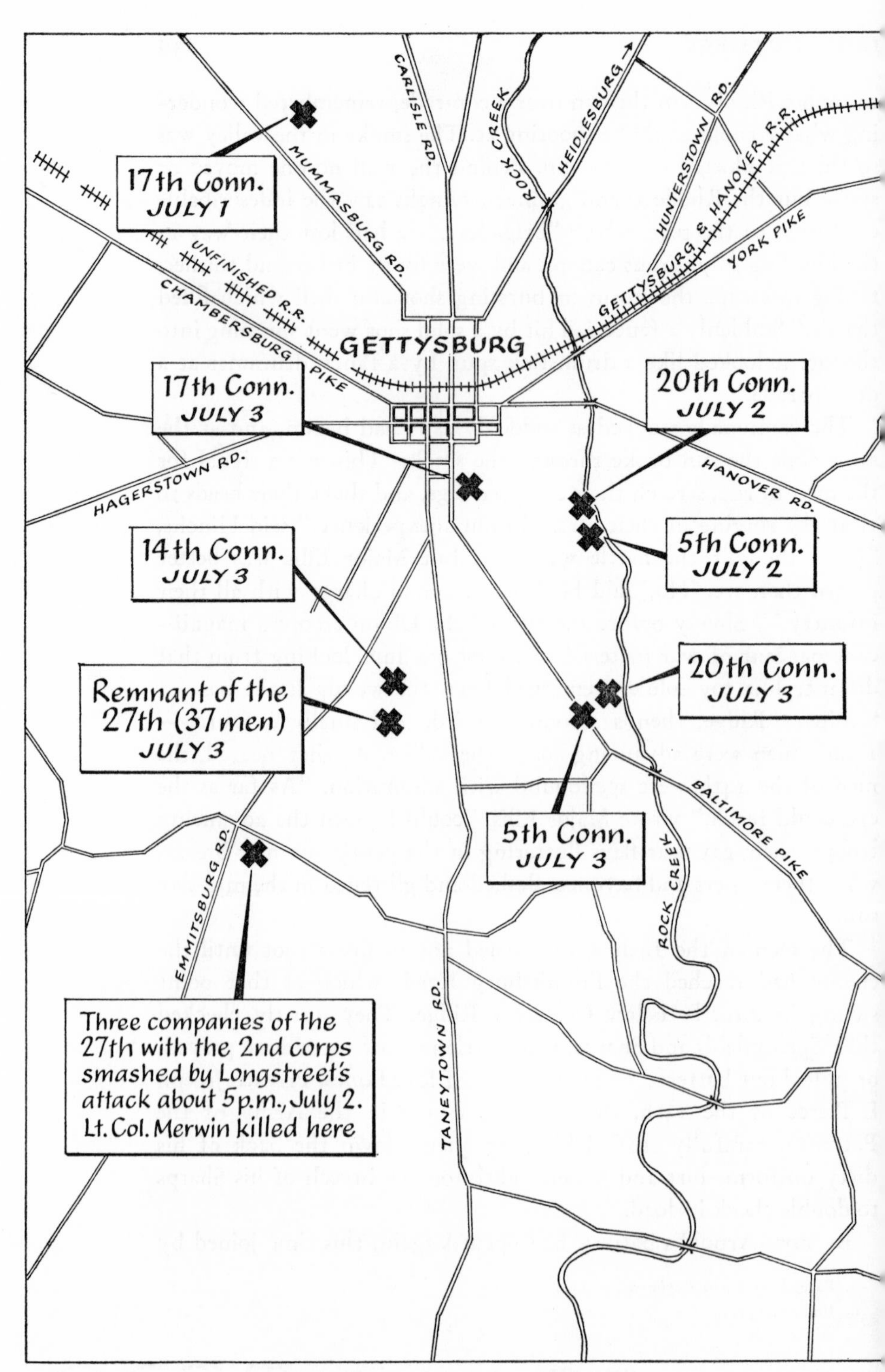

11. Gettysburg, July 1–3, 1863.

all the front-line batteries. Gaps were appearing in the line of the advancing enemy and the sky was clotted with the white puffs of exploding shells. Nothing, however, stopped the steady tread of the Confederate infantry. The mile-wide line seemed as solid as ever. When it reached the fence that marked the Emmitsburg Road, all along the Union line rattled the orders "Fire! Fire! Fire!" Tyler had brought up his reserve artillery, over 200 cannon, double-shotted with canister. Guns then added their deeper rumble to the high-pitched crackle of 25,000 rifles and muskets. The pageant in front quickly dissolved as the entire Confederate line was blown away, but the Connecticut boys were too busy pumping shots to be aware of anything except the mechanical rhythm of loading and firing. Sergeant Hincks, his sleepy eyes bright with sustained excitement, was using two Sharps, one his own, the other belonging to a comrade wounded earlier in the day. Lieutenant William Hawley was loading for him. Hincks was the best rifleman in the outfit, a cool soldier who made every shot count. Despite the continuous fire, the Confederate line came within fifty yards of the 14th's position, where a Tennessee color-bearer defiantly planted his flag before he was shot. That was the end of the great charge as far as the 14th was concerned, and indeed, the end all along the line. Shell-shocked survivors were now surrendering or running away. Over the walls and down the slope went the cheering Union lines, collecting battle flags, souvenirs, and prisoners among the heaps of Confederate dead and wounded—over 5,000 of them along the base of Cemetery Ridge alone. The 14th collected 5 battle flags and 200 prisoners, 2 prisoners for every member of the regiment in action.

It was now late in the afternoon. Longstreet's artillery on Seminary Ridge checked the Union advance, and both armies settled down for the night. The next day, when it was discovered that Lee was in full retreat toward Virginia, Meade cautiously advanced his lines; but it was not until the following day that he sent the fresh 6th Corps in slow pursuit, and several days more before the army moved forward. Meade's army was worn out. It had suffered frightful casualties, and thousands of stragglers had to be collected and sorted out. Thus the commanding general decided to hold his men in the Gettysburg vicinity, where they could clean up, rest, and refit. Even hardened veterans were shaken at the shambles in front of Cemetery Ridge. "Everywhere between the two lines," wrote a shocked Colonel Buckingham, "were found the same ghastly scenes—dead horses and dead men, the latter with ghastly staring eyes and over whose bodies the unclean birds of the air were already hovering—exploded caissons, trees severed in twain and so on." [7] Many of the dead were found in such realistic postures that gun-shy burial squads were constantly being startled. "Look out! there's a Johnny aiming at you," shouted one of the soldiers of the 20th, "and sure enough," reported his comrade, "there he was, with his musket in position and his face down on the breech. He had been struck in the forehead in the act of firing and was instantly killed." [8]

All Connecticut volunteers had fought well at Gettysburg, but for sheer energy and resourcefulness, none could match a civilian from Norwalk, A. H. Byington. As a reporter for the *New York Tribune,* Byington had arrived at Gettysburg on the evening of July 2. He was quick to recognize that he was witnessing the decisive battle of the war. But how would he get the news through? He was told by other reporters that the enemy had cut the telegraph lines and destroyed all the instruments for miles around. The enterprising Byington, however, was determined to see for himself. He hired a horse from an army teamster and spent several hours combing the countryside. To his delight, he discovered an operator who had hidden his instrument from enemy patrols. The next problem was far more difficult. Telegraph lines had to be repaired. Making liberal use of *Tribune* funds, Byington managed to employ enough army stragglers to repair several miles of cut line between Hanover Station and Baltimore. Army officers going to and fro were so busy with their own problems that they paid no attention to the several hundred soldiers who were repairing the line. Probably those who witnessed the operation thought that it was being done under orders. At any rate, no one reported him, and he got his one-man telegraph line going just after the repulse of Pickett's charge.

Standing behind the operator, Byington dictated his dispatch to the *Tribune,* prudently directing it to the attention of Gideon Welles, Secretary of the Navy. It went clicking over the line to the

7. Storrs, *Twentieth Connecticut,* p. 103.
8. Ibid., p. 102.

War Department at Washington, where it made a sensation. When he finished his dispatch, back came the questions, "What about this battle?" "Who is Byington?" But "Who are you?" Byington impudently asked. "Abraham Lincoln," came the reply. "Ask Secretary Welles," Byington telegraphed. There was a brief silence on the line while Lincoln sent word to Welles, who had just left the War Department, asking if he could identify the reporter. Welles promptly vouched for Byington. Then the anxious President telegraphed to Hanover, "send us more." But Byington was too much of a reporter and too much of a Connecticut Yankee to let it go at that. He asked Lincoln to give his dispatch an exclusive to the *New York Tribune*, "as soon as read." "Agreed!" was the prompt response. For the remainder of the action at Gettysburg, the *New York Tribune* had a monopoly on the news of the battle. Even the chronically irritable Meade was so happy to have open communication with Washington that he interposed no objection to Byington's informal arrangement with the President.

After Gettysburg four of the five Connecticut regiments with the Army of the Potomac were detached. The remnant of the 27th went home to be discharged. In August the 17th shipped south to participate in Gillmore's siege of Charleston, and in late September 1863 the 5th and 20th went west with the 12th Corps to reinforce the Army of the Cumberland. Only the 14th remained with Meade. For the next six months this battle-scarred regiment was to be involved in Meade's abortive maneuvers against Lee to the west of Richmond.[9] Occasionally the marching was varied with a nasty little skirmish like Bristow Station, where the 14th lost 26 men. Or the regiment would be drawn up, ready to storm near-impregnable positions such as at Mine Run, where after one look at Lee's entrenchments, Lieutenant Colonel Samuel Moore said, "Men, there is no use denying it, but three quarters of you are to be left in that marsh with your toes turned up."[10] At the last moment General Warren called off this suicidal attack. But several months later, an equally strong position at Morton's Ford across the Rapidan was attacked, costing 20 per cent of the 14th's effective force.

Morton's Ford was to have been only a demonstration to cover

9. Fiske, *Mr. Dunn Browne*, p. 297.
10. Page, *Fourteenth Regiment*, p. 202.

Judson Fitzpatrick's foolish cavalry attack on Richmond. Gouverneur K. Warren, the 14th's corps commander, Alexander Hays, division commander, and Colonel Charles Powers, brigade commander, had been drinking for hours prior to the attack. Warren was hopelessly drunk most of the day. Hays had taken enough liquor to "make him reckless and almost like a crazyman." While his brigade was fighting for its life, Powers was slumped in an armchair behind the lines. At one point Hays ordered several companies of the 14th to storm a Confederate entrenchment around the Morton house. Most of the men were captured and ordered to stand in front of the house before being marched away. Meanwhile, Hays brought up a New York regiment and a battalion and ordered them to open fire. One of the New York officers questioned the order. "General, those are our men in front of us." Hays swore that the men were rebels and ordered the regiment to fire or be charged with mutiny. The shocked New Yorkers dutifully killed and wounded many of their helpless Connecticut comrades.[11] But the men of the 14th, like all seasoned soldiers, lived from day to day. Hays' disgraceful conduct was soon forgotten, along with yesterday's other miseries. They had become used to Meade, and while no one considered him a military genius, he was thought a skillful general—one who did not needlessly sacrifice his troops. The appointment of Grant to over-all command excited more curiosity than comment, especially since Meade stayed on as their commander.

Grant's appointment was of more immediate moment to other Connecticut regiments, scattered throughout the southern seaboard. During April and May they were recalled to the Virginia theater of operations and concentrated near Fortress Monroe. Most looked forward to participation in the big show, but for the time being they were disappointed. Instead of being assigned to the Army of the Potomac, the 6th, 7th, and 10th and the 1st and 2nd Light Batteries were sent to Benjamin Butler's new Army of the James. The 8th, 11th, and 21st were already with W. F. "Baldy" Smith's 18th Corps, also under Butler's command. Initially, Butler was to have been an important element in Grant's strategic planning. While the Army of the Potomac struck at Lee's left through Hooker's old Wilderness route, Butler was to move up the penin-

11. Ibid., pp. 222–29.

sula along the James River and aim for Richmond. It was an excellent plan, but one that called for close coordination and speedy execution among the various corps' commanders. Lee would now have the benefit of interior lines; and the terrain, especially in the east, would be difficult for an attacking army. Butler has been justifiably accused of incompetence in his handling of the Army of the James. He has also been charged with a feeble advance, in spite of his superior forces. This was true earlier, when instead of seizing an almost completely undefended Petersburg he delayed and threw up entrenchments. But the Connecticut troops found that when Butler did advance, they had as tough fighting as they had ever experienced. Drewry's Bluff was no feeble affair. Beauregard's counterattack on May 16 cost the Connecticut regiments 739 casualties out of about 2,400 engaged.[12]

Meanwhile, the Army of the Potomac was moving toward Richmond from the west. Grant hoped to have it through the Wilderness area before Lee could concentrate his forces. But mistakes were made by his subordinates, divisions got lost, and as a result it took many additional hours to maneuver the unwieldy Army with its seventy-mile wagon train through the Wilderness maze. Lee caught Grant while his troops were still in the Wilderness, where Union artillery could not be used to advantage.

As had happened at Chancellorsville, the woods soon caught on fire. Thick acrid smoke, attacks and counterattacks from every direction, digging in during lulls, and constant casualties were the hideous experiences of the 14th during the battle of the Wilderness. The 14th lost almost 100 men in the two-day battle, among them the humorously sardonic Captain Samuel Fiske, the *Springfield Republican's* best war correspondent.[13] On May 7 the Army fought its way out of the Wilderness and headed for the strategic crossroads of Spotsylvania Court House, about fifteen miles away. This was the first of Grant's many side-steps to the southeast.

The 1st Connecticut Cavalry, skirmishing in front of the Army, was commanded by Major Erastus Blakeslee of Plymouth, and was

12. Croffut and Morris, *Connecticut*, pp. 542–57; W. S. Hubbell, *The Story of the Twenty-First Regiment, Connecticut Volunteer Infantry during the Civil War, 1861–1865* (Middletown, 1900), pp. 178–98.

13. Page, pp. 235–43.

part of the cavalry detachment that captured the hamlet of Spotsylvania on the morning of May 8. Dismounting and digging in, the troops held their position for two hours until dislodged by superior forces. The 1st Connecticut had a checkered past. It had suffered during the period when the Union cavalry had been mishandled by infantry-minded generals. Morale had been bad and personal strife had existed among its officers. But the regiment had been recently re-equipped, troublemakers had been weeded out, and under such spirited cavalrymen as Blakeslee, Brayton Ives of New Haven, George Marcy of Bridgeport, and Edward A. Whittaker of Ashford, the Connecticut troopers had been whipped into shape. Its job done at Spotsylvania, the 1st joined Sheridan's new cavalry corps and trotted off to the south, seeking to cut Lee's communications and if possible to corner "Jeb" Stuart.[14]

Lee had also raced for Spotsylvania and reached there in time to entrench around the village. Though tired and rain-soaked, the 14th went in with Hancock's attack on Ewell's salient, where it took more prisoners than its effective strength. Under repeated counterattacks as Lee built a new defense line farther south, the men of the 14th fought desperately in "the bloody angle." One Connecticut man thrust his bayonet into the chest of a Confederate who in turn bayoneted him in the neck. When they were found "dead against the breastworks, the guns of each served to brace them and hold them in their standing position." [15]

The desperate fighting in the tangled, burning Wilderness, where the average soldier was totally unable to see that the Army was getting anywhere, except paying its daily butcher bill, as young Oliver Wendell Holmes so acidly observed, bore very hard on the morale of the Union troops. "There is a feeling of uneasiness in the stoutest heart," commented Sergeant E. B. Tyler of the 14th. "The mystery is doubly intensified by the sudden, silent dropping dead, or fatally wounded, of men on either hand that somehow does not seem to connect itself with the constant roar of musketry that is going on." [16] And then at the height of the confusion and the slaughter the one senior general officer in whom the troops had

14. Croffut and Morris, pp. 572, 490–93.

15. Page, p. 248.

16. Ibid., pp. 241–42.

confidence—plain, dependable John Sedgwick—was killed by a sniper. No one, not even Grant himself, was less expendable at that time and place. Despite his martinet ways, Sedgwick had symbolized strength and security to the battered, bewildered soldiers. His loss was more keenly felt because his image as a wise and humane protector of the common soldier had not been built quickly; nor had he, like McClellan or Hooker, sought to kindle affection or court popularity. To the men he was simply plain "Uncle John," square of face and feature, grizzled, blunt, and direct, a Litchfield County farmer who had been in Mexico, California, and all over the country in between, yet never doubted that his native town surpassed any place he had ever seen. "Is there another spot on earth so beautiful as Cornwall Hollow?" he asked one of his adoring nephews during a home leave recuperating from the three wounds he had received at Antietam.

Sedgwick was only 51 years old at the time of his death, yet to his staff and, indeed, to all who followed the Greek cross, the 6th Corps' identification badge, he seemed an indestructible, patriarchal figure.[17] But he did have a boyish, playful side to his nature, which was evident when he watched his men at sports or played a harmless practical joke on some pompous subaltern. Outwardly a patient, modest man, Sedgwick could be sharply critical of his superiors, though rarely indulging in those unseemly public displays of backbiting that characterized army headquarters after major Union defeats. In private, however, Uncle John did not always bother to conceal his exasperation. "I know but little of what is going on," he wrote his sister in August 1862, after Pope's defeat at Second Bull Run. "No one does," he continued, "but General Halleck and the enemy." [18]

What really endeared Sedgwick to his men was not his appearance, demeanor, or even the attention he paid to their ordinary wants, such as food, supplies, medical services, and the like. Rather, it was the scrupulous care he took in making battle dispositions, a care that saved lives and could be counted on in any emergency.

17. Thomas W. Hyde, *Following the Greek Cross, or the Memories of the Sixth Army Corps* (Boston, 1894), p. 137.

18. *Correspondence of John Sedgwick, Major General,* 2 (New York, 1902), pp. 78–79.

After the battle of Salem Church, for example, when Sedgwick's corps was nearly encircled by Lee's entire army, Uncle John got his men safely across the Rappahannock. An admiring George T. Stevens, surgeon of the 77th New York, had this to say about Sedgwick during that crisis: "Personally examining every part of the ground in front and rear, riding from one end of the line to the other, now ordering a battery placed at some commanding point and now looking out a new position . . . he was everywhere present, full of energy, as determined to save as he had been to win." [19] Sedgwick was a great lieutenant, "never at fault when serious work was to be done," according to General Grant. But like all introspective men, he seemed to lack ambition and to distrust his judgment. Grant, who had a discerning eye when it came to high military officers, described him as "brave and conscientious," but noted that "his ambition was not great and he seemed to dread responsibility. He was willing to do any amount of battling but always wanted some one else to direct." [20] John Sedgwick died as he had fought, among the common soldiers, joking with them as they sought protection from Confederate sharpshooters at Spotsylvania. His last words before the fatal shot were, "What are you dodging for? They could not hit an elephant at that distance." [21]

As much as they mourned the passing of Sedgwick, as much as their sense of security had been shaken, the men of the 6th Corps continued doggedly to do their duty, which at Spotsylvania meant constant death or injury in the smoke-laden, rain-soaked woods. For Lee had succeeded in establishing his new line. After two weeks of futile hammering, during which he suffered 40,000 casualties, Grant again started his army east. Lee followed on parallel lines. The forces met briefly along the North Ana River, but Grant quickly side-stepped when he discovered that his army was divided by a deep bend in the river. His new objective would be Cold Harbor, another dreary crossroad, commanding the last natural defense line before Richmond. There Grant would face an enemy as

19. George T. Stevens, *Three Years in the Sixth Corps* (Albany, 1866), pp. 205–06.

20. Ulysses S. Grant, *Personal Memoirs* (New York, 1886), 2, 214, 540.

21. George R. Agassiz, ed., *Meade's Headquarters, 1863–1865, Letters of Colonel Theodore Lyman from the Wilderness to Appomattox* (Boston, 1922), pp. 107–08.

strong as, if not stronger than, at the beginning of the Wilderness campaign. Butler had been bottled up in Bermuda Hundred, northeast of Petersburg; and Franz Sigel had been defeated in the Shenandoah Valley. These Confederate successes had released almost 30,000 troops to Lee's army.

The Army of the Potomac had also been reinforced during the Spotsylvania battle. Grant had withdrawn W. F. Smith's 18th Corps from Bermuda Hundred. These troops, which included the 8th, 11th, and 21st Connecticut, would join the Army of the Potomac on June 1. The General-in-chief had also stripped the Washington defenses to fill his depleted ranks. The 2nd Connecticut Heavy Artillery, which had thus far fought the war from comfortable Washington billets, had arrived on May 20 and was marching as an infantry regiment with Emory Upton's brigade of H. G. Wright's 6th Corps.

Colonel Elisha Strong Kellogg commanded the 2nd Connecticut, or the "heavies," as they preferred to be called. The heavies never could decide whether they loved or hated him, but all agreed that the regiment had been his personal creation. Big, burly, red-faced Kellogg was strangely complex, as if contradictory traits warred for control of his personality. He was a bully on the parade ground, "a horrid, strutting, shaggy monster," who humiliated his officers and drove his men to the brink of mutiny. He was also given to impulsive gestures of kindness and understanding that would compel the devotion of all. As Adjutant Vaill put it: "The men who were cursing him one day for the almost intolerable rigors of his discipline, would in twenty-four hours be throwing up their caps for him, or subscribing to buy him a new horse, or petitioning the Governor not to let him be jumped." [22] Kellogg's prewar career had the same inconsistent pattern of irresponsible adventure balanced by responsible family life. He had served before the mast in the British merchant service; he had been a forty-niner in California and a first-rate mechanic and a good family man in the little factory town of Winsted. Tough, blustering, kindly, and resourceful, Kellogg was fiercely proud of his men, and pathetically anxious

22. Theodore F. Vaill, *History of the Second Connecticut Volunteer Heavy Artillery, Originally the Nineteenth Connecticut Volunteers* (Winsted, Conn., 1868), pp. 326–27.

that they live down their reputation as "a band-box regiment." [23] They were soon given the opportunity.

Lee chose a strong position at Cold Harbor. With his right flank buttressed by the Chickahominy River and his left by the Totopotomoy, his army could not be turned. Therefore, Grant resolved to try a massive frontal attack, hoping to drive Lee into the deep Chickahominy. It took all day to perfect arrangements for a two-corps reconnaissance in force, a time lag that Lee improved by strengthening his already formidable entrenchments. The 2nd Connecticut, completely played out after its all-night march from Spotsylvania, was drawn up near an old Union breastworks to the right of the Nine Mile Road to Richmond. About 200 feet in front of the regiment lay an open field that extended several hundred yards to a line of enemy rifle pits with a thin belt of pine trees beyond; then another field, narrower than the first, adjoined the main line of the enemy. This consisted of trenches guarded in front by heavy abatis of brush and sharply pointed pine logs. The enemy line stretched for miles to the right and left, and was studded with artillery emplacements.

Colonel Kellogg had assembled his regiment—over 1,800 men—in three battalions. Climbing up on the log breastworks, he gave last-minute instructions, which were repeated by the three battalion commanders. "Now men," he said, "when you have the order to move, go in steady, keep cool, keep still until I give you the order to charge, and then go in arms a-port with a yell." He warned them not to fire a shot "until we are in the enemy breastworks." The battalions were to go forward at intervals of 100 feet; muskets would be uncapped. At 5 P.M. Emory Upton ordered the advance, and the first battalion was under way, following its burly, blue-coated Colonel as he swung along on foot, with his pillbox garrison cap on the tip of his outstretched sword. Across the field it went in close order, found the first line of rifle pits abandoned, and moved through the scrubby pine, down into a hollow, and up to the ominous abatis front. Through the gaps in the obstacles the men caught a momentary glimpse of musket barrels and slouch hats twenty yards away, before they were caught "in a sheet of flame, sudden as lightning, red as blood—so near that it seemed to singe

23. Ibid., p. 329.

11. The Regiment had been his personal creation: Colonel Elisha Strong Kellogg of the 2nd Connecticut Heavy Artillery. Connecticut Historical Society.

12. His regiment was one of the first to be engulfed by Stonewall Jackson's flank attack at Chancellorsville: Colonel William H. Noble of the 17th Connecticut. Connecticut Historical Society.

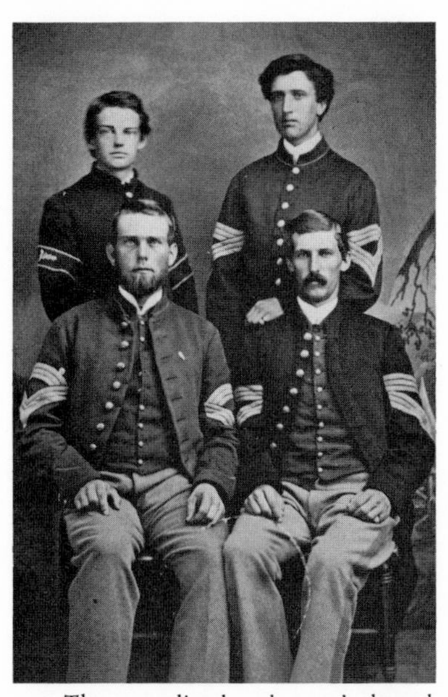

13. They re-enlisted and served through to the end: (standing, left to right), Hospital steward James J. Averill, Commissary Sergeant Franklin J. Candee: (seated, left to right), Sergeant-Major Bushrod H. Camp, Quartermaster Sergeant Edward C. Huxley—all of the 2nd Connecticut Heavy Artillery. Connecticut Historical Society.

14. A camp tin-type for the folks at home: Private George Meech of the 21st Connecticut in full marching equipment, including hardtack. Connecticut Historical Society.

the men's faces." The rebel fusillade was high; few were hit. The battalion dropped to the ground in time to escape a second volley. At Kellogg's command, the men leaped up to clear the abatis, just as the entire left of the Confederate line opened on them. Two hundred were shot down in a few minutes.[24]

"About face," shouted Kellogg, who had been wounded in the face. He had scarcely given the order when he was hit twice more in the head and fell dead upon the abatis. Three hundred Connecticut boys were milling around like sheep and being cut down in droves. "Wild and blind with wounds, bruises, noise, smoke and conflicting orders, the men staggered in every direction," said Adjutant Vaill. They were finally brought to their senses by Upton, whose strident voice somehow carried over the din. "Lie down," he shouted, an order that was instantly obeyed. It saved what was left of the first battalion and most of the second and third, who were crowding forward. From then until dark, the survivors worked their way back to their old breastworks, where they helped repel a Confederate counterattack. From an observation post behind the advance line, Martin McMahon, adjutant general of the corps, was shocked at the carnage. "The second Connecticut Heavy Artillery . . . had joined us but a few days before the battle," he wrote, "its uniform was bright and fresh; therefore its dead easily distinguished where they lay. They marked in a dotted line an obtuse angle, covering a wide front, with its apex toward the enemy, and there upon his face, still in death, with his head to the works, lay the Colonel, the brave and genial Colonel Elisha S. Kellogg."[25]

The following day Grant tried again. This time he hurled his entire army against Lee's six-mile line in column by divisions closed in mass. Each division was both a massive battering ram and a perfect target as 6,000 men advanced in three waves on a front of about 1,500 feet. The 8th, 11th, and 21st went in with Smith's corps and in five minutes suffered 171 casualties. Colonel Griffin Stedman of the 11th, who closely resembled McClellan in physical appearance, had a moment of dismay when he saw the open field ahead, the smoke-sprouting enemy line curving round it—"a

24. Ibid., pp. 61–66.

25. Johnson and Buel, *Battles and Leaders*, 4, 219.

wicked red-green gash of piled up earth and felled pine trees." "I bade farewell to all I loved," wrote Stedman. "It seemed impossible to survive that fire." He escaped injury, though he led his regiment to within thirty yards of the enemy lines. But every member of his staff was mortally wounded and eighty more in the ranks were hit.[26] In five minutes the brigade lost 600 men out of 2,000. Grant's grand assault had been pounded to pieces.

Stubborn as the General-in-Chief was, he would not try again. The men dug in and held their position for several days, while headquarters drew up orders for another end run. This time Grant was to move the entire army to the Petersburg area some fifty miles away. It was to be a vast and complicated maneuver, and if it were to achieve a success worthy of its daring, a most important preliminary objective had to be gained. The city of Petersburg had to be in Union hands before Lee understood Grant's new intentions. Petersburg was the key to the Richmond defenses in the southeast and to Lee's major supply lines with the interior. Success here not only would ensure the capture of the Confederate capital but would cripple, perhaps critically, the Army of Northern Virginia.

For the vital Petersburg assignment, Grant chose Baldy Smith and his 18th Corps. Smith took his troops out of the Cold Harbor Lines at dusk on June 12. They joined Butler at Bermuda Hundred two days later. The remainder of Grant's army, corps by corps, moved south and east, crossing the Chickahominy and the James. By June 16 the Army of the Potomac was closing in on Petersburg from the east. Grant's maneuver had been handled so skillfully that Lee decided it was only another side step. Thus he concentrated his forces between White Oak swamp and Malvern Hill, one day's march from Petersburg. But Smith did not attack fast enough. The Petersburg fortifications looked imposing, and he wasted several hours reconnoitering them. He finally attacked at 7 P.M., achieving almost instant success, but then he heard a rumor that Lee was sending reinforcements, and decided to hold what he had until Hancock's corps arrived. Had Smith and his 14,000 men pushed on, Petersburg would have fallen. The garrison consisted of only 2,400 troops, most of whom were untrained militia. When Hancock arrived, over 25,000 Union troops opposed Beauregard's tiny

26. Croffut and Morris, *Connecticut*, p. 597.

garrison. It was late, the troops were tired, the rumor of enemy reinforcements persisted. Both generals decided to postpone any advance until the next day. During the night Beauregard shortened his lines and shifted those of his troops that were opposite Bermuda Hundred to the Petersburg defenses. The Confederate commander had also alerted Lee, who was rushing reinforcements. Thus when the Union troops were ready to resume that attack, Beauregard had 14,000 men, enough to hang on. The opportunity was lost; Grant ordered the army to entrench.

For nine awful months 6,000 Connecticut troops fought in the trenches around Petersburg with Grant's army, 50 to 100 feet from enemy lines. Raids and skirmishes were frequent, as Grant constantly grappled for Lee's communications. Adjutant Vaill of the 2nd Connecticut Heavy Artillery considered the Petersburg trenches "the most intolerable position the regiment was ever required to hold." [27] Movement was possible only after dark. The long hours of summer daylight were torture to the men. Trenches were so shallow and narrow that even crawling was difficult. With a fifty-fifty chance of not being hit, the men would expose themselves briefly, for, as Vaill explained, "soldiers will take the chances rather than lie still and suffer from thirst, supineness and want of all things." Officers were always warning their men to keep down. But perhaps the worst trial for the suffering soldiers was the dead men and the horses and mules, left in no man's land after each skirmish. On at least one occasion, when both Grant and Lee were unable to coordinate their requests for a truce to bury the dead, troops on both sides ignored their commanders and held an informal burial party. Chaplain Moses Smith of the 8th described the Petersburg trenches as "a month of siege work; lying in the trenches; eyeing the rebels; digging by moonlight; broiling in the sun; shooting through a slit; shot at if a head is lifted . . . our lines endangered by shells from both sides; officers falling; comrades dying." [28]

The high command, though seemingly indifferent to casualties, did what it could to help morale. Sometimes, however, its well-meant efforts had the reverse effect. On July 28 a brass band was

27. Vaill, *Second Connecticut*, p. 74.
28. Croffut and Morris, p. 618.

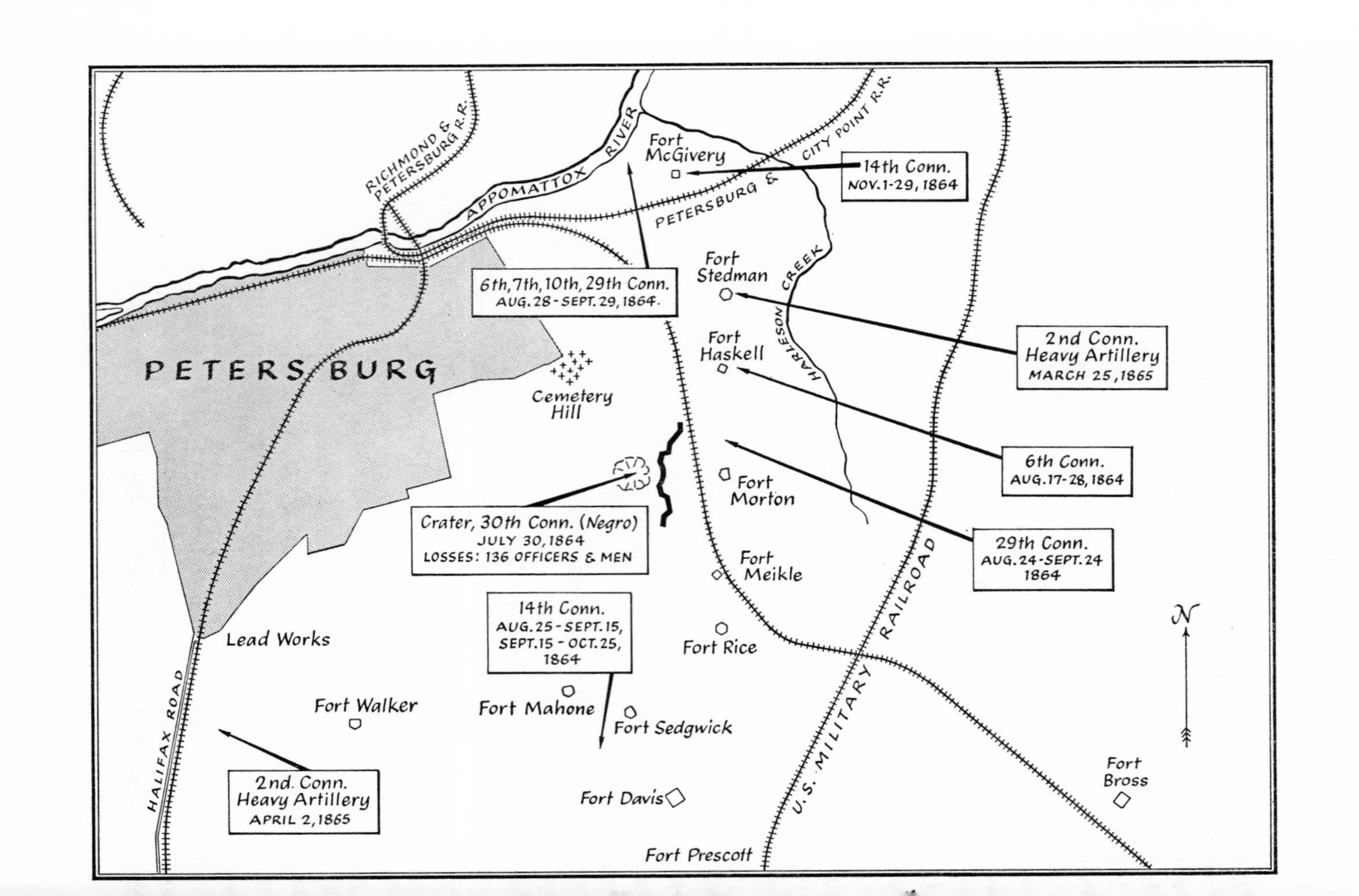
RICHMOND & PETERSBURG R.R.
APPOMATTOX RIVER
Fort McGivery
PETERSBURG & CITY POINT R.R.
14th Conn.
NOV. 1-29, 1864
Fort Stedman
HARLESON CREEK
6th, 7th, 10th, 29th Conn.
AUG. 28 - SEPT. 29, 1864.
PETERSBURG
Fort Haskell
2nd Conn.
Heavy Artillery
MARCH 25, 1865
Cemetery Hill
6th Conn.
AUG. 17-28, 1864
Fort Morton
Crater, 30th Conn. (Negro)
JULY 30, 1864
LOSSES: 136 OFFICERS & MEN
29th Conn.
AUG. 24 - SEPT. 24
1864
Fort Meikle
14th Conn.
AUG. 25 - SEPT. 15,
SEPT. 15 - OCT. 25,
1864
Lead Works
Fort Rice
U.S. MILITARY RAILROAD
N
Fort Walker
Fort Mahone
Fort Sedgwick
HALIFAX ROAD
2nd. Conn.
Heavy Artillery
APRIL 2, 1865
Fort Davis
Fort Bross
Fort Prescott

rdered to play behind General Robert Foster's position at Four Iile Creek on the right of the Union line. Hundreds of Union dead nd wounded lay unattended in front of Foster's trenches. The ombination of music and groans was too much for Private Charles Iotchkiss of New Haven. "Who is to blame for all this? May God ave mercy on us all," he scrawled in his diary.[29]

Attrition, especially among the officers, was more or less steady, unctuated by short, sharp bursts of significant blood-letting when he opposing commanders tried to seize the initiative. In the crater asco Connecticut's little battalion of colored troops, with the 31st Jnited States Infantry, lost over half its effectives; all its officers vere either killed or wounded. The 29th Connecticut, an all-Negro egiment, lost 178 men in the siege and in various skirmishes on the ight of the line. "Well you colored fellows have had a pretty ough job I reckon," said a member of the 2nd Connecticut to a oldier of the 29th. "Yes we have," the Negro private replied, "as ough as we care for. We have to die for eight dollars a month, while you get thirteen for the same business." "Was not that a easonable answer?" asked Vaill.[30] By the end of 1864 such famous, battle-scarred regiments as the 10th could muster but 100 nen; the 7th, not much larger, was commanded by the last of its riginal officers. Even Griffin Stedman, a realist when it came to attle casualties, was moved to remark: "Poor fellows—they all ie." Stedman was killed by a sniper on August 5.

Siege and battle casualties were not solely responsible for the tiny ze of the Connecticut regiments before Petersburg. Hundreds had one home after serving out their three-year enlistments. Some of he career officers, such as Colonel Henry L. Abbott of the 1st Connecticut Heavy Artillery treated discharged veterans badly. When they refused to re-enlist, he assigned them to difficult or angerous tasks as if they were prisoners under sentence of court-martial; and when their terms of service expired, Abbott refused to rovide them with discharge papers and transportation. Benjamin utler also had a bad reputation with discharged veterans. On October 26, 1864, Private Edward Griswold, his honorable discharge n his pocket, went over to see General Joseph R. Hawley before

29. Beecher, *First Light Battery*, 2, 527.
30. Vaill, pp. 72–73.

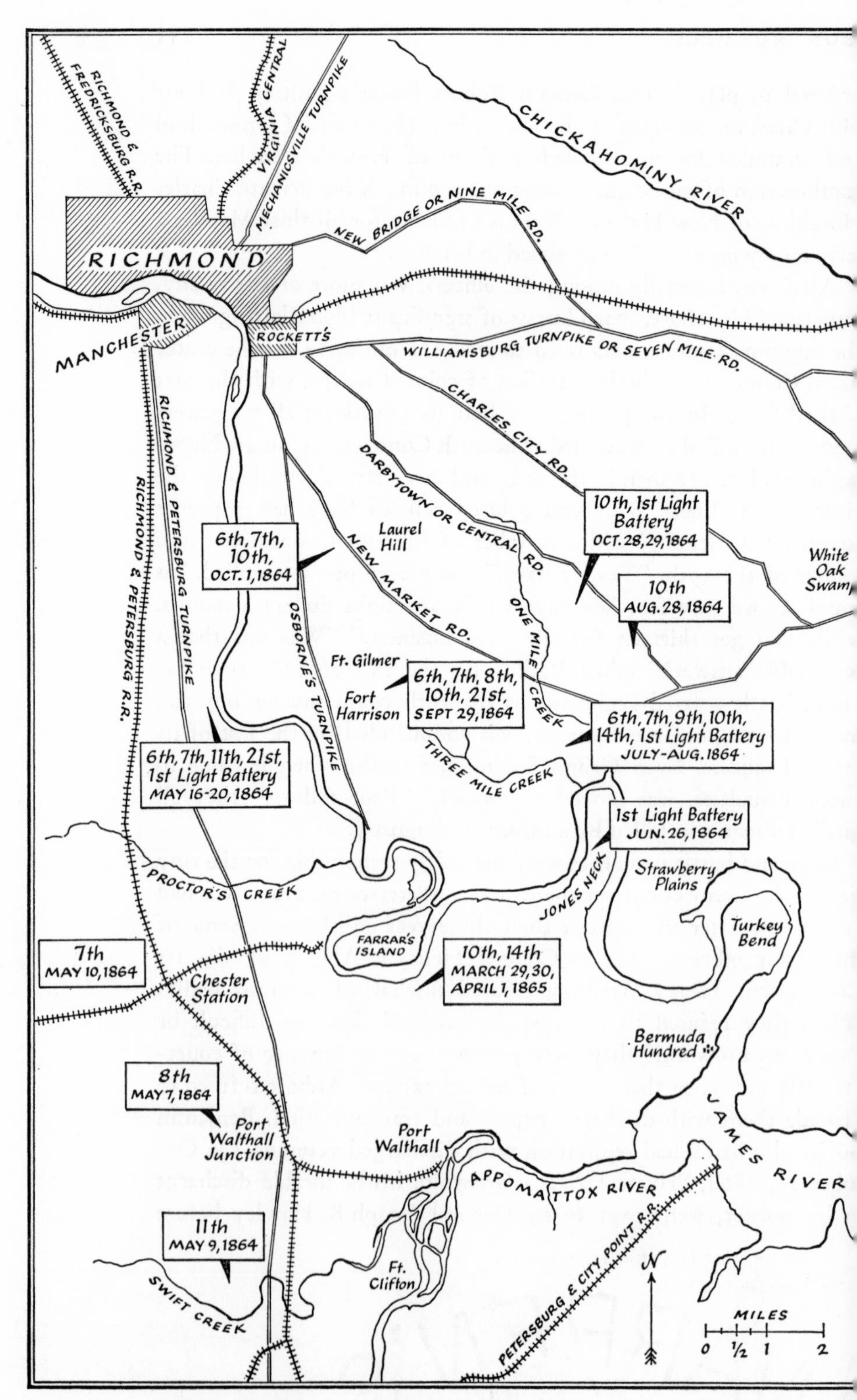

13. Richmond-Bermuda Hundred Front, May 1864–April 1865.

eaving for Guilford, Connecticut. Hawley gave him messages to arry home; then warned him to get out of the area fast. "He told s," recalled Griswold, "there would be an engagement before ight, and if General Butler found us starting he would be liable to lo as he had done before in such cases: arrest us for being within he lines as citizens without leave, and either set us to work in the renches or send us to the front." [31]

Despite the Abbotts and the Butlers in the Army of the Potonac, the ceaseless casualties in the filthy trenches, and the bloody ffairs at Chaffin's Bluff, Fort Harrison, or along the Southside Railroad, Grant's reputation among the Connecticut troops improved steadily. The General-in-Chief had a faculty for doing little hings to help the common soldier. These incidents were described nd elaborated by the witnesses, and passed by word of mouth hroughout the Army. But there was a limit to what the Grant nystique could accomplish, even with the hard-bitten Army of he Potomac. The Wilderness and Petersburg pounding had beaten lown the spirit of the troops.

John W. DeForest was dismayed at the low morale of the famous th Corps, which had joined Sheridan's campaign against Jubal Early in the Shenandoah Valley during the late summer of 1864. DeForest's 12th, the 9th Irish, and the 13th Connecticut had also een transferred to Sheridan's command after the capture of Port Hudson.) The 6th Corps camp had "no boundary lines between he different regiments, all being mixed together higgledy-iggledy, officers with the men and the brigade commander in the niddle." DeForest recorded the morose attitude of a 6th Corps rigade commander with whom he talked. "But don't you believe n Grant at all?" I finally asked. "Yes, we believe in Grant," replied he colonel. "But we believe a great deal more in Lee." [32] The 2nd Connecticut Heavy Artillery, now with the 6th Corps, was just as asual as its companion regiments. Sixty days before, the men in heir bright new uniforms had listened to their terrible tempered olonel demand that they get rid of their reputation as a "band-box egiment."

Yet it seemed that there was nothing like victory, a good hard,

31. Beecher, 2, 605.

32. DeForest, *A Volunteer's Adventures*, p. 165.

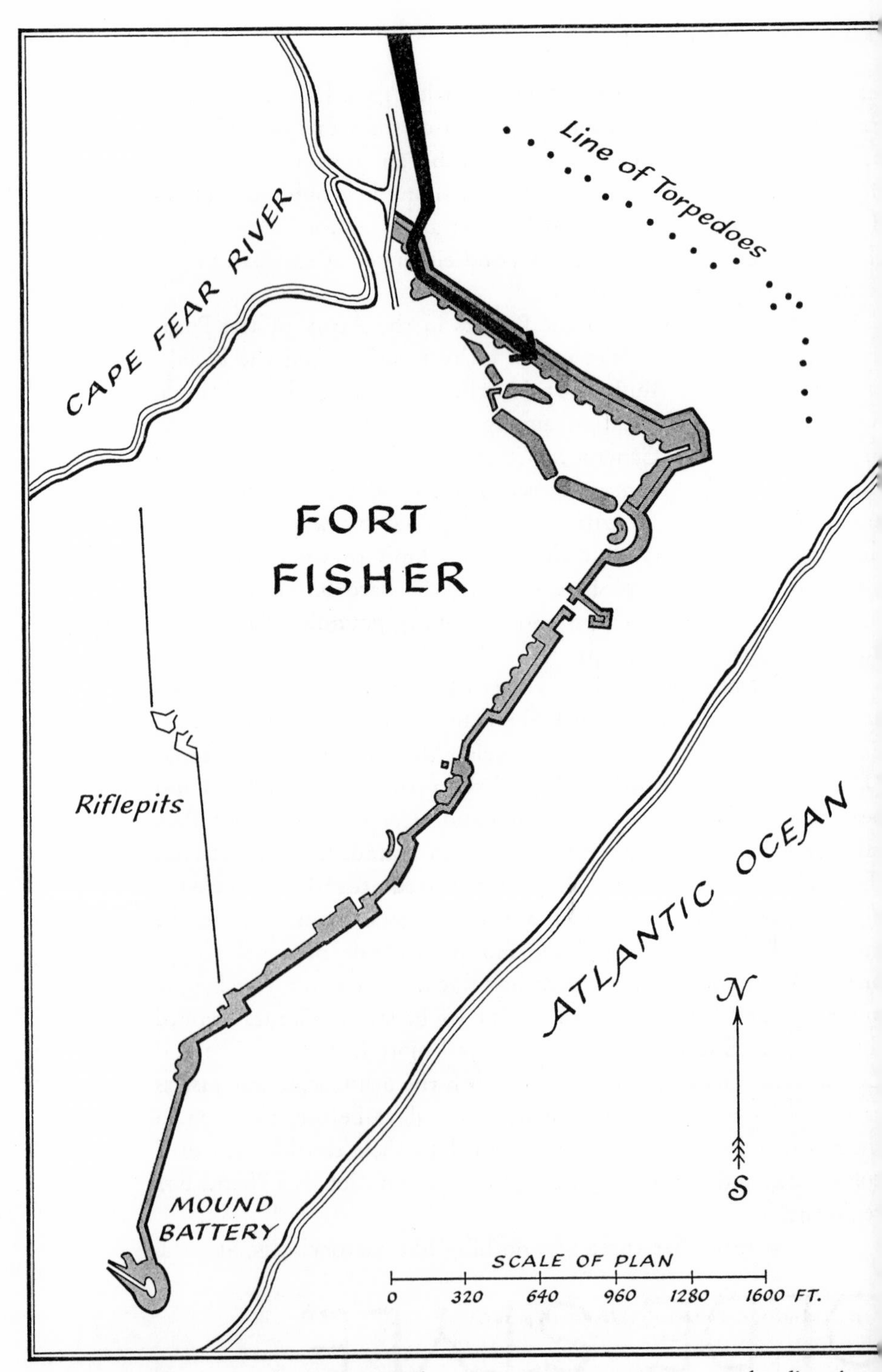

14. Alfred Terry's assault on Fort Fisher, Jan. 15, 1865. Arrow marks direction infantry attack.

smashing, visible defeat of the invincible gray army to stiffen the slumping posture of the Union troops. Sheridan drove his dispirited men unmercifully, but he led them to victory three times over Jubal Early in the valley—at the Opequon River, at Fisher's Hill, and at Cedar Creek. Though all the Connecticut regiments suffered heavy casualties, especially the 2nd Connecticut, they fought bravely and well. Sherman's dynamic march through Georgia, which followed within two months, provided additional tonic for the desperate troops around Petersburg. The 5th and 20th were with Sherman. They had already fought in six engagements and had marched 500 miles from Tennessee. Their uniforms were poor enough when they started, but when they reached North Carolina early in 1865, many were "almost naked and some entirely barefoot." Yet they, too, like Sheridan's men, marched and fought on leadership and success as much as on the "liberal foraging" of the rich Georgia countryside. The third spectacular achievement of Union arms that occurred within the space of six weeks was of particular interest to Connecticut troops. This was the capture of the formidable Fort Fisher and the city of Wilmington, North Carolina, by General Alfred Terry and Admiral David Porter—a victory that was particularly relished because of previous failure by the hated Butler. Not three weeks before, Butler had probed Fort Fisher, exploded a shipload of gunpowder off its sea face, probed again, and had withdrawn, proclaiming that Fisher was impregnable. Grant had promptly relieved Butler and entrusted the army part of a new Fort Fisher expedition to General Terry. The 6th and 7th Connecticut and three batteries of the 1st Connecticut Heavy Artillery accompanied the expedition. Terry had a force of about 8,000 men, a small number indeed, considering that General Bragg was known to have a like number in the vicinity and that the garrison of the Fort mustered some 2,000 in addition. For once the Army and Navy worked together with smooth precision. Porter softened the sea faces of Fisher with over 600 heavy guns and then lent close-in support for the combined Army-Navy assault on the river face. While 2,000 sailors and marines armed with pistols and cutlasses stormed the northeast salient of the Fort, over 6,000 soldiers poured into Fisher from its land side. The Navy assault was beaten back with heavy casualties, but in order to meet it, the garrison had been divided; and there was no resisting the flood of manpower that charged over the river batteries. The 6th and 7th were part of the second wave. When they went in, General Terry put himself at their head. Inspired by the example of their commander, they drove the defenders from casemate to casemate. Two hours after the combined assault had begun, Fisher surrendered.[33]

During the next eight weeks Grant steadily increased his pressure on the crumbling Confederate defenses. Connecticut troops fought to the very end. The night before Richmond fell, the 10th Connecticut captured forts Gregg and Baldwin, part of the outer defenses of Petersburg, but not before a desperate shooting match, which soon became a hand-to-hand combat on the parapets of Gregg.[34] The 2nd Connecticut also had hard fighting that day, and slept the night of April 3 in the muddy trenches before Petersburg's Fort Fisher, a key Confederate earthwork, "among the dying and the dead under a most murderous fire of sharp-shooters." [35] Toward dawn the sporadic firing ceased and a New York regiment cautiously worked its way to the ramparts of Fisher, only to find the Fort deserted. The New Yorkers opened a picket fire on the enemy redoubts beyond, but there was no reply: they, too, had been abandoned. Since 2 A.M. heavy explosions had been heard in the direction of Richmond. From Fort Fisher huge fires in the vicinity of the enemy capital could be seen with a glass. Still careful but with increasing confidence, the Union line moved forward over empty rifle pits, deserted bombproofs, trenches, and forts into the city of Petersburg. A few hours later, Union troops occupied Richmond.

The rest was anticlimax. Although hopelessly outnumbered, his supplies cut off, and all lines of retreat blocked, Lee hurled his starving men against Grant's army until a few hours before his surrender. In their eagerness to administer the coup de grâce, Sheridan and Custer were equally reckless of human life. On April 6, for example, the 1st Connecticut Cavalry was ordered with its brigade to charge Dick Ewell's entrenched corps. "In less than three minutes after the 'charge' was sounded," said Colonel Brayton Ives of the 1st Connecticut, "one fifth of the men and horses I led in were

33. Walkley, *Seventh Connecticut,* chap. 20; Cadwell, *Sixth Regiment,* p. 116.

34. Croffut and Morris, *Connecticut,* pp. 787–88.

35. Vaill, *Second Connecticut,* p. 161.

killed outright (my own horse among them)—all lying in one spot that could be covered by a radius of a rod."[36] Indeed, the 1st Cavalry and the 10th Connecticut were with Sheridan when he received the shock of Lee's last attack on the morning of April 9. Other Connecticut regiments saw little action during those last days, but were marched on half rations into a state of near exhaustion. Few would believe that Lee had surrendered until the men were ordered to share their scant supplies of hardtack and coffee with their former enemies. In North Carolina the Confederate commander Joseph E. Johnston had at least kept his retreating army out of contact with Sherman. Thus the 5th, 6th, 7th, and 20th Regiments endured nothing worse than marathon marches on short rations. When Johnston learned of Lee's surrender, he proposed an armistice, which was accepted on April 17, and he surrendered his army three days later. Confederate forces in Texas and western Louisiana gave up soon after.

After the capitulation, war-weary Connecticut troops thought they would be sent home immediately. Had not their enlistment papers said they were only obligated to serve for the duration of the war? But the high command, which had been in such a rush to end the war was not to be hurried into peace. Every corps commander had to have his grand review in Washington, whether the soldiers liked it or not. Moreover, there were provost duties and other military government chores to be performed throughout the South. Time was also needed for the settling of military accounts and the arranging of transportation for discharged veterans. Most Connecticut soldiers, though they grumbled, were willing to wait until the red tape was unraveled; they were less understanding about the Washington reviews. The jaundiced attitude of the 2nd Heavy Artillery and the 14th Infantry toward General Horatio Wright's 6th Corps review in Washington was typical of the resentment that boiled up in the ranks against the military brass. The men were routed out of their shelter tents at 4 A.M. "Buckled, bandaged and strapped into full dress," they were on the road by 6 A.M for the ten-mile march to Washington. With 14-pound muskets at right shoulder arms, and the temperature around 100 degrees, the men soon began to suffer. But there was no halt for a rest, no break in

36. Croffut and Morris, p. 793.

the cadenced step. Over the Long Bridge they went up Maryland and Pennsylvania avenues, every man cursing the corps commander and the mounted officers, many of whom galloped ahead for a drink in taverns along the way. "Commanding officers dared not halt," said Adjutant Vaill of the 2nd, "for fear of having no men to move on with—and when the 'head of the column' reached camp, the tail was in Georgetown and under every bush along the road. The 2nd brigade was a very long brigade." [37]

What with reviews and other chores, it was not until midsummer that the regiments began to arrive in New Haven and Hartford. The bells and salutes that greeted them may have had the same cheerful, strident clamor of Sumter days; the speeches of the notables may have been as quaint and ceremonious as they had remembered; but these lean, tanned men were a different breed from the wide-eyed innocents who had joined the colors in 1861. The romantic gloss of adventure and patriotic glory had been well rubbed off. Those who survived had been toughened and coarsened in the trials of camp life and combat. Yet something of a higher value had been gained too. More than 20 per cent of the volunteer regiments were of immigrant or Negro stock. These new citizens of the state and nation now had a common heritage to share with their Yankee neighbors: they too had fought for the Union. And the Yankee volunteers themselves had developed a deeper appreciation of their Irish and German and Negro comrades-in-arms. Friendship, respect, even kinship had been cemented on the battlefield.

All Connecticut troops, whether native born or not, had been broadened by their travels in distant places. They had seen something of other people, other customs, and if they remembered the suffering of the long marches, the horrors of Libby or Andersonville, the filth, the disease, and death, they recalled also those rare moments when they had been awed by the beauty, the richness, and the variety of their vast country. Many had enlisted to escape narrow environments, others for lofty moral purposes, and still others for money or prestige, but all had gone as Connecticut boys first, and as Northerners second. They had emerged from their ordeal with a different understanding. Union now meant nation, not state, not even North. It had taken four years of bitter cam-

37. Vaill, pp. 361–62.

paigning with 2,350 dead and almost 10,000 wounded to effect the transition. In the process, the Connecticut volunteers learned that modern war was a ruthless business, not a dashing adventure.

Meanwhile, it would take some time before the veterans could accommodate themselves to the demands and rigors of the new industrial state; for the homefolk themselves had changed in their absence. Something of the harsh realism of the battlefield had permeated society, yet without the compensating rewards of military comradeship and teamwork. Readjustment would not be easy for those whose skills had grown rusty through disuse in a society so ruthlessly dedicated to what it was pleased to call individual merit. Like the prancing field and staff horses of the 2nd Connecticut, which mistook New Haven's welcoming showers of rockets and red lights for another battle,[38] many of the returning veterans would find it difficult to believe that the war was over.

38. Ibid., pp. 365–66.

PART THREE

Home Front: The Human Resource

10. "WHY DO WE FIGHT?"

CAPTAIN CHARLES WHITTLESEY of the 22nd Connecticut had been in the Army only six weeks. As yet, no harsh campaign experience had distorted his sense of patriotism nor subdued any of his lofty motives for enlisting in a nine-months regiment. He had believed that the slavery question was one of the crucial issues of the day. As befitted a young Hartford idealist, he thought in terms of moral absolutes. Thus the war to him was a struggle between the forces of righteousness and the forces of evil, a struggle in which freedom and union were arrayed against disunion and slavery. Whittlesey was, of course, convinced that the North was fighting God's fight. He never doubted that it would eventually triumph. Yet even such a visionary as he was somewhat bewildered at the rush of events, and found it difficult to grasp the notion that such a "trivial cause" as a man's color had led to "such tremendous effects."

In early December 1862 Whittlesey had further opportunity to speculate on the importance of hidden forces in the history of the nation. He had managed a day's leave in Washington and spent his free time inspecting places of national interest—the huge, unfinished Capitol, the patent office, the Corcoran gallery. There, amid heroic statuary, patriotic paintings, and other symbols of the common heritage, Whittlesey mulled over the problem of the slave. He was struck by the fact that he had seen no representation, even indirectly, of the Negro. How ironic it seemed to him that "the small 'chattel race' existing at the dawn of our national life should in a scant thirty years have threatened the great republic with extinction." Whittlesey was reminded of Elijah's little cloud, like man's hand, that had suddenly grown into a great storm. "History," he mused, "to be faithful to itself, whether breathing in letters, on canvas or in marble, the story of our great trial hour, shall be compelled to make 'the chattel man' the great central theme and figure . . . of mighty import and interest to our time."[1] As Whittlesey sensed, the growth of antislavery sentiment had been one of the most significant developments of the first year of the war. Even in Connecticut, which was more conservative than most states, emancipation was now accepted as a war aim by a majority of people.

Freedom for the slave was not a primary aim, and it would never be admitted as such during the conflict. But if one were to consider that up to the attack on Sumter, public opinion had regarded abolition as a subversive belief, the radical change in attitude toward the Negro had been remarkable indeed. A dawning realization that the war would be long and hard had pushed the Connecticut public toward more concrete objectives. Abstract arguments about the nature of the Constitution and the Union may have served New Haven professors and Hartford lawyers as practical war aims, but they were simply not comprehensive enough for the man in the street, the common soldier, and even, eventually, the better-educated classes at home or in the field. Not that any loyal citizen had abandoned his belief in the Union cause; he merely wanted it strengthened and clarified. Emancipation of the slave would accomplish this by personalizing the conflict. Now the war for the unification of the nation was also the war for human freedom. Any taint of a partisan conflict that had disturbed the common-sense loyalists, any wrestling with the semantic problem that the Confederate Constitution did not differ fundamentally from the Federal Constitution, any queasy doubts that the Northern side of the war might be just as sectional as the Southern, would cease to be subtly disturbing factors. Emancipation restored the moral absolutes to the conflict. It rounded out somehow the incomplete argument and made the Union cause the tangible, not just the theoretical, cause of freedom.

To a people who were disturbed by the internal divisions of their own social order—the ambivalence of an incomplete industrial ethic—such an external division as posed by Sumter had come as a terrific shock. The yawning chasm of anarchy loomed before the propertied classes, who were already unsure of their status in a

1. *Hartford Courant* (Dec. 19, 1862).

changing society. Anxiety about the future was to drive most of them into extremes of political thought and behavior. And almost at once, an ideological split developed along partisan lines. Conservative Democrats argued the course of peaceful separation and co-existence; moderate Republicans and War Democrats sought a tentative solution—"the Union as it was"—by force of arms. Those of more radical attitudes argued a fight to the finish, no compromise with aristocratic slavocracy until the nation was re-established on nationalist terms that outlawed both slavery and divisible sovereignty. Their leaders held to an inflexible opinion that the Southern slave system must not be permitted to menace the future of the nation, as they felt it had been doing since the Mexican War. In their quasi-mystical concept of geographic and political totality, state, nation, abolition, enterprise, progress, and imperial future were all interchangeable terms, unconditional verities. Connecticut, itself, was but a material expression of this vision: its institutions and social order, when solidified in the new industrial ethic, was to them the pattern of what the nation must be. Meanwhile, the state had to be purged of such evildoers as Democrats who believed in the political heresy of peaceful coexistence. Essentially, the development of war aims would be a result of the ideological struggle between these extremist positions. Moderate majority opinion, ultimately dividing, would gravitate toward the opposite poles.

It was all a very confusing mixture of politics and principles, forcing massive rationalizations on both sides. Looking back from the vantage point of 1965, one finds the vexing problems of what were politics and what were principles—a Churchillian puzzle wrapped up in an enigma. But to the people of Connecticut in 1863, the vital question of American political ideology had not been settled, nor in fact had the equally vital question of American nationality. The uncertain state of such powerful social and political institutions invested one's political and social beliefs with an almost religious significance. This climate of uncertainty and division, and perhaps guilt at the awful bloodletting, would breed radical intolerance among the loyalists. As the war continued, intolerance was to foster despotic practices, xenophobia, atrocity fabrication, a coarse, even cynical materialism. Likewise, it was to push the peaceful coexistence faction to the limits of obstruction, well beyond the prescribed posture of loyal opposition. Yet a majority of Connecticut citizens were to find a viable war aim in the maintenance of the Union, which circumstances would broaden to include emancipation and a Northern concept of imperial destiny based on free capital and presumably free labor.

A sense of war aims was being formulated among opinion leaders in the state well before the firing on Fort Sumter. As early as January 1861 Leonard Bacon was branding the secession movement a revolution, with armed conflict inevitable. Declaring that the Southern leaders had seized power "with as little show of legal rights as poor John Brown," the New Haven minister stated flatly that "the revolution, thus attempted, must be achieved like any other revolution, by an appeal to arms." [2] Bacon's forthright identification of the North with the Union and the Union as the only legitimate government foreshadowed what would be the principal war aim for the first year of the conflict. Horace Bushnell of Hartford, with his vivid sense of ruthless optimism, welcomed the impending contest. Absolutely certain of the Union's moral superiority, he looked for a substantial benefit—"to see it proved that our government is only made stronger and more consolidated by it." Slavery at the same time would be "greatly moderated and weakened." "I really pity those wretched slave-holding sections of the country," Bushnell wrote his daughter in January 1861. "Between so many fears, so much pride and poverty and jealousy, so many wild tempers and so many appalling weaknesses, it must be just now, next thing to a hell upon earth." [3]

After Sumter most Connecticut citizens simply fused the cause of the Union with that of the nation.[4] Unionist opinion leaders readily accepted a Bushnell credo that civil government and the Federal Union were synonymous. Since civil government in Bushnell's logic was divinely ordained, it followed that the rebellion was not only treason but a violation of the laws of God. On a less exalted level, the South was stigmatized as the exponent of disorder

2. Leonard Bacon, "The Pulpit and the Crisis," *New Englander, 19* (1861), 146.

3. Bushnell to Mary Bushnell, Jan. 5, 1861, in Mary Bushnell Cheney, ed., *Life and Letters of Horace Bushnell* (New York, 1905), p. 443.

4. Theodore D. Woolsey, "The Southern Apology for Secession," *New Englander, 19* (1861), 731–32.

and anarchy, while the North was hailed as the champion of law and order and of Christian civilization. The Congregational clergy could not resist giving a hoary Federalist twist to their arguments. According to Bushnell and Theodore Dwight Woolsey, Thomas Jefferson had been responsible for the rebellion. In words reminiscent of his illustrious uncle and predecessor, Timothy Dwight, Woolsey charged that the sage of Monticello had always opposed the Constitution. The issue was clear-cut: lawful order against the unlawful anarchy that Jefferson had first posed in the Kentucky Resolution of 1798. To such a legalistic New England moralist as the Yale president, secession was both a criminal and an heretical movement of willful men. "It is an evil thing and a bitter," he said, "to depart in passion or in pride from obedience to the Constitution." [5]

Defeat at Bull Run amplified the Union thesis, yet curiously seems to have shaken the supreme confidence of some in a priori explanations of Northern righteousness and Southern war guilt. Attempts were made to assess war aims more realistically in the light of experience and of history. One Hartford theorist writing in August 1861 upgraded the rebellion to the status of a war and declared that the struggle was a "revolution for empire." With an attempt at objectivity, he alluded to the education of Northern and Southern youth as sectional rather than national. "Boys north," he wrote in the *Hartford Courant*, "have been educated to laugh at and despise boys of the south as great sinners by right of inheritance." He concluded that the conflict was really between "young American South and young American North." [6] Reverend Joel Hawes, the senior pastor of Hartford's First Congregational Church, told his fast-day congregation in October 1861 that the North was waging a defensive war. "It is not a war of conquest; it is not subjugation . . ." he said, "but only to stay the hand of violence, they have raised against us, to bring them back to their allegiance and maintain the government of the country." Hawes saw free institutions everywhere on trial. Failure, he prophesied, would result either in anarchy or in the establishment of "separate sovereign states," which in his opinion would be just as dire a con-

5. Ibid.
6. "Colt" in *Hartford Courant* (Aug. 23, 1861).

tingency, threatening constant war between two hostile, contiguous nations. The congregation was deeply moved when the tall, angular old man, in his old man's quavering voice, declared, "I for one should feel that the sun of freedom had gone back on the dial of time for generations and for centuries and might never regenerate." [7] Less eloquently but more succinctly, Orris S. Ferry, commanding the 5th Connecticut and soon to be elected a Republican congressman from the Fairfield district, echoed similar sentiments. "The issue," according to Ferry, "is not whether the Confederate States of America shall begin to be, but whether the great Republic shall cease to be. Consciously or unconsciously everyone understands this." [8]

What Hawes and Ferry had said was elaborated in the first of a series of significant speeches on war aims, delivered by William Wolcott Ellsworth at Sharon, in Litchfield County, on January 1, 1862. Ellsworth was one of the most distinguished men in the state. A son of the famous jurist Oliver Ellsworth and a notable jurist in his own right, he had been a congressman, thrice governor of the state, and had just retired from the state Supreme Court. Despite his reputation as a political theorist, Ellsworth was rather more hortatory than analytical in his thinking. He focused his argument on the structure and powers of government. Government is not "counsel, or admonition or entreaty or courtesy," he stated. "It is power." If "the Federal Constitution is the supreme law of the land in some areas, it is supreme in all," he argued. "Power, like sovereignty is not divisible." Ellsworth was to go well beyond John Marshall's definition that the national government was supreme only within its clearly defined limits. "The national government," declared Ellsworth, ". . . must be able to move every obstruction in the path of its progress." He asserted that governments by their very nature must be perpetual. "It is true," he said, "that rebellion may destroy the Constitution, but secession is a contradiction." To Ellsworth's sense of order and propriety, all organized society must rest upon government. Admit secession of a state and, eventually, one must admit the secession of a county or a town or, finally, an individual. He cited the experience of the Confederate

7. Ibid. (Oct. 22, 1861).
8. Ibid. (Feb. 26, 1862).

15. "A slight, frail man, tapering from head to foot": Horace Bushnell, Hartford's most eminent clergyman. Connecticut State Library.

16. "It is not a war of conquest . . . but only to stay the hand of violence": Joel Hawes, senior pastor of Hartford's First Congregational Church. Connecticut State Library.

17. Nestor of New England Congregationalism: Leonard Bacon, pastor of the First Ecclesiastical Society of New Haven.

18. Lawful order versus unlawful anarchy: Theodore Dwight Woolsey, President of Yale College, 1846–1871. Sterling Library, Yale University.

government to demonstrate that the secessionists themselves had rejected their own doctrine.

What then of the two-government, two-nation thesis argued by both the Confederacy and the coexistence advocates in Connecticut? In words similar to those of Hawes and Ferry, Ellsworth utterly rejected this possibility. Basing his rationale on "the physical and natural relations of the country," he revealed an organic concept of the nation, which was being shared by more and more of his fellow citizens. "Consider," he asked his Sharon audience, "the physical and natural relations of this country, which like ligaments bind these states indissolubly together, as well may the human body be separated and expect vitality and health. Can the hands say to the feet, 'I have no need of thee' or the head to the heart, 'I have no need of thee?' No more can this Union be divided, and our free government continued." In his citing of Pauline doctrine, Ellsworth was reminding his audience that Connecticut and South Carolina, Massachusetts and Louisiana, were all involved in an organic unity in which each part contributed to the functioning of other parts and to the proper functioning of the whole. Stripped of its property consciousness, its Anglophobia, its moral sureties, Ellsworth's primary war aim bespeaks a transcendent nationalism that would brook no interference with its ultimate fulfillment.[9] This was powerful stuff for an old-line Federalist-Whig, who had been brought up to revere the institutions of his native state.

Northern victories along the South Atlantic coast and lower Mississippi Valley sustained conservative Unionist sentiment in the state until the spring of 1862. Even Peace Democrats supported the embattled Lincoln Administration and assisted in the great recruitment drives of July and August 1862. But the collapse of McClellan's Pensinsular campaign, upon which so much had been staked, made a strong impression on public opinion. The conservative Republican press suddenly discovered that "the South hate us with an implacable deadly hatred." "Are we ready" asked *Courant* editor A. N. Clark, "to look the matter squarely in the face and say that war means burn, kill and destroy; that it means weakening the enemy by all possible methods; that it means crushing, obliterating, exterminating every available instrument by which rebellion

9. Ibid. (Jan. 9, 1862).

can be sustained and made successful?" Clearly, Clark expected an affirmative answer; yet leaving nothing to chance, he pointed out there was no alternative, for total war against the North had already been decreed by the Davis government.[10] It only remained for Horace Bushnell to put the capstone on the argument for total war by insisting that there be no mental reservation from anyone regarding the sanctity of the Union cause.

Bushnell was 59 years old when the war began, "a slight, frail man, tapering from head to foot," as a younger Hartford colleague, Reverend Edwin Parker, remembered him.[11] Persistent ill health had forced his retirement from the active ministry in 1859, but it had not curtailed his literary or polemic activities. Behind him there stretched more than a quarter century of personal controversy with both the orthodox and the unorthodox leaders of his Church. An original thinker, strongly pragmatic in his theological views, Bushnell had attempted singlehandedly to steer Congregationalism through the treacherous secular currents of mid-nineteenth-century American society. This had led Hartford's most eminent clergyman into theological positions that bewildered his less gifted colleagues. Just when liberal Congregationalists were applauding Bushnell's alleged drift toward liberal theology, he suddenly asserted that he had always been orthodox. And he backed up this statement by declaring that science and transcendentalism were merely evidences of man's depravity. No wonder theologians of such diverse thinking as Joel Hawes and Calvin Stowe should find Bushnell inconsistent for exactly the opposite reasons.[12]

But Bushnell seems to have been sublimely unaware of any doctrinal deviation. He always regarded himself as an orthodox Congregationalist and his critics as men who misinterpreted his teachings. These he would defend with great agility, and in the tight little world of the religious journal he rarely failed to bring his man down. Reverend W. L. Gage recalled that Bushnell "caught up weapons on all sides: wit, sarcasm, raillery, argument, analogy, learned authority—everything was ammunition to his gun." [13]

10. Ibid. (July 23, 1862).

11. Cheney, *Bushnell*, p. 473.

12. Henry C. Trumbull, *My Four Religious Teachers, Charles G. Finney, David Hawley, Elias R. Beadle, Horace Bushnell* (Philadelphia, 1903), pp. 91–92.

13. Cheney, p. 255.

However changeable his theology, Bushnell was consistent in two respects: a life-long interest in mechanical inventions and a passionate, even fanatical, devotion to the Northern brand of American nationalism. In both respects, whether patenting a new coal furnace [14] or denouncing as un-American the state-rights position of Jacksonian Democrats, he proclaimed his Connecticut Yankee-Federalist-Whig instincts. These, together with his curious theological instability and his appeal to emotion and experience rather than to reason or logic, would, in the ordeal of Civil War, provide Bushnell with yet another sword of righteousness.

Bushnell had been an early and busy propagandist for the divinity of Federal government thesis. But after the Emancipation Proclamation, which drove most of the conservative Democrats into organized opposition to the government's war policy, Bushnell began to ponder the problem of internal loyalty. Bloody Union defeats at Fredericksburg and Chancellorsville, the President's suspension of the writ of habeas corpus, draft riots in New York, draft disturbances in Pennsylvania and Wisconsin, Democratic party strength in Connecticut—all these ominous portents of social unrest and war weariness disturbed the intensely patriotic Bushnell.

Always the ingenious rationalizer, Bushnell brought his not inconsiderable gifts of style and feeling to the thorny question of domestic loyalty. Before he was finished with his definition, this frail gadfly of Congregationalism had produced a thesis that would suspend civil rights and civil liberties for the duration. Had his ideas been accepted and acted upon, no critic of the war policy would have been safe from arbitrary arrest, no one but the most outspoken patriot would have been free from the taint of sedition. In his zeal to rout out disloyalty, Bushnell sanctioned a "temporary waiving of the Constitution itself to save the Constitution and the nation." [15] It seemed not to concern the Hartford divine that his thesis on loyalty in the spring of 1863 was diametrically opposed to his thesis on the divine origins of the Federal Constitution, which he had promulgated two years earlier. For a devout minister and deep thinker who had worshiped the forces of law and order, such harsh intolerance and logical inconsistency can be explained only as

14. Ibid., p. 297.

15. Horace Bushnell, "The Doctrine of Loyalty," *New Englander*, 22 (1863), 568.

an emotional by-product of the extreme tensions of the times.

Bushnell approached the problem of loyalty from a moralist position. In his opinion it was completely outside any legal definition, standing "on the same footing with patriotism, honor and bravery."[16] He stated that the "civil law had never anything to do with it, till disloyalty runs to some act of public treason. And then it punishes the disloyalty as treason, never as disloyalty." In assigning loyalty to the "moral department of life," he found it to be "recognized and recognizable only by the law of God." Since man-made codes of behavior could not define loyalty, obviously they could not establish principles or penalties for it. After developing this point, Bushnell went further by declaring that "genuine loyalty is in a higher key at such times as this." "One may even be a great stickler for the Constitution at such a time," he wrote, "and be one of the more pestilential movers of sedition—more poisonously disloyal than he could be in the open renunciation of his allegiance." The worst kind of disloyalty, according to Bushnell, was that kind which keeps "just within the law and only dares not perpetuate the treason it wants to have done; which takes on airs of patriotic concern for the Constitution when it really had none." In his intense concern for the Union-nation, Bushnell made little distinction between Southern rebels and Northern Copperheads. "Let us fight our nation's enemies and destroyers," he exhorted his readers, "and then, if we can, it will be time to mend the abuses of the laws."[17] Despite his emphasis on means, even if illegal or extra-legal, Bushnell did not neglect the end he had in mind. "Events move fast—change is the order of the day," he concluded. "We shall be no more a compact or a confederation, or a composition made up by the temporary surrender of powers but a nation—God's own nation, providentially planted, established on moral foundations."[18]

Events had moved fast for the Hartford nationalist, so fast that his state of mind by early 1863 can best be described as Draconian. Sometime shortly after the battle of Chancellorsville, Bushnell met a member of his former congregation, Lieutenant George Metcalf

16. Ibid., p. 566.
17. Ibid., p. 568.
18. Ibid., p. 581.

of the 1st Light Battery, who was home on leave. "Glad to see you Metcalf. Killed anybody yet?" "I don't know as I can say that I have," the young officer replied. "Time you had," said Bushnell, "that's what you went out for." [19] The awful casualties at Antietam, Fredericksburg, and Chancellorsville had moved Bushnell, but more in anger than in sorrow. "We have no time now for heart-sickening or low regrets," he wrote his Unitarian friend, Dr. Cyrus Bartol, in June 1863, "our mourning should have thunder in it." [20] That the gentle Bushnell should have become so belligerent demonstrates the perilous condition of Connecticut society in the spring of 1863. It was well that the people of Connecticut, during those dark days before Gettysburg, were listening to Leonard Bacon as well as to Bushnell.

Bacon, who was the same age as his Hartford colleague, could not match Bushnell in originality of thought or in grace of expression. But for clarity of judgment and learned exposition the New Haven clergyman was by far the superior. Moreover, he had a much more extensive background in history and in political theory than Bushnell. Judicious rather than provocative, deliberate rather than impulsive, Bacon understood the confusing legal, social, and economic issues of the war with a lucidity unique among clergymen and unusual even among the more able statemen of the times. His 64-page reply to Professor Joel Parker of the Harvard Law School, published in the April 1863 *New Englander,* not only demolished Parker's argument on the legal implications of the rebellion but set forth skillfully Lincoln's and Seward's rationale of the Union cause, with all of its careful distinctions between the Southern states and their rebellious populations.

To Bacon's rational mind it was useless to discuss whether the Southerners were waging war or merely rebelling. The rebellion was so extensive that, practically, the Confederates had to be accorded belligerent rights. This had nothing to do with recognition of their government as a sovereign nation; nor, indeed, with any postwar settlement. "If the war shall terminate in the conquest of the rebellion, then as soon as the authority of the Constitution and laws shall have been completely established over those who have made war on

19. Trumbull, *Teachers,* p. 82.
20. Cheney, p. 581.

their country, the laws of war and the rights of belligerents will have nothing to do with the sequel," Bacon wrote.[21] It would then be the time for the lawyers to decide whether the rebels were traitors or not, "to rejoice in the prospect of trials for treason and of infinite litigation." If the Confederacy, on the other hand, should succeed in establishing itself as a sovereign state, there would obviously be no treason.

Bacon refused to be drawn into the radical position that the Southern states had lost their corporate status through secession. His frequent writings during the war demonstrated that he was a traditional and stalwart upholder of the Constitution and the laws. His concept of the President's war powers, it is true, was somewhat broad for conservative loyalists like Parker; but unlike Bushnell, he would never countenance their indiscriminate use to enforce patriotism in Connecticut or in any other loyal state. A calm, steady, careful man, Bacon saw the war as simply a defense of "ourselves, our laws, our national unity, our Constitution, our glorious heritage."[22] He would maintain this essentially moderate stand throughout the war—even during the trying times of early 1864, when the temptation to follow the radical line was strong indeed.

The development of radical war aims and radical measures of dealing with the war antedated by at least fifteen months Bacon's "Reply to Professor Parker" and Bushnell's essay on loyalty. The *Hartford Press*, edited during Hawley's absence in the Army by his close friend Charles Dudley Warner, began as early as December 1861 to agitate for a war of conquest over the South. But it was on the slavery question that the *Press* adopted a consistently radical tone. And it was the slavery question that would eventually become the cutting edge of radicalism throughout the entire state.

The tall, stooped Warner had been an early convert to the little abolition circle centered around John Hooker, Harriet Beecher Stowe, and that irrepressible reformer Francis Gillette. These parlor zealots, known collectively as the Nook Farm group, had been interested in every reform movement of the mid-nineteenth century. Women's rights, temperance, spiritualism, all were eagerly discussed and written about at Nook Farm—a tract of land on the outskirts

21. Leonard Bacon, "Reply to Professor Parker," *New Englander, 22* (1863), 232.

22. Ibid., p. 258.

of Hartford, where John Hooker had established a select community of kindred spirits. Abolition, however, had claimed precedence over other reforms at Nook Farm, and Harriet Beecher Stowe, by common consent, had been acknowledged as the leader in that cause. Initially, Warner, because of his quasi-public position, could not afford to espouse the radical abolition sentiments of his friends. But the impetuous editor chafed under the restraints during the first two years of the war and had to be admonished more than once by Gideon Welles and even by Hawley, who privately shared Warner's abolition views. Though only a handful of Connecticut citizens espoused abolition, a majority had come around to an antislavery viewpoint after the attack on Sumter. Most believed that slavery somehow had something to do with the outbreak of the war, but few had any clear understanding what that might be. The state Baptist convention in June 1861, for example, had resolved that the primary war aim was the maintenance of the Union, yet it condemned "chattel slavery" as "the bitter root" of the conflict.[23] Loyal conservative opinion, however, would not go so far as that.

One writer in the *Courant* considered that "the slave question is but the excuse, as the Greek church question was the excuse for the Crimean War." [24] Joel Hawes also denied that the abolition of slavery "was—or is—" a war aim, as had been alleged by Southern spokesmen. Hawes, like other members of the clergy, prayed for emancipation as an ultimate result of the conflict.[25] As late as January 1862 Ellsworth was restating 1860 Republican party doctrine when he shifted the burden of the war to the South for its insistence on the extension of slavery into the territories.[26] In March a contributor to the *Courant,* signing himself Republican, declared confidently that "slavery has had its death knock but we have no right to meddle with it as a state institution. Let it go to pieces of its own accord." [27] Even Bushnell, though an outspoken opponent of slavery for years, considered that it was but "proximately responsible" for the conflict.[28] Radical in his views on the

23. *Hartford Courant* (June 17, 1861).
24. Ibid. (Aug. 22, 1861).
25. Ibid. (Oct. 22, 1861).
26. Ibid. (Jan. 9, 1862).
27. Ibid. (March 7, 1862).
28. Cheney, p. 474.

nature of government, Bushnell would never identify himself openly with the radical abolitionists. During the war he was content to follow Lincoln's gradualist policy of emancipation. In this respect his stand was similar to that of Leonard Bacon, who drew a careful distinction between emancipation (legal) and abolition (illegal), until the pending 13th Amendment, which he supported strongly, was ratified by the requisite number of states. Both of these spokesmen, however, had from the outbreak of the war thrown their very real influence with the Connecticut public behind the emancipation movement.

By February 1862 emancipation was being publicly supported by all shades of conservative opinion except the Peace Democrats. On February 25 the *Hartford Courant* published in the most prominent position of its editorial page an anonymous jingle entitled "Strike," which called on Lincoln to free the slaves:

> Dread no future. Let the word
> Like the voice of fate be heard;
> Free the slave, the work is done!
> *Freedom's battle fought and won.*
>
> In the place of Contraband
> Let the name of freedom stand
> Up and act! and while you may
> Sweep a nation's curse away.
>
> Shake the horrid nightmare off
> Ere the world begins to scoff
> Take your station in the van
> Be a hero—and a MAN! [29]

Thus congressional emancipation of slaves in the District of Columbia, with compensation to loyal owners, which was approved by the President on April 16, 1862, met with a cordial reception in Connecticut. True, the *Hartford Times* and the *New Haven Register* opposed the measure, as did the radical-minded *Hartford Press.* The *Times,* though less outspoken against the war than it had been six months earlier, refused to admit that slavery was any issue at all.

29. *Hartford Courant* (Feb. 25, 1862). Stanzas 3, 5, and 6.

Radicals were against compensated emancipation because they felt that it admitted the evil and placed the government on the same level as the slaveowner. But majority opinion would accept neither the proslavery position of the *Times* nor the antislavery quibble of the *Hartford Press*. It looked upon the District Emancipation Act as a first step in what had come to mean an irrevocable contest with the South. As a *Courant* correspondent signing himself "R" remarked, "it shows the rebels clearly that they must either be victorious or utter defeat and political overthrow awaits them." [30] Most conservatives now seemed ready to discard their original aim of "the Union as it was." They had concluded that this objective could only result in the continued protection of slavery, with all its privileges in the South and all its threats to the political balance of the nation. "This nation is now in a transition state," said R. "I have no faith in permanent success until we are just without fear . . . depend upon it you must have a new policy or you will find it hard to fight God and the rebels too." [31]

Once the dike had been breeched by the District Emancipation Act, Unionist sentiment in the state moved rapidly toward a more comprehensive attack on slavery. Moderate opinion, however, was still in the majority; emancipation, not abolition, was its goal. Some favored compensation to slaveowners, others accepted Benjamin Butler's contraband thesis and urged the President to confiscate slaves as war booty. Whatever the means, emancipation had been accepted as a necessary adjunct to the Union cause and as a practical measure to assist in crippling the enemy.

Governor Buckingham, who had been opposed to slavery in principle for years, lent the power and prestige of his office to the emancipation movement. In late August 1862 he headed a Connecticut delegation to Washington, where he personally presented a petition in favor of emancipation to the President. Lincoln, at this time, was under heavy pressure to free the slaves in the war zones. Two months before, he had broached the subject of emancipation to Secretary Welles in the strictest confidence; and when Buckingham appeared with the Connecticut petition, he had already made up his mind to issue the proclamation as soon as he deemed it

30. Ibid. (July 15, 1862).

31. Ibid.

militarily and politically expedient. The harassed President had, however, become annoyed at the attempts to force his hand. He suspected, and rightly so, that the radicals in Congress were behind the public clamor, though there is no evidence that they had any direct influence on the Connecticut petition. Lincoln heard Buckingham out and then replied sharply, "Governor, I suppose what your people want is more nigger." The dignified Governor was so taken aback by the President's sarcastic retort that he found it difficult to control his temper. Lincoln immediately disclaimed any discourtesy, explained his reasons for delay, and assured the Governor that he was only waiting for the proper time to issue the proclamation.[32] When Buckingham returned to Connecticut, he communicated the substance of the President's remarks, on a confidential basis, to a select group of party leaders, journalists, and businessmen. This disclosure headed off temporarily what might have developed into a serious factional dispute within the Union party. But the mounting pressure of public opinion was disturbing to the Governor, and he was much relieved when Lincoln issued his preliminary proclamation promptly after the battle of Antietam. On September 26, 1862, four days after the proclamation had been published, he wrote Lincoln that the emancipation policy has "my cordial approval and shall have my unconditional support."

Buckingham did not read abolition into Lincoln's action, as some Connecticut radicals were doing; he applauded the new policy as a powerful war measure that would eventually wreck slavery. "Not that I think your declaration of freedom will of itself bring liberty to the slave, or restore peace to the nation," he wrote the President, "but I rejoice that your administration will not be prevented . . . from using such measures as you indicate to overpower the rebellion, even if it interferes with and overthrows their much-loved system of slavery."[33] In this respect Buckingham was reflecting the moderate views of a majority of his fellow citizens. Though some conservative Unionists fretted about possible antiproperty implications of the proclamation and worried about its legal status after the war, most loyal citizens thought as the Governor did, that it would be impossible to re-enslave the freed Negroes in the event

32. Buckingham, *Life*, pp. 261–62.

33. Ibid., p. 263.

of a Union victory. Practical-minded Leonard Bacon argued that all those who were disturbed about the postwar status of emancipation should let the future take care of itself. Quoting the Sermon on the Mount, Bacon reminded his readers that "the end is not yet; and this is eminently one of the cases in which it is wise 'to take no thought for the morrow' and in which 'the morrow will take thought for things of itself.' "[34]

Though a majority of Connecticut citizens supported emancipation with enthusiasm, they had not altered their belief in white supremacy. Negroes were regarded as an alien race of inferior status to the superior whites. It was widely held that if the freed Negroes were left to their own devices in the agricultural regions of the South, they would be massacred by the poor whites. Yet few Connecticut citizens suggested that freedmen be relocated in the North or in the Western territories. Even if the more enlightened whites of the free states and territories would not murder the freedmen, they would assert their natural superiority. Since Negroes could not possibly compete on white men's terms, such a relocation would be inhumane. The only alternative seemed to be colonization, either in Haiti or in Africa, the Negro homeland.[35]

Not all advocates of colonization were white supremacists. Reverend Asher Moore of Hartford stated the case on slightly different grounds, avoiding the troublesome distinction that some men had been created unequal. Quoting Scripture that all men were of the same blood, Moore argued before Hartford's Unitarian congregation that geography had ordained the separation of the races. "Facts prove," stated Moore blandly, "that the branch of the race to which we belong is not suited to an abode in Africa while the black race will flourish in that country." Taking note of the American Negro's long residence in the United States, Moore saw in this the hand of Providence. Here, all African savages had been civilized to some extent; and some had received the benefits of education and training to equip them as leaders of their race. In what might be styled a kind of black man's burden thesis, he saw a vision of enlightened Negroes leading their people on a vast missionary endeavor that would civilize darkest Africa. "In this way," said

34. Bacon, *New Englander*, 22, 253.
35. *Hartford Courant* (April 15, 1862).

Moore, "justice will at least be done to the poor African and the rights of humanity will be vindicated; and . . . the human race shall be carried forward in the career of advancement." [36]

Moore's thesis was bound to be popular. After the enlistment of Negro troops, the white supremacy arguments simply would not square with the facts. With Negroes fighting for the Union, the community experienced a sense of obligation, but one that merely lacquered over a deep bias against the colored man with a thin veneer of apparent altruism. Negro soldiers were now elevated to the status of "nobles of their race." The *Courant* asserted that a year of military service had done more for the Negro than twenty years of peacetime education. With a perfervid burst of humanitarian sentiment, the *Courant* editor declared that Africa would be "redeemed from barbarism. This war, perhaps, is to furnish the missionaries and the leaders. A few generations hence the wastes of Ethiopia may blossom with the flowers of high civilization." [37] It did not occur to the *Courant* editor that Negro veterans and Ethiopians might not share his high-minded program for their mutual welfare.

The concept of the black man's burden was not satisfactory to such practical moderates as William Ellsworth. Indeed, the noted jurist attacked all proposals for Negro colonization, including the President's. Ellsworth was concerned primarily about the economic future of the South, though he did have some regard for the inhumanity of uprooting and deporting Negroes. "These laborers," he wrote, "are wanted, every man of them where they now are—where they were born and have lived . . . fully acclimated and taught the labors of the plantation . . . since they now support themselves and their masters, to separate the two will distress both and do an irreparable injury to the industry of the north and of Europe."

Ellsworth was too close to the New England cotton textile industry to back any schemes that might injure its source of raw material. Yet his shrewd mixture of humanitarianism and practical economics was as opportunistic on the segregation of the races as any harebrained colonization plan. The North and West would still be a

36. Ibid. (July 24, 1862).
37. Ibid. (Jan. 1, 1864).

white man's country, and raw cotton would still supply the hungry spindles of the textile kingdom. Of course, the South would have to face up to the problem of the free Negro, but Ellsworth, ignoring any of the social aspects of race adjustment, saw the problem in purely economic terms. Once Negroes were freed and faced the necessity of working to support themselves and their families, they would react just as any other wage earner. In fact, Ellsworth asserted that after the former slaves had experienced the benefits of free labor, "they would assume a new character at once." [38]

Leonard Bacon was another influential moderate who would not accept the black man's burden. His blueprint for the future of the freed Negro anticipated, however, that a new breed, presumably of Northern entrepreneurs, would replace the "rebels, banished or emigrating in disgust." As Bacon rather smugly saw the new South: "Slowly and quietly, thought, speech, industry, enterprise, domestic arrangements and all the relations of society, will begin to be adjusted to the new basis. Instead of the relation of owner and slave, there will spring up the relations of landlord and peasant, of employer and employed, of master and free servant." [39] Thus, if Abraham Lincoln and Asher Moore would transport the freed Negroes as a solution to race adjustment, Bacon would remove the rebellious whites.

It was all very well for the ministers, journalists, and politicians to indulge in comfortable abstractions regarding the freedmen; but the soldiers who had observed the ex-slaves in their actual environment were far more realistic. Most of the volunteers had gone south to save the Union, not to free the slaves; many had never even seen a Negro in their lives. Probably a majority were vaguely antislavery as a matter of general principle, simply because slavery was not compatible with their idea of freedom and opportunity. Furthermore, slavery was a Southern institution and therefore both foreign and hostile. A few months of campaigning in the South strengthened the antislavery conviction of the Connecticut troops; yet those who thought about war aims still regarded the slavery issue as subordinate to the Union cause. In this respect they were, if anything, more conservative on war aims than the folks at home.

38. Ibid. (Nov. 20, 1862).
39. Bacon, *New Englander*, 22, 254.

"What on earth have I said to give you the idea that I am fighting not for the government, but the abolition of slavery?" asked Lieutenant Henry Ward Camp of his family in early 1862. "It is the maintenance of the government that I consider the object and the *only* object of the war; abolition, one of the means, but no more." [40]

Though against slavery, the troops were decidedly skeptical about the equality of the races. They pitied the destitute Negro families who swarmed into the Union lines; they enjoyed the services that the Negroes performed for them—the homemade pies, the laundry work, the supply of fresh vegetables. Negroes were also endless sources of amusement to the troops and, unfortunately, the butt of practical jokes and swindlers. When the soldiers were not laughing at Negro drolleries, they were vexed by their childlike evasion of responsibility. Energetic Yankee officers eventually resorted to stringent measures in their efforts to cope with the tens of thousands of "contrabands" who had to be supported. Able-bodied male Negroes were often conscripted for manual labor on roads and fortifications; when Negro troops were authorized, many were drafted into black regiments.

It took some time, however, before the enlisted men could get used to the idea of Negro troops. Officers were more enthusiastic, primarily because the new Negro regiments offered senior billets and rapid promotion. By late August 1862 DeForest reported from Louisiana that "everybody here is coming over to the notion of enlisting the darkeys. Even old Democrats, even the Hibernian rank and file of the 9th Connecticut are talking in favor of it." [41] Much latent prejudice was dispelled by the heroism of the 54th Massachusetts (colored) at Fort Wagner, but the soldiers tended not to judge colored regiments on an individual basis. There were enough incidents where the poorly trained Negro troops had proved unsteady under fire to promote the myth of white superiority among the Connecticut regiments.

Nor were the soldiers any more tolerant of the efforts being made by Northern idealists to prepare the ex-slave for his future role as a free citizen. Shortly after the Port Royal expedition, large numbers

40. Trumbull, *The Knightly Soldier*, p. 86.

41. DeForest, *A Volunteer's Adventures*, p. 40.

of philanthropic men and women with Negro uplift in mind descended on the army at Beaufort, South Carolina. The soldiers referred to them as "Gideonites," and were both amused and irritated at their antics. William Thompson Lusk, who recognized that something had to be done to educate the former slaves, was disgusted at the assumptions and the pretensions of the missionaries. In his judgment the problem was a delicate one, requiring wisdom and forbearance of the highest order. He found none of these qualities among the Gideonites. "A more narrow-minded pack of fools I rarely ever met. Instead of showing the necessary qualities for the position, they seem to care for nothing but themselves," he wrote his mother in April 1862.[42] Curiously enough, Lusk thought that the women among the Gideonites were far superior to the men, "for they mostly came down under excitement or determined to do good."[43] But in general, he thought such missionaries were beneath contempt and their letters to the Northern press "awful lies."[44]

Though the Connecticut troops tended to scoff at reformers and to regard the illiterate, ignorant Negroes as distinctly inferior, they became bitterly hostile to the institution of slavery. A New Haven officer of the Irish 9th wrote home that after witnessing some of the results of slavery, the regiment had become abolitionist, almost to a man. In a fine burst of Irish eloquence, he attributed this mass conversion to the fact that "they have seen slavery in its naked deformity . . . from the woolly head to the long soft tresses of the octoroon, from the helpless slave to the pampered toy of debauchery, from the $50 slave to the $2,500 doll and from the innocent to the sharp, self-made darkey who knows the value of free action."[45] Gradually also, Negroes gained status from the grudging white soldiers because of their unwavering assistance to escaped Union prisoners of war. Typical of the aid rendered to hundreds of escaped prisoners was the experience of captains Morse, Burke, and Robinson of the 16th Connecticut, who had been captured at Plymouth, North Carolina. After eluding the

42. Lusk, *War Letters*, pp. 141–42.
43. Ibid.
44. Ibid., p. 239.
45. *Hartford Courant* (Aug. 26, 1863).

guards at Camp Sorghum, South Carolina, the three were fed, sheltered, and passed from one Negro family to another in a sort of underground escape route, until they reached the coast, where they were picked up by a United States Navy blockade vessel.[46] "Nowhere in the South," wrote DeForest, "did I ever find or hear of one Negro who was hostile to us." [47]

Despite his antagonism toward slavery, the average Connecticut soldier had little to offer on the problem of racial adjustment. If any private had been asked whether he would approve the resettlement of Southern Negroes in Connecticut or New York or Michigan, he would probably have answered in a decided negative. More than likely, such a question would have seemed incredible to him. Nor would he have been more responsive to the colonization schemes that were being advanced at home. The average soldier, if he did think about the future status of the Negro, probably regarded him as an intrinsic part of the Southern environment, an exotic who belonged with cotton fields and cane fields, orange groves and live oaks. The Negro must be free, for no man must be a slave and the Negro was clearly a man. But the volunteer soldier would probably have agreed with Lusk, the Norwich-born officer of the 79th New York, that while "something must be done for the regeneration of the Negro, it would take time, tact, and above all, understanding."

Once emancipation had been taken for granted as a war aim, the rank and file spent little time debating the status of the Negro. As the war dragged on, however, they became increasingly concerned with the morale of the home front. To the fighting man the patriotism of the folks at home seemed to have declined drastically. Profiteering, politics as usual, the substitute mania, and the ominous strength of the Copperheads called into question the sincerity of the civilian population. As Chaplain Henry Clay Trumbull of the 10th Connecticut told an overflow audience in Hartford's Center Church, "gold rules instead of patriotism. In Hartford there are men who look upon it and are swayed by the effect it produces upon the price of goods. This spirit is not the spirit which animates

46. Blakeslee, *Sixteenth Connecticut*, pp. 87–88.
47. DeForest, *A Volunteer's Adventures*, pp. 56–57.

the soldier in the Army of the Potomac." [48] Commenting on the quota shaving of Connecticut towns and the prevailing tendency to evade the draft, Samuel Fiske described New England as "one vast mutual insurance company against the government." [49] Fiske, however, still believed that a majority of Connecticut's citizens supported the war effort. "They still cherish the Union and the Constitution. They still desire the overthrow of Davis and his whole rebellious dynasty, but they hadn't figured on the cost of educating warriors." [50]

Fiske's observation was an accurate one. In such a disorderly society as Connecticut's, the tensions of civil war were bound to strain the moral and material resources of the people. Even that lofty patriot Horace Bushnell was shaken at the terrible casualties in the Wilderness campaign. Writing Dr. Bartol after the battle of Spotsylvania Court House, he said, "what terrible throes this new campaign of Grant's is costing us! I do not feel discouraged because of the way, but it is a dreadfully hard way." [51]

Soldiers were called upon to stiffen sagging home-front morale with their votes in the spring elections of 1863 and 1864 and in the Presidential election of 1864. In all three elections they supported overwhelmingly the state and national Republican administrations. But most Connecticut soldiers remained critical of the extremist groups that developed rapidly as civilian morale declined. The radicals in the Republican party, though acknowledged to be patriotic, were suspected of irresponsible actions. Soldiers were particularly irritated at the excesses of the radical press. As early as August 1862 the *Hartford Press* and the *Bridgeport Standard* were harping on rebel atrocities and calling on the individual soldier to carry fire and sword into the South. This seemed a betrayal of war aims to such individuals as William Lusk, who thought he was fighting for law and order. "We have heard enough of rebel atrocities, masked batteries, guerillas and other lying humbugs," he wrote, ". . . are we alone virtuous and the enemy demons?" [52] Almost exactly a

48. *Hartford Courant* (May 18, 1863).
49. Fiske, *Mr. Dunn Browne*, p. 252.
50. Ibid., p. 253.
51. Cheney, *Bushnell*, p. 482.
52. Lusk, *War Letters*, p. 177.

year later, Captain Fiske attacked the atrocity fabrications in the radical press at home. "There is evil and suffering enough . . . without telling cock and bull stories to inflame the minds of antagonists to retaliation barbarities," he said. Fiske was also irritated at radical xenophobia, especially its constant anti-English campaign. "We have some few things to complain of as towards the English government," Fiske wrote in the *Springfield Republican;* "but the English people, on the whole have always been on our side and more and more as they have better understood the principles at issue in the contest." If, at times, Fiske was hard on the radicals, he reserved his most pointed criticism for the Copperheads. In his opinion they were far worse than the Southern enemy, who at least were fighting for a cause. "Others sacrifice for their country; he [the Copperhead] sacrifices his country," was Fiske's caustic description of Thomas H. Seymour and his following in 1863.[53] E. P. Nettleton, writing to Cyrus Northrup from the Army of the Potomac, claimed that Connecticut soldiers may have been divided on war aims and politics, but that all detested the Peace Democrats. "Not everyone," said Nettleton, "is a Republican or an anti-slavery man, or a lover of the present administration . . . there are those who call Africans apes—who feel above dying on the same day with a Negro—who would not associate with him in dividing the chances of a Confederate bullet . . . but there is not *one* who does not hold the Copperhead Peace Party, especially of New England, in utter loathing and contempt." [54]

Though most of the soldiers and many of the state's political and religious leaders held to a moderate course, the radical movement made steady progress during the last year of the war. By 1864 Buckingham and two of the three Republican congressmen had gone over. Senator Dixon thus far had managed to fend off the radicals, but he was under heavy attack. He would lose effective control of the state Republican organization in 1865. The *Hartford Courant* was the only influential Republican paper that was still supporting Lincoln's reconstruction plans. Warner and Hawley were abusing the President in their private correspondence and hatching schemes to curtail Dixon's patronage power. Gideon

53. Fiske, p. 261.

54. Firkins, *Cyrus Northrop,* pp. 198–99.

Welles had remained aloof from the contest, but his chief clerk in the Navy Department, William Faxon, was secretly in league with the radicals. Senator Foster was wavering between the two courses. Besides Dixon, only Congressman Henry Deming of Hartford was backing the Administration. It seems evident that the butchery of the Wilderness campaign propelled a majority of the Republicans into the radical ranks.

In January 1865 the *New Englander* carried a long article by Colonel William M. Grosvenor (DeForest's wine-drinking friend of New Orleans days) that frankly espoused radical war aims. Citing the right of conquest, Grosvenor boldly demanded that the postwar South be treated as a conquered province. He was unconcerned with the Unionist argument that the Southern states had never left the Union because secession was illegal. In his opinion they were merely phantoms. Grosvenor followed Charles Sumner's logic that states were not physical entities but creatures of law. "From the moment a state puts itself in arms against the supreme law, it ceases to have legal existence," he argued. "The state has committed suicide." [55] State rights and civil rights for all Southerners were to be banned by "untrammelled territorial sovereignty." Grosvenor would make no distinction between the Unionist minority and the rebellious majority. Since the majority ruled the rebellion, the innocent must suffer with the guilty. That such a staid magazine as the *New Englander* would feature Grosvenor's article indicated a strong radical drift among the prestigious Congregational clergy.

In its May 1865 issue the *New Englander* found in the assassination of Lincoln further evidence of Southern intransigence that called for radical measures. Reverend S. W. S. Dutton of New Haven expressed the opinion of its editors when he demanded the speedy trial and execution of Jefferson Davis, members of the Confederate cabinet, and leading Confederate generals. At the same time, a radical Republican majority in the state legislature passed the necessary legislation to present a Negro suffrage constitutional amendment for public ratification. To their utmost chagrin, however, white supremacy was still strong enough in the state to defeat the amendment at the polls. Though a majority of the people rati-

55. William M. Grosvenor, "The Law of Conquest, the True Basis for Reconstruction," *New Englander*, 24 (1865), 123.

fied the 13th Amendment to the Federal Constitution outlawing slavery and seemed to acquiesce in harsh terms toward the defeated South, they would still not admit the equality of the races.

Despite the confusing nature of the Civil War, its perplexing political and constitutional problems, and its racial ambiguities and nationalist overtones, war aims were remarkably consistent. Political extremists, though active and vocal, were never quite strong enough to interfere seriously with individual rights. War weariness was, of course, a constant threat to a social order that had not as yet established firm control. At first, it manifested itself in the protest movement of the Peace Democrats; but after their defeat in the spring election of 1863 and the Union victory at Gettysburg, any danger of a conservative coup faded away. As the Copperhead menace declined, radicalism gained in the community. Now that it seemed the war would be won, public opinion drifted toward the radical program as the best means of winning it quickly and of winning the peace. The sanguinary contest in the Wilderness convinced a majority that the Union dead must not have died in vain.

Once emancipation had been added to the Union cause, all shades of loyal opinion agreed that the supremacy of the Federal government over the state would be an ultimate result of Union victory. Such a conservative, old state's righter as Gideon Welles had come around to this point of view. "Persistence is as essential as courage," he jotted down on a piece of notepaper in 1864, "and a wise exercise of both may ensure for our country a firmer government and a more glorious Union." [56] In more colorful language Horace Bushnell expressed much the same idea in honor of Yale alumni who had died in the war. To Bushnell the war had been the blood sacrifice demanded before any nation achieved its maturity. "We had not bled enough," he said, "to merge our colonial distinctions and let out the state-rights doctrine, and make us a proper nation. And so what argument could not accomplish, sacrifice has achieved." [57]

56. Welles Papers, 1864 (HL).
57. Cheney, *Bushnell*, p. 486.

11. DISLOYAL OPPOSITION

WAR always places a heavy strain on democratic institutions, but a civil war imposes additional tensions of a unique nature. There is the problem of the war itself and there is the problem of rebellion, which makes it doubly hard for the average citizen to perceive the fine gossamer between loyalty and disloyalty. This was the case with the American Civil War. Neither government was firmly entrenched at home, and their publics had long traditions of individual rights and liberties that were potential hindrances to their respective war efforts. Both the Union and the Confederacy were presumably dedicated to the same democratic process; both announced that they were fighting for freedom as well as for the integrity of their countries. Thus each side found itself involved almost immediately in what seemed a basic contradiction, troublesome enough when fighting a foreign enemy, painfully perplexing when fighting one's own countrymen. How does a government wage war without curtailing freedom of dissent? And if dissent is suppressed, what then becomes of the cause of freedom? Senator Lyman Trumbull of Illinois stated the problem accurately when he replied to James Dixon, who had been defending the government's policy of arbitrary arrest during the fall of 1861. "I thought the Senator from Connecticut was engaged in a war to defend and uphold the Constitution," said Trumbull. "What sir," he asked, "becomes of Constitutional liberty, what are we fighting for, if this broad ground is to be assumed and to be justified in this body, and any man is to be thanked for assuming an unconstitutional and unwarranted authority?" [1]

Fortunately for the Civil War propagandists, geography was a powerful ally, the Confederacy being largely sovereign in the South and the Federal government sovereign in the North. These facts of

1. *Congressional Globe,* 1, 37th Congress, 2d Sess., 1861, 91.

physical territory enabled the Lincoln Administration to proclaim a war for national integrity, and the Davis Administration a war of defense against actual aggression across territorial lines—legitimate, tangible aims for a majority of the people North and South. Of the two opposing war aims, that of the North rested more precariously on the abstract concept of the Union. After all, Northern armies *were* operating in the Southern heartland, while only briefly did Confederate armies menace the North, and then only its borders, never its heartland. It was easier for Davis to justify war for the defense of Southern homes than it was for Lincoln to appeal to national self-interest. Lincoln never could be sure that the rebellion would not leap over its physical boundaries and either develop into a social war of citizen against citizen in the North, or force his government to sue for peace. That possible rebellion in the North had little basis in actual fact should not blind us to the genuine concern it must have caused Lincoln, especially after heavy Union defeats, when half of the Army of the Potomac were armed stragglers, or during the summer of 1863, when draft riots engulfed New York City.

One of Lincoln's dilemmas was that, at least on the surface, the sectional conflict had started as a political division. Many inveterate Democrats in the North looked upon the war as a partisan adventure foisted on the people by Abolitionists and "Black Republicans." This charge seemed plausible enough to raise lingering doubts among the public during periods of serious military reverses. A second dilemma was that much of the opposition was based on honest convictions that had enjoyed a long and respectable heritage. Was a Democrat, for instance, to be arrested if he differed from a Republican on interpretations of the Constitution? To differ on the meaning of the Constitution had been a hallowed privilege, almost a divine right, of the American citizen since the founding of the Republic.

What of emancipation? To be sure, all Peace Democrats were more or less obtuse on the moral aspects of slavery, and of course they shared the white supremacy attitudes of most Northerners. Many, indeed, hated the free Negro, a prejudice which ranged from the hostility of the poor Irish immigrant to the proslavery bias of the rich, southern-market-oriented conservative. Was the Peace

Democrat to be seized if he publicly opposed the President's policy of emancipation, when a majority of loyalists were ambivalent on the status of the Negro? Peace Democrats were fanatical worshipers of individualism, another common American trait. Were they to be arrested and denied civil rights because they spoke out for individual freedom and against arbitrary coercion of free men? Yet there was no escaping the fact that a war had to be won and a rebellion crushed. The government not only had to protect itself but had to adopt measures for the successful prosecution of its endeavors. The third dilemma, then, involved the delicate question of control. The Civil War had raised unique problems, involving cherished American beliefs and common aspirations on both sides. If the President believed in free institutions, and he pre-eminently did, he had to understand the nature of the disloyal opposition and not act with undue severity as many of the radicals were demanding. The future interests of democratic institutions would not be served by drumhead courts-martial and the imprisonment without due process of thousands of indiscreet political opponents.

Lincoln was probably too lenient in his tolerance of disloyalty, considering the crucial nature of the conflict. In Connecticut, at any rate, the Peace Democrats acted out the role of disloyal opposition with little or no interference from the Federal government. Their opposition to the war ranged from the extremes of outright treason to carefully constructed criticism of Administration measures. Examples of overt acts were rare and easily dealt with. Far more serious were the subtle innuendoes, the seemingly reasonable criticisms of the government that were so difficult to control without resort to arbitrary acts. Peace, of course, was the consistent aim of the disloyal opposition, or the Copperheads, as the Peace Democrats were called. All the arguments against blundering generals, war profiteers, arbitrary acts, and conscription of citizens were bent to this common purpose. Political action quickly became the accepted means of agitation early in the conflict; but "spontaneous" peace meetings were also organized and peace flags displayed. Such agitation followed closely the ebb and flow of Union success. Thus it achieved maximum impact on public morale. Unwittingly, the Copperheads, by their constant criticism of the war, strengthened the hand of their bitter political enemies, the radicals. For the war-weary, badgered, bewildered public tended to be drawn toward the fancied security of extremist measures.

If the Connecticut radical seemed to be giving hostages to the future, the Copperhead seemed to be a prisoner of the past. An archconservative, a localist, a strict construction cultist, the status quo in his opinion far outweighed any mystical concept of a powerful, free, imperial nation. The Copperhead's capacity for growth, for reform, for moral compassion ran smoothly along traditional grooves. Like his leader, Thomas Hart Seymour, the Copperhead was always storming Chapultepecs of centralism with his gallant Southern comrades-in-arms.

Seymour could never forget the blood-brotherhood of the Mexican War—the courtesy, the courage, the easy affability of the young Southern-born American officer. It had been the one great experience of his life. That young Americans should kill each other for what he regarded as abolitionists and political opportunists was a personal and a public tragedy to Seymour. The past also dominated the attitude and the pens of the two chief Copperhead editors in the state, Alfred E. Burr of the *Hartford Times* and Minott Osborne of the *New Haven Register*. Both had achieved local fame and fortune and personal adventure in the party battles of Jackson's day. Comfortable, distinguished members of their communities, they had found in the old Democratic party a career and a livelihood. They would oppose the war on political grounds just as their old Whig rivals had opposed the Mexican War. Peace and the Democratic party "as it was" would in their opinion soon restore the grand old Federal Union of the past. William Wallace Eaton, the fourth member of the Copperhead establishment, was another devotee of the past. A constitution worshiper of the state-rights school, Eaton resembled his passionate Scottish namesake in his penchant for lost causes. Utterly sincere in his convictions, he was the best trial lawyer in the state and a master of persuasive argument; but his resistance to change was matched only by his steadfast devotion to party regularity. These, then, were the leading Connecticut opponents of the war. Men of ability, community leaders, they refused to adapt themselves to new conditions, and were completely unyielding in their political views. On their determination to restore the past as they knew it, the Copperheads risked their reputations, their wealth, even their personal freedom. Brave, bitter reactionaries, they were loyal to a polity that no longer existed. Quite obviously, such men were as ignorant of Southern intentions as they were of Northern ones. In a very real sense they had become aliens in their own land.

Except for a handful of fanatics, most Breckenridge supporters before Sumter clung to the myth that secession was a legitimate political reaction to the political excesses of the Republicans. Even after the Confederacy was an accomplished fact, they hoped for a reunion of conservative Democrats North and South that would solate the Republicans and frustrate their alleged warlike aims. Typical of this confused state of mind was an incredible solution offered a few weeks before Sumter by Norman Brigham of Mansield, one of the leading conservative Democrats of Tolland County. Brigham regarded the Northern states as the real secessionists because they had deprived the South of its constitutional rights. If all the border states joined the Confederacy, Brigham decided that the Lincoln Administration would have to drop its coercive posture; for "it would be the height of folly for a minority to undertake to whip a majority." The Confederacy should then adopt the Federal Constitution and the American flag, and call itself the rightful government "de facto" of the United States. According to Brigham, conservative Democrats in the North would organize politically on a reunion basis. "And then," he declared, "let the northern ectional states, who now stand as nullifiers of the Constitution, come in as fast as they reject their platform and return to the Constitution, and give bonds for keeping the peace in the future." [2]

The attack on Fort Sumter shocked conservative Democrats, and the wave of national spirit that followed stunned them temporarly. Yet there had been enough prior evidences of pro-Confederacy entiment in Connecticut for the Davis government to be intersted in fostering it. Thomas Yeatman, for instance, a transplanted outherner who had lived in New Haven for six years, wrote Jefferon Davis on April 10, 1861, offering to raise locally two companies f volunteers for the Confederacy. "From present indications," said

2. Brigham to Charles Spencer, March 7, 1861, in *South Carolina Watchman* (March 2, 1862).

Yeatman, "war seems resolved upon. If this dread contingency should arise, I can, without the slightest difficulty, raise and equip from this city [New Haven] two companies of 100 men each to serve under your command, every man a Democrat upon whom you can rely." [3] Davis referred Yeatman's letter to the Confederate War Department. On April 18 J. J. Hooper, a War Department clerk, replied for the Confederate President, accepting Yeatman's offer and asking that he and his associates keep themselves in readiness for instructions.[4] No further record exists regarding Yeatman's activities. Probably he was unable to recruit any Confederate soldiers in Connecticut. But the fact that a well-connected New Haven lawyer (he was a Yale graduate and a stepson of John Bell) should have claimed that 200 New Haven Democrats were ready to fight for the South must have had something to do with the sending of Parker French, one of the Confederacy's top secret agents, to the state during the late summer of 1861.

French was a man of great personal charm and daring. He had been one of William Walker's chief lieutenants in the ill-fated Nicaraguan filibustering venture.[5] During the late fifties French had been active in such clandestine Southern nationalist societies as the Knights of the Golden Circle and the Order of the White Camelia. His Connecticut mission was to organize lodges of the Knights of the Golden Circle, which would act as secret pro-Confederate organizations. French made his way north without difficulty, and for six weeks he operated with considerable success, principally in New Haven and Fairfield counties. State and Federal authorities became aware of French when Bridgeport Unionists discovered a Golden Circle lodge in their city. Without waiting for the authorities, the Unionists took the law into their own hands. On the lodge's meeting night, July 29, 1861, they illuminated the doorway of its hall, drummed out the participants, and identified fifty frightened members. Unionists seized also a quantity of incriminating literature on the premises.[6] Federal marshals finally tracked down

3. *OR*, Ser. I, *4*, 216.

4. Ibid., p. 225.

5. *New Haven Palladium* (Nov. 13, 1861).

6. Samuel Orcutt, *A History of the Old Town of Stratford and the City of Bridgeport, Connecticut*, 2 (New Haven, 1886), 819–20.

French in the village of Branford, near New Haven. He was found to possess a record of his activities, the constitution and bylaws of the Knights, and authority from the Confederate government to organize subordinate lodges. United States Marshal David Carr, fearing that a rescue attempt might be made by French's Connecticut friends, dared not risk a trial before the United States District Court in New Haven.[7] He was hurried off to Fort Warren, where he was confined for the duration of the war.

Meanwhile, the General Assembly had taken a direct hand in discouraging subversive activity. In the May session of 1861 a stringent espionage act was passed that provided for a thousand dollar fine and from three to seven years' imprisonment for "direct or indirect written or verbal contact with a rebel, any selling or transport of war goods." [8] In addition, self-appointed Unionist "prudential committees" worked closely with both state and Federal authorities to ferret out enemy agents or those suspected of treasonable conduct.[9] The operations of these legal and extralegal Union agents and the arrest of French effectively smashed the Knights' organization. No other organized pro-Confederate conspiracy was attempted in the state. But the Democratic-sponsored peace movement of 1861, potentially more dangerous than any Confederate fifth column, raised unique problems of control. At first, neither state nor Federal government was prepared to cope with citizens exercising their constitutional right of dissent.

The conservative Democrats had found their voice after the first Bull Run disaster. The *Hartford Times* and the *New Haven Register* suggested that since the Confederacy had put a large army in the field and won a victory, it had proved that it was a viable state, not just an outlaw band. The Davis government had exercised the right of revolution and had vindicated this right by the only possible test, the success of its army. Both papers emphasized the bleakness of the future if the war continued. Immense armies would have to be formed, billions of dollars spent, thousands of lives lost, and probably in the end the Confederacy would have to be recognized. All the horrors of internecine war were presented to their

7. *New Haven Palladium* (Nov. 13, 1861).
8. *Connecticut Acts, 1861*, Chap. 69.
9. *Hartford Courant* (April 30, 1861).

readers: it was unnatural fratricide; it was un-Christian, un-American. However, the *Times* and *Register*, while urging peace, exercised considerable restraint in their attacks on the national administration. Not so the *Bridgeport Farmer*, whose editors, Pomeroy and Morse, filled its columns with scurrilous abuse of Lincoln and Buckingham, and quoted with approval long excerpts from such rabid Confederate papers as the *Charleston Mercury* and the *Richmond Enquirer*.

Besides the press, conservative Democrats found another forum in the Connecticut legislature. On the last day of the May session Thomas H. Seymour, who represented Hartford in the House, offered a series of peace resolutions. These were voted down by the Republican majority, but sixteen members supported Seymour and signed the resolutions, which were published by the conservative Democratic press.[10] In addition, they were reprinted in leaflet form and distributed throughout the state. The Seymour resolutions were the signal for conservative Democrats to organize peace meetings in as many country towns as possible. During August at least thirty of these were held. It was inevitable that some violence would develop between the Peace Democrats and local Union prudential committees. At first, the Peace Democrats were careful about their attacks on the government. William W. Eaton, who addressed the most successful gathering at Bloomfield, a town near Hartford, confined himself to the hateful effects of civil war and merely called for a national convention along the lines of the Crittenden Compromise.[11] As the campaign gained momentum, however, several out-of-state agitators appeared. Criticism of the war took on a bolder, more denunciatory tone; while at the same time prudential committees stepped up their activities. On August 16 Joseph R. Hawley, who had just completed his three months' service in the Army, led a group of discharged veterans and loyal citizens to break up a Saybrook peace meeting. A white peace flag that was flying above the Stars and Stripes on a homemade flag pole in front of Saybrook's Congregational church was hauled down. The only disturbance that occurred was a tug of war for possession of

10. *Hartford Times* (July 8, 1861).
11. Ibid. (Aug. 7, 1861).

the flag between the opposing factions, during which a local Peace Democrat was manhandled by a three-months veteran.[12]

Everyone expected that sooner or later a serious clash would occur. Hotheads on both sides started carrying arms. Finally, on August 24, three riots flared up in Fairfield County. The first disturbance on that notable Saturday occurred in the town of New Fairfield. Several hundred peace men had hoisted a peace flag and were listening to an antiwar harangue when forty Unionists arrived on the scene determined to break up the meeting. Though no shots were fired, shovels, pickaxes, and stones were used as weapons. The peace men successfully defended themselves and their flag, though not before two of their number and three Union men were hurt seriously.

While Peace Democrats and Union men were rioting in New Fairfield, a disturbance that would have much more serious results was in process at Stepney, a town ten miles north of Bridgeport. At least a thousand Bridgeport loyalists headed by P. T. Barnum and two companies of discharged three-months men surrounded a smaller number of Peace Democrats assembled on the Stepney green. Some of the more belligerent peace men drew their revolvers and threatened the portly showman as he descended from his carriage. Undaunted, Barnum warned them of the consequences if shots were fired. For a few minutes the situation was tense indeed, but cooler tempers prevailed and the would-be defenders surrendered their weapons. The peace flag was then torn down and the Stars and Stripes run up to the peak of the makeshift flag pole. Barnum and Elias Howe, Jr., the sewing machine heir, made patriotic speeches that should have terminated the proceedings. But the Union men had been aroused to a high pitch of excitement. On the way back to town, several of the veterans suggested an attack on the *Bridgeport Farmer* office. Barnum and Howe pointed out that this would be an act of mob violence and exacted a promise of orderly conduct. As the Union procession straggled into Bridgeport, it was greeted by throngs of cheering citizens who had heard about the success of the raid. That night an impromptu Union mass meeting developed in the center of the city. Speeches, patriotic

12. Newton C. Brainerd, "The Saybrook Peace Flag," *CHS Bulletin*, 27 (1961), 8–9.

songs, and bonfires soon attracted a crowd estimated at 8,000, which completely blocked Main and Wall streets. One of the speakers, carried away by the response of the crowd to his spread-eagle eloquence, closed his remarks with the injunction "To the *Farmer* office." This was instantly repeated by a thousand excited listeners. Mob psychology took over and within minutes the frenzied crowd had completely gutted the *Farmer* office. Presses were smashed, type and paper were thrown into the street, even desks and chairs were reduced to kindling wood. Co-editor Morse barely escaped with his life when he fled over the roof to an adjoining building, just as the mob was breaking down the front door.[13]

Responsible citizens were shocked at the increasing tempo of mob violence. Every Republican paper in the state, including the *Hartford Press,* condemned the destruction of the *Farmer*. The *Hartford Courant* asserted that illegal destruction of property was harmful to a just cause. "The strength of Union feeling in our midst," it noted, "is such that secessionists can be put down legally and more effectively in a quiet way than by such proceedings as those of the volunteers in Bridgeport." [14] Though the press unanimously condemned mob action, the *Farmer* had few defenders in the state. Even the *Hartford Times* thought that its editorial policy had been most indiscreet. "We are frank to say that we regretted to see that tone [bitterness of spirit] in the columns of the *Farmer* —it was calculated to irritate the public mind," commented Alfred Burr, editor of the *Times*.[15]

The *Farmer* affair alerted both state and Federal governments to the potential danger of widespread civil disorder. On August 28 William H. Seward telegraphed United States Marshal Westell Russell from Auburn, New York, ordering him to arrest Ellis Schnable, a Pennsylvania agitator, who had been the principal speaker at Connecticut peace meetings for the past month. The subversive Schnable was arrested by a Litchfield County deputy sheriff at the

13. Morse fled to Canada and eventually turned up in Augusta, Georgia, where he edited a paper until it was closed by General Sherman upon his capture of the city in late 1864. Pomeroy remained in seclusion for almost a year. In the fall of 1862 he resumed publication of the *Farmer,* though carefully refraining from any but the mildest criticism of war policy. Lane, *History of Connecticut,* p. 180.

14. *Hartford Courant* (Aug. 26, 1861).

15. *Hartford Times* (Aug. 26, 1861).

Harlem Railroad Station near Morris, three hours after Russell had received Seward's telegram. The following day he was delivered to Colonel Berry, commandant of Fort Lafayette, and confined for the duration of the war.[16] Two days later Henry L. Reynolds, another prominent peace advocate, was arrested and followed Schnable to Fort Lafayette. Reynolds' arrest proved to be an important one. His luggage contained correspondence with the Confederate government and implicated other peace-meeting agitators and organizers in the state.[17] These were promptly apprehended under the authority of Secretary Seward.[18]

Meanwhile, Governor Buckingham clarified the issue for the citizens of the state. On September 1, 1861, he issued a proclamation which reminded the public of the difference between liberty and license. "The Constitution," declared the Governor, "guarantees liberty of speech and of the press, but holds the person and the press responsible for the evils which result from this liberty; it guarantees the protection of property, but regards no property as sound which is used to subvert governmental authority; it guarantees the person from unreasonable seizure, but it protects no individual from arrest and punishment who gives aid and comfort to the enemies of our country." Buckingham ended his proclamation by calling upon all law officers of the state to proceed vigorously against anyone who disturbed the public peace or engaged in sedition or treason.[19]

Such forthright displays of government intention and action put an end to the organized peace movement in Connecticut. It had been a dangerous interlude for the land of steady habits when mob violence threatened to plunge the community into chaos. Yet the peace movement had not been without some beneficial effects. Internal disorder was feared as much by the property-minded, conservative Democrat as by the most ardent Unionist. After "foreign" agitators like Schnable came into the state, Democratic leader William W. Eaton refused to share the same platforms with them. In fact, Eaton privately advised Schnable to leave the state several weeks before his eventual arrest. The *Farmer* episode had, likewise,

16. *Hartford Courant* (Aug. 30, 1861).
17. *Norwich Bulletin* (Aug. 31, 1861).
18. *Hartford Courant* (Sept. 3, 1861).
19. Croffut and Morris, *History of Connecticut*, pp. 109–10.

proved a sobering experience to the conservative press. Democratic leaders had not, in any respect, modified their stand on the war, but they would never countenance anarchy within the state. Henceforth, they would register their opposition through the ballot box, and would be more careful about public opinion in the future. They had, in short, recognized that there was a limit beyond which disloyal opposition could not venture. The agencies of the government also discovered that prompt and vigorous action with respect to internal subversion would be supported by public opinion. As Senator James Dixon had remarked in his defense of the Lincoln Administration's policy of arbitrary arrest during the late summer of 1861, "It was precisely the right time; and it nipped treason in Connecticut in the bud." [20]

For a time during the spring and summer of 1862 conservative Democrats acted as if they were the loyal opposition. James C. Loomis, their candidate for governor, when accused of having supported secession, denied the charge emphatically. Secession in his opinion was "unlawful and justifiable, without right of equity," and the Confederacy was "a rebellion against the best government ever devised by man." [21] Though again defeated at the polls, some leading Democrats cooperated in the great Union recruitment drive of July 1862. This apparent change in attitude toward the war inspired the *Hartford Courant* to suggest Thomas H. Seymour as the commanding officer of one of the new regiments. The *Courant* soon discovered, however, that Seymour had not changed his opinions. The Hartford Peace Democrat had been elected, along with Alfred Burr, as one of the many vice-presidents of the great Union mass meeting that was held in Hartford on July 11, 1862. Seymour repudiated the honor with scorn and indignation. In a letter to the *Times* he wrote, "The monstrous fallacy of the present day, that the Union can be re-established by destroying any part of the south is one which will burst with the shells that are thrown into its defenseless cities . . . a spectacle for the reproach or the commiseration of the civilized world." [22]

When Seymour rejected cooperation, the brief ascendancy of

20. *Congressional Globe*, 1, 37th Congress, 2d Sess., 1861, 90.
21. Lloyd W. Fowler, "No Backward Step," *CHS Bulletin*, 27 (1961), 6–7.
22. *Hartford Times* (July 13, 1862).

moderate Peace Democrats like Loomis or William J. Hammersly had run its course. Apparently they had staked all on a McClellan victory and the restoration of the Union on approximately the same terms as the old Crittenden Compromise. Four massive hammer blows had wrecked their position and delivered the party into the hands of Seymour extremists. These same blows shook the moderate Republicans, too, but with the full support of the Lincoln Administration they managed to continue their party control for another eighteen months. First, McClellan's Peninsular campaign collapsed in bloody defeat; then John Pope was badly beaten at Second Bull Run. Third, McClellan's drawn battle at Antietam shocked the Connecticut public with its frightful casualties among Connecticut regiments. These military actions convinced many moderate Democrats that the Confederacy would never be subjugated except at a price that would ruin the entire nation. When Lincoln followed up the Antietam battle with his preliminary Emancipation Proclamation, it was the hardest blow of all. To their way of thinking, all hope of a negotiated settlement on the old basis was now impossible, and all hope of a quick Union victory had been likewise liquidated at the stroke of a pen. If the Union Army had been unable to defeat the Army of Virginia before emancipation, how would it ever be able to win now that the North was determined to destroy the social system of the South? Moreover, property-minded Connecticut reactionaries and constitution cultists were shaken to their very depths by what they considered to be the dangerous implications of emancipation. The incredible military disaster at Fredericksburg lent further impetus to political extremism. In such a climate of opinion Seymour had no difficulty in reasserting both his political leadership and his peace objectives. As 1863 began, a distinct resurgence of disloyal opposition was underway in Connecticut. At the same time, the radical program was claiming more and more converts from the moderate Union majority.

With morale at a low ebb among Administration supporters, Buckingham and the entire state ticket were renominated by a poorly attended Republican convention on January 21, 1863.[23] Two weeks earlier an even smaller Union convention had also re-

23. Lane, *Connecticut*, p. 220.

nominated him.[24] If the Republicans were apathetic, the Democrats by contrast were spirited. Sensing victory for the first time in nine years, they flung discretion to the winds and nominated Thomas H. Seymour for governor. Obedient to the wishes of the extremists, the convention adopted an uncompromising peace plank [25] that reflected such truculent attitudes as that of Dr. David Crary, a prominent Hartford Democrat. In making out a birth certificate for a child of a Connecticut soldier, Crary had inserted the following language: "Father—Leverett B. Owen, North Main Street. Occupation—Off South murdering as many of our brethren there as possible." [26]

The campaign that followed was long and bitter. Seymour supporters took their cue from the anti-Administration diatribes of the former Ohio Congressman Clement L. Vallandigham. The entire Democratic plan of attack shifted from the milder course of hammering on the arbitrary exercise of powers over citizens by Lincoln to a demand for peace at any price. As if to vie with Democratic ferocity, perhaps frightened of it, the Republicans countered with threats of Federal intervention should Seymour and Eaton's program be carried into practice upon a Democratic victory.[27] Politically, the Republicans had to contend with the Congressional Conscription Act of March 3.[28] To conservatives this was anathema, an unwarranted invasion of state rights; to many others its frank recognition of substitutes seemed undemocratic.[29] Seymour declared vehemently that if elected he would not enforce the draft. And when Lincoln suspended the writ of habeas corpus for any citizen seeking to avoid compulsory military duty, the Hartford Democrat declared that "if the ballot should fail to correct such enormities and preserve [individual] liberties, they [the Democrats] might be driven to look for some other remedy." [30] Ardent Democrat James Gallagher, running for re-election to the House from New Haven, was asked by a heckler what he would do about the

24. Ibid., pp. 222–23.
25. Ibid.
26. *Hartford Courant* (March 4, 1863).
27. Lane, p. 237.
28. Ibid., p. 230.
29. *Hartford Press* (July 12, 1863).
30. Firkins, *Cyrus Northrop*, p. 197.

Federal officers who would come into the state to conduct the draft. "Kill 'em, damn 'em," was Gallagher's reply.[31] But Democratic attacks did not center entirely upon national affairs. The state administration was not spared. It was accused of excessive, if not slavish, devotion to the Federal government, of mismanagement, and of general inefficiency.[32] The Republicans were quite vulnerable, though well organized, with a network of Federal appointees to support them and a host of able campaigners. With political control over the Connecticut regiments, they counted heavily upon the votes of soldiers especially furloughed for the election.[33] Against these positive sources of strength, the Democrats could count on some disaffected conservatives, but their most powerful weapon was war weariness in the state. They hoped this would bring out a large percentage of party members or sympathizers who had not voted in 1862.[34]

As the campaign wore on, however, the Republicans shifted their fire with unerring accuracy to the weakest point in the Democratic line, the name and reputation of the party's leader, Thomas H. Seymour. That Seymour was a brave man, a fighter who commanded respect, no one could deny; that he was perfectly sincere in his wholehearted opposition to the war, though not admitted publicly by the Republicans, was doubtlessly entertained in private; that he was flagrantly indiscreet in his utterances and writing, and tauntingly cynical about war aims, made him hated, feared, and easily assailable. After a month of campaigning, the Democrats sensed the mistake they had made in nominating him. Many moderates who held the balance of power might have voted for a less violent and controversial figure; few would vote for Seymour.[35]

The result of the election, however, was an uncomfortably close victory for Buckingham, under 3,000 votes.[36] In the Congressional election, the Democrats elected only James E. English from the New Haven district, giving the Republicans a three-to-one majority in the Connecticut delegation to the House of Representa-

31. Ibid., p. 198.
32. Lane, p. 230.
33. Ibid.
34. Ibid., passim.
35. Ibid.
36. Ibid., p. 236.

tives. Though unable to control either house in the Connecticut legislature, the Democrats cut down Republican majorities, securing a much stronger voice in the affairs of the state. Since they had carried their peace plank into every nomination for the legislature, Buckingham and the Republican majority faced a difficult session. Gideon Welles voiced the predominate Republican dismay and mortification at the tenuous victory when he wrote to Buckingham on April 7, 1863, that it was "a lamentable want of political independence . . . that the party should have secured so large a vote for a candidate whose avowed sympathies are with traitors, and whose platform is devoid of honest patriotism." [37]

The temper of the Democrats became apparent in the opening days of the legislative session; the keen edge of their opposition, if anything, had been sharpened by defeat. William W. Eaton, who had been elected a member of the House from Hartford, introduced immediately resolutions of censure on the arrest of Vallandigham. Happily, the Republicans and Union-Democrats were able by sheer weight and party regularity to overcome Eaton's mastery of debate and parliamentary tactics; but not before he had used the House as a forum for his views, and subjected to a searching analysis the measures of Lincoln's Administration on the national level and Buckingham's on the state. There was not a man on the Republican side who could match Eaton's eloquence or logic.[38] At one time during the extended debate the Democrats substituted Jefferson's Kentucky Resolution, changing one or two words for the sake of conformity to the situation. When this was denounced and voted down by the Republicans, the *Register* and *Times* drew a number of conclusions definitely embarrassing to the Republicans. Though finally defeated, the Democrats drained all possible publicity from the Vallandigham debate. Scarcely had the orations on this subject ceased to draw visitors to the Hartford State House when new and broader fields were opened up for opposition talents.

A Federal draft overseen by Federal officers was announced if the latest volunteer recruiting drive failed to fulfill quotas. Following this declaration, it was voiced in the legislature that the Buckingham Administration would make another attempt to adopt coercive

37. Welles to Buckingham, April 7, 1863 (Buckingham Papers, CSL).

38. Lane, p. 240.

features for a sound militia.[39] The Democrats could not stop a Federal draft; but they could wreck a militia draft by using their strength in the legislature to postpone it until it fell victim to the end-of-the-season rush. With approximately three-eighths of the lower house (94 members out of 234) and one-half of the Senate (7 out of 14) under their firm control, they were in a good strategic position.[40] Captained by superior men who were constantly on the alert to exploit weakness, the Democrats also possessed a secret ally in the influential speaker of the House, a conservative Republican and former governor, Chauncey F. Cleveland. Earnest debate did not begin until July 11, at a time when farmer members were worrying about harvest and August drought. The legislature was sweltering in the humid heat of Hartford. Protraction of argument would inevitably sap the resolution of the Republican rank and file, and the courage and discipline of their leaders. On the first day of debate William W. Eaton was ready with some crucial amendments to the reported militia bill, which were aimed at driving a wedge between the conservative and radical Republicans.[41] The first was an amendment to restrain the Governor from handing the militia over to the Federal government for a period longer than thirty days.[42] Practically, this meant, if adopted, refusal to allow active militia troops to the central government, since mobilization and transport would have consumed the entire allotted period. On the face of it, Eaton's proposal did pay lip service to the acknowledged responsibility of state militia forces to support the government.[43] Federal courts would have had difficulty construing it as unconstitutional. However, conservatives and radicals voting together defeated it.

Eaton had anticipated rebuff, but had risked it as exploratory and therefore expendable. His next amendment had been more carefully planned. It provided that active militiamen ordered into Federal service might purchase substitutes.[44] If any bill might gain conservative support, this one would; yet most radicals, if they

39. *New Haven Register* (May 10, 1863).
40. Lane, p. 236; *Hartford Courant* (April 4, 1863).
41. Ibid. (July 10, 1863).
42. Ibid.
43. Ibid.
44. Ibid.

were true to their oft repeated convictions, could not vote for an obvious class measure that placed the burden of a militia draft squarely upon those who could not afford to hire substitutes. Undoubtedly, the Democrats had noted radical discomfiture at the substitute provision in the Federal Conscription Act. The opposition of Hawley and that of his Hartford radical circle to the hiring of substitutes was well known.[45] At the height of debate, adjournment was called for the evening meal at six; but when the House reassembled two hours later, a surprising move took place.[46] Speaker Cleveland left the chair and entered debate to support the Eaton amendment. He demanded that a loophole be kept in the proposed militia law for those who wished to buy themselves out.[47] To most radicals, Cleveland's stand was apostasy. He had supported Federal supremacy in fundamental political matters, but refused to adopt what the radicals thought were the correct means of achieving it.[48] They immediately attacked the speaker, and the Democrats were treated to an unseemly wrangle among their opponents. Thereafter, it was an easy matter for Eaton to adopt dilatory tactics, enmesh the bill in parliamentary procedure, and finish it off. By July 18 the General Assembly, after the longest session on record, adjourned with no adequate militia law; it had been considered for three regular and two extra sessions with no result.[49] From a political viewpoint the militia debate had helped crack the Republican coalition, starting a fissure that would gradually widen until Cleveland and his followers would bolt the Union party and return to a political allegiance more consonant with their essentially conservative beliefs.

The year 1863 saw the political fortunes of the Democrats reach their zenith: their attacks on the Administration and demands for peace were never more strident, their audiences never larger. Though they shrank from active interference with the Federal draft, a lack of courage which was probably in large measure due to the extraordinary precautions of Governor Buckingham, they made threatening statements and freely predicted a Republican defeat in

45. Hawley Letters to Buckingham, Aug. 4, 1864 (Buckingham Papers).

46. *Hartford Courant* (July 11, 1863).

47. Ibid.

48. Ibid.

49. Ibid.

1864.[50] However, a new wave of public confidence, following the appointment of General Grant to supreme command in Virginia, strengthened Republican leadership. At the same time it contributed to the growth of radical power. Buckingham, renominated in January 1864, had little difficulty in defeating the moderate Democrat Origen S. Seymour. As in past elections, the Republicans were aided immeasurably by the votes of furloughed soldiers. But the time was fast approaching when they would not have to bring the soldiers home to vote. Over the bitter opposition of the Democratic minority, a constitutional amendment permitting absentee soldier voting had been passed at the special session of January 1864.[51] According to the difficult amendment provision of the Connecticut constitution, it had to lay over a session and again be passed by a two-thirds majority of both houses before submission to the people.[52] Thus the amendment was again introduced in the May session of 1864, and a constitutional crisis was precipitated, weakening minority power in the amending procedure.

In the Senate the large Republican majority had no difficulty in securing the necessary two-thirds.[53] But when the question came up in the House, an exact party split revealed that Republicans lacked five votes if total membership was considered.[54] Speaker Rice immediately ruled that the amendment had failed; thereupon, O. H. Platt of Meriden appealed the ruling, and in so doing, revealed the temper of the majority.[55] Platt argued that the amendment procedure requiring a two-thirds vote of both houses could be interpreted as merely those voting, not necessarily the total membership. This opened the question of whether or not a transient majority in the legislature was empowered to add or subtract from the organic law. Unfortunately for the Democrats, the constitution was not explicit on this point, and no such question had ever come up before. The inference was plain, however. If two-thirds of those voting were permitted to propose a constitutional amendment, then

50. Lane, pp. 247–48.

51. *New Haven Register* (Jan. 13, 1864).

52. Constitution of Connecticut, Art. 13, *Connecticut State Register and Manual* (1947).

53. Croffut and Morris, *Connecticut*, p. 631.

54. Ibid.; *New Haven Register* (May 28, 1864).

55. *New Haven Register* (May 29, 1964).

two-thirds of a bare quorum would also suffice. Such an interpretation opened up possible avenues of change in the constitution to those who were bold and resourceful tacticians. Platt's appeal was sustained after a day of argument, and the amendment prevailed.[56]

Since the winter of 1862–63 and the resurgence of Democratic strength, Republican leaders had realized that if they wished continued victory, they must seek other means than appeals to patriotism and the denunciation of Democrats as traitors. It was neither unusual nor implausible that they should turn to such an obvious source of political strength as the volunteer regiments. The governor, as nominal commander-in-chief of the state forces in the field and responsible for commissioning and promoting officers, exerted a decisive influence upon the political affiliations of ambitious commanders. They in turn controlled the political thinking of most of their men in the field. The only foreseeable obstacle was whether a mere legislative enactment would suffice, or whether it would require a constitutional amendment. Members of the legislature at the special session of December 1862 were undecided as to what to do and even debated a resolution asking the judges of the Supreme Court for an advisory opinion before taking action.[57] Fortunately, the legislature saved itself from taking a step which would have proved embarrassing. One member of the House understood the constitutional implications of such an unprecedented procedure when he stated: "that since the adopting of the present constitution there never had been an instance in which the legislature had called upon the judges for their opinion upon a law not yet passed.[58] The people had always kept jealously separate and independent the judicial and legislative departments." [59]

Without testing constitutional propriety, the General Assembly had passed the law and hoped for the best. This did not prevent active efforts to secure a favorable decision from the courts when the Democrats immediately set in motion the machinery for review. The Republicans were in a position to threaten two of the Supreme Court judges, Origen Seymour and Loren Waldo, whom

56. Ibid.

57. *Norwich Courier* (Dec. 18, 1862).

58. Ibid.

59. Ibid.

they suspected of conservative tendencies that would lead to a strict construction of the state constitution. Both judges were to come up for re-election in 1864. Regardless of previous scruples on the independence of the legislature, prominent radical members thought it not inconsistent with the theory of the separation of powers to demand of the doubtful judges a prior opinion favorable to the constitutionality of the soldiers' voting law.[60] Since Seymour and Waldo would not give such advice, it was made plain to them that they could not expect re-election if they sought to nullify the law.[61] Despite Republican threats, both judges refused to be intimidated. When the law came before the Supreme Court (largely through their vote and influence), it was declared unconstitutional.[62] Though a constitutional amendment was passed in the special session of January 1864 and in the May session of 1864, the Republican legislative caucus did not forget its rebuff.[63] Seymour and Waldo were purged, and men of more radical tendencies were appointed in their places.[64] Thus by the exigencies of the moment the independence of the judiciary had been seriously curtailed. Connecticut's highest tribunal had suffered a loss of prestige from embittered Democrats as well as from headstrong Republicans.

Soldiers voting from the field were useful but, unfortunately, temporary expedients to elect a Republican state administration and congressional delegations. Some Republican leaders, who were looking ahead to peacetime and were desperately anxious, even in 1864, to preserve the fruits of victory, knew that once the artificial constraints of army life were removed, many former soldiers would probably return to their former political allegiance. To men who had already broken minority bulwarks in the amendment procedures, the enfranchisement of Connecticut Negroes represented an excellent alternative, a political stake worth fighting for, and one that would appeal to humanitarian interests. The entire adult male Negro population of the state was small, but an accretion of 1,500 votes well distributed and pro-Republican might well be the measure between victory or defeat in the closely fought New Haven

60. *Norwich Aurora* (April 2, 1864).

61. Ibid.

62. *New Haven Register* (May 13, 1864).

63. Croffut and Morris, pp. 629, 631.

64. Ibid.

congressional district, or as an offset to Irish Democrats in the cities of the state. Even with a placid judiciary, the Republicans dared not enfranchise Negroes by law. The radicals saw no way around the explicit suffrage requirements of the state constitution except by amendment. This was going to be more difficult to achieve in the 1864 legislature than the soldier voting amendment had been.

Buckingham and the Republican state ticket had won by an overall majority of 5,658 votes, even though the Democrats had nominated former Judge Origen S. Seymour, an able moderate, as their candidate for governor.[65] In the contests for the legislature, the Republican victory had also been impressive, but not quite impressive enough to shape the constitution to their own partisan ends. With full attendance on both sides, the Republicans would lack three votes in the House for the necessary two-thirds.[66] Furthermore, they were by no means sure of every vote from their Union majority on a question fraught with racial prejudice. Outraged by an earlier highhanded procedure, the Democrats could be expected to utilize every effort to keep their House attendance high. Lastly, a very special problem immediately asserted itself. In 1855 the legislature, dominated by Know-Nothing sentiment, had passed—and the people had accepted—Amendment Nine to the Connecticut constitution, which imposed a stringent literacy requirement on suffrage.[67] This had proved of incalculable value to the Republicans in reducing the Irish Democratic majorities of the cities. How could the Republicans enfranchise enough Negroes to make a difference in the state vote and yet circumvent the provisions of the literacy amendment? Certainly, the Democrats would willingly sacrifice their racial prejudices in the interests of equality of opportunity if the Republicans gained a paltry of 1,500 votes, while they gained three to four times that number. When the amendment motion to omit the word "white" from Article 6, Section 2, came before the House on June 22, the Democrats moved to amend by striking out the so-called "illiteracy clause." As one Democrat put it, "I am for impartial action and would give the franchise to the men, illiterate though they may be, who are fighting the battles of

65. Lane, *Connecticut*, p. 270.

66. *New Haven Register* (April 13, 1864).

67. Connecticut Constitution, Art. 11, *Connecticut State Register and Manual* (1947), p. 54.

our country." The Republicans immediately saw through this scheme, and the amendment passed as originally proposed, by resorting to the same means they had employed on the soldiers' vote amendment—namely, a two-thirds majority of those voting.[68]

While the amendment waited its session, events in the military sphere moved from the bloody stalemate of Grant's army before Richmond to the successes of Sherman further south and the dawning realization by November 1864 that the war was in its last stages. Connecticut gave Lincoln a 2,406 majority over McClellan, to which little significance could be attached.[69] Despite the employment of high bounties and other attractive offers, the near impossibility of securing additional recruits from among the native population indicated that a profound war-weariness still persisted.[70] With the coming of the new year, however, the change in public opinion was electric. Even the most critical Democrats did little but murmur at the ratification of the 13th Amendment. When Congressman Augustus Brandegee of New London, a bit warmed with alcoholic beverages, harangued the Negro waiters at Willard's Hotel in Washington with abolitionist remarks, Democrats merely considered him vulgar.[71] A year earlier they would have excoriated the mildest of pro-Negro sentiments from a responsible public servant. The few months of the war that remained were times of heightening anticipation. Buckingham won his last and greatest victory by again defeating Origen Seymour, this time with a majority of 11,035 votes in a lackluster campaign.[72] The people were too interested in the fact and rumor surrounding the crumbling Confederate government.

In Connecticut, on midnight of Sunday, April 9, the momentous news of peace had to wait and not disturb the rest of the citizens in the "land of steady habits."[73] Promptly at daybreak on Monday, with a cold April rain lacing the windows,[74] bells and cannon heralded the event throughout the state. Not a few of the people as

68. In the House, June 22, 1864. *New Haven Register* (June 23, 1864).

69. Lane, p. 240.

70. *Hartford Courant* (Jan. 15, 17, 1864); "Governor's Annual Message," *PDLC* (1864), pp. 12–15.

71. *Norwich Aurora* (Feb. 11, 1865).

72. Lane, p. 301.

73. *Norwich Aurora* (April 15, 1865).

74. Ibid.

they listened must have recalled a similar storm-lashed April day four years before—the image of all the young men, the pathos and the excitement and the glory, the nightmare from which they were now awakening.

Three years of acrimonious political controversy had left scars which would remain visible for a decade. Though the Democrats, by and large, had refrained from open subversion, their actions had frequently been intemperate, their press abusive, and their obstructionism to Administration manpower policies unceasing. The Knights of the Golden Circle in Connecticut may have been speedily destroyed and the handful of fanatic pro-Southerners confined in Federal prisons for the duration, but the articulate Democrats who had walked the narrow line between bitter partisanship and outright treason were both numerous and harmful to the successful prosecution of the war. Not all Peace Democrats were Copperheads, and not all opposed the war measures of the Lincoln and Buckingham administrations for partisan or pro-Southern reasons. Many were localists, sincere believers in strict constitutional principles. They had disapproved of the war in the beginning, and deplored the wide use of executive powers to continue what they considered a bloody, senseless conflict. Few Connecticut Democrats cared for the Negro, few were moralists. In fact, they were decided adherents of white supremacy, a belief that went with the times and was by no means confined to the Democratic party.

The more intense the disloyal opposition, the more vigorous became its political opposite, the radical movement. Radicals were not disloyal, but they were not altogether loyal either, at least in their constant sabotage of Administration war policy. They may not have damaged public morale in the same way or to the same extent that Peace Democrats had, but they confused the public, irritated the soldiers in the field, and frequently played the opposition's game with their constant clamor, their carping criticism, and their impatience with individual rights. Many moderates, who had not believed the charges of a Democratic-slaveholder conspiracy that were voiced early in the war, must have revised their opinions after reading the legislative record of the Vallandigham debates or reflecting upon Democratic opposition to a strong militia law or to the absentee soldier franchise. As for the radicals, a foretaste of their freehanded methods and lack of constitutional scruples was evident from 1863 to 1865. Between these determined enemies, the moderate Unionists managed to conduct the war effort in Connecticut with a considerable degree of success, but failed to establish a nucleus of vital political thinking that would carry over into the reconstruction era ahead.

Beneath the political ferment was a society of deepening contrasts, both physical and ideological. Restless and ambivalent, it was responding with a kind of impulsive dedication to the dynamics of a wartime environment. The folks at home were in a busy, prosperous, objective mood, in which emphatic individualism was the common denominator for everything except politics.

12. THE FOLKS AT HOME

TO THE AVERAGE CITIZEN who had lived in a wartime environment for four years, it seemed almost unbelievable that peace had come. He had grown so used to casualty lists, blue uniforms, inflation, substitute brokers, bounty jumpers, war profiteers, wretched train service, high prices, and high wages that the war was an integral part of his everyday life. The newspapers, the periodicals, and the books he read, the songs he heard or sang, were all influenced in some way by the great conflict. He had become accustomed to abnormal times, when there was good fortune for some, despair for others. Everyone had lived through a period of constant tension, whether this meant the scanning of casualty lists, the rumors of Confederate naval attacks on Connecticut ports, or the unremitting pressure from the government for more troops, more munitions, more speed in meeting delivery dates on war contract items.

Whatever their calling, their sex, or their status in life, whether among those who had opposed the war or among those who had supported it, the folks at home had been personally involved. No other war in American history had been or conceivably could be so close to the civilian population. In Connecticut, as in other Northern states, it was pre-eminently an individual's war. The men who fought, or who materially aided the war effort, did so from a sense of either personal obligation or personal gain. If they organized themselves, they organized on a voluntary basis. No government apparatus existed to regiment the people in a total war—to ration scarce materials, to establish price controls, to tax excess profits. Even within its appropriate jurisdiction, the government was never adequately equipped to provide what we would regard as essential services for its military arm. This meant that volunteer assistance from the home folks was an important function of the war effort.

Much of wartime social life, therefore, revolved around "soldiers' aid" in its many guises—the furnishing of medical and food supplies, the support of soldiers' families, care of the wounded, burial of the dead.

Such emphatic individualism brought out the best and the worst in the folks at home. Frequently those who profited the most contributed the least, and those who contributed the most profited the least or even suffered for their generosity. Millionaire P. T. Barnum counted himself patriotic by purchasing three substitutes instead of the required one—paltry, to say the least, when compared to the sacrifice made by a soldier's wife and family. In the inflation economy of wartime Connecticut, a volunteer's monthly income could barely sustain his family on a subsistence level. If a soldier husband was killed or incapacitated, there was no insurance, no pension. If he was captured, as thousands were, both state and Federal pay were stopped until he rejoined his regiment. The *Hartford Courant* reported in December 1864 what was undoubtedly an extreme case but one that emphasizes the economic insecurity of the average soldier's family. In this instance a soldier's widow and her two children were found in a Hartford tenement weak from hunger. The family was destitute and had eaten nothing for the past week but "a little meal and a few potatoes." [1] During the winter of 1864–65 an estimated 70 per cent of the charity cases in Connecticut cities were soldiers' families. David Hawley, the city missionary of Hartford, reported that he had aided 359 family groups in that period, of whom 233 were families of soldiers at the front. Most were of native stock—215 families; 54 were Irish; 36, German; 12, English; and 6, French and Scottish.[2] Citizens' mass meetings, fairs, and benefits for soldiers' families did what they could, but private contributions were never enough to make up the difference. Large bounties and substitute fees were paid after 1863. In the curious, uncertain values of wartime Connecticut these went generally not to the best—those brave, patriotic young men who had enlisted for three years—but to the worst—criminals, adventurers, drifters from the city slums. This was not a deliberate policy but an expedient one, a function of the extreme individualism of

1. *Hartford Courant* (Dec. 23, 1864).
2. Ibid. (June 5, 1865).

the times and of unpreparedness and inexperience in organizing massive citizen armies.

As soon as the war began, soldiers' aid societies sprang up all over the state. Staffed principally by women, these volunteer community groups served an important social function from the very beginning. The women enjoyed the gregarious activity of rolling bandages, picking lint, knitting mittens, and packing preserves and other delicacies for the boys in the field. "Who ever imagined," mused F. E. Holcomb, a citizen of Granby, "that *girls*, 'a parcel of young silly girls' could by any means be brought down to anything half so sensible and useful as knitting socks, veritable socks? Great men's socks, heavy coarse and vulgar in the extreme?" [3] In addition to these activities, every Thanksgiving and Christmas, community leaders supervised the preparation, collection, and shipment of tons of holiday food for the volunteer regiments. These, too, were large-scale voluntary endeavors, paid for either in work or in money by private individuals in towns and cities. Early in the war, when the regiments were being raised in the state, camps formed the focal point of community social life. Again the townsfolk supplied many services to the recruits and enjoyed their company, particularly at dress reviews and other military functions. Young ladies of the community also made the regimental colors, which were presented with great fanfare by the Governor or some other important political figure. Later during the war years more ambitious social functions, sanitary fairs, *tableaux vivants*, promenades, benefit plays, and the like were organized for the benefit of the troops.

Another facet of social life during the war years were the hundreds of individual and group missions to the Connecticut regiments. These too were inspired by meaningful, frivolous, or quite simply selfish motives. Among the meaningful missions were those which provided a variety of services—emergency pay for the soldiers, distributing and collecting ballots, transporting provisions from home, caring for the sick and disabled, bringing home the dead. Many citizens, however, went merely for the adventure. Somehow they managed to procure a pass and spend what amounted to a brief vacation in the camps, where they could enjoy military life

3. Ibid. (March 7, 1862).

vicariously. But even vacationers were of positive benefit to the soldiers, who always welcomed news of home. On July 30, 1863, for example, Colonel C. H. Prentice, J. G. Rathbun, J. A. Case, and J. S. Brooks of Hartford paid just such a visit to the 16th at Camp Tennant in Virginia. Lieutenant Blakeslee of the 16th recalled that the troops were happy to see the Hartford junketers "as nearly the entire regiment was acquainted with them." [4] The visitors inspected outposts, played cards, and generally enjoyed themselves. When they were soaked by a sudden downpour, they were temporarily outfitted in uniforms, to the great amusement of the regiment. "Colonel P. was so large and tall," said Blakeslee, "that the soldiers' sizes could not be gotten half on, and therefore with a cap and coat half on and pants that reached a little below the knees and with a huge pair of brogans, he looked so badly that he stayed in the colonel's tent and played euchre all day and night." [5] When the troops were in winter quarters or standing garrison duty, wives and relatives flocked down to see them. Some of the women set up housekeeping in camp. Harriet Hawley spent most of 1862 with her husband at Port Royal, Hilton Head, and Beaufort. Colonel Burnham's mother visited him for several months at the 16th's winter quarters in Virginia during 1863.[6] All of these visits tended to bring the war very close to the home folks. Civilian travelers wrote about their experiences in the press and talked about their adventures sometimes on the platform, more frequently to friends and acquaintances on an informal basis.

Junkets or volunteer war work may have dominated the lighter side of social life, but there were grimmer aspects which brought the folks at home face to face with war in all its ugliness and sorrow. Until the frightful and well-nigh continuous carnage of Grant's Wilderness campaign of 1864, army and government authorities were lenient about permitting civilians to care for their wounded relatives or remove their own dead and bring them home for burial. In fact, even the practical Grant relaxed his restrictions on occasion if the presence of large numbers of civilians behind his lines did not hinder troop movements. As a result, after every

4. Blakeslee, *Sixteenth Connecticut*, p. 43.
5. Ibid.; see Fiske, *Mr. Dunn Browne*, p. 127.
6. Blakeslee, p. 45.

great battle in Virginia, Connecticut newspapers reported the long roll of worried or bereft parents and relatives who had departed from the towns and the countryside to search for their loved ones. Indeed, it was part of the regimental adjutant's job to inform the press at home of who was killed and where buried, and who was wounded, how seriously, and where hospitalized. After Antietam, for example, John B. Burnham, adjutant of the ill-fated 16th, personally supervised the burial of its dead and sent explicit directions to the *Hartford Courant* as to where they were buried. How poignant it is to reconstruct his sad duties from his own account. An earnest and devoted young officer (he was only nineteen), he wrote the following for the folks at home: "All the bodies lie near a large tree standing alone, and which I had blazed on all sides so that it can be easily discovered. With the exception of Captain Manross who was killed earlier in the fight and carried to the rear, they all lie together and lie as follows." He then listed in sequence south of the tree, and north, some forty names. Individual graves were also located by Burnham, all marked with rough headboards.[7]

During the last week in September relatives of the dead and undertakers from all over the state converged on the Antietam battlefield. From then until mid-October over 200 funerals were conducted. Some were impressive ceremonies, with the Governor in attendance, such as those held at Middletown for old General J. K. F. Mansfield. But the great majority were simple affairs, like the Congregational service for Private Gilbert Crane, "buried from his mother's residence" in Hartford.[8] Antietam was the first direct contact of the Connecticut public with heavy casualties; thereafter, it was the mournful procession of relatives to the battlefields of Fredericksburg, Chancellorsville, Gettysburg, and the Wilderness; and always the funerals were somber reminders that the war was very close indeed.

After the bodies, came the wounded, hundreds of them, not just Connecticut boys but casualties from other state regiments. The New Haven Hospital, which had been enlarged by Governor Buckingham, was soon filled to overflowing with the wounded from Michigan, Pennsylvania, and New York. Sarah Chauncey Woolsey,

7. *Hartford Courant* (Sept. 30, 1862).
8. Ibid. (Oct. 13, 1862).

who was doing voluntary nursing at the hospital, noted in June 1862 that 240 wounded had arrived from the Peninsular battles, "all dreadfully neglected and needing attention of every kind." They had been transported by ship to New Haven, with "only one surgeon on board to care for them, no nurses and hardly any provisions; the wounds of many had not been dressed for nearly a week when they got here." The authorities would not permit any of the young New Haven girls to enter the hospital for several days because of the "sights and sounds." [9] Daughters of the best New Haven families, such as Sarah Woolsey, Harriet Terry, and Rebecca Bacon, worked long hours as volunteer nurses at the New Haven Hospital. Though all came from carefully sheltered homes, they overcame the skepticism and the prejudice of the hospital authorities and proved that they could cope with any of the "sights and sounds." At times it was an ordeal for them. Sarah Woolsey wrote of "an awful boy with no arms, who swears so frightfully (all the time he isn't screeching for currant pie, or fried meat, or some other indigestible) that he turns you blue as you listen." [10] But they did essential work and set an example that feminine society in New Haven was happy to follow.

New Haven was the only city in the state which had made any provision for systematic care of the wounded. Elsewhere, those who came home or were brought by relatives and friends were nursed by their own families. At first, nothing was done for their reception. A delegation of Hartford volunteers, consisting of Treasury office clerk William T. Elmer, O. D. Seymour, a Unionist cousin of Colonel Seymour, and Sheriff Goodrich, brought four badly wounded men of the 16th and one of the 11th home from the Antietam battlefield. The men arrived in Hartford late at night and could find no one competent to look after the medical needs of their charges. Transportation and temporary lodgings were found only after considerable difficulty and delay. The *Courant* was concerned about a lack of personnel and facilities in Hartford. "Quite a number of badly wounded will arrive today," said the *Courant*, "and on almost every train for days to come. They should be met at the

9. Sarah Woolsey to Georgeanna Woolsey, June 1862, in Bacon and Howland, *Letters of a Family*, 2, 417–18.

10. Sarah Woolsey to Georgeanna Woolsey, July 22, 1862, ibid., 462, 463.

depot by agents of the Aid Society, or by a committee of citizens, and those who are in transit to their homes should be provided with temporary quarters, and others who have no good home to go to, should be taken to our hospital."[11] This advice was well received and was acted upon by the citizens of Hartford and other cities and towns in the state.

Once the initial shock of the Antietam casualties had made its impression, strenuous private efforts were made to receive and care for the wounded. It was a difficult task, however, and complaints were voiced throughout the war that the community was not living up to its obligations. But the problem lay beyond state and local authorities. Large drafts of wounded could be, and were, handled well by the home folk once they had been informed of the impending arrival. Unfortunately, the voluntary system broke down precisely where its services were needed most—the reception and care of the wounded who had somehow managed to make their own way home. They would arrive singly or in small groups, unattended, without prior warning, at all hours of the day and night. Most were exhausted, many so dazed, weak, or feverish that they wandered off to back alleys and byways where some would not be discovered for hours. Soldiers' aid committees seemed never able to organize themselves for these unscheduled tasks; nor were the overworked municipal police forces large enough to add these responsibilities to their regular tasks of maintaining law and order. The burden fell upon the casual passer-by, and as a result, confusion and delay invariably followed, before some responsible citizen had taken charge. This same sense of individual and personal involvement characterized the home folk's attitude toward the badly wounded who could not be moved. Relatives traveled to the field hospitals or private houses near the battlefields to supplement the meager care the government provided. During the sixteen-day ordeal of Captain Fiske before he died from a chest wound, he was nursed at a private home in Fredericksburg, Virginia, by his wife, sister, and brother. The faithful, sorrowing little family group then brought his body home for burial.[12]

Even those with no direct personal ties or contact with the

11. *Hartford Courant* (Sept. 29, 1862).

12. Fiske, *Mr. Dunn Browne*, p. 24.

battlefield were constantly reminded of the war by the large numbers of uniformed soldiers and sailors on the streets. Connecticut had the appearance of an armed camp from Sumter through Appomattox. When new regiments were not being recruited, replacements were always being marched to and from camps in the various cities. Convalescent soldiers, soldiers home on leave, soldiers on special duty, sailors, and deserters seemed everywhere. There were so many young men away from the inhibitions of the family circle, perhaps for the first time in their lives, that drunken and disorderly conduct on a large scale soon became a disturbing factor in the community. The strict discipline administered in the three-months regiments had kept those volunteers well in check. But discipline began to slip among the three-year regiments and became very lax among the nine-months men.

The Irish 9th Regiment, for example, had caused so much trouble in New Haven that the city fathers had demanded its removal from the area. And Norwich had its share of disorder during the brief period when the 26th was billeted in that city. Elizabeth Lusk, writing her son in November 1862, noted that "the twenty-sixth Reg't left last Thursday, to the relief of our citizens. They were in town at all hours and a hundred or more at once would run past the guard, and rush to their tents when they pleased." [13] The Governor himself had some embarrassing run-ins with the undisciplined nine-months men. On at least one occasion he was surrounded by a "groaning hissing" group from the 22nd Regiment on Chapel Street in New Haven and followed by them all the way to his office at the State House. The men were angry because the Governor would not authorize payment of the $50 state bounty that had been paid to three-year volunteers.[14]

Military misconduct, however, did not raise any serious community problem until 1864. Starting in the spring of that year, reenlisted three-year veterans on furlough and veterans who had been brought home to vote soon showed the home folks that army life had relaxed conventional restraints. A wave of drunkenness, tavern scuffles, shootings, and beatings made certain areas of Bridgeport, New Haven, Hartford, and even Norwich and New London un-

13. Lusk, *War Letters*, p. 227.
14. *Hartford Evening Post* (Oct. 18, 1862).

safe for civilians at night. Substitutes and bounty men, their pockets stuffed with money, contributed to the general rowdiness. Slum areas and taverns were not the only scenes of disorderly or destructive conduct. During the winter of 1864–65 the trains to and from Connecticut were jammed with drunken soldiers coming home on leave. Since no military police accompanied the roistering veterans, civilian travelers, especially women, had to put up with profanity, horseplay, and petty annoyances. In a letter to the *Courant*, a traveler from New York who had escorted two ladies on the Hartford train complained of the soldiers' "vulgarity, profanity and obscenity." He related that two days before on the same train his two daughters had endured a similar experience. "The state of things now appears to be such," he wrote, "that no lady can travel between Hartford and New York without being exposed to annoyances to which no decent female should ever be subjected."[15] Trains from New York to New Haven and Hartford were the most disorderly, but even local lines had their share of military exuberance. A squad of veterans from the 6th Regiment, while riding between Norwich and New London, broke all the windows in their car, refused to pay their fare, and played coarse practical jokes on the civilian passengers.[16]

Many of the volunteers were openly contemptuous of civilian men, whom, in typical soldier fashion, they regarded as slackers and war profiteers. Their general attitude, their brawling, and their insulting remarks soon generated friction. Inevitably, violence occurred on the main streets of the cities. On February 22, twenty-five members of the 6th and 7th Regiments were walking down Chapel Street in New Haven. One of their number was accompanied by his wife. John Reilly, a civilian bricklayer, who was standing on the sidewalk as they passed, called out after them that "no one but a ——— would go through Chapel Street with a soldier." He was immediately mobbed and beaten badly by the angry soldiers. Managing to escape, he ran into Edward Malley's dry goods store, but was followed by the soldiers, who smashed their way in. During the fracas, Reilly was stabbed fatally.[17] Several of the soldiers were held by the police, but since the actual murderer could

15. *Hartford Courant* (Feb. 18, 1864).
16. *Norwich Bulletin* (Feb. 23, 1864).
17. *New Haven Register* (Feb. 22, 1864).

not be identified, they were all released after agreeing to pay for the damage to the store. Another ugly incident occurred in Hartford some six weeks later, when an intoxicated veteran of the 12th commandeered a wagon on Central Row and threw its Negro driver on the street. It took two policemen, who had witnessed the scuffle, several minutes of rough and tumble before they could subdue the veteran and drag him off to jail. Meanwhile, a crowd of from 150 to 200 soldiers had collected, most in various stages of intoxication. Vowing they would rescue their comrade, they stormed the jail and released him. "It was useless to stem such a torrent of men, who were as a general thing, mad with liquor," said the *Courant*, ". . . they had matters their own way, neither their own officers nor the policemen having any control over them." [18]

Not all disturbances were caused by veterans. The Fort Trumbull garrison at New London seems to have been an unruly lot. After numerous street rows between soldiers and civilians in the city streets, the *Norwich Bulletin* charged that the Fort, "as managed now, is a great, grinning granite humbug, whose only use is to furnish an avenue for deserters to crawl out of the army and another for cripples to crawl in. The former get their bounties and run away; the latter get theirs and crawl into the army hospitals to be paid off, guarded and cared for by the government." [19]

Chaplains of the various regiments warned the home folk that returning veterans would indulge in some unseemly displays and asked forbearance from the community. Chaplain Moses Smith of the 8th Connecticut noted that "the army has many evil influences and not a few of the sons of Connecticut have been injured in morals if not in limbs." Chaplain Smith declared bluntly that furloughs at home, free of army discipline, could have disastrous consequences in many cases. "Make home attractive," he asked the Connecticut public. "Make these thirty days to be full of noble, honorable and if possible Christian enjoyment. Leave nothing untried to show how much you appreciate the heroic deed your friend has performed in giving himself anew to the great work of our nation's redemption." [20] Some of the folks at home were not as considerate or as grateful as Chaplain Smith would have wanted.

18. *Hartford Courant* (April 9, 1864).
19. *Norwich Bulletin* (Feb. 1, 1864).
20. *Hartford Courant* (Feb. 3, 1864).

Enlisted men, particularly, found themselves stigmatized as unruly, boisterous elements not fit to associate in polite society. Private William M. Fowler of the 1st Light Battery had the mortifying experience of being denied a stateroom by the purser of the *Elm City* simply because he was an enlisted man. When he asked for a first-class ticket to New Haven, the purser said "we don't allow private soldiers on deck nor give them staterooms. There is a place downstairs good enough for you!" [21]

Such inexcusable conduct we may hope was rare; but at a time when so many able-bodied young men were permitted to purchase substitutes, when towns made a practice of shaving their draft quotas, when profiteers and speculators gloried in their new-found wealth, prejudice arising from a sense of personal guilt among civilians must have been just beneath the surface. For there was another side to wartime society—a brutal, materialistic side, where there was plenty of money for the opportunist, the political promoter and fixer, and the skilled craftsman, and never enough for the unskilled worker, the recent immigrant, or the soldier's family. Society in Connecticut ran to extremes. Never before had there been such a contrast between growing riches and increasing poverty, between neat, prosperous homes and crime and disease-ridden slums, between new splendor and old shabbiness.

Wartime Connecticut presented a helter-skelter appearance, in which exuberant individualism was supreme, and in which a sense of social responsibility had not as yet made much of an impression. Railroad lines ran directly through the center of the cities. Crossings were unprotected and soot and sparks from the inefficient, soft-coal burning locomotives rained down on the houses, stores, and people. Until the city of Hartford began grading for Bushnell Park in 1861, the New Haven Railroad's engine house, repair shops, and water tanks occupied part of the site. The remainder was bordered on the south by the new Park Street Church, which overlooked the city dump, and on the north and northeast by a row of filthy tenements (with outhouses projecting over the Park River), a soap factory, two old tanneries, and a decaying gristmill. The whole area has been described by Horace Bushnell as a "gehenna without fire—shavings, under-bed fillings, tin wastes, leather cuttings, cabbage

21. Beecher, *First Light Battery*, 2, 619–20.

19. Hartford during the Civil War: State House dome (center right). The old, covered bridge across the Connecticut River (upper right). Connecticut Historical Society.

stumps, hats without tops, old saddles, stovepipes rusted out, everything in short, that had no right to be anywhere else."[22] This wasteland was near the heart of the city of Hartford. Factory villages and market towns had the same casual aspect, in some instances division being more obvious between order and chaos, wealth and poverty, than it was in the bustling little cities. The more traditional rural society was cleaner and more orderly, though it had its share of tumbledown shacks, community dumping grounds, and tree-stump littered, eroding hillsides.

Some progress had been made in urban improvement when the war brought most municipal projects, private as well as public, to a standstill. Projects that had been started before the war, like the New Haven Hall of Records or Bushnell Park, were completed, but no further programs were to be undertaken until the postwar period. Such important functions of city life as mass transportation, water, and sewage systems languished in an undeveloped state during the war years. Only Hartford and New Haven had horse-railroad lines, and these were short, primitive affairs. The New Haven line, which ran three miles to suburban Fair Haven, was opened to the public on May 7, 1861,[23] the day the third of the three-months regiments left for Washington to avenge Fort Sumter. Throughout the war, it ran six round trips each day and was immensely popular;[24] yet no one was interested in expanding service to other areas of the city. The Hartford and Wethersfield horse railroad had been incorporated two years earlier but was not opened for travel until 1863, and then only on Main Street. The Hartford public grumbled so frequently over chaotic schedules, high fares, and interference with private transportation interests that even this limited service hung in the balance. Better management and spirited newspaper support, however, eventually stilled criticism. Several factors restricted significant expansion of horse-railroad lines. Rival transportation interests—omnibus companies, hackmen, livery stables—defended themselves vigorously against the new carriers. The strong individualism of the people expressed itself in a

22. Cheney, *Horace Bushnell,* p. 314.

23. *New Haven Palladium* (May 8, 1861).

24. During 1863, for example, the line carried half a million passengers. *Hartford Courant* (Sept. 18, 1863).

general suspicion, not ill founded, that corrupt "rings" would monopolize valuable franchises. An enterprising group of Norwich promoters, for example, sought to build a horse railroad in that city during 1864 but were thoroughly routed by community opposition. Norwich citizens were not to enjoy the cheaper, faster, more comfortable rides of a horse railroad until 1870.

The twin capitals were also the only cities in the state to have municipal water systems. Hartford had been the leader in this improvement. In 1855, after eight years of planning and argument, a 25-inch piped water system driven by a Woodruff and Beach steam engine began to make available a tenuous supply of impure Connecticut River water to Hartford dwellings. The distribution pipes were so small and the system so imperfectly engineered that users frequently had to wait as long as an hour before they got a small supply of water. And on Mondays—washday in Hartford households—it was "not uncommon," said the *Courant*, "for whole neighborhoods to find the supply fail." [25] Despite these inconveniences, piped water was an instant success, and its consumption tripled over a period of six years.[26] After a brief period of organization and profiting from the experience of Hartford, what was known as the Old Company signed a twenty-year franchise with the city of New Haven. By the spring of 1862 the ancient town wells, which had been the scene of much social activity for many years, were on the way out, and by the end of the war were only being used in poorer neighborhoods.[27]

Neither city, however, made much progress in macadamizing its streets. In 1861 a beginning had been made in New Haven, and each year some further work was done, but resurfacing was so slow that six years after the war only four miles of the city's more than ninety miles of streets had been paved.[28] Street conditions in Hartford were just as bad. A young lady complained in a letter to the *Courant* of the "awful clouds of dust raised by the whirling carriages from the depot to High Street." "It is even worse," she said,

25. Ibid. (June 20, 1860).

26. J. Hammond Trumbull, ed., *The Memorial History of Hartford County, Connecticut* (Boston, 1886), *1*, 437.

27. Edward E. Atwater, ed., *History of the City of New Haven, 1784–1884* (New York, 1887), p. 412.

28. *New Haven Register* (Jan 6, 1871).

"than the smoke and pickpockets of New Haven." [29] Other Connecticut cities were not to have paved streets or piped water until the middle seventies. City and country dwellers alike walked along dirt roads that were "clouds of dust" in dry spells or quagmires during winter thaws and spring rains. If they could afford it, they traveled by stage between towns and by omnibus within city limits. Both these modes of transportation were too expensive to attract a high volume of traffic, while hacks for hire and private carriages were only for the well-to-do. It is safe to say that a majority of the state's population had to depend upon their own legs to move about cities and towns, a major reason perhaps why factories, shops, and workers' homes were always located in near proximity to each other.

No doubt more would have been accomplished for the improvement and convenience of urban and suburban life had not the war intervened. Labor and materials rapidly became so expensive and wartime taxes increased at such a rate that cities, towns, and individual promoters were reluctant to undertake projects of a public character. A more significant deterrent was that most available capital and organizing ability had been diverted from enterprises of a public nature. Businessmen who had shown some interest in promoting such improvements as horse-car lines, paved streets, and water and gas companies before the war now found the profit potential of government contracts or the booming civilian market far more attractive outlets for their energy and their capital.

Yet for the first six months after the attack on Sumter the economic future seemed uncertain indeed. It was a period of economic dislocation, with sporadic unemployment. Particularly hard hit had been those industries that depended on the Southern trade: carriage manufacturing in New Haven, cotton textiles in southeastern Connecticut, and the agricultural implement industry in Hartford and Middlesex counties. Unemployed skilled and unskilled workmen moved to New Haven, Hartford, Norwich, and Middletown, where the munitions industry was booming. But the arms industry already had more labor than it needed for existing facilities. Though production facilities were expanding rapidly, new capacity would not be ready for another six months. A temporary labor surplus in the cities soon caused considerable hardship. Tenement

29. *Hartford Courant* (Jan. 8, 1858).

landlords, responding to unprecedented demand, raised rents from 12 to 25 per cent.[30] An inflationary spiral in food and clothing costs was just beginning. Even skilled mechanics had to take whatever jobs were available to support their families. This meant working as farm hands or joining one of the volunteer regiments. Either occupation resulted in a sharp reduction of family income. A machinist, who had lived in Hartford four months, explained to a meeting of tenants that he walked from 20 to 25 miles a day with his scythe, picking up odd jobs from neighboring farms. Even with his wife supplementing the family income by long hours of home sewing, he could not afford the high rents of Hartford. Samuel Dyer, another unemployed mechanic, declared he would enlist if "somebody gave him security for his family." An estimated thousand tenants attended this meeting and passed a resolution calling for a 25 per cent reduction in city rents.[31] Similar meetings were held during the fall of 1861 in other cities. Nothing came of the rent meetings, however, and by early October enough new jobs had been created to take up the slack.[32] Army manpower requirements helped ease the situation, but a more important factor had been the construction industry, particularly factory construction, which had reached a stage where machinists, boilermakers, carpenters, and joiners were needed in quantity to install machinery and put the finishing touches on the new plants. Labor was soon in short supply, and for a brief time it too would share in the largesse of lucrative war work.

From now on, government contracts produced a chain reaction in the economy. It was estimated, for example, that Hartford factories in January 1862 were disbursing in payrolls above $150,000 monthly; New Haven plants were paying out over $200,000 a month; while factories like Wheeler and Wilson (sewing machines) in Bridgeport, or Coe Brothers (brass products) in Waterbury were working their expanded labor forces on a two shift, twenty-hour-a-day basis.[33] The languid carriage business in New Haven was pick-

30. Ibid. (Aug. 20, 1861).
31. Ibid.
32. Ibid. (Oct. 7, 1861).
33. Ibid. (Jan. 10, 1862).

ing up, and by 1863 was manufacturing more luxury vehicles than it had in the boom carriage year of 1860.[34]

All this sudden prosperity brought in its wake a lively real estate and building boom, which also bid for scarce workers in the labor mart. Stimulated initially by factory construction, the boom moved into urban development—mansions and large homes for the newly affluent, as well as stores and office buildings. The economic difficulties of 1861 and the subsequent urban real estate boom were mirrored in the tax rolls. From 1860 to 1865 the value of taxable real property in Connecticut advanced 21 per cent. But the counties of Hartford and New Haven more than doubled their assessed valuation. In 1860 Hartford had an assessed valuation of $24,813,190, while New Haven's was $25,750,820. By 1864 the value of real property in Hartford and New Haven counties had risen to almost $55,000,000 each, which amounted to 45 per cent of the grand list for the entire state.[35] Real property values in the city of New Haven, which had dipped more than $1,000,000 between 1860 and 1861, began to rise, slowly at first, then more rapidly. From May 1863 until May 1865 almost $6,000,000 was added to the city's taxable property, approximately half of this sum occurring in the last year of the war. For the entire state, Governor Joseph Hawley noted in his 1866 message to the legislature, total taxable wealth had increased 25 per cent during fiscal 1864–65. Of course, by this time property values were responding to inflation, but if the millions of dollars invested in tax-exempt securities were included, the increase in real dollars would have been close to the amount Hawley had given.[36]

Anyone visiting the busy urban centers of Connecticut during the war would not have needed these statistical indices to have been convinced that a building boom was in progress. As early as 1862, despite the labor shortage, the streets of the busy little cities and towns were bordered with scaffolding. Carpenters, bricklayers, and masons seemed as plentiful as mechanics or soldiers. An average of

34. *Report of the Commissioner of Internal Revenue, for the Year Ending June 30, 1865* (Washington, 1865), p. 23.

35. *Geer's Hartford Directory, 1861*; *Benham's New Haven Directory, 1862–63*; *Hunt's Merchant's Magazine* (April 1864), p. 259.

36. "Governor's Annual Message, 1866," *PDLC* (May Sess., 1866), p. 6.

300 new buildings a year were erected in New Haven during the war. Hartford's building activity was just as vigorous. In the city of Meriden thirty new buildings were finished during August 1863.[37] Even Middletown, which had a reputation for economic conservatism, was burgeoning with construction activity. At the end of May 1864 the *Sentinel and Witness* estimated that business activity in Middletown had increased 40 per cent in the past 18 months, much of this due to new construction.[38] Had labor and materials costs not risen so rapidly, substantially more construction would have been undertaken. By 1863 the price of brick had advanced from $4.75 to $8.00 a thousand, and that of white lead from 9 cents a pound to 18 cents a pound, window glass from $2.25 to $3.50 a box. And wages in the building trades had gone up about 60 per cent over prewar averages.[39] Some tenement construction was undertaken, but never enough in the lower-rent categories. There was such a brisk demand for apartments of the better class that few builders would bother with the needs of lower-income groups. Even that pre-eminent workers' town of Bridgeport had a persistent shortage of lower rental housing during the war.

Bridgeport, or more correctly, East Bridgeport, as the industrial section was then known, was a city of small houses, tenements, and new factories. With but one-third of New Haven's wealth and one quarter of its population, it had almost as many dwelling houses in 1862. This had been due largely to the speculative foresight of P. T. Barnum and his associate William H. Noble—soon to be commander of the 17th Connecticut. As early as 1850, Barnum and Noble had started purchasing large tracts of farm and woodland east of Bridgeport along the banks of the Pequonnock River, where they hoped to build a model industrial community. Barnum moved his ill-fated Jerome Clock Company from Litchfield to East Bridgeport in 1852, and later persuaded Wheeler and Wilson to purchase a parcel of the property for its new factory. But it was the war boom that really prospered the venture. In 1864 Barnum offered to lend workmen mortgage money at what were then extraordinarily generous terms—6 per cent interest and up to 80 per

37. *Hartford Courant* (Sept. 7, 1863).
38. *Middletown Sentinel and Witness* (May 29, 1864).
39. *Hartford Courant* (May 15, July 14, 1863).

cent of the value of their new houses and land.[40] He also anticipated modern real estate practice by developing and donating park land and church sites. Barnum's credit policy attracted industrialists as well. Such prosperous enterprises as Winchester Arms, Bridgeport Brass, and the Union Metallic Cartridge Company were persuaded to build in East Bridgeport. Barnum and Noble, of course, made enormous profits on their real estate development, on some parcels as much as 2,000 per cent.[41] Despite all this encouragement and promotion, the *Bridgeport Standard* in February 1865 noted that tenement rentals had risen another forty to fifty dollars a year because so few had been built.[42]

If the profit motive retarded construction of low rental housing, public buildings, and the like, it tended to accelerate the already heavy demand for expensive dwellings. Unlike New York City, few grandiose mansions were erected in Connecticut during the war. This was to be a postwar phenomenon associated with the piping prosperity of the late sixties and early seventies. However, thousands of substantial brick and brownstone town houses and country "villas" in the $10–25,000 class were built for the busy, prosperous, growing middle class. New Haven and Hartford, of course, led in this construction as they led in all economic and social activities, yet Norwich and Bridgeport at the war's end also had rows of fine new houses, which compared favorably with any constructed in the state.

The countryside was never far away from any Connecticut city in the mid-sixties, nor indeed was the new industrial age. Both old and new flourished in close proximity and in mutual dependence. Visitors to Hartford during the war were as agreeably impressed by the tree-lined avenues, busy shops, and fine new residences being built in its western section as they were with the carefully tended vegetable and tobacco farms that encircled the city. No one seemed to mind that the ugly, smoke-belching factories that housed the machine tool, boiler, leather, and firearms industries, with their outriding tenement belts, had crept along both banks of the Con-

40. *Bridgeport Standard* (Feb. 17, 1864).

41. P. T. Barnum, *Struggles and Triumphs: Or, Forty Years' Recollections* (Hartford, 1869), pp. 554, 559.

42. *Bridgeport Standard* (Feb. 17, 1865).

necticut River and were within short walking distance of shops and homes.

The most dazzling residence in Hartford and, indeed, one of the most picturesque in New England was "Armsmear," Samuel Colt's baronial estate on Wethersfield Avenue, close to the factory district. This massive, rambling mansion built by Colonel Colt in the middle fifties was a blend of Italian, Moorish, and Gothic architecture, with domed conservatories and a prominent watchtower. Receptions, promenades, and garden parties for as many as 200 guests were regular occurrences at Armsmear. On clear, summer nights, when Mrs. Colt was entertaining, its gardens and fountains were illuminated by gaslights and expensive, multicolored lanterns. Firework displays startled the estate's private herd of deer but were enjoyed by the working population who lived less than a mile away. Nothing in New Haven could match the exuberant luxury of "Armsmear." Elm-lined Hillhouse Avenue and Elm Street, with their mélange of colonial mansions, elaborate Tuscan façades, and new three-story brownstone gothics, however, bespoke solid material comfort and graceful living. Golden Hill in Bridgeport, and the villas and parks of New York commuters in Stamford, were all noted as points of interest and evidences of progress in the travel literature of the times. An appreciative observer of Washington Street and Broadway in Norwich concluded rapturously that the new mansions were "like the creation of Arabian tales, the scene . . . continually changing." One residence that he singled out for special praise was a two-story affair "of handsome cornices, dormers . . . with French roof . . . angular and circular pediments and piazza in the Italian style." Another commentator on Norwich elegance had an eye for the lawns and gardens, which he thought "looked glorious with their quaint rustic tete-a-tetes, their urns, statues and fountains." [43]

The eclectic architecture masked conventional interior arrangements of spacious comfort. In 1864 William S. White and A. B. West of Windsor Locks, machine tool manufacturers who were investing wartime profits in speculative building, constructed a block of granite-faced brick houses on Buckingham Street in Hartford, which was typical of city housing in the $12–15,000 range.

43. *Norwich Advertizer* (July 22, Nov. 10, 1867).

20. Spacious comfort of conventional interiors: Bishop and Mrs. Thomas C. Brownell of Hartford at home in the early sixties. Connecticut Historical Society.

21. The cities presented a helter-skelter appearance. This old, ramshackle building stood on State Street, New London, during the Civil War. Connecticut State Library.

A visitor to one of White and West's three-story brick fronts would cross a wide belt of lawn (the houses were set back to avoid street dust) and enter the house through "a vestibule" paneled with solid black walnut. If the visit were a formal one, he might be entertained in the front parlor. More than likely, however, he would be escorted through black walnut folding doors to the sitting room beyond, where four-pane windows of imported French plate glass overlooked flowering borders. Should the visitor be taken on a tour of the household, the hot and cold running-water taps in the kitchen would be pointed out, as would be the servant's pantry and the large Mott's cast-iron coal range. A trip to the cellar by back stairs from the kitchen would have disclosed "one of Magee's hot air furnaces," which overheated and certainly dried out the entire house. White and West had also provided marble manteled fireplaces in every room except the kitchen and the servants' bedrooms for additional space heating and the aesthetic appreciation of open fires. Bedroom suites for adults were on the second floor, single bedrooms for children and servants on the third. Every bedroom had a marble washstand. Bathrooms with tubs and water closets were installed on the bedroom levels.[44]

As the White and West development suggests, new middle-class housing was making use of technical and muncipal improvements for additional comfort and convenience. Ten years before, similar housing would not have been equipped with hot and cold running-water, water closets, or central heating. Ranges and furnaces had been in limited use since the early forties, but it was not until the Civil War that they emerged from the curiosity phase to become a fixture in prosperous households. The wartime expansion of the foundry industry provided the production base. Wartime prosperity created the market demand.

In other aspects of family life the prosperous Connecticut citizen was enjoying more creature comforts than ever before. To be sure, salaries for servants had increased substantially and competition from labor-short industry would seem to have made them more temperamental than usual. In April 1864 a rich New Haven citizen complained humorously about the servant problem. He told the editor of the *Journal and Courier* that "on Friday last, Margaret

44. *Hartford Courant* (March 22, 1865).

gave a week's warning, stating as a reason that where she worked before the family invariably had tenderloin for breakfast and she was not the girl to come down to sausages and hash!"[45] There was more than mere caprice to Margaret's saucy independence. Among the expansive middle classes, food and drink was taking on that lavish variety which had formerly been enjoyed by only the very rich or the very important persons in Washington. No longer did a prosperous citizen need to maintain his own livestock or journey to a market center like New York to purchase a meat supply and superintend its butchering, packing, and shipment.[46] Although this had been customary procedure in the Connecticut of the fifties, improved transportation and the growth of retail specialization in the cities and larger towns had made seasonal shopping trips to distant points unnecessary.[47] Even that fixture of casual urban life before the war, the family milch cow, was disappearing.[48] New Haven and Bridgeport were being supplied with fresh milk from the dairy farms of the Housatonic Valley, where many farmers had formed themselves into cooperative distributing associations during the war and were shipping dairy products into those cities every day,[49] over the Housatonic Railroad. The New Haven and Hartford Railroad performed a similar service for Hartford from the dairy farms of Hartford and Middlesex counties.

Tropical fruits and out-of-season vegetables for a brief time were casualties of the war, even for the richest families, because of the disruption of the Southern trade. But new sources of supply for citrus and other exotic fruits were developed by New Haven, Norwich, and New London shipping interests, which had reopened the old West Indies trade. And as soon as the Sea Islands and southern Louisiana were captured by Union troops, these productive citrus and early vegetable areas began shipping their crops again to the Northern speciality markets. Indeed, the temporary scarcity of tropical fruits and out-of-season vegetables promoted a vogue for conservatories among the new rich, where in true Yankee fashion

45. *New Haven Journal and Courier* (April 20, 1864).

46. MS Diary of Judge Asa Fish (Mystic Marine Museum).

47. Ibid.

48. Thomas S. Gold, "The Age of Agricultural Science," *Connecticut Magazine*, 9, (1899), 233.

49. *Bridgeport Weekly Standard* (Feb. 7, March 21, 1868).

one could make an expensive, prestigious hobby into a profitable operation. The greenhouses and conservatories of "Armsmear," like the mansion itself, were the most lavish in the state. Two of Colt's greenhouses were devoted exclusively to pineapple culture, another raised only figs, others were reserved for flowers. Oranges, lemons, and nectarines were among the "exotic" fruits grown on the estate. Mrs. Colt also raised vegetables during the winter, and after the family's wants had been met, shipped the surplus off to market. The chief gardener at Armsmear told a *Courant* reporter that "these greenhouses afford a comfortable income."[50] But with oranges fluctuating in price between 50 and 75 cents each, early cucumbers at 75 cents each, and preseason asparagus at $1.50 a bunch, winter fare even among the prosperous middle class had little variation. Despite an expansion of retail marketing facilities, flour and oysters continued to be purchased by the barrel, potatoes and other root vegetables by the bushel, and bacon by the side. In more modest dwellings home-canned perishable vegetables or the new commercially canned products, which were just becoming available, provided some relief from seasonal dictates. Comfortable, even luxurious, houses and more varied menus were generally the results of prewar developments that had been accelerated by wartime prosperity. And the trend had been toward the satisfying of individual wants rather than community needs, more in the direction of luxuries than necessities.

Yet one notable advance in urban living during the war years which served rich and poor alike was gas lighting. Rare indeed was an urban workmen's tenement that did not possess at least one gas fixture in the parlor by 1865. Streets in all the cities and most of the larger towns may have been unpaved, but they were illuminated by gas lamps. Country towns, suburban areas, and the poorer classes in factory towns continued to rely for home illumination upon candles, whale oil, and, toward the end of the war, kerosene or a particularly explosive petroleum product known as "burning fluid."[51]

Besides material things, the new prosperity derived aesthetic sat-

50. *Hartford Courant* (May 22, 1862).

51. Osterweis, *New Haven*, p. 317; Atwater, *New Haven*, pp. 408–09; J. H. Trumbull, *Hartford County* I, 452.

isfaction from patronizing the arts. The era of the sixties was the golden age of native American landscape and portrait art, a period when few of the 150 artists residing in Connecticut had any difficulty in disposing of their canvases at good prices.[52] The huge romantic landscapes of Frederick Church or the fish paintings of Gurdon Trumbull were particularly prized by such art fanciers as Congressman James E. English, rich New Haven manufacturer and real estate developer; Marshall Jewell, of the great Hartford leather family; Mrs. Samuel Colt; and James G. Batterson, of the Travelers' Insurance and Westerly Granite. English was not only an avid collector but a great patron of artists, many of whom would study in Europe after the war at his own personal expense.

Music was well patronized too, largely through the devoted efforts of the German-born population in the cities. New Haven had its Mendelssohn society and Hartford its Beethoven society—groups of music lovers, performers, and local impresarios who put together symphonic programs that played to packed houses. On December 1, 1863, all east-west trains out of Hartford were held over to carry home the crowds from Rockville, Manchester, and New Britain that had visited Hartford's Allyn Hall for a performance of *Elijah* by the New Haven society.[53] Generally, however, concerts had to be entertaining rather than cultural. Musical evenings depended upon traveling artists who specialized in light dramatic pieces or virtuoso performances. Clara Louise Kellogg, daughter of a Birmingham, Connecticut inventor and manufacturer, dazzled New Haven and Hartford audiences with her intricate coloratura style and the range of her clear soprano voice. In 1864 New Haven's rather stiff society greeted her rendition of the "Swiss Echo Song" with such deafening applause that she encored with the "French Laughing Song." Madame Varian, who was billed "as one of the sweetest concert singers in the country," headed a list of New York performers who appeared in all Connecticut cities during the winter of 1865. At Hartford's Allyn Hall, Madame Varian sang selections from *Der Freischütz* and encored with Sontag's "Echo Song." George Simpson, of the Grace Church chorus in New York, lilted through "Come into the Garden, Maud" and

52. Henry W. French, *Art and Artists in Connecticut* (Boston, 1879), pp. 12–14.
53. *Hartford Courant* (Nov. 30, 1863).

various sentimental Scottish ballads. A cellist, a pianist, and two violinists completed the program with such scale-splitting exercises as *The Carnival of Venice* and selections from Franz Liszt.

The stage, too, profited from a war-enhanced interest in entertainment. Heavy melodramas vied with atrocious pun-studded comedies as the favorite dramatic fare of Connecticut audiences. Again performers were esteemed for versatility rather than quality. J. E. McDonough, for example, who played Mrs. Pluto, eccentric queen of the underworld in *The Seven Sisters,* a gaudy presentation of the old fable, was far more successful than the able Shakespearean actor, Edward L. Davenport, in his great role of Richard III. But the most popular entertainers by far were juggler-acrobat troupes, minstrels, and New England folk singers. Over 1,000 Hartford citizens jammed Allyn Hall for three nights in succession to watch Charles Shay's Quincuplexal and Celestial Troupe perform juggling, magic acts, gymnastics, songs, and dances.[54] The so-called Fakir of Ava always had a capacity audience at New Haven's Music Hall, Breed's Hall in Norwich, or Touro Hall in Hartford. Doubtless the Fakir's popularity was assisted by the hundred prizes, ranging from "articles of parlor and bedroom furniture down to a pair of stockings," he gave away each night to lucky ticket holders.[55] George Christy's Minstrels, including his "famous live pig," could always count on a full house. The Huchinson family singers and Father Kemp with his "family of old folks" were popular entertainers. "If you wish to have a real old-fashioned time go [hear Father Kemp] tonight," puffed the *Courant* in November 1862.

Until the failure of McClellan's Peninsular campaign, war themes were standard stage attractions. On April 17, 1861, for example, the Touro Theater presented the rather incongruous double-bill—"Ten Nights in a Bar Room" and "Major Anderson, the Hero of Fort Sumter."[56] But toward the end of 1862 the public would seem to have lost interest in the war as a dramatic stage subject. By then, the sanguinary conflict had probably become too realistic for such romantic gilding. However, popular music contin-

54. Ibid. (March 11, 1863).
55. Ibid. (Nov. 16, 1864).
56. Ibid. (April 17, 1861).

ued to dwell on war themes, some comic, like Henry Clay Work's "Grafted into the Army"; most, nostalgic or sentimental. Madame Varian usually included in her concerts the lachrymose "Oh, Why Did You Die, or the Lament of the Irish Mother." [57] Even the patriotic and military airs turned out in such profusion by Hartford-born Henry Clay Work during 1861–62 lost their appeal until a new wave of Union optimism began in late 1864, after Sherman's march through Georgia. The melancholy "Vacant Chair" and the wistful "Tenting Tonight" were the style of songs Connecticut sang during the awful days from Fredericksburg through the Wilderness.

Popular literature also emphasized war themes, to the immense profit of authors and publishers. Dr. Ashbel Woodward's illustrated $1.00 biography of General Nathaniel Lyon, published by Case, Lockwood of Hartford, sold thousands of copies in Connecticut during 1862. Joel T. Headley's popular history of the war and Horace Greeley's first volume of *The American Conflict* were extremely well received, and so were the sketches of Connecticut's war heroes that were rushed into print after their death on the battlefields. None of these books, however, had such instant success as Emma E. Edmonds' account of her adventures as a nurse and a spy for the Union Army. Hurlburt and Williams of Hartford published Miss Edmonds' book under the title *Nurse and Scout,* in November 1864. Within four months 50,000 copies had been sold and sales during March 1865 were increasing at the rate of 1,000 a day.[58]

Newspaper circulation reflected the public's passion for war news, instruction, and entertainment. By 1865 all of the larger city dailies had acquired one or more of the Hoe steam-driven cylinder presses to meet the public demand. This new-found prosperity of the press had not been achieved, however, without sharp increases in publishing overhead. Outlays for telegraphic news and for paper showed the greatest increase, but wartime taxes on newsprint, ink, and type were substantial too.[59] Publishers were forced to raise advertising rates and newspaper prices several times during the war.

57. Ibid. (Oct. 8, 1864).
58. Ibid. (April 1, 1865).
59. *New Haven Register* (Dec. 17, 1862).

Despite these increases, in many instances amounting to 100 per cent, circulation continued its upward course.

Public lectures on wartime subjects attracted large and interested audiences. Indeed, Anna Dickinson, Wendell Phillips, and Parson Brownlow always spoke to a capacity crowd when they toured the state during the war. The outspoken Miss Dickinson was particularly enjoyed for her slashing, freehanded attacks on important military and government figures.[60] Both New Haven and Hartford had privately supported Young Men's Institutes, which sponsored a lecture series during the winter months. In addition, church organizations and local subscription agents brought in colorful or famous speakers, such as John B. Gough, the eloquent lecturer on temperance; Fred Douglass, the great Negro orator; or Dr. Augustus Schubert, a Prussian-born physical fitness zealot, who addressed the German population of New Haven and Hartford on "The Physical Decline of Civilized Man in the 19th Century; its Causes, Consequences and Cure." [61] The large sums spent for entertainment or cultural improvement during the war years argue that increasing numbers of Connecticut's working-class population were patronizing leisure time activities. Yet this was due more to full employment than to any substantial improvement in real wages. Escalating costs of living outstripped wage increases, so that by the end of the war even highly skilled workmen were earning about what they had four years earlier.

To be sure, labor had strengthened its position since pre-Sumter days, especially in union organization. In February 1861 there had been so little interest in union activity among workmen in the First Congressional District that it was decided not to send a delegation to the National Labor Union's Philadelphia convention.[62] But the union idea rapidly became popular as the persistent manpower shortage improved labor's bargaining position. William Sylvis, of the International Iron Molders, and Alfred W. Phelps, of the New Haven Carpenters' and Joiners' Union, managed to triple the number of unions in Connecticut between 1861 and 1865.[63] Although

60. *Hartford Courant* (May 2, 1864).

61. Ibid. (Feb. 21, 1863).

62. Ibid. (Feb. 20, 1861).

63. From two unions in 1861 to six unions in 1865. John R. Commons et al., *History of Labor in the United States*, 2 (New York, 1918), 19.

general wage levels increased, the lion's share went to the smallest segment of the labor population. Journeymen tailors, for instance, at the top of the scale, refused an average wage of $16 a week in March 1864, while railroad longshoremen, after unsuccessful strikes during 1863, were still earning $7.50 a week.[64] Iron molders, typesetters, harness makers, carpenters and other skilled trades were averaging about $15 a week at the end of the war, a wage increase of approximately 60 per cent. Semiskilled and unskilled averaged about 20 per cent increase, but large numbers of women who had entered such industries as cartridge and textile manufacture were paid far less than the men they had replaced in 1861. An unmarried woman worker wrote in April 1864 that "board and washing cost at least $3.25 a week, and I would ask, how can a woman support herself on four dollars, or four and a half, a week?" [65]

Meanwhile, inflation canceled out wage gains for all but the most highly skilled. Moulton's index of real wages using the years 1824 to 1842 as a base shows a decline from 152 in 1861 to 104 in 1865. The average worker's income in 1865 was equivalent in purchasing power to what it had been in 1832 and was 21 per cent less than the average real wage from 1840 to 1861.[66] By May 1863 a barrel of flour that had cost $7.50 in 1861 was now retailing for $11; black tea had gone from 42 cents a pound to 80 cents a pound; rice from 5 cents a pound to 30 cents a pound, and even that homely staple salt codfish had almost doubled in price. Drugs had advanced by a third, clothing by 40 per cent; and coal had become so expensive that cooperative companies were being formed in the cities in an effort to reduce prices.[67] Clearly, wartime luxuries were not for the multitudes, but full employment did give an air of surface prosperity to Connecticut cities and towns. It also contributed to drunkenness and crime, which seemed to flourish under wartime economic and social conditions.

Hundreds of unstable individuals who had previously found difficulty securing employment now had money to spend for liquor or other vices. Not a few steady workmen must have sought alco-

64. *Hartford Courant* (March 14, 1864); *New Haven Register* (Jan. 8, June 9, 1863).

65. *Hartford Courant* (April 26, 1864).

66. Deyrup, *Arms Makers of the Connecticut Valley*, pp. 242–43.

67. *Hartford Courant* (May 15, 1863).

holic refuge from the vexing problem of long work hours at pay scales that never seemed to purchase better housing or better food and clothing. Juvenile delinquency would seem to have been an increasing problem during the war and was no doubt in part the result of wartime inflation. Many soldiers' wives in the cities and towns, particularly those of immigrant stock, found it necessary to augment their inadequate income by either sewing at home on piece rate, or working in the mills or as domestics. Whatever the task, these women were unable to care properly for their families. Hordes of ragged urchins roamed the streets of New Haven, Hartford, Bridgeport, Norwich, and even New London during the war. They engaged in mischief, petty larceny, and rowdiness, and were especially annoying around the theaters and music halls, where they would congregate in the evening to badger those going in or out.[68] From 1862 through 1865 juveniles contributed substantially to urban crime rates, which rose sharply each year.

The nearness of factory districts, dram shops, and houses of prostitution to better residential and shopping sections brought poverty and crime into close proximity with the social and cultural centers of the cities. Not four blocks from Yale College and the well-kept green were the overcrowded, crumbling tenements of New Haven's working population. In Hartford only a well-armed individual would venture into the east side of the city or along the Connecticut River wharves after dark. Carousing lumber-barge crews, river sailors, and a motley of ruffians defied the inadequate control measures of Hartford's twenty-three man police force. Bountymen and Negro regiments were irresistible lures for gangs of thieves, who found easy marks among the ignorant or the gullible soldiers. Pickpockets infested trains, railroad depots, and busy streets, and were most ubiquitous at large public affairs such as state funerals, Union mass meetings, or recruiting drives. One's personal possessions were never safe from these resourceful thieves. Even the Governor had his pocket picked twice during the war. Police forces were never enlarged fast enough to cope with the increasing crime rate; nor were they supplied with essential equipment to perform their law enforcement duties properly. City policemen carried clubs only at night. During the day they had to depend on their fists to

68. Ibid. (March 14, 1864).

assert their authority. Patrol wagons would not be furnished police departments until the seventies. A not uncommon sight in the cities of Civil War Connecticut was a burly patrolman pushing his subdued prisoner along the street in a wheelbarrow—the usual vehicle for transporting the unruly who could not be walked to the station house.

On the surface the war seems to have made a lasting impact on citizens had some sort of personal involvement in it either directly, through actual participation in the armed forces, or indirectly, through friends or relatives, government contracts, war work. Cer- Connecticut society. It is an obvious fact that a majority of the tainly the way in which the North mobilized its manpower and natural resources had exaggerated individualism as a dominant social theme, and had condoned, if not encouraged, the growing disparity between individual progress and mass poverty. The war had also tended to delay by at least five years urban improvement and those public conveniences which would characterize the new industrial North of the seventies and eighties. Leisure-time activities, whether pure entertainment or of more serious import, were shaped in many ways by the wartime environment.

But basically, the war played a minor role in the formation of lasting social values. These were being evolved by the maturing industrial revolution well before the attack on Sumter. The war was more of a transient phenomenon, a violent and destructive interlude, which delayed rather than hastened the difficult adjustment to the dominant industrial society. As a catalyst in the industrializing process, as a creator of new capital, the war was important. Yet even in these significant respects it promoted some disorderly economic growth, some resultant social problems. Railroad development, so essential to a mature industrial economy, was neglected; while the munitions industry, of little use in the postwar era, was expanded far beyond even wartime needs.

In the rise of Connecticut's munitions industry may be witnessed the economic impact of the war at its most dramatic. For the times and the state of the managerial art, the industry was a magnificent display of mechanical muscle and ingenuity that converted the state into an arsenal of war production, but at the same time unbalanced the maturing economy.

PART FOUR

Home Front: The Material Resource

13. MOUSETRAPS TO MUSKETS

NOTHING like it had ever happened before in the United States. In the brief space of a year's time a new firearms factory with half the capacity of the government's Springfield arsenal had been established and was in full production at the small Connecticut city of Norwich. The new armory had been such a spectacular demonstration of the North's productive might that *Harper's New Monthly Magazine* commissioned the famed travel writer and illustrator T. Addison Richards to describe the Norwich phenomenon for the March 1864 issue.

It had all started in January 1862 when James D. Mowry, a small manufacturer of cotton flannelette, received a government order for 30,000 Springfield muskets. Mowry, like other Norwich textile men, had been forced to shut down his factory when the war cut off his supply of raw cotton. An enterprising individual with important political connections, he borrowed some additional capital in New York and formed the Norwich Arms Company. Then he visited his good friend and fellow townsman Senator Lafayette Foster in Washington. Through Foster and Alfred Burnham, his congressman, the War Department was persuaded to award Mowry the contract. As yet, the only production facility possessed by the Norwich Arms Company was Mowry's inoperative factory in suburban Greenville.

Many influential members of the Norwich business community scoffed at Mowry's bravado and predicted an early collapse of his ambitious venture. Arms manufacture was one of the most sophisticated of American industries. It demanded large production facilities, highly skilled manpower, intricate machine tools. And the government, though a lavish customer, was a harsh taskmaster. Rigid inspection may not have been required of foreign-made imported arms, but it emphatically was required of American-made weapons. Moreover, the War Department insisted that manufacturers meet their contract delivery schedules or suffer harsh penalties. How could the inexperienced Mowry manufacture precision firearms, much less deliver such a gigantic order on time? It seemed the wildest of speculations. But the Norwich skeptics were underrating both Mowry's organizing ability and the productive capacity of their own city.

Norwich had once been the center of a promising firearms industry. By 1861 all but one of the arms plants had moved to Worcester or New Haven. Yet this enterprising little city of 14,000 had a substantial base of machine shops, boiler works, and iron-rolling mills that had grown up in response to the machinery needs of local woolen, cotton, and paper mills. A deep water river port some twelve miles inland from the Long Island Sound, Norwich was the southern terminus of the Norwich and Worcester Railroad, which tapped the traffic and markets of a dozen little factory towns along its 42-mile route to Worcester, Massachusetts. In addition, a spur line to New London connected Norwich with the Shore Line to New Haven and points north and west. The Norwich Arms Company could therefore count on good rail transportation, besides an efficient coastal shipping route through a steamboat company owned by the Norwich and Worcester. Since Norwich capital controlled the railroad, it was reasonable to assume that Mowry would receive preferential freight rates.

Perhaps the most important reason for his enterprise's astonishing success was the cotton famine. When the cotton mills closed down or went on reduced time, satellite machine shops, boiler works, and the like had to curtail production or seek other markets. Mowry could rely on a surplus of machine shop capacity and of highly skilled labor that could be readily converted to firearms production. And this is just what he did, until he had the time and the experience and had earned sufficient capital to organize all the diverse skills and equipment required for arms-making under the direct control of his new company. Mowry had the gunlocks made at C. B. Rogers and Company in the West Chelsea district of the city; barrels were rolled and rifled at Cole and Walker's machine shop on Franklin Street. He auctioned off the spindles and looms of his Greenville factory and installed in their place those complex wood cutting and shaping machines known as stockers, which somehow he had managed to obtain in a scarcity market. Thus the gunstocks were made under Mowry's supervision, and he personally directed the assembly and proving of the weapons. The Norwich Arms Company fulfilled all the terms of its original contract. When it received a second quantity order for muskets, Mowry had already recapitalized the company for $600,000, had leased the machine shop on Franklin Street, and was constructing next to his original factory a complex of lock rooms, rolling mills, mechanical forge rooms, and smithies. By October 1863 the Norwich Arms Company was producing 1,000 muskets a week. Four months later, production had risen to 1,200 muskets, not counting 3,000 bayonets, 2,000 locks, and several hundred breech-loading Kentucky rifles and carbines, which were also being manufactured each week. At this time the company payroll amounted to $28,000 a month.[1]

Mowry had solved the problem of labor scarcity by substituting machine processes for manual labor whenever possible and by rationalizing the "more than 400" operations made on the 49 separate parts of a musket so that "no two of which are performed by the same hand, and are, indeed, all so distinct in character that the artisan employed upon one . . . generally has no knowledge whatever of any other." Swaging machines, or drop forges, as they were more commonly called, performed 150 of these operations for each barrel. Rifling, the most lengthy and most skillful operation, took thirty minutes for each barrel, but even here, one workman and one unskilled helper or apprentice tended a battery of barrels mounted on a flatbed iron frame. Assembly of the completed weapon took ten minutes, as skilled workmen moved rapidly among the cases of hammers, triggers, screws, and bands, and the racks of finished barrels and stocks. Watching them at work, Richards was reminded of compositors, setting type, deftly picking up "the several parts from their separate cases or racks and skillfully adjusting springs and inserting screws." [2]

All workmen at the Norwich Arms Company were paid by the piece according to the value of the part on which they worked.

1. *Hartford Courant* (Oct. 20, 1863); *Harper's New Monthly Magazine*, 28 (1864), 451.

2. *Harper's New Monthly Magazine*, 28, 461.

Thus barrelmakers and riflers received the highest rate per piece, barrels being the most expensive item in the weapon, while those who turned out ramrod spring-wires, valued at one-tenth of a cent each, received the lowest rate per piece. Any flaw in workmanship that resulted in the scrapping of the part was born by the workman held responsible.

The Norwich Arms Company operated the largest, most successful new firearms factory in the state, if not in the nation. It was soon imitated by numerous similar ventures, most of which relied on subcontractors, at least until they had fulfilled the terms of their original contracts. William W. Welch, a Norfolk physician and a politician, like James Mowry seems to have envisaged a completely integrated arms factory from the very beginning. He incorporated the Connecticut Arms Company in the fall of 1862 and then received a government contract for 18,000 muskets. Since he had no suitable plant, Welch depended on subcontractors for three months until he could remodel and equip an inactive machine shop for his new factory. In another five months' time, he was producing and shipping 1,400 muskets a month.[3]

But most of the new arms manufacturers during the first year of the war either did not have the capital or were unwilling to take the risks of expanding as quickly as Welch or Mowry. More typical was the course pursued by the Eagle Arms Company of Mansfield. Until the fall of 1862 it made nothing but bayonets and assembled rifles. Parts were manufactured elsewhere. Barrels had been reamed and finished on Middletown lathes; locks had come in from Philadelphia; while Hartford and New Haven had supplied all other components. Out of the first year's profits and with a new contract at hand for 25,000 Springfields, the company decided to concentrate all branches of rifle manufacture at Mansfield. Harford and New York interests, who owned the new corporation, bought enough buildings to serve as a suitable armory. With a labor force of 500 men working two shifts of twelve hours each, the Eagle Arms Company was soon producing 300 rifles and 400 bayonets a

3. *Norwich Courier* (Oct. 9, Dec. 2, 1862); *Hartford Courant* (July 15, 1864); Theron W. Crissey, *History of Norfolk, Litchfield County, Connecticut* (Everett, 1900), p. 240.

day.[4] At the war's end, not less than forty large and small factories were producing firearms exclusively.[5] Yet several of the established concerns found it advantageous to rely on subcontractors for a part of their work throughout the war.

The Joslyn Arms Company of Stonington, a small prewar manufacturer of firearms, adopted this more conservative policy. Even large arms companies like Alsop and Savage of Middletown utilized the local machine shops of Ira Johns and Peter Ashton for gun barrels and locks.[6] Alsop and Savage turned out a major part of Middletown's firearms production, which was valued at about $700,000 a year from 1861 to 1865. Since barrels and locks were the most expensive components of a musket, the subcontractors played an important role in generating this volume of business. Although many small factories took on substantial subcontracting business, they often pursued profitable side lines in rifle equipment on their own. The Union Machine Company of Norwich, while working night and day to fill $100,000 in orders for gun barrels, locks, and springs, secured a prime contract for 75,000 bayonets.[7] Charles Parker of Meriden, Pierpont and Tolles of Unionville, and Denslow and Chase of Windsor Locks were a few of the scores of Connecticut manufacturers who did both subcontracting and prime-contracting on the same premises.

Despite the output of the new firearms companies, the industry was still centered upon the big five that had been established before the war. These were the plants of Eli Whitney, Jr., and Oliver Winchester in New Haven, Sharps' Rifle Company and the Colt Patent Fire Arms Company of Hartford, and the Middletown works of Alsop and Savage. All these factories had been doing a heavy volume of business since mid-1860; and all had completed ambitious expansion programs by the fall of 1861, in most instances doubling their manufacturing capacity. Even this new plant capacity fell far short of government demands, which explains the rise of new arms manufacturers in the state and the

4. *Norwich Courier* (Jan. 9, 1863).
5. Deyrup, *Arms Makers*, pp. 221–26.
6. *Norwich Courier* (Oct. 9, Dec. 2, 1862); *Hartford Courant* (July 15, 1864).
7. *Norwich Bulletin* (May 8, 1862).

widespread conversion of the consumer goods industry to firearms production.

Well before Bull Run, for instance, Governor Buckingham had ordered the recruitment and organization of five additional regiments. The equipment required by these regiments, in addition to large Federal contracts, provided more work than the factories of the state could handle. By August 15 Colonel Samuel Colt had 1,100 men employed, with over 500 carpenters, masons, and laborers, building an addition that would double facilities and production.[8] During the first six months of the war all this new capacity came into production, yet there was still a severe shortage of firearms.

Sharps' rifles and Colt's revolving rifles were so scarce that only the flank companies of the Connecticut three-months regiments received them, the remainder being equipped with smooth-bore muskets.[9] The bidding of the War Department and the state adjutant generals doubled the price of all weapons, even the despised Enfields, on the open market.[10] When the War Department tried to confiscate Connecticut's rifles after the battle of Bull Run, Governor Buckingham put pressure on the Administration for their return. The President and Secretary of War Cameron reluctantly acquiesced. Agents of the state journeyed to Washington, gathered up the 800 precious Sharps, and brought them back.[11]

In such an emergency, state and nation were fortunate to have had the services of Colonel Sam Colt. His ideas, energy, and capacity for labor were blocked out on a Byronic scale, far beyond the limits of his physical endurance. In fact, he was to work himself to death in 1862.[12] Colt's great weakness was his egotism, causing him frequently to clash with the press, the people of Hartford, and the Governor.[13] But he had generous qualities as well, which, in a man of his dynamic personality, took the form of a benevolent paternalism. No businessman in Connecticut, if not in the entire Union,

8. Ibid. (Aug. 15, 1861).
9. Croffut and Morris, *History of Connecticut,* p. 67.
10. Ibid.
11. *Norwich Bulletin* (Oct. 18, 1861).
12. J. H. Trumbull, *Hartford County,* 1, 565.
13. *Hartford Press* (Jan. 10, 11, 1862); Marvin, *Fifth Regiment,* pp. 17–19.

was more conscientious in providing employee services than this magnetic man with his clipped brown beard and flowing hair. Colt saw to it that the various contractors he employed paid their men the highest wages in the arms industry. His sprawling brownstone factory was equipped with steam heat, gaslights, and running water, conveniences few workmen enjoyed in the Connecticut of the early sixties. The work rooms were large and well ventilated; lofty sixteen-foot ceilings were standard throughout the factory.[14] Colt was also most solicitous of his employees' welfare and cultural improvement. Near the factory he built model homes for his workers and charged them nominal rents in comparison with other privately owned housing in Hartford. Interested in the leisure time activities of his employees, he built a library and a public hall on the armory grounds, where free lectures, concerts, and socials were enjoyed by the workers and their families. The Colt band, which he organized and fitted out with instruments and uniforms, was the pride of Hartford.[15]

The Colt Armory at Hartford in 1861 covered acres of former marsh land, which the Colonel with shrewd business sense had purchased very cheaply in 1850.[16] He had promptly erected an enormous two-mile dike to protect his property from Connecticut River floods, and drained the land. This South Meadow Improvement, as it was known, was one of those monumental tasks in which he gloried, risking large amounts of capital that mocked the caution of his conservative neighbors. Whatever the odds, it was a most successful undertaking. Much to the amazement and perhaps the envy of the business community, a three-story armory rapidly took shape on the 250 acres of reclaimed land.[17] Colt surmounted the vast works with an onion-shaped blue and gold cupola, topped with a rampant colt.[18]

The Hartford gunmaker was a mechanical genius, a great improviser, and a prodigious worker.[19] By 1861 the interior of his factory was stocked with one of the finest assortments of machine tools

14. Deyrup, p. 164.
15. Wilson and Fiske, *Appleton's*, I, 694.
16. J. H. Trumbull, I, 566.
17. Ibid.
18. *Hartford Press* (Jan. 10, 1862).
19. J. H. Trumbull, I, 566.

in North America. Many of them were of his own design or the work of his versatile assistant, E. K. Root.[20] Furthermore, Colt was an apostle of interchangeable parts and mass production, substituting machine for hand labor, and unskilled for skilled, wherever possible.[21] He had been a keen observer of Eli Whitney and Seth Thomas' pioneering in that field and a not too scrupulous borrower of those old masters' methods.[22] Constantly improving and improvising new techniques in the interest of faster, cheaper, and better production, his restless brain pushed machine techniques far beyond Whitney's beginnings.

Colt shaped his production force upon a widely copied idea: a division of labor that involved three levels—management, contractors, and workmen. He negotiated a separate contract for each individual part of his rifle and revolver with a different middleman, stipulating the price, quantity, and production schedule. Colt furnished the factory space and most of the machinery, power, and samples; the contractors purchased the raw materials and labor and sold him the finished product.[23] He retained under his direct supervision only the assembly of the standardized parts.[24] This procedure, actually a refinement of the old domestic system, was perhaps the only way in which so many diverse machine activities could be carried on under one roof without the moving assembly-lines of the future.[25] Its one great weakness, which frequently interfered with production, was the complex interdependence of the work force, whose management was split up among scores of individual contractors. Were one contractor to fall behind in his schedule, everyone else was halted until the parts pipeline began flowing evenly again.[26] Fortunately, most of Colt's contractors were exceptionally able men, who would later make their mark in the rising machine-tool industry. At least one, Dwight Slate, must

20. Ibid. Root is credited with the invention of the drop forge.

21. J. H. Trumbull, *I*, 569.

22. Rachel M. Hartley, *The History of Hamden, Connecticut, 1786–1936* (New Haven, 1943), p. 262; John E. Parsons, ed., *Samuel Colt's Own Record of Transactions with Captain Walker and Eli Whitney, Jr., in 1847*, CHS (Hartford), 1949, pp. 108, 110, 195.

23. J. H. Trumbull, *I*, 569.

24. Ibid., p. 569.

25. Ibid.

26. Deyrup, p. 164.

rank with Colt and Root as a mechanical genius. Slate, a weather-beaten figure with a full beard and quizzical eyes, was one of those self-taught Yankee mechanics whose energy, creative ability, and perseverance were developing the industrial revolution in the North. While at Colt's, he rifled 120,000 muskets on contract, with only ½ of 1 per cent being rejected by government inspectors.[27] To accomplish this production feat, Slate utilized special tools of his own invention. Some of these, like the taper lathe, were to prove invaluable when adapted to the needs of the new machine-tool industry.[28]

A visit to Colt's factory would have disclosed an acre of trip hammers and drop forges arranged in rows, and deriving their power by means of belts and wheels from heavy-duty steam engines in the basement. Sears, triggers, and springs were shaped in sequence, collected, sorted, and sent to spacious assembly rooms. Should a machine break down, machinists were ready to repair it, for the factory had a completely equipped machine shop.[29] Bottlenecks or work stoppages due to machine failure were rare. So extensive a calamity as the destruction of half the works by fire in 1864 daunted not the superior organization Colt had developed during his short business career in Hartford.[30] It took only eight months to repair damage estimated at two million dollars and bring production up to the 1861 level.[31] The Colt factory alone manufactured enough rifles during the war years to outfit the Army of the Potomac and enough revolvers to equip all the Union armies.[32]

Christian Sharps' Rifle Company under the capable management of John C. Palmer, though far behind Colt's in output, achieved an impressive production schedule. Assembly of rifles rose in a steady curve until, by the first half of November 1861, a thousand rifles a month were being manufactured, with plans set for twice this production rate.[33] The wartime output of the Whitney and Winches-

27. Davis, *New England States*, 2, 852–53.

28. Ibid.

29. Charles E. Hanson and Frank A. Belden, *A History of the Colt Revolver and Other Arms* (New York, 1940), pp. 352–62.

30. Ibid.

31. Ibid.; *Hartford Courant* (Feb. 8, 1864).

32. 673,000 rifles and 414,391 revolvers. Hanson and Belden, p. 120.

33. *Hartford Press* (Nov. 18, 1861).

ter armories in New Haven was each approximately equal to Sharps'. Oliver Winchester, however, would seem to have been more interested in improving rifle design than any other arms maker in the state.

Formerly a large-scale shirt manufacturer, Winchester had invested a part of his fortune in the arms industry three years before the war, when he bought out the Volcanic Arms Company and purchased Eli Whitney's old factory for his original production facility. Winchester, a restless, aggressive businessman, not only plowed back wartime profits into plant expansion but launched an extensive development program, which eventually resulted in the famed Henry Rifle. Henry Rifles employed fixed ammunition in place of the cumbersome ball and paper cartridge combination. A breech-loaded Henry, using a brass case cartridge with a conical fixed head, was much more accurate and more easily loaded than the regulation Springfield and far outranged the breech-loading Sharps. It was to rank with the Spencer repeater as a revolutionary weapon in infantry tactics. Henry Rifles were little used during the war, however, because of arch conservatism in the War Department.

Large profits accruing to the arms makers—Sharps, to cite an example, declared dividends equivalent to 24 per cent on the market value of its stock during the third quarter of 1862—permitted the luxury of experimentation and product improvement, increased facilities, trained a skilled labor supply, and stimulated other industries.[34] The development of the Henry Rifle, for example, and the numerous imitators that followed, created a heavy demand in postwar years for brass cartridge cases, giving impetus to special branches of the flourishing brass industry in the Naugatuck Valley. Lyman Coe, one of the partners of the Walcottville Brass Company, bought out and perfected a Smith and Wesson patent for brass cartridge cases.[35] The company began volume production of them for the Henry Rifle in 1863, scarcely a year after that weapon had proved its worth on the range of the Winchester Armory.[36]

34. *Hartford Courant* (Nov. 10, 1862).

35. William G. Lathrop, *The Brass Industry in the United States: A Study of the Origins and Development of the Brass Industry in the Naugatuck Valley* (Mount Carmel, 1926), pp. 107–08.

36. Ibid.

Even with the expanded production of established arms plants and the host of new arms makers, demand for rifles, muskets, and revolvers continued to mount during 1862. As the experience of the Norwich Arms Company suggests, the roaring government market for firearms and munitions of all kinds inspired a rapid conversion from consumer goods to war production. Connecticut was eminently well prepared to make the transition. For its size and population no other state in the Union had such a diversity of skill and industry. In 1860 Connecticut manufactured more firearms and brass and paper products than any other state. Besides these important industries, all of which were to deal directly or indirectly with weapons production, such useful industries for the supply of military equipment as rubber, machine tools, hardware, and leather were all well established and growing rapidly. A large share of the nation's shipbuilding was carried on in Connecticut, as well as the manufacture of sewing machines, clocks, textiles, and silverware. In addition, hundreds of small factories producing a variety of merchandise from pianoforte keys and mousetraps to carriages and cotton gins made an ideal industrial plant for conversion to badly needed items of war material. It was not to prove difficult for a factory like the Collins Company, which produced the best axes in the United States, to adapt itself to the manufacture of sabers and bayonets. In fact, L. T. Richardson, a contractor for Collins, with one helper, made 10,000 bayonet blades during the month of October 1863.[37] Nor was the departure from the manufacture of carriages to the production of army wagons, or from the casting of ornamental bronzes to the casting of artillery accessories, to be troublesome. The rapid conversion of Connecticut's consumer goods industry to war production and a remarkable expansion of the munitions industry contributed significantly to the crucial struggle for material supremacy, a struggle that had been determined in favor of the North long before Gettysburg.

Whether manufacturing firearms and bayonets directly or by subcontract, the consumer goods industry made a rapid conversion, considering the state of managerial competence in 1861. Of course, in many instances the presence of machine shops permitted a comparatively easy conversion to a kindred industry such as fire-

37. *Hartford Courant* (Nov. 7, 1863).

arms. But there were innumerable instances of successful conversions where the former product bore little or no relationship to musket manufacture. Side by side with the waffle irons, coffee mills, wood screws, and piano stools manufactured by the remarkable Charles Parker at Meriden were rows of rifle stocks, barrels, and other parts ready for assembly on the premises. In little more than a year he too had erected a new factory solely for firearms manufacture, and was conducting both his war and consumer goods business with his accustomed efficiency.[38] The old Pierpont and Tolles factory, which had produced at one time or another since 1832 an astonishing variety of goods such as clocks, rivets, spoons, and mousetraps, found no difficulty adding gunstocks to its current production of hardware and cutlery.[39] Nor apparently was it much of a problem for Frederick Curtis, a noted Glastonbury manufacturer of silver plate, to turn out a substantial quantity of rifles.[40] Forming the Connecticut Arms and Manufacturing Company early in the war, he assembled rifles and made rifle parts under subcontracts.[41] At Windsor Locks, Denslow and Chase leased a cotton gin factory that had been ruined by the loss of its Southern market and converted it into a highly successful small armory.[42]

In another important industry, the manufacture of ordnance, conversion made a notable contribution to the war effort. Northwestern Connecticut had long been famed for its deposits of high quality hematite ore. Since colonial days, mines and smelters, bloomeries and forges had flourished near the towns of Sharon and Salisbury, in the southernmost spur of the Berkshire Hills. Salisbury iron had been cast into ordnance for Washington's army, and during the early nineteenth century it had supplied the principal needs of the gunmakers of Connecticut Valley. Long before the war, however, the quality of Litchfield County iron had started to decline. Though quite adequate for heavy castings or rough forgings it was considered too impure for the more precise requirements of small arms. Private and government armories had therefore shifted to foreign sources for their iron and steel. But wartime interrup-

38. Davis, 2, 1079, 1808.

39. J. H. Trumbull, *Hartford County*, 2, 199.

40. Ibid.

41. Ibid.

42. Ibid.

ions of commerce created an acute shortage of high-grade im-
orted iron; so again there was a heavy demand for Salisbury iron,
articularly for the manufacture of artillery and of solid shot and
hells.

Early in the war years Hotchkiss and Sons of Sharon converted
heir factory entirely to the production of artillery shells. It had
een forging from local ore such malleable iron products as garden
akes, wagon shaft couplings, monkey wrenches, and mowing ma-
hine fingers. However, Andrew Hotchkiss, a crippled son of the
ounder, who was something of an inventive genius, patented in
860 a new type of explosive shell. This projectile, in many ways a
rototype of modern artillery shells, was an instant success on the
Army proving grounds.

The Hotchkiss shell was an oblong, conical projectile with a loose
itting brass cap on its propellent end. Above this cap was a lead
and, so that when the shell was fired, the cap forced the lead band
nto the rifled grooves of the barrel, imparting the necessary twist
or accuracy. The conical part of the shell was hollow and con-
ained the bursting charge. A chamber bored through the point of
he shell carried a slender iron primer tipped with a percussion cap
nd filled with fulminate of mercury. A threaded brass plug acted
s a stopper. The tube was machined so that it would slide smoothly
within its chamber. During shell flight, inertia carried the tube and
ap back in its chamber. Upon impact it would be carried forward
gainst the plug, exploding primer and charge.[43] This rifled pro-
ectile was one of the first practical explosive shells based on the
nertia principle to be used by the Union artillery. Cast and ma-
hined to fit a variety of field artillery cannon, the shells were
rdered in such quantities that Hotchkiss and Sons converted their
ntire factory to munitions production during 1862. In 1863 the
ompany was forced to move to larger facilities in Bridgeport. But
t continued to draw on Salisbury iron for raw material and for
ough shell castings. Lawrence Van Alstyne, a Sharon supplier of
astings for the Hotchkiss Company, recalled that "every gray iron
oundry for miles around made shells for them." [44]

43. Lawrence Van Alstine, "Manufacturing in Sharon," *Pogunnuck Historical Society's ollections, #1, Lakeville Journal* (1912), passim.

44. Ibid.

Besides novel artillery ammunition, the old Salisbury ironmasters who had been written off in the fifties by army ordnance experts, a well as by the small arms factories of the Connecticut Valley, wer producing by late 1862 some of the most advanced cannon in th world. The Ames Iron Works in the little town of Falls Village, fo instance, was leased by the Federal government, and in the shor period of five months produced five 5,600-pound wrought-iro rifles capable of firing a 56-pound projectile five miles.[45] Bot Barnum and Richardson of Lime Rock and the Holley Iron Work at Salisbury, besides their usual production of pig iron and stee were also delivering large quantities of newly developed light artil lery rifles toward the end of 1862. Connecticut's iron industr would have converted to war production much sooner had it no been plagued by an acute shortage of skilled ironworkers and mold ers.[46] In fact, Alexander Holley made a personal trip to England i search of skilled labor. By means of attractive offers he secured considerable number of ironworkers under labor contract, thoug not enough manpower to meet his own demands, without eve considering the requirements of the industry.[47] The ordnance in dustry of Connecticut could not compare with the gigantic found ries of Pennsylvania and New York, where Columbiads and Parrot guns designed to fire projectiles of over 1,000 pounds were cast. Ye the partial conversion of Litchfield County's venerable iron indus try to artillery production was not the least of Connecticut's con tribution to the battle of supply.

Conversion to the production of associated military equipment— wagons, uniforms, canteens, bayonets, harnesses, leather belts, car tridge boxes, and many other items deemed necessary to equi soldiers and sailors—was both rapid and spectacular. The Collin Company, one of the leading producers of edged tools in the Unite States, probably set the first wartime production record in Connect icut when it delivered 7,500 sabers to the War Department les than thirty days after receipt of the order.[48] Carriage companies i the New Haven area, which had been reduced to near bankrupt

45. *Norwich Courier* (Sept. 11, 1862).

46. Davis, *New England States*, 1, 380.

47. *New Haven Palladium* (Jan. 5, 1863).

48. *New Haven Journal and Courier* (May 16, 1861).

22. Typical of Connecticut's war industry. Alfred Vaughn's Iron Foundry of Norwich, Connecticut, produced ornamental iron fencing, and did job work for armories, shipyards, and munitions plants. Connecticut Historical Society.

y the loss of their Southern customers, suddenly found that they ad so many orders for army wagons that they could not meet ivilian demands, which had begun to mount sharply. During the ummer of 1861 a small Walcottville carriage factory set the pace vith twenty-eight complete wagons in fifteen days.

Former merchant tailors with state and Federal contracts rapidly dapted themselves to machine-cutting techniques and achieved an mazing output. One such company in Hartford (the Charles Day Company) actually delivered 20,000 uniforms between April 5 and August 5, 1861, though most were of poor material and mperfectly sewn.[49] Button factories in Waterbury, Naugatuck, nd Ansonia perfected suitable dies, hired more help, and while naintaining a stream of bone, glass, and jet buttons for their regu-ar trade, manufactured millions of brass buttons for uniforms.[50] This unprecedented expansion of the civilian button industry timulated the dynamic brass industry of the Naugatuck Valley, vhich was already at a frenzied tempo of production as it worked o complete large government contracts for artillery accessories and ll manner of rolled or drawn brass products.[51] The demands of he cavalry regiments and horse-drawn transport converted a part f the New Britain saddle equipment and hardware industries into pecialized military production, which consumed much of the out-ut of the booming Jewell tannery and leather factory in Hart-ord. Army demands for rubber blankets, ponchos, and boots rovided a profitable market for Connecticut's thriving rubber ndustry. The Hayward Rubber Company of Colchester, whose irection was in the hands of Governor Buckingham (no conflict of nterest in those days), the Goodyear Rubber Company of Nauga-uck, and the Candee Rubber Company of New Haven together onstituted the second largest producers of rubber goods in the ation.[52] Though these companies manufactured millions of dol-ars worth of equipment for the armed forces, they still succeeded n supplying adequately an accelerating home market for rubber oods.

49. *Hartford Times* (Aug. 7, 1861); *Norwich Courier* (Aug. 8, 1861).
50. Lathrop, *Brass Industry*, pp. 24, 108.
51. Ibid.
52. *Compendium*, Ninth Census, 1870, p. 878.

Another established industry that rivaled any in production wa the manufacture of gunpowder in Hartford County. Since colonia times, powder-making had been carried on along the Hockanum River and its tributaries at the towns of East Hartford, Canton and Enfield. Factories in each of these localities manufactured 15,000 tons of powder annually during the war years.[53] The largest of Connecticut powder factories—and, indeed, one of the largest in the country—was the Hazard Powder Company at Enfield. Founded in 1843 by Augustus Hazard, who had made a fortune in merchandising and shipping, it had expanded continuously under his personal management until it rivaled the arms factories in size and output.[54] Hazard, like Colt and Whitney, had done a thriving business with the South prior to Sumter. In fact over 60,000 pounds of his powder, which had been convenientl stored at Lynchburg, Virginia, awaiting distribution to Southern customers, was confiscated by Governor Letcher when Virginia seceded from the Union.[55] This loss, however, was soon replaced thousands of times over through the sale of powder to the Federal government and to the loyal states. A marked similarity characterized the manufacturing methods of both Colt and Hazard. Every process in the manufacture of gunpowder at Enfield was performed in his factory complex of 125 buildings. This included the manufacture and repair of the presses, rollers, and granulato at the company machine shops. By utilizing machine techniques and by constantly enlarging his facilities, Hazard produced over twelve tons of powder daily, with an annual output valued at over a million dollars.[56]

Although the Hazard Powder Company and other powder factories carried production one step further and manufactured cartridges, still a substantial share of their output was consumed by the many wartime ammunition plants that sprang up in response to an unlimited demand. Little more than shops, with a working force consisting mainly of women, they specialized in paper cartridges that were cut, filled, and crimped by hand. Robert Chadwick, for

53. This is an estimate derived from ibid., pp. 850–80; Eighth Census, 1860, *Manufactures*, passim; J. H. Trumbull, *1*, 210; *2*, 75, 98, 158.

54. J. H. Trumbull, *2*, 161.

55. *Norwich Courier* (May 9, 1861).

56. J. H. Trumbull, *2*, 157–58.

example, organized a cartridge factory in Hartford in the summer of 1861, drew his labor force from unemployed female textile workers, and was producing eight tons of waterproof paper cartridges a week by September of that year.[57] This was typical of the innumerable low overhead cartridge plants that were hastily established in industrial centers and swelled the munitions output of Connecticut to unprecedented proportions. The wartime market for cartridges soon awakened the interest of Connecticut inventors and mechanics in the possibility of developing automatic cartridge makers. Dozens of mechanical contrivances that would shape, fill, and crimp the watertight paper cartridge casings were submitted by Connecticut citizens to the Patent Office during the war. Perhaps the most practical of these, and certainly the only cartridge machines that were used in any quantity, were those invented by T. W. Webb of Hartford. Webb developed a semiautomatic cartridge header and a trimmer. Both were self-acting and feeding devices. Working on continuous lengths of cartridge paper, the two machines in tandem were capable of producing 3,000 completed cartridges per hour. According to the Hartford *Courant*, they were easy to operate—the header, for instance, requiring the labor of one boy.[58] Cartridge machinery, however, came late in the war, and by the time it was perfected, brass had supplanted paper as cartridge casing.

All this industrial activity in the munitions field meant a frenzied search for government contracts, a search that was often marred by influence peddling and political favoritism. The rush was on to Washington and Hartford: the lobbies of Congress, the General Assembly, and the offices of state and Federal officials were crowded with business agents, lobbyists, and a newer breed of individuals best described as middlemen or contract brokers. At first, it was not too difficult to obtain a contract; but as the war continued, more orders went to fewer concerns. Without either money or political influence, small factories and shops were forced to divide their profits with contract brokers or to subcontract from middlemen who had gained the ear of a military purchasing agent. Ambitious businessmen even utilized church membership as a means of

57. *Hartford Times* (Sept. 16, 1861).
58. *Hartford Courant* (March 11, 1865).

seeking out those who were in a position to bestow favors. So successful was a ring of Hartford Baptists in prevailing upon the sentiments of fellow church members Adjutant General Williams and Quartermaster General Hathaway that it would seem to have garnered a lion's share of the state contracts until both those officials were dismissed by the Governor for negligence or misconduct.[59] In New Haven the firm of C. and D. Cook and Company, closely associated with N. D. Sperry, the New Haven postmaster, secured large contracts for battery carriage work, 20,000 pairs of army shoes, and quantities of knapsacks and haversacks. Such an assortment of orders to a carriage factory shows the extent that political influence played in the war effort.

Members of the legislature also entered the scramble for war work. Dr. William W. Welch, a former Republican representative from Norfolk and a local politician of considerable influence, secured a War Department contract for 18,000 Enfields, though he possessed no factory for their manufacture. Similarly, the Hotchkiss brothers of Middletown had potent political influence. Julius Hotchkiss, the leading Democratic politician in Middlesex County, was President of Alsop and Savage, which produced enough rifles and made enough money to acclimate itself to the perils of peacetime production.[60] Others had indirect contacts with the War and Navy Departments or with Lincoln himself. James Dixon made it possible for Horatio Ames of Falls Village to meet the President and present his plans for wrought-iron cannon manufacture. The friendship that the New Haven entrepreneur Cornelius S. Bushnell enjoyed with Gideon Welles laid the basis for the *Monitor* construction contract in which he and Postmaster Nehemiah D. Sperry each

59. "Clothing contracts went to C. G. Day & Co. of South Baptist Church, for canteens to Bronson & Co.—poor canteens it was said but good Baptists made them—H. Griswold & Co. of the South Baptist made the haversacks. Sundry small positions like quartermasters and paymasters have gone to the inevitable Baptist . . . this is the general everyday talk in the streets. A while ago Major Hathaway, the Quartermaster General was supposed to be looking outside for clothing contracts. This was taking the cash out of the Baptists' pockets and immediately charges of defalcation were made which have never been proved. He resigned, and the position was given to Jonathan B. Bunce who probably means well, but has opened his administration by giving a blacksmith in Willimantic a contract to make a hundred military coats." *Winsted Herald* (Oct. 21, 1861).

60. *Norwich Courier* (March 20, 1862).

held a fourth interest.[61] The rotund, literary Congressman Henry Deming of Hartford, assisted by Julius Strong, soon to occupy Deming's seat, and the Hartford postmaster Edward Cleveland, all acted as contract commission agents and influence-peddlers for the Sharps' Rifle Company of Hartford and the Norwich Arms Company. As the war continued, their political influence became so strong, declared Charles Dudley Warner, that they were able to force rifles on a reluctant War Department even when army stockpiles of surplus ordnance were bulging in early 1863.[62]

Despite laxity in procurement methods and the consequent growth of favoritism, if not downright rascality, in contract awards, few Connecticut factories capable and desirous of performing war work were neglected. Considering the circumstances and the lack of procurement experience, there was a high degree of efficiency in utilizing the state's industrial potential. The firearms industry alone probably produced enough rifles and pistols to equip most of the Union armies—a phenomenal achievement. Another striking quality of the Connecticut munitions industry was its ability to produce in quantity almost everything required to make war. Brass buttons, sabers, uniforms, rubber goods, blankets, bayonets, cannons and mounts, brass products, wagons, harnesses, firearms, shells and warships all poured forth in great volume from shipyards, shops, factories, foundries, and forges. At the same time, the state was developing into an important financial and insurance center and was producing millions of dollars worth of agricultural products and consumer goods despite the fact that over 15 per cent of its total manpower was serving in the armed forces. The economic capacity of Connecticut, as expressed in its productive power, was impressive indeed, yet the reasons for such astonishing vigor are not difficult to explain.

Connecticut in 1861 was well advanced in the industrial revolution. Since the 1820s her enterprising people, with the assistance of abundant waterpower and capital derived from shipping, had been engaged in diversified industry. Conversion, which was the single most important factor behind the development of her wartime mu-

61. Dixon to Abraham Lincoln, Sept. 8, 1863 (Lincoln Papers).

62. Warner to J. R. Hawley, Dec. 4, 1864; Jan. 15, 1865 (Hawley Papers, LC).

nitions industry, was a relatively simple adjustment. Inventive managers and skilled workmen, though well versed in the techniques of machine production, had not yet become rigidly specialized. Although the output of Connecticut industry during the war would have delighted a Carnot, there was little or no organization and probably no conscious effort on the part of the participants. To most it was merely the addition or substitution of another product for the two or three being manufactured, with the profit motive and patriotism determining the emphasis. It should also be remembered that the weapons and equipment of the Civil War were by and large of simple design, easily fabricated and assembled with such well-understood machine tools as drop forges, steam hammers, lathes, and traditional casting, rolling, and machine techniques.

The munitions industry was undoubtedly a major achievement, but by its very nature fleeting. In one respect, however, it could claim a measure of permanence. It developed capital as well as managerial skill for all branches of industry, whose importance in peace would ensure a continued advance in a troubled economic future. The war had created a large munition industry with its demand for a type of goods and skill which Connecticut was particularly well equipped to supply. However, there were other products manufactured in the state that were needed just as desperately by both the military and civilian population and whose production had occupied some of its best business talents and enterprise for over half a century. These were textiles to be made into uniforms, tents, blankets, and clothing for the military and the civilian population. Wartime Connecticut may have been a land of machine shops, foundries, and rolling mills; it was also a land of spindles, jacquards, and looms.

14. TEXTILES IN WARTIME: WOOLENS, COTTONS, AND SILKS

IN APRIL 1861 Connecticut was one of the leading textile centers in the United States. With 129 cotton factories, it ranked third in the manufacture of that commodity, exceeded by Massachusetts and Rhode Island, and was second only to Massachusetts in the manufacture of woolens. In the production of that indispensable though commonplace item—thread, Connecticut was well ahead of all contenders. Its silk industry at Manchester and Rockville was as progressive as any in the nation.[1] This extensive industrial plant had not been achieved in a brief period, but bore every evidence of carefully tended growth by skillful managers.

Connecticut possessed many natural advantages which had assisted early textile entrepreneurs. Like neighboring New England states, it was endowed with several large rivers and scores of swiftly flowing tributaries. Its geographic position between two great commercial centers, with the sheltered Long Island Sound as an inland sea along the southern border, provided inexpensive water transportation. The same sheltered coastline, studded with good harbors, had also fostered the early development of commercial enterprises and the accretion of maritime wealth. Thus, when commerce was interrupted by the Napoleonic Wars, much of this capital flowed into such domestic channels as the infant industries of the day or early transportation projects. Since the textile industry was the first to profit from the machine techniques of the dawning industrial revolution, it received a substantial share of this diverted maritime capital. Textile manufacturing, as a result, got its start in Connecticut between 1809 and 1815, when American commerce fell victim to the war policies of France and England, though the first woolen mill in the United States had been erected at Hartford in 1788 and

1. Eighth Census, 1860, *Manufactures*, passim.

some cotton factories had been established during the 1790s.[2]

Except for isolated instances, the manufacture of woolens predated that of cottons by thirty-five years. David Humphreys, a picturesque squire with a philosophic bent, founded the Connecticut woolen industry.[3] After importing some choice Merino sheep from Spain, inaugurating a Merino craze in New England, he established the first successful woolen mill in the town of Derby.[4] Shortly thereafter, two emigrants from Yorkshire, the Schofield brothers, built and operated several small woolen mills in southeastern Connecticut. The production of these early factories was confined exclusively to the finer materials such as broadcloth and cassimere. But as such fabrics were decidedly inferior to English varieties and more expensive, the infant industry would have failed had not the maritime difficulties of the Napoleonic Wars given it a large share of the domestic market. In fact, the Jeffersonian Embargo and the War of 1812 not only saved the Connecticut woolen industry from imminent destruction but developed it out of all proportion. What amounted to a blockade of the United States from 1809 to 1815 created such a scarcity of broadcloth and cassimere that the existing mills were swamped with orders and many new mills were built or projected. No less than twenty-six woolen companies were chartered in Connecticut from the declaration of war to the Peace of Ghent. When the normal channels of trade were restored after the war, however, English goods again invaded the American market, with disastrous results for the new industry.

The bitter lesson of foreign competition inspired woolen manufacturers to agitate for a protective tariff. Although not powerful enough to secure adequate protection from the Tariff of 1816 or even to enlist the support of commercially minded Connecticut congressmen, they were more successful with subsequent tariff legislation.[5] National tariff policy from 1824 until 1861 was in the

2. J. H. Trumbull, *Hartford County*, I, 196; Davis, *New England States*, I, 119–20, 195–96.

3. Davis, I, 205.

4. J. H. Trumbull, I, 565. Although the Hartford Mill had been built in 1788 and had manufactured cloth including the material from which the inaugural suits of President Washington and Vice-President Adams were made, it was not a financial success.

5. Frank W. Taussig, *The Tariff History of the United States* (8th ed., rev., New York, 1931), chap. I.

main favorable to the woolen industry in Connecticut, but by no means went as far as the manufacturers desired.[6] The principal reason for this was an economic conflict between native producers of raw wool and the manufacturers. American wool production had also expanded during the trade interruptions of the Napoleonic period and had become in a very short time an important industry, especially along the frontier in northern New England and in the Western Reserve. Unlike American raw cotton, which enjoyed a virtual monopoly of the market at an early date, native wool producers had to compete with western Europe, where sheep raising had been one of the most important industries since the Middle Ages, and where near optimum conditions, economic and geographic, existed for the production of raw wool.[7] Furthermore, raw wool was not of uniform quality, ranging from the very coarse, suitable for carpets and cheap flannels, to the very fine, from which expensive broadcloths and cassimeres were made. American wool, though inferior to the European product and more expensive, was of the fine variety, thus directly competitive.

Naturally, American wool manufacturers wanted free access to the cheapest and best raw materials, as well as protection from foreign cloth in the home market, while American wool producers wanted protection from foreign wool. The history of the tariff prior to the Civil War reflected the opposing views of these groups. By complicated schedules involving mixtures of ad valorem and specific duties on both types of commodities, the tariff was generally, though modestly, beneficial to both. Wool producers were favored in the Tariffs of 1816, 1824, and 1828. Although duties had been levied on woolen cloth imports in every one of these tariffs, corresponding duties on raw wool imports canceled out most benefits to the woolen manufacturers. Likewise, the Compromise Tariff of 1832 had been partial to the sheepherders; but in 1842 the duties on fine wool were lowered, stimulating the manufacture of fine broadcloth and blankets. The Walker Tariff, however, restored these duties five years later, severely crippling such manufacture. What has been regarded as the high point of free trade in the United States, the Tariff of 1857, was, oddly enough, the first na-

6. Ibid., pp. 37, 65, 143–54.
7. Ibid.

tional tariff act to favor woolen cloth interests.[8] To be sure, duties on imported cloth were reduced, but raw wool was admitted practically free of duty.[9] The outcry from sheep raisers was especially intense, and the not inconsiderable raw wool interest in Connecticut joined its brethren of the West and North in denouncing it.[10] It was in response to these interests, as well as to raise revenue, that the great war Tariffs of 1862 and 1864 embodied the principle of compensation whereby high duties were reimposed upon foreign wool; but the manufacturers were compensated by correspondingly higher duties on imported cloth of all types.[11] Needless to say, the American consumer of woolen goods, which included the military as well as the average citizen, had to pay exceedingly high prices for cloth during the war period. Nor was it of good quality. With compensating duties added to normal protection rates and burdensome wartime excise taxes also imposed, fine English cloth became prohibitive in price and the inferior domestic product very nearly so.[12]

An encouraging tariff (at least on the cheaper varieties of cloth), better transportation by way of railroads, and an expanding market—all acted to stimulate the development of woolen manufacture in Connecticut. On the whole, it had enjoyed a substantial though not spectacular prosperity, with the period of greatest prewar growth occurring between 1840 and 1860. On the eve of the war the Connecticut woolen industry was one of considerable wealth, somewhat backward in machine techniques and chronically short of skilled workers, yet accustomed to hard competition, both domestic and foreign. The mills were small by postwar standards, employing an average of 50 to 100 employees and operating about the same number of looms.[13] Though scattered throughout the

8. Ibid., p. 151.

9. Ibid.

10. Daniel L. Phillips, *Griswold—A History; Being a History of the Town of Griswold, Connecticut* (New Haven, 1929), pp. 164, 204. In 1850 Connecticut raised 174,181 sheep, which produced 497,454 pounds of wool. In 1860 it raised 119,807 sheep, and the clip for that year amounted to 335,986 pounds of wool. *Wool Report to the Boston Board of Trade for 1862*, p. 13.

11. Taussig, pp. 195–97.

12. Victor S. Clark, *History of Manufactures in the United States, 1860–93* (Washington, D.C., 1916), 2, 30.

13. *Compendium*, Ninth Census, 1870, 630.

state wherever adequate waterpower was available, the industry was showing definite signs of concentration in specific areas by the early sixties.[14] The towns of Rockville and Torrington in Tolland County had the largest mills and produced the greatest amount of cloth in the state.[15] Rockville itself had eight large mills employing 1,500 operatives.[16] In 1864, Hartford and Tolland counties boasted 44 woolen mills with the majority of them in Tolland County.[17] Next in importance was the Norwich area, followed closely by Stafford Springs and Montville. Nearly all of these mills manufactured some broadcloth and fine cassimere, but the mainstays of their production were coarse satinets, and flannels, much of which until the outbreak of the war was marketed in the Southern states.[18] Carpet manufacture was also important and was represented by the Hartford Carpet Company at Thompsonville, a close neighbor of Augustus Hazard's powder works. In 1860 it was just beginning to turn out the new Wilton and Moquet carpets, which would adorn the homes of the wartime nouveaux riches.[19] Only in the seven years between 1857 and 1864 did the woolen cloth industry in Connecticut enjoy what might be called a truly favorable tariff, and then only by application of compensation duties that at best were thinly disguised subsidies to the manufacturers. But the manufacture of cotton had received beneficial treatment in tariffs almost from its establishment as an industry.

Cotton manufacture in Connecticut, like that of wool, prospered mightily during the commercial difficulties of the Napoleonic period. The first mill, erected at Pomfret in 1806 by that indefatigable Briton Samuel Slater, was followed by fifteen large and many small mills in the next ten years. Similarly, the overexpanded cotton industry suffered when the Peace of Ghent was followed by a flood of English cloth that poured into the American market.[20] In sharp contrast to woolen cloth interests, cotton manufacturers did secure adequate relief by virtue of the minimum valuation

14. Davis, *New England*, 1, 250.
15. *Compendium*, Ninth Census, 1870, 630.
16. *Hartford Courant* (Aug. 11, 1863).
17. Ibid. (Feb. 20, 1864).
18. Ibid.
19. J. H. Trumbull, 2, 156–57.
20. Forrest Morgan, ed., *Connecticut as a Colony and a State*, 3 (Hartford, 1904), 225–26.

principle in the Tariff of 1816. Since there was no raw material problem, they were able to maintain the principle in later tariffs and enjoy protection.[21] Although Massachusetts and Rhode Island quickly developed a much larger cotton industry than Connecticut, production charted a steady expansion, particularly in the output of coarse sheetings and shirtings. According to the statistical survey of the state made in 1845, cotton cloth was second only to woolens among the various industries.

The center of this growing industry was southeastern Connecticut, in the counties of New London and Windham, a region of wild beauty, where swiftly flowing streams inspired local romantic poets and attracted practical entrepreneurs to sources of unexploited power. Yet these power sites remained largely undeveloped for twenty-five years because of the preoccupation of the textile magnates, who were expanding the potential of Massachusetts and Rhode Island, and the unexplained apathy of local capitalists. From the beginning, Connecticut capitalists had been quite indifferent to the cotton industry. The earliest mills had been built by Rhode Island manufacturers and were conducted as subsidiaries to their home mills. In 1845 the largest cotton mill in the state, the Quinnebaug Company, which was capitalized at $1,000,000, was owned and operated by the Lippett brothers of Woonsocket, Rhode Island.[22] The Slaters conducted the affairs of their prosperous mills in Jewett City through an agent, as did the Masons at Thompson.[23] By the early 1850s, however, Rhode Island manufacturers had exploited most of the water-power sites of that state and had begun to look upon their Connecticut investments with greater interest. At the same time, they explored the water-power potential in southeastern Connecticut and made preparations to purchase choice sites. Eastern Connecticut capitalists, who had so long ignored the possibilities for an expansion of cotton manufacture in the Norwich area, also caught the fever, with the result that the decade of the fifties was the prelude to development on a large scale.

21. Taussig, *Tariff History*, p. 190.

22. Jarvis M. Morse, *A Neglected Period of Connecticut's History, 1818–1850* (New Haven, 1933), p. 223.

23. Davis, *1*, 160.

Fittingly enough, the invasion was inaugurated by the greatest of all Rhode Island cotton manufacturers, Governor William Sprague. Sprague purchased Lord's farm, an 8,000-acre tract of land along the Shetucket River, about fifteen miles northeast of Norwich. There, in the spring of 1856, he started construction of a very large cotton mill—enormous by the standards of the day.[24] Sprague died in October of that year, bequeathing the enterprise to his capable nephews, Amasa and William Sprague, who completed the project. The Sprague mill was constructed of substantial gray stone; it was 954 feet long and 4 stories high; and its machinery was powered by 6 waterwheels, each with a diameter of 31 feet, which developed in all 950 horsepower. The capacity of the Sprague mill was estimated in 1862 to be almost one million yards of cloth a month.[25] Clustered about the factory was a well-planned workers' town of 100 identical cottages complete with company store, shops, a school, and a combined town hall and church. Furthermore, the Spragues gave notice that they were planning another factory as soon as the first went into production. They expected when all was complete to have 1,300 workmen employed.[26]

One year after William Sprague bought the Shetucket privilege, Westcott and Pray of Norwich built an 8,000-spindle mill at East Killingly; and in 1858 other Norwich men formed the Griswold Company to utilize the power of the Pachuag River near the town of Griswold.[27] On the eve of the war another group of Norwich capitalists formed the Attawaugan Company and built a mill with a capacity of 10,000 spindles in Killingly.[28] Plans were under way for the erection of more mills in the Norwich vicinity and the enlargement of established ones, when the war interrupted to cut off all supplies of raw material, dislocate the market, and threaten the existence of the entire industry.

The first impact of the war on cotton manufacture was not an immediate shortage of Southern raw cotton. Anticipating trouble,

24. *Norwich Courier* (Nov. 27, 1862).

25. Ibid.

26. *Norwich Bulletin* (May 28, 1861); *Norwich Courier* (May 28, 1861).

27. Davis, 2, 1009–10.

28. Ibid.

Connecticut manufacturers in late 1860 had stocked large quantities of the raw staple. To be sure, some, attracted by the sudden rise of raw cotton values, emptied their warehouses, and speculators ran up the price; but ample stocks for at least one year's full production were in factory warehouses.[29] It was rather the loss of the Southern cloth market and the temporary tightening of credit that hurt the industry. Particularly hard hit were those mills which specialized in coarse sheetings, shirtings, and denims for the slave population of the South. Many must have shared a fate similar to the Union Manufacturing Company of Marlborough, which never recovered when its denim trade with the South was severed.[30] But a majority of the larger mills followed the example of the Spragues, who put their mills in Baltic on half time in June 1861 because of a dull market.[31] This action was only of brief duration, for a strong cotton-cloth demand soon reasserted itself, imposing a heavy drain on existing stocks. During 1862 the dwindling supply of raw cotton was reflected by sharp advances in the price of all cloths. By May 1863 raw cotton had practically disappeared from the market, and what remained was so expensive that it was scarcely profitable to manufacture. Further discouragements to the manufacturer were the Federal excise taxes levied under the Revenue Act of 1862 on both the production and the sale of textiles. In addition, the inflationary financial policies of Treasury Secretary Salmon P. Chase helped price cotton cloth out of the market. Brown cottons in mid-1863 were up 400 per cent over 1860; bleached sheetings and prints showed a 300 per cent increase. With almost no demand for cloth at such prices, the six mills in Griswold stopped all operations. John F. Slater's mill was the last to close, but when raw cotton rose to 67 cents a pound he, too, bowed to the inevitable.[32] What occurred in Griswold was duplicated throughout eastern Connecticut.[33] The famine was on.

These were dark days for the cotton industry, though not without the promise of future profits for those manufacturers who

29. *Norwich Courier* (June 4, 1861).
30. J. H. Trumbull, *2*, 265.
31. *Norwich Courier* (June 4, 1861).
32. Phillips, *Griswold*, pp. 204–21.
33. Hurd, *New London County*, passim.

THE ADVANCE OF COTTON CLOTH PRICES IN NEW LONDON COUNTY[34]

	1860		1863	
Brown Cottons	8¾¢–9¼¢	per yd.	36¢ –46¢	per yd.
Bleached	12½¢	" "	38½¢–47¢	" "
Prints	7½¢–9¢	" "	23¢ –26¢	" "
Delaines	16¢	" "	32¢	" "
Coates' Thread	42½¢	" pkg.	$1.25	" pkg.

could hold out. Grant's successful Vicksburg campaign had just been concluded and Port Hudson had surrendered. Such victories assured Northern control of the lower Mississippi Valley with its vast potential of raw cotton. Indeed, cotton seized by the armed forces was already beginning to trickle into trade channels. Manufacturers could reasonably anticipate considerable supplies of the staple after the 1863 crop was harvested in the late fall, and if they had faith in the continued success of Union arms, a larger amount from the 1864 planting. It did not take a very discerning businessman, whether he was an established cotton manufacturer or a successful war contractor, to assume that investment in cotton textiles would shortly prove very profitable. The "cotton famine" was beginning to break and the public was desperately short of cheap cotton cloth. Consumer demand had been building up for two years. Merely the restoration of normal raw material supplies and relief from wartime excise taxes should create the greatest market in the history of the industry.

Garnishing this repast for the investor were rich side dishes offered by the Tariffs of 1862 and 1864. Though these acts had been passed to raise revenue, they were most beneficial to cotton manufacturers. By 1861 the New England cotton industry had advanced sufficiently in machine techniques to compete on even terms with foreign producers, and in the manufacture of coarse goods had exported sizable quantities abroad.[35] The Tariff Act of 1862, which laid a duty of one cent a yard on foreign cottons, and the Tariff of 1864, which increased this impost to five cents a yard, meant that manufacturers could raise their price accordingly in the domestic market and pocket from four to five cents on every yard of their output in addition to their normal profits. Conditions were

34. *New London Daily Star* (March 16, 1863).

35. Taussig, *Tariff History*, p. 193.

ripe for a renewal of plant expansion in eastern Connecticut, an expansion which would more than double the spindle capacity of that region during the next ten years.

With such powerful forces at work, the industry needed only to secure general flowage privileges similar to those granted in Massachusetts and Rhode Island in the place of the old individual charter grants. General flowage privileges would allow textile interests to condemn land for water-power purposes, and were essentially at variance with property rights because they involved the application of eminent domain for private rather than public use. Since such privileges might ruin farm lands adjoining water-power sites, the proposed legislation aroused opposition from the farmers.[36] After much lobbying from the textile interests, however, the legislature granted a comprehensive flowage law in 1864, which embodied all that the manufacturers demanded.[37]

Even before the flowage question had been settled, capital was beginning to pour into the cotton industry of eastern Connecticut. The Governor himself was one of the first to gamble on its future profits. At the head of a syndicate of Norwich capitalists, Buckingham obtained a charter for the Ashland Cotton Company from the 1863 legislature.[38] Having added largely to his fortune from the lucrative wartime business of the Hayward Rubber Company, he had already perceived tokens of a market glut in rubber goods and recognized in the peacetime potentialities of cotton manufacture an opportune field for investment. The new company purchased a thousand acres of marshy land for flowage between the Pachaug and Glasgo rivers near the town of Griswold, and within a year had erected a new four-story mill together with tenements for thirty families.[39]

Another officer of the Hayward Rubber Company and a close friend of the Governor, Lorenzo Blackstone, who had formed the Attawaugan Company before the war, also converted his wartime rubber profits into cotton investments. Blackstone had barely com-

36. *Hartford Courant* (June 12, 1861); *Norwich Courier* (June 20, 1861).

37. *New London Chronicle* (June 14, 1864); *Public Acts* (May Sess., 1864), chap. 34.

38. Davis, 2, 1005–06; Hurd, p. 405.

39. Phillips, pp. 221–22; Davis, 2, 1028.

pleted his first mill in 1862 when the cotton famine forced him to suspend operations; but his faith remained unshaken, and in 1864 he had the temerity to increase Attawaugan's capacity by 8,000 spindles.[40] The following year he purchased Leonard Ballou's mill on an adjoining privilege, built a new mill with 18,000 spindles nearby, and in 1866 was operating something over 60,000 spindles in all.[41] At the height of the cotton famine and wartime financial uncertainties, this Norwich group had expanded New London County's cloth production by over 100,000 spindles, yet their enterprise was unabated. In the fall of 1864 they formed the Occum Company to develop another water-power site on the Shetucket River.[42] The Occum Company purchased 950 acres and all the magnificent privileges on the Shetucket between Greenville and Baltic, which for some reason the Spragues had chosen to ignore. At any rate, other Rhode Island and Massachusetts cotton interests were not so diffident. The Occum Company soon sold about two-thirds of its holdings to Cyrus and Edward Taft, who represented themselves, the Slaters, and the Massachusetts manufacturers Edmunds and Little, of Lawrence.[43] Shortly afterward, this combine began construction of the extensive Ponemah Mills, which would rival the Sprague mills at Baltic and were to rank among the greatest textile producers of New England.[44]

Although the Norwich locale was the center of largest growth, an important expansion of cotton manufacturing was occurring to the north, in the county of Windham. Perhaps the most notable development during these years was at Thompson, where Dr. William Grosvernor, who had purchased the Mason mills, added 19,000 spindles in 1864, bringing his plant capacity to an aggregate of 46,000.[45] Under the aggressive leadership of Austin Dunham and a coterie of Hartford insurance men, new additions were made to the rambling Willimantic Linen Company, which had done a roaring business in cotton thread during the war. This mill, one of the

40. Davis, *2*, 1008.
41. Hurd, pp. 361–62.
42. Ibid.; Davis, *2*, 1005–06.
43. Davis, *1*, 163.
44. Ibid.
45. Ibid.

largest in the nation in 1861, had prospered mightily from the dual effects of the wartime tariff acts on foreign threads and an unlimited demand for its products.[46]

All in all, about half a million spindles were put into operation in eastern Connecticut from 1861 to 1866, more than two-thirds of which were installed during the last two years of the war.[47] So great was over-all expansion by 1870 that the Long Island Sound area was ahead of Lowell in cotton production. Proximity to New York markets, good water and rail transportation, the reliance of the cotton industry upon inelastic waterpower—all these factors had made such a change in geographical emphasis inevitable.[48] The accumulation of large quantities of capital, much of it derived from war contracts and the foresight of its owners to risk their gains in the development of cotton manufacture, had lent the necessary impetus.

Connecticut's cotton industry after 1862 played little part in the war effort or in the supply of cloth to the civilian population. Except for thread, which rose sharply in price but remained in supply, the cotton famine rather effectively removed all types of cotton textiles from the market. Deprived of cotton, both military and civilian customers sought relief in woolens; and, of course, the demand for woolen uniforms and blankets was insatiable. The Connecticut woolen industry enjoyed the bonanza days of 1812 multiplied many times over.

At first, the woolen mills were unable to supply the needs of the rapidly mobilizing armed forces. With state and Federal governments bidding against each other in the open market, broadcloth, cassimere, and blanket material vanished in a matter of days. What remained was either the coarse satinet or cassinet of the poorest quality, worked up from worn-out fabrics and known as shoddy. Much justifiable criticism was leveled at woolen manufacturers throughout the war period for selling shoddy to the military at fancy prices. Inferior woolens, which wore out after as little as a week of campaigning, were sold to the Army by unscrupulous con-

46. Ibid., pp. 164, 165.

47. *Norwich Courier* (Oct. 7, 1865).

48. Jacob H. Burgy, *The New England Cotton Textile Industry: A Study in Industrial Geography* (Baltimore, 1932), pp. 4–5.

tractors with political influence. Some of these profiteers were Connecticut manufacturers. But sufficient high quality fabrics were simply unavailable during the early war years, while the better grades of shoddy were not always as poor as its detractors claimed. The War Department quickly recognized its place in the war effort by permitting its purchase for uniforms,[49] and the Connecticut legislature refused to prohibit its manufacture in 1863 despite frequent complaints from the field.[50] An expanding market, high tariffs on both raw wool and finished cloth imports, and the excise taxes that were passed on to consumers drove up the prices of scarce domestic woolens to a point which demanded the use of poor cloth.[51]

With such encouragement, it was not surprising that the Connecticut shoddy industry grew rapidly. War contractors and speculators entered the field, purchasing or leasing idle mills and installing machinery.[52] Even an established woolen factory like the Hopeville Mill at Jewett City found shoddy manufacture so profitable and raw wool so expensive that it produced little else from 1863 on.[53] Though never a suitable replacement for genuine woolens, shoddy did achieve a better quality as the war progressed, while that produced by experienced manufacturers at Rockville or in the Norwich area was reasonably good from the beginning.[54]

Profits in the wartime shoddy industry were large. The Lathrops, owners and operators of the Hope Mills, who had enjoyed moderate prosperity in the manufacture of good woolens before the war, quickly shifted to shoddy and by 1863 paid the heaviest income taxes in Griswold.[55] Colonel Francis Loomis of New London, perhaps the largest and certainly one of the most successful wool operators in wartime Connecticut, made an immense fortune in both shoddy and genuine woolen cloth.[56] With mills scattered through New London, Windham, and Tolland counties, he employed 1,200

49. Clark, *History of Manufactures*, 2, 30.

50. Buckingham, *Life*, p. 294.

51. Phillips, *Griswold*, pp. 221–22.

52. Hurd, pp. 670–81.

53. Phillips, pp. 221–22.

54. J. R. Cole, *History of Tolland County, Connecticut, Including Its Early Settlement and Progress to the Present Time* (New York, 1888), pp. 816–17.

55. Ibid.

56. Hurd, pp. 238–39.

workers day and night on government orders. Some idea of the wealth Loomis gained in these and similar ventures and a testimonial to his patriotism is provided by a dramatic offer he made to President Lincoln in 1864. In an effort to help the government furnish trained men for Grant's army, he agreed to replace the garrison at Fort Trumbull, guarding New London Harbor, with a thousand volunteers whom he would raise, equip, and maintain for a hundred days at his own personal expense. Counting the cost of bounties, equipment, subsistence, and pay, Loomis must have been willing to spend close to a million dollars. Though the President acknowledged this princely gift with a graceful response, he declined to accept it for military reasons.[57]

Profits in legitimate cloth were less fantastic owing to the high prices of domestic fleeces, but the market was excellent and had more permanence.[58] T. M. Allyn, who reported the largest income in Hartford from 1862 to 1865, earned most of this from his Tolland County mills, which manufactured mainly from virgin woolens.[59] Indeed, a majority of mill owners, and particularly those who had been in the trade for some time, preferred to avoid the stigma and uncertainty of shoddy. Even Colonel Loomis pursued shoddy merely as a profitable sideline, manufacturing genuine cloth at his largest mill in South Coventry.[60] The same was true of the mills in Rockville and Norwich. With such a heavy demand for good woolens, established manufacturers could afford to be circumspect, leaving most of the ephemeral shoddy to speculators and new operators.

Despite this booming market, there was little over-all plant expansion except that represented by the new shoddy mills.[61] But a notable expansion of individual facilities, especially through the addition of machinery and labor, did take place. In many instances

57. Loomis had made the offer on April 28, 1864, and the President replied on August 12. He wrote that "it seems inexpedient at this time to accept this proposition, on account of the special duties upon the garrison mentioned." Lincoln to F. B. Loomis, Aug. 12, 1864, in Henry J. Raymond, *The Life and Public Services of Abraham Lincoln* (New York, 1865), p. 524.

58. A. H. Cole, *American Woolen Manufacture, 1*, 380.

59. J. R. Cole, p. 817.

60. Hurd, p. 238.

61. Davis, *1*, 235; *Compendium,* Ninth Census, 1870, p. 850. There were 93 establishments in 1859, and 103 establishments in 1870.

the mills were driven far beyond their capacity, which probably accounted for some of the disastrous fires that occurred during 1864 and 1865. It is significant that after these fires, new mills of much greater capacity replaced those which had been destroyed. Along with this expansion went a further concentration of the industry in those areas where it had become firmly rooted before the war.[62] There was no significant shift to other centers, and though a handful of new factories was brought into operation or converted from shoddy to better grades of cloth in 1865, the industry was still controlled by established manufacturers after the war.

One of the most remarkable aspects of the war period was that few of the great cotton mills changed over to woolen manufacture, despite the rigors of the cotton famine and the high profits to be made in genuine woolens and shoddy. Such factors as cost of re-equipment, shortage of skilled weavers and dyers, and the comparatively short duration of the cotton famine must have argued strongly against change. Furthermore, with every prospect of a handsome market for cottons in the near future, why enter an unfamiliar, highly competitive industry? Even a newcomer like Lorenzo Blackstone, whose first large mill was completed in the middle of the famine, let it remain idle, making no attempt to enter woolen manufacture. There seems to have been considerable conversion from cottons to woolens in Massachusetts, but no significant change-over took place in Connecticut.[63]

One other aspect of textile development during wartime was the expansion of the silk industry. Though not directly connected with the war effort, it exemplified the enterprise and the industrial versatility of the state. Furthermore, the industry was organized, at least in part, by creative capitalists who plowed back much of their wartime profits not only in new property, plants, and equipment, but in the continuous improvement of manufacturing methods and the quality control of the products. Prior to the outbreak of hostilities, one of the largest silk mills in the Union was operated by the Cheneys at Manchester and Hartford. These mills were the product of continuous experimentation in methods of working silk and of

62. Henry A. Baker, Comp., *History of Montville, Connecticut, from 1640–1896* (Hartford, 1896), pp. 625–35; Davis, 2, 1011–13; J. R. Cole, pp. 817–20.

63. A. H. Cole, *1*, 379.

careful business management since the early forties. Capitalized at $1,000,000 in 1854, the Cheney assets were many times that figure in 1861.[64] Yet previous business was Lilliputian compared with wartime demand for luxury items. The four mills that made up the Cheney aggregate worked on a 24-hour schedule and underwent constant enlargement without ever keeping abreast of sales. In the fall of 1861, faced with mounting problems of coordination between their mills in Manchester and in Hartford, the Cheneys had the American Telegraph Company install a private communication system that involved over thirty miles of line.[65] Profits were so large that in addition to reinvestment the Cheneys were able to finance costly experiments in spun silk.[66] Ranging farther afield, they backed the experiments that led to the design of the famous Spencer rifle. Although Manchester outstripped all other communities in silk manufacture, mills were built or converted to silk production in Rockville, Windham, and the New Haven area.[67]

Indeed, the wartime profits in silk for a time provoked a veritable mania in Windham County. Governor Wilbur Cross, whose boyhood was spent in the small Windham village of Gurleyville, recalled that prosperous farmers and sawmill owners talked of little else when together.[68] Countless small establishments for the manufacture of silks and for the cultivation of silkworms were founded there and in other localities nearby. Like all speculative ventures inspired by wartime markets, almost all of them disappeared at the war's end. But their output, together with that of the larger mills, swelled the volume of Connecticut textiles to a position of dominance and assisted in the growth of capital for later industrial development.

All branches of the textile industry were affected similarly, though in varying degrees, by wartime conditions, tariff legislation, and scarcity markets. All were faced by shortages of raw materials; but where domestic virgin or reclaimed wool was always in supply, and silk, as a luxury item, could enjoy an excellent market even at exorbitant prices, cotton had neither a prestige value nor a firm

64. J. H. Trumbull, *Hartford*, 2, 256.

65. *Hartford Courant* (Oct. 19, 1861).

66. Davis, 2, 1058.

67. J. R. Cole, p. 825.

68. Wilbur L. Cross, *Connecticut Yankee; an Autobiography* (New Haven, 1943), p. 10.

source of supply. Raw cotton stocks became tight in early 1862, and by 1863 had practically disappeared. While woolen and silk mills were working to capacity, the great cotton centers of eastern Connecticut lay idle. Yet certain of a great future, cotton manufacturers not only resisted the temptation to turn to woolens, but before the end of the war actually began to expand their plants. They could not be tempted by the surface glitter of the woolen industry, a judgment eminently correct, attesting to their sagacity as well as their restraint. For the textile market from 1865 to 1873 was to prove to be the reverse of what it had been during the war. In 1865 the woolen industry was overexpanded, the market was glutted with a surfeit of cloth, and the War Department aggravated the situation when it auctioned off huge stocks of army woolens in 1866. Woolen interests in Connecticut suffered along with those in other New England states and constantly importuned Congress in the postwar period for higher tariffs. Though the woolen industry languished, the Connecticut cotton industry enjoyed the greatest market in its history, a factor that accelerated postwar expansion.[69]

The development of the textile industry was but another facet in the industrial revolution, which was approaching maturity in Connecticut during the early sixties. With an industrial history reaching back to the latter part of the eighteenth century, the state had benefited much from an expanding population, from machine techniques and the growth of capital, from a usually favorable government policy—exceptionally favorable during the Civil War—and from a parallel growth in transportation. In the production of textiles and munitions Connecticut excelled; and measured by the potential of these alone, she could lay claim to being a great industrial state. But little of this great potential would have been realized by a nation in peril if the instruments of transportation had not been available—railroads and ships that carried the products of Connecticut factories to market centers and returned with essential raw materials; a shipbuilding industry that could keep pace with wartime demands.

69. *Report of the Special Commissioner of the Revenue, 1868,* Washington, D.C., 1870, passim; H. R. Feleger, *David A. Wells and the American Revenue System, 1865–1870* (New York, 1942), chap. 6.

15. SHIPPING AND RAILROADS, 1861–1865

CONNECTICUT IN 1861 had a transportation network that was still inadequate for the needs of a new industrial economy, much less for the unique demands of wartime. The first surge of railroad building during the 1840s and early 1850s had lost its momentum when the depression of 1857 put an abrupt stop to further expansion. Much had been accomplished; much remained to be done. All the major cities were linked together and there were through connections with Boston and New York, but most towns and villages had no rail service. Few of the roads were over fifty miles long. Inefficient single-track affairs, they depended upon cumbersome ferry service over navigable streams.[1] Uneven roadbeds and rudimentary grading meant uncomfortable, even dangerous, passenger travel and slow expensive freight service. In every respect the railroad net of the state was a rickety affair of many impecunious small railroad companies. Most of them, even when joined in a through route, were competitive and annoyingly independent on such matters as rates, exchange of rolling stock, or the scheduling of traffic.[2] As a result, Connecticut was heavily dependent upon shipping for the transport of all types of goods, and wholly so for the cheap, bulky raw materials that she consumed.

Like the railroads, the Connecticut shipping and shipbuilding industries were in the early stages of technological change. Sailing vessels were beginning to give way before steamers, which were rapidly becoming more efficient as knowledge accumulated about hull design and propulsion. Side-wheelers and some screw steamers had largely replaced sail on the Connecticut River and on Long Island Sound. But for ocean trade, both coastwise and foreign, com-

1. "Ninth Annual Report of the Railroad Commission," *PDLC* (1862).

2. "Fifth, Sixth, Seventh Annual Reports of the Railroad Commission," ibid. (1857–1860).

mercial interests still relied upon large sailing vessels. They were more economical to operate because of the high price of coal, and they represented a heavy capital investment. Furthermore, most shipowners were convinced that steamers could not withstand long voyages, a state of mind that was influenced by a deep-rooted tradition of sailing ships.

Along with agriculture, shipbuilding and commerce had been the earliest occupations of importance in colonial Connecticut.[3] Magnificent forests of hard woods and conifers, and a shore serrated with protected bays, inlets, and navigable rivers flowing in north-south directions to the Long Island Sound, provided all those natural elements so conducive to mercantile development. To be sure, the products of these first endeavors had been little more than fishing shallops or an occasional small brig, merely a necessary adjustment to the environment. But on the sloping banks and sheltered channels, where keels could be laid down and ships launched safely, a seafaring tradition fast established itself.[4] The development of the West Indies trade, in which all seaports and many of the Connecticut River towns were interested, brought commercial wealth and gave further impetus to shipbuilding. From New London, shipyards crept both east and west, managing to retain both their skills and capital despite the commercial handicaps of the American Revolution, the Jeffersonian Embargo, and the War of 1812.[5] By 1860 ships were being built all along the Connecticut River and the northern confines of the sound in Stonington, Mystic, New London, Stratford, Guilford, New Haven, Fair Haven, Derby, and Bridgeport on the coast, and in Essex, Haddam, Portland, and Glastonbury on the river.[6] Whaling, sealing, and guano had developed the already extensive New London complex and pushed capital and facilities to Stonington on the Rhode Island border.[7] The West Indies trade, which had once been important in

3. Carl C. Cutler, *A Brief Summary of the Early Shipping Industry in the Northern States* (Mystic, Conn., 1932), pp. 71–72.

4. Carl C. Cutler, *Mystic: The Story of a Small New England Seaport* (Mystic, Conn., 1945), pp. 137–38. Boston had 20 yards to New London's more than 40.

5. Hurd, *New London County,* chap. 15.

6. Pliny L. Harwood, *History of Eastern Connecticut,* 2 (New Haven, 1931–32), 480–85.

7. Hurd, chap. 15.

New Haven's economy, also created a sizable shipbuilding industry in nearby Fair Haven. Though all such pursuits except seal fishing had become stagnant by 1860 because of competition from better and cheaper substitutes, these enterprises had built the yards and trained the men. Wealth derived from them had assisted in making the magnificent American clipper ship era possible.[8] When the tall ships went down over the horizon, their owners and builders, practical yet visionary men, were ready for steam.

The increasing use of steam vessels for short hauls, however, received a temporary setback with the advent of war. Indeed, the little steamers that had formerly been so plentiful suddenly disappeared. Anyone who journeyed between Hartford and New Haven along the old River Road or traveled on the single-track Hartford and New Haven Railroad might have thought that the age of steam was giving way to the age of sail on the Connecticut River. This busy artery, connecting the interior of the state with Long Island Sound when not frozen over, had accommodated thousands of tons of shipping, and by 1860 much of it was steam. But the government needed ships for transports and for conversion to blockade cruisers or river gunboats. Steamboat owners found that they could sell their vessels at a handsome profit. Cannier ones deemed it even more desirable to lease to the government for the duration at rates that varied between $150 and $700 a day. Thus they would avoid risk and responsibility and at the same time earn an excellent profit on their original investment.[9] Schooners, sloops, and brigs took over much of the state's carrying trade; short hauls by water became slower, less reliable, and more expensive.[10]

Nor were replacements immediately forthcoming. Government orders monopolized the extensive shipyard facilities of the coastal towns. Almost every steam vessel large enough to mount guns either on the stocks or in operation was sold or leased to the services. At first, so great was the demand that little thought was given by the builders or the Navy Department as to whether the ships were constructed properly for heavy duty. C. H. Mallory and Company, prominent shipbuilders of Mystic, for example, sold the propeller

8. Cutler, *Mystic*, 1, 146–50.

9. William H. Mallory, MS Diary, Aug. 20, 1865 (MHA).

10. *Hartford Times* (Nov. 5, 1861).

Varuna to the government, and she was subsequently armed with ten heavy guns.[11] Four days of moderate gales, during which she nearly foundered, disclosed that her frame was entirely too light to bear her extra burden and still remain seaworthy.[12] The *Varuna*, like many other peacetime vessels pressed into service, had been built for the coastal passenger and freighting business. She was totally inadequate for the rigorous demands of naval warfare except with the lightest of armaments, and then only fit for river duty. Her builders and George D. Morgan, Secretary Welles' New York procurement agent, were culpable, it would seem.[13] Yet the absolute unpreparedness of the Navy Department in 1861, the scarcity of warship designs and naval architects, and, above all, the pressing need for a large navy made questionable purchases and conversion necessary.[14] It should be noted also that not all of the hastily converted ships were to perform as poorly as the *Varuna*. The tiny 221-ton sound-steamer *New London* was heavily armed in New York during the chaotic summer of 1861. She left there on November 5 and cruised on blockade duty off southern ports for a full year, broken only by a ten-day period during which her boilers were overhauled. Despite the unpreparedness of the Connecticut shipbuilding industry in 1861, it responded handsomely to the pressing need for ships. New tonnage doubled between 1861–62 and trebled the following year. And this high level of construction was maintained through the year 1864. Oddly enough, one of the major centers of shipbuilding activity was the small town of Mystic, in the southeastern corner of the state.

With a population at the onset of hostilities of about 2,000, Mystic had for the past twenty-five years enjoyed a modest prosperity.[15] Though the town had some favorable characteristics for the industry and was connected by rail with Boston and New York, it did not have the site, position, or population of other

11. See Welles' letters to Congress, Committee on Government Contracts (May 8, 1862, House Select Docs. No. 3). The *Varuna* had been owned jointly by the Mallorys and C. S. Bushnell of New Haven. She cost the government $125,460.

12. *Norwich Courier* (March 13, 1862); Cutler, *Mystic*, *1*, 158. The *Varuna*, however, did give a good account of herself in the Mississippi River warfare.

13. The *Varuna* was Morgan's first purchase for the Navy Department.

14. *Norwich Courier* (Nov. 27, 1862).

15. *Connecticut State Register and Manual* (1947), pp. 451, 453.

shipbuilding centers. What Mystic did have in abundance, and what other towns lacked to some extent, was a dominant group of capable, shrewd, hard-working shipbuilders. Former shipwrights or sailors, accustomed to taking chances, they were as familiar with an adz or a construction estimate as they were with navigation or commercial ventures. These were the men who had owned and manned the clippers that had established records for some of the fastest voyages to California.[16] The Mallorys, the Greenmans, and others no less skillful, who owned the yards, were able to meet stringent production schedules for the government, yet at the same time make substantial deliveries for commercial interests.

The Mallorys, father and three sons, were among the leading shipbuilders of the nation. Though they had spent their lives building sailing ships, they were not, like Donald McKay, the great Boston clipper ship designer and builder, wistful about their passing. While McKay was vainly trying to sell the government on fast sailing cruisers for the Navy, the Mallorys had been converted to steam.[17] When McKay, near the war's end, finally became convinced of his error and managed to produce four steamers for government service, the Mallorys had already built, equipped, launched, and delivered on lease twenty-one steamers, each averaging about 1,500 tons.[18]

Charles Mallory, the elder, who established the business in Mystic, had sprung from the humblest of beginnings. He had learned the trade of a sailmaker, by dint of a grueling apprenticeship, and had known poverty and hardship; but he had a flair for calculating risks and for managing such a complex business as shipbuilding, in which a trivial design error or construction fault could ruin a firm's reputation. Mallory's lean, sharp face, hollow cheeks framed by white whiskers, and piercing, light blue eyes under a heavy white thatch of eyebrows bespoke shrewdness and wiry strength.[19] Charles H. Mallory, the most enterprising of his sons, though never having experienced poverty, knew physical danger and hardship as a sailor at the age of fifteen and as a captain at

16. Cutler, *Mystic,* I, 155.

17. Ibid.

18. Hurd, *New London,* p. 693.

19. Ibid.; Cutler, *Mystic,* I, 144–51.

twenty-one on his father's ships. Round of face and portly of figure, he gave every appearance of the placid businessman (though his diary proclaims him as nervous and moody), yet he was as shrewd in business deals as his father and even more daring.[20] With a small administrative staff, the father and sons personally supervised every detail of their integrated business: they operated their own rope walks, sail lofts, and saw mills; they purchased and supervised the installation of machinery; and they negotiated contracts with Navy purchasing agent George D. Morgan or middleman C. S. Bushnell.

During the summer of 1862 the Mystic yards built five propellers, one of 1,500 tons, the others slightly smaller; one master sailing ship; three steam tugs; and two lighters.[21] The output of Mystic for the United States Navy from 1861 to the close of the war in April 1865 was fifty-six steamers.[22] For both the Navy and civilian ownership, Mystic yards also launched six schooners, three brigs, two barks, and three ships, the smallest of these displacing 300 tons. A total of over 50,000 tons of shipping was constructed by this town, whose entire population, swelled by war workers, could not have exceeded 3,600. Indeed, Mystic launched more steamers than the great maritime states of Massachusetts and Maine combined.[23]

Other cities and towns contributed vessels both directly for government use or indirectly to assist the railroads in circulating raw material and finished products for both civilian and military consumption. The ironworks and shipyard at Norwich built and equipped five steamers during the war, three of which were sold to the Navy.[24] Every yard in Fair Haven, a suburb of New Haven, worked to capacity from late 1862 on.[25] The yards along the Connecticut River from Middletown to Saybrook, many of them inactive since the decline of the West Indies trade in the thirties, were refurbished and were soon crowded with new construction. Only two, however, produced shipping of any size—the Gildersleeve Yard at Portland and the Goodspeed Yard at East Haddam.

20. Hurd, pp. 693–94.
21. *Mystic Pioneer* (July 12, 1862).
22. Cutler, *Mystic*, 1, 158.
23. *Connecticut State Register and Manual* (1947), pp. 451, 453.
24. Caulkins, *History of Norwich*, p. 653.
25. *New Haven Journal and Courier* (Sept. 18, 1862).

On October 21, 1861, Sylvester Gildersleeve and George E. Goodspeed launched sister gunboats for the United States Navy, the *Cayuga* at Portland and the *Kanawha* at East Haddam.[26] Gildersleeve and Goodspeed, like the Mallorys, had built up their facilities on prewar business.[27] Both firms would build additional gunboats for the government, but the bulk of their wartime business was for commercial customers.

In addition to yards in the state, Connecticut capital controlled some extensive facilities in Brooklyn and Philadelphia. The most important of these was the Continental Iron Works in the Greenpoint area of Brooklyn. Thomas Fitch Rowland of Fair Haven owned and operated the Brooklyn yard, and in association with Cornelius Scranton Bushnell, a rich New Haven grocer and railroad president, Nehemiah D. Sperry, New Haven's postmaster, and New York speculator Daniel Drew, built John Ericsson's original *Monitor*.[28] Bushnell and Rowland later constructed a number of additional monitors and ironclad gunboats for the Navy at Greenpoint.

The wartime career of Bushnell illustrates the driving energy and the uncertain business ethics of that period. A merchant and a commission agent, he was a resourceful promoter rather than a shipbuilder. In the early summer of 1861 he formed the New Haven Propeller Company, which promptly went into the profitable business of supplying the Navy with new charter vessels. Associated with Bushnell in this venture were several New Haven men, the most prominent being Henry W. Benedict. Bushnell, however, retained a controlling interest—one third of the capital stock—in the new company. New Haven Propeller's first important deal was the purchase of the *Stars and Stripes*, a new steamer still on the stocks at the Mallory yard in Mystic. The company paid Mallory $36,000 for the vessel and then chartered her to the Navy for $10,000 a month. Under charter terms, New Haven Propeller paid all operating costs, which averaged $1,800 a month, leaving a net profit for the month of $8,200. The *Stars and Stripes* was in charter service for only thirty days when Bushnell, without consulting his

26. *Harford Courant* (Oct. 19, 1861).

27. *New Haven Journal and Courier* (Sept. 18, 1862).

28. George L. Clark, *A History of Connecticut, Its People and Institutions* (New York, 1914), pp. 387–88.

directors, sold her to the Navy for $55,000. He then demanded a $10,000 commission from the company for his valuable services. Anticipating opposition from the board, Bushnell seems to have left the impression with the directors that he had spent the money in Washington to purchase influence with the Navy Department. This he was to deny when later questioned by a House Select Committee investigating government contracts. At any rate, the directors accepted his explanation but scaled down his fee to $8,000. Even with this pay-out, they were well satisfied with profits of $19,200 over a thirty-day period on one small-scale investment.

In December 1861 Bushnell was pressed hard by Congressman Elihu Washburne of Illinois, who was trying to unravel his transactions with the Navy Department. The New Haven businessman claimed that he had used his special commission to help defray the cost of designing a unique war vessel that would soon be launched. This was an oblique reference to the *Monitor,* still a secret project, but one well known to the investigating committee. "You thought it justifiable to take $8,000 from the stockholders of your company and expend it that way," asked the persistent Washburne. "Absolutely," was the bland reply, "it is [sic] the proudest moment of my life; I took the money from a company that had been abundantly fortunate." [29] The committee was also highly critical of Bushnell's $25,000 commission, which he had earned for his role as middleman on the sale of the *Varuna* by the Mallorys to the Navy Department. Despite his posture of selfless devotion to his country, the New Haven promoter was to be well recompensed for his patriotic investment of the *Stars and Stripes'* commission in the development and construction of the *Monitor.*

Another commission agent who was active in Connecticut during the early days of the war was Richard Chappell of New London. Secretary Welles himself designated Chappell and George D. Morgan, his New York agent, to purchase laid-up whalers in New London, Mystic, Stonington, and New Bedford for the so-called "stone fleet" that was to bottle up Southern harbors. The venerable ships were to be filled with granite blocks (actually Chappell and Morgan used stone walls for the purpose) and sailed by volunteer crews in convoys of six each to the headquarters of

29. 32d Congress, 2d Sess., *House Report* #2, Pt. I, pp. 23–24; Pt. II, pp. 17, 682.

the South Atlantic blockading squadron.[30] Morgan and Chappell performed their work with dispatch. Twenty-five whalers were purchased (and crews were engaged) and loaded with stone within twenty days of the Navy Department's initial order.[31] Eight of these came from the New London vicinity, the remainder from New Bedford. Each ship averaged 333 tons burden and cost roughly $4,000. All were in bad condition, and it was one of those minor miracles of the war that their masters and crews managed to sail them to Port Royal, South Carolina, without major mishap. The Navy sank them off Savannah, and a later batch of twenty off Charleston.[32] These obstructions were soon washed away by tide and storm. The stone fleet accomplished nothing of military value, but it did anger the British as a flagrant example of Yankee high-handedness and it did permit a half dozen New London, Mystic, and Stonington shipowners to unload a dozen old hulks on the government.

Apart from such early warship ventures as the stone fleet, the Mystic-built *Galena* (another Bushnell project), and the *Varuna*, most Connecticut yards concentrated on the building of vessels for the merchant service or for civilian-operated supply steamers for the armed forces. The rapid expansion of the nation's economy and the increasing production of Connecticut industry overloaded all transportation facilities. With ship tonnage substantially reduced by the employment of so many former merchant vessels in the government service, shipbuilders were never able to satisfy the needs of the commercial interests—an important reason for the shortages and high prices of all consumer goods during the war. Although many, if not most, of the Connecticut shipyards were crowded with government transport work, they still launched an impressive amount of tonnage for purely commercial use. The Greenman brothers at Mystic, for example, built three large square-riggers for John A. McGraw, a New York merchant, and several steamers for the California trade.[33] The *United States*, 1,600 tons, the largest propeller ever launched on the river, was built by Syl-

30. *OR, Navies* Ser. I, *12*, 416–17.
31. Ibid., p. 417.
32. Ibid., pp. 420–21.
33. Hurd, *New London*, pp. 667, 716.

vester Gildersleeve for Wakeman and Damon, New York merchants, in 1863.[34] Other shipyards along the river launched countless brigs, schooners, and sloops, which helped to ease the acute shortage of river and sound shipping in the early years of the war. During the spring and summer of 1863, for instance, the river yards built twenty vessels averaging from two to three hundred tons burden, and during the winter months the following vessels were being finished: "two [large schooners] at Gildersleeve and Son's yard at Portland, one for the Middlesex Quarry Company and the other for Captain J. J. Worthington; two at D. B. Warner's yard, East Haddam, for captains Frank Boardman and Henry Hill; two at Essex for captains J. D. Billard and Charles Vibberts, each about 200 tons burden; at Dennison's yard, Deep River, one for Captain Leonard Fox . . . Belden of [Middletown] has one nearly completed for Meade of Portland." [35] The increased production of small vessels like these was one of the many indications that new competition was entering the sound and river trade.[36]

Scarcity of shipping during the first year of the war had opened a profitable enterprise to anyone who had some knowledge of the inland waterways of the state and possessed the relatively small amount of capital necessary to acquire a brig or a schooner. Though welcomed by hard-pressed manufacturers and commission agents, these interlopers in the short-haul traffic were resented by a well-knit group of established shipping lines, a resentment which soon brought countermeasures. Since 1860 local shipping lines had acted in concert to prescribe rates and divide the traffic to their mutual advantage. Under the terms of this agreement or shipping conference, the ruinous rate wars that had followed the depression of 1857 were curbed and new competitors were ruthlessly excluded. The conference had been in effect scarcely a year when the war broke out, bringing with it new conditions. By 1862 a second conference was deemed necessary.[37] Rates needed readjustment in the light of wartime prosperity, and, above all, the members viewed with alarm the growth of independent competition, particularly

34. *New London Star* (Nov. 23, 1863). Her 1,000-horsepower engine was furnished by Woodruff and Beach's Hartford Engine and Boiler Works.

35. *Middletown Constitution* (Nov. 12, 1863).

36. Harwood, *Eastern Connecticut,* 3, 480–90, for total shipyard production figures.

37. *Norwich Courier* (April 24, 1862).

after the shipyards began to make steamboat deliveries, permitting an expansion of their business. Accordingly, the second conference, when it did meet at New York City in April 1862, struck directly at the independents by doubling passenger rates but adhering to the 1860 schedule of freight rates. Since few passengers were carried by small sailing vessels, it would appear that the member steamboat lines, by keeping freight rates low, hoped to undercut their competitors and make up the losses on their passenger traffic.

Yet even this action failed to drive out competition. In 1865 the powerful Hartford and New York Steamboat Company, which had enjoyed a virtual monopoly of the river traffic prior to the war, was forced to seek legislative assistance in its struggle with independent shippers. Disguised as an act to improve the navigation of the Connecticut River, a discriminatory tax of two cents a ton was levied on the cargo of all shipping, sail or steam, above fifty tons in burden, except the Hartford and New York, which was to pay a token tax of one thousand dollars.[38] This legislation hit back hard at independent river shippers, particularly when it was combined with the low freight rates that the conference prescribed during the war. The greater operating efficiency of the steamboat lines also counted against independent shipmasters. Outside competition at once began to lessen and would cease to be a threat in the postwar era. That independent shippers managed to do business in the teeth of concerted opposition from the steamboat lines after 1862 can only be explained in terms of a market which was expanding more rapidly than transportation facilities. Nor is the wartime development of local shipping the only evidence of the gap between market demands and available transport. Similarly, Connecticut railroads were being operated to capacity and, despite their inefficiency, were proving indispensable to the transportation needs of an industrial state at war.

The railroads were distinctly weak economic organisms in 1861. They had been painfully recovering from the effects of the Panic of 1857, when the market dislocations that attended the outbreak of

38. House, July 29, 1865. *Hartford Times* (July 30, 1865). Judge Munson, Democrat, of Seymour, objected in the House. He said: "It is unjust to many sailing masters along the coast, whom it purposes to tax for the benefit of the steamboat company, whose large steamers are exempted."

the war drove many of them back to near bankruptcy. Total railroad receipts fell off by 17 per cent in 1861. Only with the utmost difficulty were the managers able to operate a minimum service. It was not until 1862 that the Shore Line, for example, was able to grope its way out of receivership under the ministrations of trustees for the first mortgage bondholders. The New Haven and Northampton was still in the throes of bankruptcy.[39]

But under the stimulus of a wartime market and an inflation economy, traffic began to increase. Like the independent shipping interests, the railroads profited from the dearth of steamers among their shipping line competitors at a time when an expanded wartime industry clamored for raw materials and markets for its finished products. And the government—state and Federal—added its demands for the transport of troops, horses, and munitions. Indeed, in the short space of a year after Sumter, the railroads had fully recovered. The Norwich and Worcester Railroad, which tapped both eastern Connecticut and east central Massachusetts, showed a small gain over the previous year on its railroad operations of $2,795 for the year 1860–61.[40] Earnings of $8,350 for September 1862 were three times the earnings of the corresponding month in the preceding year.[41] After the 1857 panic the Norwich and Worcester had a $647,733 debt over all available assets.[42] In 1865 the entire debt had been extinguished, a 3.5 per cent dividend was voted to stockholders, and the treasury bulged with a net surplus of $144,174 after all expenses.[43] The Housatonic Railroad was showing a similar infusion of profit as its principal customers, the iron interests of Litchfield County, drew in coal and wood and shipped out pig iron, cannon balls, shells, and cast cannon for the government's war machine.[44]

That never-failing barometer of profit or loss the stock quota-

39. "Eighth Annual Report of the Railroad Commission," *PDLC* (May Sess., 1861)

40. *Norwich Courier* (April 17, 1862). Net earnings March 1860–61 were $21,454. The Norwich and Worcester incorporated in 1832 and the oldest railroad in the state, for years a cornerstone of Norwich's prosperity, became one of the longest and most profitable. Its total earnings for 1861 show the low financial condition of the Connecticut railroads at the beginning of the war.

41. *Norwich Courier* (Oct. 16, 1862).

42. Ibid.

43. *Norwich Aurora* (Sept. 23, 1865).

44. Ibid.

tions disclosed that the Hartford and New Haven Railroad was also sharing in wartime largesse. In November 1862 Hartford and New Haven Railroad stocks were up $20 a share over the preceding year and were selling to eager buyers at from $127 to $145.[45] Five months later, in April 1863, they had jumped another $40 a share to $185, and it was difficult to purchase Hartford and New Haven Railroad bonds at $8–$10 above par.[46] Railroading in the state entered its golden period of profits in mid-1864. Despite higher operating expenses, the net income on the paid-in capital of slightly over $19,000,000 was $1,694,730, an increase of more than $400,000 over 1863 and a percentage earning of about 12 per cent.[47]

At least a part of these earnings reflected a rapid rise in freight rates and passenger fares. As transportation grew tighter after 1862, the railroads charged higher rates and invariably passed all wartime taxes, state as well as Federal, onto the public.[48] Though profits climbed proportionately, service and upkeep declined. Rarely did managers or directors utilize their new wealth to improve their lines or even in most cases to make minimum repairs on overstrained rails and rolling stock. A series of disasters, causing the injury or death of hundreds of people during the war years, was directly traceable to this irresponsible policy. The absence of effective state laws regarding safety appliances or inspection of rolling stock and roadbeds showed that little thought was being given by the legislature for the protection of the public.[49] The Shore Line Railroad, running between New London and New Haven, was in a deplorable condition by 1864, after three years of very heavy traffic and almost no repairs or maintenance of way. A Norwich lawyer told the New London correspondent of the *New York Herald* that he had stood on the end of a section of rail at Clinton and felt it "rise and fall as when boys play on a board over a saw horse."[50] The *Herald* correspondent was visiting the scene of a wreck on the

45. Ibid.
46. Ibid. (Nov. 6, 1862).
47. *Hartford Courant* (April 28, 1864).
48. "Governor's Annual Message, 1864," *PDLC* (May Sess., 1864), pp. 6–8.
49. *Norwich Aurora* (Nov. 18, 1865).
50. Letter dated Nov. 6, *New York Herald* (Nov. 7, 1864).

23. "Our constant travelling companion": Connecticut railroad accidents resulted in 52 deaths and 117 injuries during 1865. Travelers' Insurance Company.

Shore Line, in which sixty soldiers had been killed or injured on October 15. He noted that "in many places the chairs are broken, the ties are rotten, the iron is poor, the rails are loose." [51] In 1865, with railroad net earnings up 25 per cent over 1864, there were 52 deaths and 117 injuries—a sharp increase.[52]

Frightful accidents, wretched service, and exorbitant rates soon

51. Ibid.

52. "Governor's Annual Message, 1865," *PDLC* (May Sess., 1865), pp. 5–6.

led to a public outcry for legislation to strengthen the superficial regulatory powers of the railroad commission.[53] Public opinion was well expressed by the *Norwich Aurora,* which called the railroad commission "a humbug." "No one will deny," said the *Aurora's* editor, John W. Stedman, "that the *Bulletin* [Republican] is right in saying that the Board of Railroad Commissioners is a simple political contrivance whose only use is to give some politicians a small office, with no great pay to be sure but with no duties whatever."[54] Criticism of railroad management reached such proportions by 1864 that the Joint Legislative Committee on Railroads was compelled to hold an investigation. The railroads were able to postpone any major repairs until after the war by pleading scarcity of labor and materials, but on the question of rates they narrowly escaped complete state control and then only after a bitter struggle.[55]

The movement to control rates originated in Bridgeport, which had suffered perhaps more than any other city from the dictatorial policies of the railroads.[56] Three times between 1862 and 1865 the New York and New Haven Railroad increased its rates in such a manner as to discriminate in favor of New Haven. Since Bridgeport was dependent upon this road for its rail connections with New York as well as the Connecticut Valley, a group of local capitalists headed by P. T. Barnum attempted to capture its management in order to modify both its rates and policy.[57] Barnum and his allies were also interested in forcing the New York and New Haven to send spur lines into a vast real estate tract north of the city, which they were trying to develop. When their efforts proved unavailing because of the astute maneuvers of the New York and New Haven management, they carried the battle to the legislature.[58]

Barnum secured election as a representative from Bridgeport to the 1865 session, where he promptly introduced a series of measures aimed particularly at the New York and New Haven but also

53. *Norwich Aurora* (Nov. 19, 1865).

54. Ibid.

55. *Hartford Times* (July 13, 14, 1865).

56. Phineas T. Barnum, *Life of P. T. Barnum Written by Himself Including His Golden Rules for Moneymaking* (Buffalo, 1888), pp. 208, 233.

57. *Hartford Times* (July 13, 1865).

58. *New Haven Register* (July 13, 1865).

applying to all other roads in the state.[59] With a wealth of stratagem and bluster characteristic of his exuberant personality, he secured the first control legislation since the beginning of the railroad era. By sponsoring a law that would remove any member of the railroad commission who was "employed by a railroad corporation, either directly or indirectly," Barnum paved the way for the establishment of a vigorous, honest commission.[60] Then he introduced a bill giving the commission broad powers to regulate passenger fares and freight rates. Though the freight provisions of his bill were defeated, passenger fares did pass under commission regulation.[61] Barnum may not have been motivated by any high idealistic purpose, and his legislation may have had political as well as narrowly local overtones, but it had state-wide application and it served notice on the railroads that they owed a measure of responsibility to the public.

Though the war years were barren ones for railroad upkeep and improvement, they were formative years for future development. Heavy wartime traffic wore out rolling stock and roadbeds that were obsolescent to begin with, but equally heavy wartime revenues canceled debts, piled up surpluses, and prepared the railroads for the future. War-born capital would finance new equipment, expansion, and consolidation that would repair the traffic-weakened iron links and weld them into a stronger, more efficient chain.[62]

Many difficulties and obstacles stood in the way, for the railroad era was still very new in Connecticut. Railroads were fiercely competitive. Towns and cities that had often subscribed liberally to railroad capital were jealous of the trade brought to them by the carriers. Ambitious towns feared that economic advantages might accrue to other areas should the roads be linked, allowing profitable traffic to be diverted in through hauls. Even if local partisans did not actually sit on the boards of the railroads, they were quick to assert their rights in the legislature by opposing any additions or exemptions to charters that might permit such action. Thus two

59. Barnum, *Life*, pp. 232–33.

60. *Hartford Times* (June 1, July 13, 1865).

61. Ibid. (July 6, 14, 1865); *Public Acts, State of Connecticut, May Session, 1865.*

62. For railroad prosperity during the war years, see "Annual Reports of the Railroad Commissioners," PDLC.

forces were at work that would vitally affect the course of railroad expansion. One was the infusion of capital during the war years favoring expansion, and the other was the opposition of interested areas or the competition of the railroads themselves, both of which obstructed. The two consolidation attempts and the one new railroad project launched between 1862 and 1865 bear witness to future railroad development, even as they foreshadow some of the difficulties that would be encountered.

Paradoxically, it was the shakiest railroad in the state, the New Haven and Northampton, lately bankrupt, which accomplished the first and only successful consolidation. With the assistance of a powerful tonic in the form of wartime revenues, it had recovered sufficiently in a few months to devour a valuable spur line, the Hampden and Hampshire.[63] However, some months later, when the powerful New York and New Haven Railroad attempted a similar consolidation scheme, it ran into a hornet's nest of opposition. It controlled the Harlem Road and thus had a profitable through route to New York. Maintaining special arrangements with the Hartford and New Haven, it was the most efficient connection between the two greatest cities in the state and the New York metropolis. The object of its solicitude was the temptingly close Housatonic Railroad. During 1862 it had purchased secretly a controlling interest in the Housatonic, and then laid plans to build a five-mile connecting spur line from its main track near Bridgeport. If the legislature approved, the New York and New Haven would control all the valley trade northward to the Massachusetts line.[64]

In 1863 and 1864 the New York and New Haven repeatedly introduced legislation that would permit it to consolidate with the Housatonic, and on every occasion was roundly defeated.[65] Unlike the more fortunate New Haven and Northampton, the respective locations of these two roads made their consolidation a matter of economic rivalry between two growing cities: youthful, ambitious Bridgeport and vigorous, equally ambitious New Haven. The Housatonic had long been regarded as Bridgeport's own, an important

63. *Hartford Courant* (May 23, 1862).
64. Ibid. (June 13, 1863).
65. Ibid. (May 1, Aug. 1, 1863).

factor in its development, and a key to future prosperity. There were sound economic reasons for this point of view. The Housatonic had been completed in 1842, largely through the assistance of Bridgeport capital.[66] But Bridgeport investors had received few dividends through the years, and the principal recompense had been the trade that the railroad brought from the small manufacturing towns of the Housatonic Valley. Bridgeport interests, therefore, were exceedingly hostile to any move whereby the Housatonic was either tapped or controlled by the New York and New Haven, diverting the valley trade to New Haven. They were also loath to see a railroad built by Bridgeport money managed by outsiders.[67]

Bridgeport was not alone in its opposition to this consolidation project, nor was the economic rivalry of two cities the only motive that figured in the conflict. Fear of monopoly was certainly a factor, especially with farmer members of the legislature. Another factor of some importance was a deep antipathy felt by many citizens toward the New York and New Haven road.

The New York and New Haven was undoubtedly the soundest, best equipped railroad in Connecticut; but its management was aggressive, arbitrary, and independent.[68] These unpopular traits were well illustrated by an incident in the spring of 1862. When 112 Massachusetts and 45 Connecticut soldiers, all wounded, some seriously, attempted to board the New York and New Haven Railroad in New York for transport home, James H. Hoyt, the superintendent of the road, refused to allow any on the cars until each man had paid a full fare. In demanding an immediate reckoning of the soldiers, he chose to disregard the fact that their attending doctors had travel orders signed by General Burnside. Considerable delay and confusion ensued until Connecticut's New York agent, Colonel Almy, could arrive with the required funds for tickets.[69] Typical of the comments that Hoyt's action inspired in the press was this angry remark of a Massachusetts merchant: "there are other ways of going to New York besides going on that road. I

66. Sidney Withington, *The First Twenty Years of Railroads in Connecticut* (New Haven, 1935), pp. 19–20.

67. *Hartford Times* (June 1, July 13, 1865).

68. *New Haven Journal and Courier* (March 15, 18, 1862).

69. *Norwich Courier* (March 27, 1862).

frequently go to New York over that road but for the years to come, at least, they shall not get one dollar of my money—not if I am compelled to go round to New York by way of the North Pole on crutches." [70]

If the legislature refused to allow a merger that would probably have been beneficial, it rashly granted a charter to a speculative railroad scheme that not only involved consolidation on a much larger scale but also new construction. This was the incorporation in 1863 of the Boston, Hartford and Erie.[71] With little in the way of capital or anything else except extravagant promises and a powerful lobby, the project would piece together existing railroads in Massachusetts and Connecticut, and where necessary, construct connective links to provide a new through route to the Hudson River and the West.[72] Apparently attracted by its glittering prospectus, neither the legislatures of Massachusetts nor Connecticut bothered to examine its assets with any care. They merely accepted the incorporator's pledge of $10,000,000 for construction, one-fifth of which was to be spent before July 4, 1866.[73] Two months after receiving its charter, the Boston, Hartford and Erie purchased the Hartford, Providence and Fishkill with borrowed funds and initiated a long-range plan of stock watering, which was to cost the taxpayers and investors of both states almost $20,000,000 over a ten-year period of gross financial mismanagement.

Although the Connecticut railroad system was far from complete in 1861, financially unstable, and for the most part inefficiently managed, it had nevertheless been a mighty adjunct to the war effort. During the last year of the war the railroads carried over one million tons of freight and close to five million passengers.[74] Of course, this implied a heavy burden on railroads that had entered the war with indifferent equipment and roadbeds; yet scarcely any improvement, replacement, or expansion occurred. As could be expected, the strain showed itself in declining service and soaring accident rates. The Hartford and New Haven Railroad

70. *Hartford Courant* (March 15, 1862).

71. *Norwich Aurora* (Aug. 29, 1863).

72. Davis, *New England States, 4,* 1815.

73. *Norwich Aurora* (Aug. 29, 1863).

74. "Governor's Annual Message, 1865," *PDLC* (May Sess., 1865), Docs. 1, pp. 5–6.

24. Spectacular washout on the Connecticut River during the sixties. Badly ballasted roadbeds and lack of adequate maintenance were features of Connecticut railroads. Connecticut Historical Society.

may have carried 856,355 passengers during 1864, but 7 of these were killed and upward of 50 were injured.[75] With little expenditure for improvement, rapid increase in rates, and a constantly expanding business, the railroads raised themselves from the edge of economic disaster in 1861 to a peak of prosperity in 1865. Besides canceling their debts and paying large dividends, they piled up heavy surpluses that were to be available for postwar expansion and improvement. Such an individualistic policy, however, aroused public enmity, which was expressed in attempts to bring the railroads more effectively under public control.

By 1865 the legislature had reconstituted the railroad commission and had given it powers to control passenger fares. This was a small price to pay for the financial security that the war had brought. By providing capital for future expansion and by establishing beyond doubt the necessity of railroads in an industrial state, the Civil War period had been one of great formative value. This was not the case with shipping, the great rival of the railroads. Connecticut commercial interests also enjoyed substantial profits from the expanded volume of the wartime carrying trade. But the effects of such prosperity stimulated overexpansion, which in their case was to prove disastrous.

When the war broke out, military demands and a sharply increased consumer market soon resulted in an extreme shortage of steamers on the river and sound, and even in the coastwide trade. So taxed were Northern shipyards in attempting to fill government orders that they were unable to make sizable deliveries of commercial steamers until early 1863. Thus, during the early years of the war, countless small sailing vessels appeared on the river and sound. Established steamship lines were confronted with sharp competition from scores of independent shippers. Retaliatory action in the form of a sustained rate war and discriminatory legislation, together with deliveries of new, more efficient steamers after 1864, re-established shipping line supremacy.

The shipping industry, in both its building and transportation phase, had been sharply stimulated by the war. Connecticut shipyards turned out over one hundred ships of all types for the government and for private interests. Though some were sailing vessels,

75. Ibid.

the great majority were steamers, side-wheel or screw, reflecting the modern outlook of Connecticut shipbuilders. Commerce enjoyed a corresponding expansion. River and sound trade developed enormously in a very short period; the seal and guano trade picked up; even whaling and the long moribund West Indies trade became profitable. Whalers again fared forth from New London under the flag of Williams and Havens. New Haven shipping interests began to prospect South American ports. Long Wharf in that city, after twenty years of inactivity, became for a time the center of a bustling commercial prosperity. This war-inspired renascence bred overconfidence in dying industries, like whaling or the West Indies trade. Both shipbuilding and commerce, responding to what they must have considered unlimited demands and heedless of the changing economic scene—a scene in which tariff policy and the growth of rail transportation would work against them—expanded out of all proportion to the needs of a peacetime adjustment. The war brought vigor to the youthful railroads, enabling them to expand their horizons often at the expense of shipping. It also brought vigor to the shipping industry, but it was the vigor of false strength that consumed available resources far too rapidly and hastened the inevitable decline.

The shipping industry, the railroads, and the production of munitions and textiles—the basic components of Connecticut's wartime economy—could not have grown as rapidly as they did without an adequate supply of capital. Thus the financial policies of the state and Federal governments, and the management of capital by such private institutions as the banks and insurance companies, form the next important episode in the history of wartime Connecticut.

16. FINANCING THE WAR EFFORT

AFTER THE FIRST YEAR of war, a general prosperity was evident in all economic activities. Credit sources—like banks of deposit and exchange, savings banks, and insurance companies—were unable to accumulate nonreserve funds for investment rapidly enough to accommodate the needs of an expanding war economy. To be sure, money in the form of greenbacks had become much cheaper after the Legal Tender Acts of 1862 and the National Banking Act of 1863, but these experiments in inflation merely aggravated the credit shortage. Discount rates continued to rise proportionately almost as fast as the price of gold.[1]

Though credit grew more expensive, industry and finance maintained a high level of prosperity. Neither heavy Union reverses in the field during the greater part of the war nor a burdensome state debt seemed to impair confidence in industrial securities or in state bond issues. In fact, overconfidence and speculation were ever-present dangers. Favorite securities at the Hartford exchange were rarely under par and usually well above, while Connecticut state bonds only once fell below premium. Such war-born prosperity and inflation, both directly traceable to the financial policy or lack of policy at the state capitals and at Washington, unleashed powerful forces that generated a host of problems.

From the onset of the conflict up to the very end, worried citizens saw $2,000,000 each year added to the state debt with a monotonous regularity. The outfitting, pay, and support of the first five Connecticut regiments and general mobilization had cost the state $1,866,097 by May 1861.[2] A special bond issue of $2,000,000

1. *Hartford Courant* (Oct. 2, 1862); Mallory Diary, passim.

2. "Report of the Comptroller of Public Accounts," *PDLC* (May Sess., 1862), p. 30. Breakdown of state expenses of $1,886,097 for war-effort 1861 drafts on state Treasury for the year ending March 31, 1862, as follows: Quartermaster's Dep't., $1,164,788; Paymaster General, $403,330; Commissary General $65,421; town authorities for bounty

was voted in the May session of the legislature to meet these expenditures. It was marketed easily at an average premium of 1.5 per cent with Connecticut citizens or institutions purchasing over half the issue.[3] But no sooner had the session adjourned than Congress imposed a direct tax of $20,000,000 on the states and levied a Federal income tax. Connecticut's share of the direct tax was $308,214.[4] However, one feature of this new levy must have proved attractive. If the state assumed the burdens of administration and collection, a 15 per cent deduction would be allowed, an invitation for patronage in the appointment of collectors.[5] The Governor lost no time in convening a special session of the legislature, and it quickly approved a list of state agents to collect the tax.[6] How to apportion the tax was a thornier question. Buckingham had compromised with this delicate issue by proposing a modest tax increase on the grand list and meeting the balance from a new bond issue.[7] With no more than a perfunctory hearing, a bill authorizing the second $2,000,000 bond issue passed both houses; but the tax measure immediately developed heavy opposition from farmers and small freeholders. They objected to additional taxation when railroads, insurance companies, and especially savings banks remained untouched.[8] Though a new bill was originated in the House, levying a ⅓ per cent tax on the annual business of the railroads and the deposits of financial institutions, and one mill on each dollar of the grand list, it was defeated by savings-banks partisans in the Senate. With neither side willing to recede, the entire measure perished. This forced the state to pay its share of the Federal tax from borrowed funds.[9]

Apparently the legislature hoped to dispose of the Federal income tax in the same manner, for it instructed Connecticut's congressional delegation to work for repeal and to urge as a substitute the

to families of volunteers, $110,099; for volunteer outfits, $40,635; for imported arms, $76,832.

3. *Hartford Courant* (Dec. 21, 1861).

4. "Governor's Message, Special Session, 1861," *PDLC* (1861), pp. 1–7.

5. Ibid.

6. *Norwich Courier* (Oct. 17, 1861).

7. "Message, Special Session, 1861," *PDLC*, pp. 1–7.

8. *Norwich Bulletin* (Oct. 17, 1861).

9. Ibid.; *Norwich Courier* (Oct. 24, 1861).

adoption of the very convenient direct tax.[10] Scenting more patronage, the Governor was also eager to have the income tax administered on the state level. As he explained in a letter to Secretary Chase: "Connecticut has adopted a system of taxation in accordance with the views, usages, and business interests of her citizens, a system altogether better for her people than any which may be adopted by the general government, and she will even prefer meeting her pecuniary obligations to the government through her own officers rather than through assessors and collectors appointed by Federal authorities." [11] The plaint of the Governor and legislature fell on deaf ears. Chase, at this time, had patronage visions of his own and doubtless was happy to relieve the state from the burden of appointing assessors and collectors.[12]

Obviously, some logical system of finance had to be inaugurated, new sources of revenue secured, taxes increased. Connecticut could not continue to meet her mounting obligations with borrowed capital at high rates of interest. However, Governor Buckingham was not sufficiently disturbed to recommend a positive taxation program in his 1862 message to the legislature. He estimated an expenditure of $1,133,384 for 1862, and after subtracting all claims against the Federal government, foresaw a deficit of over $1,500,000. Buckingham suggested that the legislature finance the deficit by either loans, taxation, or a combination of both, but he neglected to indicate which course should be taken.[13] Thus the May session of 1862 was confronted with a most difficult financial problem, and could expect neither leadership nor advice from the executive branch.

The experience of the 1861 special session had taught that real estate owners would permit no tax increases unless the burdens were equitably distributed. Yet the dogged obstinacy and political power of the financial institutions had defeated such attempts. Furthermore, savings banks and mutual insurance companies, the greatest source of nonreal wealth in the state, were exceedingly difficult to

10. *Norwich Courier* (Oct. 24, 1861).

11. Buckingham to Salmon P. Chase, Dec. 4, 1861 (Buckingham Papers).

12. See Dixon to Abraham Lincoln, July 14, Aug. 1, 1862, on Chase's very definite plans to appoint his own men to Connecticut internal revenue jobs. Also, Dixon to Frederick Seward, July 17, 1862 (Lincoln Papers).

13. "Governor's Annual Message, 1862," *PDLC* (May Sess., 1862), p. 5.

tax by their very nature. Both held funds of small depositors and investors, as well as large; both had invested much of their deposits in real estate mortgages. Unless interest rates were rigidly controlled, an impossibility under the ineffectual usury law, any tax might be passed on to the credit consumer in the form of higher interest rates. To complicate the problem, United States bonds, various state bonds, and some railroad securities enjoyed tax immunity, though none except railroad securities were considered blue chip investments until 1864. This led to fear on the part of many that if deposits were taxed, wealth might leave the banks and the burden would fall on the small depositors.

Despite these difficulties, the legislature did succeed in framing a law that taxed savings banks half of one per cent on their deposits and three-quarters of one per cent on their stock, if capitalized in Connecticut, with a half of one per cent tax on the business of railroads, telegraph, express companies, insurance companies, and all other companies and associations.[14] Almost concurrently, it doubled real estate taxes[15] and voted another $2,000,000 bond issue. With a final burst of energy, the legislature established a sinking fund to finance the debt repayment, a needful measure that had been carelessly delayed to the detriment of the state's credit.[16] Connecticut seemed finally to be moving toward a systematic and reliable financial policy; but expenses were far outstripping income, and an unfunded debt of $6,000,000 had elements of danger. These became evident in 1863 when, even with higher taxes, there was a deficit of over $1,000,000. Nor had the sinking fund, after a year's trial, afforded any relief. Members of the legislature were told that it had been created out of borrowed funds and had not contributed one penny toward extinguishing the debt.[17] Higher taxes or more bond issues were the two alternatives, and the legislature seemed disposed to adopt the latter course.

The chairman of the joint committee on finance recommended a continuation of the two-mill levy on the grand list, the same tax on corporations and financial institutions, and another $2,000,000

14. *Hartford Courant* (July 11, 1862); *Connecticut Laws, May Session, 1862*, chap. 55.

15. From one mill to two. *Hartford Courant* (July 14, 1862).

16. "Governor's Annual Message, 1862," *PDLC* (May Sess., 1862), pp. 6–7.

17. *Hartford Courant* (May 17, 1863).

bond issue carrying the usual terms—5 per cent interest and a twenty-year maturity. Such a display of debtor philosophy, however, was too much for some of the more conservative members of the legislature: they decided to challenge the wisdom of the state's financial policy in its entirety. No doubt partisan motives were an element in their thinking, for their spokesman was William W. Eaton, Democrat and inveterate foe of the war. But Eaton spoke for a much wider circle than his own political following when he said, "it is our duty as we can to pay as we go." [18] To achieve this, he proposed a simple two-point program that would fund the debt in ten years rather than twenty, and increase taxes twofold on real and business property.

Since the first bond issue in 1861, the legislature had followed a financial policy based on a long-term principle. The finance committee had stated frankly that the debt should be spread out so as not to fall with a crushing burden upon the present taxpayers.[19] As further justification of this course, it had pointed to the lower interest rates that could be expected on longer term debts.[20] Conditions, however, had changed rapidly. The state debt had increased much faster than had been expected, and an inflation economy had developed throughout the country.

Thus it seemed the height of folly to Eaton and others of his persuasion that the debt should be incurred in cheap money and paid off in dear money after the war, when a deflation was bound to set in. "Money is so plentiful that it is seeking investment," claimed Eaton. "Would it not be better to raise more by taxation now, and thus in part at least pay as we go and not make such large bond issues? Let us not cast this debt wholly upon our children." [21] Such a long view may have been sound, but it was not popular with the majority. "T'wont do to say money is plentiful in every man's pocket," replied the chairman of the finance committee. "Let us go on as we have reported it. In eight years if things in the country generally come round as we hope, the two mills tax will pay off the whole funded debt." [22] Those who agreed with his short-term pol-

18. *Hartford Times* (July 11, 1863).
19. *Hartford Courant* (May 17, 1861).
20. Ibid.
21. *Hartford Times* (July 11, 1863).
22. Ibid.

icy of deficit finance argued that "this war is for the benefit of posterity as well as for us." They refused to raise taxes or refinance the debt. All they would do was to vote another $2,000,000 bond issue with the usual terms.[23]

The results of this policy at once disclosed its fundamental weakness. When State Treasurer Coite put up for sale $1,000,000 worth of the newly authorized 5 per cent bonds, the offers were so limited that none was accepted.[24] True, the money market had declined in the fall of 1862; a more important reason for lack of faith in the state government, however, was the mistrust with which the banks viewed the state's credit policy. As a partial countermeasure, Governor Buckingham recommended to the special session of January 1864 that the interest rate be raised to 6 per cent, making the 1863 bond issue more attractive. He also urged that the State Treasurer be allowed to sell bonds as the needs of the state required and to accept any offer not below par value. Both houses supported Buckingham's recommendations.[25] On January 23 Treasurer Coite again accepted bids, which this time elicited lively competition, with offers ranging from par to 5 per cent over par. For reasons known only to the state administration, Ketchum and Sons were awarded the entire issue on a very low bid of one dollar over par.[26] The acceptance of such a low bid surprised state capitalists and aroused a violent outburst of criticism from the Democratic press. It was charged that Governor Buckingham was a bidder, that he had offered a mere one to one and a half per cent over par for a part of the issue, and that a low bid coming from a man in his position had damaged the value of the issue.[27] New York State bonds at

23. Ibid.

24. "Governor's Message to Special Session, Jan. 16, 1864," *PDLC* (May Sess., 1864), p. 9.

25. *Hartford Times* (Jan. 16, 1864).

26. *Norwich Aurora* (Jan. 30, 1864).

27. *New Haven Register* (Feb. 9, 1864). The *New Haven Register* was especially scathing. "The Connecticut 5%'s," it said, "three or four months ago went readily at ten% premium on the market and sometimes as high as 11 or 12%. But when the last state loan was offered for sale our own citizens, prominent among whom was the Governor of the state, made depressing and damaging offers of from 1–2% only for the new loan. . . . Such an offer made or about to be made from one in his position, so thoroughly acquainted with the monied concerns of the state and nation whispered about among the knowing ones, as such things generally are, could have no other than a damaging effect upon the state's public credit."

this time were selling on Wall Street at a premium of from 14 to 16 per cent. The new Connecticut 6 per cents, immediately after the sale, rose from 101 to 106, netting $100,000 for the Ketchums.[28] Furthermore, they continued to rise. On March 21 Democratic newspapers duly reported them at 115 to 118, with the brokers' profit around $300,000.[29]

Evidently the Governor and the Treasurer had grossly underestimated the credit of the state. Whether or not Buckingham had made the damaging bid, the low premium accepted for the bond issue is abundant evidence that the state administration was not now in accord with moderate taxation and immoderate bond issue. In his message to the members of the legislature in May 1864, the Governor reminded them that the state had a funded debt of $8,000,000 and an ominous unfunded one of $1,249,660.[30] Buckingham anticipated a call for more troops and foresaw more heavy payments of bounties as a consequence.[31] His stand on financial policies now was exactly the same as Eaton's had been in 1863. Though poles apart on politics, their thinking on the proper course for financing the war effort was practically identical. Somewhat belatedly, the Governor was ready to throw his influence behind some sort of pay-as-you-go program.[32]

Though responsible public opinion was worried about a large state debt and staggering town debts,[33] heavy Federal indirect taxation and the inflation economy was oppressive to the laboring and farming population. The *Norwich Aurora* did not agree with the Governor that the times were favorable to increase direct taxes. "It may be for him and those like him," said the *Aurora*, "but there

28. *Norwich Aurora* (Feb. 13, 1864).

29. *New Haven Register* (March 21, 1864).

30. "Governor's Annual Message," *PDLC* (May Sess., 1864), p. 4.

31. Ibid., p. 5.

32. Ibid. He said, "The present inflated condition of the currency . . . affords a time peculiarly favorable for meeting money obligations. I would recommend largely increased taxation."

33. *New Haven Register* (June 23, June 24, 1864). Towns began floating bond issues without legislative authorization as early as 1863 to finance their bounty and other war expenses. Manpower requirements mounted steeply after the battle of Gettysburg and so did town financial commitments, far surpassing what they were willing to tax themselves. By 1864 almost every sizable town and all of the cities had voted bond issues, so the legislature of that year was presented with a *fait accompli*. It validated the issues late in June.

never was a time when the laboring men of the state could so poorly afford to have direct taxes piled upon them in addition to the crushing weight of indirect taxation to which they are subject and which they cannot escape." [34] Arguments like this were plentiful in the press; but with the credit of the state at stake, and businessmen and bankers alarmed at the prospects, a four-mill real estate tax and a one-quarter to one per cent tax across the board on all types of industrial and financial business were finally wrung from a reluctant legislature.[35]

Even the additional taxation brought in hardly enough funds to pay the interest on the debt.[36] This exasperating situation began to intrude itself early in 1865 after a summer of heavy expenses for bounties, support for volunteers' families, emergency hospital facilities, state agents, and other drains on the Treasury. The *Hartford Times* painted a very gloomy and distorted picture in February 1865. Estimating the state debt in the neighborhood of $12,000,000, and anticipating an added $3,000,000 for the year, editor Burr calculated that should the grand-list levy be tripled to the unheard-of rate of twelve mills, it "would raise slightly over $3,000,000, and this will do no more than carry us along with one call for troops a year." Without war expenses he figured a four-mill levy would take years to bring the debt within manageable proportions. "We have been borrowing money to pay the interest on the state debt," he asserted, "and the debt has been rolling up so rapidly for the past three years, the time will come when this will not answer any longer. The people must pay the current expenses of the state and the interest on their debt by direct taxes or their credit will suffer." [37] To a certain extent the credit of the state had been suffering since the summer of 1863, but had rallied when bond interest was raised by the special session of January 1864.[38] Under the adroit manipulations of the Ketchums, Connecticut 6-20's had risen to a high of 112–15.[39] Thereafter, they had declined steadily.

34. *Norwich Aurora* (May 6, 1864).

35. *Connecticut Laws, May Session, 1864,* chap. 74.

36. *Hartford Times* (Feb. 1, 1865). $720,000 annually for interest, and a four-mill tax brought in about $1,000,000.

37. Ibid.

38. *Hartford Times* (Jan. 14, 1864).

39. *New Haven Register* (March 12, 1864).

In February 1865 they were down to 99, with few sales, and gave every indication of declining further.[40]

But the critics of the state financial policies had failed to take into account the fabulous increase of real and industrial wealth. The grand list each year during the war disclosed an average increase on real and personal property valuation of $10,000,000, and the trend was constantly upward. When the war ended and it was possible to make a recapitulation of past expenses as well as a business-like estimate of the future, the picture was far better than the prophets of gloom had sketched. Governor Buckingham, who, it appears, had been a victim of the same wartime psychology, must have felt a trifle guilty in the summer of 1865 when he told the legislature that the grand list had increased $17,477,243 during the fiscal year.[41] The entire debt was slightly over 4 per cent of the grand list and two-thirds less than its annual increase.[42]

With the final triumph of the Union armies and faith in the government restored, the legislature experienced a change of heart and discarded its debtor philosophy. The heavy four-mill tax on the grand list[43] was continued, and taxes were raised to one per cent on the annual business of the railroads and deposits of mutual insurance companies, 2 per cent on the business of telegraph and express companies, and a half per cent increase on the business or deposits of all other corporations, including savings banks.[44] It was not to be supposed that such stiff taxes were levied without the usual opposition or lobbying activities. On hand were the guardians of corporations who argued that such special taxes discriminated unfairly against them when compared with individual taxation.[45] But $3,000,000 had to be raised to carry the $10,523,113 funded and floating debt besides military expenses, which, though sharply

40. *Norwich Aurora* (Feb. 25, 1865).

41. "Governor's Message," *PDLC* (May Sess., 1865), p. 6.

42. Ibid.

43. *Norwich Aurora* (July 24, 1865).

44. *Connecticut Laws, 1865*, chaps. 43, 116.

45. *Hartford Courant* (July 15, 1865). Benjamin Douglas, a Republican member of the lower house, of the wealthy Middletown pump and machinery family, and H. K. W. Welch made a serious though unsuccessful attack in the 1865 session. Douglas attempted to establish the argument that government and state taxes were so burdensome on manufacturers that they more than counterbalanced the high tariff. As a result, he pictured a renewed and successful invasion of the American market by British firms.

cut, were still impressive.[46] A new bond issue would account for $2,000,000; the remainder had to come from taxation.[47] Landowners were paying four times as much in taxes as before the war. It was both necessary and just that corporations, heavy with war profits, should contribute their share. The course pursued by many powerful corporations, notably the mutual insurance companies and certain manufacturing corporations, had been anything but patriotic. They had ignored the taxes assessed on them by the 1864 legislature, compelling the State Treasurer to undertake a series of expensive litigations, all of which were to drag on for a number of years, finally ending in complete success for the state.[48]

One other source of capital had thus far escaped taxation—the estimated $10,000,000 invested in government bonds paying 7.3 per cent interest. Though most members of the legislature must have been familiar with the taxation immunity these securities enjoyed, a bill sponsored by the Democrats which would levy a one per cent tax on their dividends actually passed in the House.[49]

The national banks of the state seemed not to have anticipated this action, but they acted promptly when they learned of it. President John L. Bunce of the Phoenix National Bank of Hartford at once requested information of the United States Treasury Department as to the constitutionality of the proposed legislation.[50] A prompt reply was received from the Federal comptroller, Freeman Clarke, who put the subject on a political base by branding any state attempt to tax United States bonds as a Copperhead action. "It is a source of regret," he said,

> that any Northern State should for a single moment countenance an attempt to repudiate or nullify a constitutional act of Congress and one, too, that was deemed necessary to preserve the integrity of the nation. In one aspect it is fortunate as it

46. "Governor's Annual Message, 1865," *PDLC* (May Sess., 1865), p. 4.

47. *Norwich Aurora* (July 29, 1865). The legislature acknowledged that the credit of the state was in a perilous condition by again trying to make the 1865 $2,000,000 bond issue more attractive to prospective purchasers. The interest rate was continued at 6 per cent, but income derived from them was made tax free.

48. See legislature's authorization for suits, in *Hartford Times* (May 20, May 25, July 6, 1865), and Treasurers' reports, *PDLC* (May Sess., 1865–68), passim.

49. *Hartford Times* (July 15, 1865).

50. *Norwich Aurora* (July 24, 1865).

> will serve to show the people that it will not be safe for the government to allow the southern states to be so reconstructed as to permit their being represented in Congress as a unit, as they would be by men who would be but too willing to unite with northern men such as those favoring the measure to repudiate the National debt [by taxing it] if not by direct action by an equally destructive want of action in providing the means of payment.[51]

Armed with this letter, Bunce and his colleagues had no difficulty in pledging the Senate to defeat the House measure. On January 19 the Senate unanimously rejected it.[52] That the Federal bond tax issue was largely a partisan move was demonstrated a few days later when the Democrats suddenly announced that they had always stood for the taxation immunity of United States bonds and decried any talk of a conspiracy on their part to embarrass the national government. Pains were taken to point out that the taxing of government bonds on the state level was more a Republican movement than a Democratic one. Had not the Republican-dominated New Hampshire legislature recently passed such a measure? Had not Connecticut's heavily Republican lower house done the same? [53] Democrats did not believe that wealth invested in government bonds should go untaxed, but recognized that the constitutional opinions of Marshall governed the question and bowed to the inevitable.[54] Thus the question was buried for the time being, but such a lively issue with its economic and class implications could not be suppressed. It would continue to assert itself in Connecticut politics for several years to come.

Quite apart from the partisan motives of government bond taxation, many must have been worried about the credit of the state, or a measure of such obvious unconstitutionality and embarrassment to the Federal government would not have gained, even for a moment, wide acceptance in the legislature. This new-found con-

51. Ibid. (July 29, 1865).

52. Ibid.

53. Ibid.

54. Ibid.; *New Haven Register* (July 24, 1865). Arguments over its constitutionality in both the *Aurora* and *New Haven Register* implied a full realization of McCulloch vs. Maryland.

cern over the credit of the state was also born out by the serious proposal to reinvest the school fund in Connecticut bonds. The school fund had resulted from the sale in 1793 of 500,000 acres of land held by Connecticut under colonial charter rights in the Western Reserve.[55] It had been carefully administered and the interest had been distributed annually to the towns at the rate of two dollars for each child of school age. Though the educational level of the state declined because the towns had been able to slough off taxation and depend on the fund, its revenue had become so important to them that the new constitution adopted in 1818 fixed it in the organic law of the state.[56] The fund had become equally important as a lending agency. With its loans restricted to 6 per cent and with most money bringing much higher interest during the war years, it had been a very attractive source of low-cost money, especially for urban borrowers.[57] Interests like these viewed with alarm any attempt to absorb the fund into the state debt and remove it from the Connecticut money mart. A bill permitting the Treasurer to call in all school fund loans and reinvest in state bonds was instantly challenged on constitutional grounds [58] and defeated by a close vote late in the session.[59]

Having failed to develop any new sources of revenue or to strengthen the state credit, the General Assembly was in no mood to add any more burdens to the Treasury. A proposition for a constitutional amendment to guarantee $5,195,877 in debts incurred by the towns for war purposes met short shrift.[60] Members of the legislature were acutely aware that if such an amendment were passed, it would have been speedily ratified by the people. So repugnant was this proposition, however, that even members from the

55. George T. Clark, *A History of Connecticut,* p. 213.

56. Constitution of Connecticut, Art. 8, *Connecticut State Register and Manual* (1947).

57. *Hartford Times* (July 6, 1865).

58. *Norwich Aurora* (July 15, 1865).

59. Ibid. David Gallup of Plainfield, a Republican member of the House, of considerable prominence and a consistent advocate of farmers as against urban financial and industrial interests, spearheaded the forces that favored allowing the School Fund Commissioners to invest in state bonds. He charged that Hartford borrowed 70 per cent of the fund.

60. Croffut and Morris, *History of Connecticut,* p. 849.

cities which would have gained from such legislation voted unanimously with country members against it.[61]

Inflation figured largely in Connecticut's financial policy, even as it was of primary importance in the Federal government's management of the extraordinary wartime expenditures. The effects of this basic policy on state financial institutions and their consequent transmission of it to the local economy had spectacular results. Connecticut banks, whether they were aware of it or not, were the agents of both the Federal and state governments; and though at times they pursued an independent course and often seemed to have little faith in the ultimate victory, their maintenance of credit was imperative to the war effort. As expressions of governmental economic policies and as arbiters of Connecticut's industrial destiny, the banks occupied a unique position during the war period and made their impression upon the history of the state.

Despite the financial problems brought on by the depression of 1857, Connecticut banks were surprisingly strong at the outbreak of the war. The financial assistance that the Governor received from them in the early and chaotic days of mobilization was backed up with substantial hard-money reserves and sound investments. But at first the emergency fiscal measures sponsored by Secretary of the Treasury Salmon P. Chase temporarily shook the public confidence in the solvency of the banks. So tempting were the new three-year gold notes that the banks oversubscribed, drastically impairing their gold reserves. In July 1861 the legislature was forced to permit a suspension of specie payment,[62] which shocked those conservative citizens who well remembered the ruinous suspensions of 1837.[63]

Of more telling effect to the man in the street was the disappearance of fractional currency, which had rapidly followed gold into oblivion after the first issue of inflationary greenbacks in February 1862 and their precipitous decline in value during the spring and summer of that year.[64] Change became so scarce in Hartford that

61. *Hartford Times* (July 6, 1865).
62. *Hartford Courant* (July 11, 1862).
63. Davis, *New England States*, 2, 669–70.
64. Croffut and Morris, p. 849.

on July 19 over $900 worth of postage stamps were sold at the post office as a temporary expedient.[65] A few days later the Aetna Bank in Hartford cut its one dollar bills in half and stamped them so that each half could be used in lieu of a fifty-cent piece. The bank announced that it would redeem them either in stamps or in whole bills.[66] About $20,000 in these cut notes had been circulated before David Carr, United States Marshal for Connecticut, called attention to the illegality of such expedients. According to the Congressional Act of July 27, 1862, private agencies were forbidden to issue currency in denominations of less than one dollar.[67] Aetna at once stopped circulating them and began to redeem all in special one dollar notes.[68] Yet no relief was in sight. As the new greenbacks sank lower, the premium rose on specie of all kinds, even down to copper cents. Speculators in Hartford and New Haven scoured the countryside during October, paying from 23 to 25 per cent premium, and packed off the coins in bags to New York for sale.[69] Merchants all over the state, whose daily business demanded large amounts of ready cash, experienced great inconvenience. Private firms and individuals began to issue their own fractional notes.[70] For several weeks these shin plasters, as they were immediately nicknamed, were in general use. Of course they were illegal, and their values fluctuated wildly because of the prevailing tendency to counterfeit or issue them without restraint.[71] Their presence in great numbers only made the trade situation worse, and it became almost impossible to do business.[72] Everywhere merchants besought local authorities to aid them in their plight. In Norwich, on October 27, the common council met to consider how the city government might ease the situation. At hand was a resolution for the city to engrave plates and circulate on its own authority small denominational notes from 5 cents to 50 cents, the issue not to exceed $20,000 in value.[73]

65. *Hartford Press* (July 20, 1862).
66. *Norwich Courier* (July 24, 1862).
67. *Congressional Globe,* 37th Congress, 2d Sess., 1861–62, Pt. 4, p. 413.
68. *Norwich Courier* (Oct. 9, 1862).
69. Ibid.
70. *Hartford Courant* (Oct. 13, 14, 1862).
71. *Norwich Courier* (Oct. 30, 1862).
72. Ibid.
73. Ibid.

Governor Buckingham attended the meeting, yet his influence barely succeeded in preventing the council from violating the Federal law. The plea of expediency made by the handsome young lawyer H. H. Starkweather was so impressive that it almost carried the council.[74] Starkweather felt that the coining of fractional money did not violate the spirit of the law. While Federal law may have prohibited banks from issuing fractional currency, it said nothing about corporations, especially public corporations, such as a city government. The Norwich lawyer contended that public demand for such an issue was so great that no suit would ever come before the courts. "If anybody thinks the law is violated, let him get an injunction!" he remarked. The presence of the governor and others who were reluctant to take the law into their own hands restrained the more impetuous. A few more weeks of fiscal chaos and the Federal government belatedly came to the rescue with a plentiful supply of paper currency in small denominations. By the end of November, Connecticut banks were well supplied and the crisis was over.[75]

However, the pressure of an expanding economy was not to be reduced so easily. It continued to force state banks to higher circulation in ratio to their deposits. In midsummer of 1862 the 75 banks of discount and deposit had in circulation a little over $9,500,000 based on liquid assets, mostly state and United States bonds of $6,079,203, an increase of 17 per cent in circulation and 20 per cent in assets of 1861.[76] By December 1862 the legislature allowed them to expand note circulation another 25 per cent of their deposits, which afforded temporary relief.[77] Thereafter, the state banks received no further grants to expand their note circulation, but they found another way of accomplishing the same thing, until the bank commissioners intervened.

Not a few of them, tempted by the soaring price of gold in terms of greenbacks, sold their specie deposits at enormous advances, a practice that naturally cheapened their issues. To guard against speculation, Connecticut law had long required that note circulation of state banks should never exceed ten times the amount of

74. Ibid.

75. *Hartford Courant* (Dec. 1, 1863).

76. "Bank Commissioners' Report, 1862," *PDLC* (May Sess., 1862), pp. 3–20.

77. *Norwich Courier* (Dec. 18, 1862).

specie in their vaults. The bank commissioners had repeatedly warned that this ratio must not be exceeded.[78] During 1862 and 1864, however, many financial agencies secretly speculated in gold, deriving large profits; and some like the Aetna bank of Hartford openly flouted the commissioners. Vowing that the replacement of gold by legal tender did not violate "the spirit of the law," Aetna sold $20,000 worth of gold at a premium of 150 per cent early in 1864. For once the commissioners acted decisively: refusing either to be bullied or purchased, they gave the bank the alternative of suit or settlement at the hands of the legislative committee on banks. Aetna chose the latter. When the committee ordered repayment in full, it meekly agreed to do so.[79] Thoroughly chastened by this example, other commercial banks curbed their speculative tendencies and respected the law.

Still, restrictive legislation could do little to regulate the personal honesty of bank officials. The bank commissioners had neither the staff nor the funds to track down the worth of every investment. Even if this had been possible, it is doubtful that they would have considered investments with the New York financial house Ketchum and Sons a bad risk. Nevertheless, the old State Bank of Hartford was nearly ruined in a combination of gold speculations by its own cashier and Edward Ketchum, who held about $300,000 of its deposits. Both individuals gambled away about $500,000 of the bank's deposits before their speculations came to light.[80]

Gold was not the only field for speculation, nor were commercial banks the only lending agencies that sought a wider field of investment and were, in turn, besieged by an expanding industry desperate for credit. Savings banks, which constituted the greatest single source of capital in the state, were also assailed by the speculative fever. Required by law to invest 75 per cent of their deposits in real estate, and with new deposits increasing at the average rate of about $2,000,000 a year, they chafed under restraint. In December 1862 the legislature was sufficiently receptive to allow them to invest half their deposits outside of real estate, but in a moment of rare wisdom insisted that not more than 15 per cent of any bank's capital stock

78. "Bank Commissioners' Report, 1865," *PDLC* (May Sess., 1865), pp. 4–5.

79. Ibid., p. 11.

80. *Hartford Times* (Sept. 1, 1865).

be lent to one man or one company.[81] Nor were savings banks permitted to invest in government bonds until after Appomattox, when the Federal debt had been properly secured and the National Banking System had become firmly rooted.

Indeed, the financial policies of the Federal government were regarded with suspicion during the entire war period. When one considers the specie stringency, the low value of greenbacks, and the poor showing of United States bonds on the market, such distrust is not surprising. Furthermore, many influential Republicans disliked Chase, and their views were no doubt communicated to the bankers. Thus state banks were reluctant to enter the new national system when it began to operate in 1863, even though permitted to do so by state legislation. Connecticut bankers were especially critical of that feature of the National Banking Act which compelled them to base their note circulation in a fixed ratio on the market value of government bonds. Men of individualistic business instincts opposed the idea of being forced to buy more bonds if they depreciated merely to keep up their note circulation. The broader concept of being a party to the credit of the United States made little impression, especially as few bankers prior to late 1864 were inclined to risk their entire capital on Union victory. But some businessmen grasped the fact that national bank notes would certainly be better secured than the state issues. Self-interest of member banks would compel them to support the government bond issues and hold down depreciation.[82]

Shortly after President Lincoln signed the National Banking Act on February 25, 1863, five prominent businessmen—James E. English, then the only Democratic member of the state's congressional delegation, Harmanus M. Welch, mayor of New Haven, Amos F. Barnes, Daniel Trowbridge, and Elisha N. Welch of Bristol—met together and decided to petition for a national bank charter. Subscribing $300,000 of their personal funds, a major portion of which would be used to purchase government bonds as prescribed by law, they drew up articles of association and forwarded them to Washington. Twelve days later they petitioned the Treasury Department, asking that the proposed bank be named "The First National

81. *Norwich Courier* (Dec. 18, 1862).
82. Ibid. (Aug. 29, 1863).

Bank of New Haven."[83] Actually the New Haven group was the first in the nation to file for incorporation, and would have received Charter No. 1, had not English graciously relinquished this honor to Jay Cooke, the Philadelphia financier and the nation's leading salesman of government bonds. Cooke's Philadelphia group was thus granted the first charter, the New Haven bank being accorded Charter No. 2. The First National of Stamford received Charter No. 4, giving Connecticut two of the first four national banks established in the country.[84] After less than a year of operation, the First National of New Haven reported resources and liabilities of over $800,000. "One need not be an economist," said the bank's historian, "to sense the dynamic, healthy implications of the details of this quarterly report, especially the $386,000 in the loans and discounts item."[85]

Despite such evidences of profitability in the new national system, only four state banks, with a combined capital of about $2,000,000, had joined it by May 1864: the Merchant's and Manufacturer's Bank of Hartford, Elm City of New Haven, Farmers' of Bridgeport, and the Exchange Bank of Norwich.[86] The rush to enter came early in 1865, when nineteen more with a capital of $7,850,880 suddenly realized that, with victory assured, a national banking system could be viewed in a more profitable atmosphere.[87] Forty-nine banks still retained their state charters.[88] The transfer of so many of the state banks to national control raised a taxing problem that compelled a reform of some features of the state tax system; otherwise, a smooth transition was made.[89]

All financial institutions prospered during the war, particularly

83. "Bank Commissioners' Report, 1864," *PDLC* (May Sess., 1864), pp. 3–10. See Rollin G. Osterweis, *Charter Number Two: The Centennial History of the First New Haven National Bank* (New Haven, 1963), pp. 14–18.

84. Osterweis, p. 14.

85. Ibid., p. 15.

86. Ibid., p. 21.

87. "Governor's Annual Message, 1865," *PDLC* (May Sess., 1865), p. 8.

88. Ibid.

89. Ibid. The Banking Act of 1863 permitted the state to tax the stock of national banks, but insisted that it be taxed in the town where the bank was located and at the same rate as other monied institutions. Connecticut laws taxed the owners of bank stock where they resided and at the local rate assessed independently of other towns and not uniform.

after 1863, when state restrictions on investment were relaxed.[90] Deposits bounded upward each year, and interest rates remained high.[91] Feeble attempts of hard-pressed debtors to invoke usury were casually brushed aside. Indeed, far from accepting a usury ceiling on mortgage interest rates, the banks managed to raise the customary 6 per cent by adding to it both taxes and insurance.[92] Investments of practically every kind, including much suspended paper that had been considered worthless since 1857, paid high and sustaining dividends.[93] Though the mortgage mart became somewhat depressed due to the absence of so many potential home owners in the armed forces, savings banks were able to make up this loss by the relaxation of investment restrictions at the close of 1862.[94] In 1864 they had invested $7,907,442 in loans outside of real estate, principally in long-term high interest bearing securities.[95]

On the whole, Connecticut banks were well managed, considering the unusual demands made upon them, the sudden, bewildering prosperity, the absence of effective restraint, and the speculative mood of the business community. There were no bank failures and only two flagrant speculations, despite the constant temptation of gold. If anything, the banks were too conservative, at least in their support of the state and Federal governments. Their rather selfish attitude regarding taxes is a case in point. But their caution regarding the national banking system and the purchase of state and government bonds reflected a latent hostility to inflation as much as a lack of confidence in the government.

For want of a sound pay-as-you-go policy, Connecticut paid heavily in future dollars. At the war's end the state debt, including

90. "Bank Commissioners' Report, 1865," *PDLC* (May Sess., 1865), p. 9.

91. "Governor's Annual Message, 1865," ibid., p. 8. By 1865 about one-fifth of the state's entire population, or 121,682, had savings accounts.

92. See *Connecticut Laws, May Session, 1862,* chap. 21. Section 1 of this law stated: "No contract heretofore or hereafter made shall be deemed usurious by reason of the borrower paying or agreeing to pay the taxes assessed and paid upon the sum loaned or the insurance of the estate morgaged to secure the loan."

93. "Bank Commissioners' Report, 1864," *PDLC* (May Sess., 1864), p. 8.

94. *Norwich Courier* (Dec. 25, 1862).

95. "Bank Commissioners' Report, 1864. Despite the fact that they were permitted to invest 50% of their deposits in securities, real estate mortgages still absorbed the greatest share of their investment capital, $12,850,258 in 1864.

that portion incurred by the towns, stood at upward of sixteen million dollars, of which about one quarter was a collectable claim against the United States Treasury. The debt was large but not staggering, and the war had brought large increases in wealth—almost sixty million taxable dollars between 1861 and 1865.[96] If moderate and consistent taxation had only tempered immoderate and inconsistent bond issues, Connecticut taxpayers would have been spared the extravagance of selling bonds for cheap money and retiring them later for dear money. The state treasurer, for example, had sold the 1864 and 1865 issues, five million dollars worth of bonds, at from par to one above par; yet when the state sinking fund really began to operate after the war, Connecticut 6-20's rose proportionately, costing the state millions of dollars, most of which further enriched the banks and insurance companies.[97]

Indirectly, however, the state financial policy, by pouring wealth into these agencies, did help to strengthen local credit facilities. Such timely, if unplanned, assistance was a factor in stimulating industrial growth at home and elsewhere. Ahead lay the economic readjustment during which this new accretion of capital would seek out investment possibilities. Much would go into the new cotton industry, and much more would finance railroad development, exploit wartime inventions in firearms and machine tools, and inaugurate large-scale urban development.

96. "Governor's Annual Message, 1866," *PDLC* (May Sess., 1866), Doc. 2, pp. 3–5. This estimate does not include a large amount of capital invested in United States bonds, state bonds, and certain tax exempt railroad securities.

97. *Norwich Aurora* (Feb. 13, 1864).

PART FIVE

Conclusion: The Problems of Peace

17. READJUSTMENT

APPOMATTOX raised serious problems of economic and social adjustment for the people of Connecticut. The sudden end of the great war had caught everyone unawares. As is typical of such an individualist society, peace had been expected and welcomed, but no one had done anything to prepare for it. Thus all classes at first felt a trifle insecure in what seemed to be an unfamiliar environment.

The transportation and discharge of 35,000 men was the last important war measure to be undertaken by the state administration. It was directed with the same foresight and ability that had characterized Governor Buckingham's wartime leadership. A network of state agents, under the control of the Reverend William A. Benedict and the Washington Sons of Connecticut, arranged for the transportation of the Connecticut regiments from the front. In New York the ever-faithful Almy expedited their passage through the city.[1] For three years these groups had gained experience in coping with the affairs of Connecticut soldiers, and Governor Buckingham had cautiously assisted them by adding personnel to their organization, despite the charges of political jobbery the Democrats leveled at each appointment.[2] In a caustic editorial of March 23, 1865, the *New Haven Register* remarked: "one of the leaks in the state treasury is found in the money spent for the support of state agents at various points, ostensibly to look to the affairs and wants of Connecticut soldiers. They are paid more than they could earn at home besides their expenses . . . [are] busy looking up soldiers of the right stamp to be sent home, and last winter some of them were living at Washington hotels at the people of Connecticut's expense, engaged in trying to lobby some favorite scheme through

1. Croffut and Morris, *History of Connecticut*, pp. 833–38.
2. "Governor's Annual Message, 1865," *PDLC* (May Sess., 1865), p. 9.

Congress."[3] At home the adjutant general's office was under strict orders to furnish war records upon request, and to search and negotiate claims to pensions, back pay, and bounties.[4] In addition, every effort was made to bring sick and wounded soldiers to hospitals in or near their native state so that they could be near their families. Governor Buckingham built five new pavilions for the New Haven Hospital to accommodate the expected excess.[5] Indeed, the state administration discharged its demobilization duties with such efficiency that the local labor market was flooded at a time when the abrupt termination of war contracts was creating widespread technological unemployment. Although no veterans were reduced to begging in the streets, a situation endured by some of their forebears after the Mexican War, jobs were scarce and poorly paid.[6] Compounding the unemployment problem, inflationary pressures continued to drive up the cost of living.

Early predictions that the rise of greenback values would automatically result in a lowering of commodity prices had not materialized. The suffering consumer was more deeply involved in an arcanian wilderness of inflated commodity prices in 1865 than he had been during the worst days of the war. During 1865 the cost of food, clothing, and shelter advanced from 12 to 15 per cent.[7] All commodities were expensive, but coal was exorbitant, and the usual cooperative remedies were applied in a vain attempt to lower prices.[8] Several cooperative companies were formed in the summer of 1865: some were fraudulent and bilked Connecticut investors of thousands of dollars; others of more honorable intent were brought to an early end by shipping and labor difficulties.[9] Another flurry of speculation happily confined to stock manipulators was the curi-

3. *New Haven Register* (March 23, 1865).

4. "Governor's Annual Message, 1865," *PDLC* (May Sess., 1865), pp. 9–10.

5. Ibid.

6. James Gallagher's speech before the legislature, June 7, 1861; *Hartford Courant* (June 18, 1861).

7. *Norwich Aurora* (Jan. 21, Dec. 30, 1865).

8. *Hartford Courant* (May 6, 1865).

9. See, for example, the sordid and fortunately brief career of the Charter Oak Mutual Coal Company of Hartford—a simple confidence scheme that cost its investors thousands of dollars, but whose promoters went unpunished because of a weakness in the joint stock laws of the state. *Hartford Press* (June 27, 1866); *Norwich Advertizer* (Aug. [illegible] 1866).

ous attempt to mine and process Connecticut peat as a substitute for coal.[10] Not one of these experiments, either with substitutes or cooperatives, proved to be a lasting solution to the problem of high fuel costs or of food prices, for that matter, and many of them had played upon the gullibility of the public, adding to the general pattern of frustration. When some relief in the high cost of living was realized in the late fall of 1866, it was not from oppressive fuel prices but from high food costs; nor was it in any way due to cooperative action but simply to an oversupply of meat, which tumbled beef and pork about three cents a pound.[11] As if shortages and high commodity prices were not enough to bear, the working population had to contend with an acute housing shortage.

Housing for the working population may not have been plentiful during the war, but at least it had been adequate. Actually, low-cost dwellings barely kept pace with demand, and little or no funds had been invested in replacement or upkeep; but a combination of circumstances peculiar to wartime had postponed an incipient tenement shortage. Although many workmen and their families, attracted by war industries, swelled the population of the cities and towns, the absence of so many young men in the armed forces had produced a counterbalancing effect by checking population growth.[12] The excess of births over deaths in 1865 was only 657, as compared with 4,271 in 1860, and though an average of 9 per cent more males than females had been born every year during the war, there were 8,150 more women than men in 1865, with 60 per cent of these in the 15–30 year age group.[13] Since boys up to the age of fifteen outnumbered girls by 1,274, this disparity between the sexes could not be attributed to the higher infant mortality of boys.[14] Two other factors had also been responsible for a postponement of the housing shortage: the rapid development of the factory village, which the war had stimulated, and the prevailing tendency of village mill owners to provide housing for their employees. Then, too, an agricultural boom inspired by the war

10. *Norwich Aurora* (April 28, 1866); *New Haven Register* (June 16, 1866).

11. *Norwich Aurora* (Nov. 24, 1866).

12. Their numbers must be subtracted from the population, for their absence from home cut down on marriages and lowered the birth rate.

13. "Annual Report of the State Librarian," *PDLC* (May Sess., 1865), passim.

14. Of course, migration to the Western states must also be considered as a factor.

economy and rising food prices, together with a shortage of agricultural labor, had diminished country to city migration, easing to some degree the population pressure on urban areas. Most of these conditions were reversed after 1865.

The demobilization of the Army helped create a housing shortage as returning veterans began to establish families. Industry was expanding and specializing under the impetus of the maturing industrial revolution; a renewal of emigration, both native and foreign, added its share to the ranks of the home-seekers. Thus a housing shortage immediately developed that was to continue for years. There was no rent control and almost no new construction except in business or industrial buildings and expensive houses for families with high incomes. In the spring of 1867 the *New Haven Register* noted: "First quality nine rooms from $500 to $900 a year; second class, $300 to $500 a year; third class, three stories and up from $100 to $175." Not wishing to encourage those who might wish to pay even these exorbitant rents, the *Register* added, "Not one in the above catalogue can be obtained at any price . . . a house advertised to rent is besieged by an army of renters from daylight to the hour of midnight. What people are going to do is more than we know." [15] Clearly the public had been misled by the newspaper opinion that when military demands tapered off, large surpluses of commodities and raw materials would bring down prices. What had been overlooked were inadequate transportation facilities.

The demands of an inflated economy and a public starved for consumer goods strained available transportation, which had been temporarily aggravated by the independent behavior of coastwise shipping.[16] With the sudden reopening of normal Southern trade, Connecticut shipowners crowded every possible ocean-going vessel into the rush for Southern pine and cotton. This resulted in a heavy surplus of these particular commodities, but everything else remained scarce and expensive, including, of course, most building materials. For a brief period Connecticut shipowners did a greater volume of business than during the war. Twenty to twenty-five thousand dollars profit for an easy voyage from Connecticut ports to New Orleans by way of New York was a frequent occurrence.

15. *New Haven Register* (April 16, 1867).
16. *Bridgeport Standard* (Oct. 14, 1864).

The merchant service expanded rapidly, absorbing ships faster than the Federal government could auction off its surplus or return charters, faster than the shipyards could build new vessels. Departing from his accustomed melancholy, Charles H. Mallory happily noted one profitable voyage after another, and the arrival of his steamer, the *A. J. Ingersoll,* from Mobile moved him to sheer delight. "She has made a good trip," he noted, "earning $26,000." [17]

Temporary unemployment, high commodity prices, and shortages in practically everything were some of the more obvious effects of social imbalance as the economy began adjusting itself to peacetime conditions. There were bound to be strains and dislocations when the powerful psychic and economic stimuli of the war were suddenly withdrawn. Fortunately, the new industrial society was fundamentally vigorous enough to cope with the readjustment. After a brief period of transition, complicated by the short depression of 1866, a notable surge of economic growth absorbed the labor surplus, ironed out the cost of living problem, and ushered in a seven-year period of solid prosperity.

The boom in the Southern trade was short-lived, however. A few months after Mallory had chronicled the trip of the *Ingersoll,* he was again complaining about the prevalence of competition and wondering whether he could maintain all his ships. The political disturbances of radical reconstruction had depressed the Southern market, while the high tariff and a shipping surplus made it difficult for shipowners to adjust.[18] By the spring of 1866 the yards of Gildersleeve and Goodspeed, as well as those of Greenman and Company, Hill and Grinnell, and Maxson and Fish, were almost idle. In Mystic one bark of 600 tons, one ship of 1,100 tons, and a small schooner smack for Southern fishing were all that occupied ways that a few years before had held a dozen keels.[19] The freighting business, especially to Southern ports, had declined sharply because of the scarcity of Southern capital and plethora of raw cotton.[20] Mallory's New York to Galveston line did a fair business but, but could obtain no more than one-half to three-quarters of a

17. Mallory Diary, April 30, Nov. 7, 1865.

18. Decline of Connecticut commerce, see United States Treasury Department, Director of Statistics, *Reports, 1866, 1867, 1870,* passim.

19. *Mystic Pioneer* (May 30, 1866).

20. Mallory Diary, Oct. 4, 1867.

cent a pound for cotton on return.[21] Grain freights to Europe were more profitable, yet the tariff made return freight rates so low that they scarcely paid fixed charges without considering a profit.[22] Under such unfavorable circumstances shipmasters were lucky if they could obtain a full return cargo.

In the space of two years, depression had overtaken commercial and shipbuilding interests. Stagnation in Mystic was nearly complete, and what applied to this once busy little port was true elsewhere. Mallory was a keen enough businessman to see that the small Connecticut seaports did not have adequate facilities or trade potential to withstand at the same time the competition of Boston, New York, and Philadelphia, and the high tariff policy. While he filled the pages of his diary with complaints of hard times, he was cautiously shifting his base of operations to New York, and by 1868 he was to be conducting his entire business from that city.[23]

The sudden boom and equally sudden depression of Connecticut's commerce, though unsettling to industry in general, was of positive assistance to railroads. When much of the coastwise shipping was diverted to the Southern market, most of the burden of supplying an inflated home economy fell squarely on railroads that were ill equipped to handle the additional strain. They had expanded little during the war, and because of a shortage of labor and materials, had not even made the necessary repairs to their roadbed and rolling stock. A temporary materials and fuel famine, which arose from this situation, prompted many a manufacturer to seek improvements in existing rail transportation and to furnish capital for expansion. The foundations of an ambitious railroad net, which was already laid when shipping became plentiful again in 1867, was to be too firmly rooted to be checked, even though commercial interests fought hard to stifle its growth. Then, the commercial depression appeared. This was to sap the vitality of interstate shipping and either transfer mercantile capital from the state or channel it into other industries, including the railroads.

One of the more striking developments of the readjustment phase was the rapid disappearance of the arms industry. As early as

21. Ibid., April 4, 1867.
22. Ibid., Aug. 1, Dec. 14, 1867.
23. Ibid., March 3, 1868.

Лay 1862 the armaments industry had shown signs of overproduc-ion in rifles and pistols when Colt's reduced from two shifts to one. 'his brought considerable hardship and uncertainty to Colt's vorkers and their families—some 10,000 people.[24] By the close of 863 a pronounced glut of rifles and military equipment had uined the market. Prices of such equipment were a mere fraction f what they had been in the peak demand year of 1861.[25] The pectacular Norwich Arms Company, heavily in debt by 1864, was ankrupt a few weeks after Appomattox.[26] Even the old established harps' plant at Hartford could not stand the strain of peace for nore than a few months. On October 14, 1865, it closed down ompletely, never to regain its former prosperity.[27] Colt's was nore fortunate, or perhaps better managed by General William B. 'ranklin, who succeeded E. K. Root upon the latter's death in 865. At Franklin's instigation, the greater part of the factory was eased to various machine tool companies. Only one building was etained and six to seven hundred workmen employed for the nanufacture of revolvers and breech-loading rifles.[28] The New Iaven and Bridgeport arms industry made a better adjustment han that of Hartford. Oliver Winchester's wartime development rogram in breech-loading rifles had helped in this regard. Henry Lifles were to enjoy a substantial peacetime market, particularly in he Western states and territories. Winchester Arms was the only ifle manufacturer in the state that expanded its production in the ostwar period. Volume sales for Winchester's new twenty-shot reech-loading rifle stimulated the brass industry in Waterbury nd the new brass cartridge industry in Bridgeport and New Ha-en.[29]

The wartime concentration of the brass industry in New Haven nd Fairfield counties was an important factor in persuading he brothers Sargent to establish their hardware factory in New Iaven. By 1871 the Sargent Company employed 2,000 workers. Vinchester Arms and the Sargent Company were easily the largest

24. *Hartford Evening Post* (Jan. 14, 1862); *Hartford Courant* (May 1, 1862).
25. *New London Daily Star* (Dec. 3, 1863).
26. Corr., *Boston Traveler* (Dec. 6, 1866), in *Norwich Aurora* (Dec. 22, 1866).
27. Davis, *New England States*, 2, 828.
28. J. H. Trumbull, *Hartford County*, 2, 569.
29. Barnum, *Life*, pp. 556–57.

factories in the city.[30] The New Haven-Bridgeport industrial complex owed a large measure of its successful readjustment to wartime development of new products that would have a peacetime consumer demand. Similarly, Hartford and Norwich had been responsive to future markets. But investments in new products, in new manufacturing facilities, or in new development programs did not always prove feasible. Horatio Ames demonstrated this perilous aspect of the postwar readjustment.

The sooty little town of Falls Village, in the Salisbury Hills, was almost depopulated when Ames' new gun factory went out of business. Ames, one of the great ironmasters of the Housatonic Valley had invented and manufactured what proved to be the strongest cannons yet tested by Army and Navy ordnance experts.[31] Their acceptance, however, came too late to save Ames, who had risked his entire fortune in perfecting them.[32] His failure in 1865 shook the entire iron industry in Litchfield County, and decreed an agricultural future for that part of the state. Other industries whose foundations were not firmly rooted in the past or whose management was not able to cope with the market difficulties of peace experienced extreme difficulty in adjusting to the production of consumer goods. Not a few followed in the path of the Reliance Machine Company of Mystic, which collapsed utterly in the fall of 1864, inspiring Charles Mallory as one of the receivers to "realize how frail and treacherous human prospects are." [33]

The owner of the Reliance Company, Isaac Randall, had made an easy and profitable transition from cotton gin manufacture to engine and boiler production for Mystic-built ships during the war His failure presaged the sharp decline for ship engines that had set in before the war's end. It was an irony of fate when Mallory was appointed receiver, as he and other shipbuilders, by temporarily outproducing the market, had unwittingly caused the demise. The greatest engine and boiler works in Connecticut, the Woodruff and Beach Company of Hartford, had also gained substantial profits during the conflict; and when demand slackened, Samuel Wood-

30. Osterweis, *New Haven*, pp. 352–53.
31. Chard P. Smith, *The Housatonic Puritan River* (New York, 1946), p. 369.
32. Ibid., pp. 365–66.
33. Mallory Diary, Jan. 2, 1865.

ruff, unlike his Mystic counterpart, made strenuous efforts to invest in other fields. He became involved in the Putnam Insurance Company of Hartford, but instead of enlarging his fortune was to become a bankrupt in 1871.[34]

The widespread effects of cutbacks in war production, already well advanced in 1865, had a decided economic effect on the cities and towns, an effect directly proportional to their size and the diversity of their output.[35] Although Hartford and the greater New Haven area experienced considerable hardship in readjusting, their problems were simple in comparison to smaller, isolated communities. If the sudden emergence of a war industry had catapulted a country village into the machine age, so its abrupt departure after four years of furious activity brought grave social dislocations. Tragic was the fate of a town like Canton. Its chief industry, powder manufacture, but a step removed from the household stage in 1861, burgeoned during the war. When munitions production ended in 1865, the economic heart of the community was destroyed. The population of Canton was forced either into subsistence agriculture or migration.[36] Another example was East Hartford, an agricultural community before the war. It reverted to agriculture after the war; but vacant powder mills, an empty shoddy factory, and a discontented population marked the brief passage of a transient industrial prosperity.

The war-enhanced industries of towns like Canton and East Hartford made no attempt to readjust. Probably nothing could have been done that might have reconciled their unfavorable economic characteristics with the free-for-all competition ushered in by peace. A satisfactory readjustment came rather in those areas where the industrial revolution was in full tide before the war; where capital and labor were relatively abundant and cheap power available; where transportation, though inadequate, still existed. It took the form of a more highly developed division of labor by industry and by area, which in turn was created by market demand, competition, and the speed-up given to industry by war

34. Davis, 2, 822.

35. Grace P. Fuller, *An Introduction to the History of Connecticut as a Manufacturing State*, Smith College Studies (Northampton, 1915), pp. 59–63.

36. J. H. Trumbull, 2, 75.

production. The demands of a peacetime economy and the crescendo of the industrial revolution practically forced capital into consumer goods specialties, often with an apparent disregard for long-range consequences.

The sure, quick profits of the postwar textile industry enticed so many capitalists in eastern Connecticut that by the mid-seventies the economy of the area was to suffer from overspecialization. Norwich provides one of the best examples. Since the building of the Norwich and Worcester Railroad in the late 1830s, a comprehensive machinery industry had grown up that was soberly cumulative in economic growth. With a skilled labor supply expanding every year, and a steady accretion of capital, Norwich, unlike her sister city New London, avoided the fatal error of pivoting on one industry. When New London's whaling industry fell before kerosene and gas lamps, Norwich continued to flourish.[37] But the war brought hectic development to its diversified interests, spawning too much paper capital and developing a far greater labor force than was necessary for its industries and importance. Following the example of the Rhode Island textile empire, which had already worked its way westward along the magnificent water privileges of the Yantic and Shetucket Rivers, Norwich capital poured into the manufacture of cotton cloth. It is somewhat ironic that the industrialists and the bankers of the area, old in years and experience, who had built up a healthy industry in Norwich, should be the first to succumb to cotton manufacture. By 1867 the economy of Norwich revolved on textiles, as New London's never had on whale oil. There had been romance and daring in whaling; yet in cotton there was naught but a transitory profit and a permanent legacy of social ills.[38] Specialization, however, as a distinct feature of Connecticut's adjustment to peacetime conditions, was in most instances of long-term benefit to the economy.

Meriden and Wallingford had been specializing in the production of silver-plate ware since the early fifties, and the few war plants in the area had not disturbed the industry's steady growth. While other towns were producing munitions, Meriden capital was

37. *New London Daily Star* (Jan. 2, 1866).

38. For postwar concentration of woolen and cotton mills in the Norwich area compare figures in Eighth Census, *Manufactures* with figures in *Compendium*, Ninth Census; also *Seventh Annual Report*, Boston Board of Trade.

building new silver-plate factories and preparing to supply a national market. On the very day that the battle of Gettysburg began, Rogers Brothers broke ground for their largest factory; that same year they established a sales branch in New York to handle the increased volume of trade. By 1868, with agencies in San Francisco, Chicago, and London, Rogers Brothers would be in a position to bid for the international market and to control the distribution of their product.[39]

Another industry that tended strongly toward specialization was the manufacture of machine tools at Hartford. However, its development had been of far more recent origin, almost synonymous with the war itself. In fact, the industry was an outgrowth of firearms production, with the Colt factory as an amazing educational institution from which graduates went forth after a few years of training in machine techniques to establish their own plants. Certainly the most successful alumnus of Colt's was Francis A. Pratt, who had been employed as an assistant manager from 1852 until 1854. Colt and Root communicated their ardor for machine tools to the youthful Pratt, enabling him to see other applications and an enlarging market in other industries besides firearms. During the war he formed a partnership with Amos Whitney, an expert mechanic, and the two men rented a room where they began production of machine tools for the arms and sewing machine industries. Their initial work schedule struck a nice balance between the uncertainties of a war market and the less profitable, but safer, production of goods that were essentially of the civilian variety. Perhaps this was why Pratt and Whitney made substantial, though not phenomenal, profits in the war years, when phenomenal profits were the rule rather than the exception.[40] More likely, the reason why greater profits were not made was that the era of wholesale application of machine tools would not reach full tide until after the war. From 1866 to 1868, Pratt and Whitney made a profit of $100,000, which they prudently reinvested in their business, and by 1869 they incorporated with a paid-in capital of $300,000.[41]

If Pratt was the most successful Colt graduate, Charles E. Bil-

39. Davis, 2, 938, 940–46.

40. About $75,000. Ibid., p. 835.

41. Ibid., p. 844.

lings was the most ingenious. As the single-minded proselyte of the drop forge, which would revolutionize the machine-tool industry in the postwar period, Billings was first employed as a die sinker in Colt's forging department.[42] His principal task at Colt's was to keep the drop forges in good repair, an apprenticeship that made him a passionate advocate of the device. After six years at Colt's he went to the Remington Arms Company, resolving to establish there a similar system of forging. The Remington Company was in the midst of full war production at that time. Thus it took a good deal of persuasion as well as true devotion to a cause before the management would permit a complete overturn of its accustomed methods of manufacture. But Billings had his way: he built a shop for the manufacture of drop forges. With the improved designs that he introduced, Remington's was able to make great savings in labor costs on government contracts.[43]

Except for an ill-fated venture in the manufacture of sporting rifles, Billings' connection with the arms industry ended in 1865, when he devoted his talents to the production of sewing machines. As superintendent of the Weed Sewing Machine Company of Hartford for the next three years, Billings applied the drop forge wherever possible with outstanding success. At first he concentrated on bobbins, which then consisted of four pieces of metal brazed together by hand. By using a drop forge and a die, a stronger bobbin was stamped out in one simple operation. The process was applied to other parts of the Weed machine, so that by 1869 practically every movable part was a die casting.[44] In 1870, when Billings formed his own machine tool company, his pioneer production techniques not only were in general use among sewing machine manufacturers but were common practice in other industries that produced both complex and simple machinery.

Spurred on by the success of these pioneers, the manufacture of machine tools easily shrugged off its wartime dependence upon the arms factories to emerge as one of the most profitable industries in the state. The fact that Billings was able to concentrate solely on the production of machine tools, and that Pratt and Whitney con-

42. Ibid.
43. Ibid., p. 845.
44. Ibid.

stantly enlarged their facilities in the middle sixties, was indicative of revolutionary changes in production. It took no great skill to operate a drop forge, and the product was cheaper, better, and more durable. On the other hand, as new machinery was developed and dies and forges to make the parts became more complicated, the machine-tool industry demanded higher skills from its labor, greater ingenuity from its designers.

A most vital consideration in the expansion and localization of the Connecticut machine tool manufacture was the parallel development at Hartford of the leather-belting industry. The transmission of power by means of leather belts was far more efficient than the cumbersome series of cranks and levers and gears that had served the early industrialists. Pliny Jewell, a tanner who had emigrated from New Hampshire to Hartford in the 1840s, had been one of the first in the United States to recognize the future in belting as a power conveyor.[45] Assisted by his four sons, all tanners and businessmen of exceptional ability, he undertook to educate factory owners in the merits of his product. Though the Jewells managed to build up a prosperous business during the fifties, it was the Civil War that established beyond doubt both the efficiency of the belt drive and their own personal fortunes.[46] The wartime expansion of the munitions industry, with its dependence upon high-speed machine tools, created an enormous market for leather belting. In 1863, crowded beyond capacity by orders, the Jewells purchased another larger factory building in Hartford, and equipped it with the new shoe-cutting and stitching machinery they had adapted to their own requirements. The rise of the machine-tool industry in the postwar period would furnish a profitable local market for their products. In addition, it ensured the further development of leather belt manufacture at Hartford.[47]

Far more important than leatherware or machine tools in terms of long-range economic significance was the concentration of the insurance industry in Hartford. Insurance had been a Hartford specialty long before 1861. Marine insurance dated back to 1798

45. J. H. Trumbull, *Hartford*, 1, 571.
46. Davis, 2, 825–32.
47. Ibid.

and fire insurance to the second decade of the nineteenth century. Life insurance was already a flourishing industry when Edmund Ruffin touched off the first gun against Fort Sumter. But it was the war itself that elevated insurance to the status of big business and established Hartford's absolute supremacy as the center for the industry in the state and a challenger for first rank in the nation. Prior to the war, New Haven and Norwich, for a time, were would-be rivals. Speculation and mismanagement ruined the New Haven industry in the postwar period, while the Norwich business community diverted its capital into other enterprises. The Hartford companies, however, enjoyed a remarkable succession of able managers, an entire generation of perhaps the best business brains in the state, who had guided successfully the infant industry through the perilous, depression-studded years between 1840 and 1861, and were ready to capitalize on postwar opportunities.

At first, the war administered a sharp setback to industry in Hartford and elsewhere. Premium revenue from the South, which accounted for a substantial share of the life insurance business and a lesser but still not insignificant part of the fire insurance business, ceased abruptly, forcing the industry to reorient its market policy. Connecticut Mutual, for example, wrote 1,275 policies in 1859, more than in any previous year of its existence, but in 1861 wrote only 959 new policies, a decrease of approximately one fourth.[48] Only three of the nine fire and life companies in Hartford—Aetna, Hartford Fire, and Connecticut Mutual—declared dividends during the third and fourth quarters of 1861.[49] The new Union Insurance Company surrendered its charter, divided up its capital among the stockholders, and went out of business. Two other prospective companies, the National and the Safety, unable to organize because of economic uncertainties, also gave up their charters.[50] By 1862, however, the insurance industry had more than made up its loss of Southern business in the booming economy of the Middle West. Indeed, life insurance entered a period of spectacular growth that was to be sustained for the next twenty years. Wartime psychology, a broad level of prosperity, and a profitable sales device

48. Ibid., p. 563.
49. Ibid., p. 253.
50. *Hartford Courant* (Aug. 29, 1861).

known as the premium note seemed an irresistible combination for the growth of the industry. Of all these factors, the premium note was probably the most influential, for it brought policies within the reach of the masses and at the same time permitted the insurance companies to enjoy a most lucrative personal loan business with negligible risks.

As a business technique, the premium note was simplicity itself. It was an arrangement by which a policyholder gave notes in lieu of premiums and still maintained his policy, providing he kept up the regular interest payments on his indebtedness.[51] Should the risk have to be paid by the insurance company before the notes were extinguished, the indebtedness of the policyholder was withheld from the settlement. Thus, in addition to normal profits from policies, the life companies were enjoying 6 to 7 per cent interest on their premium notes with little or no possibility of loss.[52] Premium notes had been introduced when fire insurance was in its infancy and when the manufacturing interests of the state were feeble. As a convenient method of keeping policies in effect during bad seasons, the premium note had been beneficial to all concerned. Its usage quickly spread to life insurance, where it proved invaluable in canvassing for small policies.[53] So important were premium notes for Connecticut Mutual that by 1870 they were valued at $12,000,000, or fully one-half of its assets. In that year, Aetna held over $6,000,000 worth of premium notes, while Charter Oak and Phoenix held nearly $3,000,000 each.[54] But the premium note was more than an instrument to expand business or even a device to secure rich profits: it was a recognition of the spirit of the age. Like a harbinger of modern times, the premium note represented a symbolic understanding of the dynamics of a new industrial society in which large increases in sales and profits might be gained by responding to the insurance needs of lower-income groups. The sale of insurance on the installment plan was the principal reason for the great success of life insurance in Connecticut during the sixties and seventies, a success that would dwarf all previous triumphs.

51. Davis, 2, 563.
52. *Hartford Times* (July 5, 1871).
53. Davis, 2, 562–63.
54. "Treasurer's Report, 1871," *PDLC* (May Sess., 1871), Doc. 12, p. 3.

Connecticut Mutual alone, by liberal resort to the premium note, wrote 5,090 policies in 1863 (five times as many as in 1861), 8,045 policies in 1864, and the amazing total of 14,151 in 1867. During those years the tide of its assets surged from $3,300,000 to $22,-500,000. Other life insurance companies gained proportionately.[55] The decade of the sixties also witnessed a large increase in new companies (almost concentrating the life insurance business of the state in Hartford) and the introduction of casualty insurance.[56]

The appearance of accident insurance was similar to that of life a generation earlier. In 1863 James G. Batterson, a wealthy quarry owner and successful speculator in Hartford real estate, discovered accident insurance while traveling in England. Examining the business with his accustomed penetration, he decided it might prove profitable in an America that was fast becoming dependent upon rail travel.[57] Shortly after his return, Batterson and other Hartford capitalists incorporated the Travelers' Insurance Company to write travel policies payable upon death or personal injury on railroads, steamers, or "other modes of conveyance in the United States and other countries." [58] At the onset, the new, inexperienced company had trouble with risks and with competition when five Western states chartered a host of accident companies. But the sagacity and the wealth of Travelers' founders and particularly the masterful management of Batterson soon eliminated both the risk problem and the competitors. Forming a pool of seven accident companies in June 1865, he made savage war upon the interlopers. In 1866 this informal arrangement was merged into a single group, the Railways Passengers' Association, with Batterson and the Travelers' directorate in firm control. Against such a combine, enjoying all the benefits of large assets, single management, and uniform risks, independent companies were plowed under so rapidly that by 1867 not one remained. Eventually, Travelers' bought out its associates and

55. Davis, 2, 563.

56. The 1860s also witnessed the formation of the Hartford Steam Boiler Company, first company to insure against boiler explosions in America. Davis, 2, 262.

57. Ibid., pp. 15–16.

58. Ibid., p. 604.

forged a near monopoly of accident insurance in the United States.[59]

Besides the amazing development of life insurance and the first appearance of casualty underwriting, fire insurance shared in the prosperity of the sixties and was cast into new molds by a war-imposed acceleration of the industrial revolution. The westward shift of Connecticut fire companies, which resulted from the loss of Southern business, had been most profitable, so profitable in fact that dangerous concentrations of risks were allowed to develop in certain urban areas. By virtue of its size and wealth, Chicago had attracted a preponderance of these underwriting liabilities, yet no other Western city had grown so rapidly or had become so susceptible to the dangers of widespread conflagration. Throughout the war and the postwar period, agents of Aetna, Hartford Fire, Phoenix, and other Connecticut companies diligently wrote policies in Chicago, and the directors at home urged them on.[60] Such a concentration of risks in one area was to have disastrous consequences when the great Chicago fire of 1871 dealt a heavy blow to Connecticut's fire insurance industry. But this was far in the future, and meanwhile, the influx of premium revenue was providing a solid cushion of new capital that would help support the economic readjustment.

Thanks largely to the increasing tempo of industrial change, the creation of substantial new capital, and the ebullient drive of the new entrepreneurs, significant progress was made in urban improvement during the postwar period. Much of the untidiness and inconvenience formerly associated with urban life was fast disappearing as horse-car lines, paved streets, and public utilities were extended and improved. A rapid development of railroads not only cut down travel time between distant points, but brought dozens of country towns within easy reach of population and trade centers. Little improvement, however, occurred in the living standards of the labor force and the farm population. The long work week continued to remain in force despite various attempts by the

59. Ibid., pp. 605–06.

60. "Seventh Annual Report of the Commissioners of Insurance," *PDLC* (May Sess., 1872), pp. 6–10.

union movement to enact a legal eight-hour day. A renewal of heavy European immigration after the war and increasing migration from farm to city served to cheapen the labor mart. Real wages did not increase even though the economy was expanding rapidly. Indeed, after the Panic of 1873, real wages started a long period of decline.[61]

For Connecticut the postwar decade witnessed a maturing of the industrial revolution, highlighted by a spectacular advance in railroad construction. In 1864 the state possessed 540 miles of railroad trackage. Seven years later it had 866 miles, half again as much as at the war's end.[62] Four new routes had been completed and were in operation. Under the aegis of the Vanderbilt interests and the adroit management of William D. Bishop, the leading railroad man in the state, the New York and New Haven, the Hartford and New Haven, and the Shore Line had been consolidated into one system. The battle for the bridging of navigable streams had been won by the railroads against the opposition of commercial interests and jealous localities. Railroad travel between New York and Boston had become faster, safer, and cheaper; and the building of new routes and the construction of new spur lines had eased much of the prewar isolation that made farm and small-town life so narrow and monotonous.

But with all the hustle and bustle, a certain neighborly warmth in the character of the people seemed to have left the "land of steady habits." As early as 1865 Frederick Sheldon, a frequent contributor to the *Atlantic,* sensed this change of attitude, this preoccupation with one's own affairs. "The brisk little democratic state," he wrote, "has turned its brains upon its machinery. Not a snug valley with a few drops of water at the bottom of it, but rattles with the manufacture of notions, great and small—axes and pistols, carriages and clocks, tin pans and toys, hats, garters, buttons and pins." [63] In that half-humorous, half-sardonic vein, much admired by his Boston-Brahmin audience, Sheldon charged that "there are no poets known to exist there, unless it be that well paid band who

61. Layer, *Earnings of Cotton Mill Operatives,* pp. 52–53.

62. "Report of the Railroad Commission, 1872," *PDLC* (May Sess., 1872), pp. 4, 6.

63. Frederick Sheldon, "The Pleiades of Connecticut," *Atlantic Monthly,* 15 (1865), 187.

write the rhymed puffs of cheap garments and cosmetics." [64] As unfair as Sheldon was in his whimsical strictures upon Connecticut's apparent obsession with "the busy marts of trade," there was some truth in his observations.

Even the sacred portals of Yale College were not immune, it seems, to the profane and secularizing influences of the railroad men, the stock jobbers, and the real estate speculators. Professor Cyrus Northrop, in the early 1870s, found it appropriate to explain style, in his literature classes, as an example of commercial exchange. "Thought," he remarked, "is the article manufactured. You are the producers. I am the consumer. The problem is to transport this commodity, thought, from your mind to mine at the least expense and with the least wear and tear of the commodity." [65] Gideon Welles, when he returned to Hartford after eight years in Washington, acknowledged the city more prosperous, more comfortable, and more beautiful than he remembered it in 1861. But he missed the mellow cordiality and the friendly, intimate character of the little country town-city he had known. To that morbidly sensitive yet astringent critic of man's foibles, Hartford seemed a rather cold, preoccupied place. "In looking around in the few days I have been here," Welles wrote in his diary, "I learn that hearts which I valued have passed away. They are cold in the grave; others colder are out of it." [66]

As the economy moved boldly ahead into the harsh competitive era of the late sixties and early seventies, society followed closely in its well-defined wake, leaving behind those traits of rural innocence and narrow convention that had comforted the old folks and vexed the young. Whatever irritation, even disgust, the volunteer soldiers had felt about the old fogies who enjoyed singing psalms through their noses at drafty prayer meetings or who insisted upon the observance of the blue laws, many felt a twinge of nostalgia for the good old days. It was no more than a twinge, for the past now seemed so pale and fine of outline as to be scarcely remembered at all. The great war that had started so gaily and romantically in the spring of '61 had ended in the charnel houses around a devastated

64. Ibid.
65. Firkins, *Cyrus Northrop*, p. 225.
66. Morse, *Welles Diary*, 3, 583.

Richmond, a brutalizing period that was to leave its horrid scars for a generation. But the war had only been an episode, a tragic, irrational release of social pressures that had been mounting for thirty years. Once the release had occurred, the memory of the war's inhuman side began to fade, as veterans sought to recapture the fun, the companionship, and the glory, and to forget the privation, the misery, and the gore. Meanwhile, the problems of adjusting fully to the demands of the new industrial state were far too strenuous to permit more than an occasional backward glance either in humor or regret or criticism of things past.

"What I chiefly lament," wrote that inveterate New England traveler Samuel Drake, as he mourned the passage of rural Connecticut, "is the disappearance of the Yankee—not the conventional Yankee of the theatre . . . but the hearty yet suspicious, 'cute,' though green, drawling, whittling, unadulterated Yankee, with his broad humor, delirious patois and large hearted patriotism. His very mother tongue is forgotten . . . Railway and telegraph, factory and workshop, penetrating into the most secluded hamlet, have rubbed off the crust of an originality so pronounced as to have become a type." [67] Connecticut in 1860 had been a composite of the old and the new, with rather more of the old in its make-up; Connecticut of 1870 was to present a character quite different in tone, which fancied it owed little to the past, and was already in heavy debt to the future.

67. Samuel Drake, *Nooks and Corners of the New England Coast* (New York, 1875), pp. 442–43.

BIBLIOGRAPHY

Manuscripts

THREE outstanding manuscript collections dealing with American nineteenth-century political, social, and intellectual life are the work of Connecticut men: Mark Howard, Joseph R. Hawley, and Gideon Welles. Indeed, the Welles Papers, at the Library of Congress, New York Public Library, Huntington Library, and Connecticut Historical Society are certainly the most voluminous and one of the most significant of American manuscript collections. Welles' manuscript diary, which he kept intermittently from the late 1820s until 1862, and faithfully from August 1862 through May 1869, is one of the most complete sources for the Lincoln and Johnson administrations. Howard's Papers, at the Connecticut Historical Society, and his correspondence that shows up in many other manuscript collections are exceedingly rich in specific Connecticut material. Similarly, the Hawley papers, also at the Library of Congress, are valuable sources for local politics, social history, and life in a Connecticut regiment. Charles Dudley Warner, a close friend of Hawley and co-editor of the *Hartford Press,* provides us with the best sources for the state of mind of the Connecticut Radicals during the war. His long letters to Hawley and his own personal papers at the Trinity College Library, Hartford, form a mercurial, delightfully ill-tempered chronicle of Connecticut wartime politics. The James G. Batterson and James Dixon Papers, at the Connecticut Historical Society, are also important sources for Republican politics in Connecticut. Both men, though Dixon reluctantly, supported the President when he was renominated in 1864. Batterson, more than anyone else, got out the Lincoln vote in the state. Apparently much of William A. Buckingham's private correspondence has been lost or remains in private hands. The collection at the Connecticut State Library is fragmentary, though Buckingham letters appear in such papers as those of Welles, Hawley, R. T. Lincoln, and John A. Rockwell. His official letter-books, also housed in the State Library, are complete and of great value in assessing his wartime administrative policies. Of some significance, particularly for 1860 and 1861, are the Bacon and Baldwin Family Papers, Sterling Library; the R. T. Lincoln Papers, Library of Congress; the Phineas T. Barnum Papers and the James Beeckman Papers, New York Historical Society; and the John A. Rockwell Papers, Huntington Library.

It is unfortunate that none of the Democratic politicians or those of conservative political instincts have left a comparable body of papers. The Thomas Hart Seymour Papers, at the Connecticut Historical Society, are the best and the most complete. William J. Hammersly, sometime Democratic mayor of Hartford and prominent bookseller, has left a large body of papers, also at the Connecticut Historical Society, but it is of minor importance.

Good manuscript diaries and journals dealing with the political and social history of the period are quite rare. Gideon Welles made some important diary entries beginning in the fall of 1860 and ending in January 1861. The William H. Mallory Diary, Mystic Marine Museum, is useful for economic trends; the Judge Asa Fish Diary, Mystic Marine Museum, has some interesting social material, but useful only for background. Of major significance is the Yale Civil War collection, Sterling Library, which has an impressive collection of manuscripts, soldier diaries, and letters. An example is the vivid journal of William Bishop of New Haven, a yeoman aboard the ill-fated *Cumberland*. Yale also has the valuable wartime correspondence of Major General Alfred H. Terry, his brother, Brevet-Colonel Adrian Terry, Captain Theodore Bacon of the 7th Connecticut, and Major General Joseph R. Hawley.

Newspapers, Periodicals, State and Federal Documents

The most influential newspapers in the state were those published in Hartford and New Haven. Both cities had several morning and evening daily newspapers, all of which published weekly editions for the countryside. The venerable *Hartford Courant*, edited by A. N. Clark and the *Hartford Evening Press*, edited by Hawley and Warner prior to the war and by Warner, alone, after Hawley volunteered for military service, had the largest circulation and were the most influential of Hartford's Republican papers. The *Courant* was conservative and frequently a spokesman for Senator Dixon, while the *Press* early espoused the Radical movement. The *Hartford Times*, formerly the organ of Jacksonian democracy in the state, had, under the editorship of Alfred E. Burr, swung into conservative Democratic ranks. The *Hartford Evening Post* represented the War Democrat viewpoint from 1861 to 1865.

The *New Haven Palladium*, edited by James F. Babcock during the first year of the war, reflected that editor's conservative Republican stand. When Cyrus Northrop took over, he swung the *Palladium* into the Radical camp. The *New Haven Journal and Courier*, edited by John B. Carrington, became increasingly Radical after 1863. On the conservative Democratic side, Minott Osborne's *New Haven Register* was a vigorous critic of both Buckingham and Lincoln, though never as intemperate as William S. Pomeroy and S. N. Morse, the editors of the outspoken Copperhead daily, the *Bridgeport Republican Farmer*. Bridgeport also maintained a Republican paper, the *Standard*, which wielded considerable influence in Fairfield County. Other significant papers were the *Norwich Bulletin* (Republican), edited by that able and sulphurous journalist Isaac "Ike" Bromley, and the *Norwich Aurora* (conservative Democrat), edited by capable John W. Stedman. Connecticut material, mainly descriptive, turns up in the *Atlantic Monthly* and *Harper's Magazine*, but the best contemporary periodical source is the *New Englander Magazine*, the most influential journal of the Congregational Church but also reflecting the more secular interests of its editor, William L. Kingsley. On the state level, committee and commission reports and governors' messages provide statistical information and policy recommendations that are indispensable sources for both military and administrative history. Entitled *Public Documents of the Legislature of Connecticut*, complete files are located in the Connecticut State Library and the Sterling Library, Yale University. In this collection the only accurate source for Connecticut military manpower statistics is the *Record of Service of Connecticut Men in the Army and Navy of the United States during the War of the Rebellion*, compiled by the Adjutant General's Office and published as a state document (Hartford, 1889).

The only sources for legislative debates, miscellaneous documents, and laws are the daily press during the regular session of the legislature in May, and during the special sessions—November and December. On the Federal level, Senate and House debates are in the *Congressional Globe,* for the appropriate Congress and session, while such valuable sources as testimony developed during congressional investigations of Army and Navy procurement are in House Report, Vol. 2, Pts. I and II, 32d Congress, 2d Session, and in the multivolume joint House and Senate reports of the Committee on the Conduct of the War. The *War of the Rebellion, a Compilation of the Official Records of Union and Confederate Armies,* published by the War Department from 1880 to 1900 in four series, with a total of 128 volumes, has all official correspondence of the Connecticut regiments as well as their division, corps, and army commanders. Confederate correspondence included in this monumental work has interesting material bearing on the sale of munitions by Connecticut manufacturers to the various Confederate states and the Confederate government itself. Details on the "stone fleet" and on ships in government service that were built in Connecticut yards can be found in the *Official Records of the Union and Confederate Navies in the War of the Rebellion,* published by the Navy Department in two series, a total of 30 volumes, between 1894 and 1914. William M. Lytle (comp.), *Merchant Steam Vessels of the United States, 1807–1868* (Mystic, 1952), has a complete list of steamers built in Connecticut yards during the war.

Printed Diaries, Reminiscences, Memoirs, Correspondence

Much valuable source material is contained in published works of a personal or autobiographical nature. To be sure, such sources must be used with some care. The editors, usually relatives or close personal friends of the subjects concerned, have, on occasion, altered the meaning intended or have by careful selection presented only one side of an issue. Autobiographies, unless based upon diaries or letters, are frequently only as accurate as the author's memory. There is abundant material of this nature that deals with Civil War Connecticut, though less than one would imagine concerning the domestic scene. Despite its preoccupation with medical affairs, I found Georgeanna Woolsey Bacon and Eliza Woolsey Howland, eds., *Letters of a Family during the War for the Union, 1861–1864* (2 vols. New Haven, 1899), a remarkable collection of perceptive letters with many astute observations on local society in the grip of a great war. The first eight chapters of John W. DeForest's *Miss Ravenel's Conversion from Secession to Loyalty* (Harper, New York, 1939) contains superb description and incisive commentary on the social life of the New Haven élite during the early months of the war. Since the novel is largely autobiographical and is a contemporary work (submitted for publication in 1865), I have deemed it a first-rate source not only for the local scene but for its realistic portrayal of army life. Also of interest to students of wartime Connecticut is Mary Bushnell Cheney, ed., *Life and Letters of Horace Bushnell* (New York, 1905). Bushnell, as Hartford's most renowned theologian and man of affairs, dominated the cultural life of that city for fifty years. The letters, anecdotes, and biographical material in this substantial volume are invaluable sources for the social and intellectual history of the state during the middle period of the nineteenth century. John Hooker, *Some Reminiscences of a Long Life* (Hartford, 1899), is a light and charming foil to Bushnell's polemical, frequently blunt correspondence. Rambling, anecdotal, and witty, Hooker makes Connecticut seem a lighter, brighter place than the new Jerusalem of Bushnell or the new Canaan of Leonard Bacon and Theodore Dwight Woolsey. The early editions of Phineas T. Barnum's autobiographies are useful for both economic and social history. *Struggles and Triumphs: Or, Forty Years' Recollections* (Hartford, 1869) cover the period 1850–68. Mainly political but also an occasional comment on Connecticut social mores is the *Diary of Gideon Welles,* ed. John T. Morse (3 vols. Boston, 1911); ed. Howard K. Beale (3 vols. New York, 1960). The Beale edition is somewhat harder to use, but is a faithful reproduction of the manuscript diary. Another significant printed collection whose Connecticut material is exclusively political or military is Roy P. Basler, ed., *The Collected Works of Abraham Lincoln* (9 vols. New Brunswick, 1953–55).

The published reminiscences and the correspondence of military personnel are more abundant, though much of this material is reprinted in regimental histories or in letters to the various home newspapers. However, several important special works deserve mention. The best of these is John W. DeForest, *A Volunteer's Adventures: A Union Captain's Record of the Civil War*, ed. James H. Croushore (New Haven, 1946). This is a realistic account of army life in Louisiana and Virginia as related in home letters to his wife or in articles that DeForest published in *Harper's New Monthly Magazine* or *Galaxy*, 1864 through 1868. Another excellent collection of letters and memoir material is to be found in Henry Clay Trumbull, *The Knightly Soldier: A Biography of Major Henry Ward Camp, Tenth Connecticut Volunteers* (Boston, 1865). Though organized as a biography, this volume contains more than 300 letters written by Camp, commenting on camp life, battle scenes, religion, politics, war aims, and Southern prison life. Equally significant is Samuel Fiske, *Mr. Dunn Browne's Experience in the Army* (Boston, 1866), a series of letters that Fiske wrote under the pseudonym of Dunn Browne for the *Springfield Republican*. A captain in the 14th Connecticut, Fiske was a talented humorist, a sharp critic, and a good reporter. *The War Letters of William Thompson Lusk, Captain, Assistant Adjutant-General United States Volunteers, 1861–1863* (New York, 1911) reveals also a sensitive, highly critical observer. Though serving in a New York regiment, Lusk regarded himself as a Connecticut man. Some interesting local Connecticut material can be found in letters to Lusk from his mother, who lived in Norwich during the war. *The Correspondence of John Sedgwick, Major General* (2 vols. New York, 1902) has some Connecticut material but is principally concerned with upper echelon matters and with important military and political figures.

Regimental Histories

All Connecticut regiments, cavalry units, and artillery batteries have some sort of published history. These range from elaborate illustrated two-volume works like that of the 1st Light Battery to the mere skeleton outline of the 26th (nine-months) Regiment. A few are excellent, well-written narratives with a wealth of detail and description. Many are rambling, discursive compilations in which one must pick one's way with care to sift out bits and pieces of significant material. All the accounts have more or less inaccurate statements on matters of detail, and include gossip that passes for fact; but they are most rewarding if one has the interest and the patience to study them carefully. And they are, of course, an essential source for Connecticut's military participation in the Civil War.

W. A. Croffut and John M. Morris, *The Military and Civil History of Connecticut during the War of 1861–1864* (New York, 1868), is the only comprehensive work that seeks to chronicle the home front build-up as well as actual campaign participation. Though an indispensable source, Croffut and Morris bares evidence of haste in compiling: indeed, much of the material is a scissors and paste job of contemporary newspaper accounts, published letters, and reminiscences. It must be used with care, as there are many errors and some distortions to fit the political and moral biases of the authors.

Of specific regimental histories the following, arranged alphabetically by the principal author, are representative. Herbert W. Beecher, *History of the First Light Battery Connecticut Volunteers, 1861–1865* (2 vols. New York, 1901), is the most ambitious and in some respects the most interesting of Connecticut regimental histories. Anecdotal and descriptive, it abounds with rollicking humor, vivid realism, and, alas, exaggeration. Where Beecher's work is overly elaborate, Bernard F. Blakeslee's readable *History of the Sixteenth Connecticut Volunteers* (Hartford, 1875) is too abbreviated, but is excellent for Antietam and the capture of Plymouth, North Carolina. Charles K. Cadwell, *The Old Sixth Regiment, Its War Record, 1861–65* (New Haven, 1875), is also a readable and useful history but too brief. Alvin M. Crane and others, *The Story of the Twenty-First Regiment, Connecticut Volunteer Infantry during the Civil War, 1861–1865* (Middletown, 1900), is an oddly disjointed book written by six members of the regiment whose differing style and approaches make for difficult reading. It is the best source, however, for the battle of Drewry's Bluff and for Butler's operations at Bermuda Hundred. Almost a documentary history, Edwin E. Marvin, *The Fifth Regiment Connecticut Volunteers, a History* (Hartford, 1889), has valuable diary material and personal correspondence interspersed with routine dispatches and official orders. Thomas Hamilton Murray, *His-*

tory of the Ninth Regiment Connecticut Volunteer Infantry, "The Irish Regiment," in the War of the Rebellion, 1861–65 (New Haven, 1903), is well written, with some useful documents, profiles of members, and a general index. Another ambitious, well-illustrated work is Charles D. Page, *History of the Fourteenth Connecticut Volunteer Infantry* (Meriden, 1906). Uneven in style, frequently careless on details, it nevertheless contains fine descriptions of Antietam and Gettysburg. Best for the nine-months regiments is Winthrop D. Sheldon, *The Twenty-Seventh: A Regimental History* (New Haven, 1866), which has particularly good accounts of Fredericksburg, Chancellorsville, and Gettsyburg. Also an admirable work is Homer B. Sprague, *History of the 13th Infantry Regiment of Connecticut Volunteers during the Great Rebellion* (Hartford, 1867), a lively, anecdotal, well-organized, carefully constructed narrative. John W. Storrs, *The Twentieth Connecticut: A Regimental History* (Ansonia, 1886), has excellent realistic material, largely based on the war diary of Colonel Philo Buckingham. It contains an especially moving account of the sufferings of the abandoned Union casualties after Chancellorsville. Less satisfactory is Sheldon B. Thorpe, *The History of the Fifteenth Connecticut Volunteers in the War for the Defense of the Union, 1861–1865* (New Haven, 1893). More a scrapbook than a history, it has some valuable material. Elnathen B. Tyler (Frinkle Fry), *"Wooden Nutmegs" at Bull Run* (Hartford, 1872), is the only lengthy treatment of a three-months regiment and the only Connecticut regimental history written in a humorous vein—more entertaining than useful. In my opinion Theodore F. Vaill, *History of the Second Connecticut Volunteer Heavy Artillery, Originally the Nineteenth Connecticut Volunteers* (Winsted, Conn., 1868), is the best of Connecticut regimental histories. With excellent narrative and valuable profiles of officers and men, it is comparatively free of digressions, undigested documents, and digested moralisms. William C. Walker, *History of the Eighteenth Regiment Connecticut Volunteers in the War for the Union* (Norwich, 1885), is valuable primarily for its statistical survey of the regiment, and Stephen W. Walkley, *History of the Seventh Connecticut Volunteer Infantry, Hawley's Brigade, Terry's Division, Tenth Army*

Corps (Hartford, 1905), for its documents, useful maps, and well-developed narrative.

General Secondary Works

For general military history, the superb maps in Vincent J. Esposito, ed., *The West Point Atlas of American Wars* (New York, 1959), are indispensable to any understanding of the campaigns. Bruce Catton's memorable trilogy—*Mr. Lincoln's Army* (New York, 1951), *Glory Road: The Bloody Route from Fredericksburg to Gettysburg* (New York, 1952), *A Stillness at Appomattox* (New York, 1953)—is the most colorful, comprehensive history of the Army of the Potomac yet published. R. U. Johnson and C. C. Buel, eds., *Battles and Leaders of the Civil War* (4 vols. New York, 1884–85), however, was my principal source for over-all strategy as well as specific battle accounts. The series of pamphlets published by the Connecticut Civil War Centennial Commission were helpful, particularly J. Doyle Dewitt, *Lincoln in Hartford* (Hartford, 1962), and Stanley B. Weld, *Connecticut Physicians in the Civil War* (Hartford, 1963), which has invaluable profiles of the medical volunteer officers and substantial extracts from Dr. Nathan Mayer's memoirs. In this connection, George Worthington Adams, *Doctors in Blue, the Medical History of the Union Army in the Civil War* (New York, 1952), provides essential background material.

Principal sources for social and cultural history are the contemporary newspapers and periodicals, and published and manuscript letters and diaries. To a lesser extent, town, city, and county histories contain useful information or comment. But two biographies deserve special mention: Oscar Firkins, *Cyrus Northrop: A Memoir* (Minneapolis, 1925), and Waldo H. Dunn, *The Life of Donald Grant Mitchell "Ik Marvel"* (New York, 1922). Firkins' is the better book, a well-written treatment of a prominent politician, newspaper editor, and Yale professor. The author quotes extensively from Northrop's personal papers and thus provides valuable social and political material bearing on prewar and wartime Connecticut. The Mitchell biography is a solid, rather wooden book about a charming humorist, essayist, and novelist, who was one of the most popular writers of his day. Dunn also makes elaborate use of Mitchell's personal papers. Such essay material as Nathaniel Shipman, "A Memoir of Joseph R. Hawley and Arthur Shipman," *Hartford Times* (Jan. 28, 1938), and Thomas F. Weaver, *Historical Sketch of the Police Service of Hartford* (Hartford, 1901), contain colorful descriptions. Chapter 1 of Kenneth Andrews, *Nook Farm, Mark Twain's Hartford Circle* (Cambridge, 1950), has some interesting information on the Hookers, Stowes, Hawley, and Warner. *Benham's New Haven Directory, 1860–1865* and *Geer's Hartford Directory, 1860–65* are major sources for facts on population and industrial growth. Less valuable for social and cultural history but useful are George A. King, S.J., *Theodore Dwight Woolsey: His Political and Social Ideas* (Chicago, 1956); Theodore D. Bacon, *Leonard Bacon: A Statesman in the Church* (New Haven, 1931); and Henry W. French, *Art and Artists in Connecticut* (Boston, 1879).

For state politics in wartime, Jarlath R. Lane, *A Political History of Connecticut during the Civil War* (Washington, 1941), is the only specific treatment. A noninterpretive work of impressive scholarship, it is an extremely valuable source for facts, but does not deal with motivation or attempt any political analysis. William B. Hesseltine, *Lincoln and the War Governors* (New York, 1955), a much more significant work, unfortunately does not deal adequately with Connecticut. Harry J. Carman and Reinhard H. Luthin, *Lincoln and the Patronage* (New York, 1943), has a better coverage and is particularly illuminating for the patronage quarrels between Senator James Dixon and the "state" faction in Connecticut politics. The *Welles Diary*, also, has important references to this and to other political issues in the state. Other works useful for political background are Carroll J. Noonan, *Nativism in Connecticut, 1820–1860* (Washington, 1938); Jarvis M. Morse, *A Neglected Period in Connecticut's History, 1818–1850* (New Haven, 1933); and Samuel G. Buckingham, *The Life of William A. Buckingham, the War Governor of Connecticut* (Springfield, 1894).

Indispensable for the industrial buildup of wartime Connecticut is William T. Davis, ed., *The New England States: Their Constitutional, Judicial, Educational, Commercial, Professional and Industrial History*, Vols. 1 and 2 (Boston, 1897), and the various town, city, and county histories. The best of these are J. Hammond Trumbull, ed., *The Memorial History of Hartford County, Connecticut* (2 vols. Boston, 1886); Edward E. Atwater, ed., *History of the City of New Haven, 1784–1884* (New York, 1887); Rollin G. Osterweis, *Three Centuries of New Haven, 1638–1938* (New Haven, 1953); and Frances M. Caulkins, *History of Norwich* (Hartford, 1866). A number of monographs are mines of information. Among the more significant are Felicia J. Deyrup, *Arms Makers of the Connecticut Valley, a Regional Study of the Economic Development of the Small Arms Industry* (Northampton, 1948); Charles T. Hansen and Frank A. Belden, *A History of the Colt Revolver and Other Arms, Made by Colt's Patent Fire Arms Manufacturing Company from 1830–1940* (New York, 1940); William G. Lathrop, *The Brass Industry in the United States: A Study of the Origins and Development of the Brass Industry in the Naugatuck Valley* (Mount Carmel, 1926); Jacob H. Burgy, *The New England Cotton Textile Industry: A Study in Industrial Geography* (Baltimore, 1932); Robert G. Layer, *Earnings of Cotton Mill Operatives, 1825–1914* (Cambridge, 1955); Arthur H. Cole, *The American Woolen Manufacture* (2 vols. Cambridge, 1926); Sidney Withington, *The First Twenty Years of Railroads in Connecticut* (New Haven, 1935); Carl C. Cutler, *Mystic; The Story of a Small New England Seaport* (Mystic, 1945); Rollin G. Osterweis, *Charter Number Two: The Centennial History of the First New Haven National Bank* (New Haven, 1963). Much economic history can also be gleaned from such general histories of the state as George L. Clark, *A History of Connecticut: Its People and Institutions* (New York, 1914); and Norris G. Osborn, ed., *History of Connecticut in Monographic Form* (4 vols. New York, 1925).

INDEX

Italicized page numbers indicate principal entry